P,o

FITZROY
MACLEAN

FITZROY MACLEAN

Frank McLynn

JOHN MURRAY

For Pauline

First published in 1992
by John Murray (Publishers) Ltd.,
50 Albemarle Street, London W1X 4BD

A catalogue record for this book is available from the British Library

ISBN 0-7195-4971 X

Typeset in 11½/12 pt Baskerville by Colset Private Limited, Singapore
Printed and bound in Great Britain by
Cambridge University Press, Cambridge

Contents

Illustrations

(*between pages 210 and 211*)

All photographs are reproduced courtesy of Sir Fitzroy Maclean from his private collection.

MAPS

Preface

I first made the acquaintance of Sir Fitzroy Maclean as a result of our both having written biographies of Bonnie Prince Charlie. With lives of H.M. Stanley and Sir Richard Burton aslo under my belt, I was looking around for a modern adventurer who continued that tradition into the twentieth century. I hope the reader will agree that I found one. Fitzroy has generously made available the few diaries he kept and, more importantly, has provided me with dozens of hours of taped interviews. Although this biography was written with his full co-operation, at no time did he seek to influence or alter anything I wrote, but contented himself with pointing out factual errors.

I also owe a debt to scores of other individuals who consented to talk to me about Fitzroy. Their help ranged from, at the minimum, merely answering questions that closed avenues of enquiry to, at the maximum, providing six-hour taped interviews. It would be invidious to single out those people who helped me most, but they know who they are, and I am especially grateful to them.

Accordingly, my thanks are due to the following: Julian Amery, Sir John Astor, Richard Bates, Lady Sheila de Bellaigue, Ralph Bennett, General Georges Berger, John Blelloch, Alan Brien, Lady Bullard, Lord Bullock, Philip Burleigh, Nancy Cameron, Sir Peter Carey, Robert Chenciner, Colonel John Clarke, Jeanne Clissold, Colonel John Cooper, Ian Curteiss, Basil Davidson, Sir William Deakin, Sir Douglas Dodds-Parker, Pamela, Lady Egremont, Douglas Fairbanks Jr, Patrick Leigh Fermor, Dominic Flessati, Professor M.R.D. Foot, Lady Antonia Fraser, Allen Garnett, Admiral Sir Morgan Morgan-Giles, Michael Gill, Lady Caroline Gilmour, Sir Ian Gilmour, Sir Alexander Glen, Lord Henniker, Christian, Lady Hesketh, Alan Hoe, Dr John Hemming, J. Bittenfeld von Herwarth, Sir Reginald Hibbert, Thelma Holt, Jean Howard, Tony Isaacs, Lord Jellicoe, Lord Jenkins of Hillhead, Sir Richard Keene, Lawrence Kelly, Hilary King, David

Lambie MP, Sir John Lawrence, Barbara Leaming, the late Michael Lees, John Linklater, Colonel Franklin Lindsay, Charlie Maclean, Jamie Maclean, Lady Maclean, Sheila MacPherson, Ella Maillart, John Massey-Stewart, Lord Mayhew, Alistair Milne, Brigadier Peter Moore, John Mortimer, Suki Paravicini, Mike Parker, Brigadier Jeremy Phipps, John Purdie, Erina Rayner, Sir Frank Roberts, John Roberts, Nicholas Shakespeare, Colonel David Smiley, Annette Street, Colonel David Sutherland, Dr Han Suyin, Count Nikolai Tolstoy, Vladimir Velebit, Dr Mark Wheeler, Baron Wyatt and Will Wyatt.

As always, my wife Pauline gave me invaluable advice and help during the writing of this book.

Twickenham, 1992

CENTRAL ASIA

North Cape

Murmansk

Archangel

Dvina

LONDON

Leningrad

Baltic Sea

Volga

PARIS

BERLIN

Negoreloye

MOSCOW

Kuiybyshev

Warsaw

Kiev

Kharkov

Dneiper

Volga

ROME

Belgrade

Odessa

Rostov

Don

Volga

Stalingrad

Astrakhan

Georgian Mil. Highway

Caspian Sea

Caucasus

DAGHESTAN

Black Sea

Ordzhonikidze

Makhach Kala

Mt. Kazbek

GEORGIA

Mts.

Derbent

Istanbul

Ankara

Batum

Tiflis

AZERBAIJAN

Trebizond

ARMENIA

Kura

Baku

Mediterranean

Sea

TURKEY

Erzerum

Erivan

Krasnovodsk

Julfa

Araxes

Lenkoran

Tabriz

Elburz

Benghazi

Beirut

SYRIA

Kazvin

Hamadan

Qum

Lebanon Mts.

Damascus

Khanaqin

Kermanshah

Alexandria

Jerusalem

IRAQ

Baghdad

TEHRAN

CAIRO

Euphrates

Tigris

Basra

Red Sea

Persian Gulf

BAHREIN

miles

0   500   1000

0   800   1600

km

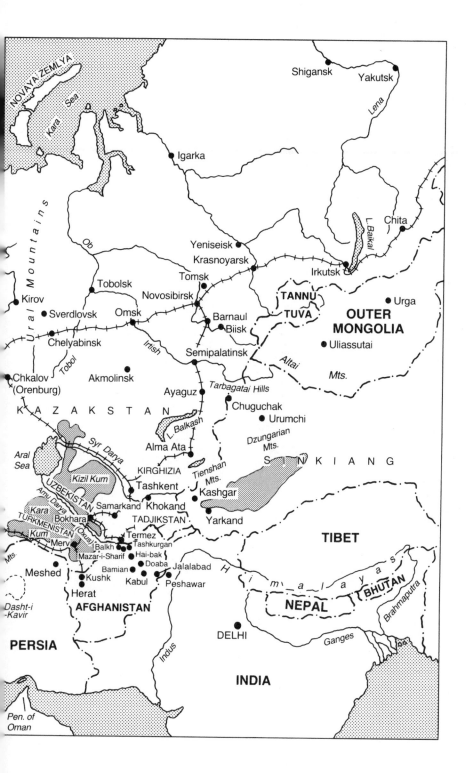

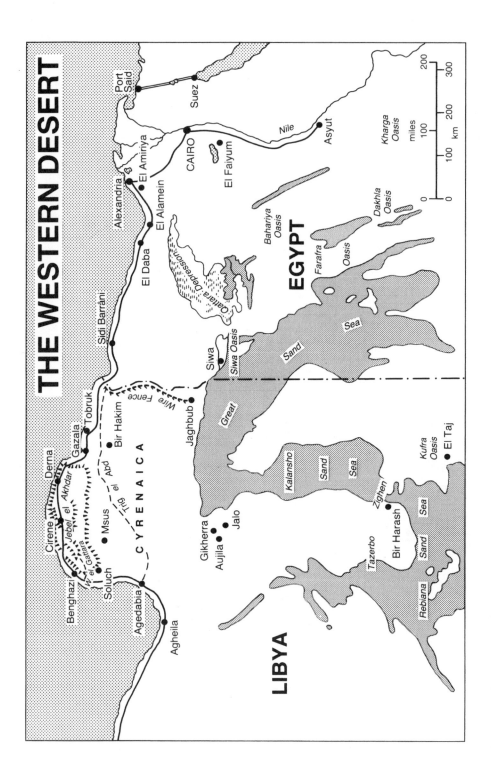

THE WESTERN DESERT

Port Said
Suez
Nile
Asyut
CAIRO
El Faiyum
El Amiriya
Alexandria
El Alamein
El Daba
Sidi Barrani
Qattara Depression
EGYPT
Bahariya Oasis
Farafra Oasis
Dakhla Oasis
Kharga Oasis
miles
km
Siwa
Siwa Oasis
Great Sand Sea
Jaghbub
Bir Hakim
Wire Fence
Gazala
Tobruk
Derna
Cirene
Jebel el Akhdar
W. el Gattara
Trig el Abd
Msus
CYRENAICA
Benghazi
Soluch
Agedabia
Agheila
Gikherra
Aujila
Jalo
Kalansho Sand Sea
Zighen
Bir Harash
Tazerbo
Rebiana Sand Sea
Kufra Oasis
El Taj
LIBYA

200
300
200
100
100

0
0

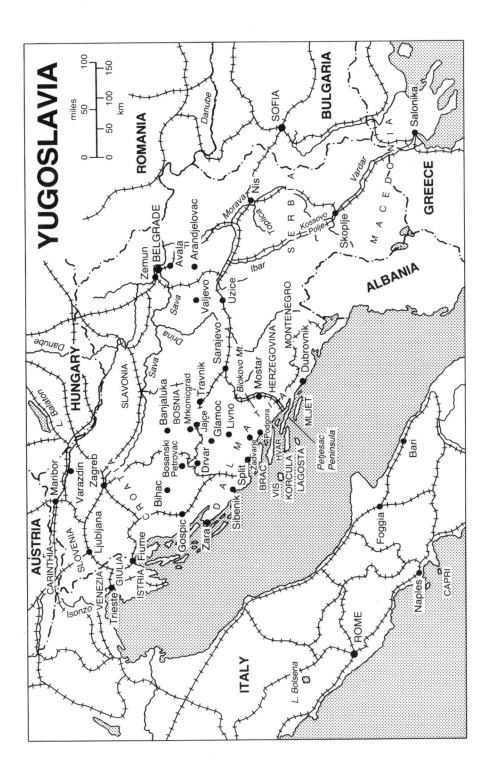

1

Childhood and Youth
1911–1933

'THANK God I am a Maclean' is the motto of the Maclean clan, and one in which Sir Fitzroy Hew Royle Maclean, soldier, statesman, diplomat, MP, traveller and media man believes implicitly. Love of Scotland and of his clan is probably the most important public emotion in his life. He was born on 11 March 1911 to an inheritance that has always been to him a source of the utmost pride. In the beginning was spirit, St John's Gospel tells us, and in the life of the man history has come to know as the 'Balkan brigadier' it is the spirit of his clan that has haunted and inspired him. The weight of ancestry, tradition, Highland ideology and expectations of how a Maclean should live rests on his shoulders. Yet not the least remarkable feature of his life is the way he has managed to escape the coils of determinism which have bound so many aristocratic Highlanders to a life of unexciting duty and *noblesse oblige*.

Fitzroy Maclean is a scion of the clan Maclean, the 'sons of Gillean', whose territory was the western shores of Argyll and the isles of Mull and Coll. The Macleans trace their origins to a thirteenth-century warrior, Gillean of the Battle-Axe, and commanded the territories of Duart, Lochbuie and Ardgour. The Duart Macleans traditionally supply the chiefs of the clan, and Fitzroy can trace his descent from Maclean of Ardgour.[1]

Yet Highland lineage is never a simple matter, and from earliest times intermarriage with other clans has complicated the picture. Until the mid-sixteenth century the Macleans pursued a policy of alliance with the MacDonald Lords of the Isles, and took wives and husbands from among the MacDonalds. They combined to support the great Macdonald in 1481 when his son Argus Og rebelled against him, and many of them were butchered though the chief's life was spared. But in 1493 James IV of Scotland declared the Lordship of the Isles forfeit and annexed it to the Crown,[2] and the Maclean chiefs began to feud with the various branches of clan Donald, as both sides vied to fill the vacuum thus created. In particular, the clans fought for the islands of Jura and Islay, which controlled the trade route with Ireland. The MacDonalds and Macleans wore themselves out by feuding and, after the disastrous battle of Tráigh Ghruineard in Islay in 1598, the Campbells of Argyll emerged as *tertius gaudens*. Although the Macleans now began to intermarry with the Campbells, the latter increasingly posed a threat to the Macleans' survival: by 1670 the Maclean chief owed the Earl of Argyll 200,000 marks, and there was a full-scale clan war when Argyll tried to make good his claim to Morvern, Mull and Tiree in lieu of payment.[3]

The Macleans were a notably martial clan ('the Spartans of the North'), and after the Scottish Stewart kings became monarchs of England also, in 1603, consistently expended their valour in the cause of the House of Stuart. In 1651, at the battle of Inverkeithing, 800 Macleans entered the fray under their chieftain Hector Maclean of Duart. By nightfall 760 of them were dead, including Duart himself and two sons of Maclean of Ardgour. The Maclean slogan 'Another for Hector' is said to have been uttered by the clansmen who died in heaps around their chief. During the Jacobite period (1689 to 1746) the Macleans gave valiant service to 'James III' (the 'Old Pretender' to the Whigs) and his son Charles Edward Stuart ('Bonnie Prince Charlie'). Their allegiance was not unconnected with the Campbells' support for the 'Glorious Revolution' of 1688 which expelled James II and later for the Hanoverian succession. The defeat of the Jacobites under 'Bonnie Dundee' at Killiekrankie in 1689 enabled the Campbells to invade Mull and take Duart Castle, which had held out against them for most of the century. In the '15 rising Sir John Maclean of Duart brought his clan out for James. At the battle of Sheriffmuir in 1715, as the Macleans faced their hereditary enemies the Campbells, Maclean of Duart made a brief speech of exhortation to his men: 'Gentlemen, this is a day we have long wished to see. Yonder stands MacChailein Mor for King George. Here stands Maclean for King James. Gentlemen, charge.'[4]

In the 1745 Jacobite rising the Macleans played a conspicuous part. Sir John's son Hector of Duart, the 5th baronet (created Lord Maclean in the Jacobite peerage), was a driving force until his imprisonment in Edinburgh castle. Of all the Scottish chiefs whom he saw in Paris before the launch of his great adventure, it was Sir Hector Maclean who most impressed Prince Charlie; indeed, the Prince's original intention had been to land on the island of Mull, until Hector's unlucky capture by the English forced him to change his plans.[5]

'Though poor, I am noble', runs an old Maclean saying, particularly relevant to Fitzroy whose father, as a cadet member of the clan, was not in line for any great inheritance. But Charles Wilberforce Maclean did establish impeccable credentials as a war hero by winning the DSO. Born in 1875, he was in the same year at Sandhurst as Winston Churchill, and both cadets passed out very near the bottom of the list. When Charles Maclean obtained his commission, Winston Churchill was the first of his friends to write to him. 'Many congratulations', he wrote, 'on becoming an officer and a gentleman. Don't let the double promotion go to your head.' Charles was soon seconded from his regiment, the Cameron Highlanders, to service with the Egyptian government. During hostilities in Sierra Leone in the 1890s he took a bullet through the mouth – or, rather, not so much a bullet as a slug from an old-fashioned 'Brown Bess'. The wound troubled him, but the slug eventually fell out during a polo game. In 1898 he was at Fashoda with Kitchener, facing down the French in one of the famous flashpoints of the 'scramble for Africa'.

After his service with the Egyptian government, Charles returned to the Cameron Highlanders. He was in the trenches in France early in the First World War and was badly wounded in the leg. For eight years he was in continual pain and for the rest of his life suffered poor health. From France he was transferred to the Western Desert – to the very area where his son was to win laurels twenty-five years later. Charles Maclean commanded a detachment sent to Siwa oasis to raise the desert tribes against the Turks, who had landed in Libya. In 1942 Fitzroy and the SAS penetrated to Siwa oasis, and found not only the tracks of that detachment's vehicles still in the sand, but the remains of their rusty bully-beef cans. Nobody had been there in the intervening years. Fitzroy remembers: 'My father had often told me when I was a boy about a Greek temple at Siwa with a spring that fed a bathing pool. In 1942 I swam in the same pool he had swum in twenty-five years earlier.'[6] For his desert exploits Major Charles Maclean was awarded the DSO, and he went on to accompany Allenby in the liberation of Jerusalem in 1918.

Fitzroy's mother was born Gladys Royle. Her father had been a career sailor in his early life, serving on the China station in the 1850s and 1860s. A talented amateur draughtsman, he sketched some memorable scenes of action between Royal Navy gunboats and armed Chinese junks. When he was over forty he retired from the Royal Navy and trained as a barrister. In this capacity he fought and won a lawsuit concerning claims by the firm of Lambert Brothers in connection with the newly constructed Suez Canal. He then entered the permanent service of Lambert Brothers in Egypt, where he met his future wife, and set up house. It was there, in 1882, that Gladys was born; and it was there, in the first decade of the twentieth century, that Major Maclean met and married her.

Fitzroy, their son, was conceived in Inverness, born in Egypt in 1911, spent his first two years in Scotland, his next two in India, and his youth from the age of eight in Italy. Such a rootless childhood (resembling that of Sir Richard Burton) was always likely to produce a lover of the exotic, a globetrotter. Yet this particular 'Magian rover', to use Herman Melville's phrase, also had countervailing impulses towards stability and tradition, and these clearly distinguish him from the great nineteenth-century travellers with whom he is often compared. From birth he was enmeshed in clan loyalties and hereditary attachments. Even his given name was significant. Fitzroy was a traditional Maclean name: Sir Fitzroy Maclean, 10th baronet of Duart and a centenarian, had as a Hussar colonel ridden with the Light Brigade in the Crimean War. Scotland and the Army were crucial in forging Fitzroy's public persona.

Fitzroy was brought up an adored boy in luxurious upper-class surroundings: in contrast to Tito, the man with whom he will always be linked historically, reared in dire poverty as the seventh of fifteen children, eight of whom died in infancy. Fitzroy was brought up in an atmosphere of great affection but, he claims, with a measure of discipline. When he refused to eat his egg 'because it had a bone in it' his nanny stood no nonsense.[7] Being a spoiled only child is likely to produce egocentricity, of which Fitzroy has often been accused, but it also engenders the feeling that anything is possible, that no doors are closed. In the late 1980s Dennis Healey remarked to Fitzroy that the most important thing in life is to get yourself a really good father and mother. Fitzroy certainly achieved that. 'I had the most idyllic childhood,' he says, and it seems to be entirely true. His wife Veronica comments: 'Fitz is basically a simple character in that he thought his parents were wonderful – which they were – but that's unusual. Even if his parents had been less than perfect, I doubt if Fitz would have noticed. He's very uncritical of people, rarely unkind.'[8]

Christian Hesketh remembers Fitzroy's mother as a *maîtresse femme*, who seemed forbidding, elegant in black and extremely houseproud. Fitzroy's stepdaughter Suki Paravicini paints a more sympathetic portrait: 'She was blonde as a girl and very tall, though never fat. She was statuesque, not exactly beautiful in a modern way, but she had a lovely open face and a very well-defined nose and mouth, wide-apart eyes and magnificent hair. She never made one feel she was old, as she had this incredible bearing and used to stand up beautifully straight. When she came to stay she was always very nice to me and I used to chat to her at her dressing table with lovely silver brushes as she plaited her terribly long silver-blonde hair.'[9] Fitzroy's wife adds: 'She was a wonderful woman, very stiff and shy at first meeting but with a great sense of humour. She was cosmopolitan and there was nothing she didn't know about human nature. She would cap one's lurid stories and was immensely generous. Of course, her only son was the apple of her eye.'[10]

It was from his mother that Fitzroy imbibed his love of languages. 'As there were lots of servants in those days, my mother spent all her time educating me.'[11] She taught him French at an early age and used to read to him from French children's books, to the point where he remembers French nursery classics better than the English ones. She also influenced his taste, steering him away from Sir Walter Scott – the usual diet for a Highlander – to more exotic fare. Although Fitzroy remembers being given Stevenson's *Treasure Island* for his sixth birthday, reading Bulldog Drummond during his first school holidays and later tackling John Buchan's thrillers, his early reading had a distinctly intellectual tinge. 'From a very early age I was reading lots of French and German, and some of the authors are ones I still return to, such as Anatole France and Thomas Mann. Later, in English, I enjoyed Aldous Huxley and Lytton Strachey, and as a classical scholar I was influenced by Thucydides. I don't know that any of these books had a deep effect on my character but they all served as models of English style, as did P.G. Wodehouse, and Evelyn Waugh, whom I later knew.'[12]

The stability provided by his mother was important, for in Fitzroy's early years the family were frequently on the move. Born in Egypt, he was back in Inverness at six weeks. In 1913 his father was posted to India. Fitzroy has vague memories of his eighteen months in Poona: riding a pony, nearly dying of dysentery. The outbreak of the First World War brought the Cameron Highlanders back to Europe post-haste. Fitzroy remembers the troop-ship, where all the children played together on deck, offspring of officers and sergeants alike. Once into the Mediterranean, the ship was chased by the German cruisers *Goerben* and *Breslau*, part of a challenge to British supremacy in the Mediterranean mounted with Turkish help.

Two impressions of Gibraltar etched themselves on the mind of the little boy, now three and a half. First there was a line of terribly mauled battleships at anchor, survivors of the Battle of the Falklands. Then came news that virtually the entire 1st Battalion of the Cameron Highlanders had been wiped out in the early trench warfare in France. This was a terrible blow to Fitzroy's parents, as many of their best friends had perished.

The troop-ship carrying the 2nd Battalion put in at Southampton early in autumn 1914. Fitzroy's father was ordered up to Winchester and it was from the windows of the George Hotel there that Fitzroy remembers seeing the Camerons, following a review by George V and Lord Kitchener, march down the High Street on their way to the

Western Front. Fitzroy's maternal grandmother took a house near Bournemouth during the war and the family lived there while Major Maclean was at the front. The smell of his father's Army greatcoat and musty goatskin hat conjure up for Fitzroy a Proustian recall of his father's rare leaves from France; he remembers, too, the talk of death that pervaded the household, especially his mother and grandmother discussing the drowning of Lord Kitchener.

Although his father finished the war crippled, he was lucky to have survived at all. His doctors prescribed a hot climate to minimize the effects of his wound, and Major Maclean decided that on his army pension the family could enjoy the best standard of living in Italy. At the age of eight Fitzroy travelled out to Florence with his maternal grandmother. They were in Paris on 11 November 1919, the anniversary of Armistice Day, and went to church at the Madeleine. His grandmother told him that she had been in Paris through the Franco-Prussian war and the Paris Commune; she pointed out where machine-gun fire had chipped the columns of the Madeleine during the suppression of the Communards.

Between the wars Fitzroy's father was honorary consul in Florence. At first the family lived in the Villa Passerini in the village of Arcetri, rented from the father of Harold Acton, with whom Fitzroy sometimes went to children's parties. Then in 1924 they bought their own house, the Villa Arrighetti near the Torre al Gallo. Except for fleeting visits, Fitzroy saw nothing in the 1920s of the land of his forefathers.

From the age of eight Fitzroy lived between two worlds: term time as a boarder at Heatherdown preparatory school in Ascot, with holidays in Italy, imbibing the culture, speaking the language. His inbuilt sense of hierarchy may derive partly from his early life in this highly stratified society, but Fitzroy is adamant that the influence of the Army was paramount and profound.

> I always wanted to be a soldier. My nanny was the wife of a sergeant in the Camerons. During the war she and my mother both had husbands fighting and they were very close. All my toys were guns – I even had a toy battleship. Also, in a way, the regiment carried on the traditions of the clans. All that, for a five-, six-, seven-year-old, was enormously important. All the early photographs of me show me dressed up as a soldier. It seemed both obvious and predetermined that I should follow in my father's and grandfather's footsteps. But my mother could not bear the idea that her son might suffer the same fate as his father – in virtually constant pain to the end of his life – so she very firmly pushed me in the direction of the Diplomatic Service. Also, my father said it was not much fun being a soldier in peacetime. Soon I found I liked the idea of being a diplomat. At some stage I read books like *Some People* by Harold Nicolson and I thought it sounded great fun, which it was.[13]

Fitzroy was perhaps catapulted too soon into the adult world, for he remembers that from a very early age he was included in family discussions. 'I always tried to stay awake until my mother and father came to bed, when I would nip out of my room and say, "Here I am" – the last thing they wanted to see.' Although his father, mother and grandmother were all very tall, Fitzroy did not begin to shoot up towards his height of 6 ft 4 in until his late teens. That Fitzroy came, uniquely, to combine the macho warrior and ladies' man was perhaps because, unusually, he had intensely loving feelings towards *both* parents. 'My father was a very strong influence. I had enormous admiration for him in all ways, as man and soldier. To my mother I was a grateful, devoted and admiring son. I was always very much concerned about what they would both think of me.'[14] In these early years were laid the foundations for the unity of thought and action he was later to achieve as 'warrior-cardinal' (to use Harold Macmillan's phrase). From his mother he took a love of languages and an interest in the diplomatic corps; from his father he derived an ambition to be a war hero, despite the suffering he could see it might involve. Suki Paravicini, who saw the effects of the war wound on Major Maclean later, testifies: 'Fitzroy's father was a very gentle, sweet man, smaller than his wife partly because of the wound in his leg. Almost certainly in the modern era he would have had the hip operation. He had one leg that went out in a curve, which fascinated us as children. He limped and walked with a stick but never complained.'[15]

Such was the snobbery at Heatherdown school that pupils were discouraged from putting in for an Eton scholarship, lest it should seem that they needed the money; consequently, Fitzroy entered Eton as an Oppidan rather than a Scholar. But he had no real quarrel with Heatherdown as a preparation for public school: both his sons went there before Eton.

Fitzroy was at Eton from 30 April 1924 until July 1929. The 'house' system obtains there, and Fitzroy opted for Crace's. John Foster Crace was then 47 years old and a classics teacher who had been at Eton since 1901 and a housemaster for just a year when Fitzroy arrived; he was a reticent, reserved and inhibited bachelor with a reputation for being overfond of some of the boys.[16] As a classicist he sided with Athens against Sparta, hated games, and as a boy himself at Eton lived like a hermit. But he was very musical and ventured out of his shell sufficiently to produce Shakespeare's plays at the school. Though a good teacher, he was not very successful as a housemaster: the *Eton Chronicle* summed up his failings in its 1960 obituary: 'The crudities of lower boys and *l'homme moyen sensuel* at any age were always something of a mystery to him.'[17]

Fitzroy, however, got on well enough with Crace and, more generally, enjoyed Eton, which he found a very good preparation for life.

When he became a private in the Cameron Highlanders he was struck by how much better prepared for 'roughing it' he was than the superficially tougher Gorbals kids. 'There was lots of unfair beating at Eton, but delivered by the boys rather than the masters. One of my sons got an official flogging, but I was never flogged by the Head. Once or twice I was beaten by the other boys, but this was a good preparation for life, which is often unfair. There were quite a lot of potentially criminal elements, but also good intellectual company, and you were left to yourself quite a lot.'[18]

Eton specialises also in the development of 'effortless superiority'. Lord Soames, sometime ambassador in Paris and governor of pre-independence Rhodesia, said: 'I think that Eton in particular dispenses a certain *savoir-faire* in the world which no other school, in my opinion, not even one of the other "sacred nine" [Eton, Harrow, Winchester, St Paul's, Shrewsbury, Westminster, Merchant Taylors, Rugby and Charterhouse] can teach . . . Not so much *savoir-faire* as *savoir-vivre* – a unique grace in relations one has with other people. I think it is Eton's secret. I don't know how it is done but it is done.'[19]

Fitzroy's parents left him free to decide on his specialization. John Lawrence, three years older than Fitzroy but whose brother George was an exact contemporary, remembers Fitzroy as very artistic, with a penchant for old prints and books.[20] Fitzroy himself remembers hundreds of his contemporaries, including Randolph Churchill. 'My first memory of Randolph is of coming into a room at Eton and seeing an excited small boy with golden hair and shining eyes leaning over a bewildered master's desk and arguing with him – arguing, clearly, for the sake of arguing, and arguing with no holds barred.'[21]

Fitzroy worked hard and at this stage was interested in the military, as Eton's was the only cadet force whose regiment had seen action, in the Boer War. In evidence very early was a talent for what would now be called lateral thinking. He combed the Eton Calendar to find obscure prizes for essays on Italian art or Renaissance culture, which he would then win by default, as no one else knew of their existence. He also performed extremely well in the 'public' prizes. He showed distinct academic promise very early, with a flair for modern languages. A string of prizes fell to him: the Lower Boy French Prize in December 1924, the Duke of Newcastle's Italian Prize in March 1926, the King's French and German Prize in 1927, plus a succession of 'firsts' in the Holiday Task Prize competitions. In the summer of 1928 he scooped the Reynolds Scholarship in an examination called the 'Grand July'. Two hundred pounds' worth of books – a substantial prize in 1928 – was given to whoever scored the highest mark in the July 'trials'. The most distinguished scholar in Eton at the time was A. J. Ayer, who felt that he had the measure of his fellow scholars and looked forward confidently to winning. But from the despised 'Oppidans' came Fitzroy to pip him at the post: 'a studious Oppidan and a specialist in modern languages', as Ayer later somewhat ungraciously remembered his rival.[22] Certainly there was an irony in that the most abstract-minded of men should have been overhauled by one of the least so minded; indeed, their penchant for women apart, it is difficult to think of anyone more remote in sensibility from Fitzroy than the future Wykeham Professor of Logic at Oxford.

The *Eton Chronicle* recorded Fitzroy's academic progress through the school with admiration. Reviewing the academic year 1927 to 1928, it declared: 'At least one remarkable performance deserves to be mentioned. Fitzroy Maclean apparently won all the prizes for which he was allowed to compete.'[23] He wound up 1928 by winning a scholarship in Modern Languages to King's College, Cambridge, the natural berth for academically distinguished Etonians. Living in Florence had enabled him to hone his Italian. As for French, he knew it well as a child, though he cannot remember learning it other than by osmosis: his mother spoke excellent French and conversed with him in the language, as well as seeing to it that he had French governesses. At Eton he had made great strides in German.

Although Eton's official records give the date of Fitzroy's departure as July 1929 – the end of the academic year – in fact he left the school as soon as he had won his scholarship. Here John Foster Crace must be allowed some influence. Like all classical scholars, Crace was convinced that his discipline alone was a test of the 'first-class mind'. Somewhat snobbishly he remarked to Fitzroy that the trouble with modern languages was that any waiter could speak them, and that a First in classics alone was the measure of true intellectual calibre. Stung, Fitzroy decided to enter for Part One of the Classical Tripos at Cambridge, and put himself through a crash course of Latin and Greek at Marburg University in Germany. From January to September 1929 he did Latin and Greek proses and unseens into and out of German – a linguistic feat which enabled him to land a First in his Classical Tripos in 1931, and put paid to Crace's sneers.

Veronica Maclean is illuminating on her husband's time at Marburg. 'His parents were wonderfully trusting in that they left educational decisions to him. After he got his scholarship to King's, he could have stayed on and got all the relaxed glory of the final year at Eton. But Fitz wanted to go to Germany, so to Germany he went.'[24] Fitzroy himself adds: 'I organized the whole thing myself, booked the tickets, found myself lodgings. My German became very good indeed . . . I wasn't just a foreigner learning German, but was on the full course, doing classics. In those days it was traditional for German students to go to two or three different universities, not just one. Most of the foreign students were Swedes, there were no British or Americans. T. S. Eliot had done the same thing I was doing.'[25]

Fitzroy loved Marburg so much that he returned from Cambridge every long vacation, and still goes back to this day. His attitude to Germany, coloured by his own wartime experiences and those of his father in the First World War, can be summed up by saying that he hates the sin yet loves the sinner. He agrees with Thomas Mann that there was something in the German personality that made Hitlerism almost inevitable, given the disastrous Treaty of Versailles.

> I have no doubt that if it hadn't been Hitler it would have been someone else – von Papen, Hindenburg or one of the other right-wing people. The threat of Germany was something I was very much brought up on. My mother's favourite uncle and her favourite cousin were both killed and my father made a cripple for the rest of his life, so she didn't love Germans. When she started teaching me German, she told me how awful they were, but what a lovely language. So I was very conscious of the dark side, despite the blonde blue-eyed girls and the jolly drinking in the *bierkellers*. I also sensed the German limitations. They always had a slight sort of inferiority complex towards the outer world in general and perhaps especially the French. The French are maddening in many ways, but they do have a terrific intellectual quality.[26]

After nine months in Marburg, Fitzroy found Cambridge rather a disappointment. 'In Marburg one was treated much more as a grown-up and was much freer to work as one liked . . . To that extent, I found Cambridge rather like going back to school.' But he worked hard and had very little social life, his sole relaxation riding and going out with the Cambridgeshire hunt.

Fitzroy also disliked Cambridge's leftist political orientation. This was the era of Burgess, Philby and Blunt, and what Fitzroy calls 'a silly and shallow left-wing tendency', when his fellow-students were 'woolly-minded and earnestly progressive'.[27] He reacted to it in his usual 'spirit of contradiction'. Though a conservative in all matters and a member of the Establishment since his twenties, Fitzroy has often swum against the tide of orthodoxy.

In his third year Fitzroy switched to History and achieved a Second in Part Two of his Tripos. His first thought was to return to Marburg – graduates of Oxford and Cambridge commonly went abroad for further study in those days. Fitzroy went through the formal matriculation procedures, intending to pursue a doctorate in either Greek or History. While deciding on a subject for a thesis, he found lodgings and set about recording his impressions of Germany four years after his first visit.

As Fitzroy covered the countryside on the long walks that became a lifetime habit, he was forever coming on groups of earnest German youths with wooden rifles: a portent of things to come, as were the gliding classes – obviously the Nazis' surreptitious way of training fighter pilots. In January 1933, Hitler came to power. 'When I first went to Germany, in 1929, nobody was concerned about Hitler – they all thought he was a joke. But by 1933 it was quite clear to me that a war was coming, which cast quite a blight on things. What was extraordinary was that the people who had said in 1929 or even in 1932 that Hitler was a joke were in 1933 suddenly all appearing in Party gear.'[28]

Even less a joke was the reaction of the Jewish professors at Marburg. Two committed suicide by lying on the railway track. 'Professor Friedlander, with a good Iron Cross in the First War, suddenly found himself surviving only because he was made an honorary Aryan.'[29] The rise of the Nazis increased Fitzroy's conviction that political ideologies and systems of abstract thought always have baneful results, and he is fond of quoting Hans Castorp in Thomas Mann's *Magic Mountain* to that effect. What Nazism did reinforce was his growing belief in *realpolitik*: 'People have sometimes accused me of going where the power is, but *realpolitik* is what politics is all about. I admire Bismarck and Machiavelli for their realism in this regard. I was a child in Italy when Mussolini came to power, a student in Hitler's Germany, and my second posting was in the Soviet Union. All these are examples of what power is. If you leave that out of account, you'll live in a dream world.'[30]

The rise of the Nazis led Fitzroy to feel that he should abandon his idea of an academic career. In the autumn of 1933 he entered instead the stiffly competitive examinations for the Diplomatic Service. In the written examinations he swept the board, and in the French and German papers scored 97 per cent – the highest marks ever recorded for a would-be entrant. But his spectacular showing went before a fall in the interviews, where he managed to drop 40 or 50 marks. He was ill-prepared for rough treatment at the hands of Lady Violet Bonham-Carter. Given that the balance of power in Europe depended on equilibrium between France and Germany, Lady Violet shot at him, which side was he on at the present juncture? Fitzroy replied that, on the basis of what he had just seen in Germany, and the likelihood of another war, he would have to opt for France. Lady Violet bridled. 'You hold very reactionary views, Mr Macleen,' she said, adding insult to injury by mispronouncing his name. Thereafter it was downhill all the way.

There was a further revelation in store. Fitzroy was a member of Brooks's Club and repaired there for lunch. He found himself sitting next to one of the examiners, who had no idea that he was a candidate. The examiner explained to a neighbour that he had spent all morning interviewing young men and it was all he could do to focus his attention to distinguish between the 'brown ones' (applicants for the Indian Civil Service) and the 'white ones' (Home and Diplomatic Service). Fitzroy remembers: 'I thought, you bastard, you might have just wrecked my life.'[31]

However, he had been accepted. Even better, he had been requested by the head of the Consular department, David Montagu Douglas-Scott, a friend of his father's from the First World War. Scott was one of those curious mandarins – Orme Sargent was another – who never served abroad; in the days of the old Diplomatic Service not a single FO official could be sent abroad without his consent. In the 1930s the Service was also a very small circle, only about 250 people at home and abroad, all of whom knew each other. After five or six years a newcomer was on first-name terms with everyone in the Service, regardless of age or rank. 'It was a very happy, united family, and all my friends were anti-German and anti-appeasement later on: Cranborne [Lord Salisbury], Duff Cooper, Orme Sargent.'

The diplomatic service had a profound influence on Fitzroy, and he admits that the effects remain with him to this day. 'We were trained to be precisians and to have a reverence for accuracy. Nowadays people are not meticulous and don't try to get it right the way we used to. Nowadays I expect people to get facts and figures wrong. Also, my life as a diplomat made me like working with the Establishment and its rules. The rules go very deep. It always amuses me that on the very day Donald Maclean bolted with Burgess, before he wrote explaining his motives, he cleared his in-tray and out-tray and left everything neat and tidy. The diplomatic training had left its mark!'[32]

Fitzroy spent just under a year in the Consular department. He confesses that he felt very happy and delighted with himself. After about six months' service he had received a circular asking where he would like to be posted. Thinking there was no chance of such a posting, he wrote 'Paris'. Most of the other recruits reckoned it was more politic not to reveal their ambition, so opted for postings to Outer Mongolia or Bolivia. The next thing Fitzroy knew was that his first tour of duty was to be in the British Embassy in Paris.

2

Paris

1934–1937

———

IN *Eastern Approaches* Fitzroy recalls three distinct memories of these years in Paris. The images can stand for three aspects of the man himself. The first sums up the fun-loving Fitzroy, though he is careful to stress that champagne was only part of the story. 'Though I have had a lot of fun out of life (and still do), I would sooner not appear too much of a Hooray Henry!' The second shows the serious young diplomat and potential academic. Fitzroy is not a typical intellectual – he is far too impatient of abstract ideas – but he is erudite, widely-read and deeply serious, though a puckish sense of humour sometimes disguises this. The third, I think, breathes the spirit of the man of action.

All the different lights and colours and smells and noises of Paris at night. Big official dinner parties, with white ties and decorations. Small private dinner parties, with black ties and that particular type of general conversation at which the French excel. The best-dressed women, the best food, the best wine, the best brandy in the world. Parties in restaurants. Parties in night-clubs. The Théâtre de Dix Heures; the chansonniers; jokes about politics and sex. The Bal Tabarin; the rattle and bang of the can-can; the plump thighs of the dancers in their long black silk stockings. Week after week; month after month. An agreeable existence, but one that, if prolonged unduly, seemed bound to lead to chronic liver trouble, if to nothing worse.

There was the broad sweep of the Champs Elysées and the Avenue du Bois; the magnificence of the Place Vendôme and the Place de la Concorde; the grey stone of the buildings gilded by the sunlight; the green of the trees; the life and noise of the streets less overwhelming, more intimate than the roar of the London traffic. There were those pleasant walks on summer evenings along the banks of the Seine, under the trees, to the Ile de la Cité; friends' houses with their cool panelled rooms; the lights reflected in the river, as one went home by night.

And then there was the enjoyable sensation of being permanently at the centre of things. Something was always happening; somebody was always arriving or leaving. We lived in an atmosphere of continual crisis. It might be

Mr Ramsay MacDonald and Sir John Simon, looking a little shaken after a rough crossing, on their way to talk things over with Signor Mussolini at Stresa; or Sir Samuel Hoare, always so neat and tidy, come to see Monsieur Laval, intelligent, olive-skinned and leering, with his discoloured teeth and crumpled white tie; or Mr and Mrs Baldwin, hurrying home from Aix-les-Bains, the serenity of their summer holiday disturbed by talk of sanctions and the threat of war; or Mr Eden, travelling backwards and forwards to Geneva; or Mr Churchill, then a private Member of Parliament, unfashionably preoccupied with questions of defence, come to talk to the French soldiers about their eastern frontier.

Another memory from those days is of a vast crowd, many thousands strong, sweeping along towards the Place de la Bastille on July 14th. Above it waves a forest of red flags with here and there an isolated tricolor, and, borne aloft on the shoulders of the crowd, immense portraits of Stalin, brooding over the proceedings with benign malignity, and the French Communist leaders; Maurice Thorez, square and bloated-looking who, when war came, was to run away to Moscow; Gabriel Peri, the frail intellectual who was to become a resistance leader and be tortured to death in a Gestapo prison; Jacques Duclos, spectacled and cunning; André Marty, the mutineer of the Black Sea fleet; Marcel Cachin, who had become the Grand Old Man of French Communism. Out in front a tall, pale girl in a red shirt strides along, her black hair streaming out behind her. From time to time sections of the crowd start to sing and the lugubrious strains of the 'Internationale' rise and fall above the tumult. Then as the singing dies away, there is a shrill cry of 'Les Soviets!' and thousands of hoarse voices take up the rhythmic refrain, 'LES SOV-I-ETS PAR-TOUT, LES SOV-I-ETS PAR-TOUT'.[1]

Ah, but what of Fitzroy the lover of women? A sentence in his *Take Nine Spies* is significant. He quotes Miyake Kanako, mistress of the master-spy Victor Sorge, as saying: 'Isn't it natural for a famous man to have several mistresses?' 'There's always been a female interest,' he admits, 'but in those days there wasn't this idea of having a steady live-in.' Fitzroy is reticent. Apart from his patrician disdain of 'kiss and tell', many are still alive who might object to intimate revelations.

France was in deep social and economic crisis when the 23-year-old Fitzroy arrived in Paris. As Third Secretary it was his principal job to compile intelligence digests on internal affairs. From the very start he was pitchforked into the inferno. In an amazingly short time he built up a list of impressive contacts. Almost his first luncheon engagement was with the outstanding journalist Alexander Werth and other members of the press corps. They nursed him through the first few months. He could soon distinguish a Laval from an Herrier at a hundred paces. The French politicians, for their part, were delighted to have links with the British embassy. Dinner invitations piled up. The *éminences* of the Chambre des Députés confided their hopes and fears to the young man, who wrote up the latest gossip for his reports. Among the Communists Fitzroy targeted were Gabriel Peri Marcel Cachin and Maurice Thorez. Another eminent political contact was Paul Reynaud, later premier, once closeted with Fitzroy for three hours over a champagne lunch on a train journey.

Also invaluable was Sir Charles Mendl. Scion of an old Jewish corn-merchant family, Mendl had been in France during the First World War and drifted into Paris journalism. He then got a job at the British Embassy as Press Attaché under Lord Derby, a position which was eventually transformed into the grand-sounding *Conseiller Spécial*. From 1926 to 1940 Mendl briefed each incoming ambassador on who was who on the French political scene. As he was permanently based in Paris, while an ambassador served a tour of three years on average, he was the British diplomatic anchor. He also produced a weekly in-house bulletin called 'Charles's Comic Cuts', full of political scandal and gossip, but accurate.

Mendl was wealthy in his own right and married to the American designer Elsie de Wolff, who had made a fortune in New York as an interior decorator. Fitzroy remembers her as 'small, curious but glamorous, with blue-rinsed hair and the latest fashions'. The Mendls had a house in Versailles where they entertained lavishly. Typical guests might include Maurice de Rothschild, the Bibescos, the Windsors (after 1936: Elsie scandalized diplomatic circles by curtseying to the Duchess of Windsor after the abdication), and also unsavoury denizens of café society, whom Fitzroy refers to as 'international white trash'. Elsie had a glamorous flat in the Avenue d'Iéna, where she entertained separately. Charles did likewise, in what would nowadays be called a 'love-nest' not far from the Embassy, away from Elsie's inquisitive eye. Here he used to give informal lunches twice or three times a week. He would invite a couple of people from the Embassy, then throw in three or four French politicians or journalists and complete the mixture with four or five of the prettiest women in Paris – without their husbands, of course. The food served at these lunches was always the same: haddock soufflée and white wine, followed by shepherd's pie with claret and burgundy. Mendl worked on the theory that the bouquet of the finest wines was enhanced by the plainest of food. After two hours of cuisine and conversation, Fitzroy would be back at his desk by 3.30 in the afternoon. 'One heard more here of what was going on than at a dozen formal gatherings. It was an enormous education in all kinds of ways.'[2] The Mendls were based in Paris until its fall in 1940, after which they retired to Hollywood, where Evelyn Waugh encountered them in 1947.[3]

If Fitzroy quickly made his mark with the key man *de facto* in the Embassy, his early relations with the *de jure* incumbent were uneasy. Sir George Clerk was an unusual choice for ambassador. It was common

Diplomatic Service gossip that he had hated the French ever since the Fashoda crisis in 1898, when as a 24-year-old resident clerk he received a cable falsely announcing the sailing of a French invasion fleet from Brest towards the English coast. A career diplomat of the old school, Clerk had been disappointed with his progress before the surprise Paris posting. He had been Lord Curzon's private secretary, then ambassador in Istanbul. His appointment to the embassy at Brussels seemed to herald the end of a not very distinguished progression, but then he had a stroke of luck. The ambassador in Paris, Lord Tyrell, was taken seriously ill and the FO found itself without an obvious replacement. Shunting Clerk over from Brussels seemed the thing to do in the circumstances. He was bowled over by his luck.

Clerk used to say quite openly: 'I've got a first-class staff; they do the work and I enjoy myself.' Lady Clerk was artistic and temperamental, and effectively the couple were separated, though they kept up appearances. Clerk spent many of his days on the golf-course and his evenings in Paris's night-spots, though because of his over-correct demeanour, rumours of his forays among the fleshpots tended to be discounted. On one occasion Queen Mary read out to George V an item from a gossip column to the effect that Clerk had been seen in a Paris night-club. 'Nonsense, my dear, that's no more credible than to say *I* have been seen in a night-club!' replied the monarch.

Fitzroy got off on the wrong foot with Clerk. In those days there was a standard Diplomatic Service dress code. Secretaries were expected to appear in a white starched collar, a sober tie, sponge-bag trousers and a black homburg hat with a curled-up brim. Outside the office it was *de rigueur* to carry a tightly-rolled umbrella (the umbrella was abandoned only after 1938, when it became for younger diplomats a symbol of Chamberlain and appeasement). Many years later Fitzroy still remembered the unwritten sumptuary laws of his Paris posting. 'There were those pin-striped suits from Scholte; those blue and white shirts from Beale and Inman with their starched collars; those neat, well-cleaned shoes from Lobb; the dark red carnation from the florist in the Faubourg Saint Honoré.'[4]

Always one to trump an ace, Fitzroy noticed that Clerk wore a Homburg, a monocle and a carnation in his buttonhole. He adopted the same outfit. The result is related by Fitzroy's colleague Frank Roberts. 'Clerk took this amiss and thought Fitzroy was trying to guy him. A Junior Secretary was usually on hand to accompany the ambassador to football matches, et cetera; I was eager to pass on some of these chores to Fitzroy, but Sir George was not keen on the idea. But finally he had to go somewhere and his Homburg had gone astray. Fitzroy was on hand and was able to lend his. From that time relations between them eased.'[5]

Fitzroy describes the improved relations. 'Paris was full of beautiful

White Russian princesses and *émigré* generals. Sir George liked that sort of romantic thing very much. He was a very good-looking man. When we had to work late at the Chancery, he used to send us a magnum of champagne. He was a bit of a joke really. We used to go and play golf at one of the courses outside Paris. Then we'd have at least one bottle of champagne for lunch, then another eighteen holes, then out to dinner, and so on. This was all very glamorous, which between the ages of 23 and 27 one appreciates.'[6]

Next to Clerk in the hierarchy at the Paris embassy was the Minister, Hugh Lloyd Thomas, who later broke his neck while on a practice gallop for the Grand National, which he had intended to enter as an amateur rider. First Secretary and Head of Chancery was Oliver Harvey, who had a distinguished diplomatic career and wrote two valuable volumes of diaries. Charles Peake, later ambassador in Athens, was the Second Secretary. Peake and Harvey tended to work hand in glove, and later annoyed Clerk's successor Sir Eric Phipps by arranging Parisian press contacts for Anthony Eden without informing him or Mendl.[7] But a man with great influence on Fitzroy was the outgoing Third Secretary Frank Roberts, who was clearly going places and in fact ended his diplomatic career with the highest honours.[8] Having completed his three-year tour he had been posted to Cairo, but had a three-month hand over period in Paris in which to teach the newcomer the ropes. Born in Argentina but educated at Rugby and Cambridge, Roberts was diminutive. A keen sportsman – hockey, golf, football – he impressed Fitzroy most by his energy and his incisive mind. He blue-pencilled his trainee's draft despatches, teaching him to cut out all superfluous verbiage.

The pupil prospered under this regime. At the end of three months Roberts gave him the nod. 'You'll do. But what you have to remember is that this is the room where the real work is done. Peake, Harvey and Lloyd Thomas, they're all very good in their way, but you're the key man here.'[9] Though well satisfied with his protégé, Roberts frankly admits that he underestimated Fitzroy at the time because of his penchant for *la gaieté parisienne*. 'Nobody could have predicted Fitzroy's subsequent career and if they did, would have been laughed to scorn.'[10] Roberts, like so many, stayed in touch with the charming young Etonian and later became a close friend, as did another Third Secretary, Armine Dew, who came out to Paris in 1935 to bring the embassy up to full strength. Son of an administrator in the Indian Civil Service and distinguished by his Nordic good looks, Dew died in 1945 when the plane bringing him back from the Yalta conference was shot down over enemy territory.

One of Frank Roberts's last favours before he departed for Cairo was to introduce Fitzroy to an exclusive luncheon club. This used to meet every Wednesday in different restaurants. A *mélange* of Quai d'Orsay diplomats, journalists and businessmen, the club was a further transmission belt between the French élite and the diplomatic corps. After lunch the gourmets would send for the manager and go through the meal course by course. 'Liked the wine, hated the *hors d'oeuvres*, that sort of thing. By 3 in the afternoon one was totally sated and able to take a detached view of gastronomy. Very useful at that time to be in close touch with French yuppies.'

In Paris Fitzroy burned the candle at both ends. In the main, he did the legwork and the senior staff appended their names to documents. Only rarely did Fitzroy get the chance to sign official documents, and then it was usually because his superiors considered the subject *infra dig*.

A pattern began to take shape in Fitzroy's daily life. After breakfast he would stroll along the Champs Elysées or perhaps ride in the Bois de Boulogne. Then to the office, where he would spend the morning drafting telegrams and despatches on thick blue paper. In those days all the drafting was done by hand and Fitzroy's large, clear and elegant handwriting came into its own. Telecommunications were still in their technological infancy, so that the telephone between Paris and London was used only sparingly and for emergencies. 'Occasional visits to the Quai d'Orsay, the smell of beeswax in the passages; the rather fusty smell of the cluttered, steam-heated offices; *comment allez-vous, cher collègue?*'[11] After an extended break for luncheon, there was more drafting until six in the evening, then a bath and a drink took one to dinner-time.

Although Fitzroy refers offhandedly to the Quai d'Orsay, and remembers Clerk as popular with the French and the British Embassy as a social magnet for *le tout Paris*, there was a deal of anti-British prejudice to overcome, both in the French Foreign Ministry and elsewhere. There were many Anglophiles among French diplomats, like Alexis Léger, but others, such as René Massigli, the conference director at the Quai d'Orsay, were defeatist and would go to any lengths to avoid irritating the dictators. Roughly speaking, Establishment France could be divided into a pro-British half and a pro-Italian half. The alliance with Britain was nominally accepted by everybody, but there was great dislike for England, especially on the Right. Henri Berant's vitriolic attack during the Abyssinian crisis is typical of the sort of thing the British Embassy had to combat: 'England must be reduced to slavery . . . I hate England by instinct and tradition.'[12]

The British Embassy in the 1930s consisted of the Residence, formerly the palace of Princesse (Pauline) Borghese, plus the Chancery, set to the side of the entrance gate. The Minister's office was downstairs, while the Secretaries were on the first floor, looking out onto the extremely noisy rue de Provence. On the top floor was the Commercial

Counsellor. The Military and Naval Attachés were housed across the
street in a modern building; the consulate and the alleged Passport
Control Office were located elsewhere. It took Fitzroy just twenty minutes to walk home: from the Place de la Concorde across the Pont de
Concorde to his flat at 5, Place du Palais Bourbon. Here he had rented
from an English woman, Kay Norton, a most magnificent apartment
– way beyond the means of the average Third Secretary. The Mount-
battens had stayed there and Douglas Fairbanks, Sr had been a tenant.
The apartment was in a beautiful eighteenth-century house, but the
interior had been modernised by one of Paris's top interior decorators;
a balcony looked out onto the gardens of the Ministry of War. Here
the 23-year-old Fitzroy began to give glittering dinner parties, like the
Mendls'.

What with the Wednesday lunch club, Sir Charles Mendl's gatherings and his own soirées, Fitzroy's circle of social contacts became
ever wider. A new avenue was opened up at the end of 1934. On New
Year's Day 1935 Sir George Clerk threw a luncheon party for all members of the British mission in Paris. 'That meant everybody, typists, the
man who took the bag to Calais, everyone.' They all sat down in the
great state dining-room in the Residence. The table seated sixty, but in
1935 the total staff came to less than that (nowadays, it is upwards of six
hundred). Fitzroy found himself next to a dazzling, lavishly-dressed
American blonde. Since he had met only the Diplomatic Service personnel hitherto, he asked her what she did. She replied that her husband
was a clerk in the Passport Control Office. 'I was so innocent then, I
didn't know what that meant.'[13] His companion introduced him to her
husband and the couple invited him to dinner a week later. June
Dunderdale, *née* Morse, had been a *vendeuse* at Malbêche and was the
grand-daughter of the inventor of the Morse code; her husband was
Commander Wilfred Dunderdale.

Dinner proved an eye-opener for the young diplomat. The Dunderdales lived in a magnificent first-floor flat near the Eiffel tower, with a
vast marble entrance hall. Twenty-four people sat down to dinner,
and champagne flowed. After dinner Dunderdale took his guests to
a night-club run by an *émigré* Czarist general. The general greeted
Dunderdale effusively. 'This is my friend Maclean,' said Dunderdale.
'He must have free champagne whenever he comes in here.'[14] The
party stayed in the night-club until dawn. Then Dunderdale suggested
a boat trip down the Seine. Fitzroy thought he meant a *bateau mouche*,
but when they arrived at the Seine, there was a private cruiser, all
mahogany and brass. The company was piped aboard in great style.
'More champagne, with dawn coming up – I thought, I'm really seeing
life.'

Stumbling, bleary-eyed, into his office, Fitzroy encountered the military attaché, related his adventures and speculated how a mere clerk could afford such a life-style. The attaché laughed. 'Don't you know what the Passport Control Office is? Standard euphemism for SIS.'

Since Fitzroy has sometimes been identified as Ian Fleming's model for James Bond, it is interesting to recount his meeting with the man who really was. Dunderdale was a spy who had joined the Secret Intelligence Service from Naval Intelligence in Constantinople in 1924. From 1925 to 1939 he was SIS representative in Paris. He boasted that he had never assassinated anybody (unlike Bond); on the one occasion he had been asked to 'terminate' a man by pushing him into the Channel from the boat train, his victim failed to show.[15] Fitzroy could never work out how much of the Dunderdale life-style was financed from private income and how much from the Secret Service account, but he was fascinated by the couple and flattered to be included in their inner circle. Dunderdale, it turned out, had been born in Odessa of British parents and spoke Russian like a native. Hardly surprisingly, most of his contacts in Paris were White Russians, and it was thus Fitzroy was first introduced to the Slav charm that yielded such a rich harvest later. It has been said that the glamorous June was an even bigger asset to the British Secret Service than Dunderdale himself. It saddened Fitzroy when the marriage broke up after the war.

Third Secretaries had to meet visiting dignitaries at the station, and feed them in the Residence. Many such men passed through Paris on their way to the League of Nations in Geneva, and Fitzroy early came to know all the leading figures in British political life. One of the first was Winston Churchill, destined to be a key figure in Fitzroy's life. Churchill, in Paris to consult with the French chiefs of staff, was being put up by Clerk in the Residence. In the Third Secretaries' room Churchill confided some of his fears for the future. Hitler's accession to power in Germany and his repudiation of the Versailles treaty made war inevitable, he thought, but neither the French nor the British government seemed capable of drawing the obvious inference. Fitzroy could clearly sense the frustration of the prophet preaching in the wilderness.[16]

He was less impressed by Stanley Baldwin, who came out on a couple of occasions during the Abyssinian crisis. Baldwin was usually in such a rush to get to Aix-les-Bains to take the waters that he could hardly be bothered to read even 'Most Secret' briefs on important issues. He would arrive in Paris at eight in the morning, and preferred to walk in the park while waiting for his connection to Aix, rather than read telegrams in the embassy.[17] Sir John Simon, however, who was Foreign Secretary in 1935 and came to Paris for talks with Laval, evoked 'great admiration'. But his visit taught Fitzroy a lesson in the value of an interpreter, even in cases where a politician spoke a foreign language fairly well. 'Simon had conversations with Laval at which I was present. He was a very good speaker, being a lawyer, and he thought he knew French very well. He insisted on having his conversation with Laval, who ran rings around him. Simon was also a language snob, but he wasn't making the right points with the right nuances to Laval. I thought it rather dangerous. Also, to retain an interpreter gives you thinking time.'[18]

Fitzroy shortly began to give signs of formidable powers of imagination and originality. One morning he did not appear at his desk and had left no message. When his excuses arrived, they bore the dateline Boulogne-sur-Seine. What had happened was this. Alexander Werth, the *Manchester Guardian* correspondent and Thomas Cadett, the Reuters stringer, had told him of their plans to report the strike at the giant Renault works in Boulogne from the inside, and invited him along. Dressed as workers, Fitzroy and his two friends slipped past the pickets at the gate. They wandered through a labyrinth of workshops converted into dormitories as the occupying comrades, male and female, bedded down for the night on the luxurious cushions of half-finished limousines. Fitzroy managed to interview the Strike Committee in the Managing Director's office, where they had made their headquarters. He found them defiant but despairing. The unreality of their surroundings affected Fitzroy as dreamlike: 'The luxuriously furnished room was draped from floor to ceiling with red flags, plentifully adorned with hammers and sickles. Against this improvised background sat the strikers' leaders, unshaven, with berets or cloth caps on their heads and cigarettes drooping from the corners of their mouths, presided over by a massively formidable woman whose deftly flicking knitting needles struck me as symbolic. From this nerve centre, as we watched, orders went out by messenger or telephone to different parts of the works.'[19]

Fitzroy points out that this episode broke no Embassy rules, nor did his later journeys in Russia. 'People nowadays usually don't realize how things were done in those days. They have the idea that you were sent for by the Head of Chancery or the Ambassador and told what to do and what not to do, and that in this case the ambassador would have been appalled if he'd heard that I'd been in the Renault factory. On the contrary, he was very glad.'[20] Sir George Clerk was indeed impressed by the energy and enterprise of his Third Secretary.

After a period of titanic class struggle, Léon Blum's Popular Front came to power in 1936. Fitzroy was sufficiently abreast of affairs to be at once stimulated by the ferment of ideas and cast down by the political divisions becoming daily more evident in France. There was nothing a foreign embassy could or should do about the internal affairs of a sovereign state, other than report events. Only in the field of foreign policy was there scope for real influence.

Moving in the reverse direction from Scott's hero, Fitzroy turned from thoughts of (civil) war to love. At a party he was introduced to more Slav charm in the shape of Iya, Lady Abdy, a White Russian, daughter of a theatrical impresario in the Czarist years. Iya had left Russia when the Bolsheviks took power, but her father stayed on and became the head of the Leningrad Theatre. Fitzroy was bowled over and his fascination was visible. A fellow diplomat reported an exchange between the ambassador and his wife. 'That new secretary spends all his time goggling at the most beautiful women in Paris,' Lady Clerk remarked, no doubt with her own husband partly in mind. 'It will do him nothing but good,' replied Clerk who, after all, should have known.[21]

All roads, whether from the Dunderdales or Iya Abdy, seemed to lead towards Russian *émigrés*. Less than twenty years after the Revolution there were hundreds of White Russians in Paris, mainly on the fringes of *la vie bohème*, driving taxis, running night-clubs and so on. From early on Fitzroy entertained especially warm feelings for the Georgians, though amusedly cynical about their aristocratic pretensions: 'before World War One about one in seven of the population of Georgia was a prince or princess!'

It was an *émigrée* Georgian princess who was the first great love of his life. For some time Fitzroy had been navigating a perilous social course between two rival *grandes dames*. One was Violet Trefusis, who ran a thriving salon in Paris. The other, her deadly enemy, was the novelist Daisy Fellowes, 'a terrific character, half grand French and half Singer Sewing Machine.'[22] One evening Daisy Fellowes took him to a party where the Georgian contingent was much in evidence. Even in such glittering company Fitzroy's eye was soon caught by the glamorous Madame Sert. As Fitzroy now recalls, it was a *coup de foudre*. The two became engrossed in conversation. When the time came to leave, Madame Sert offered him a lift to the Place du Palais Bourbon in her dark-blue Renault convertible: it turned out she lived next door to him. They agreed to meet again.

During the next few weeks, as a besotted Fitzroy courted this quintessence of Slavic charisma, Madame Sert, or Roussi, as Fitzroy quickly came to call her, revealed more details of her life. *Née* Mdivani, she had fled Russia as a teenager after the Revolution with a sister and two brothers. Some of the clan remained in Georgia and took their chances with the new regime; one, Gulyu Mdivani, even became People's Commissar. There was a persistent legend in the family that Stalin's father had been General Mdivani's cobbler. For this and because he was a general and had been an ADC to the Czar, Roussi's father was a marked man, but by 1920 he had got his brood safely to Istanbul. Roussi learned to paint and made her way to Paris, 'where all good White Russians went'.

The 18-year-old Roussi then took a giant step up the social ladder. A natural adventuress, she targeted the Spanish painter Sert – then well-known for having adorned the inside of the League of Nations building with frescos of elephants, black boys and African scenes. Seeing a stunning girl forever parading outside his house, Sert one day invited her in: though married, he scented an easy conquest. But Roussi quickly turned the tables. Somehow she inveigled him and his wife into a round-the-world cruise. When the trio returned, Roussi had displaced the former Madame Sert as the painter's wife. Curiously, the two women seemed nonetheless to be on excellent terms.

Sert rented a house in the Place du Palais Bourbon from the Moghul family. There he and Roussi established an 'open marriage'. Sert laid down certain ground rules; these apart, Roussi could go her own way. Most importantly, she had to be home every night at eight, and surround the dinner-table with bright young things, especially pretty girls. If Roussi did not return by eight, Sert promptly phoned the police.

Roussi and Fitzroy soon became intimate. She introduced him to her brothers, and it was not long before Fitzroy realized what a ruthless operator he was in love with. Roussi's principal preoccupation in life was to see her two brothers married to heiresses. Alec was the brother who made the greater impact, hitting the headlines with his marriage to Barbara Hutton. An ineffable aura of glamour enveloped Alec. His luggage alone was said to glow with the sheen of millions. He would set off on voyages with a travelling office, complete with pigeon-holes, drawers, files, writing materials and a gold-plated typewriter; his impedimenta even included a folding pigskin armchair in which to recline while writing. Someone who knew him at the time recorded: 'He was the embodiment of wealth and health and carefree youthful hedonism . . . I have never seen the like of it since. Alec Mdivani, brimming with class, had been put through Cambridge by the combined resources of his two brothers and two sisters and then financed by the same syndicate on a tour of America's haunts of the rich. The notable success of this family gamble had in no way spoilt Prince Alec, who succeeded in retaining the fresh charms of youth in spite of it.'[23]

Through the Mdivanis Fitzroy met Aly Khan and other members of their set. 'I remember giving Roussi lunch at the Paris Ritz. At the next table was Alec with a whole lot of girls. By then he had married Barbara Hutton, but was tired of her and looking out for another millionairess. Roussi ran the whole family. It was difficult to know which way to look for glamour. At the lunch was the wife of Krupp von Thyssen, the armaments millionaire, one of the most beautiful women I'd ever seen. Roussi was setting it up for Krupp's wife to elope with Alec.'[24]

But disaster was stalking the Mdivanis. One of their close friends was killed at the wheel of his car. Soon afterwards Roussi suggested that she and Fitzroy make up a foursome with Alec and Krupp's beautiful wife and drive down to a house she owned near Barcelona. But there was a crisis at the Embassy and Fitzroy could not get away. Alec and his girl went to Barcelona alone. On the way down he drove into a tree. He was killed immediately; she survived, but with one side of her face destroyed. Press headlines became sensational when it was discovered that she had been travelling with some fabulously valuable Krupp diamonds, which disappeared. The Krupps sued. As Fitzroy says, with characteristic understatement: 'It was all rather unedifying.'

The disaster gradually unhinged Roussi, by which time Fitzroy was in Russia. When he visited her in Paris in 1938 she was dying. He recalls a final, dispiriting meeting with her in the Hotel Prince de Galles. Roussi was in bed, in a bad way from drink and drugs. She had been deeply distressed by her brother's death. Other writers have suggested that Roussi was not as straightforwardly heterosexual as he had assumed. Nor was the first Madame Sert, which explained the puzzling cordiality between the two women. Here was a sentimental education with a vengeance, life far removed from the usual orbit of a young diplomat.

The Spanish Civil War in July 1936 was a major test of British nerve. If Britain were serious about facing the dictators, now was the time to act, for Hitler and Mussolini poured arms and *matériel* into Spain to support Franco. Russia's support for the Republican government was an excuse for inactivity, but Russian aid to Azaña and his beleaguered regime was, comparatively, a trickle: Stalin was already too busy with his purges to have much time for Spain.

Already scourged at the pillar of social and economic affairs, Blum's Popular Front was then presented with a Spanish crown of thorns. Blum tried to help the Republicans while heading off a general European war and a backlash at home. The French Right saw in the Spanish Civil War a golden opportunity to topple him. Blum sought help from the British. He and his Foreign Minister saw Eden, with whom Blum always enjoyed good relations, and came away encouraged. But the Baldwin government had no real intention of helping. In this they were encouraged by Charles Corbin, the French ambassador in London. Of the extreme Right and so absurdly anglophile that he was known as the 'English ambassador in London', Corbin later pretended that London never put any pressure on France over the Spanish Civil War.[25]

The reality was different. Two weeks after Blum's meeting with Eden Sir George Clerk called on the French Foreign Minister, Yvon Delbos, at the Quai d'Orsay in order to be 'more certain' about the French attitude to Spain. Clerk raised the subject of the French planes and other armaments ordered before the outbreak of hostilities by the Azaña government. Delbos replied that he had no basis in international law for refusing delivery. Clerk declared that he was far from certain the Azaña government was the legitimate government of Spain. Was it not simply a screen behind which the anarchists were operating?[26]

Clerk did not rest content with this broad hint. Next day he delivered a virtual ultimatum. If France did not ban the export of war materials to the Republicans, and if a war with Germany ensued, Britain would consider herself absolved of her obligations under the 1925 Locarno treaty to aid France.[27] This touched Blum on a raw nerve: it was his abiding nightmare (*cauchemar* was a word much on his lips during 1936 and 1937) that Baldwin might actually in the end make common cause with Germany against France. He had no choice but to capitulate. All further military aid to Spain was suspended.[28]

Although British writers and intellectuals overwhelmingly supported the Republic, the Foreign Office attitude was circumspect and officially evenhanded, but with a strong undercurrent of hostility to the Republicans; it was convenient to describe *all* Republicans as communists, and cry 'a plague on both your houses'. The British ambassador to Spain, Sir Henry Chilton, an unimaginative diplomat of the old school, set up his embassy in a grocer's shop at Hendaye, on the French side of the International Bridge. The French Minister in Spain, Jean Herbette, refused to reside at Madrid, and set up his quarters in San Sebastian and San Juan de Luz. Since these were almost immediately occupied by Franco's forces, he was really ambassador to Franco rather than to Madrid.

The Foreign Office attitude to the Civil War is clear from the following remark, also sometimes attributed to Chamberlain and Baldwin: 'We English hate Fascism. But we hate Bolshevism just as much. If there is a country where Fascists and Bolshevists are killing each other, then that is a great gift to humanity.'[29]

This is the context in which Fitzroy's rather Olympian *au dessus de la mêlée* judgement on the Spanish Civil War should be understood. He had no time for either side. With the hindsight of forty years he speaks of 'the utter cynicism with which the Great Powers regarded it'.[30] Fitzroy has been criticized for not taking a more resolute anti-Franco stance. Whence the selectivity, it is asked, whereby he excepted Falangist Spain from his general condemnation of fascist dictators? Is there a judicious conclusion? It is true that Churchill changed his mind on the Spanish Civil War, but Fitzroy did not. In 1936, presented to the Republican Ambassador in London, Churchill muttered 'Blood, blood, blood' and refused to shake his hand. But in 1938 he recanted, became a convinced Republican supporter, and even conversed amicably with the man whose hand he had refused to shake two years before. It is thought that his conversion was the work of his son-in-law Duncan Sandys, who visited Barcelona in the spring of 1938.[31] In not denouncing Franco, Fitzroy can be accused of double standards. But even George Orwell, who was wounded while fighting for the Republican cause, finally became disillusioned with leftist faction fighting and with the cynicism of the Moscow-directed Spanish Communist Party.

Had the British helped Blum against his enemies instead of giving them comfort, we might well have had a stauncher ally at the time of Munich. Blum later declared he would have forged an alliance with the Soviet Union rather than sign the Munich agreement.[32] Are we then justified in agreeing with Fitzroy's critics, who say that his position was inconsistent, and that one could not logically oppose appeasement while continuing to regard Communism as the greater enemy, though Fitzroy and his friends at the Foreign Office carried this attitude even into 1940?

We should remember that for part of the time when a comprehensive study of Spain might have teased out its deeper implications, Fitzroy was in the Soviet Union witnessing some of Stalin's worst excesses. There he had not the time to study Spain; nor, psychologically, would he have been disposed to favour a side that Stalin supported, however just its cause.

On the other hand, Fitzroy was not in the Soviet Union when the Spanish Civil War began, and his anti-Communism became pronouced only when he had seen it at close quarters. In January 1937 his attitude was still 'wait and see'. But he was already pressing hard to be sent to Russia. Business frequently took him back to London, and as the end of his three-year tour approached the question of his next posting was raised. In those days appointments were controlled by the Foreign Secretary's private secretaries. Fitzroy told them he was very sensible of the privilege of having been sent to Paris for his first posting: now, however, he would like to go to Moscow. The secretaries were stupefied. In the thirties Moscow was regarded as a hardship post: for instance, no British women were employed in the embassy there. Moreover, a Moscow posting would take Fitzroy out of the 'fast lane'. He would miss his place in the *cursus honorum*, whereas, if he left it to them, the secretaries would see that he obtained another comfortable billet on the 'inner circle'. 'You'll never have a nasty post as long as you live,' said Sir Nigel Ronald, the senior among them.[33]

But Fitzroy has always been actuated by what he calls the 'spirit of contradiction'. He would accept no substitute. Secretarial shoulders were collectively shrugged.

It must already be clear how wide of the mark the labels 'hedonist' or 'playboy' are as descriptions of the young Fitzroy. He has always made difficult choices, and plumped for the unconventional option. It took courage for a novice diplomat, not yet 26, to fly in the face of received wisdom and thus, perhaps, mark himself down in the Diplomatic Service as 'unsound'. But why Russia, and why then? Fitzroy explains.

> Having had three enormously happy years in Paris, my thoughts turned to Russia. I had been in love with a beautiful Georgian princess and had fallen completely for Slav charm. I had been excited and stimulated by the Eisenstein films I had seen in Paris and wanted to see Russia for myself. Paris comes into it, too. These were the years of the *Front Populaire*, of strikes and massive left-wing demonstrations. For these reasons Russia, the biggest country in the world, Communists and Communism were very much to the forefront of everyone's mind. This made me want to see them for myself. I guessed, too, that Russia might feature in a future war. Also, my generation was Philby, Blunt, Maclean. We were fascinated by Russia and tended to think this was the future of the world. I had a feeling before I went there that it wouldn't turn out to be utopia. But a lot of people, then, without being Communists, thought that was where the future lay. Lincoln Steffens said, 'I've seen the future and it works', having come back from the USSR.[34]

Another aspect of Fitzroy's personality is that he constantly sets himself new challenges. As he confessed in *Eastern Approaches*: 'Already I was beginning to get a little set in my ways; perhaps, I reflected in my rare moments of introspection, even a little smug . . . I have always relished contrasts, and what more complete contrast could there be after Paris than Moscow? I had seen something of the West. Now I wanted to see the East.'[35]

The motives of this complex man are always complex. In his Paris years one can sense the different drives and impulses: towards pleasure but also towards danger; towards thought but also towards action: seemingly a Bertie Wooster when the champagne corks popped, but an Isaiah Berlin when it came to drafting despatches. This complexity was to be fully tested as he made his way towards the heart of darkness that was Stalin's Russia.

3

The Years with Stalin

1937–1939

T HE atmosphere of fear and mutual suspicion in Moscow [under Stalin] was horrendous. Children were denouncing their parents to the NKVD [People's Commissariat for Internal Affairs] and parents their children. Everyone lived in terror of the knock on their door at 3 a.m. From the big new block of flats made of lavatory brick near the Embassy there was a nightly carting-away of top people – by the score. There were thousands living there then, and they were picking them up, twenty or thirty every night. If you look now, you'll see a monument to Marshal Tukhachevsky, which was where they arrested him. We naturally always assumed that all telephone conversations would be tapped, all our rooms bugged and anything one said to a Russian immediately reported back to the NKVD. Diplomats were in practice almost entirely confined to the company of other diplomats. The Kremlin parties (when they happened) were in fact fascinating. Plenty to eat and drink. The Tsar's gold plate. Litvinov tangoing with his alleged adopted daughter. English-born Ivy Litvinov's reckless remarks did them both credit, all against a background frieze of terrified Marshals uneasily fingering their tight uniform collars.

Fitzroy laughs at the mania of the secret services for bugging. He tells of bugs in the beak of an American eagle in the US Embassy, and in the Virgin's hand on a cardinal's desk in the Vatican. 'We used to go round with a clipper, clipping odd wires. In the US embassy NKVD agents actually hid between the ceiling and the floor above but, being Russians, left empty sardine tins behind.'

'For Fitzroy to choose Russia in 1937 showed foresight,' his old friend Sir Frank Roberts commented. 'Also, he prepared himself by learning the language – many diplomats didn't.' Here Fitzroy showed himself a professional in a world of amateurs. His most enduring legacy from these years is his love of the Russian language; even today, he reads a page of Russian each night. Fitzroy is a great believer in the importance of languages. When he arrived in Yugoslavia in 1943 the first thing he did was to work out with Tito what language they were to speak in. Tito spoke better Russian, Fitzroy better German so at first they spoke in German although eventually they conversed in Serbo-Croat.

> France was a good place to learn Russian in, once I'd made the decision. There were so many glamorous 'dictionaries'. I learned as much as I could in Paris. When I arrived in Moscow I could speak a bit and could read the papers. It was very difficult to get a tutor in Russia, but there was this lady licensed to teach foreigners. We also had a translator/interpreter who lent a hand. A man who was half-Scots and half-Russian. He talked a mixture of both languages in a half-Scots, half-Russian accent. A nice old man from one of those Scottish families, long settled in Russia.

The Bukharin trial remains with Fitzroy as a ghastly memory. 'One of the most extraordinary experiences of my life. One of the most exciting things recently was a conversation I had with Bukharin's widow, amazingly still alive. She told me they were living in the Metropole hotel in the thirties (still the best hotel in Moscow) which was occupied then by the party élite. Her father was a Bolshevik contemporary of Bukharin. As a teenager she fell in love with this Bolshevik revolutionary who lived upstairs. She wrote love poems to Bukharin. One day she went out and saw a man passing and asked if he'd mind delivering a letter to Comrade Bukharin. The man passing was Stalin, so he acted in that case as a Cupid.'

Of all the Russians he saw between 1937 and 1939, Fitzroy claims to have been most impressed by Bukharin and most disgusted by the prosecutor at his trial, Andrei Vyshinski. In 1989 he took part in the making of a *Timewatch* film on the trial.

Twenty years after the Revolution the Soviet Union was in crisis, the root cause of which was that all the actors, Stalin included, were having to make up the script as they went along. 'It wasn't supposed to happen like this' was the subtext. But while veteran Bolshevik theorists agonized, Stalin acted, and his actions were usually murderous.

It was Stalin who proposed the feasibility of 'socialism in one country'. Classical Marxist theory envisaged the collapse of capitalism in the most advanced countries as the entire proletariat acquired revolutionary consciousness in the very act of class struggle. Lenin modified the theory, introducing the idea of the Communist Party as 'vanguard', since, impatient with Marx's Hegelian metaphysics, he doubted that the proletariat could acquire true political consciousness without the aid of an intellectual leadership. But Marx and Lenin were at one in believing that unless revolution swept simultaneously through the countries of Europe, disaster would result. Lenin, early in 1917, thought that he would not see the revolution in his lifetime – but when his chance came in October 1917 he took it, regardless of the theoretical unsoundness of his position. Orthodoxy required revolution to break out in, say, Germany first and Russia last, but he rationalized that it did not matter much if the position were reversed *provided* there actually was general revolution in Europe.

But revolution was arrested in Europe. Indeed the Western powers, in alarm, launched armies into the wide spaces of Russia and did their best to help the 'White' counter-revolution. This hostility from Europe added a layer of paranoia to the perplexity felt by the Bolsheviks because the world was not proceeding in accordance with the revolutionary handbook. The Lenin period (1917 to 1924) sees the first appearance of the dreaded secret police (*Cheka*), who originally derived legitimacy from the presence on Soviet soil of White Russian invaders.

Lenin's claim to greatness was twofold. He was a revolutionary genius, able to abandon his own theories and improvise to bring about premature revolution in 1917. And he was prepared to throw away the strait-jacket of ideology and introduce modified capitalism (the New Economic Policy) when circumstances required it. He doubted the feasibility of socialism in Russia alone. Stalin, who fancied himself as a theorist, boldly embraced the idea of 'socialism in one country', and to this end began to industrialize the nation in a series of Five-Year Plans. He aimed to exact the money for investment in heavy industry from the peasantry. When the rich peasants (the *kulaks*, and even the small-holding middle peasants) resisted this, Stalin turned his machine-guns on them.

Now was fulfilled the prophecy of the Russian Menshevik theorist Plekhanov, that a premature revolution in one country alone would lead to 'Inca despotism'. The theoretical excuse for Stalin's dictatorship was that military aggression and the economic blockade by the Western powers made it impossible for Russia to advance beyond the 'dictatorship of the proletariat' – an interim stage on the road to true socialism. If the Soviet Union was frozen in the ice of dictatorship, that was the fault of the myopic West. And now, too, first became manifest the snag in Lenin's idea that the party was the vanguard of the proletariat. If the working class was as much in tandem with the Party as the right arm with the left arm – so claimed Stalin the theorist – then it followed that the Secretary of the Party must himself embody the 'objective' interests of the proletariat. Ivan the Terrible and Peter the Great had never been able to think of such ingenious arguments to bolster their tyranny.

Meanwhile, Soviet society became ossified. As Trotsky pointed out, the very backwardness of Russian society meant there was no educated middle class, and thus few technicians and administrators. Yet such people were essential to transform Russia into a modern industrial state, and their co-operation had to be acquired with differentials and privileges. But the privileged realized that their status and perquisites could be guaranteed only if the temporary situation became the permanent one, that is if the 'emergency' dictatorship of the proletariat became an institutionalized one-party state.

The sickness Fitzroy observed in the USSR from 1937 to 1939 was doubtless partly due to an unconscious guilt over betrayal of the revolution; it helped to foster a sense of chaos which Stalin exploited to the full. Why did Russian society not rise up against the tyrant? The answer seems to be that there was a powerful élite in the bureaucracy, the secret police and (later) the Army, whose aspirations were satisfied by Stalinism. Those who opposed Stalin and all his works were disorientated, as they had no theoretical model of the sort of society that should replace the new Russia and were immobilized by depression about 'the revolution gone wrong'.

Chaos, anarchy, terror, madness: these are the characteristics of the Soviet Union in the 1930s. The liquidation of the *kulaks* is the sort of lunacy that results when theoretical goals are implemented at the administrative level. Santayana defined fanaticism as redoubling one's efforts after losing sight of one's aims. The most frightening aspect of totalitarian regimes is the way inhumanity becomes routinely processed through the administrative machine. So the Final Solution in the mind of a Reinhardt Heydrich becomes a necessary aim, not because of blind hatred or anti-Semitism as such, but because the gas chambers appear the most administratively *convenient* solution.

Such was the situation in Russia when Fitzroy boarded the trans-Europe express at the Gare du Nord in February 1937. His itinerary lay across the flat north European plain: northern France, then north Germany and, by dusk on the second evening, Poland. In the middle of the night the train crossed into Russia. An encounter with Customs officials confirmed to Fitzroy that his time with the glamorous 'dictionaries' had not been wasted. But what struck him most was the unique smell of Russia. Part of it was 'black bread and sheepskin and vodka and unwashed humanity. Now to these were added the more modern smells of petrol and disinfectant and the clinging, cloying odour of Soviet soap . . . Since leaving Russia I have smelt it once or twice again, for Russians in sufficiently large numbers seem to carry it with them abroad, and each time with that special power of evocation which smells possess, it has brought back with startling vividness the memories of those years.'[1]

Next morning the landscape, too, proved a revelation. What Fitzroy wrote many years later, when treating of the spy Alfred Redl, can clearly in a sense be applied to himself. 'On a young man of intelligence and imagination . . . this first journey to Russia, remote, mysterious and equivocal, was bound to make a strong impression . . . Along the

railway line the silver birches were brilliantly green; in every direction the vast Russian plain stretched endlessly away and the gilded
onion-domes of the Orthodox churches standing out above the roofs
of the peasant houses, lent the landscape a different, more exotic
look.'[2]

The train reached Moscow in the afternoon of 19 February, in a
snowstorm. Fitzroy was met at the station by Dan Lascelles, the First
Secretary, who had been in Russia for eighteen months. On the way to
the Embassy the car stopped at Red Square, the Cathedral of Saint
Basil and the Kremlin. And in his very first hour in Moscow he saw for
himself the reality of the purges that were decimating the top echelons of
Soviet society: further delay was caused by the State funeral of Commissar Ordzhonikidze, a Georgian and one of Stalin's oldest and
closest associates. It is now known (though naturally it was not in 1937)
that Stalin gave Ordzhonikidze the choice of a State trial and a bullet in
the back of the neck, or suicide and a State funeral. Ordzhonikidze
chose the Roman way.

Arrival at the Embassy was a sobering business. Fitzroy began to
realize how unlike his life in Paris this posting was going to be. For a
start, he would have to live 'above the shop'. The Embassy was an
extraordinary edifice, built in 1910 by a sugar millionaire regardless of
cost. It faced the Kremlin across the river and had two wings, large
stables or garages and an extensive garden. The millionaire had had
each room in the mansion decorated in a particular style: one would
be François I, another Louis XV, another Gothic, and so on. The
Embassy proper was housed in the right wing, and the accommodation
was on the left. 'It used to drive Stalin mad. He'd wake up and see the
Union Jack fluttering there and bawl out to his aides, "Get them out of
there!" We agreed to leave ten years ago but Gorby and Mrs T. swung
it back.'[3]

In the residential wing Fitzroy had the ground floor flat and Dan
Lascelles the flat above. Each of the apartments contained four spacious
rooms and was very comfortable. Lascelles warned him that every room
was bugged. Years later Fitzroy recalled his impressions. 'For two years
in the 1930s I lived directly across the river from the Kremlin, looking
out at it throughout the day and again every night when a floodlit flag
flapped blood-red above it and the luminous red stars, which had lately
replaced the old Imperial double eagles on its gates and towers, shone
out like beacons on an unregenerate world. Each night at the stroke of
twelve the chimes of the great clock above the Spasski Gate would play
the old Internationale, that sad and yet somehow triumphant melody,
which in those days still doubled as the Soviet National Anthem and call
to world revolution, summoning the poor and oppressed of all nations
to rise and cast off the chains.

'The Kremlin was then still closely guarded and relentlessly closed to all comers. In it lived Stalin, cocooned in mystery and paranoia. Sometimes, as you were passing the Spasski gate, suddenly red lights would flash, and the bell would ring menacingly and insistently and a convoy of three or four long black limousines with windows of semi-opaque green bullet-proof glass would shoot out across the Red Square at high speed and disappear down hastily emptied streets to some mysterious destination in the country. Through the thick green glass, you could, if you were sufficiently quick or endowed with a lively enough imagination, sometimes catch a glimpse of an eagle nose and drooping, Asiatic moustache. But that was the closest view most people ever got of the Kremlin or its inmates. And so it remained, remote and mysterious, a treasure-house full of marvels which one could never hope to see.'[4]

The first thing for Fitzroy to do was make the acquaintance of the Embassy personnel. The two significant incumbents were the Ambassador, Lord Chilston, and Lascelles, the First Secretary. Chilston, like Clerk, was another 'hands off' envoy. His chief object in life was to get back to the delights of Chilston in Kent and potter in the garden. His wife was a much livelier character, very interested in the arts and the theatre.

But it was the diminutive, moustachioed Lascelles who intrigued Fitzroy. Born at the turn of the century, he was old enough to have served as a midshipman in the First World War. He was a truly great linguist, not just in the sense of being fluent as a speaker, but in that he knew the grammar and origins of his languages in detail. When he was in Ethiopia, the Abyssinian Ministry of Foreign Affairs actually used to check with him that their memoranda were correctly written in Amharic, which he knew better than most natives. He was a wartime Minister in Beirut, and later ambassador in Athens. Yet he seems to have been very far from the conventional diplomat, as Fitzroy recalls: 'An extraordinary character but enormously neurotic. He could not bear Moscow and was driven wild by the regime. He thought he was being poisoned. Smoked a hundred cigarettes a day. He had every sort of hang-up you can imagine. He was highly intelligent but his extreme reserve didn't allow for close contact with other people. His conscience did not allow him to wear any sort of fur coat, but without a fur coat one froze. He was a good painter and a good pianist. He used to play the piano until 3 a.m. He didn't like his colleagues, either, so he was driven back on his own resources. But we were friends.'[5]

Social life in Moscow invariably meant one's fellow diplomats, so it was to these, especially the Americans, that Fitzroy gravitated. He very soon made the acquaintance of the two Charlies, Thayer and Bohlen. Charlie Thayer was a young East Coaster with ruffled hair and a strong

Philadelphia society drawl. Fitzroy was drawn to him by his 'naughty boy' image and his outrageous sense of humour, which masked a deep seriousness. Thayer's sister Avis was married to the other Charles, 'Chip' Bohlen.

Bohlen and Thayer, together with other young American diplomats such as George Kennan, later the State Department's *éminence grise* in matters Soviet, had rented a *dacha* some twelve miles south of Moscow. Avis Bohlen was the heart and soul of the place, with sterling support from an old factotum, George, and a popular Russian peasant, Panteleimon. The summer house had a tennis court and stables with horses, and became the Mecca of younger members of the diplomatic community – Americans, British, French, Italians and Germans. Ironically, for an outpost of capitalism, a form of communalism was practised there. All 'members' chipped in what they could: the Germans brought beer and sausages, the British Scotch whisky, the Italians wine, the Americans peanut butter (which quickly became one of Fitzroy's favourite delicacies).

The stables contained the only privately-owned saddle horses in the Soviet Union, and on them Fitzroy and his young companions ranged far and wide over the green, rolling countryside. In those days, twelve miles took one well outside the Moscow city limits; fifty years later this Arcadia has been eaten up by urban sprawl. When snow made riding impossible, the young diplomats would ski on the slopes, with more enthusiasm than skill. Fitzroy remembers his times at the summer house as an idyll. 'In the evenings, after a hard day's exercise, we would congregate round a roaring open fire in the *dacha* and Avis would dispense frankfurters and peanut butter and corned-beef hash and other unaccustomed delicacies, washed down by plenty of good American coffee and equally good Scotch whisky. Then we would lie about and talk and play the gramophone until it was time to go home. As we drove back to Moscow the air was icy and the stars shone down frostily on the sparkling snow.'[6]

At the *dacha* Fitzroy made a close study of his American hosts. The USA had established diplomatic relations with the Soviet Union only in 1934. Initially there were just four American diplomats in Moscow: ambassador William C. Bullitt, Joseph Flask, George Kennan, and Charlie Thayer. Kennan actually met Thayer in the bar of Moscow's National Hotel (next to the US Embassy on the Mokhovaya) while Thayer was collecting material for a book; he took to him, and put him on the payroll, at first as 'messenger'.[7]

Kennan and Chip Bohlen were the first professional Russian specialists. Bohlen, born in 1904, was well known later as wartime adviser on the USSR, and trained as a Sovietologist in Paris; his monthly reports from Moscow were particularly admired. Kennan, who had learned his

Russian while serving in Berlin, called Bohlen 'a man of exceptional native brilliance, for whom Russian communism was to constitute a central interest throughout a long and distinguished professional career'.[8] Kennan himself was a deeply serious individual with a lighter side disclosed mainly in his relationship with his Norwegian wife, Anneliese, and his guitar-playing. He took a great interest in the Russian musical scene, was fascinated and amused by their approach to jazz, and knew many Russian and gypsy songs by heart.

Bohlen, Thayer and Kennan were the basis of the US diplomats' burgeoning reputation. In Kennan's words: 'By the end of 1936 [the American Embassy] was developing, we felt, into one of the best-informed and most highly respected diplomatic missions in Moscow, rivalled only by the German, which was at all times excellent.'[9] By the time Fitzroy got to know the Americans, their diplomatic strength had been enhanced by Elbridge Durbow, Loy Henderson and Norris Shipman. But, to the dismay of career diplomats, at the end of 1936 President Roosevelt appointed the Democratic politician Joseph E. Davies as ambassador. He became notorious as Stalin's apologist, and took the line that those purged in the great trials of 1937 and 1938 were almost certainly guilty as charged. Tension between Davies and his staff was palpable.

Ambassador Davies, who died in 1958, still provokes strong emotions. Although he served in Russia less than two years, his account of his embassy, *Mission to Moscow*, became a best-seller and was turned into an accomplished movie by Warner Brothers, starring Walter Huston and directed by Michael Curtiz (who in the same year turned out the classic *Casablanca*). The film was widely shown in the USSR during the Second World War, and Roosevelt actually sent Stalin a personal copy with a covering note in which he referred to Davies as 'my old friend'. On 18 May 1945 Davies was awarded the Order of Lenin, the only foreign diplomat in the history of the USSR to be so decorated. But during the McCarthy era, Jack L. Warner was forced to recant publicly and to declare that making the movie had been a 'mistake'.

Davies was controversial not only for his blinkered support of Stalin. In the early 1930s one could buy tickets for foreign travel in Moscow and pay in roubles. Because of the special rouble rate at which diplomats could exchange foreign currency (representing the true market rate of the rouble), one could use deflated roubles to buy tickets for travel all round Europe. By extension, diplomats could make a 'killing' buying up books and antiques in this way. During the purges Davies bought up entire museums with black market roubles. His purchases were so huge that the black market price for roubles all over Europe was driven up. Fitzroy, not surprisingly, has little good to say about Davies.

He was a corporation lawyer on the make who had married the Post-Toastie heiress, who I think was the sixteenth richest woman in the world. He was really an exceedingly sharp corporation lawyer who by large contributions to the Democrats had got himself made Ambassador to Moscow. *Mission to Moscow*? I saw the movie with Churchill at Chequers after the war. In the movie Davies comes to see Winston and tells him all about Russia and how great it was. One of the funny things in the movie was that Mrs Davies was also the frozen food queen, and in 1937 nobody had even heard of frozen food! Davies was so appalled at the thought of having to live in Russia that he had the whole of his yacht filled with frozen delicacies, and never touched Russian food the whole time he was there. He lived on his yacht on the Black Sea or the Baltic most of the time. In the movie he arrives at the frontier, gets out of the train and there is a hot-dog stand. He buys one, eats it and says, 'Gee, you can't get anything like that in the States'! He wanted the court of St James's, which Joe Kennedy got. After Moscow he wanted *some*where with a court, so he got himself Brussels. He had quite nice children who used to give lots of parties at the Embassy, which I went to quite a lot.[10]

Davies apart, these years in Moscow sowed the seeds of the pro-Americanism which is so obvious a part of Fitzroy's profile. 'The Americans were very important,' he concedes. 'Their *dacha* saved our lives. Also, before the purges it had been possible to meet Russians. Bill Bullitt, the first ambassador, had raked a lot of them into his net, and when I arrived three years later there were still some of these Russians left, who would come out to the *dacha*. That was how I had a few native contacts.'[11] It is certainly significant that although a number of top British diplomats overlapped with Fitzroy in Moscow – William Hayter, John Russell and Noel Charles, later the outspoken ambassador in Rome – of English-speakers (with the single exception of Dan Lascelles), it is the American colleagues that he most frequently mentions. But he did make one very important friend in the German embassy.

Hans von Herwarth von Bittenfeld, always referred to by Fitzroy as 'Jonny', had been at the German embassy in Moscow since 1931 and remained there until the outbreak of war in 1939. His problem was that as a 'non-Aryan' he could not be transferred to a more important post, and was safer in the obscurity of Moscow than somewhere where the Nazis might take an interest in him. Fitzroy explains:

. . . a great friend, Jonny von Herwarth [was] my opposite number in the German embassy in Moscow. He was 75 per cent upper-crust Prussian aristocracy, with a lot of field-marshals, et cetera, in his background, and 25 per cent Jewish, with an Italian grandmother. He was almost an honorary Aryan type. So you've got this man who's 75 per cent very grand and 25 per cent Jewish – highly intelligent, very nice, one of my greatest friends. In order to keep him out of sight, he'd been kept in Moscow after 1933. They thought that this was the one place where Hitler and Co. would not spot that they had a man who was 25 per cent Jewish working for them. He became a very experienced Moscow hand and was in this awful situation where he could see the war coming – better than any of us. One half of him was a patriotic German but the other half was violently opposed to the regime. His wife was a cousin of Stauffenberg and in the end he was very much involved in the Stauffenberg plot.[12]

Charlie Thayer added some touches to the portrait. 'I'd known Jonny von Herwarth since 1934. He was one of the seeded favourites in the Moscow game of guessing what the Russians were going to do next, and he could spend hours arguing with anyone who would argue back about the meaning of this decree or that speech. Why was Molotov's picture closer to Stalin's than Kalinin's? What had happened to Mikoyan's standing since he became Commissar for Food? How much of a fake was the "Stalin Constitution"? Why had the Kremlin suddenly forbidden abortions?'[13]

Von Herwarth for his part was not impressed at first sight with Fitzroy. 'He looked like a dandy with his ornate evening dress and outsize cummerbund. I thought, this man won't survive the rigours of Moscow diplomatic life. I could not have been more wrong!'[14] Soon he had him singled out as one of the best-informed diplomats on the Russian scene. 'At his famous dinner parties he excelled as a brilliant host and raconteur. His German was excellent.'[15] The half-humorous, half contemptuous Maclean attitude to established channels and protocol was already in evidence. It was the custom for all diplomatic limousines to fly pennants, and von Herwarth remembers how bitterly the Russians detested the swastika fluttering on the German vehicles. Fitzroy decided on an early form of UDI and ran up the *Scottish* flag on his car.[16]

Von Herwarth soon had a sample of Fitzroy's brilliant improvisation when in danger or under stress. All the diplomats who went out to the American *dacha* were profoundly irritated by the unremitting NKVD surveillance, and went out of their way to tweak the Russians' noses. A favourite ploy was for four people to drive to the *dacha*, then for two of them to lie down in the car on the way back, so the secret police would think that a couple had slipped the leash. One night Fitzroy devised a refinement. A trio of cars set out from the *dacha* towards Moscow. First was 'Jonny' in his car, behind him were the NKVD in the inevitable Ford saloon, and last of all came Fitzroy in a third vehicle. At a point where they knew there was a police post, von Herwarth and Fitzroy drew in to the side of the road, as did their tail. Fitzroy got out and complained to the police that his diplomat friend ahead was being harassed by hooligans who were following him in a late-model Ford. A police officer approached the 'hooligans' and began to caution them prior to arrest, only to discover to his horror that it was the NKVD he was tangling with.[17]

But von Herwarth's abiding preoccupation in his relationship with Fitzroy was to warn of the danger of war. Although by 1936 some of his colleagues already regarded him as a zealot and alarmist, von Herwarth pressed on with his one-man mission, reiterating that 'World War Two is as sure as the Amen in Church'. In the milieu of the *dacha* – 'a kind of Masonic lodge or Mutual Admiration Society', as he termed it – he looked around for like-minded colleagues. Some of the diplomats would have none of it: Kennan, for example, was at that time sceptical of any supposed German threat to the USSR and thought that, if there was a threat, it would come from Japan. The ones whose views von Herwarth found most congenial were Chip Bohlen and Fitzroy. He remembers an argument in which all the others were at one in thinking that the Soviet economy would eventually catch up with the capitalist West; only he and Fitzroy maintained that it would always lag behind.

As his confidence in Fitzroy grew, von Herwarth started to leak to him and to Bohlen snippets of top secret information from the German archives, all in the forlorn, Tolstoyan hope that if evil men can band together for evil purposes, so can good men for good ends.[18] His first briefing of Fitzroy, in August 1938, was to the effect that German career diplomats would like to see Britain taking a stronger line over Czechoslovakia, since Hitler believed he could invade that country with impunity.[19] Fitzroy passed the information on to London, where his superiors printed it as follows: 'Maclean had a not uninteresting conversation yesterday with the German Ambassador's Private Secretary, with whom he is on quite intimate terms and who had asked specifically if he might come and have a talk with him.'[20]

Ambassador Chilston also relied heavily on Fitzroy's talks with von Herwarth for his assessments of Soviet foreign policy. It was a permanent motif in von Herwarth's prognostications that Hitler and Stalin would one day dish the West by striking a deal. So it was that in 1938 the first whisperings began to be heard of a Soviet–German *rapprochement*, which led to the Molotov–Ribbentrop pact in August 1939. Hitler's insane hatred of Bolshevism, it had been said, stood in the way of a deal between the two great totalitarian powers.

Von Herwarth would have been shot if caught. 'I should perhaps stress', he wrote, 'that in leaking information to Maclean and other foreign diplomats in Moscow, I acted on my own initiative and without the knowledge of anyone else in the Embassy, least of all Schulenburg; leaking official secrets and publicizing one's private dissent from the policies of the government for which one worked were not viewed with favour in Berlin. Not wishing to lay others open to the charge of high treason, I preferred to act on my own.'[21]

Even before Fitzroy's contacts with von Herwarth established him as a rising star, his superiors had him marked as 'one to note'. In June 1937 he was sent to Paris on 'special leave' to test the impression made on French public opinion by Stalin's purges, and in particular by the recent execution of eight top Red Army generals. He interviewed Paul Reynaud, whom he found disillusioned. French opinion on the purges was that either the accused were guilty, in which case the Red Army was honeycombed with corruption and would be no use as a military ally to France in the event of a European war – not least because all its secrets would be known to the Germans – or that they were innocent, in which case it was clear that the USSR was being run by madmen. Fitzroy was particularly briefed to interview a French politician codenamed 'Pertinax', who until the purges had been a strong advocate of a Franco-Soviet alliance. Fitzroy found 'Pertinax', too, disgruntled and pessimistic.[22]

Fitzroy's diplomatic life went on at a hectic pace. In July 1938 he was back in London for a short visit, where he met an old friend, Oliver Harvey. 'I have had a long talk with Fitzroy Maclean back from Moscow. He said the Soviet government under Stalin was now firmly opportunistic – Stalin with his purges was merely concerned with securing his own position. The purges, amounting to 75 per cent of the higher command in the Army for instance, and as high or higher a percentage in all other walks of life, had gravely shaken efficiency . . . Nobody's life was safe.'[23]

Few of Fitzroy's friends in London, however, were prepared to visit him in Moscow. One who did was the journalist Virginia Cowles, though she did not go out until early 1939.[24] A surprising visitor was the White Russian beauty, Lady Abdy, whom he had admired in his Paris days. 'She came out to see me – one of the very few, as by and large people didn't come out – and went to see her father. I remember taking her on a picnic outside Moscow. She got hold of a spoon, dug up some earth, put it in a bag and said, "This is Russian soil. I'm taking it back to all the poor White Russians in Paris." '[25]

Every night the Embassy staff was expected to turn out in white tie for this or that official reception, attended by diplomats only or the odd clustering of bedizened Red Army marshals, grey with fright. Fitzroy got used to the sight of the portly Foreign Minister Litvinov dancing with his 'adopted daughter' (actually his mistress). Fitzroy had a sneaking regard for Litvinov who, amazingly, survived the purges, even though he was a Jew and was sacked in 1939. He had even warmer feelings of admiration for Litvinov's wife Ivy, *née* Lowe, scion of an old leftish Jewish family in England. She was the soul of indiscretion and said exactly what she thought about the topic of the hour, regardless of who was displeased. 'When one went to the Kremlin parties, the old Czarist gold plate was there. Someone quite ready to talk to foreigners was Ivy Litvinov, who was English. She had kept up links. Not that the links were much use. Bernard Shaw, Lady Astor, the Webbs used to come out, be entertained and shown model schools, hospitals, collective farms, et cetera, kept for the visitors. They were filled up with champagne and caviare and used to say to us, "You're taking a prejudiced and jaundiced view of the country".' Almost the only visiting 'name' to win approval from Fitzroy was Malcolm Muggeridge.[26]

Official entertaining, the Litvinovs apart, was a dispiriting business, though characteristically Fitzroy found humour in the most unlikely places. 'Lady Chilston liked the arts, but Russians never came to our parties even when invited. At the Kremlin parties they were terrified of being spoken to by Westerners. The man who was head of protocol had been in the Czarist Foreign Office. He had continued in his career, as the Bolsheviks needed someone to show them how to behave with diplomats. Someone said to him, "Wasn't your father shot by the Bolsheviks during the Revolution? How can you work with these people?" He said, "If your father had been run over by a tram, would you never travel by tram?" '[27]

Fitzroy very soon saw for himself the risks Russians ran by talking to foreigners. At one of the *dacha* parties he met an attractive actress. He proposed dinner next evening, followed by a visit to the cinema. The actress accepted. They had dinner, enjoyed the film, and Fitzroy dropped her off at about eleven in the evening. Next morning her distraught mother came on the phone. 'They came for her at three in the morning.' There was no need to say who *they* were. The girl was never seen again.

Fear was everywhere. No one, no matter how humble their job, could be sure of escaping the drag-net. Fitzroy recalls:

> How frightened everyone was! A couple of middle-aged women cooked and housemaided for us in the Embassy flat. On the whole such people lived in the Embassy compound. They occasionally went out. Our cook once went out and didn't come back. We shrugged our shoulders. Six months later she returned. 'Where have you been?' we asked her. She had been inside. It was a most rewarding experience, she said. They have this great word *kulturny*. '*Kulturny*' is a clean tablecloth. '*Ne kulturny*' is a tablecloth with an egg-stain on it. It was very *kulturny* inside, she said. Because of all the other women. The wives of generals, commissars, ambassadors. Full of really cultivated people. Full of fascinating people and wonderful conversation. 'Why aren't you still there?' we asked. 'One day the commandant sent for me and asked my name. Olga Petrovna, I said. "You're the wrong woman, you should be Vera. What are you doing here?" "They arrested me." "Well" – shrug of shoulders – "they've made another of their mistakes. Get out." '[28]

What of the ultimate author of all this, Stalin himself? Diplomats did not get to see the leader, since officially he was merely Secretary

General of the Communist Party and had no duties which would require him to meet ambassadors. If ever the British formally requested an interview with Stalin, Litvinov, Commissar for Foreign Affairs, would simply laugh and say: 'Mr Stalin, he is just a private gentleman, and he does not like to see foreigners.'[29]

Appropriately, it was in Red Square that Fitzroy first saw the dictator, on May Day 1937, '. . . a squat, rather menacing figure, with hawk-like nose and downward-turned moustache, watching inscrutably as infantry, cavalry, armour and artillery swept swiftly past him.'[30] Impressed by the full-throated cheering, Fitzroy looked to see where it was coming from. But there was nobody at the parade except the diplomatic corps and thousands of soldiers. He realized the cheering emanated solely from loudspeakers placed around Red Square. Not even Chaplin in *The Great Dictator* could have trumped that for black comedy. 'Living in Moscow, even under the conditions to which we were condemned, one could in a few months find out more about the real character of the Soviet Union than one could hope to learn by reading all the books that were ever written on the subject.'[31]

What of the idea that Stalin, for all his monstrous excesses, was a great man who by sheer brute will made Russia a modern industrial power? That his energy alone brought a dispirited people to eventual victory against the Nazis in the Second World War? Fitzroy accepts none of this, but he does concede to the dictator certain qualities,

> . . . a quick and devious mind. In the Caucasus the people in the next valley may be friends or enemies. They may be of a different race and speak a different language, so in that neck of the woods people are looking out for themselves in a big way, and that was his upbringing and it came naturally. Also, they say it takes three Greeks to get the better of a Jew, but six Jews to get the better of an Armenian. Armenia and Georgia are next-door neighbours and I find, talking to Armenians, they're always two or three jumps ahead of you. They've worked out what you're going to say and their answers to that. Stalin was always a couple of moves ahead of all he came into contact with. The purge trials show you the frame of mind of a whole nation, complicated of course by ideology and Russian character. A lot of Russians take it badly if you talk about a Dostoevsky syndrome, but there is one, or was one then.[32]

So were the purge trials simply the excesses of one unbalanced individual? As Hume famously pointed out, no man can commit mass murder without support: even a crazed Caligula or Nero needed the Praetorian guard. Who were Stalin's praetorians? At first sight it is hard to see any beneficiaries, since members of every Party, State and military organization fell victim. In the Red Army three out of five marshals were executed or 'disappeared'; three out of five Army

Commanders, First Class, all ten Army Commanders, Second Class, 50 out of 57 Corps commanders, 154 out of 186 Divisional Command-ers, all sixteen Army Commissars, 25 out of 28 Corps Commissars, 58 out of 64 Divisional Commissars, 401 out of 456 colonels.[33] Such a swathe of destruction made the Wehrmacht's initial task much easier in 1941.

Meanwhile, practically the entire Soviet diplomatic corps was wiped out in successive purges. Only Litvinov and a handful of his key lieuten-ants survived (notably Suritz in France and Maisky in Britain).

> The officials at the Commissariat for Foreign Affairs [Narkomindel] became more inaccessible than ever . . . Contacts with foreigners were notoriously fatal . . . Yet it was their duty to see foreigners. If they refused, they were clearly neglecting their duty, or else had a guilty conscience. If, on the other hand, they continued to see foreigners, someone sooner or later was bound to accuse them of betraying State secrets or plotting the overthrow of the Soviet regime . . . One would ring up and ask to speak to Comrade Ivanov. 'He is sick,' an unfamiliar voice would answer nervously; 'he is busy; he has gone for a walk.' 'And who', one would ask, 'is doing his work?' 'For the time being,' the voice would reply unhappily, 'I am – Comrade Maximov.' 'May I come and see you, Mr Maximov?' one would inquire. 'It is very difficult,' would come the evasive answer. 'I also am very busy.'
>
> Next time, if one could remember his name, one would ring up Mr Maximov. And once more there would be the increasingly familiar answer. 'He is sick; he is busy; he has gone for a walk. For the time being I am replacing him.' And the chances were that that would be the last that one would hear of Comrade Maximov.[34]

Many years later Fitzroy wrote: 'I have since sometimes asked survi-vors of that period whether, even as good Communists, they did not find it and all that went with it disillusioning and hard to take. Their answer (and they include President Tito of Yugoslavia) has generally been that, though appalled by what was happening there, they still saw Soviet Russia as the Country of the Revolution, and as such, at that time the only hope for the World Communist Movement in which they firmly believed.'[35]

The most dramatic liquidation, at least before the 1938 Bukharin trial, was that of Red Army hero Marshal Mikhail Tukhachevsky, the commander-in-chief. The charge was that he had had treasonable con-tacts with the German Minister of War Werner von Blomberg during a visit to Berlin in 1936. In fact, the German embassy in Moscow habitu-ally reported Tukhachevsky as cool towards the Third Reich. The usual view is, rather, that Stalin used a pretext to purge his commander-in-chief and other top brass in the Red Army before they could liquidate *him*. One gloss on this view is that Winston Churchill, knowing of

Stalin's secret hatred for Tukhachevsky, reported the rumour of his treason to Czech President Benes, who in turn passed it on to Stalin, thus giving him the 'evidence' he needed. Certainly many mysteries surround the Tukhachevsky case.

The great purges of the 1930s defy rational analysis. Some have seen them as the destruction of political opposition; others as the extirpation of ideological heresy; others, more ingeniously, argue that Stalin's project was to get rid of all who were opposed to a deal with Hitler, and thus lay the foundations for the Nazi–Soviet pact. There are objections to all these interpretations. Devotees of Stalinist ideology perished while sceptics survived; supporters of Stalin himself were purged; and the pro-German wing of Narkomindel was destroyed alongside the Germanophobes and Anglophiles. Fitzroy himself noticed that there was no rationality in the process, that it became a self-sustaining whirlwind in which eventually the purgers were themselves purged. Also, people took advantage of the chaos to settle personal scores. 'If you wanted a man's job or his room or his wife, you denounced him as a Trotskyist or a British spy, and the chances were that he would disappear.'

Fitzroy came face to face with the reality of the purges during the third of the great trials, when in February 1938 the great Soviet ideologist and founding father Bukharin was arraigned. For eight or nine hours a day Fitzroy sat in court, in what had once been the ballroom of the Czarist Nobles' Club, along with other foreign observers. There, too, was Joseph E. Davies, with Kennan acting as his interpreter. In Davies's memoirs, as later in the movie *Mission to Moscow*, the prosecutor Andrei Vyshinski featured as a tireless campaigner against corruption.[36] The atmosphere was of Romans at the arena baying for the blood of a once-favoured gladiator. Fitzroy later recalled: 'To see this actually happening was a horrifying experience, the nightmarish memory of which has remained with me for more than forty years, being suddenly relived when not long ago I found myself in the selfsame ballroom, listening to a concert given by a celebrated American pianist.'[37]

Bukharin was indicted for espionage, sabotage, murder and high treason. Apart from Bukharin, who had the distinction of having been Lenin's close comrade, formerly Secretary-General of the Communist International and for years the Party's leading theoretician, the other prisoners at the bar included Yagoda, formerly head of NKVD and People's Commissar for Internal Affairs, Rykov, Lenin's successor as premier, and Krestinski, formerly Vice-Commissar for Foreign Affairs, plus a host of lesser luminaries.

Most of the accused pleaded guilty at once. Krestinski put up a fight and at first denied the charges, but after a twenty-four-hour adjournment he was back, pleading guilty as vehemently as the others. Fitzroy remarked sombrely: 'The words were reeled off like a well-learnt lesson. The night had not been wasted.'[38]

Vyshinski's strategy was to poison the minds of his audience against the big fish. To this end the 'small fry' were tried first, so that they could pile on the circumstantial detail of a master-plan concocted by a Trotskyist bloc in collusion with Western secret services. Some of the charges were so self-evidently absurd that they seemed to have strayed in from some surrealistic black comedy. One of the accused pleaded guilty to doctoring butter with nails and powdered glass and to having destroyed fifty truckloads of eggs. Another man was said to have tried to engineer a revolt of the middle peasants by killing tens of thousands of pigs and horses.

> Bit by bit, as one confession succeeded another, the fantastic structure took shape. Each prisoner incriminated his fellows and was in turn incriminated by them. Readily, glibly, they dwelt on their crimes and those of their companions, enlarged on them, embroidered them, elaborated them. There was no attempt to evade responsibility. On the contrary, they often argued among themselves as to who had played the more important part, each claiming the honour for himself. Some displayed considerable narrative powers; of some it might also have been said that they were eloquent. These were men in full possession of their faculties; the statements they made were closely reasoned and delivered, for the most part, with every appearance of spontaneity. It was unthinkable that what they had said had simply been learnt by heart beforehand and was now being delivered under the influence of some drug or hypnotic spell.
>
> And yet what they said, the actual contents of their statements, seemed to bear no relation to reality. The fabric that was being built up was fantastic beyond belief.[39]

Every day Vyshinski's strategy became more obvious. The leaders of the alleged Trotskyist 'bloc' were presented, not as political offenders but as common criminals, murderers, poisoners and spies. And as each prisoner incriminated himself, he managed also to incriminate Bukharin. The fact that many of Vyshinski's charges, when closely examined, contradicted each other, seemed to bother neither the prosecution nor the native audience. 'But don't you see,' the argument would run, 'the diabolical plot of the fascist hyenas and their acolytes the Trotskyists was so fiendishly cunning that they even fed in their own "contradictions" to confuse the tribunes of the people.'

By the time Bukharin himself appeared in the dock he was a doomed man and would have been so even if allowed the luxury of trial by jury. 'Methodically, the old picture of the revolutionary fighter, the Marxist theoretician, the friend of Lenin, the member of the Politbureau, the President of the Communist International, was demolished, and a new portrait substituted for it: a demon, complete with horns, hooves and tail, a traitor, a spy and a capitalist mercenary, a sinister figure, skulking in the shadows, poisoning Soviet hogs, slaughtering Soviet stallions, slipping powdered glass into the workers' butter. Lurking memories of a glorious past were obliterated. No one could have any sympathy with such a miserable wretch. Each fresh revelation was greeted by the crowd with murmurs of rage, horror and disgust. Clearly the method chosen was having the desired effect, was working satisfactorily.'[40]

It was hard to leave the courtroom at night with a firm anchorage in reality. Fitzroy felt irritable and depressed. Perhaps his black mood sometimes spilled over into momentary distaste for Russians in general, since a fellow diplomat tells a story that shows Fitzroy in an unwontedly sour mood. Sitting beside him in the theatre, Harold Eeman heard a young Russian ask politely, 'Tovaritsh, may I borrow a programme?' 'Maclean gave him a cold Caledonian look, then said, "*Ya nye vash tovaritsh*" (I am no comrade of yours) and turned his back on the abashed young man.'[41]

At last, on 5 March 1938, it was Bukharin's turn to appear. He pleaded guilty as charged, but to the general astonishment gave a reasoned defence of his 'errors'. This amounted to putting Stalin in the dock, by asserting that all his policies had been wrong. This was an obvious challenge to Vyshinski, for Bukharin was subtly conveying to his audience the clear impression that he was on trial for disagreeing with Stalin, not for high crimes and misdemeanours. As Vyshinski produced one 'star' witness after another, Bukharin tore their evidence to shreds. Patently the loser in the dialectical contest, Vyshinski laid off Bukharin for a while and instead put former NKVD chief Yagoda in the dock. From Yagoda, who appeared to have been tortured, Vyshinski wrung many damaging admissions.

Then, on 11 March, Vyshinski rose to sum up for the prosecution. He recapitulated all the details of the plots hatched by the Trotskyists and their collaborators in the foreign intelligence agencies, likened Bukharin to Judas Iscariot and Al Capone, and described him as a 'cross between a fox and a pig'. The accused then rose to defend themselves. Almost to a man they simply reiterated their guilt and threw themselves on the mercy of the court. But on 12 March Bukharin made a vigorous rebuttal of the charges. He cunningly made a fool of Vyshinski by pleading guilty to all the plots, sabotage and assassinations, whether he knew anything about them or not. He claimed to be the leader of a Trotskyist 'bloc' but made nonsense of the admission by declaring he knew no other members of the cabal. It seemed illogical, he conceded, but if the People's Prosecutor in his wisdom would have it so . . .

Why, then, was he confessing? Because, now that his faith in

Bolshevism was shattered, he could not face the void. If spared the death penalty – he had nothing to live for. If executed – without repentance, his life had been meaningless. To embrace the superior wisdom of the Party and the fatherland was to commit himself to a cause in which he could die happy. This was the mode of Newman's *Grammar of Assent* or Tertullian's *credo quia absurdum*.

The final outcome was predictable. Fourteen of the defendants, including Bukharin, Rykov, Yagoda and Krestinski, were sentenced to be executed by firing squad. Fitzroy had been at the trial for ten days, eight or nine hours a day. His experiences found expression in the greatest section of a great book. Fitzroy is not usually at home in theoretical territory but his writing on the Bukharin trial, alternately stunned as he was by the nightmare world in which he found himself and tickled by the humour of an unsurpassable black comedy, plumbs unusual psychological depths and achieves a kind of Dostoevskyan grandeur. He shrewdly grasped that Bukharin's closing speech was the key to the whole enigma of his confession. Torture or drugs alone could not produce such eloquent self-denunciation; the answer to this bizarre example of human behaviour had to be sought in a general and pervasive Soviet psychosis.

In an atmosphere of uncertainty and unpredictability, where a 3 a.m. knock on the door could bring sudden death, where the Party line might require you, in a lightning *volte-face*, to believe that black was white, all order and all truth vanished. The result was a chaos of thought and an anarchy of action, where the only constant was the firing squad. The most insidious aspect of totalitarian tyranny is its ability to make people – virtually *all* people, *pace* Lincoln – willing participants in their own humiliation. The 99.9 per cent 'Yes' votes in totalitarian referenda are frightening, not because the regimes falsify the results, but because the result really is a true and accurate reflection of popular 'participation'. If the 'contradiction' of freedom is slavery, the stage beyond is slavery perceived as freedom. Fitzroy's ability to perceive this showed him a far shrewder critic than naïve observers who opted for explanations like 'torture' or 'brainwashing'.

Only one aspect of Fitzroy's brilliant reportage has aroused controversy. Fitzroy claimed actually to have seen Stalin at the trial. 'Of his interest in the proceedings we had direct proof, for at one stage of the trial a clumsily directed arc-light dramatically revealed to attentive members of the audience the familiar features and heavy drooping moustache peering out from behind the black glass of a small window, high up under the ceiling of the court-room.'[42]

Some have doubted this story, finding it just too good to be true. Here perhaps is the place to defend Fitzroy against his critics' suggestion that as an accomplished raconteur he never allows the facts to interfere with a good story. It very much depends on the story. Where the literal truth does not matter the rule of poetic licence may be allowed to apply; but where such licence conflicts with the requirements of the historian, journalist or chronicler, Fitzroy always prefers the implausible possibility to the plausible impossibility – if it is true. Here we can offer him an excellent defence. The writer Arkady Vaksberg remarks of the Stalin 'sighting': 'this sounds hardly plausible, but then, could you call the trial and everything that went with it plausible? No, it was not plausible, but it was true: in those days everything proved possible.'[43]

The Bukharin trial was not Fitzroy's only experience of the late 1930s Alice-in-Wonderland world of the Soviet Union. He had more direct encounters with it as a result of his Chancery work. An employee of the Consular Section and Commercial Secretariat, one Mlle Nina Bergson, was suddenly arrested in November 1937. When Fitzroy asked for details of charges Weinberg, head of the Third Western Department at the People's Commissariat for Foreign Affairs, replied that this was a purely Soviet matter.[44] Weinberg was an old adversary who had curtly brushed aside one of Fitzroy's earlier enquiries. An actress named Ivy Linden, a British subject, had lobbied successfully in London for pressure to be brought in the case of her relative, Eva Linden, also known as Mme Loewenberg. Eva, it transpired, was stateless; she had divorced a German and married a Russian but the marriages had not been recognized by the relevant authorities. Weinberg at once pounced on the weak point in the case. Was she a British subject, he asked? No, said Fitzroy, but her British birth gave the Embassy an unofficial interest. In that case, replied Weinberg, wrapping his answer up in diplomatic language, mind your own business.[45] A similar fate attended Fitzroy's representations on behalf of a Mrs George Fles, a British subject. Her Dutch husband was imprisoned in Smolensk, and she was campaigning for his release. Once again Fitzroy ran into a brick wall. Fles is a Dutch subject, was the reply. What is your *locus standi*? Fitzroy had to admit it was purely humanitarian. He was coldly reminded that his intervention was in that case a diplomatic impertinence.[46]

The lengths to which the purgers would go to get their victims were dramatically illustrated in the case of Rose Cohen, a long-standing British fellow-traveller who spent much of the thirties shuttling between London and Moscow. A friend of Kingsley Martin and other influential British socialists, she married the man who ran the Department of Western Culture at the Soviet Institute. Early in 1937 he was taken up on charges of spying for the Japanese and sent to the firing squad. Twenty years earlier Rose Cohen had applied, unsuccessfully, for Soviet citizenship. The file was now dug up and acted on. Fitzroy takes up the story: 'Suddenly at three o'clock one morning came the knock at the door. "Good morning, Comrade Cohen, you are now a Soviet citizen. Now come with us.'' She was never seen again. Naturally, when we said, ''we hear you have arrested the British subject Rose Cohen'', they said, ''She's not a British subject, so you have no standing in the matter.'' '[47]

It was taxing to switch from matters of high politics to the minutiae of individual cases, but early in 1939, just before Fitzroy was recalled to London, the two streams coalesced in what was at the time a *cause célèbre*. A British oil engineer called Grover, who was working in Baku, fell in love with a Russian woman. Grover wanted to marry the girl, but he was already married. So he went back to England to divorce his wife, promising his new love that he would return soonest. He had no problems over the divorce but he was refused a visa to re-enter the Soviet Union. He next applied for an exit visa for his sweetheart: this too was refused. The couple then appealed to the Foreign Office, who passed the dossier on to the Embassy in Moscow. Fitzroy applied to his old enemies at Narkomindel for a visa on compassionate grounds; NKID refused. Fitzroy then reapplied and NKID re-refused. The charade went on and on. Then: 'One day we get a note saying, ''The People's Commissariat sends its compliments and has the honour to inform His Britannic Majesty's Embassy that the British subject Grover has violated Soviet airspace.'' '[48]

What had happened was that Grover had gone to Copenhagen and taken six lessons in flying a plane. On the sixth lesson, 'Solo Flying', he had simply pointed the plane in the direction of the USSR and decamped. When the fuel ran out, he crash-landed in a field.[49] Peasants ran up with billhooks and arrested him. He was taken to Moscow and housed in the notorious Lubyanka jail, where Fitzroy went to visit him. Many years later Fitzroy made his only public statement about this visit, and a cryptic one it is: 'The only time I was ever inside the Lubyanka, my surroundings struck me as somehow less horrific than might have been expected. But then, I went there merely as a visitor, on business that was quickly discharged.'[50]

Fitzroy now takes up the story. 'I was shown into the room. With Grover were two goons – what we used to call anthropoids from the Urals. I ask Grover if there's anything I can do. Grover says he's being looked after very well. Oh dear, I thought, that sounds bad. ''But I'd be glad if you could manage a little Navy Cut,'' he goes on. ''Are you all right otherwise?'' ''Yes, these two kind gentlemen look after me very well.'' He explains that he's hopeful of getting his wish to marry his girl. At this stage the apes intervene and say, ''No more speaking English, from now on you speak Russian.'' The conversation then continued in halting Russian.'

Fitzroy began by pointing out how serious it was to give up a British passport. He started to tell Grover the story of Rose Cohen. 'I hadn't got far when the two apes said to me, ''You're cheating, that's not a fair story to tell. Rose Cohen was not yours, she was one of ours and we can do with her what we like.'' But Grover was anyway impenetrable. He repeated that all he wanted was to marry this woman and settle down in a job. ''Job?'' I said to him. ''You'll be lucky if you get a job breaking stones in a Siberian salt mine.'' But the more I said things like that, the more he insisted.'[51]

At this stage there occurred a twist in the tale. At the beginning of 1939, Rob Hudson, then a Tory Under-Secretary to the Department of Overseas Trade and later Minister of Agriculture and Fisheries, came out to Moscow to re-negotiate an Anglo-Soviet trade agreement.[52] It was expected that the Grover imbroglio would ruin these talks, or that the Russians would use him as a bargaining counter. Hudson arrived with a cohort of newspapermen. Ian Fleming was covering the story for *The Times*, and for the *Express* there was Sefton Delmer, of whom Fitzroy says: 'He had been thrown out of Germany and Italy and his one object was to get thrown out of the USSR too.'[53]

The talks with Anastas Mikoyan, Commissar for Foreign Trade, began unsatisfactorily. Hudson claimed with a flourish, to the vexation of the new British ambassador, who knew nothing of it, that he had a political brief as well as an economic one. Additionally, the bilingual half-Russian interpreter who usually steered British negotiators through the maze of Soviet dickering fell violently ill, so that Fitzroy had to assume the role of interpreter, as well as briefing Hudson.

Just before Hudson arrived, it had been announced that Grover's trial was imminent. British spirits plummeted when Grover was assigned the defence counsel who had failed to do anything for Bukharin. It looked as though the Soviets were limbering up for a major story of British sabotage in the Baku oil wells. But to general astonishment, the prosecutor made a speech that would not have been out of place in a schmaltzy Hollywood movie. Love made the world go round, he declared, and it was clear that Grover had been lured into his foolish conduct, not just by his passion for a single Russian woman, but by his love for Mother Russia. Grover had already spent three and a half weeks in jail, so that the People's justice required a sentence of – just three and a half weeks. Grover was free! The Soviets thus secured a brilliant propaganda triumph. Grover's fiancée was picked up in Baku and flown to Moscow where, instead of the expected firing-squad, a *dacha* outside Moscow was put at her disposal. With consummate showmanship the Russians arranged to have the world's press on hand as Grover loped through seven-foot snowdrifts for a joyful reunion with his beloved. Next day Fitzroy put the couple on a train bound for the West and home, and gave them a magnum of champagne as a farewell present.[54]

Meanwhile the Hudson negotiations had started. 'Mikoyan, who was very tough, says, we are satisfied with the present agreement and see no reason to change it. Hudson asked me to translate that he was a "tough egg". I did this rather haughtily, but Mikoyan said, "I'm fairly tough too and I don't want a new agreement." Apart from being Armenian and six times as clever as any of us, Mikoyan was reputedly the twentieth Commissar of Baku – it's alleged that the British shot nineteen commissars in Baku while helping the Whites in the Civil war and that Mikoyan's brother was one of them; Mikoyan himself escaped, and consequently never liked us.'

But when Hudson revealed that he had a political remit as well, Mikoyan at once saw a chance to outwit the Germans, with whom the Soviets had been negotiating the non-aggression pact which finally surfaced as the Molotov–Ribbentrop pact in August. In fact, all Hudson had was an anodyne message of encouragement from Lord Halifax, but the promise of a political deal enabled both sides to work on a communiqué. Litvinov and Mikoyan were pleased, as they thought this would put pressure on the Reich. The time came when the communiqué was distributed for publication. Fitzroy takes up the story.

> That evening Hudson and wife are going to the Gypsy Theatre. Mrs Hudson says to me, when I take her out to dinner at the National Hotel, 'I do wish I could meet the nice Mr [Ian] Fleming. As he's staying in this hotel, couldn't you see whether he wouldn't like to join us for dinner?' I go upstairs and find Fleming in bed with a girl. I have to come back and say, he's very, very busy. Anyway, after dinner we're on our way to the Gypsy Theatre. As I'm on the way out of the door – Hudson has gone ahead in car number one – they say, there's a 'Most Immediate' telegram. The telegram instructs the delegation to stick to commercial negotiations and in no circumstances to broach any political matters whatever.
>
> Having got this deciphered, I join Hudson at the theatre. It is full of NKVD apes and commissars. You can see the ankles of the gypsies flickering under the curtain. The thing is already five minutes late. The audience is furious at the delay. I whisper in Hudson's ear. He comes out of the theatre, to the rage of the audience, as the play is now further held up. We go into the manager's office and try to ring the Kremlin. Easier said than done, not only because of the intrinsic inefficiency of the service but because of the delays and breakdowns caused by the bugging devices. We don't get anywhere. Eventually I get into the Ministry of Foreign Affairs – again far from easy at eight at night – and find the Press Release man.[55]

Fitzroy pointed out what had happened and asked that the communiqué be scrapped. The Press Officer said this could not be done without the say-so of Litvinov. The problem was that it was Friday evening and Litvinov had gone to his *dacha* for the weekend. After a flurry of activity, an irate Litvinov was haled back into Moscow. When told the news, he

replied acidly that he had thought he was dealing with a pleni-
potentiary, but now found that he was a second-rate office boy. Scorn-
fully he agreed to the cancellation of the communiqué. Fitzroy raced
back to square things with the Soviet Press Officer, only to discover
a new snag. By now it was 10 p.m. Moscow time, which meant 6 a.m.
Vladivostok time, which in turn meant that the newspapers bearing
the communiqué were already on the streets. Fortunately for Hudson
and the British, Mussolini had chosen to invade Albania, so the papers
were full of that and the communiqué was forgotten. Fitzroy bundled
the Hudsons onto the Leningrad-bound Red Arrow at midnight, complete with imperial gold dining room, champagne, and fox furs and
perfume for Mrs Hudson. But not before Hudson had committed one
last *gaffe*. At the Embassy before leaving for the station Hudson was
distraught and virtually in tears. Shaking his head with disbelief, he
went into the courtyard leading to the double doors of the Embassy.
' "It's a disaster, that's the end of my career," he boomed. Looking
around, he saw the entire foreign press corps assembled there, waiting
for his reaction to the cancelled communiqué.'

It was on this note of farce that Fitzroy bowed out of his diplomatic
career in Moscow. His work in Russia had won him golden opinions
from the Foreign Office mandarins, who needed a 'safe pair of hands' at
the Russian desk in London. What had most of all convinced them of
Fitzroy's calibre was the series of journeys he undertook in the Soviet
Union in 1937 and 1938, his greatest achievement in those two eventful
years, to be surpassed only by 1943 to 1945.

4

Magian Rover

1937–1939

———

'BY miles my most important achievement while in Moscow was to make three or four long journeys on my own to places no foreigner (and certainly no foreign diplomat) had been to since before the Revolution.' Nobody in his right mind would attempt to cap the brilliant description in *Eastern Approaches* of Fitzroy's forays into Soviet Central Asia. But some people have got hold of the wrong end of the stick and, perhaps partly because of his friendship with Wilfred Dunderdale in Paris, assume that Fitzroy was working for the Secret Intelligence Service. He scoffs at such a suggestion. 'I want to emphasize that I have never been involved in espionage, and in fact wouldn't touch it with a bargepole.'

None the less, having visited Samarkand, Fitzroy did report to his superiors what he had seen there. That is a normal part of a diplomat's job. Beyond that? 'The Russians thought I was a spy, though they thought anyone who went for a walk in the park was a spy.' Was he, perhaps, manipulated by hidden puppetmasters who exploited his boyish naïveté? Was Fitzroy, who has sometimes been accused of duping Churchill and Eden, gulled in this way by some minor functionary in MI6?

I considered myself to be working, continuing my career and enjoying myself on my Russian travels. It is true that I had the full support of the Ambassador in Moscow and of the Foreign Office, but they were sceptical that I would reach my destinations. It's normal practice for a career diplomat to travel around the country he's in and report. There was not such a big difference in principle about Russia, just that it was impossible to do so. I took photos with a Leica camera given me as a present by Jonny von Herwarth, which was risky. No sketches but he still has the negatives. I don't think SIS was getting anything out of Russia at the time. That was why all my reports were circulated under FO print, to King–Cabinet Committees.

There seems no good reason to doubt Fitzroy's word. He makes a clear distinction between Signals Intelligence, for which he has a great deal of respect (and how not, considering what is now known about the role of Ultra in World War Two?), and the espionage carried out by agents, about whose usefulness he is broadly sceptical. The world of agents, as le Carré memorably said, is largely that of civil servants playing Cowboys and Indians. 'The Foreign Office has no secrets,' said A.J.P. Taylor. Nor, in any significant sense, has MI6 or MI5. Huge dossiers are held on trade union leaders and other significant leaders of the Left, and the details of many tawdry political deals are stored up ready for possible use. But the idea that the actions of a single agent can change the history of the world is a fantasy of espionage fiction.

In the 1930s British diplomats were trying to 'second-guess' Stalin's likely policies towards Nazi Germany, or towards Japan in the Far East. But even if Fitzroy had managed to smuggle himself into some plant in Soviet Asia banned to foreigners, what could he have proved? Only that the USSR was in a state of readiness to face various contingencies – which everyone knew. No, the idea of Fitzroy as spy is fantastic, and also rather anachronistic. Significantly, in his *jeu d'esprit*, *Take Nine Spies*, he makes the point that the most effective agents (like Yevno Azef) are men of ambiguous loyalties, double or triple agents. And there could be no more eloquent expression of Fitzroy's essential contempt for espionage than the following passages in that book:

> This is not the right place, nor am I the right person, to attempt a detailed study of the inner workings of the Secret Service during the war or at any other time. Quite apart from other considerations, such a study would, I think, be about as interesting to the average reader as a parallel account of the wartime workings of the Ministry of Food, Agriculture and Fisheries – in fact, probably a good deal less so. Though fascinating to those personally involved, the intrigues and petty jealousies from which no government department is entirely free, have a limited appeal for the uninitiated. [A propos the MI6 spies smuggled into Albania in the late 1940s but greeted with machine-gun fire because the Russians had been tipped off by Philby, he says:] . . . just what they could have achieved had they ever reached their destination is to me, at any rate, far from clear.

Sir Douglas Dodds Parker says: 'Fitzroy was down on espionage throughout his life, because he wanted to do rather than to be. He was essentially a soldier, and SIS is as far away on the spectrum from military action as you could get. Espionage is all reaction, not original action. SIS reacts, SOE takes clandestine action, SAS takes paramilitary action, and the regular forces just fight.'

To follow Fitzroy's Soviet travels, we have to return to the early days of his Moscow posting, in 1937. Turkestan had been his objective even before he set foot in Russia. The Foreign Office had poured cold water over his enthusiastic ideas of travelling there. Turkestan? No foreigner had visited it for twenty years.

All through the spring of 1937 Fitzroy puzzled over the problem of how to get there. No direct rail ticket from Moscow to Tashkent would be issued without a letter of authorization from the authorities. The same obstacle confronted a rail traveller trying to use a roundabout route. Fitzroy therefore decided to set out for the oil town of Baku on the Caspian Sea, a city open to foreigners, and then try to get across the Caspian to Soviet Central Asia.

He made an uneventful three-day journey to Baku by first-class sleeper. Baku, once described by H. M. Stanley as the 'Paris of the Caspian', had long since lost whatever charm it possessed. It seemed so uninviting that Fitzroy checked into a hotel and went to bed early, but was soon awakened by the cacophony of a Soviet jazz band. The Party line had changed: such (previously) 'bourgeois decadence' was now in favour. He dressed, and spent the night observing the locals at play in the ballroom. Quite apart from the repertoire, which was ten years behind the West, he was amused to see people trying to dance Cossack-fashion to the beat. Evidently he made a mark, for thirty years later, when he revisited Baku, the same hotel manager recognized him.[1]

Fitzroy bought a ticket on a steamer bound for Lenkoran near the Persian border. There he hired a horse and went riding towards the mountains. Almost at once he found himself surrounded by NKVD cavalry, commanded by a shifty-looking Tartar. The sequel, in which Fitzroy pleaded diplomatic privilege, is described in *Eastern Approaches* with characteristic good humour. Fitzroy asked the Tartar if he knew what a diplomat was. 'To this he replied, his foolish face suddenly crafty, that he knew only too well and that if I went on arguing he would shoot me on the spot instead of waiting till we got home. I said that if he did the consequences would be very unpleasant for him, to which he replied that they would be even more unpleasant for me. This argument struck me as convincing and I relapsed into a gloomy silence.'[2]

Back at NKVD headquarters Fitzroy discovered that his captors were all illiterate. Producing a pass for the May Day parade in Red Square, Fitzroy 'translated' it as a general *laissez-passer*. His Tartar captors were profusely apologetic and released him. Next he got a berth on a Baku-bound steamer; from Baku he took a train to Tiflis (Tbilisi), the Georgian capital. After some days there he travelled by truck over the Caucasus mountain passes to Ordzhonikidze, then took the train to Moscow, arriving forty-eight hours later. He at once wrote a report on his travels, so lucid that it was sent on to London, where it was also well received, and judged worthy of reproduction in the 'Confidential Print'. Fitzroy's colleague Laurence Collier sent his congratulations on such 'vivid accounts'.[3]

At the end of the summer of 1937 Fitzroy tried again to get to Central Asia. This time his plan was to take the trans-Siberian railway, get off somewhere *en route*, and make his way south. The risk, of course, was that the authorities would spot him getting off, and arrest him.

He left Moscow on 21 September, his arsenal of official-looking documents reinforced with an old bill from a shop in London that had 'By Royal Appointment' stamped on it: 'You know, they were by appointment to the Duke of Connaught or Queen Mary or someone – and it was covered with impressive coats-of-arms. That took in everybody. It was a marvellous bill, that. I paid it in the end, too.'[4] For days the train rolled along over the steppes while Fitzroy read Simenon. He got off the train at Sverdlovsk, on the far side of the Urals, then cheekily visited the local NKVD to get a pass enabling him to stay in the 'élite' section of the local hotel. Thirty-six hours later he took a train to Novosibirsk, a further two days' journey eastward. There he queued for ten hours before getting the last ticket to Biisk, two or three hundred miles south, at the foot of the Altai mountains. His euphoria evaporated when he discovered he was being followed by two NKVD men, who dogged his heels throughout the rest of his journey.

Biisk he found to be little up on a Klondike gold-rush town; the unpaved streets had become a quagmire of mud. Worse, with the onset of autumn all the passes into the Altai range were closed. He set off in a train again, intending to get to Alma Ata via Altaisk and Barnaul. Hitherto he had secured berths in sleeping compartments or 'soft' trains, but now for the first time he had to suffer the rigours of Russian 'hard' trains – a form of transport as Spartan and uncomfortable as the nineteenth-century 'emigrant cars' in the USA.

At Barnaul Fitzroy was questioned by the NKVD there, but once again turned the tables and ended by securing their help in getting a 'soft' berth on the train to Alma Ata. So far the landscape had scarcely changed: '. . . strictly Siberian: a dead flat plain covered with grey-green moss, occasional clumps of silver birches and an occasional magpie sitting on a stump.'[5]

But at Semipalatinsk, two nights out from Barnaul, the travellers crossed the dividing line between Siberia and Central Asia. They were now running through a desert far more desolate than the Siberian tundra. The train made painfully slow progress on the single-track Turksib line and took all day to cross the first stretch of desert. Yet next morning Fitzroy caught his first glimpses of the snow caps of the Tien Shan – the Mountains of Heaven – in Chinese Turkestan. That evening he came to Alma Ata, at the foot of the range.

Fitzroy failed in his initial attempts to get into the Dom Sovietov, the only good hotel in town, even drawing a blank with the NKVD. They referred him to the 'Diplomatic Agency', and the official there was so overjoyed to see a real foreigner that he quickly whipped the Dom Sovietov into line.

Eventually Fitzroy managed to wheedle a tourist car and some petrol from the local Town Soviet, and his two NKVD shadows (who had tailed him all the way from Biisk) watched in amazement as he drove off from the hotel accompanied by a local official and a Kazakh dragoman. Climbing to 6000 ft, the travellers spent the night in a hut on the shore of Lake Issik. They then drove back to Alma Ata, where Fitzroy entrained for Tashkent. His plan was to proceed from Tashkent to Samarkand, which lay in a forbidden zone. Amazingly, this last lap into Samarkand proved the easiest of the trip: he took the dawn train, and entered the city of Tamerlane in the late morning.

He reeled intoxicatedly through the mosques and minarets, marvelling at the ubiquitous glazed tiles of deep blue and vivid turquoise, sensuously drunk on the chiaroscuro. 'In all other parts of the world light descends upon earth,' says an old Muslim proverb. 'From Holy Samarkand and Bokhara, it ascends.' He spent the entire day in Samarkand, then flopped exhaustedly in a crowded 'hard' carriage for the overnight journey back to Tashkent.

This journey to Samarkand might have seemed achievement enough for most young men, but already Fitzroy's sights were set on Bokhara, 200 miles further south-west. As he wrote: 'I had seen Alma Ata: I had seen Tashkent; best of all I had seen Samarkand. I had done what I set out to do and, having done it, immediately I conceived new ambitions.'[6] After Bokhara, Sinkiang and Chinese Turkestan beckoned.

But first he must satisfy his political masters. He had exceeded his leave and, unless he headed back to Moscow with all speed, might be granted no more. He need not have worried. His superiors were once again delighted with his achievement, and Lord Chilston sent Fitzroy's official record of his journey to Eden. 'Mr Maclean is indeed an enterprising young man', reads one minute, and another, most revealingly: 'When this has been printed I suggest that we might consider communicating a copy of it to the US Embassy, as part of our effort to meet the State Department.'[7]

What were Fitzroy's motives in undertaking these journeys, apart from impressing his superiors? In part it was the 'spirit of contradiction'. In part it was the Everest syndrome: 'because it's there'. More mundanely, they provided an opportunity to meet real Russian people. However imperfect the interdiction on Russians talking to foreigners, and whatever the opportunities at the theatre and other social gatherings, urban Russians were forever looking over their shoulders to see who would denounce them for 'congress with the enemy'. In the wilds of Central Asia, much of this inhibition was shed.

I spoke demotic Russian when I made my trips. In those days it was the kiss of death for any educated Russian to talk to you, but I talked to people on my trips and of course it was a question of getting from place to place and getting fed. I learned a lot of demotic Russian and in fact in Central Asia I spoke better Russian than most of the natives. Quite a lot of them thought I *was* Russian.[8]

I was determined, partly from a spirit of contradiction, to get to Soviet Central Asia, which I had been told was impossible. I was intellectually curious about remote areas of the Soviet Union. Also, Peter Fleming, a friend of mine, had recently won fame with *Brazilian Adventure* and *News from Tartary*. My journeys were a romantic idea of my own, *inspired* by Peter Fleming and his journeys across China . . . one, I retraced a few months ago . . . to Peking over the Karakorams from Gilgit. We went in jeeps, but in those days Peter went by pony with Ella Maillart.[9]

Wasn't he afraid, though, to make such trips when xenophobic paranoia was at its height? Afraid of being arrested, or framed on trumped-up charges? Fitzroy thinks this would have been unlikely. 'What they might have done, which I believe was done to someone else, was push me out of a train going through a tunnel and say I was drunk. They were so interested to see where I was going, especially as they lived in a fantasy world where all foreigners were spies. There was an element of chaos in Russia, then as now.'[10]

It was the summer of 1938 before Fitzroy was able to head east again. By this time the Russians had gained control of Sinkiang province in China, taking advantage of the confused situation in the Chinese heartland, where warlords battled with Chiang Kai-shek and Mao Tse-tung, Nationalists with Communists and, intermittently, the Chinese with the invading Japanese who were now in control of Shanghai, Nanking and most of the eastern seaboard. The Russian hegemony in Sinkiang severed the lifeline of the Indian traders there and made the position of the British consul-general untenable, and Fitzroy was sent as the ambassador's personal representative to secure better treatment for the consul and the Indians. Because this was an official trip he could not improvise, but had to seek formal Soviet visas and passes and obtain entry into Sinkiang from Chinese officialdom. Ironically, the Russian denial that they had any influence in Sinkiang made it easier for Fitzroy to get a passport from the Chinese authorities.

He left Moscow on 6 June and reached Alma Ata in five days. From there to Ayaguz, a 400-mile journey north, took twenty-four hours on a slow train. At Ayaguz it transpired that the NKVD knew all about his journey: they laid on a primitive bus to get him to the Soviet frontier town of Bakhti. Here again the local NKVD made straight the ways, and Fitzroy was soon in Chinese territory. But at the Chinese frontier post he met Oriental prevarication. After endless waiting and fobbings-off, the Chinese official finally admitted that he would not be allowed to proceed any farther, as no instructions had arrived from Chungking (the Chinese capital since the Japanese invasion) or from the provincial capital, Urumchi. There was nothing for it: Fitzroy must return to the Soviet side of the frontier until the matter was cleared up. But the Soviets had something else up their sleeve. Since Bakhti was in a pro-hibited area, Fitzroy could not wait there – he must return to Alma Ata. It is hard not to conclude that all the diplomatic courtesy masked a subtle revenge for the way Fitzroy had tweaked the noses of the authori-ties in 1937.

In Alma Ata, in the course of his shuntings between the Chinese con-sulate and the People's Commissariat for Foreign Affairs, a Chinese official at the consulate let the cat out of the bag by telling Fitzroy that he knew for certain the Soviet government was opposed to him setting foot in Sinkiang province – striking circumstantial evidence of the collusion of the Russians and Chinese.

Later that night the Russians revealed their hand. A sheepish Chi-nese official informed Fitzroy that permission to proceed to Urumchi had been refused. At the same time the NKVD requested his immediate departure from Alma Ata. All Fitzroy's protests were in vain. He took revenge by insisting on a first-class sleeper back to Moscow, which forced the NKVD to evict Party officials from an already full train. He fumed. 'I had been scored off heavily and all the way back to Moscow I turned over in my mind ways of getting even with the NKVD. Long before I arrived, I decided that I would come back to Central Asia before the end of the year, whether they wanted me there or not. And next time I would not make them a present of my itinerary in advance.'[11]

By the autumn of 1938 it was clear that, because of the international situation, Urumchi would have to wait at least until spring. Fitzroy therefore decided to attempt a journey from Moscow to Kabul through Soviet Central Asia, the Oxus valley and Afghan Turkestan, using an ordinary exit visa which, for the Diplomatic Corps, was valid for all frontier points. Accordingly, he obtained an exit visa for Afghanistan. His principal aim *en route* was to visit Bokhara.

Fitzroy left Moscow on 7 October, on an express train with a restaurant car, bound for Askhabad, the capital of Turkmenistan. Wherever he went, he was dogged by a pair of NKVD men. On the third evening he reached Orenburg, by the middle of the fifth night he was passing through Tashkent, and on 13 October in the morning he came again to Samarkand. Resisting the temptation to linger among the scintillating minarets, he changed trains at once and travelled westward to Kagan.

Finding that there were no through trains to Bokhara, Fitzroy made an abortive attempt to hitch a ride on the back of a lorry loaded with cotton bales.

A short sprint and a flying jump landed me head first in a rather loosely packed bale of cotton, from which I emerged to see one of my NKVD men running after the lorry, which he obviously had not a hope of catching, while the other disappeared into the door of the Militia guardroom, presumably in order to get help. Meanwhile, the lorry, with me on board, was heading for the open country and showing a pretty turn of speed. The situation, I felt, was fraught with amusing possibilities.

At this point the lorry suddenly stopped for no apparent reason, and a few seconds later a breathless NKVD man landed in the next cotton bale to mine. I felt reassured and hoped that his colleague would not now persist in his intention of turning out the guard and that I should be able to complete my journey to Bokhara undisturbed in this providential vehicle.

But this was not to be. The sight of two people jumping on to a lorry had put the same idea into a number of other heads. There was a rush and we were trampled over and rolled on as the lorry filled with a variegated crowd of Uzbeks, kicking and biting, as only Uzbeks can, in their efforts to get themselves on and their friends off.

All might have been well, had not the driver, who had let in the clutch and was moving off again, at this point put his head round the corner and caught sight of this multitude of uninvited passengers. It was, he said, overdoing it. One or two might pass, but not a whole crowd. We must all get off at once. There ensued a general argument which ended in the driver letting down the sides of the lorry and pushing off as many of his passengers as he could reach, while others climbed in again on the other side.[12]

At this point Fitzroy noticed a police car coming down the road. He jumped off the lorry and ran for cover, closely followed by his NKVD shadow. The police car, containing the other NKVD man and a State Security official, stopped the lorry. A full-scale 'strip search' of the vehicle followed; finding nothing, the Security officer abandoned his NKVD companion and drove back to town. Fitzroy decided that he would walk to Bokhara. The NKVD tail fell in unhappily behind him.

Fitzroy followed a caravan of Bactrian camels and came in sight of the walled city of Bokhara at about two o'clock, in the moonlight. He spent the night sleeping under some bushes, and his weary NKVD escort was obliged to do the same. Next day he explored the crumbling ramparts of the ancient city, the cavernous tunnels of the covered bazaar, the intricate labyrinths of narrow lanes, the high crenellated walls with eleven gates and eighteen watch-towers. Above all rose the Tower of Death, a minaret more magnificent even than the domes of Samarkand.

Here were a myriad wonders to which Fitzroy vowed he would one day return. But his time was limited, so he decided to continue his

journey to the Oxus, much to the relief of his NKVD tail. First, Fitzroy
and his reluctant companions took the Emir of Bokhara's toy-town train
back to Kagan. Then Fitzroy faced the problem of how to board his next
train, since expresses usually hurtled through this halt full to the brim.
He explained the problem to his shadows, who had been maintaining
the fiction that they were simply travellers, too, who just coincidentally
happened to be going everywhere he went. They got hold of the sta-
tionmaster: the next southbound train was halted for them, but they all
had to travel in a 'hard' coach.

The rambunctious Tajiks in the train, bound for Stalinabad, the
capital of Tajikstan, would allow Fitzroy no sleep, and seemed determined to turn the journey into a party. Vodka and pink sausages were
produced. Fitzroy describes the upshot: '. . . the sausages and vodka
had begun to have their effect. A little further up the carriage a group of
travellers had formed themselves into what is known in the Soviet
Union as an *ansambl* or concert party, and were giving spirited render-
ings of various folk-songs and dances. Vodka flowed more and more
freely and soon pandemonium was let loose . . . Several members of the
party were entirely overcome by their exertions and we had to hoist
them like sacks on to the top shelves, from which at intervals they
crashed ten feet to the floor, without any apparent ill effects. When we
reached my destination, Termez, an hour or two before dawn, the party
was at its height.'[13]

Termez, in eastern Turkmenistan, is on the Russian bank of the
Oxus, the river celebrated in Matthew Arnold's *Sohrab and Rustum* and
once described by Lord Curzon as 'that famous river that, like the
Euphrates and the Ganges, rolls its stately burden down from a hoar
antiquity through the legends and annals of the East.'[14] On the far side
of the river was Afghanistan, journey's end. After the usual interminable procrastinations and tergiversations, the authorities gave
Fitzroy permission to cross to the far bank, escorted, in a boat. Once in
Afghanistan, Fitzroy hired horses and set off with a guide. The riders
emerged onto a desert and, after many adventures, arrived in Mazar-i-
Sharif, capital of Afghan Turkestan. Here Fitzroy continued his
journey towards Kabul by truck, through Tashkurgan and Doaba.

In Doaba there was a rest-house built by the Afghan government and
reserved for travelling Europeans. By this time a bath and clean sheets
represented to Fitzroy the height of luxury. He next presented himself
to the British Minister, and found himself among good friends. 'In Mrs
Fraser-Tytler I found a fellow clanswoman with whom my friendship
dated back to the days of my childhood in Inverness, while from her
husband I learned more about Afghanistan in forty-eight hours than I
should otherwise have learnt in as many days.'[15]

He then proceeded to Kabul, where he heard news which wrecked his plan to return to Moscow overland: a cholera epidemic was raging throughout Soviet Central Asia. He therefore had to cross the Khyber pass to Peshawar, then travel via Delhi, Baghdad, Basra and Teheran to Tabriz, capital of Persian Azerbaijan, where he spent forty-eight hours arguing with the local governor about his visa before setting out on the last stage of his journey. There were the usual frontier delays at Djulfa on the Araxes, but soon Fitzroy was on his way to Erivan, capital of Soviet Armenia. As he boarded the train, he was joined once more by the inevitable NKVD escort, this time a couple of Armenians. From Erivan he went by train to Batum, hoping to take ship to the seaside resort of Sochi, but storms on the Black Sea prevented that. Finding Batum a depressing place, despite its untypically neat, bourgeois appearance, Fitzroy returned to Tiflis. His journey was nearly over but, as Odysseus warned, the worst dangers lie in wait for the traveller as he nears voyage's end.

It was now 12 November. In the late afternoon Fitzroy decided to visit the British Military Cemetery. On his way there he was roughly challenged by a sentry, who asked what he was doing. Fitzroy's reply that he was a British diplomat seemed to make matters worse. The sentry ordered him to put his hands up and threatened to shoot him if he lowered them. In this excruciating stance Fitzroy remained for a full hour, from 5.45 to 6.45 p.m. Finally he was hustled at gunpoint to a nearby military post. The officer, after examining his documents, said he had no authority to release him and would have to refer the matter to a representative of the People's Commissariat. Fitzroy remained under close arrest for another hour until two officers of State Security arrived. After examining his diplomatic card they, too, declined the responsibility of releasing him. A further hour passed. Then two senior officials of State Security appeared on the scene and, after cross-questioning him, released him without apology. The dauntless Fitzroy, bent, as ever, on having the last word, asked if he could now proceed with his original intention, to visit the cemetery. If you do so, you will be shot, he was told.[16]

Determined to shake the dust of Tiflis from his feet as soon as possible, Fitzroy found space in a lorry leaving for Ordzhonikidze by the Georgian Military Road. The route lay through snow-capped mountain passes and even clothed in the entire contents of his kitbag Fitzroy shivered and froze. When he reached Ordzhonikidze he was glad to escape into the overheated stuffiness of the Moscow train. He arrived in Moscow late at night a couple of days later.

Next day the Embassy swung into action on behalf of their slighted secretary. The official protest to Litvinov referred ironically to the NKVD agents: was it not extraordinary that they should not have intervened to clear up the 'misunderstanding'? 'HM Embassy cannot but

5

Foreign Office Doldrums
1939–1941

———————

F ITZROY now looks back on his two years at the Russian desk of
the Foreign Office's Northern Department in London as a rather
boring interlude between the Russian travelling and the military
experiences to come. 'Rather dull and dry stuff, I'm afraid,' he says.
But this quiet period reveals his talents as diplomat. Between 1939 and
1941, the years of the Nazi–Soviet pact, there were two pressing questions for Sovietologists. What were Stalin's long-term intentions? And
what military options did Britain have if Russia came into the war on
the German side?

It has sometimes been suggested that Fitzroy is 'soft' on the Soviet
Union. Any such view should be dispelled by his work during these
years, which shows him on the contrary to have been the most hawkish
of hawks. Fitzroy explains his plans for dismembering the USSR thus.

The Soviet Union had a pact with an enemy and was providing the Germans
with oil. Our project was to bomb Baku. On the strength of my expertise in
Central Asia, I was asked if there was any way to make trouble with the
Russians by stirring up minorities. I saw some people, *émigrés*, et cetera,
and reported that there were many ways. The RAF was going to bomb Baku
from Syria. The thing was thought to be a bit of a joke at the time and quickly
forgotten. Events of 22 June 1941 [when Hitler invaded the Soviet Union]
subsumed all this. But I wrote it all down and talked to the French. The
document the *Independent* reproduced [26 February 1990] was supposed to be
secret beyond thirty years. The Public Record Office let it out but has now
withdrawn it. The French felt the same way in 1939 and 1940. After the fall of
France, the Germans picked up the copy of the document I had taken over and
thought this was a good way of stirring up trouble between the UK and the
USSR.

Fitzroy sticks to his belief that at some deep level the destinies of
Germany and Russia are linked.

Twenty years or so ago I would have been alarmed at the prospect of a united Germany, especially as I think it'll eat Austria before long, but I'm not alarmed now as I think they have a virtually insoluble problem which they'll be tempted to take on, which is to sort out the Soviet Union. There's this love-hate relationship between Germany and the Soviet Union and they have some of the qualities the Russians lack: efficiency, organizing ability, decency, application and the capacity to work hard. Historically they have always been the people who pulled the Russians together and the Russians now need pulling together more than ever before in their history.

In 1939 Fitzroy travelled back to London via Berlin, convinced that European war was inevitable and that Germany and the Soviet Union would be allies in that war. Throughout 1939 'Jonny' von Herwarth continued to light on evidence that a pact between Stalin and Hitler was probable. With Fitzroy gone, he fed the information to Armine Dew, who succeeded Fitzroy in Moscow as he had in Paris.[1] Von Herwarth, Charlie Thayer and Fitzroy were all determined to get into their respective armies if war came, and all three eventually succeeded. Thayer was a West Point graduate; for 'Jonny' the Prussian heritage was important. Fitzroy's pride in his clan ancestry and his family's long military tradition was his deep motivation, but it seems that he may have underplayed this in conversation with the other two, for von Herwarth writes: 'Maclean was guided by the feeling that in wartime one should be in the army and that army life would be, to quote the title of an American edition of his memoirs, *An Escape to Adventure*.'[2]

It was an incident in Moscow in 1938 that crystallized Fitzroy's conviction that war was coming and that he must get into it. He was at the theatre with the ambassador's wife, Lady Chilston, when the Munich agreement was announced in the interval. Lady Chilston told him her husband had wanted to fight in the First World War but had been unable to because he was a diplomat and thus in a 'reserved' occupation. He had bitterly regretted ever since his failure to see action. Fitzroy was determined not to live a life of regrets himself.

Fitzroy's reputation as a Soviet specialist made the Russian desk at the Foreign Office inevitable. Here he wrote the initial assessment reports on incoming material from ambassadors and these, with the incoming cables and letters, would ascend the hierarchy for further minuting by senior officials. Very quickly he sensed pressure to adhere to one or other of the 'party' lines on the USSR. 'It was interesting, coming back from Moscow, when not many people knew Russia, that I was pounced on by all kinds of people. Some people expected me to say it was a workers' paradise, while a lot of others were delighted when I said it was most certainly *not* a workers' paradise and who said, "don't you think we ought really to forget about everything else and go in with Hitler against Russia'', which I was equally disgusted by.'[3]

Two bizarre encounters brought home to Fitzroy that 1939 was not a year for nuanced discriminations and diplomatic subleties. The first was with his namesake Donald Maclean. There was occasional confusion over the two Macleans – though not in the FO typing pool, where Donald was known as 'Fancy Pants', and Fitzroy as 'Fitzwhiskers' after the Cossack moustache he had grown in Russia. Fitzroy had first met Donald at a débutante's ball at the Savoy Hotel in 1934, where he was introduced to a golden-haired 21-year-old who was about to take the Foreign Office examinations, 'long-haired, light tie, droopy appearance. I was pursuing some girl and the last thing I wanted was to talk to him but anyhow we had five minutes' conversation . . . he said to me, "I'm a member of the Communist party". His adoring mother was present, Lady Maclean, widow of Sir Donald, who had been a Liberal Cabinet Minister. "Yes," she said, "Donald is even more of a radical than his dear father was." '[4] Fitzroy imagined that Donald was merely posing, as it was fashionable then in some circles to pretend to be a Communist. He thought no more of the incident until 1939, when he bumped into Donald Maclean in the Foreign Office corridor. 'For want of anything better to say', he asked Donald if he were still a Party member. 'Maclean, who would have had no difficulty in finding a bantering answer if he had been asked the question in a night-club, was evidently embarrassed; he dismissed his former allegiance.'[5] Somewhat flustered, he said sharply to Fitzroy: 'That was simply a childish aberration. I can assure you that now I am well to the right of you (which he correctly assumed was some way to the right of centre).'[6]

The other encounter was with Winston Churchill, at this time still a voice crying in the political wilderness. Fitzroy was quite friendly with Churchill's niece Clarissa (who later married Anthony Eden) and had indeed taken her to her first night-club, during his Paris period. Now she rang up and invited him to lunch at Chartwell the next weekend. On a glorious day in June 1939 he drove her down. She explained that Churchill wanted to talk to someone with first-hand experience of Russia. They arrived to find a big party gathered in the garden under the trellis. Mrs Churchill was there, of course; Randolph, 'who always made a lot of noise'; Ian Colvin, the *News Chronicle* correspondent in Berlin; and a number of others.

Soon Churchill came to the point. Brooding on the fact that the government had just offered guarantees to Poland and Romania, he asked Fitzroy whether the Russians would come in on the British side in the event of war. Fitzroy, armed with his knowledge of the secret dealings between Berlin and Moscow, replied that he was quite certain they would not.

At this he exploded, and all at once I found myself a target for the full flood of Churchillian eloquence. If I couldn't count on the Russians, he said, and when we were totally unprepared for war ourselves, would I please tell him why I had guaranteed Poland and Romania? Why was I so calmly sending thousands of British boys to certain death in what was clearly a forlorn cause?

At twenty-eight I was even less articulate than I am now, and it was an altogether alarming experience. But I was quite determined not to be blamed for a policy of which I disapproved as strongly as he did, and with the formulation of which I had had nothing whatever to do. When I could get a word in edgeways, I replied that I had not been responsible for guaranteeing Poland or indeed Romania and had no wish to send any British troops to their death. But with the best will in the world, I did not think Stalin was likely to do something which he quite clearly regarded as against his interests. In that case, Winston replied, why in heaven's name . . .? And off he went again. I was thankful when lunch came to an end and Mrs Churchill took me for a walk in the garden. When he said goodbye to me later in the afternoon Winston said he was sorry he had been so explosive, but he was desperately worried and frustrated at the way things were going. I said so was I.[7]

During nearly two years at the Foreign Office Fitzroy worked from a coherent set of principles, deeply influenced by what he had learned from von Herwarth. It could be said that he regarded Nazi Germany and the Soviet Union as the two horns of a single, totalitarian ram. The two dictators would sign a non-aggression pact, he thought, and it would hold. Thus, following any declaration of war against Germany the USSR would be an enemy in all but name. There were two main strands to Fitzroy's thinking. The first was that Stalin and Hitler and the regimes they represented 'coupled' naturally. Fitzroy was an early exponent of the view that it is the total power available to the centre, through technology, that defines a totalitarian system.[8] Trotskyists and others on the Left tended to see property relations and modes of production as all-important; according to their view, there was a natural harmony between the fascist regimes of Germany and Italy, plus the Western democracies, on the one hand, separated by a crevasse, on the other, from such political systems as that of the USSR, which had abolished private ownership. A third wheel on this wagon of theory was added by the fascist theorists, who saw both the Western 'plutocracies' and the Soviet Union as corrupt and unregenerate.

So much for theory. But Fitzroy thought that there was also a historical correspondence of interests between Germany and Russia: there had been a tradition of collaboration between the Prussian and Russian monarchies from the Napoleonic period. Fitzroy pondered, too, the lessons of the Rapallo treaty of 1922, which reversed existing diplomatic alliances and provided for the development of economic relations again between Germany and Russia, as well as the renunciation of all war reparations claims. The 1920s saw a spectacular growth in Soviet–German economic, military and political co-operation. Both Germany and the USSR hated the provisions of the Treaty of Versailles; both detested the newly-created Poland; both wanted to break out of the common isolation imposed by the Western powers. Quite apart from the direct benefits of trade and military co-operation, the Germans and Soviets hoped to turn their alliance to advantage in their relations with Britain and France.

It is easy to see why Fitzroy thought a pact between Stalin and Hitler was feasible, and likely to be durable. This view was largely shared by his erstwhile colleagues in the Moscow Embassy, who surmised that in the event of a European war the Soviet attitude would probably be one of 'nervous neutrality', designed to avoid antagonizing Germany. The military aid attaché, Colonel Firebrace, thought that Russia would in any case be incapable of a telling offensive against the Reich, though he did predict a formidable resistance against any invader.[9]

Soviet suspicions of the West never recovered from Munich. All Russians, from ambassador Ivan Maisky in London through Molotov to Stalin, shared the belief that British policy had the unalterable aim of bringing Germany and the USSR into collision.[10] Their response to Chamberlain's 'peace in our time' showed that Stalin and his acolytes could deploy a pleasing gift for repartee when not pursuing their murderous designs at home. Chamberlain quoted Hotspur in Henry IV:

> . . . out of this nettle, danger, we pluck this flower, safety.
> (Henry IV, Part 1, Act 2, Scene iii, lines 11–12)

But Chamberlain had not carefully noted the context of his quotation. *Izvestia* struck back with:

> The purpose you undertake is dangerous; the friends you have named uncertain; the time itself unsorted; and your whole plot too light for the counterpoise of so great an opposition. (Ibid, lines 13–16)

– the letter Hotspur is reading from during his soliloquy.

There were certainly grounds for Stalin's suspicions. In its determination to destabilize the Nazi–Soviet pact the West considered many desperate remedies during the winter of 1939. One was the formation of an anti-Comintern pact, which would detach Italy, Spain and Japan from Germany and thus unhinge the Molotov–Ribbentrop accord.[11]

Two anti-Soviet projects very much in the air even before Fitzroy returned from Russia became so closely associated with his name that they are sometimes, unfairly, regarded as his personal hobby-horses. (In fact, while Fitzroy did have certain clear and fixed ideas about the Soviet Union between 1939 and 1941, he was in a sense always devising a libretto for a score already written in the Foreign Office.) The first project was a bombing attack on the Soviet oilfields at Baku. This had been broached early in 1939 with the French, but Military Intelligence in the War Office opposed it except as part of a general war on Stalin's Russia. And about the same time, Fitzroy's old friend Oliver Harvey was collecting information on the separatist movement in the Ukraine with a view to fomenting trouble for Stalin there.[12]

Once the Molotov–Ribbentrop pact, signed in August 1939 and followed within two weeks by the British declaration of war against Germany, made a solution to the Soviet problem imperative, Fitzroy threw himself into his work with gusto. On 28 October he produced a ten-page memorandum devoted to the proposition that the Soviet Union might have to be destabilized. He started from the premiss that the USSR might use the opportunity provided by the 'phoney war' in the West to spread its tentacles into the British Empire in the East. Historically, Fitzroy argued, Russia had used the East as an outlet for its energies in times of adversity; this had been, after all, one of the causes of rivalry with Britain in the nineteenth century – the 'Great Game'.

The obvious strategy for the British, if tensions should heighten this way, was to make a pre-emptive strike in Soviet Central Asia. 'So long as the situation in the Middle East remains stable and existing frontiers are kept intact, subversive activities directed against Soviet rule in Central Asia and the Caucasus would be uncalled for and almost certainly impracticable.' But, 'it does not follow that this would be the case if the situation once became fluid.' And, Fitzroy wrote, warming to his theme, 'The independent national republics of Georgia, Armenia and Azerbaijan which had arisen in the Caucasus were invaded by the Red Army, *gleichgeschaltet* and *angeschlossen* [swiftly subjected and annexed], without any regard for the wishes of the population, and attempts to rebel against Soviet rule were met with savage repression.'

To this there was an obvious objection: if the Stalinist terror was as formidable as many (including Fitzroy) made out, the chances of destabilizing the Soviet Union were surely nil? This, he thought, overlooked one important factor: 'It is, however, not impossible that certain religious communities, notably the Mahometans in Central Asia and Trans-Caucasia and the Armenians, still maintain clandestine relations with their co-religionists outside the frontiers of the Soviet Union. It is believed that, at any rate until ten years ago, the Tajiks in Soviet Turkestan had contacts with their fellow-adherents of the Aga Khan across the border in Afghanistan, while, until his death two years ago, the Katholikos of the Armenian church all over the world resided at Etchmiadzin, near Erivan.'

Fitzroy turned to consider possible bases from which disaffection among religious and nationalist communities could be fomented.

Sinkiang, the most promising of all, was ruled out, since foreign agents there would be spotted and arrested immediately. That left Afghanistan, Turkey and Iran. Afghanistan and Iran had the advantage that 'use could be made of the natives of the frontier regions of Afghanistan, who are practically indistinguishable from the corresponding tribes on the Soviet side of the frontier'. These people could establish contact with disaffected elements in the Soviet Union, ready to fan the flames of revolt over the widest possible area.

Fitzroy recommended that an agency be set up at once to foment trouble; pending closer investigations in Iran and Afghanistan it should be based in India, under the direction of Military Intelligence. Nationalist and religious leaders should be offered independence from Moscow, a liberal system of government, private enterprise, ownership of land by individual peasants, freedom of worship and political amnesty. And, recognizing the universality of 'the old Adam', Fitzroy felt that 'an opportunity of venting their hatred on their oppressors would be bound to have a certain popular attraction, provided always that it had sufficient chance of success to be convincing.'[13]

Fitzroy's controversial memorandum made many converts within the diplomatic sevice. Much heartened, he produced another which argued that, since Soviet ambitions were Asiatic rather than European, the British should make an alliance with Turkey.

> We should no longer be faced with the alternative of either relying largely on indirect methods, or of embarking, at a most inconvenient time, on vast military operations with the object of driving the Russians back beyond their own frontiers. Instead we could with the support of Turkey concentrate on the Caucasus, and in particular on the oil wells of Baku and the Batum–Baku pipeline. With Turkey as our active ally, we should be able to send a force into the Black Sea and should also stand a much better chance of stirring up a rebellion in the Caucasus. With the Caucasus in a state of turmoil and the oil supplies cut off, we should have little to fear from the Russians anywhere else.[14]

Fitzroy was becoming a thorough-going hawk. In a minute dated 24 December 1939 but lacking in Christmas spirit he wrote: 'It is not at present our intention to declare war on the Soviet Union, for we have nothing to gain by doing so . . . It is, however, quite possible that sooner or later the moment will arise when our interests will be served by an open conflict with the Soviet Union.'[15] This was too much for some of Fitzroy's senior colleagues at the Foreign Office. One of them, Laurence Collier, minuted sceptically: 'I suppose it is natural for diplomats in countries adjacent to the Soviet Union . . . to regard Stalin as a greater menace than Hitler, but I am convinced that it is *not* true, and that to state that if we beat Stalin, we would have no fear of Germany is, to speak frankly, nonsense.'[16]

Was Fitzroy's sabre-rattling a manifestation of the frustration he felt at not being able to get into the war personally? September 1939 was a black month for him. The day after the war started he sought an interview with the Permanent Under-Secretary at the Foreign Office, Sir Alexander Cadogan, and asked permission to resign so that he might enlist as a fighting man. Cadogan was not pleased. He pointed out sharply that this apparent surge of patriotism masked a deeply unpatriotic spirit. The Foreign Office had trained him for six years. Now that he was beginning to be a useful member of the service, he wanted, to satisfy his personal vanity, to go off and play soldiers. Had he not heard of duty, of responsibility? In any case, his resignation was not accepted. The new Defence Regulations gave the Secretary of State power to compel him to remain at his desk. Fitzroy decided to press the point. What if he just went out and enlisted? In that case, said Cadogan severely, the War Office would be asked to send him back. In chains, if necessary.

A gloomy Fitzroy soon appreciated how the wheel of fortune had spun round. That winter he had another encounter with Churchill, who was again First Lord of the Admiralty, as he had been at the beginning of the First World War. Fitzroy was asked to supper at Admiralty House, an eighteenth-century building heavy with memories of Hawke, Rodney and Nelson. Churchill looked twenty years younger. In contrast to Fitzroy, all his frustrations had disappeared at the prospect of action. Mrs Churchill took Fitzroy over to her husband. ' "Here", said Mrs Churchill, "is Fitzroy. Do you remember how rude you were to him last time you saw him? What's more, he was right. And you were wrong." At which Winston gave a characteristic grunt and went back to run the war at sea, while Mrs Churchill and I went off to the theatre together.'[17]

Fitzroy did not see Churchill again until August 1942, when they met in Cairo just before the battle of El Alamein. Churchill had many other things on his mind by then, but he did recall the lunchtime conversation before the war and its sequel at Admiralty House. By this time, of course, Russia was in the war on the Allied side, so Churchill was able to get in a Parthian shot. 'In the end we were both right,' he said.

Meanwhile Fitzroy, chained to his desk, found a further focus for his anti-Soviet belligerence. One of the most dramatic incidents in the 'phoney war' of 1939 to 1940 was the winter campaign by the Red Army against Finland. Expecting to 'roll over' the Finns in a matter of days, the Russians ran into surprisingly stiff opposition and came close to military disgrace. Soviet reverses in Finland produced an anti-Moscow euphoria among British diplomats. Some urged war against the Soviets to prop up Finland; among these was Fitzroy.

Soviet ambassador Maisky was confused by British policy over

Finland. From wanting to embroil Russia and Germany in war, it now seemed that, by urging war on Russia, the Foreign Office wanted to push Stalin and Hitler into an even closer embrace. Maisky's conclusion was that some in Britain had concluded that war with Russia was the lesser evil: the USSR would be weakened by such a conflict, and meanwhile it would still be possible for the West to strike a deal with Germany which would leave the Soviets face to face with the entire capitalist world. In fact the Allies' real aim was pre-emptive. Reckoning that the war might spread to Scandinavia anyway, they intended to occupy the Swedish iron ore fields, believed to be vital to Germany.[18]

Accordingly, the British and French governments began to plan a war on two fronts. First an Allied expeditionary force would be sent to Finland, thus sparking a general Scandinavian war; then the Baku oilfields would have to be bombed. Fitzroy's particular interest in supporting the Finns was to prolong the war in the north and thus avert the threat to British interests in the Near and Middle East. In more ways than one, British foreign policy in 1939 and 1940 revived the diplomacy of the Crimean War. Some historians expressed amazement that the Allies should even have contemplated such ventures when they were having to fight for their lives in the West. 'The British and French governments', A.J.P. Taylor comments acidly, 'had taken leave of their senses.'[19]

Early in 1940 the British examined meticulously a French plan for bombing the Soviet oilfields long-range, from Tunisia. But the Chiefs of Staff were dubious: they doubted the benefits of a war with Russia and feared being sucked into the Balkans. Fitzroy set out to combat such 'weakness'. In the first of his 'blockbuster' memoranda on the Finnish war, written on 17 January 1940, he tried to refute the notion that confrontation with the Soviet Union would drive Stalin closer to Germany. Fitzroy incorporated these arguments and enlarged upon them in an even lengthier paper on 2 February. There existed, he held, a Russian threat to the British Empire via Persia and Afghanistan. To blunt this, the best British option was action against the Russians in Finland; this would decrease rather than increase the Soviet threat, since if the Russians were tempted by Iran and Afghanistan they would attack there *whatever* the British did in northern Europe. With Turkey as an ally, British armed forces should be able to knock out the Soviet Union without too much trouble, and even without Turkey considerable damage could be inflicted by air alone. Bombers could set out from bases in Iraq to destroy the oil wells at Baku and in the northern Caucasus, plus their distribution centres and linking pipelines. Above all, it was necessary to prevent Finland from collapsing, because after such a collapse it would be much easier for the Soviet Union to keep Germany supplied. Naturally, there were dangers in helping Finland, but no more risk would be incurred by attacking Russia in the north than by remaining inactive.[20]

Fitzroy also had to weigh the impact of the 'winter war' in Finland on other potential British allies, of which the key one at this stage was Turkey. He warned that although reverses in Finland were having a chastening effect in Moscow, this should not be taken to mean that Turkey would be tempted to intervene in Romania.[21] As the Russian grip on Finland tightened, Fitzroy advised forthrightly that the possibility of active Turkish co-operation with the Allies was evaporating, though 'they are . . . prepared to exchange views on the possibility of subversive action in the Caucasus and might also agree to discuss plans for eventual military action.'[22]

The ensuing Russian victory in Finland depressed Fitzroy, both in itself and in its consequences: 'The capitulation of Finland and our failure to prevent it will, I am afraid, have a dampening effect on the Turks . . . The Soviet reasons for wishing to conciliate Turkey at this moment are obvious.'[23]

Now the Finnish horse had bolted, the Allies decided to close the stable door. On 1 March 1940 Fitzroy received a sudden and urgent message to attend a meeting of the War Cabinet's Joint Planning Sub-Committee that same day. Chamberlain announced there that the War Cabinet had now decided to examine in detail the implications of war with Russia. The result was a lengthy War Cabinet Paper, and thereafter war with the Soviet Union began to look more likely. When Fitzroy's old contact Paul Reynaud replaced Daladier as Prime Minister in France in March 1940, there was strong French pressure to send an Allied fleet to the Black Sea to interdict Russian oil supplies to Germany. Churchill, as First Sea Lord, liked this idea: it had echoes of the Gallipoli strategy after which he always hankered. He had put a pilot version of such an idea to the War Cabinet in October 1939 and now returned to the fray with renewed vigour. But Cadogan was sure the Turks would not allow a Franco-British fleet free passage through the Straits.[24]

Reynaud also raised at the highest level the idea of bombing Russian oilfields, with or without a formal declaration of war. But Foreign Secretary Lord Halifax feared antagonizing the Turks by such action. The War Cabinet decided to prevaricate: they would tell the French to draw up a blueprint for bombing Baku, without committing themselves definitely to the policy.[25] In April Halifax conferred with British diplomats from south-east Europe and with Sir William Seeds, the newly retired ambassador to Moscow. Seeds believed the project to be inadvisable: in the first place it would not work, and in the second, it would be impossible to justify to public opinion an unprovoked attack on Russia. The Baku plan was therefore shelved, until the autumn.[26]

The period between September 1939 and April 1940 was one of acute frustration for Fitzroy. He was not allowed to join the Army and he saw his favourite projects consigned one by one to the Cabinet waste-paper basket. This no doubt accounts for a certain peevishness in his minuting on mundane matters passing across his desk. When information was received via the Soviet ambassador in Sweden in December 1939 to the effect that Russia would not sign a treaty with Japan because of the latter's likely adherence to the Anti-Comintern pact, Fitzroy wrote dismissively: 'I don't think that we need pay too much attention to what Madame Kollontai says.' It was the same story in January 1940 when Halifax reported a conversation with the Romanian minister in London, Virgil Tilea. Again, Fitzroy wrote witheringly: 'I don't think that we need pay much attention to what M. Tilea says about these matters.' On 2 January he minuted that Sir William Seeds's departure from Moscow proved the impossibility of co-operation with the Soviets.

Tension was also evident in his dealings on anti-Soviet propaganda in the Middle East with Brigadier Penney at the Ministry of Information. Fitzroy was particularly angered by the way Soviet ambassador Maisky used favourite contacts to place stories sympathetic to the Soviet Union in the press. A particular *bête noire* was Sir Bernard Pares at the Royal Institute for International Affairs. On 29 January 1940, after making a précis of a conversation between Pares and Maisky, Fitzroy wrote: 'I can't help thinking that it is about time that something was done about Sir B. Pares.' Again, on 27 March he minuted: 'It must be amusing for M. Maisky to find someone who swallows his accounts of Soviet policy as completely as Sir Bernard Pares appears to.' When in April Pares gave his views on Anglo-Soviet relations to Laurence Collier, Fitzroy exploded. 'Shockingly wrongheaded. Sir Bernard Pares ought to be subsidised by M. Maisky rather than HMG. It is very hard that we should waste money on having dangerous stuff of this kind put about. Could not Sir Bernard Pares be got rid of?' Next day found him in sunnier mood: 'I have spoken to Mr Leeper who tells me that Sir B. Pares is to be removed from the RIIA in the immediate future, which is most satisfactory.'[27]

In May 1940 the German *blitzkrieg* swept through the Netherlands and Belgium. Just before the fall of France Fitzroy was back briefly in Paris, as the panzers advanced. On 15 May he lunched at the British Embassy with the former Czech Minister in Moscow, M. Fierlinger, who was known to have pro-Soviet sympathies. Fierlinger explained Soviet policy towards Germany as a mixture of contentment with close trade relations, fear of the Nazis, desire to avoid hostilities at all costs, and happiness that the Reich and the West were weakening each other. Fierlinger also endorsed the line put forward by Andrew Rothstein, the influential Reuters correspondent and friend of Maisky, that Russia was not happy with German subjugation of small nations, and would like to see Dominion status for India. Reporting his conversation with Fierlinger, the implacable Fitzroy minuted: 'The question is, how unhappy and what is she prepared to do about it?' As for India and Dominion status: 'A British or a Soviet Dominion?'[28]

While in Paris Fitzroy also paid a visit to Wilfred Dunderdale and saw his personal safe, booby-trapped to explode in the faces of the Nazis who would probably open it when Paris fell – and it was clear that this would be any day now, for Fitzroy could hear the guns booming in the distance. Dunderdale's staff were toiling like the *Nibelungen* to extract the last second of advantage before the inevitable occupation. 'He threw open a door to reveal a lot of people at desks, looking like watchmakers with those things screwed into their eyes, forging passports.'[29]

The genesis of James Bond was already under way. On 17 March Robert Bruce Lockhart (Deputy Under-Secretary at the Foreign Office and Director General of the Political Warfare Executive from 1941 to 1945) had Fitzroy and Ian Fleming to lunch. Fleming reported that the Admiralty considered Churchill their best First Lord ever, and that he was in good shape, giving the lie to those Tories who claimed that he would not be able to stand the strain of being Prime Minister. After the fall of France Lockhart had another lunch party with Fitzroy and Ian Fleming, this time including Dunderdale as well. Lockhart wrote in his diary, 'Dunderdale attractive (a little sleek – 100 per cent convinced that Russia and Germany are agreed on common plan at any rate for several months ahead).'[30] The theory of a harmony of interests between Russia and Germany was clearly current coin in Fitzroy's circle. It is interesting also to observe Dunderdale, the model for James Bond, and Fitzroy, who certainly also contributed to that character, at the same table with his creator. Only a surname was lacking. This belonged to an SIS officer called Rodney Bond who operated in Crete in 1941; Peter Fleming, who was there too, later suggested it to his brother.[31]

There was another pointer to the future in a memorandum Fitzroy wrote back in London, on 29 May, about the intentions of Stalin and Hitler in the Balkans. 'There has been a good deal of evidence to show that the Yugoslavs tend to overestimate the readiness of the Soviet government to stand up to the Germans. It is only natural that the Russians should not welcome German penetration in the Balkans. It is not, however, clear what they could do in such an event. As far as can be seen, the most likely Soviet reaction to a German invasion of the Balkans would be simply to seize Bessarabia and anything else that came to hand.'[32] What is interesting about this is not Fitzroy's perennial cynicism about the Russians, but his willingness to take Yugoslavia seriously. This was not an attitude widespread among Foreign Office mandarins. Cadogan, for instance, noted in his diary in March 1941:

'The Yugoslavs seem to have sold their souls to the devil. *All* these Balkan peoples are trash.'[33]

An interesting visitor to Fitzroy's department at the Foreign Office in mid-1940 was the 59-year-old Alexander Kerensky, who had headed the ill-fated Petrograd government in Russia in the early part of 1917. Violently anti-Soviet, Kerensky had been ousted from France (whither he fled after October 1917) by the Nazi invasion. He was now on his way to Australia. On the afternoon of 4 July Kerensky bearded Fitzroy in his den and delivered a lengthy harangue in Russian on the evils of Soviet foreign policy. He argued that world-wide Soviet propaganda attacks on Britain had helped the German cause, and that in France Communist propaganda had been largely responsible for the collapse of the French armies. This was too much even for the hawkish Fitzroy. He minuted in the margin of his report: 'I doubt this.'[34] It is amusing to see what happened to Fitzroy's minute as it ascended the hierarchy. Sir Orme ('Moley') Sargent added that Kerensky was very prejudiced on the subject of Russia, while a more senior official opined that he was totally unreliable. Fitzroy encountered Kerensky again later, but never thought much of him; he considered that his 'talents as an orator greatly exceeded his gifts as a statesman or administrator.'[35]

After the fall of France Britain abandoned for a time all thoughts of bombing Baku, and sought to get closer to the Soviet Union by diplomacy. Where Finland and Turkey had been a possible *casus belli* between Britain and Russia early in 1940, Britain now looked to exploit gathering Russo-German tensions in the Balkans, and to see if there was any leverage in Far Eastern politics that could be brought to bear against the Soviets there.

In 1940 the USSR became very interested in a possible tripartite division of the Balkans with Germany and Italy. Yet in fact the Balkans proved the rock on which the Molotov–Ribbentrop pact foundered. The root cause was Germany's determination to settle the future of south-east Europe without consulting the Soviet Union. Between September 1940 and April 1941, relations traced a steep downward curve.

On 27 September 1940 the three Axis powers, Germany, Italy and Japan, signed the Tripartite Pact, promising a declaration of war if any one of them was attacked by another power not then at war. In November Molotov went to Berlin to discuss Russia's accession to the Pact. Ribbentrop insinuated that, as the real purpose of the pact was dismemberment of the British Empire by southward expansion into Africa, India, the Middle East and South East Asia, there was no need for formal adherence by the Soviet Union; they should simply join in the feeding frenzy on the carcase of the British Empire. Refusing to be diverted, Molotov insisted on knowing what Germany's intentions were towards Greece, Romania, Yugoslavia, Bulgaria and Turkey.

Meanwhile a formal Soviet reponse to the Tripartite pact was handed to ambassador Schulenburg in Moscow on 25 November. As has been well said, 'Stalin's response . . . was in every sense a test of Hitler's intentions: the Soviet terms for joining a four-power pact amounted to giving Hitler full freedom in the West only at the price of foreclosing his option to make a successful war against the Soviet Union.'[36] No German reply was ever received. Maisky reported to Molotov that the Germans and Japanese were very keen to push Russia in the direction of the Persian Gulf and India. But the reason Hitler made no response was that he had already made up his mind to invade the USSR. On 18 December 1940 he signed the directive for Operation Barbarossa.[37]

Failing to elicit a reply from Hitler, Stalin decided to resist Germany in the Balkans, attempting to draw Bulgaria into the Soviet orbit. The Russians made Yugoslavia their stalking-horse. They signed a trade agreement in April 1940, a bilateral economic pact in May, and established diplomatic relations in June. The process of friendship with Yugoslavia continued throughout 1940 – all the more important when Germany was forced to intervene in Greece after the Italian débâcle there. Stalin skilfully avoided a crisis in January 1941: the Soviets denied passage through Bulgaria to German troops, but when Bulgaria at once joined the Tripartite Pact, the USSR limited itself to diplomatic protests.

German pressure also stymied Russian aims in Turkey, which were continued Turkish neutrality, the closure of the Straits to foreign warships, and the establishment of Soviet military bases on the Dardanelles. But when Germany advanced into the Balkans, Russia abandoned its dreams of controlling the Straits in return for an assurance that Turkey would not threaten the Soviet southern flank.

How did Fitzroy attempt to unravel this complex skein? There is some evidence that he was aware of changing German attitudes to the USSR, but he was inclined to attribute them to the heroic resistance put up by the RAF during the Battle of Britain. On 24 September he wrote: 'The improvement in the Soviet attitude towards Iran can, I think, be attributed to the misgivings which our resistance to Germany must have inspired in the minds of the Soviet government.'[38] A little later we find him taking the view that the Soviets had probably calculated that Germany was unlikely to gain a complete victory over Britain. But he then draws the opposite conclusion from what might have been expected. 'If so, they will be less likely than ever to intervene on our side.' In particular, he dismissed the popular idea that the inclusion of Bevin and Attlee in the War Cabinet made it possible for socialist to talk to socialist: Stalin was always first and foremost a Russian nationalist.[39] He thought it likely, as was indeed the case, that Hitler had given Stalin a free hand to intervene in Persia. Convinced, as before, that Russia always perceived its real interests to lie in the East rather than the West, Fitzroy wrote: 'As regards the Middle East, it is quite possible that the Russians would in the first place confine themselves to an attempt to gain control of the Persian oilfields and access to the Persian gulf. Afghanistan would be left till afterwards, and the conquest of India until a still later stage of proceedings. The fact remains, however, that Russian control of the Persian Gulf would constitute a severe threat to our position in Asia.'[40]

What about Turkey, earlier in the year one of Fitzroy's prime interests? He now considered it unlikely that Turkey loomed large in the scheme of Russo-German *entente*. Most likely, Germany wanted to keep the Straits for herself, palming the Russians off with a naval base at the Black Sea end. 'It is, however, doubtful whether the Russians would oppose by force a German effort to seize the Straits, or indeed any move, short of an invasion of Soviet territory.'[41]

Throughout 1939 and 1941 Fitzroy worked on the thesis that Stalin had decided to throw in his lot permanently and wholeheartedly with Hitler, even at the cost of German economic domination and exploitation. Britain would in such a case face the problem of how to dislocate the Soviet machine so that Germany would be forced to prop it up, a task of which she would eventually tire. It was clear that no isolated air attack on Baku would be enough; co-operation would be required from Turkey also, to allow Britain to operate in the Black Sea. As that prospect in turn faded, Fitzroy and others in the Northern Department were drawn to consider encouraging Japanese imperial expansion at the expense of the Soviet Union, thus diverting the Russians to the defence of Vladivostok. Some Foreign Office officials toyed with the idea that a successful attack on Baku might in turn tempt the Japanese to attack the Soviet Union. But others argued that Japan was already too embroiled in China to have any margin for other ventures. Either way, the British could secure Japanese co-operation against the Russians only if they abandoned Chiang Kai-shek, and to do so would incur the enmity of the USA.

By the autumn of 1940 we find Fitzroy increasingly taken up with the Far Eastern implications of Soviet relations. He considered the possibility that Japan and the Soviet Union would agree to an amicable division of China, but concluded that Japanese designs on Sinkiang, north-west China and Outer Mongolia were not very serious, as those regions could play no effective part in the Greater Asian Co-Prosperity Zone which was the prime aim of Japanese policy.[42]

One way and another it was proving singularly difficult for the British to dent the carapace of the Nazi–Soviet pact. It was desperation as much as anything that led them to send a mission to Moscow under Sir Stafford Cripps. The Russians demonstrated at once that they had the whip hand by refusing to accept Cripps as a special envoy; they insisted he was merely another ambassador.[43] Ostensibly Cripps went to Moscow merely to negotiate a trade agreement, and Fitzroy's desk was immediately inundated with letters from British subjects with financial claims against the Soviet government.[44] But Fitzroy was aware that the real intention was to drive a wedge between the Gemans and the Russians. The fact that he thought this a vain hope was just one of the reasons for his hostility to the mission. He also thought Cripps veered too readily between unwarranted optimism and equally unjustified pessimism. Fitzroy even had the audacity to contrast the Foreign Office approach unfavourably with that of the State Department. 'The American attitude towards the Soviets is perfectly logical. The US government realize that the Soviet government are pursuing a policy of co-operation with Germany, and, in order not to help Germany, even indirectly, they are denying key commodities to the Soviet Union, and are treating visiting Soviet engineers as potential spies. It must also be borne in mind that the Americans, remembering Poland and Finland, tend to regard the Soviet Union as an aggressor state.'[45]

Fitzroy's doubts about Cripps were political. In the first place, '. . . no one could accuse him of being unsympathetic to the Soviet Union.'[46] In the thirties Cripps had been associated with a succession of left-wing movements, and after the rise of the Fascist dictators had joined in rallying the Left to form a 'Popular Front' to oppose Chamberlain and Appeasement. This brought about his expulsion from the Labour Party in 1939 and forced him to sit as an Independent MP throughout the war. He was therefore, in Fitzroy's view, perhaps 'unsound'. Fitzroy's misgivings were shared in the Foreign Office. His old colleague Dan Lascelles was sent back to Moscow, '. . . to keep an eye on Stafford Cripps, about whom the Foreign Office were deeply suspicious. When Cripps was there, they thought they had to have a really first-class Russian speaker there as Minister.'[47]

But, as a romantic Tory hedonist, Fitzroy was also put off by the asceticism and austerity of Cripps's approach to life, which became notorious after 1945, when it was said that 'Cripps was like other men in that he favoured short skirts for women, but unlike them in that his reason was the saving in textile supplies.'[48] The tension between his personal dislike and the necessity to be, in a sense, Cripps's handmaiden in London manifested itself in one of Fitzroy's notorious practical jokes. He concocted a telegram, complete with all the authenticating marks and call signs, as if from Lascelles, which read:

AMBASSADOR IN GRIP OF SEVERE DELUSIONAL PARANOIA HAVE PLACED HIM UNDER HOUSE ARREST AND TAKEN OVER. AWAIT FURTHER INSTRUCTIONS.

It so happened that on the evening when the telegram was received, Fitzroy was at a Foreign Office dinner in company with two junior and two senior colleagues. A flushed resident clerk appeared, brandishing the telegram. After reading it, the two senior colleagues conferred in whispers – Fitzroy, of course, was too junior to be let in on the secret. In the end he was forced to confess. Next morning a very senior mandarin appeared at his desk and threw down the telegram: 'What's the meaning of this?' Fitzroy mumbled apologetically that it was a joke. 'What!' said the mandarin. 'Lascelles has had to put the ambassador under restraint and you call that a joke?' It taught Fitzroy that some things are more easily started than stopped.[49]

In due course Cripps reported to London that his protracted negotiations were leading nowhere. 'It is beyond question that there is not the slightest chance at the present time of producing any kind of rupture in German–Soviet relations.'[50] He first raised with Molotov on 7 August the idea of a Soviet–British non-aggression treaty, and on 22 October made a formal proposal for an Anglo-Soviet pact. On 11 November he was informed that the proposal was unacceptable; there was no further meeting with Molotov until February 1941, when the Soviet Foreign Minister formally rejected the proposal. Molotov at the time had bigger fish to fry, for his abortive visit to Berlin, which took place in November 1940, marked a decisive turning point in Soviet–German relations and led to Hitler's final decision to attack Russia.

Fitzroy's memoranda during the period of Cripps's mission to Moscow constitute a sustained attack. Sometimes, it seems, Cripps is damned if he does and damned if he doesn't. In August Fitzroy minuted that a threat to withdraw the mission would be counterproductive, as it would be a public admission that the British attempt to drive a wedge between Hitler and Stalin had failed. Yet he opposed Cripps's policy of making an improved offer to Russia and agreed with Cadogan's estimate: 'Cripps argues that we must give everything – recognition, gold, ships – and trust to the Russians loving us. This is simply silly.'[51] He also took vehement exception to Cripps's claim 'that he was only prevented from achieving a rapid *rapprochement* with the Soviet Union by the collapse of France.'[52]

When the Russians slighted Cripps, Fitzroy accused him of being too easily discouraged; when they talked to him, he called Cripps over-sanguine. He poured scorn on his 'amaterurism'. When Cripps reported to Halifax that his being assigned to meet Mikoyan rather than Molotov meant the Russians were stalling, Fitzroy minuted magisterially: 'Mr Mikoyan, who is a member of the Politburo and a Caucasian, is no less able to take decisions than M. Molotov, who is also only a mouthpiece.'[53] Cripps also aroused Fitzroy's ire by suggesting that Britain improve relations with the Soviet Union by *guaranteeing* that the

British would neither attack Baku nor make probes via Iran and Turkey.[54] When Cripps gloomily concluded that the Soviets would continue to support Germany, Fitzroy minuted: 'It is a little disappointing that Sir Stafford Cripps should be so easily discouraged. Personally I see no reason to suppose that there has been a change in Soviet foreign policy.'[55] But a month later he noted: 'In the light of these telegrams, I am unable to share Sir Stafford Cripps's optimism. They seem to me to show that we have nothing to hope for from the Soviet Union, and therefore nothing to gain by attempting to bribe the Soviet government with rubber and non-ferrous metals, of which they stand in need; *or*, for that matter, by forcing Turkey to give them control of the Straits.'[56]

However, it would be wrong to suggest that all of Fitzroy's time in the second half of 1940 was spent in a vendetta against Cripps alone. He also expressed scorn for those gullible enough to accept statements put forward by the Soviet ambassador, Maisky. Particular and consistent targets for his wrath were the Dean of Canterbury and Andrew Rothstein, late of Reuters, now of Tass. The *News Chronicle* also seemed to him especially prone to echo the Maisky line. In general he found the British press polarized into pro- and anti-Soviet factions, when what was needed was for the media to be long on facts and short on interpretation.[57]

Fitzroy departed from the Foreign Office in March 1941, having been there for nearly two years. His spell had almost exactly coincided with the period of the Nazi–Soviet pact. At about the time he left, Ultra intercepts were making ever clearer Hitler's intentions towards Russia. Bruce Lockhart's diaries show the extent to which the British were forewarned. Writing on 3 June 1941, nineteen days before Operation Barbarossa, he commented: 'The Joint Intelligence Chiefs and the Chiefs of Staff are now certain that Germany will attack Russia. Yet a few days ago we were talking of bombing Baku. I doubt if Germany will invade Russia, though if she wants supplies and thinks this is the only way to get them she must hit soon to give herself time before the winter.'[58]

Why did Stalin apparently not read the runes correctly, when he had been tipped off both by Churchill and by the Soviet spy Victor Sorge in Tokyo? One possibility is that he was convinced that all intelligence reaching him of an imminent German attack was part of a British plot to embroil him with Hitler. The other is that the warnings received by Stalin before 22 June could have been interpreted as meaning that Hitler intended to issue an ultimatum to the USSR, demanding territorial concessions.[59]

Fitzroy still holds to the view that the Nazi–Soviet pact showed the two nations at their most clear-headed, and that Barbarossa was an aberration.

If Hitler had not been so frightfully stupid, Germany might well have won the war. Jonny von Herwarth went into Russia with the German advance in 1941. He said that when they went into the villages of the Ukraine they were greeted as liberators. Only the idiotic behaviour of the SS and their massacres turned the people into fighters in the Great Patriotic War. This made it clear to the Russians that [Hitler] was worse than Stalin. If Hitler had said to Stalin in spring 1941 in the right way and at the right level, we have two hundred divisions on your frontier, but what we want is the Ukraine and the oil in Baku: that's what we want and we're prepared to save your face, but if you don't give it in a friendly way we'll come and get it, I have very little doubt that Stalin would have agreed to that.[60]

This is a view typical of a man who believes in *realpolitik* and is suspicious of ideology. The most recent scholarship, however, does not support him.[61] Alan Bullock, author of *Hitler and Stalin*, comments:

I am sure . . . Hitler would never have looked at [such a deal]. All the evidence on the German side points to the fact that Hitler refused, not once but on many occasions, to consider sounding out the possibility of a deal with Stalin. Ribbentrop in particular was very keen to repeat his performance in getting the Nazi–Soviet pact signed, but Hitler always put him off by saying that he would only consider a peace offer when he had won a great victory – and everybody knew that if he ever did win a great victory, nothing more would be heard of a peace offer. This remained his attitude right through to the final days in the Bunker.[62]

One final point remains to be made about Fitzroy's work between 1939 and 1941. The bombing of Baku, one of his favourite schemes, remained a live issue right up to and beyond 22 June 1941. Detailed contingency plans were discussed between the Foreign Office and Military Intelligence. It was agreed that, whether the Russians caved in under the German onslaught or resisted, Geman occupation of the oilfields was something that would have to be prevented by British bombing. Some apprehension was expressed over having to violate Turkish or Persian territory – more over the worry that the Commander-in-Chief in India or a local commander in Basra might take action without informing London.[63] The ghost of Baku was to haunt Fitzroy for a while yet.

The first ten weeks of 1941 saw Fitzroy 'phasing out' of the Foreign Office. He had found the loophole he required. A minute study of FO Regulations revealed that anyone wishing to enter politics had to leave the service. A triumphant Fitzroy sought a second interview with Cadogan, '. . . enlivened by the fact that he hated all politicians.'[64] Cadogan grumpily consented to his resignation. Fitzroy handed over a neatly-typed letter, requesting that his resignation take immediate effect. Then he swept from the room. He was free and could keep the faith of his fathers and do justice to the warrior blood that coursed in his veins. No one would ever have to make apologies for him in the future.

6

The Turning Point
1941–1942

T HE third of Fitzroy's great friendships, only surpassed by those with Churchill and Tito, was with David Stirling, the founder of the SAS. Stirling was a controversial figure, who in post-war years moved further and further to the Right and became associated with eccentric schemes for removing Labour governments by military coups. One of the failed exploits attributed to him was to bring the detested race of politicians into hatred and contempt by flooding the House of Commons with sewage. But when Fitzroy first met him in 1942, this lay far in the future: Stirling was then on the point of finding the perfect niche for his talents.

Most would agree that some of Fitzroy's comments on Stirling display enormous admiration; face to face, he always maintained a sturdily equal relationship with him, subject only to the requirements of rank. On the other hand, some have doubted whether the two were indeed close. Lady Hesketh comments: 'I knew them both well and I can't see that Fitzroy and David had much in common. Both were adventurers, but in very different ways. Stirling was a great Catholic and Fitzroy, his [Catholic] wife notwithstanding, tended to be anti-Catholic, though I will concede that this was probably merely a traditional posture. In those days in aristocratic circles it was not quite the ''done'' thing to marry a Catholic or a Jew.' Fitzroy's stepson Brigadier Jeremy Phipps tends to agree:

> Fitzroy stumbled into the SAS through boredom. By chance he met the Stirlings, who seemed to be having a good time and were actually *doing* something, at a time when Cairo was stagnant. The similarities between Fitzroy and Stirling were superficial. Sergeant Fred Seekings [of the SAS] said the trouble with them both was that if you dropped a match in front of them, both would have fallen over. They were both physically clumsy people, too. But Fitzroy was a good administrator, as Stirling was not, so that, as well as being brave, he added some sanity to the operations. Certainly a lot of the early SAS operations

were badly planned and had administrative problems. Take the Benghazi raid, where every boat was punctured and the pump didn't work. Fitzroy laughs about it now, but because he was such a true professional, he was critical at the time. He wanted to get things right and not just be tearaways, like the Stirling brothers.

The Stirling connection is also interesting in the way it reflects the social scene in wartime Cairo. Lord Henniker, later one of Fitzroy's comrades on the mission in Yugoslavia, remembers: 'Everyone knew everyone else in the officer class in the Western desert. It was like an intimate club. And since everyone was from the same social class, they related informally to each other, like members of a family.' Fitzroy explains how this made possible the rise of the SAS: 'What I think has to be remembered is that, in those days, if you had good contacts and were reasonably resourceful, there was no end to what you could do. Remember that David Stirling, an unknown subaltern in his twenties with no military experience, managed to get General Auchinleck to let him raise the SAS, in much the same way that my father-in-law (his uncle) raised the Lovat Scouts in the Boer War.'

After Fitzroy had passed his medical, he swore the oath and was given the King's shilling and a railway warrant to Inverness. He had ful-filled a dream. He was in the Cameron Highlanders, his father's old regiment.

It took guts to go from the plushy comfort of the Foreign Office to an Army barracks as a wartime private. How was he able to make the transition from the cloistered diplomatic existence to 'roughing it' with the Camerons?

> Because it was what I wanted. If it had been against my will, I wouldn't have enjoyed it. The time I spent as a Jock in the Camerons was of great importance to me and a very important part of my all-round education. I felt delighted with myself for having brought it off and entered into it wholeheartedly, polishing the brass knobs on the urinals with as much diligence and enthusiasm as I had previously polished the prose of my diplomatic reports. Had I been a conscript, my feelings might well have been different.[1]

He arrived in Inverness to find himself in a clutch of several hundred new recruits, most of them nineteen-year-olds from Glasgow. In the gaunt, dank and damp surroundings of the barracks, the NCOs swooped in on their prey. The tiros were divided into squads and doubled into their barrack-rooms. Then began the process of licking them into shape. Kit was issued; knife, fork, spoon, blankets, boots, bonnets, et cetera. 'Don't fucking lose them' was the opening salvo in the sergeants' reign of verbal terror. 'Use your fucking initiative.'

'Scrub the fucking floor.' So it went on for a week. The army in 1941 clung to the old maxim about breaking men before you start to mould them. So it was that Fitzroy and his comrades were doubled all over the barracks. They heaved coal, peeled potatoes, cleaned lavatories, scrubbed floors.

Then they were set to military drill proper. First came bren-gun practice, then rifle practice. A fractional hesitation in finding the right part when reassembling the guns drew down a storm of expletives. Naturally, the NCOs had never seen such a shower in twenty years – when have they ever? Functioning like an automaton would have taken its toll of a much younger and less intelligent man than Fitzroy, but he stuck grimly to his task. Fitzroy's previous firearms experience had been limited to rifles; he had always been a good shot, but as a member of the Foreign Office had been debarred from joining the Territorials. His ramblings around the Soviet Union had however kept him fit, he had done a lot of riding, and in 1940 while in the Foreign Office he had managed to get away on an early commando course under Bill Stirling and Lord 'Shimi' Lovat, both important figures in his later life. A group of anti-Appeasement Scots had set up a special training centre at Lochailort and got the whole area from Arisaig to Glenfinnan declared a prohibited area. The idea was to form the nucleus of a force that could carry on guerilla warfare against the Germans if Britain was successfully invaded. The centre was commanded by Lieutenant-Colonel Brian Mayfield; Bill Stirling was his chief instructor, with the rank of major, and Lord Lovat, with the same rank, was fieldcraft instructor, assisted by Peter Stirling's younger brother, David. Also present as Assistant Chief Instructor was Spencer ('Freddie') Chapman, later to win fame as a guerrilla fighter in the jungles of Burma.[2] Fitzroy enjoyed the experience. 'We were all over the Bonnie Prince Charlie country . . . We climbed a lot of hills together. Freddie fell in love with some local lady – a great drama. He used to come and weep on Rosie Lovat's shoulder.'[3]

In Inverness, like the rest of the recruits, Fitzroy used to live for the next mealtime, a welcome respite from the incessant bawlings of Regimental, Company and Battalion Sergeant Majors. But there was no let-up in the arduous business of turning Gorbals corner-boys into crack troops. 'Week by week the training became more arduous and the distances greater, until, plodding along the road behind the pipes, or ranging over the moors in sleet and rain, we seemed to have covered most of the north of Scotland.'[4] The naïve recruits gradually became more sophisticated, devising ways to beat the army 'system': how to get out of the barracks, avoid work, evade detection, escape punishment. It seemed there was much wisdom in the constantly reiterated exhortation to 'use your own fucking initiative'. Soon they were 'Jocks' in the full sense. 'Effortlessly we fell into the linguistic habits of the army; every other word in our conversation was the same meaningless and monotonous, yet somehow satisfying, expletive.'[5]

How did the privileged Etonian with the Foreign Office background relate to the products of Glasgow tenements and Gorbals slums? Except that he was clearly a 'nob', they knew very little about him. 'I got on awfully well with them and made lots of friends. The other thing was that, having been to Eton, one was far better able to look after oneself in any circumstances than they. They were very soft. Quick with a razor-blade but soft otherwise and – do you know? – they weren't accustomed to sleeping on the floor. At Eton, you know, there is a tougher ambience. For example, the boys in the camp would get everything stolen from them. I was the only one who had two of everything from the start, two mugs, et cetera, and kept them.'[6]

Access to higher-level contacts than his official rank seems to warrant has always been a feature of Fitzroy's life. So it was in Inverness. In the locality were a number of retired soldiers who had been in the Camerons with his father, and who invited him out. Eyebrows were sometimes raised in the hut when a message arrived saying that General So-and-So was inviting Private Maclean to lunch. A particular 'father figure' was Cameron of Lochiel, who had served with Fitzroy's father.

For all the cordiality of his fellow rankers, it was the friendship of Eddie McIntosh that mattered most to Fitzroy. Originally thrown together because their names were next to each other on the list, the two formed a bond on the discovery that McIntosh's father had also been a Cameron. Fitzroy responded warmly to McIntosh's good nature and enthusiasm, so his death in Burma while fighting with the 1st Battalion of the Cameron Highlanders was a bitter blow.

McIntosh and Fitzroy, both more highly motivated than their peers, were soon promoted to Lance-Corporal, giving them the power to ladle out food, order the peeling of potatoes, accompany officers on NAAFI inspections, and put people on charge. In town they were hailed by young ladies as 'Corporal' rather than 'Jock' – a change of status that Fitzroy, with his eye for the fair sex, relished. The ultimate accolade was their invitation to mess with the sergeants. In many different ways Fitzroy flourished under a military regime. As he recalled:

I found that it possessed unsuspected tonic qualities. Despite, perhaps because of, its limitations, it had a stimulating, a humanizing, a rejuvenating effect. All of a sudden, I felt very much younger, both physically and mentally. For years, I had led my own life, seeing my own circle of friends and following my own tastes and inclinations; doing on the whole what I felt like doing. In detached fashion, I had dealt with ideas and ideologies, tendencies and trends, situations and relationships. Now, plunged suddenly into this new life, among companions assembled by the hazards of conscription, I was dealing at close quarters with people and things. And I was thoroughly enjoying it.[7]

The combination of Fitzroy's success as a soldier and his 'officerly' background soon brought him to the attention of the Board of Commissions. After nine months of his recruit training he was told he had been selected for an immediate commission by OCTU, whose job was to identify corporals and sergeants with officer potential. Selection under this procedure meant that one skipped the normal officer training. Fitzroy was asked to name three regiments he would like to join. He was interested only in the Cameron Highlanders, but knew that nobody really wanted infantry subalterns aged thirty. With a heavy heart he listed first the Camerons, then the Life Guards, and last the Grenadiers. The resulting interview went quite well.

> 'March in, Corporal Maclean. Sit down.' The one in the middle, the President of the Board, was a Grenadier. They asked me various questions. 'Would you mind explaining your choice of regiments, Corporal Maclean?' I said, 'Well, sir, my one object is to get into the Camerons. My father used to be in it, and I'm in it now, though not as an officer.' 'How about the other two?' I said, 'I've always liked horses, which is why I put down the Life Guards, and (significant glance) I've heard the Grenadiers are a very good regiment.' He smiled and said, 'It's all right. No need to worry. You're in the Camerons.'[8]

Fitzroy's promotion to subaltern in the 1st Battalion was viewed gloomily by his fellow NCOs. ' "Poor Corporal," they said pityingly. "He's away to the 1st Battalion to be a fucking officer." "But cheer up, Corporal," they said consolingly, "all you'll be needing is bags and bags of fucking patter." '

More was to be feared from his former employers. As autumn 1941 approached, the new subaltern heard that his failure to go into politics had not gone unnoticed, and steps were being taken to secure his return to the understaffed Foreign Office. Quickly he got in touch with Conservative Party Central Office, where 'Rab' Butler was his principal contact. Informed that there would soon be a by-election in Lancaster, and that nobody had as yet been adopted as Conservative candidate, he applied for a couple of days' leave from his colonel and departed to try to win over the local Association.

Although Fitzroy had some influential friends in London, he was aware that any attempt at string-pulling would be resented in Lancaster. Randolph Churchill's election the year before in the neighbouring constituency of Preston was widely felt to be the result of nepotism, and when Churchill's son-in-law Duncan Sandys was given a job in the War Office, someone in the House of Commons taunted Churchill, 'What about Vic Oliver?' – referring to

Churchill's other son-in-law, the well-known bandleader.[9]

But luck, as so often, was with Fitzroy. There were already two very good and well-known local candidates in the field, on whose merits the local Association was split down the middle. The driving force in the Lancaster Association was Mrs Cooper, a colonel's wife, of Fitzroy's parents' generation, a leading light in the affairs of the regiment as well as of the Conservative Association. Fitzroy thought her first-class in intelligence, organizational talent and speech-making ability; fifty years later he was sure she would have been not merely a Tory MP herself, but a leading Cabinet Minister. Mrs Cooper took an immediate liking to Fitzroy, and his cause was not harmed by the fact that Colonel Cooper's regiment, the King's Own, had fought at Culloden.

Fitzroy arrived as a rather naïve second lieutenant in a kilt, knowing next to nothing about politics. The redoubtable Mrs Cooper took him under her wing and soon swung the local Association in his favour. She advised him to be utterly frank in his desire to pursue military life first and political life second. Fitzroy's frankness went further: it extended to pleading ignorance to most of the questions the Executive Committee put to him. When they retired to deliberate, he felt the reverse of confident. But Mrs Cooper proved as good as she seemed. To his astonishment, Fitzroy was adopted.

Wartime politics, with a Coalition government, was not supposed to include parliamentary elections. The three main parties had agreed in 1939 to a truce by which any vacancy in the Commons would be filled unopposed by a candidate from the party holding the seat. The problem, as ever with such pacts, lay at local level. The Lancaster Liberal Association repudiated Fitzroy, on the grounds that the Lancaster Conservative Association had not consulted them. They threw their support behind Lieutenant-Colonel W. C. Ross, standing as an Independent.[10]

Seeing that there was now a free-for-all in progress, the Independent Labour Party (to the left of the official Labour Party) sent the veteran campaigner Fenner Brockway up to contest the election. Brockway, a lifelong pacifist, had hit the headlines in 1939 after a bruising clash with Randolph Churchill in a debate at the Gray's Inn Union. Brockway's intervention increased the focus on the military angle: the press had already speculated that one candidate, a lieutenant, might have to salute another, a colonel, and here was a further twist. Fitzroy was entering politics as a means of getting into the fighting – but it was Brockway's anti-war campaigning in the previous war that had led to the recognition of conscientious objection in this one. Brockway later paid an amused but magnanimous tribute to Fitzroy.

Lancaster was old ground – I had fought it in 1922 – but now conditions were very different. The Labour Party had joined the coalition and my opponent,

Fitzroy Maclean, was endorsed by three party leaders. He was an officer in a Highland regiment and excused himself from speech-making on the ground that his uniform prohibited him from political utterance. I am sure his uniform won him more votes than his speeches would have done; he had a fine figure and his short kilt revealed splendid legs; he would wander round my open-air meetings, and women would pay more attention to him than to my speeches. He even turned up for nomination in uniform, dumbfounded when the returning officer told him that his papers could not be accepted whilst he was in Army dress. Eventually he was permitted nomination on condition that he removed his belt.[11]

It is almost (but not quite) true to say that Fitzroy never made speeches. He admits he had never made one before, and knew about politics only what he had read in the newspapers. There is a distinct flavour of Richard Hannay in *The Thirty-nine Steps* about his recollections. 'People used to ask questions about health, housing, education, et cetera. I used to say, "That's an interesting question. Would you like to come up afterwards and we'll talk about it?" '[12] But one day a questioner slipped under his guard. He was asked how he felt about Chamberlain and Appeasement. Since this was the first time he had been asked anything of which he knew something, he spoke from the heart. He disapproved utterly of Munich. 'So the not-very-well-intentioned questioner said, suppose we elect you, and something like that happens again. Will you obey your conscience, or the party whip? I said I would vote against any government that did such a monstrous thing.'[13]

Still ignorant of the workings of the party machine, Fitzroy was surprised next day to find a caller at the flat he occupied over the Constituency Office, who introduced himself as Mr Pott, from Conservative Party Northern Central Office in Manchester. Pott said Manchester had heard about the remarks on defying the party whip, and didn't like them one bit. Though young and inexperienced in politics, Fitzroy was never one to be easily browbeaten. He informed Pott that he resented being spoken to like that, and he added that Manchester had better be careful, since he had already received letters of support from Churchill, Attlee and Clement Davies, the leader of the Liberal Party, wishing him success. It might be better if Mr Pott returned to Manchester. No more was ever heard of the matter.

The by-election took place on 16 October 1941. Only 43 per cent of the electorate turned out, but they secured Fitzroy a comfortable overall majority: 15,783 votes against Colonel Ross's 6,551 and Fenner Brockway's 5,418. On 21 October, still wearing the kilt of a Cameron Highlander, Fitzroy took his seat in the House as MP for Lancaster.[14]

Fitzroy then returned to his platoon, but soon perceived that there was something in the wind. He was sent, along with other officers, on a crash Russian course, directed by Elizabeth Hill (later a Cambridge Professor and Dame Elizabeth). The military head of the course was the Duke of Wellington, one-time envoy to Czarist Russia. He told the officers that in future they would be able to say they had served with Wellington.

The following week Fitzroy completed a route march across the Yorkshire moors, covering a hundred miles in two days with full pack and rifle and ending at Richmond. It was Fitzroy's job at the end of the day to '. . . check that the men's feet were all right and that they got their dinner. Then you had to make sure *you* were all right.'[15] He had no sooner completed this chore than, about nine in the evening, a high priority despatch rider arrived with a signal from London requiring Fitzroy's immediate presence there. The colonel made available his staff car, in which Fitzroy drove at speed to York. It was the first time he had been there, and he remembers admiring York Minster in the moonlight.

He took the overnight train to London and next morning sped to the War Office to see David Margesson, the Secretary of State. To Fitzroy's amazement, the Baku oil wells were under discussion again. It might have been thought that with the Russians as allies, this particular preoccupation would have been shelved, but now, the argument ran, there was a danger that the seemingly unstoppable Germans, with six months of almost continuous victory behind them, might seize the oil in the Caucasus. Since Fitzroy was one of few with first-hand knowledge of Baku, he was to be seconded to a special Middle East-based squad to draw up plans for taking out the refineries. Fitzroy had had a bellyful of the oil wells by this time, but the opportunity to be based in the Middle East was too good to miss. The 1st Camerons were sent into front-line action in Burma almost immediately after his departure.

Axis fighters over Europe and the short range of aeroplanes in the early 1940s turned Fitzroy's flight to Cairo into an odyssey. From Poole he flew to Shannon in neutral Ireland. 'We stopped wherever the crew thought it fun to stop. They said with a tremendous grin on their faces that they had to stay in Ireland to get the plane shipshape. So we were stuck in Ireland for a week. Great fun because of course the food in Ireland was unrationed and plentiful.'[16] Next to Fitzroy in the plane was the commander of the Army Equitation Centre at Weedon. Discovering that Fitzroy rode, he invited him hunting. There followed three spectacular days in and around Limerick, over high stone walls – which Fitzroy had not jumped before. All the British officers were in plain clothes and carried civilian passports, but everyone in the Limerick hunt knew who they were. They were treated royally and given the best horses.

After a week Fitzroy flew on to Lisbon. Portugal was also neutral, and he remembers that they landed next to a German plane. His air-craft did not have the range to fly across the empty spaces of the south-ern Sahara, beyond the war zone, so from Lisbon it was necessary to fly to Dakar in West Africa, then to Freetown, Lagos and the Cameroons, before heading towards the Belgian Congo and the heart of Africa. This was Fitzroy's one and only visit to Africa south of the Sahara, and he remembers the experience as extraordinary and dreamlike. It is curious that he never returned, particularly in the light of his father's early military career, but perhaps there is something in the thesis of the African traveller Peter Matthiessen that Eastern European specialists do not care for Africa.[17] After touching down at Stanleyville, the pilot flew them low enough over the Congo that they could observe the landscape clearly. Fitzroy remembers seeing hippos and pygmies. There were further stopovers at Entebbe, Nairobi, Juba in the Sudan and Khartoum before the seaplane landed in the Nile at Cairo, where Fitzroy had been born thirty years before. He comments on his 8,000 mile trip: 'I joined the *Army* and saw the world.'[18]

Fitzroy reported as ordered to Rustum Buildings. 'Ah,' said the taxi driver, 'you want Secret Service.' At SOE Fitzroy met Colonel Terence Airey, who was full of the plan to blow up the Baku oil wells. Already Fitzroy was coming to the conclusion that the whole idea was idiotic. If it was necessary to destroy the wells, the Russians were perfectly capa-ble of doing it themselves, but would hardly take kindly to their new supposed allies invading their territory to sabotage the wells without consultation.

Fitzroy's scepticism was increased by consultations with his brother-officers. It was the Grand Old Duke of York all over again. The team had been stood-to at twelve hours' notice, then stood down again; lieutenants had been promoted to major, then demoted to captain. There had been concentrated munitions training, and danger money and special allowances had been paid out. Then nothing. *Parturient montes, nascetur ridiculus mus* (Horace: 'The mountain will give birth, and a ridiculous mouse will be born'). In charge of the operation was the brother of Henry Cotton the golfer. No doubt sensing Fitzroy's growing disaffection, he had him promoted to major and sent him to Persia on a reconnaissance trip. There Fitzroy met Christopher Sykes, a Persian specialist, and with him went into the Soviet zone at Tabriz and fraternized with the new allies. Finding nothing doing in Persia he flew back to Cairo, where it soon became obvious that he would be hanging around indefinitely. He therefore handed in his resignation and requested a transfer back to his regiment: the SOE expressed dis-may and disappointment. This was the first *contretemps* in a relationship that was eventually to explode into outright antagonism.

It was now Fitzroy's intention to join the 2nd Battalion of the

Cameron Highlanders, then in the Western Desert. But on his way over to the Adjutant-General's office at GHQ to do the paperwork, he literally bumped into David Stirling, on his way to meet his brother Peter who was working at the Cairo embassy. Hearing his sorry story, Stirling invited Fitzroy to join the Special Air Service Brigade. What was that? Just half a dozen officers and twenty or thirty rankers who hoped to emulate Lawrence of Arabia. You needed to be able to handle explosives and to parachute out of aeroplanes. Fitzroy accepted on the spot.

Behind David Stirling's 'soft sell' lay a remarkable story. In 1941 Stirling was a quietly-spoken, unassuming 25-year-old subaltern with the Scots Guards, distinguished mainly by his height – he was 6 ft 5 in tall. Quoting Byron's *Don Juan*, Churchill later called him 'the mildest mannered man that ever scuttled a ship or cut a throat.'[19] He had come round the Cape in early 1941 with the early commando unit Layforce, under Bob Laycock. Among Laycock's commandos was Evelyn Waugh, who described Stirling as 'a gentleman obsessed by the pleasures of chance. He effectively wrecked ludo as a game of skill and honour. We now race clockwork motor-cars.'[20] But Layforce performed disappointingly during the invasion of Crete, and its arrogant members became bored in the fleshpots of Cairo. Morale drooped, especially when three of Laycock's major operations were called off at the last moment. One wag suggested the name be changed to 'Belayforce'. During the Cretan campaign of May 1941 it was discovered that someone had scrawled on the troop-deck of their assault ship, HMS *Glengyle*: 'Never in the history of human endeavour have so few been buggered about by so many.'[21]

Reflecting on the disappointing performance of the commandos, Stirling saw that the root of the problem was the inability of hit-and-run raiders to make successful ship-to-shore landings, and felt that there was anyway something absurd about commandos relying on the Navy in a *desert* campaign. The spectacular success achieved by the German parachute landings in Crete, albeit at the cost of heavy casualties, gave Stirling the idea of parachuting men into enemy territory to destroy planes, airfields, ammunition dumps and storage depots. He secured an interview in Cairo with the Commander-in-Chief General Claude Auchinleck who, after hearing his ideas, promoted Stirling to captain, gave permission for him to start recruiting, and allocated an area in the Suez canal zone for his training camp.

Fitzroy has always regarded Stirling as one of the most remarkable men he knew, and comments:

Ahead of anyone, David saw the unique opportunity for a small, well-trained, well-led force to carry out surprise attacks on the rear of the formidable but fully extended Afrika Korps, while using the empty desert to the South as Lawrence used the Arabian desert, to emerge out of and then fade back into. What is more, possessing, as he did, quite exceptional powers of persuasion and being by nature immensely determined, he somehow succeeded, as an unknown subaltern, in winning the personal support of . . . Auchinleck, and then in placing himself directly under the latter's command – in itself a very shrewd tactical move . . . That's the sort of thing people nowadays don't understand fully. He was able to persuade Auchinleck to let him raise a unit in wartime, when there are always shortages of good officers and weapons and equipment – to get authority to raise a unit like that on his own and operate on his own equally, picking his own targets.[22]

But Stirling had a hard time of it at first. Parachute training was rudimentary. In the early days his recruits jumped off lorries moving at thirty miles an hour, or jumped from the top of a fifteen-foot tower. Naval ratings from the nearby camp at Kabrit jeered as commandos bruised themselves, or broke legs and arms. In the end RAF Ringway lent the SAS a plane for part of each day. The first two trials, in which Stirling participated, were successful. But on the third, while Stirling was on the ground watching, two men fell to their deaths when their 'chutes failed to open. Typically, next day Stirling made sure he himself was the first to jump. When he launched his first airborne operation against the enemy, it was a fiasco. Only eighteen out of fifty-four men and four out of seven officers dropped behind enemy lines returned.

While retaining the parachute training base at Kabrit, Stirling moved his headquarters to Jalo, an oasis 150 miles inland. This was a base he shared with the Long-Range Desert Group, about whom he had been initially sceptical. Now he reconsidered. The LRDG was the brainchild of Major Ralph Bagnold, who between the wars had per- fected desert navigation and driving techniques, using a sun compass, special mats, and ladders. Bagnold made the pioneer automobile cross- ing of the Great Sand Sea, previously accessible only by camel. He had his first success in January 1941, when Layforce was still labouring round the Cape. Twenty-five men in five trucks, in collaboration with the Free French, attacked the Italian base at Murzuk in Western Libya, destroyed the airfield and blew up ammunition dumps. Unfortunately, another attack that same month on Kufra, an oasis in Libya 700 miles west of Wadi Halfa, went disastrously wrong.[23]

Meanwhile, another buccaneer had arrived on the scene – the man who had travelled with Bagnold in the thirties, Vladimir Peniakoff, a middle-aged Belgian sugar manufacturer resident in Egypt. His hand- picked force of Arabs and British troops came to be known as 'Popski's Private Army'.[24] Stirling's SAS hoped to build on the twin foundations of the Layforce commandos and the ideas of LRDG and Popski, avoid- ing the pitfalls of Layforce while evolving beyond the purely desert role of the two private armies. But Stirling learned from the LRDG and followed their practice of taking as troopers officers who had deserted after the battle of Tobruk, on the understanding that if they excelled themselves, their army records would be doctored later. There was a distinct whiff of the Foreign Legion about the infant SAS, as well as of the commandos.

By the time Fitzroy met Stirling the new policy of co-operation with the LRDG was paying off. Stirling had had second thoughts about the efficacy of parachutists in the desert and had instead opted for back-up support from the LRDG, operating deep within enemy lines in camouflaged trucks carrying their own petrol and water. The best targets were aerodromes, hundreds of miles inside enemy territory but lightly guarded. During January 1942 the newly promoted Major Stirling had the LRDG take his raiders to the closest possible spot to their targets. His men then slipped under the wire at night and placed charges on the planes, timed to go off fifteen minutes later when the raiders would already have a two-mile head start. In three weeks the SAS destroyed 90 aircraft and caused massive damage to storage depots and petrol dumps in the town of Buerat. To protect their rear against a handful of men, a few pounds of light explosive and a few hundred rounds of ammunition, the enemy pulled back more and more front-line troops.

Fitzroy, assigned first to training at Kabrit, travelled down to the Canal Zone with two sergeants in a truck full of tommy-guns, high explosive and parachutes. 'It was a long bleak drive. A bitter wind filled one's eyes with sand and chilled one to the bone. On either side of the narrow tarmac road, with its never-ending stream of cars and trucks, the desert stretched away dismally. From time to time we passed camps and dumps: huts and tents and barbed wire and sign posts and clouds of flies, an uninviting smell of food rising from the cookhouses; the sickly smell of disinfectant arising from the latrines.'[25]

When he arrived Fitzroy was assigned a tent belonging to a man thought lost on operations, but had no sooner settled in than this Enoch Arden of the desert arrived to claim his own, having trekked across two hundred miles of wilderness, staying alive by drinking rusty water from the radiators of derelict trucks. Impressed, Fitzroy went about his training with relish, doubling with full pack of explosive over rocky ravines and sandy desert, carrying the minimum of food and drink. In the intervals the men had weapons drill, physical training and practice in demolition and navigation. Bill Cumper, twenty years in the ranks but recently commissioned, licked the whole camp into shape in two weeks of intensive instruction. His unrivalled command of Cockney slang and his wonderful gift of repartee appealed strongly to Fitzroy.

Fitzroy survived the lorry- and tower-jumping parts of his parachute training, but found the instructor on the Wellington bomber somewhat tiresome. Peter Warr believed in shouting, both on the parade ground and in the air. It was scarcely ideal preparation for an unnerving experience. From Randolph Churchill to Anthony Crosland, all who went through it later maintained that they hated parachute training. Fitzroy, however, soon got his 'wings' for six successful jumps. 'Few of us, I think, enjoyed jumping, at any rate not after the first jump; but it was agreeable to think about afterwards.'[26]

The first three months of 1942, while Fitzroy went through his SAS training, were the most sombre of the war. On the Russian front the Wehrmacht seemed to be carrying all before it. No serious dent had yet been made in Rommel's Afrika Korps. In the Far East the Japanese had swept through south-east Asia like a torrent, and by their capture of Singapore dealt the credibility of the British Empire a blow from which it would never recover. Yet on the personal front there was much to be satisfied with, for Fitzroy made three important friendships, which were to last for the next fifty years.

Following an interview between David Stirling and General de Gaulle, permission was given for Free French officers to be trained in the SAS. The first to arrive at Kabrit were Captain Berger, later a general, and Lieutenant Jordan, later ambassador in Vietnam. Fitzroy took to them both. Berger, from the south of France, was excitable and mercurial, a true product of the Mediterranean; Jordan, a northerner, was saturnine and phlegmatic. Fitzroy's linguistic talents marked him out for liaison officer between the French and the British. As Berger later remarked, 'His sympathy for France and the French during a tragic period in our history, his perfect knowledge of the French language and culture, his independence of judgement and character, his open-mindedness and political sense, all these characteristics caused me to feel immense admiration for him.'[27]

The third important contact was David Sutherland, then a 21-year-old lieutenant in the Black Watch. The Caledonian connection drew them together initially, as Sutherland recalls. 'I was wearing Black Watch undress kilt, and there was this tall, thin, dashing, distinguished-looking chap in Cameron kilt and bonnet. He came up to me and said, "Hello, who are you?" "Sutherland, sir, training in small boats. What do you do?" "I'm Fitzroy Maclean. I'm godmother to the French." '[28]

During his three-month induction into the SAS, Fitzroy was able to study closely the personalities of David Stirling and his Number Two, Paddy Mayne. Stirling was a depressive who needed constant action to keep the 'black dog' at bay. 'David did nothing but get into action. He sacrificed an awful lot to that because he left the administration to anybody prepared to do it. His one object was actually to get into action himself.'[29] Though Stirling was personally criticized·for the security breaches that led to the later débâcle at Benghazi,[30] Fitzroy does not hesitate to call him great.

> Wars have a way of throwing up exceptional men. Of no one is this truer than of David Stirling. The war served as it were to concentrate, to focus qualities which up to then had largely been employed in causing uproar and mayhem. To the planning of operations he brought remarkable vision, resourcefulness and imagination. In their execution his personal courage and determination were unsurpassed. He also possessed what to my mind is the ultimate gift of leadership: the ability to carry with him those he led on enterprises which by any rational standards were bound to fail, and to convince them that they were certain to succeed. Having been so convinced by him a number of times against my better judgement, I speak from first-hand experience. There are people who pride themselves on showing a proper appreciation of the art of the possible. David was a specialist, if ever there was one, in the art of the impossible. Even after fifty years of friendship and a number of shared experiences that are not easy to forget, David's character remains a difficult one to assess. There was about him, as about many great men, an element of mystery, an intangible quality, akin perhaps to what Lawrence called 'the irrational tenth, like the kingfisher flashing across the pool' – an irrational tenth that sometimes confused GHQ Middle East every bit as much as it confused the enemy.[31]

Paddy Mayne was, like Stirling, a giant. Several inches taller than Fitzroy and massively built, he had been a Northern Ireland rugby international. He was a Belfast lawyer in peacetime, in so far as that expression held any meaning for him: he was one of those tricky customers who are happy only when brawling. Despite his quiet manner, Mayne was the kind of veteran who finds adjustment to post-war conditions very difficult, and it was no surprise when he killed himself in a car crash in the 1950s. He achieved a ferocious reputation as a hand-to-hand fighter, and it was said that he once swung an Italian soldier round his head and dashed his brains out against a wall. He would go into Cairo on terrific binges with a friend, Ian MacGonagle, before MacGonagle's death in the December 1941 parachute disaster. Depressed by the loss of his fellow Irishman, Mayne sought solace in fighting with his own side, causing havoc in Cairo night-clubs until the military police were called, then trying to do to them what he had done to the Italian soldier. Fitzroy remembers:

> He used to sulk phenomenally if David Stirling did something he didn't like, or if he thought he wasn't being fairly treated. He used to disappear into his tent and not get up for a week. But on the other hand, he blew up a hundred enemy aircraft on the ground simply by walking up to them and putting a charge of high explosive under the wings and walking away. Any RAF pilot in a very expensive Spitfire or Hurricane who shot down half that number was a wartime

hero. Yet Paddy destroyed twice as with his own hands and a little high explosive, on a captain's pay.[32]

When not training or on operations, Fitzroy made the most of the
'rest and recreation' facilities of Alexandria and Cairo. The SAS, and
especially its later offshoot the SBS (Special Boat Squadron), often sent
its men to Alexandria to liaise with the Royal Navy there. In Alexandria
a British colony of prosperous cotton merchants made the officers
welcome, and through them Fitzroy made contact with a number of
wealthy Greek women who owned magnificent houses. Using his 'living dictionary' approach, first perfected in Paris, he began to hone his
modern Greek, using the classical Greek he had studied at Cambridge
as a basis.[33]

But Cairo, 'the Clapham Junction of the war', was the principal
magnet. Because the Axis controlled the heartland of Europe, all visiting dignitaries, whether military chiefs, diplomats or political figures,
were routed via Cairo for their trips to the USSR, India, the Far East
and Australia. It became a symbol of the British Empire at play. The
hotels, clubs and embassies were more active than the military posts,
and far surpassed their London counterparts in comfort as they were
free of austerity and rationing. There were no blackout restric-
tions, champagne corks popped, dice rattled, and pretty girls were
everywhere. The hedonism was summed up in a cynical contemporary
verse:

> We fought the war in Shepheard's and the Continental Bar,
> We reserved our punch for the Turf Club lunch,
> And they gave us the Africa Star.

The most notorious sybarite in Cairo was Randolph Churchill. He
would sit in Shepheard's Hotel openly with a bevy of girls 'obviously
. . . not chosen for their conversational power', and browbeat the staff
with displays of appalling rudeness.[34] But he overreached himself when
he took his 'ladies' to the Muhammad Ali Club, the most select and
luxurious of all Cairo's night-spots. Officers of good reputation could be
reasonably certain of getting into the Turf Club or the Automobile
Club, but only the élite became members of the Muhammed Ali. It had
the best restaurant in the city, was the only noteworthy Cairo club
where the entertainment was on the roof – and as a 'den of Pashas' was
naturally suspect to British Intelligence. Randolph had blustered and
bullied his way in on the strength of his father's name, and repaid the
concession by entertaining his girl-friends in a room where women were
not permitted. When another member pointed this out, the outburst
shocked even veteran Randolph-watchers. The club changed its rules

forthwith: members had to sign in their female guests, which helped keep out the *filles de joie*.

Of course Cairo was not just champagne and *grisettes*. Poverty, disease, misery and beggary were the lot of most of its inhabitants, and there were times when, even for a British officer, this side of things became as trying as the climate. In high summer Cairo was a place to avoid during the day. Overcrowded, hot, noisy and garish in other seasons, the city by midsummer was oppressed by a humidity that made work impossible for Europeans. Most offices closed from midday until early evening, and this included the military establishments. The lucky European was merely depressed and listless; the unlucky might in addition suffer diarrhoea, other stomach disorders, heat rashes, boils, swollen feet and eye-strain. It was no wonder that, as Alan Moorehead remarked, 'Few people who had tried both GHQ and the desert would have chosen a permanent job in Cairo.'[35]

Fitzroy soon threaded his way to the top of the social heap. Membership of the Muhammad Ali Club followed, as did invitations to dine with the great and good. Fitzroy describes the Muhammad Ali as 'the best club I ever went to. A marvellous head waiter who was presumably spying on everyone, and the best food in the world. Best everything.'[36] The British Ambassador, Sir Miles Lampson (later Lord Killearn), invited Fitzroy to dinner on 28 March 1942. Lampson remembered reading Fitzroy's despatches to the Foreign Office about his travels in Central Asia in 1937 and 1938. 'I should imagine he is rather a remarkable person,' Lampson wrote in his diary.[37]

Fitzroy, for his part, was fascinated by Lampson. At the beginning of the Abyssinian crisis in 1935 the ambassador was a widower. One of his daughter's schoolfriends, Jacqueline Castellani, aged 18, came out to stay and caught 'flu. Lampson used to read to her while she was convalescing; the two fell in love and married. This caused much fluttering in Foreign Office dovecotes, since Lampson's bride was the daughter of Mussolini's leading military physician. 'The ambassador had just married the 18-year-old daughter of practically an enemy alien.'[38]

When in Cairo Fitzroy often stayed with Michael Wright, a diplomat, but tended to gravitate for meals to the house of Brigadier John Marriott, who commanded the Brigade of Guards in the desert. He was married to Mona, daughter of multimillionaire Otto Kahn, 'Momo' to the 'in' circle, and described by Fitzroy as the 'hostess with the mostest'. She entertained lavishly in an enormous house she had rented: 'When one came back from the desert, the great thing was to stay and have a hot meal there. Plenty of glamorous young ladies. Lots of beautiful Italian women whom they didn't bother to intern, and a lot of indiscreet top brass.'[39]

Another important friendship begun in Cairo was with Hermione

Ranfurly. Born Hermione Llewellyn, she had married the Earl of Ranfurly in 1939, and accompanied him when he went out to the Middle East. Hermione was like Fitzroy in refusing to take an official 'no' for an answer. When the Army decided to evacuate military wives from Cairo in August 1940 she pulled strings to engineer her return from South Africa to Egypt, pleading the utility of her secretarial skills. The Army tried to force her out again, but she charmed Lampson (evidently susceptible to a pretty face), who took her under his wing and gave her a resident's visa.[40]

She got a job with SOE as secretary to the operational director George Pollock. Again like Fitzroy, she soon became disillusioned with SOE and what she called its 'good-time Charlies'. When her husband was taken prisoner by the Germans, her disillusionment turned to bitterness. She was later suspected of having passed files exposing SOE's incompetence to the military.[41] What is certain is that she buttonholed Anthony Eden on the subject early in 1941. Using her pull with Lampson (with whom Eden was dining), she finagled a private interview with Eden, at which she complained of the chaos and waste of money in SOE.[42]

But the most famous meeting point for Fitzroy and all other SAS officers when in Cairo was Peter Stirling's flat, a large, shabby apartment in the Garden City quarter on the first floor of an apartment block overlooking the Embassy at 13, Sharia Ibrahim Pasha Naguib, shared with diplomat Charles Johnston. To complete the *ménage*, Stirling also gave a room to the inveterate gambler Julian Lezard, whose proud boast it was that his father had 'kept a pack of cards' in the country; Lezard also featured as a witness in the famous Erroll trial in Kenya's 'Happy Valley' in 1941.

This flat soon became a port of call for a floating population of SAS officers, among them David Stirling and Fitzroy. The Stirling brothers did not impress Johnston as swashbucklers; to him they seemed modest, quiet-spoken and self-effacing. Only their great height and alarming skill as revolver shots marked them out as SAS men. Peter was an even better shot than David, and the walls of the flat were riddled with holes resulting from their target practice. Peter Stirling seemed to Johnston an even tougher character than David and, like so many Scottish Catholics, a hard man in every way: '. . . in sophistication and panache he outdid his brothers and everyone else in sight . . . equally at ease in a louche nightclub or an Embassy garden party.' Johnston remembers Peter Stirling saying to Fitzroy in a slow, magisterial drawl, 'Really, a mixture of soldiering and politics is the *only* form of total war.'[43]

One of the most celebrated aspects of the Stirling flat was the presence in it during the day of the *sufragi* Mohammed Aboudi, popularly known as 'Mo'. A scion of the Aboudi family of Luxor, who had a tradition of acting as guides for Thomas Cook, Mo was famous for his fractured English. 'Mo had stripped the English language to its bare essentials; so his speech made up in vigorousness and directness what it lacked in syntax.'[44] Fitzroy was a great favourite with Mo who, noting the young officer's fondness for the fair sex, would often engage him in conversation about girls. Fitzroy soon slipped into Mo-speak: referring to the party he was looking forward to that night, he told the *sufragi*, 'Catch-it bint, make-it ball'.[45]

Contemporary descriptions of the Stirling apartment speak volumes for Mo's forbearance, though he was probably distracted by a running vendetta with Mahmoud the cook over the latter's use of hashish. The dull brown sofas in the sitting-room were pitted with cigarette burns and filthy with the sweat from a hundred greasy heads. 'The sitting-room had sofas round the walls, like the salon of a medium-grade bordel, and curtains torn by girls climbing up them at parties.'[46] Whenever the landlord came to inspect his premises, Stirling and Johnston would hurriedly paste up photographs of the Royal Family, cut from magazines, to conceal the bullet-holes. The hall was used as a *poste restante* by dozens of transient officers, who would arrive at all hours of the day and night, breaking in when necessary through a frosted glass window just to the right of the front door (Mo went home every evening). On the wall by the telephone in the hall were the graffiti of a hundred hastily pencilled telephone numbers. At the end of this passage were three bedrooms and two bathrooms. The bathrooms were piled high with uniform cases, captured German ammunition and a gigantic pair of elephant tusks. The bedrooms were like Left Luggage offices. 'Peter himself slept in comfort in the large bedroom, surrounded by camp beds huddled together in conditions which would have caused a mutiny in any normally-run transit camp.'[47]

The parties held in this flat became legendary, functioning as safety valves for men whose next operation might be their last. Famous for their food and drink, the Stirling/Johnston revelries sucked in all the most exciting people in Cairo. 'In spite of the dated dance records and battered furniture, the flat was considered one of the smartest places to be seen in Cairo.'[48] Commenting on the fact that the main interests of one of his flat mates were gambling and horses, while everyone else's seemed to be drinking and girls, Johnston once wrote to England: 'For goodness sake please keep this description very quiet, because I think people at home would be horrified if they knew how unaustere Cairo was.'[49]

In the flat above lived Adam Watson, a diplomat and later a professor, and the best German-speaker in the Embassy. Until fairly lately Olivia Manning and her husband had lived there. Fitzroy describes how Watson would be drawn into the riotous living, willy-nilly.

7

The Year of Living Dangerously
1942–1943

F ITZROY has been criticized for many things, but no one has ever questioned his physical courage or the fact that he is an authentic war hero. What, then, is courage? It is sometimes said that valour of the kind that wins a VC is a momentary aberration, a temporary insanity perhaps. A surge of adrenalin can lead to flight, or heroism: there is really not the thickness of a sheet of paper between bravery and cowardice. True courage consists, perhaps, of a cold-blooded weighing of the risks, followed by a determination to proceed anyway – the quality that characterized Fitzroy's wartime exploits.

Questioning Fitzroy on the subject does not take one very far. What is courage? Fitzroy smiles a trifle wearily, as always when abstract subjects are raised. 'That reminds me of a story,' he says, in best Abe Lincoln manner. Pinned down, he has three explanations. One is the Sartrean idea of *l'autrui*, that we perform courageously when we are under the critical gaze of others, when our reputation is on the line; this theory eliminates secret bravery in wartime. The second explanation is that one usually doesn't have time to be afraid. I asked him how he felt about parachuting out of a plane. Did the thought of a 'roman candle' ever give him pause as he was about to leap into the unknown? 'For all these reasons you don't hover about . . . On your first jump it's a new experience anyway. After that, on operations, I was too busy worrying about what I would find when I reached the ground.' His third explanation is optimism. 'There were some close shaves in the war. But I've always believed it's not going to happen to me. I never took bigger chances than I thought I had to. Dodging about behind enemy lines is not just more exciting, but safer than being shot at in the front line. Compare my experience with that of my father in the trenches, where the life expectation of an officer was weeks only.'

Throughout 1942 the Italian-held city of Benghazi obsessed David

Stirling. It was the principal supply port for the Afrika Korps, but RAF bombing consistently failed to interdict the route. Stirling felt that the SAS could succeed where the flyers had failed. In March he planned the first of three assaults on the city. He intended to enter the main town and make his way to the harbour, where he would launch a collapsible boat and plant limpet mines on the ships at anchor before making a quick getaway. But the raid was called off when it was found in practice that rough weather made the canoes unseaworthy.

The next mission was to be a reconnaissance in force. Stirling ringed on the calendar a moonless night in the second half of May 1942. By this time Fitzroy's training was complete, so Stirling picked him as one of the assault party. First Fitzroy and Bill Cumper managed to get hold of a pair of black inflatables – 'Boat, reconnaissance, (Royal Engineers)' – each holding two men and their equipment, so the SAS did not need to call on their colleagues in SBS for help. Then Bill Cumper trained the men in laying limpet mines. Two crews were formed: Stirling with Corporal Seekings, Fitzroy with Corporal Johnny Cooper. The two teams spent hours on the Great Salt Bitter Lake, inflating the dinghies and paddling them around in the dark until they had mastered the art of handling them. Reasonably satisfied with their progress, they drove to Suez for a dress-rehearsal, which involved attaching dummy limpet mines to a tanker. For the sake of greater realism, Stirling decided not to inform the Port Authorities of his plans. Once inside the Suez docks, the SAS group began to inflate the boats. Fitzroy's eye and ear for the absurdity of things was keen, as usual. 'A gunner from a nearby Anti-Aircraft site strolled across and stood watching us. "What are you blokes on?" he inquired in a friendly way. "Never you ——ing mind," we replied offensively. "You —— off." "All right; *all* right," he said in an aggrieved tone, "I didn't mean no harm," and walked sadly away. Would a German, we wondered, have been as easy to get rid of?'[1]

Planting the mines at Suez must have accounted for one of Fitzroy's nine lives. When Stirling asked the stupefied Port Authorities to return the limpets, he was told that the security forces in the harbour often dropped man-sized depth charges into the water to deter saboteurs and were inclined to spray the surface with machine-gun fire if they saw anything suspicious. Stirling's two teams could have been wiped out.

That consideration apart, the trials were a complete success. Last-minute preparations for the raid now began. Meanwhile Randolph Churchill, who had been left high and dry after the disbanding of Layforce, got wind of the operation and begged David Stirling to be allowed to go. He had not completed any training and the battle-wagon was already overcrowded, but Stirling allowed him to accompany the assault groups on the first part of the trip, on condition that he stay behind with the LRDG when the assault proper began. Fitzroy had no qualms on the score of Randolph's courage – 'he was far too brave' – but shared Stirling's misgivings about his fitness. Randolph set himself the task of getting into proper shape within three days. 'For the next two or three days, wherever one went to our base camp, one met Randolph puffing strenuously but stertorously about.'[2]

The assault party left the training base in mid-May. The SAS's magnificent seven comprised Fitzroy, Randolph, Stirling, Corporals Seekings, Cooper and Rose, and Lieutenant Gordon Alston, who had accompanied Stirling in the earlier attempt on Benghazi. He was especially valuable, since he had commanded a detachment in the town when the British last had it in their possession. The outfit's pride and joy was David Stirling's 'blitz-wagon' – a converted Ford Utility painted dark grey to resemble a German staff car and fitted with special mountings for four machine-guns.

The party stopped at the Naval Intelligence Office in Alexandria to study maps, photos and a model of Benghazi. They then drove along the coast to Mersa Matruh and struck off south-west into the desert. Two days later they were at the LRDG Headquarters at Siwa oasis. From there, under the guidance of the LRDG, in shorts and Arab headdresses, living on tinned fish and fruit, they edged across the desert towards their target. At night a fire was lit in a sand-filled tin sprinkled with petrol. A frugal supper would be followed by fitful rest in sleeping bags. This was Fitzroy's first real taste of the broiling days and freezing nights of the desert. Temperatures could rise to 112°F and sandstorms could literally flay the skin. It was well known to the troops in the Eighth Army that if sand got into the foreskin it would incapacitate; the Army Medical Corps recommended circumcision with a local anaesthetic. Desert flies were a constant menace, and there were other perils. One night Fitzroy killed a snake as it was crawling into his sleeping bag.

When they were parallel with Gazala, where the Eighth Army and the Afrika Korps were facing one another, the raiding party entered enemy territory. They switched to travel by night and sleep by day – a sleep made next to impossible by the flies and the scorching sun. On 20 May they arrived at the Jebel mountains, forty miles south-east of their objective. From the edge of a scarp they gazed across the coastal plain to the limpid Mediterranean, where they could just make out the white walls of Benghazi. They settled down to wait for the following night, when there would be no moon; their main task was to camouflage the trucks. The night sky was lit up by intermittent flashes as the RAF carried out a preconcerted bombing raid on Benghazi.

Next morning Randolph had a stroke of luck: Corporal Seekings injured his hand with a detonator. Stirling declared him not fit enough to be in the raiding party and, yielding to Randolph's importunities, allowed him to take Seekings' place. The raiders set out in the late afternoon, the LRDG escorting them the fourteen miles to the Benghazi road, which took five hours of jolting, nerve-tangling tension. Fitzroy was in front in the blitz-wagon, alongside Stirling and Gordon Alston; Randolph and Corporals Rose and Cooper were in the back.

In the moonlight they could see the line of the road ahead, with the silhouettes of telephone poles stretching away into the distance. Stirling ordered Cooper to shin up the nearest pole and cut the wires. The four strands of wire parted with a loud twang that would certainly have alerted any enemy in the vicinity. Once back in the 'buggy', Cooper was nudged by Randolph. 'You could do with a drink after that, Corporal.' Cooper uncorked the bottle, took a swig and spluttered chokingly – the bottle was full of neat rum. Stirling swung round in his seat, grabbed the bottle and hurled it into the night. 'Captain Churchill, we never drink on ops,' he said icily.[3]

When they got out onto the paved road to Benghazi, the car began to screech like a banshee. Pulling over, they discovered that the wheels had been knocked out of alignment by the jolting in the desert. One of the corporals tinkered under the vehicle, but when they started off again the screech was even louder. 'We could hardly have made more noise if we had been in a fire engine with its bell clanging.'[4] Since their schedule did not allow for delays, they had to press on. Fortunately the road was deserted and the noise did not affect the performance of the car, which ate up the miles to Benghazi.

It was an evening of unpleasant surprises. As they drew into Benghazi, they saw a red light swinging in the middle of the road. Stirling slammed on the brakes. The car juddered to a halt before a heavy wooden bar on which a lantern was perched. An Italian sentry, sub-machine-gun at the ready, asked who they were. 'Staff officers in a hurry,' barked Fitzroy in Italian. The man looked puzzled. The six SAS men faced the possibility of a shoot-out and armed pursuit. But the sentry merely pointed out that they should have had their headlights dipped. Fitzroy dealt with this as an Italian patrician faced with 'other ranks impertinence'. The sentry shrugged, saluted lackadaisically, and raised the barrier.

Once in Benghazi there were further heart-stopping moments. A car they had passed earlier turned round and started tailing them.[5] A high-speed chase developed. Stirling drove at top speed into the city centre, then turned up a side street and switched off his lights. Seconds later the pursuing car shot past into the darkness.

They had scarcely recovered from this shock when sirens began to wail and rockets exploded in the sky. It could not be an air-raid, as the RAF had orders to keep clear. What was it, then? Had the Italians been tipped off? Was their presence in the city known somehow? Stirling thought quickly and decided to blow up the troublesome 'blitz-wagon'.

After placing a thirty-minute fuse among the explosives in the car, the six men set off into the night.

They found themselves in the Arab quarter, a maze of narrow streets, bomb craters and gutted buildings. Spotting an Italian *carabiniere*, Fitzroy asked what all the noise was about. 'Oh, just another of those damned English air-raids,' said the man. 'Not British ground forces?' Fitzroy queried. Hardly, said the policeman: the British had all been penned back inside Egypt.

Once the man had gone, Stirling held a quick conference. The original plan might be possible after all. They rushed back to the blitz-wagon. There were five minutes to go before the explosion. Johnny Cooper remembers: 'I have never been so scared in my life as when I struggled in the dark to place the safety pin back into the ten-minute time pencil and remove the detonator from the Lewis bomb.'[6] But at last he defused the explosive and threw the detonator over a wall. A few minutes later it went off with a crack, just like the one that had injured Corporal Seekings' hand that morning.

Stirling thought it unwise to approach the harbour in their strident, ululating car. Telling Randolph and Corporal Rose to hide it, he, Fitzroy, Cooper and Alston filled a kitbag with explosives and set off for the harbour with one of the rubber dinghies. On reaching the wire fence surrounding the harbour they were stopped by a sentry. Fitzroy bluffed him into letting them pass. Once out of sight they slipped through a hole in the fence. Ducking and weaving between cranes and railway trucks, they arrived at the waterfront. Stirling left Fitzroy and Cooper to inflate the rubber boat while he and Alston toured the docks.

Crouching beneath a low sea wall, Fitzroy took a pair of bellows from the kitbag and started to pump. Nothing happened. He tried again. Still the boat failed to inflate. Finally a sentry on one of the boats asked him what he was doing. Mind your own business, was the reply. But it was obvious the dinghy was punctured.

Fitzroy returned to the car for the second boat. Randolph was still trying to find a hiding-place. Fitzroy extracted the second dinghy, but on returning to the harbour wall he discovered that this too was punctured. With some difficulty Fitzroy found Stirling in the dark and consulted. Dawn was near. Rather than pointlessly destroy some railway trucks, it would be better not to prejudice any later assault. That meant removing all traces of their presence. Fitzroy returned with Stirling and Cooper to the waterfront to recover the useless boats. On the way they were challenged by a black soldier, an Italian subject from Somaliland. In irritated Italian Fitzroy asked the sentry what he wanted. '*Non parlare Italiano*,' he said, prodding Fitzroy with his bayonet.

This gave me an opening. I have always found that in dealing with foreigners whose language one does not speak, it is best to shout. 'Non parlare Italiano?' I yelled, working myself into a fury. 'Non parlare Italiano!! And you a Caporale!!' And I pointed to the stripe on his sleeve.

This seemed to shake him. He lowered his bayonet and looked at me dubiously. My confidence returned. Trying to give as good a representation as I could of an angry Italian officer, I continued to shout and gesticulate.

It was too much for the black man. With an expression of injured dignity, he turned and walked slowly away, leaving us to continue our progress down to the water's edge.[7]

But they had no sooner seen off the Somali than two more sentries fell in behind them. The SAS retrieval mission looked doomed. Fitzroy again set about bluffing their way out.

Assuming as pompous a manner as my ten days' beard and shabby appearance permitted, I headed for the main gate of the docks, followed by David and Corporal Cooper and the two Italian sentries. At the gate a sentry was on duty outside the guard tent. Walking straight up to him, I told him that I wished to speak to the Guard Commander. To my relief he disappeared into the tent and came out a minute or two later followed by a sleepy-looking sergeant, hastily pulling on his trousers. For the second time that night I introduced myself as an officer of the General Staff, thereby eliciting a slovenly salute. Next, I reminded him that he was responsible for the security of this part of the harbour. This he admitted sheepishly. How was it, I asked him, that I and my party had been able to wander freely about the whole area for the best part of the night without once being properly challenged or asked to produce our identity cards? He had, I added, warming to my task, been guilty of a gross dereliction of duty. Why, for all he knew, we might have been British saboteurs carrying loads of high explosives (at this he tittered incredulously, obviously thinking that I was laying it on a bit thick). Well, I said, I would let him off this time, but he had better not let me catch him napping again. What was more, I added, with a nasty look at the sentry, who winced, he had better do something about smartening up his men's appearance.

Then I set off at a brisk pace through the gate followed by David and Corporal Cooper, but not by the two Italians, who had shuffled off into the shadows as soon as they saw that there was trouble brewing. My words had not been without effect. As we passed him, the sentry on the gate made a stupendous effort and presented arms, almost falling over backwards in the process.[8]

The disconsolate raiders staggered back to the others before dawn, having achieved nothing. Randolph and Rose had finally managed to back the car into a hole in the wall of a half-demolished house. The upstairs proved to be deserted, and there the six holed up for the rest of the night and the whole of the following day, taking turns to sleep and stand guard. Stirling gave each of them a sphere of responsibility, advising them to catnap as necessary. Fitzroy, who could speak Italian and German, was to overlook the main street; Randolph was posted on the stairs; Rose and Cooper were in the back room and Alston and Stirling himself in the main room. It was a nail-biting time, for their hideout proved to be almost directly opposite a German Sub-Area Headquarters, and sentries were posted on the pavement just fifty yards away.

Predictably, the sole incident occurred during Randolph's watch. He had been given the longest stint, 'to teach him not to be lazy', Stirling said. At about five in the evening Stirling woke up to hear Randolph grunting, 'as he always did in moments of intense excitement when about to gamble way beyond his means'. It turned out that an Italian sailor had come nosing about the building, looking for somewhere to sleep, but at the sight of a hirsute, tommy-gun-wielding Randolph had decamped at speed. Randolph tried to catch the interloper, but got only his cap. Stirling at once gave Randolph a dressing-down. 'What on earth's the use of having you around?' he asked.[9]

After an early supper of rum and bully beef, Stirling decided on another massive bluff: they should stroll through the town as if they owned the place. They linked arms and careered down the main street, whistling and laughing like Neapolitan conscripts. On reaching the harbour, they decided on impulse to blow up two torpedo boats moored there. They returned to their 'safe house', got the car out and drove back. Stirling's plan was to lob Lewis bombs at the German MTBs as they passed – Rose, having identified the trouble as a bent track rod, had managed to quieten the car's screech. But at the harbour they found the guard being changed and concluded, sensibly, that an attack would be suicidal. They decided, reluctantly, that it was time to cut their losses and head for the Jebel rendezvous without further delay.

Driving out of Benghazi, they got caught up in a traffic jam caused by a convoy of enemy trucks. At the road-block Fitzroy again used his Italian to bluff their way through. On the way back to the rendezvous they managed to blow up a large petrol dump with the limpet mines and Lewis bombs, then they raced to reach the Jebel mountains by daybreak. They got there at 6 a.m. to find that, though they were twenty-four hours late, the LRDG was still there. With Fitzroy, after stress comes food and he remembers, with joy, 'Hungrily we threw ourselves upon mugs of tea and steaming mess tins of porridge.'[10]

The journey back to Siwa was uneventful, but returning from there to Cairo Fitzroy certainly used up another of his nine lives. On 27 May the blitz-wagon got stuck behind a long convoy of lorries some forty miles from Alexandria. As Fitzroy has commented, ruefully, 'David Stirling's driving was the most dangerous thing in World War Two!'[11] Speeding to overtake the convoy, Stirling 'winged' the last lorry. The car spun off the road and landed upside down in a ditch. With them was the *Daily Telegraph* war correspondent Arthur Merton, whom Stirling had given a lift from Siwa. He was dragged bleeding and unconscious from the wreckage and died a few hours later. Corporal Rose fractured his arm. Stirling cracked a bone in his wrist. Randolph dislocated a vertebra and was in hospital for a month. But, next to Merton, the worst casualty was Fitzroy. He was knocked out by the crash and did not regain consciousness for nearly four days.

Hospital is always an ordeal for restless men of action. Fitzroy had the additional burden of a querulous Randolph in the same hospital. Fortunately, almost alone of those who knew Randolph, Fitzroy had conceived a strong liking for him, which he never relinquished. Even an angry altercation in the desert, which arose when Fitzroy 'borrowed' some of Randolph's high-quality lavatory paper, had not dampened his affection. He sums up: 'I began to realize what a marvellous companion Randolph could be. Maddening, of course, in a dozen different ways, but endlessly stimulating and entertaining. Sitting round the fire under the stars where we stopped to brew up and open one of our precious bottles of whisky, the conversation ranged over a score of subjects on all of which Randolph held (and expressed) the strongest and the most controversial possible views.' But even Fitzroy admits that: 'As a patient Randolph was not at his best and the nurses were on the whole glad when he was sent back to London for further treatment.'[12]

Fitzroy left hospital to convalesce in Alexandria at the beginning of July. There he was visited by Berger and George Jellicoe, who were just about to set off by submarine for an operation in German-occupied Crete. 'Jellicoe at this stage of his career was about 23 years old, brown as a nut, with a nose like the Iron Duke's, and an extensive capacity for irony. He was acting second-in-command to David Stirling, and was one of the few people, apart from Major Paddy Mayne, who could cope with that diverse and volcanic personality.'[13] While in Crete Jellicoe and Berger were betrayed to the enemy. Jellicoe got away, but Berger spent the rest of the war in German prison camps, ultimately in Colditz, where he was reunited with David Stirling.

Finally, Stirling himself appeared in Alexandria; having perfected his plans for another, large-scale raid on Benghazi, he had been invited to meet Churchill and the top Army chiefs in person to put his plans before them, and needed Fitzroy's advocacy to help him sell the idea. Fitzroy returned with him to Cairo and there on the evening of 8 August they dined at the Embassy with Churchill and a glittering array of Army bigwigs. Among Sir Miles Lampson's other guests were Chief of the Imperial General Staff Alanbrooke, General Alexander and General Smuts. Stirling and Fitzroy could not but be impressed. With a twinkle in his eye Churchill introduced Fitzroy to Smuts. 'Here is the young man who has made a public convenience of the Mother of Parliaments.'

Smuts, who continued to wear his Boer War medals on his Field-Marshal's uniform, impressed Fitzroy as one of the few who could stand up to Churchill. At 72 he was four years older than the Prime Minister, and liked to tease him. 'Whatever will you do when we win the war?' he asked after dinner. 'You'll be out of a job, and you won't like that.'[14]

Stirling sold his plan for a second Benghazi raid with surprising ease: an older and shrewder Fitzroy would certainly have been more suspicious. Nothing now seemed to stand in the way of a major venture against Benghazi in September. Much had happened since the last raid. The fall of Tobruk in the summer of 1942 was the major crisis point for Churchill's wartime government; Rommel's advance to El Alamein brought the Afrika Korps to within ninety miles of Alexandria. The LRDG were forced out of Siwa. The Eighth Army needed time to regroup to face Rommel's next offensive. The raid on Benghazi was a rare opportunity to divert the Axis armies.

Some two hundred men would be involved in the operation, but because Siwa was now in enemy hands, the base this time would have to be Kufra, 800 miles south of Benghazi. Much detailed planning and the utmost secrecy would be necessary if several dozen vehicles and two hundred men were to cross this stretch of desert unobserved.

In September Fitzroy and Stirling made an uncomfortable, bumpy flight in a Hudson bomber to Kufra via Wadi Halfa. Their men had already been assembled. The plan was to 'take out' the garrison of the fort at Benghazi in a surprise attack, and then to destroy everything of any conceivable value.

Next day Fitzroy set out for the Jebel mountains with the advance party; Paddy Mayne commanded this detachment. It was a considerable motorized convoy and therefore had to travel by night. From Kufra to the Jebel they had to pass through the Sand Sea, waves of parallel dunes hundreds of feet high. The lorries and trucks became bogged down in the sand, engines revving impotently as wheels spun. Each time, they had to be dug out and reversed over sand mats onto *terra firma*.

The convoy squeezed through the Jalo gap, where there was an Italian garrison, by passing at midday when the heat haze made visibility poor. Their abiding fear was attack from the air: if spotted in the open desert, such a large body of vehicles would make an easy target. But four days after leaving Kufra they reached the cover of the Jebel mountains and made contact with a British agent, Bob Melot. Melot sent an Arab spy into Benghazi, who returned with news that the garrison was forewarned – the Italians even knew the date of the attack, 14 September. When Stirling arrived with the main column, Fitzroy gave him the bad news. Stirling sent a signal to GHQ, but the answer came back to proceed as the original plan.

By the afternoon of 13 September preparations were complete. The RAF bombed Benghazi to 'soften it up'; on the ground Stirling's men got into battledress. The plan was for the first assault group to attack the fort; the second wave, containing Fitzroy, had a list of targets in the harbour area. The SAS crept to the outskirts of Benghazi. The first wave peeled off to attack the fort; Mayne's detachment proceeded up the paved road. This time there was no red light and no sentry, but all around the road mines had been laid, so to stray from the tarmac surface was hazardous in the extreme. This had the effect of funnelling any attack along the narrow strip of road. The minute the SAS approached the first road block, pandemonium broke loose. Mayne's men came under heavy and sustained mortar and machine-gun fire. After a brief but ferocious gun battle, Stirling decided that, with the element of surprise gone, the enterprise was hopeless. And it would be fatal to be caught in the open in daylight. He gave the order to retreat.

Next morning the SAS were caught at the foot of the Jebel escarpment by waves of planes, angry as hornets. A chance hit sent up a column of fire from a stricken lorry. Italian and German planes could now 'bracket' them, and spent the day methodically bombing and strafing the wadis. By a miracle they missed the one where the SAS force was clustered, but it was a shaky and demoralized platoon that greeted the dusk. The one consolation was that there was no sign of ground forces.

As soon as night fell, the long 800-mile drive back to Kufra began. Fitzroy's detachment was soon joined by the first assault group, which had successfully stormed the fort and even taken three prisoners, but at heavy cost. There were badly wounded men among the survivors. Fitzroy had hoped that camouflage would protect them against aerial attack next day, but a foolish jeep driver raised a cloud of dust and betrayed their position. Fitzroy lay amid the inferno of exploding vehicles, trying to calculate the minimum number of trucks required to get the party home. 'As truck after truck disintegrated before our eyes, it became clear that it would be a tight fit.'[15]

When the sun went down, Stirling inspected the damage. He concluded that if all but the bare necessities were jettisoned, and if every jeep and truck were loaded to maximum capacity, there would be just enough transport to get everybody home. The shortage of food and water was a major worry, as was the prospect of travelling by day and exposing the wounded to the ravages of a broiling sun. In the end it was decided that a medical orderly and one of the Italian prisoners should go back to Benghazi the next day under a Red Cross flag, to bring an ambulance out for the casualties who could not be moved. A few walking wounded opted for the trek to Kufra rather than a Benghazi hospital and an Italian prisoner-of-war camp. Fitzroy remembers the decision to abandon the badly wounded as the toughest of all the decisions they had to make in the desert.

The shortage of food and water meant they had to travel non-stop, day and night. Fitzroy describes the ordeal:

> With seven or eight of us to a jeep it was not easy to relax, even when one was not actually driving. The sun blazed down relentlessly from a brazen sky. Occasionally someone would go to sleep and fall off, and we had to stop, waiting irritably, while he picked himself up and climbed back on again. The tyres, too, were beginning to feel the strain after so many hundreds of miles of rough going under a hot sun, and punctures came with increasing frequency. Changing a wheel, or digging the jeep out of the soft sand, began to seem more and more arduous as we grew weaker. Our throats were dry and it required an effort to speak. We counted the hours and minutes which separated us from the blissful moment when we could next allow ourselves to take a pull at the rapidly dwindling supply of warm, dirty, brackish water in our water-bottles.[16]

By dusk on 18 September they were near Jalo. Fitzroy, in command of two jeeps, went out to see whether the oasis was still in enemy hands. He found a full-scale battle for possession in progress between the British and Italians, and had to take cover. But he found an Arab, at whose well his men filled their water-bottles. He also bought a vegetable marrow with a thousand-lire note. He and his companions sat down to this unusual breakfast, only for tempers to flare over whether it was a marrow, a cucumber or some other vegetable. In the desert, the real cause of stress could not be faced head-on, so men used trivial pretexts to relieve their feelings. Since the marrow induced violent stomach cramps in all of them, they soon had more urgent matter for complaint.

During a lull, Fitzroy's party made contact with the British attackers. It was agreed that the SAS would join in the final assault, but before that could happen a message arrived from GHQ ordering them to break off the attack.

They still had to get back to Kufra. The force attacking Jalo, the Sudanese Defence Force, was not much better provisioned than the SAS, and for the 400 miles back to Kufra rations were still limited to a spoon of bully beef per meal. But at least they were not short of water. Forty-eight hours of misery brought the combined forces to Zighen and the oasis of Bir Harash, where they renewed their supplies of brackish water. But they still had the dreadful Sand Sea to negotiate once more – and this time they were exhausted. The tyres on the jeeps began to give out, and with no spare wheels or jacks available, each jeep had to be lifted in the air by main force while the tattered inner tube was patched and repatched. On the outward journey through the Sand Sea four men could accomplish what on the return eight were hard put to manage.

It was another forty-eight hours before the tatterdemalion party of exhausted scarecrows crawled into Kufra. Next morning, after the official reports had been made, Fitzroy and his comrades bathed in the lake, then settled down for the breakfast of a lifetime: whisky-laced porridge, eggs, bacon, sausages, bread, butter, marmalade and tinned pineapple, washed down with mugs of thick tea.

After the war, Churchill admitted to Fitzroy that he had known from Ultra intercepts that the Germans were forewarned of the raid.[17] The object of both the Benghazi and the Jalo attacks had been to make the enemy pull back planes from El Alamein, where the decisive confrontation was now imminent. This explained, too, the order from GHQ to proceed despite the loss of surprise. In military terms, Benghazi was a success. Fitzroy later wrote, with all the cynicism an uncynical man can muster: 'I was reminded of my Sergeant Instructor's admonition in the early days at Inverness . . . we were nothing but ——ing cogs in a gigantic ——ing organization. On our eventual return to civilization we were gratified to find ourselves and our operation described in the popular press in such glowing terms as to be scarcely recognizable.'[18]

Fitzroy's reputation as a desert warrior was made. Barnacles of legend became encrusted on what was already a solid achievement. One story had him setting off into the desert on a camel and sending back the message 'Returning. Rommel captured' – which uplifting announcement was later amended to 'Returning. Camel ruptured.' Yet Benghazi taught Fitzroy that, in life, luck is almost everything. David Stirling put him in for a Military Cross for his distinguished record on the two Benghazi operations, and in the elation following the El Alamein victory the medal would certainly have been awarded. However, Stirling's notorious administrative inefficiency played its part: he forgot to post the letter, and it was found on him when he was taken prisoner in January 1943.[19]

Stirling flew out from Kufra to Cairo with Fitzroy and others, turning over in his mind schemes for SAS operations in Persia and Europe. Persia had loomed large in Allied minds in the period before El Alamein, Stalingrad, and the 'Torch' landings in North Africa. It was even thought that the Germans intended a pincer movement on the Middle East, one arm probing towards Cairo, the other entering Persia via the Caucasus. While Stirling pondered whether there might not be one last operation to be squeezed out of the dying desert war, Fitzroy went to Baghdad to consult with General Maitland Wilson, Commander-in-Chief, Persia and Iraq, on the possibility of raising an additional SAS unit in Persia. He took with him Guardsman Duncan, a veteran of the last Benghazi exploit. They travelled across the Suez canal, through the Sinai desert to Gaza and Beersheba, then through Palestine to Lebanon and Syria, and from Damascus across the desert to Baghdad, all the time cooking and sleeping by the roadside.

In Baghdad on 1 November, Fitzroy conferred with 'Jumbo' Wilson, so called from his massive girth. Wilson had a weakness for large American cars and has been described as 'even less politically sophisticated than most officers of his generation'.[20] But Fitzroy found that he combined with his somewhat ponderous manner great mental alertness and a good eye for terrain. Wilson confided that Teheran was a security headache: the month before there had been a political crisis over the paper currency and a British brigade had had to stand by. There were problems over the food supply, and on top of everything was the danger of a Russian collapse in the Caucasus followed by a drive by Kleist or Manstein towards the vital oilfields at Abadan. Wilson gave Fitzroy authority to raise from the troops under his command a force of 150 volunteers, mainly officers and NCOs.

With Duncan Fitzroy next drove across the Persian frontier at Khamikin, then followed his 1938 route of Kermanshah, Hamadan, Kazvin, Teheran. He spent three weeks raising men and reconnoitring suitable country for guerrilla warfare in the event of a German invasion. Since most British troops in Persia were bored by months of inactivity, there were plenty of volunteers. Fitzroy had exacting standards, and also a strong strain of Celtic nationalism: ninety per cent of the men he chose were Scots.

A signal sent Fitzroy back to report to Wilson's Chief of Staff, General Baillon, who had arrived in Teheran from Baghdad. There was urgent work afoot. At the Embassy Fitzroy consulted with Baillon and the Minister, Sir Reader Bullard.[21] Wilson's intelligence service had become aware of a plot by a German agent, Meyer, operating in Fars province (whose capital was Shiraz). Meyer's co-conspirators included a Cabinet minister, three members of the *Majlis*, eleven generals and many senior Army officers. The plot involved a rising of the warlike Qashgai tribe, timed to coincide with a German invasion. The Qashgai leader Nasir Khan, a deputy in the *Majlis*, was heavily involved in the conspiracy, and was fomenting trouble behind British backs. The linchpin between the plotters in Teheran and the Qashgai country where Meyer was sheltering was General Zahidi, governor-general of Isfahan. Zahidi had three strikes against him: he was a grain hoarder; he was in touch with disaffected tribal leaders; and he had lines out to the German High Command in the Caucasus. If a general revolt broke out, there would not be enough British troops in the southern sector of Persia (the north was Russian-occupied) to deal with it. Something had to be done, and the obvious thing was to spirit Zahidi out of Isfahan while attracting the minimum of attention.

Fitzroy drove south from Teheran to Isfahan and consulted with the British consul, John Gault, who confirmed all Wilson's fears. With

Gault Fitzroy inspected the barracks, and Zahidi's palatial residence next door. The whole complex was too strongly guarded to be taken by a frontal assault. The only other possibility – ambushing Zahidi on a medieval bridge as he drove from his house to his headquarters – would certainly result in loss of life, as he went everywhere with heavily armed bodyguards. If the townspeople heard shooting and discovered that locals had been gunned down by British troops, it would probably provoke the very uprising Zahidi's removal was meant to prevent.

Fitzroy therefore cabled Teheran with his proposal for Operation Pongo. His plan was to gain entry into Zahidi's house by posing as a British brigadier anxious to pay his respects. He intended to arrive at the house with Duncan and a couple of other reliable aides, kidnap Zahidi at gunpoint and, with luck, get him out of Isfahan before it was realized that anything was amiss. Fitzroy asked for a platoon of infantry as back-up, just in case anything went wrong, but he was reasonably confident the Persian troops would not intervene; Zahidi had spent so much time playing politics that he had neglected his troops, and discipline was lax.

The reply came back that Pongo was approved in principle, except that it was not permissible for a mere major to impersonate a brigadier: Fitzroy would have to obtain a real brigadier from the Corps Commander at Qum, two hundred miles away; the brigadier would be temporarily under his orders.

Fitzroy collected his brigadier from Qum, together with a platoon of Seaforth Highlanders. Their orders were to intervene only if they heard shooting, in which case a flying column with Zahidi in tow would leave Isfahan at speed. Fitzroy then rehearsed the operation with the Seaforths at a ruined fort in the desert. His presence so close to Isfahan with commandos was risky; an old friend from the Diplomatic Service actually stumbled on Fitzroy and his raiders, and immediately became suspicious.[22]

D-Day was set after consultation with GHQ in Baghdad and the Foreign Office. Fitzroy also secured reluctant permission from the authorities to shoot Zahidi if he resisted arrest. On 7 December he telephoned Zahidi and made an appointment for the brigadier. After lunch a staff car set out for Zahidi's residence, in the back Fitzroy and the brigadier. In the front next the driver was a reliable NCO; Guardsman Duncan and a Seaforth Highlander crouched fully-armed under a tarpaulin in the luggage compartment at the back. Outside the gates of the military compound two trucks concealed the other Seaforths. As a last refinement, Fitzroy had an RAF intelligence officer engage the sentry in conversation just before they arrived.

The staff car was waved through by the chatting sentry, swept up the drive and halted outside the house by a pair of open French windows. A servant ushered them in. A few minutes later Zahidi himself arrived, to find himself looking down the barrel of Fitzroy's Colt automatic. Fitzroy informed Zahidi that he was under arrest; Zahidi momentarily blustered. There then followed a moment of pure farce. 'Suddenly a podgy thirteen-year-old appeared, sucking an ice-cream, and said, "Don't do that to my Daddy!" '[23] Zahidi calmed the child, and informed his servants that he was going for a drive.

Zahidi was bundled out of the open windows into the waiting car. With a gun in his ribs, he was forced to act naturally. He saluted the sentry at the gates, the car passed through without incident, and the two trucks of Seaforths fell in behind. Now Zahidi began to grow alarmed and expostulated. 'I said, "You'll have plenty of time to explain when you get to your destination." Very civilized, smooth man, who later made a good Prime Minister of Persia. I relieved him of his splendid Belgian pistol, which I coveted and was tempted to pinch!'[24] Many years later Fitzroy told Roy Plomley, 'He was certainly one of the nicest people I ever kidnapped.'[25]

During a halt outside Isfahan Zahidi requested that fresh clothes be sent after him, and that his children be taken to Teheran. Beyond Isfahan they passed a large barracks, but the Seaforths had already cut the telephone wire and there was no sign of the alarm having been raised. They drove to a rendezvous in the desert where an officer and six men took over, transferred Zahidi to another car and drove to an airfield at Sultanabad. A waiting plane took the general to Palestine, where he was interned for the rest of the war. 'Jumbo' Wilson was delighted with the success of the operation: '. . . the possibility of others being treated in a like manner put a complete damper on any further activities of the plotters.'[26]

With a platoon of Seaforths carrying tommy-guns, Fitzroy returned to Isfahan and called on Zahidi's Chief of Staff, Colonel Aslani, a well-known Anglophobe; then, using the pretext of Zahidi's request for fresh clothes, they searched Zahidi's house thoroughly. A pile of incriminating letters linking Zahidi to the Germans was generally agreed to provide ample, if retrospective, justification for Zahidi's abduction.

Two weeks later, when the dust had settled, Gault reported to the Foreign Office: 'The going of General Zahidi has had a considerable calming effect on the administration, not so much because we removed him as because he is no longer here to intrigue and make trouble. Zahidi was a man who had an iron in every fire, however small it might seem, and that was the main cause of unrest in Isfahan. The clique of rich Isfahania – some dozen men, all rascals, who are at the same time the richest merchants in the bazaar, the biggest factory owners and the biggest landowners – which Zahidi took care to cultivate for his own ends, has been taken aback and is now more subdued.'[27]

Of all Fitzroy's exploits, the Zahidi kidnapping of December 1942 is the most reminiscent of James Bond. In retrospect, it amuses him.

> Zahidi's son, the podgy 13-year-old of 1942, later popped up as an accomplished ladies' man and ambassador to the UK. He married the Shah's daughter, but divorced her later. The last I heard he was living in Switzerland. I got an invitation to lunch at the Iranian embassy. Denis Healey was there. Delicious lunch. I heard the ambassador talking about the 1940s and about his father being snatched. I didn't know whether he knew who I was or not. I asked a young lady of my acquaintance to find out. She said he did know who I was. My stepdaughter Suki used to go to his parties. She took me to one once. As we were leaving, Zahidi's son said, 'You kidnapped my father once. It's only fair I should take your stepdaughter out to dinner.' Which he did.[28]

The surrender of Marshal von Paulus at Stalingrad in January 1943 removed the military threat to Persia. Meanwhile the Allied pincer movement – El Alamein at one end of North Africa and the 'Torch' landings at the other – had brought the desert war to a close. The obvious area for SAS operations henceforth was the Eastern Mediterranean, now controlled by the newly promoted Commander-in-Chief, Middle East, none other than 'Jumbo' Wilson. Fitzroy flew to Baghdad just before Wilson left for Cairo, and got him to agree to SAS operations in his domain. He then flew back to Persia and began transferring his men to Palestine.

Meanwhile there had been many changes in the SAS. The end of the desert war deprived them of their natural habitat, so they had to adapt to new methods of fighting, on different terrain. David Stirling had been captured in January 1943: he was taken in his sleep during virtually the last North African operation of the war when an Arab betrayed him for money. This was something of a relief to his friends, who thought that he would otherwise not have survived.[29] He spent the rest of the war in a prisoner-of-war camp. Most of Stirling's men were thereafter formed into the Special Raiding Squadron under Major Paddy Mayne, but Stirling's designated Number Two, George Jellicoe, had moved across to command the SBS. Both units moved to Palestine and established their headquarters at Azzib, north of Haifa. Jellicoe started with a winter training camp by the Lake of Galilee, then in the spring moved to a summer camp at Athlit, south of Haifa at the foot of Mount Carmel, where a long stretch of golden sand led to the ruins of a crusader castle towering over the bay. The SBS tramped energetically over the thyme-scented slopes of Mount Carmel, launched folboats in the surf and navigated the offshore waters in caiques.

Here, in April 1943, Fitzroy brought his detachment, one of three under Jellicoe's overall command. 'L' detachment, from Kabrit, was headed by Tom Langton; 'S' detachment, from Syria, by David Sutherland; and 'M' detachment, from Persia, was under Fitzroy. Each detachment consisted of five patrols, ten strong, with two signallers and commanded by an officer. In addition, the leader of each detachment retained a special patrol for his own use. Total fighting strength was about 230 men. Inter-detachment rivalry was keen, compounded by inter-patrol rivalry. At Athlit one first glimpses an authoritarian side to Fitzroy. 'Fitzroy was perceived as older, wiser and with contacts to a wider world,' Sutherland recalls. 'He had some good ideas about training but was inclined to be a hard driver. I was more easy-going, like Jellicoe.'[30] Jellicoe concurs in this estimate. 'Fitzroy objected to the superficially casual slackness of the SBS – he attached a lot of importance to these things. He is "by the book" rather than à la Wingate. He almost led a little palace coup against me. "George is a splendid chap," he used to say, "but he doesn't run a tight enough ship".'[31]

In Fitzroy's defence, commanding an élite detachment was no easy task. Predictably, parachute training caused the worst problems. Among Fitzroy's men was the same Captain Lezard whose father had 'kept a pack of cards' in Leicestershire. Fitzroy takes up the story:

> I gave myself the job of supervising his parachute training. We went up in the aeroplane at five in the morning or something unpleasant like that and there was Lezard and a 'stick' of guardsmen, as we used to call it. You know, guardsmen will do anything in the line of duty as long as they don't have to use too much imagination. So there was Captain Lezard and the eight guardsmen in this plane. He was leading – jumping out first – and there was this hole you had to get over and then hold by your hands with your legs dangling. He got over the hole and then he suddenly said to me, 'Fitzroy, I'm sorry to have to tell you this but I don't think I'm going to be able to do this. Right now jumping out of this plane doesn't seem to make much sense.' There was a green light and the man saying, one, two, three. Then Lezard thought, and said, 'But what would people say if I refused? What would they say in White's?'

Fitzroy gave him to understand that he would not be viewed in the most favourable light. At that Lezard launched himself into space. But his hesitation had sown confusion. The next guardsman got himself tangled up in the rigging head downwards and had to be pulled back in. 'Then he didn't like the idea of getting out again and had to be pushed off. All the others then went out but because of the delays they ended up scattered all over Palestine instead of being in a neat stick.'[32]

Fitzroy himself got a bump on the knee while parachuting, an injury which has returned to trouble him nearly fifty years later. But this was as nothing compared with his next experience, which used up another of his 'lives'. Fitzroy went down to Baghdad to meet a brigadier who was one of his constituents in Lancaster.

> He asked me if I was a parachutist. It was obviously very important to make a good impression on him, so I said yes. 'Well, we have some Assyrians here learning to parachute. Why don't you just show them the way and give them a practice jump?' So I did. We were jumping out of quite a different sort of aeroplane. We went very, very slowly. It was a Hercules transport and instead of going at 200 miles an hour, we were going at what seemed like about 90. I remember all these grinning Assyrians. I jumped out and nothing happened. The parachute failed to open. I thought, oh dear, I've made a fool of myself, what a waste! How stupid just to have done this to impress a constituent. I pulled the emergency cord in some desperation. Then, very, very slowly and gradually, the 'chute opened. I've never felt more relieved.[33]

After some weeks at Athlit, Fitzroy moved his detachment northwards up the coast to Lebanon, in order to complete their training in mountain warfare. 'M' detachment was based at the village of Zahle, high up in the hills behind Beirut. 'Situated in a typical Alpine valley, with rushing past its half-French-provincial, half-Arab houses, a mountain stream, which the inhabitants used for cooling bottles of delicious wine from the neighbouring vineyards, Zahle sticks in my memory as one of the most agreeable places to which my travels have taken me.'[34]

A few weeks later Fitzroy was summoned to Cairo and told to stand by for an immediate operation. He visited all his old haunts, including Peter Stirling's flat. Cairo seemed to be surpassing its habitual hedonism, for the summer of 1943 saw the opening of the Auberge des Pyramides, a luxurious new night-club on the Mena road boasting a large open-air courtyard with a dance floor in the middle. Top cabaret artists were engaged; Noel Coward performed there in August.

Fitzroy soon received his orders. Four weeks before the Sicily landings it was decided that raids would be launched against German airfields in Crete. The aim was to destroy German planes that might be used during the invasion of Sicily, and to encourage the impression that Greece and Crete were the main targets for invasion. Additionally Churchill, still obsessed with his First World War dream of securing a supply route to Russia through the Dardanelles as an alternative to the Arctic convoys, thought of isolating Crete by operations in the Aegean. He cabled 'Jumbo' Wilson: 'This is the time to think of Clive and Peterborough and of Rooke's men taking Gibraltar.'[35]

But things did not work out that way. The Germans took Rhodes, Cos and Leros. The fate of Alan Phipps, a signals officer lost in the Royal Navy operation around Leros, was linked with Fitzroy's in a way that became clear only later. David Sutherland's detachment actually got ashore on Crete and did some damage, but as Fitzroy and his men were on the point of leaving Beirut, he was suddenly summoned back to Cairo. He was told that air reconnaissance now showed the Germans were no longer using the aerodrome that was to have been 'M' detachment's target.

Fitzroy then went to see Rex Leeper, who was Ambassador to the Greek government-in-exile and whom he had known in the Foreign Office, and asked whether there was any chance of being dropped into Greece for guerrilla operations. Leeper promised to cable London. Fitzroy then flew back to Zahle, where he at once received a signal from Leeper asking him to return. Fitzroy did not realize it at the time, but his niche in history was about to be secured. The cable read:

MACLEAN NOT NEEDED IN GREECE BUT IN YUGOSLAVIA. REPORT FORTH-WITH TO PRIME MINISTER IN LONDON.

8

The Battle with SOE

1943

———

T HE story of Fitzroy's turbulent relations with Special Operations Executive in 1943 has engendered differing reactions. Many feel that Brigadier Keble got his merited come-uppance. Others think that Fitzroy ruthlessly cut SOE out of the picture, without adequate acknowledgement of their excellent supply and transport work. Taking a leaf out of David Stirling's book, Fitzroy soon engineered a situation where he was directly responsible to Churchill on the political front and General Wilson on the military side. But in so doing he made many enemies. Lord Henniker comments: 'Fitzroy had a bad habit of always going too high, to Winston or to Jumbo Wilson. If you go straight to the top, you leave behind a trail of disappointed suitors. It means the next time you want a favour, the harbourmaster at Bari plays hard to get.'

Others resented Fitzroy's meteoric rise from lieutenant in 1941 (and private before that) to brigadier two years later. 'What I hold against Fitzroy Maclean is that he was to be Number Two to Brigadier Orr but wangled himself as Number One, and then ignored the instructions that a different Number One might have carried out. Orr did not go to Yugoslavia because Maclean suggested to Churchill that Randolph go as his second-in-command.' The words are those of the late Michael Lees, one of Fitzroy's bitterest critics, and they show clearly enough that once Fitzroy got the call from Churchill he was in a minefield. Much of the criticism levelled at Fitzroy seems to be pique at his proving so much more successful than SOE in establishing close relations with Eden and Churchill. He emerged as a uniquely successful player of 'Secret Army' games. Fitzroy used SOE transport and communications systems, but there was no *quid pro quo*: Fitzroy only ever came under the aegis of SOE when it suited him, and he took out insurance by having a separate communications channel through ISLD (the Inter Services Liaison Department). In fact, there are grounds for thinking that Churchill may have selected Fitzroy, foreseeing the inevitable conflict with SOE, in the hope that he would be able to geld the organization politically and strategically in south-east Europe. By dealing not with SOE but with Wilson and with Churchill, Fitzroy catapulted himself into the higher political echelons.

The story of Fitzroy's defeat of SOE abounds in ironies. Brigadier Keble and the pro-Partisan lobby in SOE opposed Fitzroy's appointment, fearing that he, a known anti-Communist, would be against the Partisans for ideological reasons. They also thought that Orme Sargent in the Foreign Office would help them fight this 'interloper', unaware that it was Sargent who had recommended him. There were thus two strands in the SOE opposition to Fitzroy: that he was inflexibly anti-Soviet, and that he was a Foreign Office man. SOE had cause enough to fear the impact of Fitzroy on their empire, since he built one of his own. But on the ideological question he proved notably fairminded. However, there can be no doubt that his experience with SOE in 1943 increased Fitzroy's cynicism towards that organization, so that – some say – he could see no good in it at all. In the interests of fairness, it is worth citing the opinion of Fitzroy's signals officer, Hilary King: 'What no one knows and has never been properly written up is the enormous part played by SOE in our Yugoslav operation right up to the end in communications and supply, with no past precedents to guide them. Whatever Fitzroy may think, I reckon they did a marvellous job – in staff work, planning, and technical management.'

Fitzroy was due to leave Cairo at dawn on 3 July in a Liberator, bound for London via Gibraltar. The night before, he received a signal from London telling him to delay his departure. Next morning the Liberator took off; on board was General Sikorski, leader of the Polish government-in-exile, together with his daughter and the rest of his entourage. After an overnight stop at Gibraltar, the plane took off next morning but crashed into the sea almost immediately after leaving the runway. The pilot was the only survivor.

The cause of the crash remains a mystery. Certainly there had been earlier attempts to sabotage planes used by Sikorski: a well-constructed bomb with a time-fuse was found on his plane over the Atlantic in 1942.[1] The issue of Sikorski's death became notorious in the mid-1960s with Hochhuth's allegation in his play *The Soldiers* of his assassination on Winston Churchill's orders. Naturally, Fitzroy indignantly denies that Churchill could have been guilty, but he accepts that the mysterious signal from London lends circumstantial credibility to the rumour.

'I did express surprise about having been taken off the flight in the light of having been sent for by the Prime Minister. But I got a free night in Cairo! Someone on the flight not taken off was Victor Cazalet, MP, an uncle of a friend of mine who is now a judge.' But assassination?

'This wasn't the kind of thing Churchill did. Philby was in the Spanish section of MI6, and I suspect him. Stalin had no love for Sikorski. But then why take me off? The Russians might have wanted me out of the way just as much.'[2]

Churchill summoned Fitzroy to London at the end of six months of hard thought about Yugoslavia and its future, beginning in January 1943 in Cairo when three SOE officers proved to him from intercepted signals that the Partisans were doing most of the fighting in that country. This was supported by three German signals deciphered by the top-secret Ultra decoder at Bletchley on 17 January.[3] Churchill decided to send a top-level mission to the mysterious 'Tito', leader of the Partisans. He wrote to General Alexander at the beginning of July that recent heavy fighting in Yugoslavia gave the Allies a chance to ignite the entire western Balkans, and decided that he needed as his right-hand man there someone who combined diplomatic and military skills. As he wrote to the Foreign Secretary, 'What we want is a daring Ambassador-leader with these hardy and hunted guerrillas.'[4] There were not many in Churchill's inner circle who had worked in the Foreign Office *and* gone on raids with the SAS. In addition, his Russian years had given Fitzroy a knowledge of Communists and their ways. Suprise has sometimes been expressed that Churchill chose a relatively obscure young officer for such a momentous task. But Fitzroy was uniquely qualified, and Churchill was shrewd enough to see it.

Fitzroy arrived in London to find plans well in hand. Major William Deakin, one of the three SOE officers who had prepared the memorandum for Churchill, had already been parachuted into Yugoslavia to see if the Partisans would accept a full-scale Allied mission. Deakin was an academic in civilian life, and had been Churchill's research assistant on his biography of Marlborough. With Deakin went Major Jones of the Canadian Black Watch and Captain Stewart of the Royal Engineers.

Fitzroy read the brief prepared by the Foreign Office in consultation with SOE, who were now officially his employers. His principal instruction was to co-ordinate the efforts of the Partisans with Mihailovic's Cetniks and bring both bodies under the effective control of Britain's Middle East Command. The ulterior purpose was to establish a democratic form of government in Yugoslavia after the Axis powers had been defeated; ideally this would be a constitutional monarchy under the exiled King Peter, then aged twenty.[5]

Fitzroy saw a lot of Churchill in the last two weeks of July. A day or two after arriving in London he was invited down to Chequers. Being at the centre of power was an exhilarating experience. Fitzroy marvelled at the flurry of activity – everywhere red leather despatch boxes, telegrams, signals, and the constant coming and going of despatch riders.

What he did not relish so much was Churchill's inexhaustible appetite for films. A movie-lover himself, Fitzroy nevertheless baulked at the sheer volume of celluloid. 'The great men stood by, waiting their turn, hoping that it would not come in the early hours of the morning, a time when the ordinary mortal does not feel at his brightest, especially if he has seen three or four films in succession, but when the Prime Minister, on the contrary, seemed filled with renewed vigour of mind and body.'[6] For those who did not like the silver screen, the process was an agony. Fitzroy's old boss, Sir Alexander Cadogan, on board HMS *Prince of Wales* with Churchill in August 1941, recorded the toll when the great man was limited to a single movie a day.

> *6 August 1941*. Film after dinner. *The Devil and Miss Jones*. Bad.
> *7 August*. Bad film after dinner. *The High Sierras* [*sic*]. Awful bunk. But the PM loves them and they keep him quiet.
> *8 August*. Film *Lady Hamilton* after dinner. Quite good. PM, seeing it for the fifth time, moved to tears.[7]

But it is due to Churchill's love of films that Fitzroy recalls exactly where he was when Mussolini's fall was announced. It was the evening of 25 July 1943. Fitzroy's description is irresistible.

> Towards midnight, in the middle of a Mickey Mouse cartoon, a memorable interruption took place. A message was brought in to Mr Churchill, who gave an exclamation of surprise. Then there was a scuffle and the film was stopped. As the squawking of Donald Duck and the baying of Pluto died away, the Prime Minister rose to his feet. 'I have just', he said, 'received some very important news. Signor Mussolini has resigned.' Then the film was switched on again.
> As we went downstairs, I reflected that it was now more unlikely than ever that the Prime Minister would find time to attend to my affairs. But I was mistaken. 'This', he said, turning to me, 'makes your job more important than ever. The German position in Italy is crumbling. We must now put all the pressure we can on them on the other side of the Adriatic. You must go in without delay.'[8]

What Churchill did not tell Fitzroy was that there had been heated and sustained opposition to his appointment, both from Eden and from Lord Selborne, the head of SOE. The immediate result of the dramatic events of 25 July was a flurry of minutes between these two, the Prime Minister and 'Jumbo' Wilson, Commander-in-Chief, Middle East.[9] Behind Fitzroy's appointment lay a long trail of interdepartmental rivalry and ideological struggle. Two things stand out: the detestation of SOE by all other departments; and the determination in many quarters that all Allied aid to Yugoslavia should go to the Cetniks led by General Draza Mihailovic.

Special Operations Executive had been set up immediately after the fall of France, with the intention of 'setting Europe ablaze' by means of sabotage, commando raids and collaboration with national Resistance groups. Hugh Dalton was its first head, sheltering under the title of Minister of Economic Warfare. Inevitably there was confusion about the respective roles of this organization and the Secret Intelligence Service (SIS) proper, especially its military branch the ISLD. When Lord Selborne replaced Dalton in February 1942, he tried to define their respective spheres of influence. The nature of their rivalry depended on the particular theatre of war and the personalities involved. Relations were good in Cairo, but rock-bottom in London. SOE could work with ISLD in the field but not with SIS in London, where it was perceived to be a creature of the FO. This rivalry often had undesirable consequences. Intercepted German signals about the Yugoslav Partisans, available to the War Office from 1941 on, were not available to SOE Cairo until autumn 1942, and not to highly-placed officers in SOE London until spring 1943.

SOE was also disliked by the military and the Foreign Office. Foreign Office bitterness stemmed from the early years of the war, when diplomats working through normal channels collided with buccaneering saboteurs. It became a reflex action for the FO to accuse SOE of political bungling, and for SOE to charge the FO with having ruined operations with their obstruction. Selborne was brought in as the new head of SOE in February 1942 because Dalton's clashes with Eden had become intolerable – not that Selborne's relations with the Foreign Secretary were much better.

SOE was aware that it was perceived as an upstart, and asserted itself accordingly. It resented the FO claiming the right to veto, say, an act of sabotage in a neutral country, and tried to circumscribe the extent to which the mandarins could interfere. Personalities in the two organizations were very different. Foreign Office men were more detached, but were remote from the everyday realities of Resistance life; SOE men tended to have more insight into the real lives of their collaborators in occupied Europe. 'Nearly all the earlier [SOE] recruits lacked the habit of subordination to a regular hierarchy; were disciplined by no mandarin ethos; and were impatient or even contemptuous of the diplomatic service and its auxiliaries. To the diplomats they often appeared brash, ignorant of things which diplomats were trained to regard as important, and at times a positive menace.'[10]

It has sometimes been suggested, because of its close ties with the American OSS (Office of Strategic Services) and from its own social composition, that SOE was a right-wing organization, and that there was therefore an ideological component in its clashes with the 'politically neutral' FO. It is true that the leadership of SOE was rightist. Lord Selborne was a deep-dyed conservative and monarchist and Gladwyn Jebb, chief executive officer of SOE, was a well-known anti-Soviet and anti-Communist. Most SOE recruits came from business backgrounds. It is also true that there was an inbuilt contradiction in SOE, since it aimed to use national liberation forces to defeat the Axis while making sure that these countries, when finally liberated, did not swing left. Further than this the argument cannot be taken. The FO had its own view of the desirable form of government – constitutional monarchy: 'There survived in the FO a remnant of the Palmerstonian belief that constitutional monarchy is the only form of government that is good for Balkan peoples.'[11] The SOE in the field was prepared to work with both left and right. In Greece it swung right and in Yugoslavia left, but the FO disapproved on both occasions.

Pressure from London limited the effectiveness of SOE. Its task was to mobilize all the anti-fascist forces in Europe, but these were overwhelmingly on the left. SOE in London was constrained by having to deal with an array of highly conservative governments-in-exile whose sole interest at the end of the war was the restoration of the *status quo ante*, and would therefore have been obliged to become a conservative force, whatever the ideology of its leaders.

Fitzroy's brief displays the conflicting pull of the two institutions. The SOE wanted to get operational control of all Resistance forces in Yugoslavia; the FO wanted to bring the Partisans under British influence and prevent the emergence of a Communist regime after the war. Fitzroy immediately saw that his instructions were ambiguous, and sought clarification from Churchill. If Britain aided the Partisans so as to ensure the defeat of German forces in Yugoslavia, the result might be a Communist regime there after the war. Was that really what HM Government wanted? Which of the two conflicting aims, military and political, had priority? Churchill's reply left no doubt.

> So long, he said, as the whole of Western civilization was threatened by the Nazi menace, we could not afford to let our attention be diverted from the immediate issue by considerations of long-term policy . . . My task was simply to find out who was killing the most Germans and suggest means by which we could help them to kill more. Politics must be a secondary consideration.[12]

The other contentious issue Fitzroy noticed concerned General Mihailovic. Some quarters in London had known about Partisan resistance to the Axis occupiers since late 1941, but for propaganda and ideological reasons the myth had been perpetuated that Mihailovic and his Cetniks were doing all the fighting. Selborne was a devoted

Mihailovic supporter; but Mihailovic preferred to fight Partisans rather than Germans or Italians. Major S.W. Bailey, one of the first British Liaison Officers (BLOs) in Yugoslavia, who had been seconded to Mihailovic's headquarters, had this to say: 'Mihailovic's policy remained one of abstention from serious action against the occupying forces, largely because he feared that consequent reprisals on the civilian population would cost him the support of the peasantry, but also to secure favourable conditions for the consolidation of his political position in the areas under his control, and time in which to extend such control to the entire country.'[13]

Bailey exhorted Mihailovic to move against the occupiers, but this proved counterproductive. On 28 February 1943, in Bailey's presence, Mihailovic unleashed an astonishing outburst against the British. He bitterly attacked Allied policy. He claimed that it was imperative for him to liquidate all his enemies: Partisans, Croats, Moslems and Ustase – in that order – before dealing with the Axis forces, and that no action or threat from the Allies would make him change. He did not need the democracies; if necessary, he would get all he needed from Italy.[14]

When a report on this effusion reached London, it lent weight to the new policy of approaching both resistance movements – Cetniks and Partisans. Churchill was shaken by an intelligence report prepared by SOE Cairo in February which showed the Partisans bitterly opposing the Wehrmacht and Mihailovic's Cetniks doing nothing. SOE Cairo now supported the Partisans, while SOE London was still unswerving in support of the Cetniks. On 11 February the Chiefs of Staff considered the memorandum, written by Brigadier Keble of SOE Cairo, which advocated aid to the resistance movements in Croatia and Slovenia as well as to Mihailovic. A week later, Cadogan at the Foreign Office ran into a veritable typhoon of opposition when discussing these ideas with SOE London. It seemed to Cadogan that they were merely protecting an ancient investment and were unprepared to look at the facts. The Foreign Office agreed with the Chiefs of Staff that, at the very least, feelers should be put out to the Partisans. SOE London's furious opposition to this idea compounded the existing institutional rivalries. As part of a rearguard resistance, Selborne told Churchill that SOE had only four old Liberators, 'on their last legs', for work in the Balkans; Halifaxes were useless, as they could not carry an effective load more than 1,000 miles.[15]

So far it was the FO which had driven SOE out of its ideological bolt-hole. But in April a gap opened up between General Wilson and SOE Cairo and the Foreign Office itself. Cairo was moving too fast in establishing contacts with the Partisans for Whitehall's liking. Particular offence was caused by the discovery that SOE Cairo had actually sent supplies to Slovenia without first obtaining assurances that these would not be used against other Resistance groups. Fearing that matters were slipping from their control, the FO backtracked and began to defend Mihailovic more avidly than the SOE had done. Gaining in confidence, Selborne now became involved in a tremendous row in July 1943 with Churchill's protégé Brendan Bracken, the Minister of Information, over a BBC broadcast which had upset Mihailovic.

At this point Churchill made his decisive intervention by sending a mission to Tito, overruling all opposition, whether from Eden and the FO or Selborne and the SOE. It was to be made clear to Tito that if he used British supplies against the Cetniks, he would be denied further aerial drops.[16] As a further sop to the Mihailovic faction, Churchill agreed to balance the mission to the Partisans by sending out another Brigadier to Mihailovic. This was Brigadier C. D. Armstrong, a regular soldier with 25 years' experience, veteran of the Dunkirk and North Africa campaigns. It may be that the FO's new bearing had been counterproductive. It was said that Churchill mistrusted the FO, one of the few departments of which he had never been the head, and suspected them of pursuing their own line, whatever British government was in power. He arranged for Casey, the Foreign Office Minister of State in Cairo, to send him fortnightly appreciations of the situation in the Balkans, thus bypassing the FO in London. And he made Fitzroy head of the political mission to Tito, instead of merely political adviser to the FO.[17]

There was one other point puzzling Fitzroy as he worked his way through the mountains of paper in London. Why was the British government's policy in Yugoslavia so very different from that in Greece? In Yugoslavia Churchill appeared prepared to co-operate with Communist guerrillas, but in Greece he had set his face against them. As far as Fitzroy could see, a number of factors were at work. Greece was militarily more controllable than Yugoslavia and was strategically more important to the traditional route to India. The British government had a strong emotional commitment to the Greek monarchy because of King George of the Hellenes' loyalty during the dark days of 1940 and 1941: there was no such sentimental attachment to the Yugoslav monarchy. Additionally, Tito's Partisans were far more powerful and effective than ELAS, the Greek Communist guerillas – at peak fighting strength Tito had 180,000 Partisans under arms, while ELAS had just 20,000; Mihailovic, in Yugoslavia, was peevish and uncooperative while Zervas, his Greek counterpart, was pliable; in general, British Liaison Officers got on well with the Partisans but badly with the ELAS guerillas; and the British believed they could break ELAS, should that prove necessary in order to restore King George; they did not imagine they could break Tito.

There was no grand British over-arching view in the Balkans. Monty Woodhouse recalled later: 'No one seems to have given much thought to the implications of the conjunction of the events in Yugoslavia and Greece. For my part, I can only say that I never even knew of the existence of Deakin or Maclean until a year later . . . The two countries might have been on Mars or Venus for all the connection that was seen between them.'[18]

Churchill's attitude was interesting. The different policies in Yugoslavia and Greece enabled him to claim an even-handedness which, in his heart, he did not feel. He told the House of Commons in May 1944: 'In one place we support a king, in another a Communist – there is no attempt by us to enforce particular ideologies.'[19] What Churchill did not admit was that he lacked the power to enforce his favoured ideology. Churchill took pleasure in appearing a tough, ruthless master of *realpolitik*, and his directive to Fitzroy – 'find out who is killing the most Germans' – concealed a parallel romantic streak. For monarchist reasons he wanted to build up King Peter of Yugoslavia, but this was also an underhand way of improving Britain's position in the country. In short, Churchill worked at two levels: both *realpolitik*, and emotional commitment to monarchy. His later actions belied his tough words. If killing Germans was the sole point at issue, what can explain Churchill's sense of failure in Yugoslavia, apparent from the autumn of 1944?

This tangled web of *haute politique* might have appeared tangential to Fitzroy's immediate role. He soon learned it was not. He was to be parachuted into Yugoslavia, and all the arrangements were to be made by SOE, who were supposed to give him every assistance. So Fitzroy reported to SOE headquarters in Baker Street and asked them to get him on the first flight to Cairo. Nothing happened. A week later he rang up to ask when he would be going, and was told that there were no flights because of bad weather.

A day or two later Churchill summoned him to Number 10. He showed Fitzroy a signal received from General Wilson saying that he considered Maclean totally unsuitable for the job. Fitzroy was somewhat pained by this, as he had always considered Wilson a good friend. Churchill then showed Fitzroy the equally uncompromising reply he had sent to Wilson, of which the gist was, do as you're told and mind your own business. Fitzroy marvelled at the great man's indiscretion, and was even more surprised when he was given a copy of the cable.

Further calls to Baker Street elicited that the weather was still bad. But one day Fitzroy ran into an old friend from Foreign Office days, Philip Broad, who told him something of the inside story of his appointment. It seemed it was Sir Orme Sargent, Cadogan's deputy, who had swung his appointment when Churchill first mooted the idea of an 'Ambassador-leader'. Broad cautioned Fitzroy against SOE, and said the FO's suspicion of SOE was such that that he (Broad) had actually been appointed to Harold Macmillan's staff in Bari 'to watch Fitzroy's back'. Further conversation revealed that Broad was flying out to Cairo in two days, and that there had been no interruption whatever to flights to the Middle East. Fitzroy therefore returned with Broad to his office, rang the Air Ministry and got a flight on a Liberator for the next day. It transpired that the Ministry had heard of Maclean, but had been assured by SOE that his request for a flight was a pure formality, that he did not really want to travel.

Fitzroy then returned to Baker Street, where he received commiseration for the continued 'bad weather'. 'Actually,' he replied, 'I've come to let you know that I'm flying out tomorrow.' Consternation ensued. 'In that case,' replied a flustered official, 'you'd better see Lord Selborne at once.' Selborne was seated behind a large desk. He jumped up, affability itself. 'My boy, I can't tell you how delighted I am that our great leader has entrusted this to you.' By now Fitzroy was taking the entire performance with a pinch of salt. Selborne suggested that Fitzroy take an oath of allegiance to SOE. Fitzroy parried. Surely that was unnecessary, since he had already signed the Official Secrets Act when he joined the Foreign Office? Momentarily baulked, Selborne swept a huge map of the Balkans off his desk to reveal two small leather cases with the letters 'DSO' in gold. 'That', he said, 'is what we do for those who serve us loyally.' Fitzroy's inclination was to say, 'I'll take one on account, Minister', but discretion prevailed. He made his excuses and left.[20]

Next day he flew out to Cairo. He at once went to see the Commander-in-chief, 'Jumbo' Wilson. Unlike most regular officers, Wilson had a keen sense of the uses to which guerrillas could be put, and Fitzroy always had a high regard for him. Also, two of Fitzroy's friends were the general's aides: his military assistant, Mark Chapman-Walker and his private secretary, Hermione Ranfurly. 'What', they asked, 'has got into the Prime Minister? Jumbo has just had a personal signal from him about you, in reply to nothing he ever sent, telling him to shut up and do as he's told.' It was clear that some outside party must have sent an unauthorized signal to Churchill in Wilson's name.

When Fitzroy went in to see Wilson, 'Jumbo' made it clear that he too suspected SOE, for whom and all whose works he gradually revealed a general distaste – hardly surprisingly, since no military commander likes dealing with an organization outside his control. He intended to find out who had taken his name in vain: meanwhile, Fitzroy was to get himself gazetted Brigadier, then report to SOE Cairo, and come back if he had any trouble there.

Fitzroy was unaware that he was about to enter a maelstrom. Rustum Buildings, housing SOE Cairo, was an inferno of backstabbing and machination. 'Nobody who did not experience it can possibly imagine the atmosphere of jealousy, suspicion and intrigue which embittered the relations between secret and semi-secret departments in Cairo.'[21] It is true that Fitzroy had entertained a healthy scepticism about SOE's military abilities ever since his time in Palestine, where the SOE training school based on Mount Carmel, overlooking Haifa, had been neighbours of the SBS at Athlit Castle. This SOE school was something of a joke. Officially designated ME 102, under its eccentric commandant Colonel Harry Cator of the Royal Scots Greys (a hero of the First World War and cousin by marriage of the Queen), it quickly became known as 'Narkover', after J.B. Morton's infamous public school in the 'Beachcomber' column. Any lingering credibility the school might have had was destroyed when a group of Jewish zealots carried off a large cache of arms and ammunition for the Irgun organization.

But no one had warned Fitzroy about Brigadier Mervyn Keble. The brigadier, a regular officer in the Wiltshires, one of the most correct 'county' regiments, had at one time been governor of a prison in Palestine. More recently he had worked at GHQ Cairo, where he headed the intelligence section that monitored Rommel's supply situation. It was said that his aide Major Enoch Powell did all his work but that Keble took the credit. After El Alamein he became the director of SOE's Military Operations, where he was described as 'the last man to hold this position who knew all that was going on all the time'.[22] He was certainly a ruthless and formidable bureaucratic in-fighter. In the summer of 1942 Lord Glenconner had taken over both branches (operations and propaganda) of SOE Cairo, as well as the Arab Bureau. But Glenconner preferred to delegate, so as not to have to spend too much time in Cairo. This suited Keble, his Number Two, perfectly. By the autumn of 1943 he had eighty separate missions at work in the Balkans, and a complete dossier on German troop movements in Greece.

At GHQ Keble had been on the list to receive intercepts of German signals. Because of an administrative error, he was not taken off the list when he moved to SOE. Early in January it became clear from decoded *Sicherheitsdienst* (German Security Service) signals that the Wehrmacht was engaged in constant battles with a group in Yugoslavia utterly distinct from the Cetniks and clearly identifiable as the Partisans. Disregarding the Official Secrets Act, Keble took his two brightest assistants into his confidence. These were Head of Section Major Bill Davidson and his assistant, Captain Bill Deakin. Davidson and Deakin plotted a map of German movements, from which it appeared that the Wehrmacht was locked in conflict with the Partisans in Slovenia, Croatia and parts of Bosnia. When Churchill passed through Cairo in January 1943 he saw Deakin, who introduced him to Keble. It did not take Keble long to convert the Prime Minister to the idea of sending help to the Partisans. Back in London Churchill's resolve was strengthened when he read three Ultra intercepts backing up Keble's information.[23]

A friendly witness has said of Keble: 'It is he who deserves the credit for making General HQ aware of the Balkans as a theatre of war. Unfortunately, Keble was an unlovable man, driven by ambition and apparently determined to build up his own little empire and to let no one into it who was not directly under his orders.'[24] That is putting it mildly. Keble irritated GHQ by his incessant demands for more staff and resources, but his sphere of influence extended across south-east Europe and the Arab world to Persia. It was his malevolent personality that most impressed itself on those who met him. Christopher Sykes, in his *High Minded Murder*, told stories of telephone tapping, poison-pen letters, libellous verses, anonymous telephone calls and even suspicions of murder which his colleagues were happy to lay at Keble's door. In October 1943 his deputy, Colonel Guy Tamplin, was found slumped over his desk, dead from a heart attack. It was known that Keble had been experimenting with a new poison for use in field operations. The consequence was a string of anonymous phone calls from staff at Rustum Buildings, congratulating Keble on his coup.[25]

Keble's vindictiveness was legendary. If he disliked a man, he would deal with him in one of two ways. A timid man he would send on what had the makings of a suicide mission. A would-be hero he would keep permanently out of action. One who had the misfortune to cross Keble was Julian Amery, a former Press Attaché in the British Embassy in Belgrade who had been working on Yugoslav affairs for SOE since 1941 and now wanted to see active service. Selborne supported him, and in March 1943 Colonel S.W. Bailey asked to take him on the mission to Mihailovic. Unfortunately, Amery's pro-fascist brother John had recently tried to recruit British prisoners-of-war into the armed forces of the Reich – a treasonable action, for which he was hanged after the war. Keble evidently did think that one was one's brother's keeper, since his reaction was to object to parachuting the brother of a traitor into enemy territory.[26] Small wonder that Christopher Sykes allegedly rounded on Keble with the memorable words: 'The trouble with war is that it puts people like you in charge of people like me. Your heart is as false as your teeth.'

Like many people with a great capacity for doing harm, Keble was hyperactive. 'The Brigadier, a globe-shaped choleric little militarist, did his best to conceal his natural and professional shortcomings by a show of blood-thirsty activity and total disregard for the agents in the field, whom he treated like so many expendable commodities.' 'His stout red figure, sweating profusely and dressed in no more than shorts and a vest, stomped about Rustum Buildings from morning till night.'[27]

It would not have taken a mastermind to predict trouble between such a man and Fitzroy. The two were in competition for the same space. Keble claimed to have as good as discovered the Partisans, and now here was the FO – for there could surely be no doubt that Fitzroy was their man, whatever his official title – muscling in. Fitzroy, as he had made clear during his interview with Selborne in London, was a cuckoo in the SOE nest. There was, additionally, a physical antipathy between the two men – one might almost call it 'hate at first sight'.

At Rustum Buildings Fitzroy was at once taken up to Keble's office. He was struck by Keble's unprepossessing appearance, the shorts, the vest, the feet on the desk. For Keble, the sight of this elegantly turned-out young brigadier was the proverbial red rag. Fitzroy saluted smartly. Keble exploded. 'What do you mean by coming in here dressed like that?' Fitzroy calmly replied that he had just been promoted brigadier and General Wilson had ordered him to appear in the appropriate uniform. Purposely keeping him standing, Keble said that he was now in the service of SOE and that next time the Commander-in-Chief sent for him he was not to go. Fitzroy replied that if sent for he would certainly go, since that was his duty as a serving officer. Trying to move the conversation out of this impasse, he then asked to be briefed on Yugoslavia.

'I'll tell you one thing,' said the irate Keble, 'you'll never reach Yugoslavia. Whatever the PM or the Commander-in-Chief says. And as you're not going, it follows you won't be briefed.' Keble announced that he had given strict instructions that this interloper, foisted on an unwilling SOE, should be shown no files, signals or anything else concerning Yugoslavia. As Fitzroy remarks, with characteristic understatement: 'To this I replied, with, I hope, becoming dignity, that I saw no point in prolonging our conversation.'[28]

On leaving Rustum Buildings after this abortive interview, Fitzroy returned to General Wilson's office. Chapman-Walker asked him to wait, as 'Jumbo' was closeted with Colonel P.C. Vellacott, Director of Political Warfare, Middle East. Vellacott's job was to spread disinformation and to institute whispering campaigns designed to wrong-foot the enemy. He was another of the self-seeking prima donnas created by the war. In peacetime a headmaster of Harrow and Master of Peterhouse, Vellacott's principal concern was his own rank, title and emoluments, and he liked to browbeat Foreign Office officials with threats to resign if his fussy conditions were not met.[29] Churchill referred to him as 'that sour usher', but most who met him were inclined to express it more strongly.

Fitzroy sat down to compose a cable to Churchill. He had begun 'CAN'T TAKE THE JOB WITH THESE APES IN CHARGE', but was asked to go straight in to Wilson's office. Turning to Vellacott, Wilson said, 'Tell

Fitzroy what you just told me.' Vellacott explained that he was under orders from SOE to spread whispers about Fitzroy Maclean. In GHQ, Shepheard's Hotel, the Mahomet Ali Club and all other likely venues, the word was to go out that Maclean was a hopeless drunk, an active homosexual, and a coward who had jeopardized David Stirling's operations with the SAS; he had taken the precaution of coming to check the story out with Wilson. 'Kill that story at once,' barked Jumbo. 'But thanks for letting us know.'[30]

Vellacott departed. Hilary King thinks he was playing his own game and, determined for his own reasons to smash Keble, may have picked something up from Wilson about the way the wind was blowing and invented the story.[31] Whatever the truth, his revelations made a deep impression. As Wilson shook his head in disbelief, Fitzroy told him about his own recent encounter with Keble. Wilson's answer was forthright. 'Don't send the cable to the PM. I'm going to smash SOE. This is just the culmination of a whole lot of trouble.'[32]

Keble's final demise did not take place until November 1943, but his star was on the wane from August 1943. Glenconner tried to pour oil on troubled waters. In the cool of an August evening on the roof terrace of the Mahomet Ali Club, he asked Fitzroy not to make his complaint against Keble official. After all, Keble was merely doing the best job he could according to his lights; admittedly, he could have behaved less abrasively, but he was at heart a good officer. Fitzroy would have none of it. As a result, Glenconner had to incorporate some of Fitzroy's comments in his annual report on Keble. It may be an exaggeration to say that Fitzroy got Keble sacked from SOE, but he certainly did his career no good. Glenconner was annoyed that he had not been able to talk Fitzroy round, and the dinner at the Mahomet Ali ended coolly.

With Keble sidelined, the SOE files on Yugoslavia were thrown open to Fitzroy. 'Now they were prepared to show me everything. A major looked after me – he'd been in the Coldstream Guards and I think they were glad to get rid of him. He'd also been involved in the Irgun fiasco in Palestine. I thought, You're a funny one to be looking after me.' Fitzroy tried to thread his way through the labyrinth of material: there were garbled signals, some from Bailey and Hudson which had been held up for six months, and even some from Bill Deakin in Yugoslavia. The gist was that there had been a lot of fighting there; he hardly needed the SOE files to tell him that. 'But there was nothing remotely resembling an up-to-date appreciation of the situation. There was also all the correspondence between SOE Cairo and Baker Street concerning my appointment, which the major had deliberately and mischievously slipped in for me to look at.' Perusing this, Fitzroy was struck by a number of references to an organization codenamed PX. It was clear that PX was the SOE's real enemy, from which Fitzroy inferred it must be the Abwehr or *Sicherheitsdienst* (SD). But he was brought up short by one reference, stating that Maclean was a creature of PX. Was this more SOE whispering? He pinged the bell, and the major reappeared. 'Tell me,' said Fitzroy, 'what does PX stand for?' 'Oh, PX,' he said, 'that's the Foreign Office.' As Fitzroy remarked: 'This revelation made things a little clearer, though scarcely any more reassuring, and I went off, pondering deeply, to be more than adequately briefed by Hugh Seton-Watson on the difference between Serbs and Croats and their respective historical backgrounds.'[33]

For Fitzroy, August 1943 was a frustrating period of waiting and slowly organizing his mission. His talent for making contacts led to a friendly association with Air Marshal Sir William Sholto Douglas, head of Fighter Command between 1940 and 1942, who had arrived in Cairo in January to take over command of the Middle East air forces from Air Marshal Sir Arthur Tedder. Evidently a man with a capacity for making friends, Douglas even got on terms with the anti-British King Farouk, to whom the Air Marshal's moderate left-wing opinions appeared as arrant Communism. Other contacts of Fitzroy's, which initially looked even more promising, were with the other three brigadiers in charge of missions in the Balkans. On one occasion all four (Fitzroy, Brigadier C.D. Armstrong bound for Mihailovic, Brigadier 'Trotsky' Davies for Albania and Brigadier Myers for Greece) met in conference in Cairo and arranged to keep each other informed of their progress, but nothing came of this.[34]

After Fitzroy had left for Yugoslavia, events moved rapidly towards the subordination of SOE to Wilson's command. In October Wilson summoned Major-General Gubbins of SOE for a showdown. The FO attempt to have SOE abolished was thrown out, but SOE was brought under Wilson's aegis – a development Gubbins actually welcomed, as he felt his organization would be more effective that way. There could be no mistaking the fate of the big fish in SOE Cairo. Glenconner was summoned to London to explain matters; reluctantly, Selborne had to sacrifice him. Keble was moved on in November to a face-saving position back in the regular Army.[35] Not everyone was pleased. An indignant Brigadier Myers wrote: 'They are being removed because they have stated facts which are distasteful to the Foreign Office. What an example of democracy! What harm to the war effort!'[36] It is interesting to note, in the interests of objectivity, that Keble always had his champions. Apart from Enoch Powell and Myers, there is this testimony from Hugh Seton-Watson: 'A gentleman whom one had mixed feelings about, but [whom] I have always had a rather healthy respect for.'[37]

Thereafter, SOE in Yugoslavia was reduced to a supply and infrastructure organization. It seems that Keble, Glenconner and the rest had had two main objections to Fitzroy's appointment. One was that he was designated both military and political head of the mission, whereas they wanted a 'real' brigadier for the military role, and had in fact earmarked their own man. The other was that Fitzroy was Foreign Office through and through. It has been well said that in war, the only fun to be had is from fighting your own side. SOE's most intelligent policy would have been to allow Fitzroy to reach Yugoslavia before they revealed their hand. As it was, they allowed him to contrive a situation where he was answerable only to Wilson and to the Prime Minister.

Fitzroy now assembled his team. As his Number Two he chose Vivian Street, an experienced regular officer from the 5th Rifle Brigade who was part of the 'Jumbo mafia' – Wilson had also started as a rifleman. Wilson reluctantly intervened to secure him for Fitzroy just when Street was on the point of being given command of a battalion. But for his early death at 58 in 1970, as a Major-General, Fitzroy is convinced he would have become Chief of the Imperial General Staff. Before Fitzroy took him on, Street had already had a remarkable escape. As an SAS major on his first operation he was taken prisoner by the Italians, but saved from a POW camp when a Royal Navy destroyer depth-charged the submarine on which he was being transported. Rescued by the Navy, Street then served out the rest of the North Africa campaign. Fitzroy thought him particularly valuable, as he combined qualities not often seen together – courage, high intelligence, and an ability to get on with all kinds of people.

Another inspired choice was John Henniker-Major (later Lord Henniker), like Street a rifleman and like Fitzroy a refugee from the Foreign Office, which he had left to see active service. Henniker describes the confusion surounding his appointment.

I was in North Africa in 1941, wounded and convalesced in South Africa and operated on for sinusitis in the Canal Zone on my return from the veldt. In the streets of Cairo I ran into Fitzroy. Nothing happened, but doubtless he pigeonholed me. I was told to report to the Canal Zone to get a movement order. My CO said he wanted a man at HQ with battle experience. I joined my battalion at Alexandria. While I was there, a message came asking me to report to Cairo. At HQ the Military Secretary said, 'In the next room I have Brigadier Maclean, who wants you in Yugoslavia. But you only go if you want to.' Fitzroy chatted me up, said I was the right man, could be his alter ago. I told my colonel. He said, 'I don't want you to go, but you'd better talk to Jumbo Wilson.' Also, I very strongly didn't want to go into SOE. So I went to Algiers, but didn't see Jumbo. Back I went to Cairo. Mark Chapman-Walker said, 'I know if you don't volunteer, Jumbo will detail you to go.' Though this did not square with what the Military Secretary had said, it was indicative of Jumbo's wishes. So I went back, told my colonel, and he said I'd better go. I then went and did my parachute jump training.[38]

As his chief of sappers Fitzroy chose an undisputed hero, Peter Moore. Moore already had a DSO and an MC, and ended his career as what is known in military parlance as a 'failed VC' – which meant he had three DSOs. Another sapper (in civilian life an electrical engineer), Mike Parker, introduced to Fitzroy by Henniker, was appointed head of supplies to the Partisans. Major Gordon Alston, Stirling's intelligence officer on the Benghazi raids, was offered the same role with Fitzroy and accepted with alacrity. Major Robin Whetherley, Sergeant Duncan, and Corporals Dickson and Andrew made up the advance party.

At the last moment this very British mission was converted into an Anglo-American one by the addition of the genial Major Linn Farish. Ever since his days in Moscow Fitzroy has had an especially warm feeling for Americans, of whom Linn 'Slim' Farish was an admirable representative. 'A large rugged man like a bear', Farish first appeared in the uniform of a major in the Royal Engineers, explaining that he had joined the British Army in 1939 and had not bothered to change armies after Pearl Harbor. However, protocol now required that he don an American uniform; on his next appearance he wore the insignia of a major in the US Engineer Corps. He was no mere token American presence; alone of Fitzroy's men, he knew how to build airfields, and so opened up a genuine prospect of bringing in supplies and *matériel* by means other than the somewhat crude aerial drops.

The mission was to be flown from Protville in Tunisia to the target area in Yugoslavia.[39] For security reasons Fitzroy's party remained in Cairo until the last moment and was then flown by SOE air transport to Bizerta. No one was supposed to know the destination, but in Cairo word soon got about that another batch of British Liaison Officers would shortly be dropping into Yugoslavia. To Fitzroy's irritation the news was actually announced in a forces newspaper, *The Union Jack*: 'Military mission to be dropped to the Partisans on 18 September.' After this there seemed little point in bothering about security, though they went through the motions of taking off 'incriminating' tie pins, and parachute badges. In Tunisia, Fitzroy and his men stood out like sore thumbs. A Bizerta barmaid expressed her opinion of Fitzroy's cover by exclaiming, when he walked into her bar, '*Tiens, voici l'amiral Suisse!*'[40]

Fitzroy's intense suspicion of SOE continued. A friend in Cairo, David Wallace, had served with SOE in Greece, and reported that many of his signals from the field to Cairo had not got through, presumably suppressed. Since Fitzroy was friendly with the SIS chief Menzies, and as Gordon Alston was to double as SIS representative on the mission, Fitzroy arranged a twin-track system whereby he would repeat to Menzies in London his signals to SOE Cairo, through a duplicate system arranged by Alston. And when SOE distributed para-chutes just before the mission members boarded the plane, Fitzroy asked for another. 'I can assure you, I did not take the first parachute that was offered me. Because one of the things SOE did to people they wanted to get rid of was put a blanket in their parachute.'[41]

On the evening of 17 September Fitzroy and his men went down to Protville airfield and boarded the huge four-engined Halifax bomber. It took off just before midnight. On board conditions were cramped, since the long cylindrical containers of supplies seemed to take up every inch of space. For the first hour of the flight Fitzroy calmly studied a Serbo-Croat grammar.[42] Then he fell into a light doze, and was awoken at 3.30 a.m. by the dispatcher and told to get ready. The Halifax lost height, the trap-door was opened, and the cylinders rolled out. Then it was time for the men. With Fitzroy on this plane were Vivian Street, Slim Farish and Sergeant Duncan. Fitzroy was the first out. In his inimitably laconic manner he describes his jump into the pages of history:

> I sat on the edge of the hole waiting, with my legs dangling in space. A glance downwards showed some points of light twinkling a long way below – fire signals. Looking up again, I saw that the warning red light was showing. The dispatcher's hand was raised. Slowly, deliberately, he started to lower it. Then, suddenly, the light turned to green and I jumped out and down, into the breath-taking tumult of the slipstream.[43]

9

First Contacts

SEPTEMBER–OCTOBER 1943

T HE historian Elisabeth Barker suggested that one motive for British interest in Yugoslavia during the Second World War was a 'T. E. Lawrence complex' – the idea that Britain could control the manner and timing of each country's liberation, as she had done with the Arabs after the First World War. Fitzroy openly admits that Lawrence of Arabia, hero of Churchill and that other 'Establishment Scot' John Buchan, was his inspiration. 'I fancied myself as a latter-day Lawrence, blowing up trains and bridges.' In his famous report of 6 November 1943 he quoted with approval Lawrence's dictum, 'We had won a province when we had taught the civilians in it to die for our ideal of freedom. The presence or absence of the enemy was a secondary matter.' In this Fitzroy was a typical adventurer of his time. Another SOE agent, Jasper Rootham, once found himself in the company of Serbian guerrillas looking down over the Danube, and recalled how 'rosy dreams of Lawrentian exploits right in the heart of Hitler's Europe swam thus over our minds. Anything seemed possible.'

But the idea that Yugoslavia was a *tabula rasa* on which British policy-makers could write their wishes was as much a fallacy then as it would be now. Tito and his veterans had ideas of their own and, as Djilas wrote in *Wartime* of Fitzroy's hero, 'We saw in Lawrence of Arabia not an idealist hero, but the perfidious arrogant champion of an empire.' In fact, Tito and his Partisans were a hundred times more formidable than Feisal and his Hashemites. In 1944, Himmler said: 'I wish we had a dozen Titos in Germany – the man never knows when he's beaten and never gives up.'

When Fitzroy parachuted in, he had little idea of what to expect. At best, perhaps a Moscow-trained Comintern hack, blinkered and dog-matic. At worst, he might be in pursuit of a phantom. 'When I was dropped in I was told variously – there is no such person: Tito is simply a committee or its acronym, International Terrorist Organisation – he is a Hungarian nobleman in disguise – he is an immensely attractive young woman.' Such was the intelligence at the disposal of the people we are now supposed to credit with having 'created' Tito!

Fitzroy remembers that he felt no fear as he floated earthwards: he thought only of the task ahead. He had read everything he could find on recent Yugoslav history, but there was much that was obscure, and remained so. To make sense of Fitzroy's mission, we must take a brief look at events within Yugoslavia from 1941 to 1943.

Yugoslavia, a nation-state created by the Treaty of Versailles, was a *mélange* of previously autonomous states. Serbia and Montenegro had won their independence from the Turkish empire in the late nineteenth century. Bosnia and Herzegovina were territories annexed from Turkey by Austria before the First World War. Croatia, Dalmatia and Slovenia had been regions of the Austro-Hungarian empire before that war. There was little sense of national identity; the country was an uneasy farrago of different loyalties – clan, patriarchal, regional, cultural, religious, ideological. The greatest tension, then as now, was between Serbia and Croatia. A fascist movement, the Ustase, dedicated to Croatian autarky, was the dominant (albeit underground and illegal) force in that province from the 1930s. Its exiled leadership was so strongly supported by Mussolini that in 1939 it dared to assassinate King Alexander of Yugoslavia in Marseilles. In 1934 the Serbs attempted to conciliate the moderate Croats by adopting a federal structure and bringing in Dr Macek, leader of the Croatian peasant party, as Federal Vice-Premier.

In the Second World War Yugoslavia lay on a dangerous three-way crossroads, between Germany, Italy and the Soviet Union. The Yugoslav leadership kept the country out of the war until March 1941. In that month Hitler sent his armies into Romania and Bulgaria and began to squeeze the Royal Yugoslav government to join the Axis. On 25 March Hitler got his way. The Regent, Prince Paul, and his ministers signed the Tripartite pact with Germany and Italy. Two days later an anti-German Air Force coup ousted the government, declared the 18-year-old King Peter of age, and installed a new regime under General Simovic which at once put out feelers to the Russians. Hitler's response was swift. On 6 April panzers rolled across the frontier, and by 17 April the Royal Yugoslav forces had capitulated. King Peter and his entourage fled to London; Hitler installed a quisling government under Nedic. In Croatia the Ustase under Pavelvic set up a totalitarian regime with Italian help and at once began a reign of terror. Serbs in particular were singled out for massacre. Estimates of the slain range from a low of 40,000 to a high of half a million.[1]

But this was not the end of Yugoslav resistance. Two separate groups took to the mountains, vowing to continue the struggle as guerrillas.

One group was the Cetniks, under General Draza Mihailovic. The Cetniks were extreme Serb nationalists in the tradition of the *ceti*, or armed bands, who had kept alive the flame of Serbian independence during the dark days of Turkish domination. Monarchist, religious and highly conservative, they cultivated the traditional appearance of the Serb warrior; long hair, flowing beards and tall sheepskin caps bearing the Royal Arms (and sometimes the skull and crossbones). They armed themselves with curved daggers, ornate firearms and Mexican-style bandoliers.

The other group was the Partisans, under Josip Broz, known to history as Tito. The Partisans were the armed manifestation of the Yugoslav Communist Party, which for twenty years under the Royalist government had been ostracized, proscribed and persecuted. Until the German invasion of Russia on 22 June 1941 the Yugoslav Communists had taken the line that the war was an unjust squabble between one branch of 'social fascism' and another. The involvement of the Soviet Union changed all that, and the Partisans embraced the opportunity to fight a genuine 'peoples' war'. Their immense long-term advantage over the Cetniks was their wider social and national base. Tito the leader was a Croat, his close associate Milovan Djilas a Montenegrin, the party's chief ideologue Eduard Kardelj a Slovene, while the organizational genius Alexander Rankovic was a Serb. The Partisans' strength was that their soldiers had no strong local attachments, even though the Partisans were an overwhelmingly Serb movement until late 1943 when large numbers of Croats joined them: Tito's *déraciné* peasants and workers were prepared to fight anywhere.

From June to November 1941 Tito tried to organize a collaborative resistance with the Cetniks against the Axis. He actually met Mihailovic once and described him as 'a nice, pleasant-mannered sort of man – a typical regular officer'. Nothing came of the meeting, for the two had contradictory plans.[2] Obedient then to directives from Moscow, Tito was willing to work with and even under any leader who was prepared to fight the Nazis. But Mihailovic had other ideas. The Great Serb nationalism he represented meant putting Serb and class interests ahead of national ones. Moreover, the Germans terrified him by threatening to kill a hundred civilians in retaliation for each German soldier killed by the Resistance; to Mihailovic it seemed as if Serbia would soon be annihilated. He therefore began making local deals with the Axis; any Partisans he encountered he either killed, or handed over to the Nazis. On 28 November 1941 Tito made his final appeal to Mihailovic to co-operate against the German invader. The Cetnik leader refused on the grounds that this would mean Serbia's extermination, and lamely suggested that each side retreat to its own mountain fastnesses.

In effect there were now three wars in Yugoslavia: resistance against the Axis, which was almost entirely a Partisan affair; the struggle of Serbs against Croats and Muslims; and a civil war between the Serb Cetniks and the Serb Partisans. Mihailovic was interested only in the last two. Tito therefore left his base at Uzice in Serbia and retreated to Novi Pazar beyond the Zlatibor range; he took terrible casualties as he went, but the move kept his options open, since once there he could either regroup and reinfiltrate Serbia, or move west into Bosnia or south into Montenegro. Mihailovic's men meanwhile were helping the quisling Nedic and the Germans to hunt down suspected Communists. In the process the peasantry suffered, and began to turn against the Partisans, whom they blamed for their woes. 'The peasant goes with whoever is strongest,' Tito said to Djilas, and suggested in anger that, if the peasants were going over to the Cetniks for fear of having their houses burned down, the Partisans would have to make sure that in future the peasants were even more afraid of *them*. This was not, however, a threat he put into effect.

The darkest days of the Partisans were those from November 1941 to May 1942. They retreated west into Bosnia. One column, under Djilas, planned to reinfiltrate Serbia, but the hostility of the peasants made this impossible, so the two wings of the Partisan army reunited at Foca in Bosnia in February 1942. For four months Tito's men were on the defensive. In Croatia the fanatical Ustase, combining fascism and ultramontane capitalism in a manner reminiscent of Franco's Nationalists in the Spanish Civil War, massacred their opponents in tens of thousands. Serbia was in Cetnik hands, east Bosnia in the grip of the Axis and the Italians, and the Cetniks were also overrunning Montenegro. An attempted counter-attack in Montenegro faltered because the brutality of the Partisans alienated the peasantry there. Tito had to order Djilas to intervene to try to prevent atrocities rivalling those of the Ustase in Croatia. The so-called 'red terror' in Montenegro in 1942 was really an extension of old hatreds, vendettas and grudges; many Montenegrins used the excuse of a 'war of liberation' to settle ancient clan conflicts and blood-feuds.

In May Tito was forced to evacuate Foca and withdraw his forces to the border of Herzegovina and Montenegro. Then the tide turned. Eight years earlier Mao Tse-tung and the Red Army had turned the tables on their enemy by an epic trek from south to north.[3] Now, in June 1942, Tito began his own 'Long March'. He ordered his men to head north into western Bosnia, on a collision course with the Ustase in Croatia. He did so with reluctance, as it meant turning away from Serbia, the key to the mastery of Yugoslavia; but it was part of Tito's greatness as a guerrilla leader that he was prepared to build slowly and take the long-term view.

The Partisans moved north, parallel to the Adriatic coast but about 40 or 50 miles inland. Tito practised the techniques that made him the world's finest leader of irregulars. He kept on the move and denied his adversary a target at which to strike; and by considerate treatment, propaganda, 're-education', and most of all, success, he won over ever larger sections of the population. The Ustase did a lot of his work for him by sacking all the villages, whether friendly or not, where the Partisans spent a night, and massacring the inhabitants. There was great joy among the Bosnians when the Partisans proved their military superiority by taking Livno in August 1942, after a fanatical Ustase defence. Livno was the culmination of Tito's Long March, during which the Partisans had increased in numbers, sophistication, fighting experience and self-confidence. For the first time since the fall of Uzice they controlled an extensive stretch of territory.

November 1942 saw the inauguration of the political wing of the Partisans, the Anti-Fascist Council and its executive body the National Liberation Committee.[4] Moscow warned Tito that he was not to present this as a rival to the government-in-exile of King Peter or to proclaim the abolition of monarchy, as this might provoke a Western backlash. Tito therefore chose a 'bourgeois' figurehead in the form of Dr Ivan Ribar. He then turned to consolidate his position. As in China, it was the peasantry, not the proletariat, that formed the revolutionary vanguard. Tito began by trying to coax the silent majority of non-Ustase Croats over to his side, suspecting that the British might try to use the conservative Croat peasants against him as (in his view) they had already used Mihailovic in Serbia.

By now the Axis had come to realize that the Partisans were no longer a mere irritant, but a major threat.[5] On 1 January 1943 the Germans launched their so-called 'Fourth Yugoslav Offensive' – Operation WEISS – to crush them. WEISS had been carefully planned in Rome by the Wehrmacht, the Italians and senior representatives of Pavlevic's Ustase. As directed by General Lohr, Commander-in-Chief, South-East Europe, the aim of the offensive was to encircle and annihilate Tito in Bosnia. Supported by Pavlevic's troops, the Germans would advance on Bihac from the north and east; the Cetniks and Italians would come in from the west and south. It was a good plan, since it anticipated Tito's obvious strategy of retracing his steps on the Long March. This was in fact the move Tito chose. His aim was to fight his way down to Montenegro and thence back into Serbia, even though he knew this would mean tough fighting and dreadful casualties. Tito realized he would be outnumbered, but reckoned that the morale of his men could be kept as high as ever if every enemy attack was answered by an even fiercer counter-attack, whatever the disparity in numbers. This was essentially the strategy of Lee before Richmond in 1862; and in this, as in his flair for guerrilla warfare, Tito revealed himself a military genius.

The decisive clash was at the Neretva river in February and March 1943. Tito feinted towards Konjic and Prozor. The Germans dug in to receive him there. Meanwhile, by forced marches Tito got his army across the Neretva at Jablanica and by mid-March the Partisans were through the ring, despite the treachery of the Cetniks who chose this moment to attack them.[6] The crossing of the Neretva rates as a supreme military achievement. WEISS had failed. Nearing desperation, the Germans launched their Fifth Offensive in May, again aimed at encirclement of the Partisans, who were now encamped on the shores of the Black Lake under the peak of Mount Durmitor, whence they had set out on the Long March the year before. Twenty thousand of Tito's men in these mountains around the headwaters of the River Driva faced a potential death-trap. As if sensing that this was their last chance to finish off the Partisans, the Germans made a supreme effort. A hundred and twenty thousand men were flung into action: Wehrmacht veterans, Italians, Bulgarians, Ustase Croats. But, employing the principle of concentration of force, Tito pierced the encircling ring at its weakest point and broke through to Kladanj in eastern Bosnia. The cost of his success was steep. The Partisans lost half their men, and had to execute all their prisoners and abandon their wounded.[7]

Although the Germans continued to pursue them, it was clear that the Partisans would now hold the upper hand in the long run. In Italy Mussolini's government collapsed, and in Sicily the Allies invaded. The troops who had failed twice to encircle the Partisans would soon be more urgently needed on other fronts. Tito moved his headquarters to Jajce in Bosnia, where he installed his command next door to a medieval church. His sights were set on Bosnia, after which it would be time to settle accounts with Mihailovic in Serbia. By late summer 1943 the Partisans had liberated a large section of Croatia between Zagreb and Bosnia.

This was the situation when Fitzroy parachuted in. But to understand his mission fully means setting it in the context of the large number of British Liaison Officers who had already been in Yugoslavia since 1941. The first important mission was that of Captain Hudson in 1941 and 1942. Hudson's instructions were to make contact with all anti-Axis forces, whoever they were, and promise them aid from the British. Hudson located the Partisans, but found that they suspected the British of colluding with the Cetniks to destroy them. He therefore left them, intending to contact the Cetniks in Serbia; but Mihailovic refused to receive anyone who had previously been in contact with the Partisans.

In mid-1942 another important British mission, headed by Major

Terence Atherton, reached Tito's headquarters. Although Atherton brought assurances of friendship, Tito was suspicious. He claimed to have proof that British agents in Yugoslavia were encouraging the Cetniks to attack the Partisans, allegedly so that eventually Britain could land troops in Dalmatia and restore the royalists; this, according to Tito, was the real purpose of the ten other British military missions already in Yugoslavia.[8] Two circumstances fuelled Tito's suspicions. His assault on Montenegro had been an embarrassing failure, and it was from Montenegro that Atherton's mission had come. Did this not prove that 'perfidious Albion' was at work again? Tito conveniently overlooked the role the Partisan 'red terror' had played in the Montenegro fiasco. Even more sinisterly, Atherton suddenly disappeared. The Cetniks triumphantly claimed that the murderous rabble styled the Partisans had killed him, although it was later proved that Atherton had been murdered by a freelance Bosnian bandit.

Other minor British missions also failed to make a mark. The first breakthrough followed the arrival of Captain William Deakin on the night of 25–26 May 1943. Deakin parachuted in with Major Jones of the Canadian Black Watch and Captain Stewart of the Royal Engineers, with such pinpoint accuracy that they met Tito at once. Deakin found the Fifth Offensive at its height, the battle raging around Mount Durmitor. Stewart was killed almost immediately; Deakin and Tito were wounded by fragments of the same bomb, which created a powerful bond between them. Deakin soon became an enthusiastic advocate for the Partisans. His reports, though they were unknown to Fitzroy when he parachuted in on 17 September, provided more nails for Mihailovic's coffin.[9]

Deakin's main task was to ascertain whether it was justifiable for London to send in a full-scale military and political mission under a brigadier. He explains himself: 'Frankly, I never thought I'd come out alive . . . My mission was purely experimental and was not sent by Churchill, unlike Fitzroy's. The idea was that if I found out anything useful, London could send in a brigadier.' Within three days he had made up his mind: it was not just desirable, but essential, if Britain wanted to play any future role in the Balkans. 'But none of the three hundred telegrams I sent were distributed. Even if they had been, Fitzroy was not on the distribution list.'[10]

While Deakin was with Tito, Marshal Badoglio announced the surrender of Italian forces to the Allies in all theatres of war. Tito was apparently not thought important enough to be informed of any of the negotiations leading up to this, but was merely notified of the bare fact after it had happened. Angrily he remonstrated with Deakin and claimed that this clinched the case against British duplicity. Deakin remembers this as the one and only time he saw Tito truly lose his temper. 'He exploded, went through the roof about it. Saw it as an insult to his Partisans. I can tell you, this made complete fools of us in Tito's eyes. The idea of one British officer taking the Italian surrender. There were thirty-one Italian divisions in the Balkans, some 600,000 men, and not a single Partisan at the surrender. I spent a difficult day trying to decide what to do. I said to Tito, "Don't attack me, I don't make policy". He said, "Are you really trying to tell me London can't keep me informed? What's the point of a mission, then? And have you really sent the identical cable to Mihailovic?" ' Deakin mollified Tito by asking if he could go to Split with him to regularize the surrender of the Italians there. 'I was trying to help the mysterious brigadier. If he'd arrived on top of this, he'd have had a damn poor start.'[11]

On the morning of 8 September a message came to inform Deakin that the mysterious brigadier was called Maclean and that he was an ex-diplomat rather than a regular soldier. There were no other details of his arrival. Next day Deakin signalled to Cairo that all was ready for the reception of the Maclean mission at the designated dropping zone. He then departed for Split, torn between a desire to be present when the brigadier arrived, and a determination to heal the rift over the Italian surrender before then.

Fitzroy landed with a jolt, released himself from the harness, hid the parachute and set off in search of the Partisans. He crossed two fields, then came face to face with a young man toting a sub-machine-gun. 'I am a British officer,' Fitzroy yelled in his best Serbo-Croat. The young man embraced him and began to shout, 'I have found the general!' Soon a large crowd of Partisans had gathered. Fitzroy and his escort made for the beacon fires – the Partisans' sign of a drop zone – which he had seen from the air. Street, Duncan and Farish were already there, but it soon became apparent that the second plane load of men had not been dropped, so that another attempt would have to be made a few nights later.

As Fitzroy stood warming himself in the circle of bonfires, a young Partisan introduced himself. This was Major Velebit, who was to escort him to Tito. Fitzroy was at first taken aback by Velebit's flood of rhetoric, but Velebit recalls that his thoughts were elsewhere. Forty years later he told Fitzroy: 'I was wondering if you would come down wearing trousers or a kilt.'[12]

The Partisans, with their comradely discipline and clench-fisted salutes, reminded Fitzroy of the heroic revolutionaries he had seen in Eisenstein films in Paris. It occurred to him that he had never witnessed a revolution in its infancy, only in its maturity when it was devouring its own children. Such thoughts occupied him as they rode on horseback to the first large village. From there they were taken by truck to the town of

Jajce, where Tito had his headquarters. On arrival in Jajce, Fitzroy was invited, 'with his chief of staff', to come to dinner with the Commander. He quickly created two such staffers, British and American, in the form of Street and Farish.

Tito's inner sanctum was in a ruined castle on a hill overlooking the town. He greeted his visitors enthusiastically. There was no problem about communication: he spoke German and fluent Russian and was very ready to help Fitzroy out in his first attempts at Serbo-Croat. Later Fitzroy wrote up his impressions of the Partisan leader.

> He was sturdily built, with iron-grey hair. His rather wide, smooth-skinned face with its high cheek-bones showed clearly enough the stresses and strains which he had endured. It also gave some indication of his character. His regular, clearly defined features were haggard and drawn and deeply burned by the sun. His mouth was ruthlessly determined. His alert light-blue eyes missed nothing. He gave an impression of great strength held in reserve, the impression of a tiger ready to spring. As he spoke, his expression changed frequently and rapidly, in turn illumined by a sudden smile, transfigured with anger or enlivened by a quick look of understanding. He had an agreeable voice, capable of sudden harshness. His dress was neat and workmanlike: a plain dark tunic and breeches without the badges of rank now worn by his subordinates; at his belt a pistol in a leather holster; in his cap a small red five-pointed star with hammer and sickle. Almost the only contrast was furnished by the fine diamond ring which he had bought himself in 1937 and which he still wore as a reminder of those bygone days.[13]

Tito and Fitzroy got down to discussing how the British could best help the Partisans. Fitzroy explained the main difficulty – lack of air bases nearer than North Africa – but pointed out that the Italian capitulation should mean a change in those circumstances very soon. Ah yes, said Tito, the Italian capitulation, and went on to remonstrate bitterly about British perfidy. The subject of Split came up, where the Italians had surrendered and where Deakin had gone. Fitzroy suggested supplying the Partisans from the sea while they still held the port – for the Germans were likely to counter-attack and capture it before long.

As initial reserve thawed out over plum brandy, Tito told Fitzroy something of his early life: his conversion to Communism, the struggle, the proscriptions, the imprisonment. He chuckled at the price of 100,000 gold marks the Nazis had put on his head. They disputed about politics: Fitzroy made it plain that he was as far to the right as Tito was to the left. Fitzroy wondered about the nickname 'Tito'. There were many explanations, the most popular being that he was so-called because he was always sending for people and telling them what to do. 'You,' he would say, 'do this; and you, that' or, in Serbo-Croat, '*Ti to, ti to'*. Fitzroy was so taken with this version that he reproduced it in his book *Eastern Approaches*. Later, however, he had ruefully to concede: 'But I am assured by Tito himself, who I suppose should know, that it is apocryphal.'[14]

On this and several successive occasions they discussed Tito's relations with the Soviet Union, for Fitzroy still worried away at the theme he had broached with Churchill: if Tito was Stalin's stooge, was the West well-advised to help him? Tito outlined something of his previous relations with the Russians. He was far from pleased that Moscow had not only recognized the Royal government-in-exile, but had reported Partisan victories as Cetnik ones. Stalin was forever nagging him to concentrate on Popular Front tactics against the Nazis and forget about the revolutionary aims of a Socialist Yugoslavia. Tito declared exasperatedly that he was tired of banging his head against a brick wall, in the form of Mihailovic's intransigence. In January 1943, at the start of Operation WEISS, Tito had begged Moscow to send him some help. There was no reply, but when, after the battle of the Neretva, Tito tried to negotiate a prisoner exchange with the Germans, he was reprimanded. At this manifestation of such a dog-in-the-manger attitude, Tito's patience had snapped. 'If you cannot help us, then at least do not hinder us,' he wrote curtly to Stalin.

Fitzroy also found it encouraging that Tito was cynical about Soviet motives. They discussed the Nazi–Soviet pact. Tito agreed that this was good business from Stalin's point of view. If he had made a pact with the West, war would have followed immediately, and he would have borne the brunt of it; the pact with Hitler held out the prospect of territorial gains against Poland and the Baltic states; best of all was the prospect that the West and Hitler might destroy each other, leaving the Soviet Union as *tertius gaudens*. Emboldened by this, Fitzroy asked Tito outright whether the new Yugoslavia would be a Soviet satellite. Tito replied with some asperity that the Partisans had not gone through all their hardships and privations, sustained such massive casualties and seen most of their country's economy destroyed, just to hand over the prize to the Russians at the end of the day. Fitzroy remembers thinking at the time that Stalin might have more on his hands than he had bargained for. The Russians had not played their cards intelligently. After all the rebuffs, the nagging and the refusal to send him a military mission, Tito had now acquired, as a result of the Italian collapse, more arms than he could ever have got from a Soviet airlift. And, with the arrival of a full-scale military mission, it was clear that the West took him more seriously than Stalin did.

Becoming more daring, Fitzroy then raised the subject of King Peter. Tito replied that questions about the royal family would have to wait until the Germans were defeated. Fitzroy asked if Tito was prepared to have Peter come out from London and fight as a guerrilla. Tito seemed momentarily 'tickled' by the idea of having the king under his command, but second thoughts soon prevailed.

After some days of talks Fitzroy summed up his impressions.

> He was unusually ready to discuss any question on its merits and to take a decision there and then, without reference to higher authority. He seemed perfectly sure of himself: a principal, not a subordinate. There were other unexpected things about him: his surprising breadth of outlook; his apparent independence of mind; his never-failing sense of humour; his unashamed delight in the minor pleasures of life; a natural diffidence in human relationships, giving way to a natural friendliness and conviviality; a violent temper, flaring up in sudden rages; an occasional tendency to ostentation and display; a considerateness and a generosity which constantly manifested themselves in a dozen small ways; a surprising readiness to see both sides of a question; and, finally, a strong instinctive national pride.[15]

Three days after his arrival, the rest of Fitzroy's team came in. John Henniker explained what had happened. 'An Australian crew at the end of their tour, thoroughly cheesed off, took us. We flew across Bosnia and Serbia and were over Bulgaria by the time the crew figured we had missed the target. We set off again a few days later with a fresh crew, found the fires and parachuted in.'[16] That sounds simple enough, except that Henniker's friend and colleague Mike Parker adds: 'We had done our training in Palestine. But training there, with blue skies and flat ground to land on, bore no relation to reality. On top of that, Henniker was the world's worst parachutist – he could never learn to turn into the wind. When we reached the ground we had to ride nags as transport – but Henniker and I are the very worst riders!'[17]

Morale in Fitzroy's team was remarkably high. Fitzroy had proved a good picker, not just in the individual excellence of his men, but in the way their personalities meshed. Parker and Henniker were old friends, while Slim Farish, with his geological background, impressed Peter Moore by predicting that one day oil would be found in the North Sea. There was none of the disaffection in the team that has ruined many a great enterprise. Many later testified eloquently to Fitzroy's leadership qualities. Mike Parker recalls: 'Fitzroy was immensely physically fit. I was 24 and I saw Fitzroy, at 32, as middle-aged. He had immense confidence, was charismatic, knew the Establishment inside out. Extraordinarily nice man. Although he was firm and clear in his aims, he never raised his voice. When he asked you to do something, it was quite clear he meant *now*. He loved peers of the realm and famous people and liked to collect them, but of course he had to have a few people like Vivian and me to do the work. We regarded ourselves as second-class citizens – not that he gave that impression.'[18] Peter Moore concurs:

> Fitzroy was a man who knew his stuff. Good man to work for. Combined professional competence with a very easy manner with everybody from the cook-sergeant to Tito. Politically Yugoslavia was a minefield, but Fitzroy did not put a foot wrong. He was a very good choice. My first impressions were very favourable – tall, athletic. Not at all a martinet – he was very good at adjusting every meeting to the right level for those present. He said the same thing to everybody but managed to say it in a different timbre that appealed to each. Fitzroy was a good delegator. He didn't interfere, just let you get on with it. The only time I ever saw him was when something big was being discussed. That's entirely as it should be.[19]

John Henniker remembers the first few days in Yugoslavia as follows: 'It was better than we expected. Comfortable food, comfortable duvet, not the Spartan conditions I was expecting. It turned out I was not Fitz's Number Two [as had been hinted] nor even his Number Three. That was OK, I was not a senior officer, knew nothing about it, wouldn't have welcomed it. I had absolutely no grouse about it. Somebody said the other day that was treacherous of Fitz. I don't think it was at all treacherous of Fitz. He simply got his team together, and the titles were assigned by Jumbo Wilson's office, whereas Fitzroy ran it all in a more informal way.'[20]

Fitzroy's men had first to acquaint themselves with their opposite numbers and to learn who was who in Tito's entourage. Although Tito was 51, most of his comrades were in their twenties and thirties. They soon became familiar figures. There was Marko Rankovic, the peasant's son from Serbia who ran the Party machine and its intelligence network; Edo Kardelj, the Slovenian schoolteacher, a stocky, pale-skinned figure with black moustache and steel-rimmed spectacles, an expert on dialectical materialism but sensible and reliable; the tall and saturnine Zujovic, Tito's deputy; and Vlado Dedijer, an enormous Serb with the physique of a prize-fighter, a former journalist and boxer, who kept a meticulously detailed diary. Others inspired Fitzroy to close description: Milovan Djilas, 'a Montenegrin intellectual, handsome, intolerant and impetuous, with a look of inspired fanaticism'; Koka Popovic, 'small, brilliant and vital', poet, philosopher and millionaire's son, the most dashing of the Partisan commanders; and Ivan Ribar, the young, energetic orator 'with the wide brow and high cheek-bones of the typical Slav'. One of Fitzroy's closest friends was Vladko Velebit. Tall, good-looking, combining a remarkably quick brain with a fine sense of humour, Velebit began his career as a pampered general's son, man about town and lawyer to the élite, until his wide reading made him a Marxist convert. Apart from Mosa Pijade, another dialectical theoretician and Tito's cell-mate in the 1930s, the Commander's entourage was most notable for the two girl Partisans, who looked after Tito's maps and signals. Zdenka was petite, pale-skinned and immensely dedicated to the 'Old Man', as she called him; Olga, tall and well-built, was the daughter of the exiled Royalist government's Foreign Minister. Tito's retinue was completed by his heavily-armed bodyguards Bosko and Prlja, 'a formidable pair of toughs' who never left his side, and his dog Tigger, a large German wolfhound captured from the enemy during the Fifth Offensive.

The one senior Yugoslav hardly mentioned by Fitzroy in *Eastern Approaches* is Tito's chief-of-staff Arso Jovanovic. Mike Parker explains: 'It was fortunate that the chemistry between Fitzroy and Tito worked so well, as it signally failed to work with some of the other top Yugoslavs, especially Jovanovic. He disliked westerners, and certainly didn't like Fitzroy.'[21] Fitzroy says: 'Jovanovic disliked westerners, it is true, but you could say he disliked Yugoslavs as well, for in 1948 he was one of the few home-grown Communists to side with Moscow against Tito. I think he suffered from a kind of guilt complex, since as a Royalist officer in the thirties he had sworn mighty oaths which he had had to disavow when he joined the Communists. Therefore he always tried to be *plus marxiste que les marxistes*, as it were, a bigger, meaner Communist than any Stalinist.'[22]

Fitzroy now pursued his primary aim, which was to estimate the fighting capacity and numbers of the Partisans. He sent his men far and wide across the areas controlled by Tito: the first to depart was Peter Moore. From his observations, there could be no doubting the enormous military achievement of the Partisans. They had progressed from near-bandits, ambushing convoys on lonely roads, to a well-disciplined army some 150,000 strong. It was soon clear to Fitzroy that Tito was a guerrilla captain of genius, and that Yugoslavia was an irregular's paradise. Everything conspired against the occupiers: their long lines of communication, their isolated garrisons, the mountainous terrain, and the hostility of the population. Above all, the Partisans were inspired by a sustaining ideology. 'Few ideas', Fitzroy remarks, 'equal revolutionary Communism in its strength, its persistence and its power over the individual.'[23]

The Partisans needed all the inspiration they could get, for the war they fought was singular in its savagery. The Geneva Conventions meant nothing here, and by the strictest standards almost everyone under arms could have been classed as a war criminal. Bosnia, where Fitzroy had his first sight of enemy-occupied Yugoslavia, seemed to him a microcosm of the country as a whole. Orthodox Serbs, Catholic Croats and Moslems were at each other's throats; the Germans were razing villages and exacting savage reprisals on the mere suspicion of harbouring Tito's men; everywhere Partisan fought with Ustase, Ustase with Cetnik, Cetnik with Partisan. Prisoners were rarely taken; civilians were massacred, women raped, villages burnt, churches desecrated, corpses mutilated.

Once, after a battle which had raged all day amid the green hills and valleys, I came on the terribly shattered corpse of an Ustasa. Seeing that capture was inevitable, he had taken the pin from a hand-grenade and, holding it against him, blown himself to bits. Somehow his face had escaped disfigurement, and his dead eyes stared horribly from the pale, drawn, disordered features. From under his blood-stained shirt protruded a crucifix, and a black and white medal ribbon, probably the Iron Cross, still hung to the shreds of his German-type tunic. Fighting for an alien power against his own countrymen, he had destroyed himself rather than fall into the hands of men of the same race as himself . . . There could have been no better symbol of the violence and fanaticism of this Balkan war.[24]

When Bill Deakin returned from Split he was able to help Fitzroy sort out his multitudinous impressions. Fitzroy, who had been expecting a rather desiccated academic, was delighted to find that Deakin looked like a very enthusiastic undergraduate, with the same mixture of brain and affability. Deakin was loud in his praise of the Partisans – their fighting qualities, their discipline, the toll they were taking of the Germans. He was also convinced that they were the only effective opposition to the Germans: he had seen with his own eyes evidence of Cetnik collaboration with the Axis. Fitzroy made good use of what Deakin told him.

Over the years many of Fitzroy's and Bill Deakin's friends and acquaintances have constructed an elaborate myth about Deakin being 'miffed' that Fitzroy did not give him enough credit for his elaborate groundwork in the four months before the brigadier's mission was dropped in. The argument is that Fitzroy appropriated Deakin's findings, and relegated him to what amounted to a footnote in his account in *Eastern Approaches*. But Deakin will have none of it. 'All attempts to drive a wedge between Fitzroy and me are quite disgraceful. Some well-meaning friends have tried to insinuate that Fitz stole my thunder. This is rubbish. So Fitzroy doesn't go on about me in *Eastern Approaches*? Why should he? It was *his* book about *his* experiences . . . I think Fitz himself was worried that I might resent his coming, but nothing was further from my mind.'[25]

By 5 October Fitzroy had amassed a file of material on the situation in Yugoslavia. He had processed the immediate Partisan application for elementary supplies, including urgently needed radio sets.[26] He had been in touch with all the British Liaison Officers in the field, had talked at length with Velebit and others – including an Orthodox priest formerly with the Cetniks, who had become disgusted by their inactivity and collaboration and fled to the Partisans. He and Deakin had also sifted through a mass of reports and signals. Slim Farish meanwhile discovered some flat land, nestling between hills forty miles from Tito's HQ, that could be converted into a clandestine airstrip. The entire population of the neighbouring village of Glamoc was pressed into service to help the Partisans construct it. Men, women and children toiled away with pick and shovel to level and smooth the surface so that Dakotas could land. When they were not working on it, the Partisans disguised the site with uprooted branches so that the excavations could not be observed from the air. At this stage in the war the Germans still controlled the Yugoslav skies, and their planes frequently appeared from nowhere, bombing and shooting anything that moved. One morning Farish arrived at the Glamoc airstrip to find a man hanging from a tree on the edge of the runway. It turned out he was a local traitor, caught trying to trade information to the Germans for food. His corpse would be cut down and fed to the pigs, and when the Germans next raided the area for food, the villagers would make sure they got the pigs in question.

Messages had come through from Cairo that the Royal Navy intended to supply the Partisans by sea, principally through the Adriatic island of Korcula. Fitzroy therefore bade farewell to Tito and, taking Street, Henniker and Duncan with him, left for the coast. They were to be passed from one Partisan band to another all the way, improvising their itinerary in the light of enemy movements.[27] Amazingly, the journey began by train. Some time before Tito's men had captured, intact, a railway engine and a number of trucks. Among their ranks they had an engine driver, guard and engineer, so that very soon they had put together a makeshift train which operated secretly up and down a short stretch of track leading towards the west coast – the train was one of the reasons Tito had chosen this area as his headquarters. Tito put his personal coach, an impressive assemblage of rolling-stock with a coke stove in the middle, at Fitzroy's disposal; he set off at night on the first leg of his journey.

Fitzroy and his group alighted from the train at Bugojno and after breakfast with the commander of the Partisan First Corps set off on foot through the enemy-occupied mountains, still a hundred miles from the coast. In atrocious weather they zigzagged from Bugojno, up and down remote forest valleys and steep exposed mountain paths, sometimes travelling on horseback, sometimes by farm cart, even in a stolen car and a captured German bus driven by an Italian tenor. They were conveyed across a swollen river on an improvised wooden raft. First they headed for Livno, which had once again changed hands. Taken by the Partisans in 1942, then recaptured, it now lay once more in Partisan control. At the village of Kupres, not far from Livno, they found the smoking ruins of a recent battle and ran into the triumphant young commander Lola Ribar. They passed on to Livno, a notorious Ustase stronghold, where Fitzroy was suprised to find local hostility and surly non-cooperativeness openly evinced.

On his way through Livno Fitzroy received a cable which read 'King now in Cairo. Will be dropped to you at first opportunity.' Fitzroy read this with consternation, for it seemed that London had jumped the gun and sent King Peter out without waiting for the mission's report. Such a precipitate step was likely to destroy all the carefully nurtured trust between Tito and Fitzroy and cause untold political embarrassment. When he later found Alston, he asked with a weary heart if the king had been dropped in yet. Alston looked at him as if he were mad. 'Oh,' he said, 'that cable wasn't about King Peter. That was about your new signals officer. His name is Hilary King.' So great was the relief that Fitzroy did not mind feeling foolish.

At Livno also occurred one of the incidents that won Fitzroy a reputation as a martinet. He was greeted by a man calling himself Major Burke, an Irishman who had risen from the ranks and been dropped into Yugoslavia as a captain; he claimed to have been pro-moted to major by SOE, behind Fitzroy's back, but what really angered Fitzroy was that he appeared to have 'gone native'. He had a red star in his beret and greeted Fitzroy with the clenched-fist salute of the Parti-sans. Fitzroy coldly ordered him to remove the red star and salute properly. Once this was done, Fitzroy looked into the question of his rank. Why did he call himself a major? Burke then changed his story, began to bluster, and claimed that his service in the Spanish Civil War and in the Middle East entitled him to the rank. Fitzroy remembers the upshot: 'I dismissed him, but then had trouble getting him out as, unfortunately, a parachute only works one way. On that sort of thing, yes, I was a martinet. There was conflict all through between SOE's irregular method of doing things, and my determination to make it a proper military operation.'[28]

Somewhat taken aback by the scale of hostilities raging between Livno and the coast, Fitzroy decided to send Vivian Street back to Jajce. If they ran into German patrols and were captured, it would be consummate folly for both the Number One and the Number Two on the mission to be caught in the same net. He and the others pressed on. The journey to the coast from Livno was supremely hazardous, but Fitzroy was in his element. If the initial idea of contacting the Partisans had seemed to him to have Lawrentian overtones, gliding past German sentries in the dark was redolent of another hero, Bonnie Prince Charlie, 'the Prince in the Heather'. It is surely not without reason that Fitzroy entitles this chapter in his memoirs 'Road to the Isles'.

When they got to Zadvarje, the worst was over. The local Partisan commander suggested that they begin their ascent of Biokovo pass at midday, since most of the coast was now in German hands. They would then arrive at Biokovo summit at dusk, ready for a descent to the sea by night. The first sighting of the Adriatic recalled a passage in Xenophon.

> Just before we reached the summit of the ridge, we were overtaken by a thunderstorm and torrents of drenching rain, and for a few minutes we sheltered in a peasant's hut by the roadside, full of smoke and smelling of garlic, like a mountaineer's hut in the Alps.
>
> Then the rain stopped as suddenly as it had started, and a few minutes later we reached the top and were looking down on the Adriatic, with the islands in the distance, the jagged outline of their mountains grey-blue against the fading red of the sunset. Neither Mitja nor my bodyguard had ever seen the sea before, and so we waited while they accustomed themselves to the idea of so much water. Then the sun sank behind the islands, and we started on our way down.[29]

On the way down they encountered only Partisan patrols. They were soon aboard a motorized fishing smack, heading out across the Adriatic towards Korcula, following a zigzag course in and out of the islands. Off Sucuraj they nearly came to disaster. The Partisans on the boat gave the wrong signal and were answered by an uncomfortably accurate fusillade of machine-gun bullets. Eventually, by shouting across the water, they were able to make contact with their jittery comrade on shore. A similar reception awaited them at Korcula, which they reached after sunrise. The man in charge of the shore battery was Rafo Ivancevic, later a close friend of Fitzroy's; he had been under the strictest orders to look out for Germans disguised as British commandos. The Political Commissar had told Ivancevic that if he brought in bogus British Liaison Officers, he would be shot. Doubtless the same fate would have been the result of killing the head of the British mission. The war in Yugoslavia was not for men of weak nerves.[30]

Korcula provided an idyllic interlude. The local commander, a ferocious Franciscan friar, lodged them in a little whitewashed house overlooking the harbour, from which steps ran down to the sea. Fitzroy and his companions first plunged into the clear blue water and swam half a mile and back across the straits dividing Korcula from the Peljesac peninsula, then dressed and attacked the enormous meal laid out for them: fish, eggs, meat, cheese, coffee, fruit, wine. After a nap, they were taken on a tour of the island. At each village they inspected the local Partisan detachment. They were impressed by the leader of the guard of honour at the first village, a tall man with flamboyant black moustaches, mounted on a great black horse. Admiration turned to puzzlement and puzzlement to mirth as they realized that the man was accompanying them from village to village – at each one a fresh guard of honour would be presented, but always under the eye of the same cavalryman. Fitzroy and his men had to keep straight faces and avoid any flicker of recognition as they took the salute.

One problem clouded the idyll on Korcula: the radio set mysteriously ceased to function, so they had no contact with Jajce. This was worrying on a number of counts, not least because German aggressiveness seemed to increase daily. Fitzroy watched as dive-bombing German Stukas carried out the first raid on Korcula. But, as so often in the Yugoslav war, tragedy had a way of alternating with farce. One night Fitzroy woke to hear a confused shouting outside his house. Bleary-eyed, he reached for his automatic, thinking the Germans had landed, but a Partisan guard irrupted into the house with three naval officers, one his old friend Alexander ('Sandy') Glen. He and David Satow, the latest addition to Fitzroy's staff, had landed on Korcula by motor torpedo boat with a cache of arms and ammunition and carrying the replacement radio requested by Fitzroy. Believing Korcula to be in German hands, they had crawled up the beach on their bellies, only to be sardonically accosted by a Detroit-born Partisan sentry. They were then taken on a hair-raising car journey to Korcula town. 'It was on the last little hill entering Korcula town' remembers Sandy Glen, 'that a rabbit took it on himself to dash into our headlights. Our driver seized my tommy gun, took feet from the pedals and hands from the wheel, fired a long volley and, seizing the brake, brought the car to a shuddering stop. He got the rabbit. Alongside us, just off the road, was some kind of a villa. Lights went on, we heard the noise of doors and windows being flung open, and then in English, "Christ, it must be the Germans!" A torch flashed, and I heard Fitzroy Maclean's quiet voice. "No, it's only Sandy." '[31]

The radio brought Fitzroy new life. Hearing that the Germans were collecting an invasion flotilla at the mouth of the Neretva, he signalled for help from both the RAF and the Royal Navy. It seemed to Fitzroy of the utmost importance for the Partisans to hang on to the Dalmatian islands, but without naval and air cover they would be helpless. Fitzroy had to leave Yugoslavia to make a personal report to Cairo, and wanted to see Tito first to discuss strategy for the islands. He therefore left for the mainland.

Baska Voda, from which the party had crossed to Korcula, was by now in enemy hands, so the Partisans took them to Podgora, further north. Half way across the straits they were nearly captured by a German patrol boat: it held them in the beam of its searchlight for a few seconds before concluding they were fishermen. At Podgora there was gloomy news of a battle raging between the coast and Jajce.

After a few days the fighting died down and Fitzroy was able to make one of his few uneventful Yugoslav journeys, back to Jajce and a final conference with Tito. Fitzroy explained that he was keen to get Allied support to hold the Dalmatian islands and must travel urgently to Cairo. Tito suggested that he take along a couple of emissaries from the Partisans, and selected Lola Ribar and Miloje Milojevic, the only official People's Hero (equivalent of a Victoria Cross holder) in the Partisan army.

Fitzroy sent a signal to London requesting permission for the two envoys to accompany him to Cairo, then departed once more for the coast, having arranged that Ribar and Milojevic would join him there once the necessary authorization from London was received. This time Fitzroy was based on the island of Hrvar. There he received a muddled and unsatisfactory answer from London. He was to come out and report, but the two Partisans were to be put 'on hold', ready to come out later if and when required. Given the tightening German grip on the country between Jajce and the coast, this was unlikely to be possible. Fitzroy cursed the cavalier attitude of a desk-bound official who obviously knew nothing of the difficulties of travel in occupied Europe.

It was Fitzroy's unwelcome task to compose a diplomatic message to Tito, asking his delegation to mark time. Even more unwelcome was the realization that the Royal Navy was only prepared to come as far as Vis to collect him; he therefore had to cross from Hrvar to Vis at night, in a fishing boat, in heavy seas. On Vis he was picked up by motor-launch and taken across the Adriatic to the newly liberated port of Bari.

There Fitzroy revelled in the plentiful food and wine and the luxury of the Hotel Imperiale, but was not permitted to enjoy them for long. He was bundled on board a plane for a circuitous flight via Malta, Benghazi and Tobruk to Cairo. There he stayed once more with his friend Kit Steel. Steel told him that most of the Foreign Office 'top brass' were in town, just back from a conference with Molotov in Moscow and *en route* to a meeting of the 'Big Three' (Stalin, Roosevelt and Churchill) in Teheran. Present in Cairo were Eden, William Strang, Oliver Harvey, and his old boss Sir Alexander Cadogan, whom he had last seen when he handed in his resignation from the Foreign Office. Fitzroy reflected that in less than three years he had come a very long way. More immediately to the point, this was obviously the time to get a decisive resolution on Allied policy in Yugoslavia.

10

The Months of Decision
NOVEMBER 1943–JANUARY 1944

W HILE Fitzroy was away in Cairo his spirit lived on among the
Partisans. That he was sorely missed is recorded by the members
of the British mission left behind in Bosnia. Mike Parker relates:

> Fitzroy always talked to Tito like a Dutch uncle when there was trouble and,
> surprisingly, Tito took it. Fitz had established enough of a relationship with
> Tito to tell him off and get away with it. We needed Fitzroy to keep the balance
> as Tito was very fiery and anything could set him off. I remember once when
> Fitzroy and Henniker were away and I was in charge with Alston. A rather
> brusque cable arrived from Jumbo Wilson to Tito, saying, 'Why didn't you do
> so and so when I asked you?' I took it down to Tito's HQ thinking that Olga
> Humo, the interpreter, could handle it. To my horror Olga was not there. Tito
> had three and a half words of English and I had three and a half words of
> Serbo-Croat, though we both had some German. I decided the only thing was
> to read the telegram aloud. As I did so, Tito frowned. He didn't get it all, but he
> got the gist. He snatched the telegram from my hand, threw it to the ground
> angrily, then turned to me with a beaming smile and said, 'Slivovic?'

All members of the mission remember the perennial cries of 'Pokret'
in the middle of the night. A later addition to the mission, Charlie
Thayer, describes his initiation to 'Pokret': 'One day Maclean and
I had come in around noon from a long morning's ride to find our
missions in a high state of excitement. I asked Bill Callanan what was
up. "Pokret", he said and darted back into the house. "What the hell's
'Pokret'?" I asked Maclean, "– the bubonic plague, or an earthquake?" "It's Serbian for 'Get going – the Germans are coming',"
Fitzroy explained.'

The impression is sometimes given that the famous Maclean report of
6 November 1943 came like a bolt from the blue. In fact from the very
earliest days Fitzroy's signals from Yugoslavia had made it clear that

beside the Partisans, Mihailovic's Cetniks and, even more, the government-in-exile of King Peter were very small beer indeed.[1] His enthusiasm for Tito had seriously alarmed his former Foreign Office
colleagues. Ralph Stevenson, ambassador *in partibus* to the Yugoslav
government, telegraphed to London that Maclean's reports necessi-
tated a drastic rethinking of the government's support for King Peter,
and that if this policy were persisted in, the king would at the very least
have to make contact with Tito.[2] Fitzroy's early messages made it plain
that it was not at present expedient to push the issue of the Yugoslav
monarchy. This worried Sargent and Cadogan at the Foreign Office,
who construed it as 'capitulation' to Tito; it was on their recommendation that Fitzroy was first ordered to come out of Yugoslavia to 'sort out
his priorities'.[3]

The mandarins' worst fears were confirmed when Fitzroy's report
was presented. It was a masterly piece of lucid analysis.[4] Fitzroy estimated that the Partisans controlled large sections of Yugoslavia and that
Tito had twenty-six divisions under his command totalling 220,000
men, of which 50,000 were in Bosnia, 15,000 in the Sanjak, 50,000 in
Croatia, 10,000 in Slavonia, 60,000 in Slovenia and Istria, 25,000
in Dalmatia, 10,000 in the Vojvodina, and 30,000 in Serbia and
Macedonia. Fitzroy's numbers in this report have been much criticized
since, but they were remarkably accurate estimates, especially given
that top-secret intercepts varied widely in their assessments. For
instance, an SOE estimate of October 1943, working mainly from SD
intercepts, put Tito's forces at 180,000 in all, as opposed to the 20,000
Cetniks of Mihailovic, and the 25,000 guerrillas the Greek Left could
muster.[5] German Intelligence sources (via Ultra) put the figure much
higher: between 160,000 and 200,000 for the Split–Dubrovnik area
alone.[6]

Fitzroy expressed himself disappointed that, despite Allied promises
of seventy aerial sorties for September and sixty for October, no more
than eleven were flown in September and thirty in October – just
eighty tons of *matériel*, or the equivalent of the cargo of a small schooner.
During the three months before this even less had been dropped, perhaps amounting in all to 150 tons. Fitzroy particularly deplored the fact
that the Partisans had controlled the Dalmatian islands for two months,
yet almost nothing had been done to reinforce them. Again, his figures
accord well with other sources. General Wilson claimed that in 1943 as a
whole the Partisans received 6,000 tons of supplies, but only 339 tons by
air.[7] Later scholarship has established that in the last quarter of 1943 the
Partisans received a mere 113.5 tons by air, and 1,857 tons by sea.[8]

Fitzroy pointed out that Tito was no mere hit-and-run guerrilla: he
controlled large stretches of territory and even occupied towns when it
was expedient; he never made the mistake of engaging the Germans in

pitched battles. Fitzroy's estimate of the number of Reichswehr divisions pinned down was modest: just fourteen. Ultra material for the same period showed thirty enemy divisions (including Croat and Bulgarian detachments) in action, mostly against the Partisans.[9] German sources tell the same story. By the end of 1943 there were fourteen Wehrmacht divisions, two SS regiments and five divisions of non-German troops under Nazi command, amounting in all to well over 200,000 men. In addition the German commander, General Maximilian von Weichs, had another 160,000 Bulgarian, Serb and Croat quisling troops at his disposal. Even so, Weichs felt he did not have enough men to subdue Yugoslavia. In October he told Hitler that Tito was the Reich's most dangerous enemy, and that defeating the Partisans was more important than repelling an Allied landing.[10]

Fitzroy reported that he found complete religious toleration among the Partisans, no interference with private property, no class warfare, no mass executions. Tito himself looked forward to a federalist solution of the 'nationalities problem'. On the other hand, there was abundant evidence of Cetnik collaboration with the enemy. 'The Partisans are between ten and twenty times as numerous, infinitely better organized, better equipped and better disciplined. Moreover, they fight the Germans, while the Cetniks either help the Germans or do nothing.' Fitzroy argued that if Britain really wanted to influence Tito and prevent him from slipping permanently into the Soviet sphere of influence, she had to abandon Mihailovic and switch to the Partisans. This made sense whichever goal, military or political, was given precedence. Support for the Partisans would yield spectacular results in terms of the war effort and, politically, recognized the reality that they would hold the ring of power after the war. Summing up, Fitzroy made five specific recommendations. Britain should drop Mihailovic, increase aid to the Partisans, start large-scale supply by sea, attack specific German-held targets in Yugoslavia by air, and make sure that controversial BBC broadcasts, attributing all Partisan successes to Mihailovic, were kept in line with the policy of His Majesty's Government.

Even before his official report, Fitzroy's enthusiasm for Tito had been well known in Cairo. After meeting Fitzroy, Ralph Stevenson reported to London that the Partisans were clearly on their way to becoming masters of Yugoslavia.[11] Oliver Harvey's diary entries for 6 and 7 November tell the same story. 'Fitzroy Maclean has turned up, just back from Yugoslavia. He reports that the Partisans under Tito are 200,000 strong as against 10,000 or so Chetniks under Mihailovic; we should put all our money on Tito . . . Fitzroy is sure that Tito represents the future government of Yugoslavia, whether we like it or not, a sort of peasant communism, and we should be wise to come to terms and try to guide them. This also has been more or less agreed on.'[12] Other analysts commented on the outstanding work being done by the signals and radio officers in Fitzroy's team, especially their early warning that Tito's cipher was insecure and being read by the enemy.[13]

Elisabeth Barker notes:

> The Maclean report of 6 November 1943 had the effect of a blockbuster. It was immediately issued by the Foreign Office as a green print – even though they did not like its conclusions on Mihailovic and the Serbs – so it hit the War Cabinet and the Chiefs of Staff with considerable impact. Churchill minuted 'most interesting' on it. The report made it much more difficult for the Foreign Office to carry on its kid-glove policy towards Mihailovic, and gave a big shove to the movement towards dropping Mihailovic which was gathering momentum throughout November and the first half of December 1943.[14]

The official sources bear out this estimate. After a Chiefs of Staff meeting on 16 November a senior official, Cavendish Bentinck, wrote the following minute:

> The Chiefs of Staff . . . expressed a desire to hear the Foreign Office comment on Brigadier Maclean's report . . . It seemed to them at first sight that Brigadier Maclean's recommendations should be carried out. The view was expressed that it was time we ceased to consider the feelings of the Yugoslav government, if considerations of them in any way interfered with our support for the Partisans, who are doing something against our enemy, unlike General Mihailovic . . . The Chief of Air Staff enquired whether Brigadier Maclean was a realistic observer, or like many people who go on such missions, a fanatic. I [Cavendish Bentinck] replied that Brigadier Maclean was a former member of this [Foreign] office, shrewd, hard-headed and rather cynical. The Chief of the Imperial General Staff praised Brigadier Maclean's report . . . they intended to make recommendations to the Cabinet on [it].[15]

That Fitzroy's views commanded bipartisan support was clear from a letter of Herbert Morrison's to Eden early in December. 'I have read with very great interest the able report by Brigadier Maclean . . . I wonder whether it would not be a good plan for the Cabinet to discuss some of the broad questions of policy, present and future, which emerge from the report.'[16] The Joint Intelligence Committee was also keenly interested in the report, and on 12 November asked for a copy. Influenced by Ultra material, which corroborated his memorandum, the JIC members sided with Fitzroy against his old colleagues in the Foreign Office in pressing for a break with Mihailovic. One particular Ultra intercept seems to have been the deciding factor for the JIC. It contained a German claim to have killed 6,000 Partisans and only fifteen Cetniks, in a period when twice as many Cetniks as Partisans had been taken prisoner.[17] General Wilson was also impressed. He took the view that Mihailovic should be left 'to rot and fall off the branch, rather than be pushed'. In November he gave Mihailovic an ultimatum: prove yourself by blowing up two bridges on the Belgrade-Salonika railway by the end of the year, or have your supplies cut off. Mihailovic ignored the message.

Why did Fitzroy's report have such an impact? In part, because his recommendation for decisive action in the Balkans chimed with Churchill's own thinking. At one stage in 1943 Churchill had conceived of a Balkan landing as an alternative to the US-backed Overlord plan for an invasion of northern Europe; not only would this be in line with the historical tradition of the Dardanelles and Salonika, of which Churchill had been such a tireless advocate in the First World War, but it held out the hope that the western powers might pre-empt the advancing Soviet army in eastern Europe. But Eisenhower opposed any removal of forces and landing craft from the Italian front to the eastern Mediterranean, and on 19 August 1943 laid down a clear directive: 'Operations in the Balkans area will be limited to the supply of Balkan guerrillas by air and sea transport, and the bombing of Ploesti and other strategic objectives from Italian bases. The Balkans are unsuitable for large-scale offensive operations, due to the terrain and communications difficulties.'[18] This was part of a continuing pattern whereby Churchill argued for large-scale Balkan operations and the Americans vetoed them.

Yet Churchill could still hope for something from his own compatriots. In October 1943 the British Chiefs of Staff supported the idea of putting pressure on the Wehrmacht via the Yugoslav Resistance movements, in hopes of forcing the Germans to leave the Balkans, or at any rate the southern half, voluntarily. But in November Churchill's suggestion of establishing bridgeheads on the Dalmation coast, with the use of the First British Airborne Division and all available commandos, was turned down by General Alexander and the Chiefs of Staff.[19] There was always considerable ambiguity in Churchill's Balkan aims. Did he want to force the Germans out of the area, or merely tie down their divisions there? Was his primary aim 'killing Germans', as he expressed it to Fitzroy, or did he want a Western toe-hold there before the victorious Res Army should arrive? Whatever the case, there can be no denying the fascination the area held for the Prime Minister, and from his clearest statement on the subject one can readily see that he had read Fitzroy's report with enthusiasm: 'Although we cannot fight a Balkan campaign ourselves, we ought to use enough force to stimulate others to do it.'[20]

Yet it would be unjust to Fitzroy to suggest that his report made an impact purely because it accorded with one of Churchill's obsessions. This would be to discount his abilities as advocate and his political skills.

He knew who the top people were and had access to them. Crucially, he spoke the language of the decision-makers in a way that, for example, the British Liaison Officers with Mihailovic did not. The historian Mark Wheeler comments: 'These people didn't have access, hadn't been to the right schools, were not part of the Establishment. A class interpretation is possible. Bill Bailey was Emmanuel School, Wandsworth; Deakin and Maclean were Winchester and Eton products.'[21]

Fitzroy was not just a better advocate, more gifted intellectually than the liaison officers with Mihailovic. His concise lucidity was peculiarly calculated to appeal, especially to Churchill. Bailey's signal from Mihailovic's headquarters, when it arrived at the end of November 1943, was chaotically expressed and sent in ninety-two different signals: it could scarcely have been worse designed for making an impact on the Prime Minister, who was a 'basic English, one sheet of paper' man. Hilary King, Fitzroy's signals officer, points out that those who postulate conspiracies to 'do down' Mihailovic, do so in ignorance of the intricacies of signals. The mechanics of sending out a 92-part signal, complete with 'corrupt groups' and requests for repetition, creates its own chaos; in such a situation, conspiracy is a redundant hypothesis. Finally, we should not discount the 'being there' factor. Bailey and the others sent out their reports by cable; Fitzroy flew out from Bari with his and accompanied it through the corridors of power in Cairo.

Fitzroy's 'blockbuster' may not have caused the switch of Allied support from Mihailovic, but it played an important role in confirming decisions already taken at the Teheran Conference with Stalin. At the Allies' Cairo Conference which immediately followed in late 1943, Roosevelt expressed a weary opinion that the Americans 'should build a wall around those two fellows [Tito and Mihailovic] and let them fight it out . . . we could do business with the winner',[22] though in Teheran he had agreed to switch to the Partisans. A crucial influence was the report he had received from Major Linn Farish dated 29 October 1943 endorsing Fitzroy's findings and, if anything, even more enthusiastic about his Yugoslav hosts. At the second private meeting at the Teheran summit, Roosevelt handed Stalin Farish's report, which spoke of the Partisans' admiration for the USA; for this, he explained, and no other reason, the Allies proposed to aid Tito. Churchill also assured Stalin that the British had no ambitions in the Balkans, but merely wanted to pin down the thirty Axis divisions in Greece and Yugoslavia. Details of the proposed aid by the 'Big Three' were then devolved to the Foreign Ministers. Eden offered the Russians an air base in North Africa; Molotov closed the deal, and it was agreed that a Soviet base would be set up in Cairo.[23]

The Russian attitude at Teheran would not have pleased the Partisans;

there was a deep-lying divergence between the policies of Stalin and Tito that eventually led them to a parting of the ways in 1948. The initiative for a further mission to Mihailovic, despite the mountain of evidence that he was militarily useless, is said to have come from the Russians, and Mihailovic for his part told the British Liaison Officers he was quite willing to accept a Soviet mission.[24] However, when Eden suggested a mission to both Tito and Mihailovic, Molotov said he would prefer a mission to neither than such a shabby compromise.[25] Although Stalin had come down in favour of a united and enlarged Yugoslavia in December 1941 and did not subsequently change tack, uncertainties engendered by earlier fluctuations in Soviet policy were pounced on by the enemies of the Partisans (and they were legion) in the Foreign Office. As Fitzroy says, 'The Russians had had different attitudes on that particular subject over the last thirty years. There was a time, prior to 1934, when Soviet policy was to split up Yugoslavia, and there were other times when it favoured a united Yugoslavia.'[26] The uncertain stance taken by the Soviet Union at Teheran and in the past enabled factions in the Foreign Office to plead, disingenuously, that detaching Serbia from the rest of Yugoslavia would not be in conflict with Allied war aims.[27] Yet such was suspicion of US intentions that when Roosevelt mooted the idea of an independent Serbia, they opposed it.[28]

After working dinners with Cadogan and Eden, Fitzroy flew back to Italy with instructions to return to Cairo in a few weeks when Churchill would be there. At Bari there was bad news. The Germans had launched their Sixth Offensive, KUGELBLITZ ('Thunderbolt') and, using fast-moving armoured and mechanized columns with air support, were sweeping into the newly-liberated areas of Dalmatia and Slovenia. They reoccupied Slovenia and in a few weeks had the Dalmatian coast in their grip, cutting Partisan communications. Using the Peljesac peninsula as a jumping-off point, they rapidly recaptured the islands of Korcula, Brac, Hrvar and Mljet. By the end of the year only Vis was in Partisan hands. The island, by mutual agreement jointly occupied by a British commando brigade and a force of Partisans, was used as a temporary base for Allied and naval operations in the Adriatic and for schooners of the Partisan 'navy'. The Germans meanwhile turned their attention to east Bosnia and began to converge on the Partisans east of Sarajevo. Despite Partisan attempts to avoid pitched battles, there was much heavy fighting. The second phase of the Sixth Offensive ran into the ground, however, when the Germans failed to destroy three of Tito's divisions north-east of Sarajevo.

Learning that Slim Farish's newly built airfield at Glamoc was in Partisan hands – but only just – Fitzroy at once saw the urgency of picking up Ribar and Milojevic. But he could find no one in the RAF who would listen to his pleas: 'They had, they said, plenty of far better uses for their aircraft than smashing them up in futile attempts to bring futile foreigners out of the Balkans.'[29] But Fitzroy found an ally in Air Marshal Sholto Douglas, who put him on to Wing Commander John Selby, a flying ace with particular expertise in night landings. He recommended using a Baltimore light bomber for the task, but stressed the need for a fighter escort. After a lot more lobbying and cajoling, Fitzroy enlisted the support of the US 82nd Fighter Group at Lecce, who used Lightnings, the very latest fighters.

When all was ready for the evacuation from Glamoc, Fitzroy signalled Deakin at Jajce with the news. The reception party gathered at Glamoc: Deakin and Robin Whetherly were to come out with Ribar and Milojevic; Donald Knight and Vladko Velebit would be at the airstrip to see them on their way; damp straw would be burned to guide the Baltimore to the landing strip by smoke signals.

Fitzroy's plane took off from Italy in limpid sunlight, with the Lightnings in close attendance. As he watched the glittering waters of the Adriatic below, he felt confident that by that evening the Partisan delegation would be on its way to Cairo. But once they were over the Yugoslav mainland, heavy clouds closed in. They found themselves flying through a blizzard in 'white-out' conditions, with an impenetrable wall of black storm clouds ahead of them. There was nothing for it but to return to Italy. Next day they tried again, but with the same result. Then the Americans had to transfer the escort of Lightnings to another theatre of war. With a determination bordering on folly, Fitzroy and his New Zealand pilot decided to make the run without a fighter shield. This time they got tantalizingly close to their objective, but in the end the weather prevailed once more. The return journey nearly ended in disaster; Lecce was shrouded in mist and they had to divert to Foggia. Conditions there were just as bad, but petrol was now dangerously low, so the pilot was forced to make a perilous semi-blind approach prior to skidding along the waterlogged runway.

Grounded by torrential rain for the next forty-eight hours, Fitzroy was close to despair when he received news that made his own predicament seem nugatory. The Partisans had captured a German plane and, frustrated by the non-appearance of Fitzroy's rescue mission, decided to fly Ribar and Milojevic out in it. Just as the passengers were about to board the plane, a German aircraft appeared from nowhere and scored a direct hit on it. Whetherly, Knight and Ribar were killed and Milojevic was wounded. It was later discovered that this pinpoint assault was the result of treachery by a Partisan informer. Even in Fitzroy's description five years later some bitterness seeps through the controlled narrative:

It was sad news indeed. In Robin Whetherly and Donald Knight I had lost two good friends and two of my best officers. In Lola Ribar the Partisans had lost yet another of their outstanding younger leaders and one who had seemed destined to play a great part in building the new Jugoslavia. For his old father, too, whose other son had been killed in action a few weeks before, it would, I knew, be a crushing blow. We had paid dearly for the two or three weeks which it had taken to reach a decision as to the movements of the delegation. Now one of them was dead and the other wounded and Cairo as far away as ever.[30]

Naturally, the Partisans blamed British dithering. Whispers circulated that Tito would never have allowed Ribar to go on such a harebrained scheme had he known about it. Deakin had to take firm action to silence these: he saw Tito and got him to confirm publicly that Ribar had told him all about the mission.[31] Bill Deakin remembers clearly the events following Fitzroy's departure.

My admiration for Fitzroy is well known, but the one criticism I would make is that he left no one properly in charge when he departed for the coast with Vivian Street. The Yugoslavs always claimed that the Ribar accident might not have happened if we'd had a clear leader. This compounded my embarrassment when the Partisans tried to go behind his back to me, on the grounds that they had known me longer. Shortly after Fitzroy left, Velebit came to me and asked me to take out a mission. I explained that Fitzroy had gone out for that reason – to get his people to accept a military mission and to resolve the Mihailovic business at Cabinet level. But Tito kept putting pressure on me to take out a mission without waiting for Fitzroy's return, and this pressure built up when Fitzroy experienced such problems getting back in. I was in a difficult position. If I refused to take out a mission, Tito might lose confidence in us. On the other hand, if I did, Fitzroy might think I had gone behind his back and exceeded my authority. Luckily, in the end all was resolved satisfactorily.[32]

Meanwhile, on the political front there were ominous developments; more seriously, a crisis blew up with the Americans. Very soon after Fitzroy departed for the coast Tito summoned a meeting of the Anti-Fascist Council at Jajce, which began by making him a Marshal, and went on to push the Partisans further along the road of conflict with Moscow. Tito cabled Stalin that the National Committee of the Anti-Fascist Council was henceforth the provisional government of Yugoslavia. He also asked Stalin to impress on Roosevelt and Churchill at Teheran that Tito did not recognize King Peter and the Royal Yugoslav government-in-exile. But he did not inform Stalin of the Jajce Council's other resolution – not to allow King Peter to return after the war. The Russians later learned of this through their spies and were very angry, fearing that the Allies would think Moscow had put Tito up to it; Moscow forbade Radio Free Yugoslavia to mention the resolution.

Fitzroy learned the gist of all this from Deakin, who comments: 'The only sequence of events not properly handled in *Eastern Approaches* is the internal situation in Yugoslavia in October to December 1943, while Fitzroy was away. Tito was pleased to get a full military mission from the British, but what he wanted above all was *political* recognition, and he wanted the British to face the issue of his Council and Committee being in competition with the Royal government-in-exile.'[33] Fitzroy felt that Tito was trying to go too fast. He had not yet decisively carried the day in getting the Allies to switch support from the Cetniks to the Partisans, yet here was Tito demanding that King Peter be abandoned on his behalf.

More immediately worrying, however, was an American threat to British spheres of influence. Behind it were layers of high politics. A treaty had been signed in September 1942 between SOE and the newly formed Office of Strategic Services (OSS – the forerunner of the CIA) which assigned SOE the directing role in the Balkans. But Roosevelt continued to pressure Churchill into allowing the OSS, under its rumbustious director General William Joseph ('Wild Bill') Donovan, to enter the Balkans freely. He claimed that the Resistance movements in south-east Europe were chaotic but Churchill brushed the suggestion aside. The British situation was complicated by the American Lend-Lease arrangements which helped finance the British war effort. SOE welcomed the largesse but wanted no interference and no American role in decision-making. Eventually, in return for tacitly accepting that the British had special interests in Greece and Yugoslavia, the OSS got operational *carte blanche* in Bulgaria and Romania.[34]

How far Donovan was an Anglophobe is debatable. Some say that as an Irish Catholic he bore grudges towards England, and that he shared Roosevelt's dislike of the British Empire. Others claim that the pragmatic corporation lawyer in Donovan was always more important than any Irish republicanism, and that in fact Britain owed him a debt of gratitude for coming down firmly against US isolationism. Fitzroy, who shared a car with him down to Chequers in 1944, found him affable enough,[35] but he was a formidable figure, with far more power in American political circles than Lord Selbourne wielded in England, and there can be no doubting his determination to break what he called 'the British hammerlock' in the Balkans.

In the autumn of 1943 the division of the Balkans between SOE and the OSS was still in the future. Donovan at that point considered he had a chance of prising Yugoslavia open to American influence because the British military missions there were being run by SOE. Although SOE were rivals, in many ways they and OSS saw eye to eye: their social composition and rightist ideology made them natural bedfellows. It was otherwise with the Foreign Office and SIS. The coming of Fitzroy therefore posed a direct challenge to Donovan, for it meant that he could no longer use the SOE as a Trojan horse for his Balkan ambitions. Something had to be done, and quickly. Donovan began by taking advantage of the ambiguity in OSS's functions. The September 1942 treaties only prevented SOE-style operations by OSS in Britain's spheres of influence – not SIS-style intelligence activities. Once Bari passed into Allied hands after the Italian surrender, Donovan gave the order for a new offensive, Operation Audrey. OSS would use American ships to ferry men and supplies to Tito directly, thus ending American dependence on British transport at Cairo and Algiers. Donovan had no authority to order this operation, but he used as his cover a declaration from the Combined Chiefs at Quebec which supported an increase in the flow of *matériel* to any Yugoslavs who were fighting the Germans.[36]

Donovan gave command of his clandestine operation to Major Louis Huot, who at once moved to Bari without consulting the British. Once there, he browbeat local British commanders by claiming to be under the personal instructions of General Eisenhower. With barefaced effrontery he set up a large-scale operation for ferrying aid to Tito. Too late the OSS headquarters in Algiers, also kept in the dark by Donovan so as to avoid Allied channels, ordered Huot to desist forthwith and hand over his supplies. He ignored all directives and set out for Yugoslavia. Without informing Fitzroy or in any way being authorized by him, he first visited the Dalmatian islands.[37] On Vis he promised the Partisans tanks, trucks and mountain artillery, in flat contradiction of Fitzroy's orders; at that time he had no authority to supply them with other than light weapons.

OSS Cairo now added its voice to Algiers and ordered Huot out of the area. He refused to obey any but a direct order from Donovan. SOE's Lord Harcourt tried to intervene, but Huot told Harcourt to 'go and fuck himself'.[38] He then departed for the mainland with the intention of seeking out Tito at Jajce: hearing that Fitzroy was on Korcula, he avoided that island.

Huot reached Jajce on 23 October at 6 p.m. and was warmly received by Tito. He hid when a British officer appeared,[39] but did make contact with Captain Melvin Benson, OSS liaison officer with Tito and a member of Fitzroy's Anglo-American mission. Benson advised Huot to put the British in the picture, lest Tito take the opportunity to play one side off against the other. Huot was reluctant, but agreed when Benson pointed out that irreparable harm would be done if the Partisans sensed there was an Anglo-American rift.

Huot spent eighteen hours in Jajce and later made his own report on the Partisans. A seven-page document described the composition, tactics, weapons, locations and strengths of the eight corps that made up Tito's principal units. It covered the Partisans' training methods and selection and training of officers; the history of the movement, its political and ethnic composition and its attitude towards King Peter; Tito's ideas on postwar Yugoslavia, attitudes to Mihailovic and relations with the British and Americans; and the Partisans' extensive German order-of-battle intelligence. The report praised Tito but deprecated British supply operations to the Partisans.

Huot then threw down a direct challenge to Fitzroy by detaching his OSS liaison officers. He sent Benson to the coast to look after the Yugoslav end of his 'Trans Adriatic Shipping Line' and took Linn Farish with him to Bari to make another report. Huot declared glibly: 'I realized that this course would inevitably require lengthy and painful explanations with Brigadier Maclean.' 'Slim' Farish, caught between two fires, rationalized desperately: 'I was sure the brigadier would be in Bari within a week and that however difficult it might be, it should be possible to square the situation with him then.'[40]

When Huot got back to Bari on 29 October, he found himself in a hornet's nest. General Colin Gubbins, head of SOE, visited his own base at Bari and found it, without his knowledge or consent, being run by the OSS. Some plain speaking ensued, but it was as nothing to what transpired when Fitzroy arrived back in Bari. Hilary King, Fitzroy's signals officer, recalls: 'Fitzroy was much exercised about Huot – almost to the point of apoplexy, if one could imagine an apoplectic Fitzroy!'[41] A later historian wrote: 'The truth was that in Maclean Huot had made a powerful enemy, one almost as powerful as Lord Harcourt, who was now Huot's commanding officer.'[42]

The insubordinate Huot, with his secret mandate from Donovan, was a tough nut to crack. He intransigently maintained that OSS had equal rights in Yugoslavia with SOE, and that the Partisans mistrusted the British. Harcourt looked for a way to get rid of this turbulent American and lit on Huot's insane promise to supply Tito with a thousand trucks. Ordering him to Algiers, ostensibly to start work on collecting these vehicles, Harcourt wrote a stiff letter of official complaint to OSS Algiers, who in turn ordered Huot to Cairo to report to the OSS Regional Director, Lieutenant-Colonel Toulmin.

Huot appealed to Donovan, who tried to intervene but was stymied by a letter of complaint from Fitzroy which reached Cairo at the same time as Huot. Donovan knew that Fitzroy was answerable direct to Churchill. Huot did not help his case by being insubordinate to Toulmin, who promptly complained to Washington that he was out of control. Joseph Smithers, Acting Director of US Special Operations, sent Huot a mild letter of admonition which, predictably, Huot ignored. But nemesis struck from an unexpected direction. Rumours of peculation and defalcation at the OSS base in Bari began to grow, and eventually Huot was sent home in disgrace and left the OSS under a cloud. Some observers have tried to exculpate this raving Anglophobe, claiming that 'Huot's main crime was to jump the gun', since aid to Tito was about to be approved.[43] Another approach is to duck the issue of Huot's exaggerated promises to Tito. 'Could Huot have delivered what he promised? He took advantage of a "window" when the coast was literally clear. Since it wasn't later, and SOE had to drop its supplies by air, the question whether Huot could or could not does not really arise.'[44]

The fact is that Huot's actions were blatantly contrary to Allied agreements; he had usurped Fitzroy's authority, and tried to make fools out of the British. He was quite aware of what he was doing, and was consistently 'economical with the truth'. Bill Deakin explains: 'Huot said he told me all about his mission. He did not; I never saw him. Benson, who had been with me throughout August and September, told me about Huot's visit afterwards, and I informed Fitzroy by cable. That was what started the explosion.'[45] Hilary King adds that Huot's apologists fail to grasp the crucial, practical grounds for Fitzroy's objections to the American's plans, quite apart from his defiance of all chains of command, hierarchies or normal courtesies.

> Available supplies for the Partisans were necessarily limited – and what was available had to be allocated to the Partisan commands where they could be used most effectively. For most of these commands, there was no early prospect of being able to supply them by sea, for onward forwarding overland. We had to rely on carefully planned air supply, directed in continuous consultation with Tito's GHQ. Huot, to secure Brownie points for himself (and, it seems, to discredit the Brits in the eyes of the Partisans), was evidently trying to grab much of the available stores for sea-shipment to the islands – where, even if not captured by the Germans, they would probably remain stuck in the coastal area.[46]

But if 1943 saw the last of Huot, Donovan himself remained as a thorn in Fitzroy's side. In a continuing attempt to rescind the British monopoly in Yugoslavia, he applied to the Joint Chiefs of Staff on 26 November for a US presence at both Tito's and Mihailovic's headquarters. He claimed that Yugoslav policy was being made entirely by the British Foreign Office and directed by 'Foreign Office representatives in uniform and ostensibly under SOE orders but in reality (as we have actually experienced) responsible not to SOE but only to the Foreign Office.'[47] At meetings with the British in Cairo and Algiers in January 1944, Donovan refused to co-operate further with the Maclean mission in Yugoslavia and announced his intention of despatching independent US missions to both Tito and Mihailovic. This was the somewhat sordid reality behind Fitzroy's laconic comment in *Eastern Approaches*: '. . . Anglo American co-operation was of the closest. It continued so when, a year later . . . the Americans decided to send in a full-scale American mission'.[48]

After the Lola Ribar tragedy the British had to get the Partisan emissaries out. It became a matter of saving face. This time the affair was given a higher priority: half a squadron of Lightnings accompanied Fitzroy's Dakota, flown by John Selby in person. After a bumpy landing at Glamoc, Fitzroy collected the wounded Milojevic and Vladko Velebit, appointed to take Ribar's place. Also on the flight back to Italy were Vlado Dedijer, Bill Deakin, Sergeant Duncan, another British Liaison Officer, Anthony Hunter, and a captured Abwehr officer. They flew to Bari, where Fitzroy was infuriated to find that no arrangements had been made for their onward journey. He therefore asked the pilot to fly them to Alexandria, where they were urgently awaited, and assured him he would deal with any disciplinary consequences at a higher level.[49] They took off again the same evening and landed at Malta, where they looted bedding from a startled British HQ and transformed the Dakota into a flying bedroom for the last lap. Finally, they came in to land at Alexandria at dawn, with the sun rising gloriously over the desert.[50]

At Alexandria a villa had been set aside for the envoys. Milojevic and Dedijer were taken to hospital, while Velebit was left to reacclimatize to civilization after two years 'in the heather'. Here, as in Bari, Fitzroy's brisk methods ruffled feathers, so that a fortnight later we find him writing offically through War Office channels to explain that everything had been done in a friendly manner and that he had *not* peremptorily ordered the Station Commander to hand over vehicles.[51]

Fitzroy and Deakin next sped to Cairo to meet Churchill, just back from the Teheran conference, and found him ensconced in a villa near the Pyramids. He was in bed when they arrived, in an embroidered dressing gown and chomping on the inevitable cigar. Fitzroy takes up the story: 'Then he asked me whether I wore a kilt when I was dropped out of an aeroplane, and from this promising point of departure, we slid into a general discussion of the situation in Jugoslavia. He had read my report, and in its light and in the light of all other available information had talked over the Jugoslav problem with Stalin and Roosevelt at Teheran. As a result of these talks, it had been decided to give all-out support to the Partisans.'[52] Churchill also told Fitzroy about the 'last chance' offer to Mihailovic to blow up the Salonica–Belgrade railway bridge. Fitzroy pointed out that Tito's certain triumph after the war meant that Yugoslavia would be a Communist country. Churchill's reply was brutal.

'Do you intend to make Jugoslavia your home after the war?'
'No, Sir,' I replied.
'Neither do I,' he said. 'And, that being so, the less you and I worry about the

form of government they set up, the better. That is for them to decide. What interests us is, which of them is doing most harm to the Germans?'[53]

The irony is, of course, that Fitzroy did live in Yugoslavia after the war; or, rather, he bought a house there. A further twist to the tale is that after hearing of this singular conversation, Tito is said to have waived the laws against private property in foreign ownership so that Fitzroy could buy a house on the island of Korcula.

But if the Mihailovic problem had apparently been solved, the infinitely thornier issue of King Peter and the Royal government-in-exile remained to rankle for another year. King Peter continued to be the focus for Britain's long-term policy towards Yugoslavia. There was in general no great sentimental attachment to the Serbian monarchy in Britain; the Karadjordjevic dynasty was too recent to have any weight of tradition behind it, and the manner of its restoration in 1903 (by murder) had horrified England. Churchill himself, though, always with a soft spot for kings and queens, was sympathetic. After the coup of 27 March 1941 he would have preferred King Peter to stay and fight; the Foreign Office, however, hoping to mould an impressionable youth to its own policies,[54] regarded him as the 'one remaining hope of a united Yugoslavia after the war.'[55]

Peter himself was an immature, ill-educated playboy with an excessive admiration for all things American. He had escaped from his mother's apron-strings, only to fall into the clutches of Princess Aspasia of Greece and her daughter Alexandra. What was needed, in the Foreign Office view, was education at Cambridge and a spell with the RAF or the Guards to put such nonsense behind him. But nothing came of these ideas. As a close observer of wartime Yugoslavia has remarked:

> King Peter's utter unsuitability for the great role in which the British cast him was rarely allowed to intrude. His devotion either to his studies or his kingly duties might be exiguous; his preference for driving fast motor-cars or carousing with his aides-de-camp might be manifest, and his occasional intrusions into his government's affairs might be unfortunate . . . yet none of this altered what the Foreign Office regarded as self-evident facts: 'that King Peter (or the dynasty) is the only real focus of Yugoslav loyalty', and that Britain had no other means at its disposal with which to promote its interests.[56]

Mihailovic's waning cause did not help King Peter's prospects, and they dipped even further when he proposed to make Princess Alexandra his queen. The Foreign Office realized that this would damage his reputation at home. Eden convinced a recalcitrant Churchill that such a marriage would be a disaster; the Foreign Office meanwhile tried to get

Peter out to Cairo and away from Aspasia. But it took an order from George VI to his nephew not to marry before Peter reluctantly postponed the wedding until 1944.

It was into this already turbid pond that the bombshell of Fitzroy's November report had dropped. This made it clear that King Peter could not be the unifier of Yugoslavia, though he might still be a way of moderating Tito towards British influence. Ralph Stevenson telegraphed to London: 'Maclean's reports of the strength and good organization of Tito's forces have impressed me with the necessity for the king of Yugoslavia establishing contacts of some kind with Tito as soon as possible.'[57]

The tone of Fitzroy's report worried the mandarins, who feared too close links with the Partisans. Sargent and Cadogan reacted with alarm to Fitzroy's statement that it would be fatal to his mission to raise the issue of the king in any form. They decided it would be necessary to 'lean on' Fitzroy, and began by reprimanding Stevenson for falling under his influence before he (Stevenson) had even had time to talk the matter through face to face. Foreign Office fears thus lay behind the mysterious order to Fitzroy to come out alone, without the Yugoslav envoys – a decision that had ended in tragedy. In a way, Tito was more justified than he knew in his feeling that the British had killed Lola Ribar.

What the Foreign Office hoped for from a face-to-face meeting between Fitzroy and Stevenson is unclear, but Stevenson came away from the encounter even more convinced that the Partisans were well on their way to becoming masters of Yugoslavia. Then, on 7 November, the day after Fitzroy had handed him the 'blockbuster', Eden met the Middle East Defence Committee; they decided to try to extirpate the National Liberation Front (EAM) and its military wing ELAS in Greece, but to support Tito. Eden told the meeting of Fitzroy's high regard for Tito. It was decided to try to induce him to see King Peter; if he refused, the British would confine themselves to meeting a strictly military Yugoslav delegation somewhere other than Cairo.[58]

Fitzroy, indeed, was in favour of concentrating exclusively on military matters, and argued that it would be better to impress the Partisans with British commitment in the shape of aid, and thus forge closer links, before getting into the tricky area of political pressure.[59] But the Foreign Office objected to Fitzroy's formulation that Tito's feelings might be hurt. 'If we adopt this attitude at the outset, we shall never get anything we want out of them; and what we most want, at present, is that they should get together with the king.'[60]

Stevenson shared Fitzroy's view and the Foreign Office, irritated, asked him to investigate the possibility of parachuting King Peter into Jajce, persisting in its fantasy that there was a secret fund of monarchism among the Partisans, and urging Fitzroy to return to Tito to initiate a bargaining process over the king: if necessary, he should offer Tito the heads of Peter's Prime Minister, Bosida Puric, and of Mihailovic, as a *quid pro quo* for an accord on Peter.[61]

Fitzroy and Stevenson were obliged to deal with the Foreign Office chimeras as diplomatically as possible, but the gist of their communications indicates clearly their feeling that the FO was in thrall to cant and humbug: 'The suggestion that the Partisans could improve their chances and the position of the country by adopting the king would be greeted with the utmost derision, and any attempt on our part to use pressure or bribes would meet with a flat refusal.'[62] The military chiefs took Fitzroy's side, on the grounds that a political wrangle over the king would weaken the Partisans' resolve to fight, but this was rejected as 'appeasement' by the mandarins[63] – somewhat extraordinarily, given the Foreign Office attitude towards dictators in the 1930s.

Fitzroy had the advantage of Churchill's sympathetic ear. On 8 December at 10 a.m. the Prime Minister was in conclave with Fitzroy and Deakin, who recalls that Stevenson and Ralph Morton, an aide, were also there for part of the time.[64] That night Yugoslavia was again the talking point at a grand dinner in Cairo hosted by Churchill. Smuts, Eden, Cadogan and Lord Killearn (the Ambassador, the former Sir Miles Lampson) represented the men of power, while the younger generation fielded a team consisting of Fitzroy, Randolph Churchill, Julian Amery, George Jellicoe, and Smuts's son, young Jan Christiaan. As a British officer serving with the Resistance in the Balkans (mainly Albania), Julian Amery had a special interest in hearing about Fitzroy's experiences. 'I went to see Fitzroy Maclean next day. He did not ask me to join his mission and I did not press him to do so. I had always advocated maintaining contact with Tito and sending him supplies. But I did not want to become involved in breaking Mihailovic, and this had become Fitzroy's main objective.'[65]

December 10 saw Churchill again grappling with Yugoslavia. Present at a working lunch were Fitzroy, Deakin, and General Gubbins.[66] Deakin comments: 'This was the second of the two meetings when Fitzroy and I are supposed to have "persuaded" Churchill finally to switch to the Partisans. But is it conceivable that there is no record *anywhere* that a decision was taken to abandon Mihailovic? In fact, Churchill told me after the war that these meetings merely confirmed what he already knew from Ultra.'[67]

The Foreign Office had finally got King Peter out to Cairo, the monarch in some dudgeon because he had not been told about the missions of Deakin and Fitzroy. Now came a further blow to his *amour-propre*: there was a Partisan delegation in Cairo, of which he knew nothing. His Prime Minister, Puric, questioned Stevenson, who in turn asked whether the government-in-exile would have consented to meet the delegation if they had known of it. Yes, answered Puric, then spoiled his case by adding, '– provided they accept us as the legitimate government'. The waves King Peter made finally secured him an interview with Churchill, from which Puric was excluded; the only other person present was Stevenson. This meeting took place on 10 December after the Prime Minister's working lunch with Fitzroy and Deakin. Churchill said he thought the king should return to Yugoslavia in about six months, but stressed that there was to be no more aid for Mihailovic because of his collaboration with the Germans. He ended by suggesting that the king see Deakin and Maclean.[68]

Peter met Deakin, and was cast down by his fervent advocacy of the Partisans. Would he fare any better with Fitzroy?

> Some time later I was introduced to Fitzroy Maclean by Stevenson, and my conversation with him followed much the same lines as the ones with Deakin. He struck me as being extremely self-confident and forceful – quite a different personality from Deakin – and put forward his point of view with irresistible force and conviction. He spoke enthusiastically of Tito, saying that he was a good man and a fine fighter. As he spoke our language he had been able to gain a fair insight into the movements. He admitted that Tito was a Communist, but preferred to support him rather than Mihailovic, whom he advised me to dismiss from office. Maclean impressed me as being a strong, silent man. He was red-headed, very tall and good-looking – a typical Scot.[69]

Fitzroy's next job in Cairo was to ginger up military preparations to defend the Dalmatian islands, or at least Vis, the nearest to Italy. To his excellent contacts 'Jumbo' Wilson and Air Marshal Sholto Douglas he now added Admiral Willis. With the expansion of his mission he also needed fresh personnel and, as always, Peter Stirling's chaotic flat proved the best recruiting centre. Without David Stirling it was not quite the hive of activity it had been, but Mo was still there to inspire confidence. 'Bugadier very fine fellow. One day he catchit scissors', was his comment on Fitzroy – a reference to the crossed swords of a Major-General.[70] At the Stirling flat Fitzroy recruited Andrew Maxwell of the Scots Guards (a cousin of the Stirlings and a veteran of the final SAS raid on Benghazi) and John Clarke, a former Adjutant of the 2nd Scots Guards, old Etonian and regular soldier. Clarke recalls the circumstances of his joining Fitzroy's mission. 'I was . . . told that Fitzroy had asked for me. I was a major at the time, a brand new staffer. I agreed to go after talking to Fitzroy in the Stirling flat. I was told I had to parachute, but didn't go on a paratrooper course. I think it was David Sutherland who told me it was a waste of time, so I learned to parachute by falling off the back of the sofa in David Stirling's flat.'[71]

Fitzroy had time for a little Christmas socializing before returning to

Italy at Churchill's urgent insistence.[72] By this time he had also agreed to have Randolph Churchill on the Yugoslav mission, but took care to leave him behind when he flew to Bari.[73] His circumspection was justified: Randolph joined him in Bari anyway, and at a dinner party given by Air Vice-Marshal William Elliott, commander of 'Balkan Air Force' and thus a man crucial to the success of the Maclean mission, Randolph made an exhibition of himself, insulted the other star guest, and ended by passing out drunk.

But there were more serious things for Fitzroy to attend to in Bari. He learned that the enemy was on the offensive in Yugoslavia and had taken Glamoc and Livno. Of the islands, only Vis remained wholly in Allied hands. As it was clearly going to be the offshore hub of British operations, Fitzroy and Velebit crossed the Adriatic by motor torpedo boat to investigate. They made a stopover at Korcula, which it was plain the Germans would overrun in a matter of days. At Vis they linked up with Vivian Street and found the RAF excited by the prospect of being able to build a first-class airfield. Velebit was quick to appreciate the potential advantage for the Partisans, since Allied fighters would then have the range to cover the whole of Yugoslavia.

It was vital to hold Vis against German attack, but this would require a garrison of two brigades. The Partisans agreed to supply one brigade, but because of demands on troops for the Italian campaign, Fitzroy could not immediately see where the Allied brigade was going to come from. Serendipity helped him. On New Year's Eve he went with Randolph Churchill to a party given by two namesake brothers, Jack and Tom Churchill, who headed the Commando Brigade. In conversation with these Churchills Fitzroy spoke of possible commando operations on the Dalmatian islands, only to find the brothers' minds already working along similar lines.[74] Whether the commandos could actually be based on Vis long-term was, however, a matter for the Prime Minister and his military advisers. As Fitzroy lobbied higher up the military echelons, he found a sympathetic listener in General Wilson's Chief of Staff, General John Harding. Harding was about to leave with General Alexander for Marrakesh, where Churchill was recovering from an attack of pneumonia. He arranged a lift for Fitzroy in the same plane and Fitzroy, sensing that Randolph might at last be useful, took him too.

The plane made a 24-hour stopover in Algiers, and Randolph took the opportunity to call on a friend. Lady Diana Cooper (her husband was British representative with De Gaulle and the Free French, and became the British Ambassador in Paris after the Liberation) was napping in Harold Macmillan's flat when she heard 'Randolph's clarion call. He had just arrived with Brigadier Fitzroy Maclean, the Partisan hero.'[75] Lady Diana bent their ears with tales of her wartime privations:

she was obliged to live in some austerity in a house with no kitchen and
no hot water; she told them how she had to sleep in her fur coat, shaking
it out vigorously to wear in the evening.

Fitzroy and Randolph flew on over the Atlas Mountains to Marrakesh
in Alexander's private plane. Mark Chapman-Walker was at the aerodrome to meet them, and told Fitzroy in the car on the way to Churchill's villa that General Wilson had just been promoted to Supreme
Allied Commander, Mediterranean to succeed Eisenhower, who had
gone to London to co-ordinate the Overlord invasion. They found
Churchill dressed in a bright blue boiler suit; he was installed in the
Villa Taylor, an ersatz Moroccan palace complete with 'paradise garden'. Fitzroy deliberately kept as far away from the formal conference
as possible: the top brass were planning the Anzio landing, and 'in a
few days' time I was due to be dropped back into an enemy-occupied
country, where the possibility of being taken prisoner could never be
excluded, and, with the Gestapo's methods of interrogation . . . it was
inadvisable . . . to know more about the future conduct of the war than
was absolutely necessary.'[76]

After the conference Fitzroy was able to discuss Yugoslav affairs with
the Prime Minister. Now, if ever, was Fitzroy's political nous underlined: Randolph was produced, like the proverbial rabbit from the
conjuror's hat, to stiffen his father's resolve against the pleas of Eden
and the Foreign Office that Churchill should soften the tone of his
communication to Tito, and refrain from offering him Mihailovic's
head on a platter. Randolph convinced his father that Deakin,
Stevenson and Fitzroy were right to reject the Foreign Office demand
for a *quid pro quo*: Mihailovic was a millstone round King Peter's neck,
and it was clear that the British would make no real progress with Tito
until the Cetniks were ditched. As a sop to Eden, Churchill did not
promise to withdraw British Liaison Officers from Mihailovic, but
simply denied him further supplies. Feeling that Tito, his back to the
wall after the recent German offensive, needed particular encouragement, Churchill wrote him a personal letter to assure him that the sole
Allied aim in Yugoslavia was to defeat the fascists; it was not to dictate
the future shape of Yugoslav politics. The Allies were giving no further
aid to Mihailovic, and hoped that the Royal Yugoslav government
would soon dismiss him. On the other hand, it would be unchivalrous of
the British to cut King Peter adrift. Churchill ended his letter by hoping
that Stalin's mission to Yugoslavia would work amicably with the
Anglo-American mission, and added: 'Brigadier Maclean is also a
friend of mine and a colleague in the House of Commons. With him at
your headquarters will be serving my son, Major Randolph Churchill,
who is also a Member of Parliament.'[77] Fitzroy was ordered to deliver
this letter in person. Churchill sent a copy to Roosevelt on 18 January,

with a brief note: 'I hope you liked my letter to Tito. Maclean and Randolph hope to jump with it tomorrow.'[78]

On 10 January 1944 Fitzroy and Randolph flew back to Bari. Ten days later they set out for the landing strip at Bosanski Petrovac in Bosnia, where Tito had relocated after the flight from Jajce. They were again in a Dakota, escorted by a dozen Thunderbolts. It was a fine clear morning, with a sparkling Adriatic beneath them but, once more, over Yugoslavia they ran into thick cloud formations. They approached the drop zone, the exit doors were opened. Fitzroy prepared to launch first into space, followed by Randolph, Sergeant Duncan, Slim Farish and two new signallers in a 'stick'. As the dispatcher told him to get into position, Fitzroy looked down and could see a village with signal fires and several figures scurrying about. Able as he was to make out such detail, Fitzroy became concerned that they were at too low an altitude for a jump. He was right. The jump was short and hard. He landed with 'considerably more force than was comfortable'. The others also crashed down with bone-shattering force within a few yards of each other; they were lucky not to be injured. It was scarcely an auspicious return.

11

Fitzroy in the Heather
JANUARY–APRIL 1944

THE three months in Bosnia from January to April 1944 were Fitzroy's longest continuous experience of Partisan life. In addition to the usual hardships, the members of Fitzroy's mission had to put up with sexual frustration, for an ascetic code obtained among the hardy Yugoslav mountain fighters. John Henniker remembers: 'We had to live a chaste life of monastic rectitude. I never slept with a girl while I was with the Partisans. It was a tough, rigorous, monkish life.' Fitzroy adds: 'It was not wise to go trysting with Partisan girls. They used to shoot any male Partisan found in bed with a female Partisan. But Tito had a mistress, and the code was not as austere in fact as in theory. One of the girls in the cave had a father who was Minister of the Interior in the Royal Yugoslav government, but she became Communist. Though very attractive she was not generous with her favours.' John Clarke inclines to Fitzroy's view. 'I am dubious about whether anyone was actually shot for sleeping with Partisan women, but it could have been the case – I made a point of keeping well away from any executions. I personally only saw one lot of German prisoners shot – at least I heard it, I didn't want to see it.'

Fitzroy came to know Tito well at this time. He thought him a great man, and still does. He also sees similarities between him and his hero Prince Charlie, and between the Yugoslav war and the 1745 Jacobite rising.

> I think Tito was probably the greatest guerrilla/resistance fighter of all time. More importantly, in 1948 he was prepared to defy Moscow, get away with it and survive. Without much exaggeration, what is happening today in the USSR and Eastern Europe was made possible by Tito, as he made the first crack in the monolith.
>
> Since 1745 there have been few real conflicts of loyalty in Britain. Reading the history of Yugoslavia, I realize how lucky we are. People nowadays who glibly talk about the British 'creating' Tito have no idea of the complexity of

events in the 1940s, of the ferocious passions, the bloodshed and the chaos. Part of Tito's greatness was imposing order on all this. But he had many other qualities. He had a natural gift for political and military leadership, a strong personality and, like David Stirling – and this is the most important thing in leadership – the ability to convince people that the impossible is possible. When you're embarking on a crazy enterprise, the people with you have to believe you can carry it off.

As the mission members picked themselves up after their drop and dusted themselves down, the inevitable Partisan guard of honour made its appearance. The Partisans provided a splendid meal, explaining that the one they had prepared the night before had been even better but when the plane did not appear they had eaten it themselves.

Towards dusk Fitzroy set off on horseback through falling snow to find Tito, accompanied by Slavko Rodic, a young Partisan commander. It was past midnight when they found Tito's secret hide-out, a series of makeshift huts deep in the woods and constructed from the surrounding trees. The Marshal was waiting up for them. Fitzroy handed over Churchill's letter, written on Downing Street paper and complete with a signed photograph. Fitzroy watched Tito's spontaneous delight as he read the letter, and his particular pleasure at Churchill sending his son out. This was a giant step for Tito: he was on a friendly footing with one of the Big Three. Fitzroy assured Tito that henceforth he would get all he needed from air drops. They spoke of the military situation and of converting Vis into an impregnable redoubt; Tito thought it would a miracle if the Allies could keep it as a base, surrounded as it now was by German-occupied islands.

It was almost dawn before Fitzroy left. He followed a soldier through the snow to the 'British' hut, where he woke up Gordon Alston and introduced himself to Hilary King. A moustachioed Partisan appeared and announced that he was to be Fitzroy's cook, batman and bodyguard. Scarcely taking this in, an exhausted Fitzroy filled with straw the canvas bag that had contained Churchill's letter and, using it as a pillow, was soon fast asleep.

After an uneventful week, Tito moved his headquarters to Drvar; Fitzroy accompanied the Marshal in the short journey on the 'Partisan express', which had survived the Sixth Offensive. A few days later Randolph Churchill, Slim Farish and Duncan joined them there. John Clarke was dropped in a few weeks later, and the villagers soon took the strange foreigners to their hearts. Tito established his headquarters in a cave 60 feet up a rock face on the far side of the valley, with a splendid view of the town; at the back of the cave was a roaring waterfall. Life there 'partook of the atmosphere of the "Robbers' Cave" in Act 2 of a pantomime',[1] masking extreme efficiency in administration and superbly confident staff work. Some of the Partisans were for trying to convert Drvar into an unassailable fortress, but Fitzroy cautioned Tito that in the short term the Allies would not be able to supply the hardware to make this plan practicable.

By February 1944 the German Sixth Offensive had spent itself; Tito went over to the attack. The Partisans were able to help the Italian campaign considerably by timing their attacks to coincide with the offensives there, thus tying down twenty divisions. With Vivian Street absent in Italy, Fitzroy made Peter Moore, just returned from Slovenia, his second-in-command. A request came in from General Alexander in Italy that the Stampetov bridge on the Trieste–Ljubljana railway be blown up. After consultations with Tito, it was decided that Moore and the Partisans should make this a joint operation. It was a complete success: Moore and the Partisans showered superlatives on each other, and Moore received a bar to his DSO.

The pace of aerial drops, usually on Bosanski Petrovac but sometimes direct on Drvar, now accelerated, but often bad weather halted them and supplies on the ground would run short. Fitzroy comments ruefully: 'Nor were these lean phases easy to explain to the Partisans, to whom meteorological conditions, often brilliantly fine locally when they were altogether impossible in Italy, meant nothing, and who were only too ready to put the whole thing down to Capitalist Intrigue.'[2]

But in compensation there was increasing evidence of Allied mastery of the skies. Sometimes RAF and USAAF air superiority was such that German bombers raiding the Partisans would suddenly be obliged to break off their attacks when a silver armada of Fortresses, Liberators and Lightnings appeared overhead. Given direct radio contact with Italy, it was possible to call up air support for beleaguered Partisan outposts and so save them from German incursions. A further stage in aerial supremacy was reached when John Selby, who had remained with the Partisans when Fitzroy brought the envoys out at the beginning of December, went out to train handpicked Partisans as a fighter squadron in North Africa.

In his spare moments Fitzroy worked at his Serbo-Croat, but did not find it easy.[3] John Henniker comments: 'In a way it's been a snag that Fitzroy never really mastered Serbo-Croat. I was better than Fitzroy at Serbo-Croat then. I don't think he's a brilliant natural linguist, but he's a good painstaking one. Besides, he didn't really have the time to learn Serbo-Croat as he was out so much, in Bari, Cairo and London.'[4] Mike Parker adds an amusing reminiscence. 'I often wondered how well Fitzroy spoke Serbo-Croat. He was all right in conversation. But I remember once, in Drvar, Fitzroy made a speech and at the end everyone clapped. I turned to Velebit and said, "What did he say?" Velebit said, "I don't know. Perhaps he was speaking patrician Serbo-Croat!." '[5]

These three months Fitzroy spent with the Partisans enable us to appraise him as a leader of men, for a dozen or so of the Anglo-American mission were in hourly touch with the brigadier in all his moods. The two immediately under him, Vivian Street and Peter Moore, saw least of him, having the not entirely welcome task of going out among the local Partisan commanders to preach the gospel according to the Geneva Convention. In this grim war of rape, murder and atrocity neither side often took prisoners, but it was felt that an Anglo-American mission must be a standard-bearer for civilized values and insist on humane behaviour. Vivian Street's widow Annette recalls: 'Vivian used to get fed up with the Partisans, their bickering, their routine brutality. To a point he could sympathize with the Russian viewpoint, that these were simply benighted barbarians.'[6] Peter Moore concurs: 'I was given the unsavoury job of trying to browbeat the Partisans into not shooting prisoners. The Partisans always regarded such representations as arrant interference.'[7] Moore and Street were able to breast the waves of Partisan brutality without serious damage, but the darkly pessimistic tone of Slim Farish's second report, dated 28 June 1944, so at variance with his optimistic memorandum of the previous 29 October 1943, suggests a man who had seen one atrocity too many.[8]

Fitzroy also rarely came into contact with the 'functional' officers, such as those in charge of supply, but when he did his interventions were usually to the point. Mike Parker remembers: 'My job was to work with the Yugoslav "Intendant". They didn't want rifles and ammunition as much as boots. "Boots for Bosnia" was the name of one of the mission's schemes. Once they've got footwear, you can bring in more advanced stuff. Fitzroy got round the Partisan brigades. He appreciated that the best manure is the farmer's boot.'[9] John Clarke has this to say: 'Fitzroy was very imaginative, very canny. He was born canny. Also, his Foreign Office training was evident throughout, not just in his outlook on life but in his prose and way of sending telegrams. I'd never encountered this before even in Sandhurst. There was a whole new Foreign Office jargon which I picked up. As far as the operation in Yugoslavia was concerned, his strongest point was choosing people and getting the best from them. He was a very demanding chap, sometimes to the point of unreasonableness. But he never bore grudges and respected one if one stood one's ground.'[10]

Fitzroy was a stickler for correct procedures but his suspicion of SOE sometimes made him react testily in the matter of radio traffic. This is his own version. 'Knowing about SOE signals, I made arrangements with Menzies [head of SIS], who was quite a friend of mine, to have separate signals with him direct, through Alston. Later it became clear my signals were not reaching Winston, so I sent duplicates through the

SIS link and said, ''You don't seem to have received following signals''. SOE went in for a lot of suppressing of signals.''[11] His signals officer, Hilary King, tells a different story.

> Fitzroy was convinced that SOE would sabotage his signals. He got this from David Wallace, who described his experiences in Greece. Wallace wrote three long reports, handed them to an SOE radio operator, then got on a plane and was enraged to find his reports were not on the desk of his superior. This was at a time when traffic was a week in arrears on non-essential messages. But Fitzroy accepted the story uncritically. Fitzroy's a wonderful man and a great leader but he knew nothing about signals. His insistence on giving SOE a wide berth caused us any amount of headache. A number of technical reasons made it fairly easy to signal from Yugoslavia to Cairo, less easy to Bari, but much much more difficult between one valley and another within Yugoslavia. For a start, different wave lengths had to be used. Fitzroy refused to have signals between missions inside Yugoslavia routed through Cairo or Bari for fear of SOE interception. We then had to use this system for communicating internally which is much less secure and moreover enabled the Germans to locate us through radio direction-finders. It was also enormously difficult technically and used up a huge number of man hours. This elaborate system collapsed like a house of cards after the attack on Drvar in May 1944, as we had to bury crystals, cipher pads, et cetera. We would have done much better transmitting our messages to other missions via Cairo or Bari, the usual SOE system. I think Fitzroy was making difficulties, and we had to accept the SOE system after the Drvar attack anyway.[12]

As for the twin-track system for *external* signals, this also seems to have been unnecessary; Elisabeth Barker has discovered that 'Maclean's reports seem to have got through without any difficulty, although normally passing through SOE channels.'[13] Mark Wheeler comments: 'The supreme irony is that both Maclean's fears about SOE interception *and* the Lees–Martin theories that information favourable to Mihailovic was being suppressed by SOE Cairo are shown to be groundless when the technicalities of signals are taken into account.'[14] Although Fitzroy's precautions seem to have been excessive, and at times almost paranoid, one can well understand why, after his bruising encounters with Glenconner and Keble, he acted as he did. His morbid suspicion of SOE is almost certainly the explanation for the tetchy tone of some of Fitzroy's signals, such as this one to Mission Liaison in Italy,

> . . . for General Stawell. I feel bound to take up with you personally the points raised in your 496 Para 1 . . . You will doubtless agree that blame does not rest with this mission . . . and that my 393 was not misleading as suggested in your 489 which I note was repeated to PM. Meanwhile please confirm correct version of my 390 and ??? has in fact been passed to PM . . . You will understand these continued muddles and delays are most disturbing.[15]

In his memoirs Lindsay Rogers, a surgeon in the New Zealand RAMC who had commanded a field ambulance in the Western Desert, presents an interestingly mixed picture of Fitzroy at this time. Rogers jumped the gun by setting out overland for Bosnia from the coast before going through channels and clearing things properly with Fitzroy – behaviour which in normal circumstances would have got a very frosty response. Rogers describes his first meeting with Fitzroy as follows:

> I saw two British officers walking in the snow, both of them with walking-sticks. When they drew abreast, I perceived that one had red tabs on his shoulder. I decided that this must be Brigadier Maclean. I saluted awkwardly, pulled the horse up and introduced myself.
>
> 'My name is Rogers from Croatia,' I said.
>
> 'Oh, you're Rogers,' he replied. 'You came in rather irregularly, you know. However, go up to my headquarters, you'll find it in a peasant's house on the south side of town, and make yourself comfortable till we meet again at dinner.'
>
> . . . I interviewed the brigadier that night, fully expecting to be reprimanded for my more or less unorthodox entry into the country, but he treated me kindly and the episode was forgotten. I asked him why Tito had asked me to come, but he didn't know.[16]

'Doc' Rogers soon acquired a considerable reputation with the Partisans. He visited all their theatres of war, organized hospitals, built up standards of hygiene to levels never dreamed of before, and evacuated the worst casualties to Italy. But Rogers always found Fitzroy aloof. He noted that Fitzroy never breakfasted in the mess, and that dinner was a rather restrained and dull affair, very different from the rough-and-tumble of a medical mess where rules counted for little and rank for less.

One can interpret the Fitzroy of these months as stiff or preoccupied, prima donna or perfectionist, martinet or complete professional, according to one's point of view. But there were no two views about his ability to handle Tito. The general consensus seems to be that Tito *liked* Bill Deakin better, perhaps because Deakin was more to the left politically in those days than Fitzroy, perhaps because they had been wounded by the same shell at Durmitor, possibly even because Deakin deferred to him more. But he respected Fitzroy immensely, and knew that he was the conduit to Churchill and top decision-making. Only later did Fitzroy mellow and establish good *personal* relations with Tito. John Henniker recalls: 'When he first arrived he was rather like a schoolmaster come to see what the new boy was like.'[17] Clarke sees the basis of the relationship as *realpolitik*: 'Tito was a very intelligent man and he realized Fitzroy's value. He was a bandit, but no more so than any other Balkan leader, whether guerrilla or king. He was then a dyed-in-the-wool Stalinist. Fitzroy made a great insurance policy for Tito. In hunting parlance, he provided a good "heel-line" to Churchill. Tito probably thought that if he made a mistake on the eastern side, he could swing to the West, knowing of their dislike for Communism.'[18] But Mike Parker thought the 'interpersonal chemistry' was right, too. 'Fitzroy was very good with Tito, having been in Russia and understanding the Slav mentality. Tito was a real autocrat but Fitzroy took no notice. It was fortunate that the chemistry worked.'[19]

Nor can there be any doubt that Fitzroy was instrumental in building up a strong rapport between Tito and Churchill even before the two leaders met. A long correspondence via the mission's wireless link followed the receipt of the warm letter Fitzroy brought in. Yugoslavia became one of Churchill's pet projects. In February he cabled Tito to tell him of his abiding interest in the guerrilla war: 'I wish I could come myself, but I am too old and heavy to jump out on a parachute.'[20] Tito responded by telling Fitzroy that Yugoslavia was bound to remain dependent on the Allies after the war, and in return for the aid he had received so far he would gladly offer Britain economic and trading concessions.[21] This part of Fitzroy's relationship with Tito eventually became so cordial that the Marshal one day suggested that, as he was tired, Fitzroy might like to compose a suitable reply to Churchill in response to the latest message. 'Don't worry,' said Fitzroy, 'I'm used to doing that already.' 'And vice versa, no doubt,' Tito added. 'Yes', said Fitzroy, and both laughed heartily.[22]

Relations with the Partisans were generally excellent, the shooting of prisoners aside, but sometimes the British Liaison Officers found the Balkan taste for expedient exaggeration wearisome. When the toll of atrocities eventually wore Slim Farish down, he remarked pessimistically: 'They love intrigue and gossip and are the most profound liars I have ever met.'[23] Parker agreed. 'Fitzroy understood the Slav propensity to embellish but it took the rest of us a long time to appreciate that they were wild exaggerators. Using a single epithet is no good with them; only after seven adjectives do they start to take notice. "A terrific battle with the Cetniks" usually meant a few bullet-holes and a single corpse.'[24]

Also tiresome was the Partisans' reluctance to take direction. 'We know all that' became a kind of litany. Mike Parker tells a typical story of the Partisans' cavalier attitude when some explosives were dropped in.

> After one drop the Partisans carried some 'sticky bombs' – glass containers with nitroglycerine – inside. Two or three had broken and the nitro was dripping all over the place. The Partisans meanwhile were smoking. I bolted from the hut. Admittedly, Cairo has to take some share of the stupidity. But the Partisans threw sticks of gelignite into rivers and stunned fish, which helped

when we were hungry. Later on Cairo packed well and sent what we asked for, but in the beginning there were many cock-ups. SOE sent supplies we didn't want – exploding turds and nonsense like that.[25]

Fitzroy also noticed that the Partisans were careless and insouciant with new weapons and explosives and apt to brush their instructors aside. Yet they learned remarkably quickly and soon adapted the big Fiat mortars to guerrilla warfare. But always there was a problem with Partisan impetuousness. Among supplies dropped from Cairo were rations of dehydrated food, which swelled to several times its original size when water was added; these had proved a particularly successful addition to the mission's diet. Fitzroy was eager to share this benefit with the Partisans and signalled for further supplies to be dropped.

On their arrival, we handed them over to the Quartermaster's department, being careful to add full instructions for their use. But these they brushed aside lightheartedly. 'We know all about that', they said, and started to distribute the sacks to various neighbouring units. We had our doubts, but thought it better not to voice them.

It was only afterwards that we heard what had happened. The dehydrated food had not been soaked, but gulped down as it was. This was dry work, or so the Partisans thought, and so they washed it down with copious draughts of water from the neighbouring brook. Then, with disconcerting suddenness, the stuff began to swell inside them until it had reached several times its original dimensions. Their ensuing discomfort was considerable, though not so acute as that of another Partisan, who at about this time ate a stick of plastic high-explosive, mashing it up with milk, under the impression that it was some kind of maize porridge.[26]

In February 1944 the long-awaited Soviet mission to the Partisans finally arrived. Its leader was the Red Army's General Korneyev, who had lost a foot at the battle of Stalingrad. He landed at Bari airsick – scarcely a happy portent. Since the Russians had no air bases within range of Yugoslavia, the task of getting them into the country fell to the RAF. It was Deakin's job to arrange the airlift of the Soviet mission into Yugoslavia, but when the Germans overran the Glamoc airstrip the operation was naturally delayed. The Soviet refusal to parachute in caused further delay: ostensibly this was either because Korneyev was minus a foot, or because parachuting was 'undignified', but following the mysterious death of Sikorski, paranoia about the British had become an epidemic. Both Deakin and the Partisans tried hard to get the general in by light plane, but incessant snowfalls made it impossible to clear a landing strip near Drvar. Korneyev insinuated that the British were dissembling and playing some perfidious game of their own. He took his frustration out on Deakin (now a colonel), treating

him with the contempt for lower ranks which was unhappily typical of
Red Army comrades. Relations with Deakin continued cool, no matter
how much he tried to reassure the Russians.[27]

Eventually the RAF borrowed two Horsa gliders from Airborne
Forces, and the convoy set out on the first fine day. Two Dakotas hauled
the gliders, and there was a large fighter escort. Excitedly the Partisans
gathered on a hilltop to watch the landing. Fitzroy was there in full
battle dress and scarlet tabs.[28] The gliders were cut adrift and circled
down to earth under the guidance of the very best pilots the RAF could
provide, who now perforce temporarily joined the Maclean mission.
The gliders turned out to contain not just Russians but cartons and
cartons of vodka and caviare which, when shared out with the British
mission, made a welcome relief from austerity.

Korneyev brought his second-in-command, Major-General
Gorshkov, an expert on Partisan warfare, and 'a quantity of colonels,
including at least one obvious representative of the NKVD.'[29] The
Russians had obviously been instructed to be on their best behaviour
with their British allies, but towards the Partisans they were arrogant;
Gorshkov made it clear that his Russian troopers were superior to the
local 'peasants'.

It was not just the vodka and caviare which announced that the
Soviets had no intention of 'roughing it'; that was made clear also by
their gaudy uniforms with gold epaulettes and tight shiny boots. At first
the Partisans ignored these signs, since they were suffused with pro-
Soviet feeling and their own propaganda had led them to believe that
Russians were bigger, braver and handsomer than decadent westerners. But the Partisans were proud people with their own heroes, and
very conscious of their status as anti-fascist fighters. They were therefore put out when almost the first question from Korneyev's aide concerned the whereabouts of the general's lavatory. 'But the British don't
have a lavatory – the British general [Fitzroy] goes behind the nearest
tree.' 'The Soviet general must have a lavatory.' The Partisans shrugged, dug a very deep hole, erected a wooden hutch over it, whitewashed
it, and left all the excavated earth in a mound. The consequence was
almost predictable. The first German plane to spot this whitened oddity
flew in low, strafed it, and finally bombed it.[30]

Tito very quickly put Korneyev in his place. He had been annoyed by
the presentation of a shiny, inscribed tommy-gun when he felt that a
thousand workaday sub-machine-guns would have been preferable
– certainly a higher priority than vodka and caviare. But he had
ample chance to show his displeasure. It was a hardship for the lame
Russian to limp up the steep winding path to Tito's cave where the
weekly conference with his allies was held; worse still, Tito's wolfhound
Tigger had taken an instant dislike to the general and always tried to

bite him. Tito would stand at the entrance to his cave laughing at this spectacle. 'An anti-Russian dog!' he chortled.[31]

Nor did the pressure relax once Korneyev was inside the cave. Tito would ask Fitzroy what were the Anglo-American plans for the next week. Fitzroy would rattle out the statistics of boots, food and ammunition to be dropped.

> Tito would say, 'Thank you very much, Mr General' – he called us both Mr General, not Comrade General, as a snub to Korneyev. Then he would turn to Korneyev. 'Now, Mr General, what can you do?' Korneyev would say something like this: 'Much as we admire your gallant struggle against the fascist aggressor we cannot do much at present because we are not within range and . . .' At which point Tito would interrupt and say, 'You mean you can't do anything?' Since this happened once a week I remember thinking, This is bound to mean trouble sooner or later.[32]

In a confidential despatch to Churchill Fitzroy hinted that Tito seemed to go out of his way to put the Russians at a disadvantage *vis-a-vis* their British colleagues:

> Marshal Tito has, in his reception of the newly arrived Soviet Mission, gone out of his way to emphasize that their status here is to be exactly the same as that of my Mission. Reconstruction and rehabilitation are urgent problems and the Partisans cannot but realise that their country is bound to depend on Great Britain and America not only for material support during the war, but for relief and the means of prosperity after the war . . . there can be no doubt that they have realised the advantages of maintaining good relations with other Great Powers beside the Soviet Union.[33]

Korneyev was baffled by Tito's coolness and seemed at sea also about the precise status of his mission. With his usual cynicism, Stalin had sent to Yugoslavia a man of whom he had no opinion. 'The poor man is not stupid, but he is a drunkard, and an incurable drunkard',[34] he remarked scathingly. Korneyev was delighted that Fitzroy could speak Russian and often used to call on him for chats. He confided that after Stalingrad he was all set for a comfortable billet as defence attaché in Washington when he was suddenly ordered to Yugoslavia instead. 'I don't know what I've done to deserve to be posted to this awful country with all these horrible Balkan peasants.' he complained. 'Who are these Partisans, anyway?. Do I command them, or do you?' Fitzroy replied that he certainly did not, but that Korneyev could try if he liked and see how he got on.[35]

If the Soviet Mission turned out to be something of a paper tiger, Donovan's Americans were a continuing problem, for their loyalties were divided between Fitzroy and their masters in Washington. Fitzroy was determined to have no more Huots, but Donovan was a tough opponent. In February 1944 he flew to London for talks with Churchill and Eden. The talks were stormy, and Donovan talked toughly to Eden about jeopardizing the Anglo-US alliance. Churchill insisted he must have complete freedom of action in Yugoslavia, but Donovan complained to Roosevelt that though the original OSS/SOE operation in that country had been a purely liaison mission, yet Maclean had been given political tasks while OSS had not; it followed that the agreement had been broken. A compromise was reached whereby an independent US intelligence-gathering mission to Yugoslavia would be permitted, provided it did not exercise political or military roles that would vitiate or interfere with the Maclean mission. The end result was that Donovan flooded the headquarters of both Tito and Mihailovic with his agents. Later, in mid-1944, when Fitzroy was out of Yugoslavia, Colonel Ellery Huntingdon brought 26 officers and 33 men with him to Vis, then Tito's temporary base.[36]

US policy in south-east Europe in the Second World War is still unclear. The Balkans were peripheral to US interests, and for that reason Donovan could dream of a grand role there. Normally US policy seems to have taken the form of reaction to the British initiatives, and there was a basic objection to bankrolling British initiatives. The only Eastern European country that really interested Roosevelt was Poland. Poland would be the test of whether the alliance with the Russians could be sustained in peacetime; more immediately, there were three and a half million Polish-American voters. On Yugoslavia Roosevelt merely had prejudices: Yugoslavia had been put together by a committee, and it would be better if Serbia and Croatia went their separate ways.

Early in 1944 Roosevelt proposed to Churchill that Donovan be made Allied supremo in charge of guerrilla initiatives in both Greece and Yugoslavia. However, Yugoslavia and Greece were perceived in London as important to Britain because they flanked the line of communications to the Suez Canal and India. An American 'supremo' would not be welcome, least of all an Irish-American anti-colonialist like Donovan. It was precisely to secure the area as a British appanage that Churchill had sent so many British Liaison Officers into the Balkans. He assured Roosevelt that the troubles in Greece were almost over; he added that Donovan's putative 'guerrilla headquarters' would prove cumbersome, since its director would need to move rapidly from one guerrilla front to another.

However, none of this constrained Donovan, and what had been annoying rivalry with the British turned into outright opposition. In January 1944 Donovan rejected a British request that all American officers destined for Yugoslavia should be sent forthwith to Tito in Bosnia.[37] Instead, he got Roosevelt's approval for sending new intelligence officers to Mihailovic.[38] These appear to have had two main aims: to secure the evacuation of American pilots shot down over Serbia; and to learn German intentions in the Balkans. Accordingly, Marine Corps Captain W.R. Mansfield arrived at Cetnik head-quarters in March 1944. Donovan's cover story was that he intended to smuggle agents into Germany and Austria. Mansfield transmitted to Donovan's staff at Bari a personal letter from Mihailovic to Eisenhower. Eisenhower, however, refused to take the bait; he told Donovan that OSS should comb the letter for any useful intelligence but that he would not be replying.[39]

Donovan and his chief supporter in Washington, Robert Murphy, State Department representative for Mediterranean affairs, also hoped to influence future events in Yugoslavia. By 1944 there was a distinct anti-Tito mood in Washington: Secretary of State Cordell Hull was complaining that the British had given Tito a free hand in Yugoslavia, both militarily and diplomatically.[40] Even so, Donovan and his sup-porters were unable to influence Roosevelt and General Marshal to put pressure on the British to change their Balkan policies, and in August 1944 the Americans actually began swimming against the flow by send-ing a new high-level mission to Mihailovic under Colonel Robert MacDowell.[41] But initiatives like this had the unfortunate and unintended consequence of making Mihailovic think that the Ameri-cans would ultimately save his bacon. The problem was that, at bottom, American decision-makers of the time were not interested in whether the Russians overran Eastern Europe. Their main target was the British Empire, which they were determined to prevent from emerging stronger than ever after the war. There was always in American plans for the post-war world a concealed economic agenda, and it was no accident that the important figures of the US corporate structure were also the important foreign policy decision-makers. It is not an exaggeration to say that corporate America was running the war – in the shape of the 'six wise men' and figures like Donovan and the financier John J. McCloy.

Such nuances were lost on Tito. He saw the Americans giving com-fort to his enemy, and made vigorous protests to Fitzroy.[42] By the end of the summer of 1944 OSS activities were blatantly anti-Partisan, and at his trial in 1946 Mihailovic testified that the Americans were not inter-ested in his fighting the Germans but preferred him to remain quietly in the hills.[43] The historian Matteo Milazzo comments: 'There is reason to believe that MacDowell did encourage the officers to think they had American backing for the pursuit of anti-Partisan projects. There is even strong evidence to suggest that MacDowell led Mihailovic to believe that the Russians would not enter Yugoslavia, and that Mihailovic took this as proof that at least part of the country would fall in the non-Communist "sphere". With that sort of external support, the Chetniks could make one last deal with the Germans, before they left the Balkans, in order to gain the upper hand in Serbia.'[44]

In Drvar Fitzroy was only vaguely aware of all these currents and manoeuvrings. His aim was to exclude all English-speaking agents not under his control, and in his determination to have no more Huots he may sometimes have exceeded his brief. [45] Until he came out of Yugoslavia a second time in April, all the Americans there except one remained under his control. During his first sojourn with Tito, the only American members of the mission were Slim Farish and Captain Benson – the man Huot hijacked. Between January and April the American members were Farish, Captains Selvig and Goodwin and Lieutenants Green and Popovich. Hilary King, who arrived in the same aircraft in December 1943, remembers Selvig well.

> I, like other Brits, was equipped with a single capacious ruck-sack. Selvig arrived with three (or more) gigantic kit-bags, each weighing about a ton. These were something of a mystery – until it emerged that they were full of American automatic pistols, each one evidently having the status of 'Beads for the Native Chiefs' . . . Fitzroy was asked by Tito one day just after he came back in January for some private, personal guidance on a problem which he put more or less as follows: 'Your newly-arrived young American came along in person to see me, very privately, and pressed into my hands a huge, heavy American pistol. How should I have responded? I already have a good German pistol, for which I can always get ammunition. I could never be sure of getting more American ammunition – unless I lug stocks around with me everywhere. And it's a tremendously heavy pistol.I can hardly give it back: but I can't really use it. Will this cause great offence to your American friends? What ought I to do?'[46]

No doubt Tito remembered General Korneyev's present.

The one American not under Fitzroy's command was Colonel Weil, before the war a top executive at Macey's department store in New York; he was at Drvar from 27 February to the end of March. Hilary King recalls: 'Fitzroy at first had some doubts about his mission at Drvar, and was only prepared to accept it as a quite separate intelligence mission with no *locus standi* in political or military liaison with, or assitance to, Tito and the Partisans. Subject to that, which seems to have been agreed, he had a high regard for Weil personally.'[47]

As more and more Americans arrived to join the mission, Fitzroy noticed that they seemed to be odder and odder, doubtless reflecting the fierce faction fighting within OSS between pro-Tito and pro-Milailovic adherents.

> The Americans sent some very weird people, and they exacerbated things by specializing in second-generation Yugoslavs, who brought in from the New

World all the old memories of ethnic, racial and religious differences. One of them was syphilitic, and he got up on a soap-box in every village and made a great speech on behalf of God knows what political party. The last thing I wanted! The trouble about working in German-occupied territory was that you couldn't sack undesirables. In Greece one of them actually murdered another. I had some weird SOE officers, but in theory at least you could sack them . . . But the Americans were trickier, since to sack one would immediately land one in the *haute politique* of Anglo-American relations.[48]

Still worse was the problem of King Peter. Shortly after his return to Bosnia in January Fitzroy gave the Foreign Office the green light to raise this issue with Tito. In a telegram to the Marshal on 5 February Churchill asked whether he would accept the Royal government's dismissal of Mihailovic in return for having King Peter in the field with the Partisans.[49] Tito drove a hard bargain. In exchange for the mere despatch of envoys to talk to the king he demanded the suppression of the exiled government and the recognition of his National Liberation Committee; Peter would also have to declare that he was at the service of the people, not vice versa – Tito explained that this was necessary to atone for past 'treason' by the dynasty, and to allay suspicions of the king in Slovenia, Croatia and Macedonia. Fitzroy advised that the king should accept this as his last chance of regaining his throne, and urged the same on Churchill. 'From what he has said to me recently, it seems as though Tito may be genuinely concerned to preserve the independence of Yugoslavia and would welcome our support in his efforts to do so.'[50]

Churchill was prepared to accept these terms, subject only to a cast-iron assurance that Peter would be allowed to see active service with the Partisans, but the Foreign Office was vehemently opposed. Churchill did insist on the immediate withdrawal of the British Liaison Officers from Mihailovic, to give him a bargaining hand with Tito. As Eden wrote, Tito's terms were presumably only the opening bid in a process in which the Marshal was doubtless 'sufficiently oriental' to be adept. Churchill's counter-proposal was despatched on 26 February: four days earlier, he had thrown a substantial sop to Tito, telling the House of Commons about the Partisan war, the Anglo-American mission and Mihailovic's disgrace; to cheers he had announced that the mission was headed by Brigadier Maclean, 'the honourable and gallant Member for Lancaster'.[51]

Fitzroy meanwhile asked Churchill and Eden how they wanted Tito to modify his demands, and mentioned various non-Communist Yugoslavs – among them General Simovic and Ivan Subasic – whom Tito would be willing to include in a coalition government. Eden replied on 9 March:

What we want is that Tito should agree to King going to Yugoslavia and there forming new Government which would replace present Puric government. New government under Tito's presidency would no doubt consist predominantly of members of National Committee of Liberation but should also contain representatives of all other Yugoslav elements opposed to the Germans. In present conditions such representatives may have to be sought for outside Yugoslavia. Simovic and Subasic seem excellent choices. We might suggest further names if asked to do so.[52]

King Peter arrived in London on 11 March in anticipation of his wedding. It was typical of the confusion and turmoil in which both his private and his public affairs were always to be found that his domineering mother had by now withdrawn her consent for the match. How could someone who could not organize a wedding without controversy hope to lead a nation?[53]

Three days later Churchill called together Eden, Stevenson and Colonel S.W. Bailey, the newly returned Liaison Officer with Mihailovic, to discuss a Yugoslav strategy. The first step was to get King Peter to dismiss his Prime Minister, Puric, so that a new government of men sympathetic to the Partisans could be formed. If Tito refused to co-operate, he should be told he would get military assistance only, not political recognition. King Peter agreed to dismiss Puric and Mihailovic, but was frightened at the thought of standing alone for an interim period, so stalled and procrastinated. In any case, he was preoccupied with his wedding to Princess Alexandra. This event, when it took place on 20 March, did not increase his popularity in Yugoslavia, and in particular his star dimmed in Serbia, where wartime marriages were frowned on as unacceptable frivolity. A popular ditty of the time ran the Balkan rounds: 'The king got wed, Whilst his people bled.'[54]

When Tito got Churchill's message, he suggested to Fitzroy that King Peter be sent to Cairo to be trained with the Partisan air force.[55] This neat counter-check infuriated the Foreign Office, since it neither got the king home nor guaranteed Tito's co-operation with him. It also demonstrated Tito's superlative political skills, since Stalin's instructions to the Partisans were to avoid coming under British influence while compromising on the issue of the king – virtually a self-contradiction.[56] The Foreign Office insisted on pressing Tito again, and this time he gave an uncompromising answer. On 26 March he stated that the return of the king was impossible, as it contravened the Jajce resolutions of November 1943. Irritated by the ham-fisted intervention of his former Whitehall colleagues, Fitzroy went on record that this sort of pressure served no purpose and that it had been unwise to force Tito to make his position so inexorably clear.[57] Churchill then had second thoughts and blamed the Foreign Office for persuading him to overrule Fitzroy.[58]

By April Fitzroy needed to come out of Yugoslavia again. It was clear that a concerted Partisan assault on Serbia itself was now possible and could not be long delayed, and Fitzroy began sending liaison officers to the Partisans operating there. Serbia was known to be monarchist, pro-Mihailovic and nothing like as hostile to Nedic's quisling movement as it should have been. Bloody battles loomed.[59] This and the long-running saga of King Peter required urgent attention. Tito, who was keen not to rock the boat with his Western allies, agreed that Fitzroy might take Velebit out with him as an unofficial envoy; officially Tito could not endorse the Velebit embassy, as London and King Peter had not met his prior conditions.

But now came a problem. Chagrined by his experiences on his first foreign trip, when he had had to depend on British 'charity', Velebit asked that he be allowed to draw proper *per diem* expenses and thus uphold the honour and dignity of the Partisans. The snag was that the Partisans did not operate on a monetary economy, but on requisitions (in the case of enemy civilians) and promissory notes (in the case of friends). John Henniker remembers that no money was given to the Partisans in Serbia, though the British paid for their own board and lodging. Money had always been taken in by the liaison officers sent to Mihailovic, and when Fitzroy was preparing to be dropped in for the first time SOE suggested he take an enormous sum in gold sovereigns. Fitzroy declined, saying that if he later found he needed money, he would send for it. Tito for his part made it clear from day one of the mission that he neither needed money nor wished the British to send gold sovereigns. Fitzroy sacked one of his officers who had money sent in, allegedly to buy mules.[60]

This asceticism now became a problem. Tito cabled Moscow for some cash. Velebit and Fitzroy were on the airstrip at Bosanski Petrovac, waiting for the plane from Italy in the gathering dusk, when a Russian aircraft touched down and a crate of dollar bills was unloaded. A Partisan stepped forward and levered off the lid with a bayonet. Velebit took out some dollars, scribbled a receipt, pushed it into the crate, and rejoined Fitzroy.[61] Soon they were airborne, in a Dakota full of wounded Partisans, winging their way to Bari and Algiers.

12

Churchillian Interlude

MAY–SEPTEMBER 1944

F ITZROY has no doubt that the two greatest men he has met in his life are Winston Churchill and Josip Broz Tito. When the two met in Naples in August 1944, Tito found Churchill 'intensely human'. Fitzroy thinks one could say the same thing about both. Like Churchill, Tito appreciated alcohol, and would lose his temper and shout at people. Like Churchill, too, he had his moments of 'black dog'. But the surest bond uniting all three men was humour, and from the period of Tito's Adriatic roaming, between June and August 1944, Fitzroy has plucked four vintage episodes.

Life with Tito is conjured up by Fitzroy's description of the crossing from Bari to Vis on HMS *Blackmore* on the night of 6 June 1944.

We sat down to dinner in the wardroom to find ourselves confronted with a menu magnificently illuminated by one of the crew and written in Serb as well as English. I noticed at once that the wine list was a formidable one: sherry followed by gin, then red, then white, then port, then liqueurs. The Marshal drank some of everything, only hesitating momentarily when a large bottle was produced, mysteriously draped in a napkin. For an instant he wavered.

'Cheri-beri?' he inquired cryptically.

'No, champagne,' said the Captain proudly.

'Ah, champagne!' said Tito, and drained a tumbler of it.

It was not till later that we discovered that by cheri-beri he meant cherry brandy, though when, in due course, that stimulating beverage made its appearance, any distrust which he might have felt for it earlier in the evening had evidently completely vanished. By this stage of dinner the Marshal, to my surprise, was speaking quite fluent English, and rounded off the proceedings by giving a spirited recital of 'The Owl and the Pussy-Cat'.

Fitzroy also describes the strained first meeting of Tito and 'Jumbo' Wilson at Caserta – a strain exacerbated by the unnerving behaviour of Tito's bodyguards Bosko and Prlja, who took up station at the luncheon table, one behind the Marshal's chair, the other with his sub-machine-gun trained on Wilson. Everyone was tense and sweating in the summer heat, even the Italian waiters.

Nobody said anything; everyone, you could tell, was trying to think of a suitable opening gambit. We were spared the trouble. The strain of passing the vegetables, under the baleful eye of a heavily armed and extremely grim-looking guerrilla warrior, who clearly did not like Italians, was too much for the Italian mess waiter. With an exclamation of despair he let a large dish of French beans crash on the table, and at once pandemonium reigned. The trigger-fingers of the bodyguard twitched menacingly; Tigger, roused from his uneasy slumbers beneath the table, let out a long wolf-like howl and started to snap at everyone's ankles; the Italians chattered and gesticulated. For a moment the situation showed signs of getting out of control.

It was then that General Wilson started to laugh. Gently, almost silently at first, and then more and more heartily, until his whole frame quaked and rocked. Mirth bubbled in his eyes. I have never known anyone with a more infectious laugh. In a flash Tito was guffawing too, and soon the whole table was convulsed with merriment. Even the Italians sniggered nervously in the background, while a grim smile spread over the stern features of the body-guard. All tension disappeared. From then onwards I could tell that, socially at any rate, the visit was going to be a success.

When Churchill came on the scene, Fitzroy had two encounters with him that were even more ludicrous. In Algiers Fitzroy was informed that the Prime Minister wanted to speak to him on the radio-telephone, routed from London via Washington. He was taken to an underground room at Allied Forces HQ and handed over to the inevitable 'glamorous blonde WAC sergeant' of US Army Signals Corps, who explained that he could talk freely as the conversation would be scrambled.

What was my surprise, therefore, on hearing Mr Churchill's well-known voice come booming over the ether, and announcing my own identity as instructed, to be told by the Prime Minister to shut up. He then asked me whether I had spoken to Pumpkin. Disconcerted, I asked him what he meant. 'Why, that great big general of mine,' he replied in a stage whisper. 'And what', he went on, 'have you done with Pippin?'

Clearly one of us was off his head. I hoped it wasn't me. But how much worse if it were the Prime Minister! In despair, I told him I had no idea what he was talking about or how all these vegetables came into it. There was a pause, interrupted only by the inhuman wailing and crackling of the ether. Then, projected over the air, first of all across the Atlantic from Downing Street to Washington and then back to North Africa, came quite distinctly an exclamation of horror and disgust. 'Good God,' I heard him say, 'they haven't got the code.' At this point, not a moment too soon, the technicians took over, arguing among themselves about whether we needed to use a code or not. A few minutes later the Prime Minister was back on the air. 'Shall we scramble?' he asked gaily. I replied that I thought I was scrambled. There was a rumbling noise followed by silence and Mr Churchill's voice came through once more. 'So am I,' he said, after which, much to my relief, we were able to talk normally and arrange for my onward journey to London. However, he continued throughout the conversation to refer to the Supreme Commander, who was a particularly portly officer, as Pumpkin, and to Randolph as Pippin, two pseudonyms which seemed to give him the greatest pleasure.

Having laid down the receiver with relief after this unnerving experience, I started upstairs, but then turned back to get something I had left behind. As I opened the door I was startled to hear my own voice coming through it. 'Pumpkin, Prime Minister?' I was saying, 'I am afraid I don't understand what you mean . . .' I looked in. The pretty WAC sergeant was playing a recording of our conversation back to herself and rocking with laughter. 'And an English accent too!' I heard her say delightedly.

During the Naples conference of August 1944 between Tito and Churchill, an urgent decision was required from the Prime Minister one afternoon but he was nowhere to be found. Rumour had it that he was out in the Bay of Naples, so Fitzroy was sent by 'Jumbo' Wilson to find him. The Royal Navy provided him with an MTB (motor torpedo boat) and the Americans with the invariable 'young lady of considerable personal attractions', as his stenographer. Fitzroy describes the sequel.

The first thing we saw as we emerged from the harbour into the wider waters of the Bay was a great fleet of ships of every size and shape steaming majestically towards the open sea – the first phase, as I suddenly realized, of the Allied invasion of the south of France. This complicated my task. Clearly, trying to find Mr Churchill in this mighty armada was like looking for a needle in a haystack.

It was then that we noticed that something unusual was happening. As we watched, one of the troop-ships slightly slackened speed, as if to avoid something. Simultaneously there was a burst of excited cheering from the troops on deck and a small, bright blue object shot across her bows. I recognized it as the Admiral's barge, and there, standing by the coxswain, wearing a boiler suit and a broad-brimmed panama hat, smoking a cigar and giving the V-sign, was the object of my search. As we watched, he swerved out and round and disappeared behind the next ship in the convoy. Clearly, there was nothing for it but to give chase. I put this to the captain of my MTB. He did not like the idea at all. It was all very well, he said, for the Prime Minister to go swerving in and out of convoys. But if he did, he would get into trouble. I said that I would take full responsibility. At this he brightened and, having once taken the plunge, acquitted himself nobly. With the sea foaming and frothing in our wake, we set out on our erratic course down the line. As we passed them, the troops on the transports gave us an extra cheer for luck, followed by a salvo of whistles as they spotted my female companion. I have seldom felt more conspicuous.

Eventually we overtook and headed off the blue barge. There followed an intricate boarding operation in a kilt and a choppy sea and I landed precipitously at the Prime Minister's feet, while the stenographer, anxious to miss nothing, hung over the rail of the MTB. Mr Churchill seemed keenly interested. 'Do you often', he asked, 'spend your afternoons careering round the Bay of Naples in His Majesty's ships with this charming young lady?' In vain I explained the object of the exercise. He would not listen. I was not to hear the last of this episode for a long time.

Militarily, the centre of gravity had moved westwards from Cairo to Algiers once the Americans became the dominant partner in the Mediterranean, and General Wilson relocated there when he succeeded Eisenhower as area supremo. In the balmy North African sun a series of talks took place between Wilson and Velebit which went more smoothly than their negotiations in Alexandria in December. After the telephone conversation with Churchill that was turned by confusion over codes into a comedy of errors, it was agreed that Fitzroy should fly with Velebit to London.

They arrived on 1 May to begin what were officially described as 'purely military talks'.[1] In London, despite the frantic preparations for D-Day, what can only be described as Yug-fever was raging. Everyone, from the press to Eisenhower, wanted to know about Tito. Fitzroy ran the gamut of experts, from service chiefs and politicians to Menzies and the 'funnies' in SIS. He saw more of Churchill in this month than ever before. On 2 May the Prime Minister summoned a meeting at Chequers of all the Yugoslav experts: not just Fitzroy, but also Colonel Bailey and Colonel D. T. Hudson, who had just returned from Mihailovic. Bailey declared that the Partisans could never penetrate Serbia and that the only way to get the Cetniks to resist the Germans was to replace Mihailovic with King Peter. Fitzroy disagreed and was sure that the incursion of the Partisans into Serbia would be successful, now that they were heavily armed with Allied hardware. Hudson considered that the Serbs could be mobilized into the ranks of the Partisans if Tito were to renounce Communist ambitions, and Fitzroy thought there was a good chance he would do this if Churchill asked him.[2]

On 5 May Fitzroy had an encounter with someone who did not share the Prime Minister's high regard for him. This is how Robert Bruce Lockhart wrote up in his diary a morning meeting at Bush House to discuss Yugoslav affairs:

. . . Today Fitzroy Maclean is an MP (Conservative) and a brigadier. He longs to be a T. E. Lawrence, has great qualities of persistence and determination, but has more courage, guts in his long frame than brains! He arrived today in a kilt, looked fit but rather thin, and his face, now clean-shaven, was fine and rather drawn. His kilt battledress was good – kilt, battle tunic, khaki Balmoral. He stayed for an hour and a half, examined our propaganda output, asked many questions and was severely and continuously critical of Cairo who, he said, had sent him nothing and had not adopted any of his ideas. He himself is very slow and hesitant in speech and is almost painfully deliberate. He does not know when to break off a conversation, and his manner is anything but soldierly. Vellacott, who was present and wanted to see me, was neither impressed nor amused. Fitzroy, however, has his virtues. He asked me to luncheon to meet General Velebit, Tito's chief of staff, and a Zagreb lawyer who speaks very good English. I said I should be delighted and should not ask any permission. Moley Sargent who was also asked was not allowed to accept by Eden! And Velebit was not allowed to broadcast by Moley! To bring him here and ignore him (leaving him to the mercy of the Left and the *New States-man*) is the height of political stupidity.[3]

Fitzroy lunched with Churchill at Chequers again on 6 May with Bailey, Hudson and Ralph Stevenson, and once more discussed means of bringing Serbia into the fight. Four days later Fitzroy briefed his fellow Members of Parliament. Hugh Dalton was there and noted in his diary:

In the afternoon hear in a committee room in the House a statement by Brigadier Fitzroy Maclean on Tito. He looks much improved since he shaved off his long drooping moustache. But he speaks very, very slowly and is very guarded in all references to matters outside his immediate mission. He says Tito has 300,000 men, organized in ten Corps which intercommunicate by wireless and by couriers. Tito, he thinks, is the greatest master in Europe of guerrilla tactics. His following is 50 per cent Serb, 30 per cent Croat and the rest Slovene and Moslem. The original driving force behind his organization was Communist, but all parties are now in it. The German reprisals are exceedingly brutal. When they come to a village from which all the men have gone up into the hills with Tito, they massacre indiscriminately all the women, old and young, and all the children. The Partisans count it a defeat unless they kill at least five Germans for every man they lose. Mihailovic is unquestionably co-operating with the Germans. This has been so since the end of 1941.[4]

Velebit meanwhile was cold-shouldered by the British Establishment. He saw Lockhart on 12 May and confirmed all that Fitzroy had said, except that he gave higher figures for Serbian participation: Tito's army, he said, was 60 per cent Serb, 30 per cent Croat and 10 per cent Slovene. Velebit told Lockhart he was disgusted that the British Government would not allow him to have a printing press at Bari, with which he would be able to appeal to the rest of the Serbs. He denied that Tito either was or ever would be a Russian vassal, and pointed out that Benes of Czechoslovakia had followed exactly the same policy of balancing East and West. Lockhart was indignant at his treatment:

He has been badly handled during his visit here and has been left alone at the Savoy while Fitzroy went round the 'high-ups'. In consequence he has been seen by many left-wingers including members of the *New Statesman* and the BBC. Some BBC reporter gave him the impression that the BBC had invited him to broadcast. This was not true but the impression stuck and the story was given to the *New Statesman*. Anthony Eden forbade Moley to lunch with him and also vetoed his broadcasting . . . Unless he was to be seen by official people here, he should never have been brought over.[5]

There was no sign of an invitation from Churchill. Velebit grew fractious. Finally, one Friday he was told by Fitzroy to be ready to fly out the following Monday. Velebit asked whether he would be seeing Churchill, but Fitzroy changed the subject. Meanwhile his meetings with luminaries of the Left, especially Kingsley Martin and Harold Laski, bore fruit. Velebit was increasingly concerned that he had spoken to no British Minister, let alone Churchill, and mentioned his unease and embarrassment to Laski and Martin, who saw the risk to future Anglo-Yugoslav relations. While Martin departed for his country cottage for the weekend, incommunicado because of his ex-directory number, Laski tackled Major Desmond Morton, Churchill's private secretary. Morton agreed that the risk of an embarrassing slight was high and spoke to his opposite number in Lord Beaverbrook's office in the Ministry of Information. That weekend Kingsley Martin was astonished to be rung up by Beaverbrook, to whom he had not given his number; he asked him rather sharply how he had got hold of it. 'When I tell my secretary I want to speak to Kingsley Martin, I speak to Kingsley Martin,' Beaverbrook boomed. 'Anyway, this chap Velebit. Nothing to do with me. But I thought I'd better tell you, it'll be all right.' On Monday morning Velebit found a flustered Fitzroy waiting for him at the Savoy, with the news that Churchill would see him that afternoon at three o'clock.[6]

The problem had been the desire of the Foreign Office, and also Churchill, not to offend King Peter. From having been under the influence of a small group of Serbian officers, he transferred in the spring of 1944 to the aegis of his Greek mother-in-law. The idea that such a man could deal on level terms with Tito was incredible. Had he joined the Partisan bands he would in no time have been under Tito's thumb. So how could the Foreign Office conceivably have thought they could use Peter to influence post-war Yugoslavia? The only conclusion possible is that the FO was swayed by crude anti-Communism and sentimental royalism.

In *Eastern Approaches* Fitzroy relates urbanely that he and Peter 'had a friendly enough conversation, which ended in a discussion of the relative merits of various brands of motor cars'.[7] But behind this suave irony lay an exasperating story of prevarication and vacillation on the young king's part. Peter had severed his links with Mihailovic but proved reluctant to dismiss his Prime Minister, Bozidar Puric – though

Tito had made that a pre-condition for establishing contact with the government-in-exile. Churchill's favoured candidate as Puric's replacement was Ivan Subasic, the Ban of Croatia, then in the USA. On this occasion Roosevelt and 'Wild Bill' Donovan sided with Churchill, against the advice of the pro-Cetnik State Department and the right-wing lower echelons of OSS; Subasic was put on a plane and arrived in London on 7 May. King Peter had an annoying habit of appealing behind Churchill's back to Roosevelt if he did not get his own way, but the President dismissed Peter's diaphanous argument that Yugoslavia was the test-case for all central Europe in the fight to escape Communism, and saw clearly that part of the king's weakness lay in his identification with Serbian nationalism. An acceptable compromise seemed to have been reached, though Fitzroy was not happy with Subasic and warned Churchill that he was Donovan's creature.[8] The world leaders reckoned without the peevish King Peter. The historian Mark Wheeler sums the monarch up thus.

> May [1944] was a bad month for King Peter. He was frightened of Churchill, disappointed in Roosevelt, terrified of Tito, indignant at Mihailovic, intimidated by the Serb politicians, distrustful of Subasic, bored by the nagging of Stevenson, and generally resentful of his lot. He sought to evade the crisis by absenting himself on flying exercises or, encouraged by Bailey, by dreaming of descending upon Cetnik headquarters to wrest command from Mihailovic. He adopted a cavalier attitude towards the dismissal of Puric and a punctilious approach to the nomination of a successor.[9]

Churchill's prevarication over whether to see Velebit was a consequence of his difficulties with the slippery young king. Acting on assurances from Peter, by mid-May Churchill thought he had resolved matters and on the 17th sent a message to Tito that Puric had been dismissed. But the king had lied. Despite categorical assurances to Stevenson, he had not actually had the courage to go through with his promise and sack his Prime Minister.[10] Eventually Churchill 'bounced' the duplicitous monarch by announcing Puric's resignation in the House of Commons on 24 May.[11] By the beginning of June Peter had been forced to accept the reality of one-man government by Subasic.

Fitzroy meanwhile completed his round of calls in London with an audience with King George VI. The king seemed well-informed about Yugoslavia, and they discussed the morality and expediency of resistance. 'The king said, "I naturally always have to think what I would have done had the Germans landed in this country and there was a resistance movement. I came to the conclusion that the right thing would have been to go to the leader of the Resistance, even if he was a Communist, and say, I'm at your disposal as a soldier, and we can discuss the post-war situation after the war." '[12]

Another meeting fraught with implications for the future took place on 11 May with senior SOE officials, including their Chief Signals Officer, Brigadier Nicholls. SOE raised the question of Partisan security, and in particular their radio communications and ciphers.[13] All the indications were that by 1944 the Germans had broken the Partisan radio code and thus discovered the pattern of recognition lights displayed on Partisan airfields when a supply drop was expected. Fitzroy now says he cannot remember that this point was discussed, for if it had been he would immediately have raised it with Tito.

Fitzroy was supposed to return to Bosnia after his talks in London, as Churchill's correspondence with Tito reveals. 'Brigadier Maclean, who is with me now, will be with you in less than three weeks, with all the views he has gathered here, and I hope that at the very least you will await his return.' But this letter to Tito was somewhat acerbic, asking him not to jump the gun in Serbia; Roosevelt advised him to tone it down. Churchill wrote:

We do not know what will happen in the Serbian part of Yugoslavia. Mihailovic certainly holds a powerful position locally as Commander-in-Chief, and it does not follow that his ceasing to be Minister of War will rob him of his influence. We cannot predict what he will do. There is also a very large body, amounting perhaps to 200,000, of Serbian peasant proprietary [sic] who are anti-German but strongly Serbian, and who naturally hold the views of a peasants' ownership community, contrary to the Karl Marx theory.

When Churchill transmitted this letter to Washington for approval, Roosevelt insisted that the last six words he deleted, as a gratuitous jibe at an ally. Churchill complied, but in a sense had the last word: the letter was printed in its entirety in his *Second World War*, with no reference to the fact that he had had to delete the offending words.[14]

What possessed Churchill to act in such an undiplomatic manner? Speculation has had it that he was influenced by Bailey into thinking he had too readily accepted Fitzroy's estimates, and that Mihailovic's power base in Serbia was more secure than he had previously imagined.[15] More likely, in the light of all we know of Churchill, he was piqued that Tito had not come meekly to heel when he whistled. Lockhart thought that Tito refused to co-operate with Churchill's plans for King Peter because the Allies were bogged down in Italy and the Russians were advancing rapidly on the eastern front.[16] Fitzroy thought Serbia was the key. 'By 1944 the whole situation had changed. By then the Partisans were stronger in Serbia. Indeed, their whole position was much stronger and they did not need to make those sort of concessions. Of course we now know that Stalin was urging him to take King Peter in order to please us, and then have him assassinated. Rather typical of Stalin.'[17]

Just as Fitzroy was preparing to fly out to the Mediterranean, dramatic news came in that German parachutists had landed in force at Drvar and had come within an ace of capturing Tito. The first indication that something was afoot was a German plane which on 22 May made a long, leisurely aerial surveillance of Drvar valley, keeping out of range of small-arms fire. It seemed obvious that this was the harbinger of a bombing raid, and Vivian Street, commanding the Anglo-American mission in Fitzroy's absence, noticed that the high-flying German photographers paid particular attention to the part of the town occupied by the mission. Concluding that a full-scale bombing assault was imminent, Street warned Tito of the danger and, having first signalled his intentions to Bari, moved the mission to the outskirts of the town.[18]

The aerial reconnaissance was actually the prelude to the Seventh German Offensive, Operation ROESSELSPRUNG ('Knight's Move') aimed at killing or capturing Tito by a paratroop assault, followed by a drag-net through the entire Dinaric Alps between Sibenik and Bihac. The plan, scheduled for Tito's 52nd birthday, was a measure of Nazi desperation, but it had the advantage of surprise and, largely because Tito felt so secure in his Drvar stronghold, it nearly worked.

On 25 May – the day the Cassino front joined up with the Anzio beach-head and preparations for D-Day entered their final phase – 'Knight's Move' was implemented. At 6.30 in the morning two German Focke-Wulfs screamed in low to initiate the attack. Soon fifty German bombers were pounding the town, their might directed at the recently evacuated mission compound. Then out of the sun came six large Junkers 52 transports. To the astonishment of the watching Partisans, they disgorged scores of paratroopers who quickly seized landing grounds for the next wave of paratroops behind them. Then came thirty or so gliders, towed by another 'wing' of planes. As the gliders belly-flopped to the ground, more men poured out with heavier arms. Soon there were 1,000 crack troops in Drvar. Around noon there was a second paratroop landing, and the Germans soon took control of the town and its environs.

The attackers seemed to know exactly where Tito's cave was located, for one of the first raiding parties tried to gain the heights, though it was driven back by a stout Partisan defence. Tito was lucky – one of the gliders crash-landed at the very mouth of the cave, but fortunately for him there were no survivors. The Germans proceeded to spray the approach to the cave with machine-gun fire, so that nobody could enter or leave. Tito and his followers managed to scramble up the watercourse of the falls at the back of the cave, which fortuitously was dry. They made their way through a tunnel in the rock to the top of the cliff, dragging the dog Tigger with them. From the top of the cliff, which

Marko Rankovic and his detachment had held against German assault, Tito made his way to the nearest Partisan unit, in the village of Potoci.

Although the Partisans counter-attacked in Drvar, the Germans called in strong motorized and armoured forces and compelled Tito to order a general retreat. At Potoci, where Tito linked up with the Russian and Anglo-American missions, the Wehrmacht tried to spring a trap but again Tito escaped. A five-mile journey on the Partisan express was followed by a hue and cry through the woods. There were many narrow escapes before Tito got clear. The Germans took out their frustration on Drvar itself, with the usual quota of atrocities.

Tito had lost all his radio equipment, and most of the mission radio and cipher equipment had had to be destroyed by the British when the alarm went up, but Hilary King managed to patch up a radio from spare parts he and others had taken away with them in the last-minute rush for safety. Street contacted Bari to request air support and within two days the RAF had cleared the Luftwaffe from the skies of Bosnia. But the situation on the ground was still desperate. For the next eight days Tito, his staff and the Allied liaison men penetrated deeper and deeper into the forests of Bosnia as four German divisions combed the area in search of them.

By 2 June it was obvious to Tito that his command structure was in disarray. He did not fear, as some have claimed, that he would be captured unless airlifted out to Bari immediately; he was sure he could dodge the Germans indefinitely in the mountains, but thought that without a firm base from which to re-establish his radio networks he would be unable to command his forces throughout the country effectively. It has been said that Korneyev strongly urged the flight to Bari, and even presented it as a direct order from Moscow, but in fact Tito's plight left him no choice: he could not direct the war while continually on the run, so he allowed his fear that without him the Partisan war would collapse to be overruled. Street contacted Bari and asked for a plane to take Tito and his entourage to Vis.[19]

Soon afterwards a DC-3 put down at the Kupresko Polje landing strip. Tito, half a dozen of his staff, Street and the inevitable Tigger climbed on board. To their astonishment the plane turned out to be Russian, piloted by the Soviet air ace Shornikov, and operating out of Bari, which by international agreement was under RAF operational control. Shortly after the Russian plane took off, six American planes arrived and evacuated 74 more people, including fourteen Russians. By midnight on 3 June Tito was safely in Bari, but there were repercussions following the Russian rescue. The Russians claimed that they hoisted Tito to safety because the Drvar attack showed the British could not be trusted; the British claimed that the Russians by underhand trickery had stolen a cheap propaganda advantage by whisking Tito out of

Bosnia under the noses of the RAF.[20] The thesis that the Russians stole a march on the British will not hold, for the simple reason that the Russians had lost all their radio equipment in the attack on Drvar: all radio messages arranging the 'rescue' were handled by Hilary King at the Yugoslav end, and by British operators in Bari. Hilary King, who has made a close study of this incident, concludes:

> To sum up, the Russians had told our people in Bari that Shornikov would be flying in to Kupresko Polje on the night of 3 June, and we knew from the Russian signals that he was under orders to make two flights, and would therefore have to start early – probably before the Allied aircraft, organized at the last minute, would be ready for take-off. To judge from the evidence available . . . we have no grounds for concluding, as many have done, that Shornikov's flight was just a dirty trick, hatched up behind our backs, solely to snatch from the RAF all the credit for Tito's rescue. I would only add two personal comments. First, the professional skill of the legendary Shornikov was so well known among members of the British Mission that, if I had been Marshal Tito, faced with the choice between Shornikov and one of several unknown Americans, none of whom had yet arrived, I should have opted for Shornikov. Second, Colonel Street said in paragraph 16 of his report that, after arriving in Bari, the attitude of the Soviet mission changed from 'extremely cordial' to merely 'correct' – as if this might have had some connection with their conduct over the evacuation. My own recollection is exactly the opposite: the members of the Soviet Mission with whom I dealt, from being 'correct' in Bosnia, and 'friendly' after 25 May, became 'extremely cordial' by the time they reached Vis, as did General Korneyev himself. I attributed this at the time to the opening of the 'Second Front' (D-Day) on 6 June, an occasion which seemed to transform the British, in the eyes of many of our Partisan friends, from useful and moderately friendly 'Quartermasters' to friends and allies.[21]

Despite his liking for Fitzroy, Tito, as an old Comintern man, never entirely abandoned his suspicions of British policy, and the incident at Drvar scarcely helped. For their part the British felt they had been duped and that the Russians had stolen a march. But the irritation expressed about this in a spate of memoirs is misguided. British officers assumed the Russian planes at Bari were under British command, but they were not. In political circles it was fully accepted, not just that the planes were *not* under British command, but that no hint that they were should ever be made, since the RAF was at that very time negotiating with the Russians for landing rights in the Soviet Union in connection with the air drops over Warsaw. Because the RAF wanted its Warsaw planes free from Soviet control, it followed they had to accept that the Russian planes at Bari should be free from RAF interference. The situation was that the Russians at Bari were supposed to liaise closely with their allies, with the single proviso that they were free to respond unilaterally to calls for help from the Soviet mission with Tito.

The most that can be conceded is that neither Tito nor the Russians handled their public relations well. Velebit thought it was particularly unfortunate that when Tito's plane landed it taxied, not to the end of the runway where the press was waiting, but to a prearranged pickup point whence Tito was whisked away in a Russian car. Tito later explained to Fitzroy rather sheepishly that it was all very embarrassing but that he had needed complete secrecy until he was installed on Vis, in case his troops thought he had given up the struggle and run away to Italy.

The so-called 'Russian doublecross' over Tito was the first of many incidents in 1944 that soured relations between Britain and the Marshal. Hilary King's careful reconstruction of the facts has put paid to a number of legends, such as the one that Tito refused to travel in a 'Western' plane because Stalin had sent him dire warnings about the British propensity to assassinate people on planes, as they had allegedly done with Sikorski.[22] Tito in any case showed no qualms about flying in a British plane to meet 'Jumbo' Wilson at Caserta a few weeks later.

More sinister were the rumours afoot at the time that the British had known all about ROESSELSPRUNG but had failed to warn Tito of the impending attack since they now regarded him as a threat to their Balkan designs. This charge was resurrected at the height of the Cold War in late 1947 when the Russians tried to dissuade Tito from turning to the West.[23] The waters were further muddied when General Wilson claimed in his memoirs that advance warning of the attack had been sent to Drvar, but had apparently been disregarded.[24] There is also some evidence, in both Yugoslav and British sources, that the possibility of a German airborne landing at Drvar had been widely discussed with Tito by, among others, John Clarke.[25]

What, then, is the truth of all this? Four main theories have emerged and are related here in ascending order of probability. The first is that the real Judas was OSS. According to this view, the Royal Yugoslav military attaché in Washington shared a mistress with one of Donovan's right-hand men and secured detailed knowledge of the layout of the Partisan headquarters at Drvar. This information was then passed on by the Royal government to Mihailovic, who in turn passed it to the Germans. To save their blushes when the truth leaked out, OSS pretended that it was the British who had tried to betray Tito. Donovan is said to have ordered an inquiry into leaks at the Washington end, but the inquiry was shelved, allegedly for lack of manpower. Tito is said to have known that he had been betrayed, and to have flown out in a Russian plane because he could not be sure whether it was the British or the Americans who had betrayed him.[26]

There are numerous objections to this theory, some of them fatal. In the first place, the Germans did not need to be told of Tito's presence in Drvar; they already knew: their problem was the logistics of capture or assassination. Then, if the Germans really had detailed knowledge of every square inch of Drvar, why did they need to fly aerial reconnaissance missions on 22 May, thus alerting Vivian Street?

The second theory is that the British were omniscient and therefore culpable.[27] After all, were not the boffins of Bletchley Park the true winners of the war? If they did not send a warning, it must have been because of the rules governing the protection of Ultra, the 'most secret source'. This theory rests on more solid foundations. A firm decision had been taken in 1943 not to pass on Ultra material to the Maclean mission. On 9 March 1944 Churchill himself wanted to override that decision, but was told that the mission's ciphers were 'not of the highest grade' – that is, not secure enough.[28] Even if the ciphers had been secure, there was a strict policy of never divulging information from Ultra to anyone liable to capture by the Germans. Against this theory are four considerations. First, SIS head Menzies ('C') had two of his own men at Drvar. He would surely have warned *them*, if not the mission, not necessarily out of consideration for his own operatives (who in certain circumstances would have been considered expendable), but because he feared what they might reveal if captured and tortured. Second, British intelligence officers at Bari were aware of a German build-up and of the movement of gliders, but interpreted it as preparation for an assault on Vis, not Drvar.[29] Third, the mission could have been tipped off without endangering the source. Fourth, the Ultra material, which is now available to public inspection, can certainly be construed as indicating an attack on Drvar – which we now know was the true interpretation – but it would have been impossible for anyone in Bletchley at the time, reading only the Ultra signals, to establish definitively that Drvar was the German target. In other words, the notion of British omniscience rests heavily on hindsight.

The third theory is that the British did not have the information and could not have predicted the attack. The Ultra files contain no direct evidence of an intended parachute attack, since the more specific telegrams were transmitted by Land Lines and were thus not available to Ultra. Ultra specialists at Bletchley made a point of not seeing intelligence from other sources, so that their decipherments might be as objective as possible.[30] The historian Ralph Bennett sums up as follows: 'There were three Ultra references to ROESSELSPRUNG before the raid, and nearly a hundred aircraft were moved to Croatia at short notice and for a limited period, but good German security saw to it that none of these messages gave the slightest clue to the meaning of ROESSELSPRUNG or hinted at any connection with Tito. A moderately complete account of ROESSELSPRUNG can be reconstructed from Ultra signals, but only with the help of hindsight and with the help of other evidence.'[31]

It is interesting to note the gulf between the omniscience posited in the second theory and the near-ignorance assumed in the third: 'must have known' versus 'didn't know, couldn't know'. The most plausible theory is one that includes aspects of the second and third theories. A single person in possession of all the material from Yugoslavia reaching Bari *and* Bletchley would have known that the attack was coming. But there was no such person. Those in Italy who saw Ultra material, like General Stawell and the Intelligence specialist Squadron Leader Allen, saw only some of it and, as it happens, saw *none* of the Ultra signals concerning Drvar. Personnel from the Maclean mission then at Bari, like Mike Parker and John Clarke, saw no Ultra material at all. Moreover, as late as the evening of 24 May no one in Bari, through one of those administrative hiccups common in wartime, knew of Street's decision to move the mission after seeing the photo-reconnaissance planes over Drvar on 22 May.

Only someone with access to all the information, both from the mission and from Ultra, could have predicted the aerial assault and thus warned Tito. Bletchley knew one set of facts, Bari another. From Ultra intelligence alone nobody could have predicted an operation against Drvar. On the other hand, those with knowledge of Bosnia, like Clarke and Parker, would almost certainly have been able to draw the conclusions had they seen it – but they didn't. The moral to be drawn is an old one. The historian working from hindsight can piece together the likely truth, but no contemporary actor in a historical drama ever possesses that level of knowledge.[32]

It has been necessary to deal with the Drvar attack at some length in order to refute the canard that the British had foreknowledge, since Fitzroy's enemies (and not just those on the other side of what was the Iron Curtain) have whispered that through his close association with Menzies he knew what was planned and treacherously colluded with the Establishment in its betrayal of Tito.[33] Clearly, Fitzroy could never have been party to any such perfidy. And those who know him are convinced that at the limit, and even if sworn to secrecy, he would have put loyalty to his men first and found some way to warn them.

The Prime Minister wrote to Eden on 31 May with more than a hint of satisfaction to say that all Yugoslav policies should go into abeyance until Tito either broke out of the German cordon or was taken prisoner. After a few days in Bari Tito insisted on moving back to Vis, so that he could claim to be carrying on the fight against Germany from Yugoslav territory; he was taken across the Adriatic by the destroyer HMS *Blackmore* on 6 June. Churchill thought that Tito would now be in a chastened, more realistic mood and easier to deal with: he was accessible and his flight from the mainland had probably diminished his influence. For very different reasons Churchill concurred with the

Foreign Office in thinking that, from the British point of view, Drvar was a blessing in disguise.[34]

On 4 June Churchill signalled General Wilson to defend Vis at all costs; there must be no more Drvars. Alanbrooke reinforced the importance of the message with a signal to Wilson to maintain his garrison at full strength, even though Ultra intercepts were indicating that an enemy assault on Vis was highly improbable. Churchill then prepared to send King Peter out to Vis, to beard Tito in his den. But here the Foreign Office and Wilson himself dissented. Wilson later wrote: 'I had grave misgivings about the wisdom of bringing King Peter into the Mediterranean so early in the proceedings and I doubted whether his presence there could be kept from reaching Tito's ears, as there were Jugoslav warships in Malta and Jugoslav soldiers all over southern Italy; should that happen it would be impossible to convince Tito that a trap was not being set for him.'[35] The FO cautioned the Prime Minister that his cards were not as strong as he seemed to think, and that it was unlikely Tito could be 'bounced' into being co-operative. The Marshal's position was still a strong one: he knew that the British did not want to lose him entirely to the Russians and that, having enforced the dismissal of Mihailovic, they could not afford to break with the Partisans.[36] Moreover, Churchill seemed to overlook the fact that Vis was not wholly in British hands but was an Anglo-Yugoslav condominium in which any attempt to impede Tito's movements would probably lead to a sort of civil war on the island: Allies against Partisans. This was quite apart from the consideration that if King Peter suddenly left London, the Serbs would say he had been kidnapped.[37]

But Churchill was delighted with Fitzroy's news that he had persuaded Tito to talk to Subasic, who accordingly was to fly out to Vis as a kind of 'John the Baptist', in Eden's phrase.[38] Churchill was in manic mood in the immediate aftermath of D-Day, as the following phrases from telegrams to Eden and Wilson show: 'God-sent opportunity . . . last chance of safeguarding the unity of Yugoslavia and whatever hopes King Peter II may have of reigning . . . Are we going to throw all this away by making little mincing steps all tabulated one after another? . . . take the Kingdom of Heaven by storm . . . Tito will not be long in our friendly hands at Vis . . . the danger is that Tito will flit; but if we agree upon policy, I expect it will be possible to make it very difficult for him to find an aeroplane.'[39] The Prime Minister, it seems, had still not taken in the force of his advisors' objections.

The more cautious Foreign Office policy prevailed. King Peter and Subasic flew to Malta and from there Subasic proceeded to Vis to make straight the ways for the young monarch. On 14 June Stevenson and Subasic were landed by destroyer and made their way to Tito's headquarters. Three days of talks ensued. An agreement signed on 17 June guaranteed mutual recognition by the rival Yugoslav governments; the question of the king was shelved until after the war.[40]

Both Churchill and King Peter professed themselves delighted with this.[41] It took the more sceptical minds in the Foreign Office to point out that Tito had completely outwitted them. Fitzroy's old friend Armine Dew and Eden himself were annoyed that Tito had deferred recognition of the king and had evaded having to meet him.[42] The cynics were right. The June 1944 agreements ultimately proved not worth the paper they were written on: in retrospect, June 1944 marked the last date at which the British were still able to cherish the illusion that King Peter could help pacify Yugoslavia and prevent it from passing into the Soviet sphere of influence.

Political negotiations took up only part of Fitzroy's time on Vis. At one end of the spectrum he had to deal with large policy questions; at the other, with minute aspects of military planning. It was perhaps significant of the growing political gulf between Britain and the Partisans that Fitzroy had his quarters a long way from Tito's, established in a cavern on Mount Hum. As Fitzroy wryly remarked, 'Despite his experiences at Drvar, Tito had not lost his taste for caves.'[43] The Soviet mission was bivouacked in tents outside the cave. Fitzroy meanwhile was settled in a comfortable villa on the south-east corner of the island at Zaravnire, right on the coast. His friend Admiral Morgan-Giles comments: 'Fitzroy liked to live *en prince*, and it was typical of him not to end up in a cave or a tent.'[44]

From a peaceful little Dalmatian island, Vis had been transformed into a teeming, bristling military base. Runways were clogged with fighters, fighter bombers, Fortresses and Liberators; narrow roads were crammed with Army trucks and jeeps; arms dumps ensnarled in barbed wire were ubiquitous; and in the harbour the Royal Navy deployed a large flotilla of launches, MTBs and landing craft. Many of Fitzroy's old friends were on Vis. Tom Churchill and his commandos were drilling in the olive groves. Among the Americans was Douglas Fairbanks Jr, of Hollywood fame, who remained a close friend of Fitzroy's after the war. Air Vice-Marshal Elliott was there, too, in charge of 'Balkan Air Force' – an Anglo-American inter-service unit which had been set up to co-ordinate Adriatic operations. Its headquarters was in Bari, where Elliott reported to Air Marshal Slessor. It was Slessor who in February 1944 had reluctantly agreed to 'yield to the urgent request of Fitzroy Maclean' and equip a couple of squadrons of Partisans. In Bari, just before leaving with Tito for Vis, Fitzroy had asked Slessor for, first, air superiority, so that there should be no more Drvars; second, increased arms and equipment for the Partisans; and third, evacuation of the wounded from Yugoslavia. The last item was the tallest order, but Slessor and Elliott performed heroically: in a single day British,

American and Russian Dakotas airlifted out of the Montenegro mountains more than a thousand wounded Partisans, under the very noses of
the Germans.[45] Additionally, since air support was now given to the
Partisans almost instantly, the Germans found it impossible to follow
up their early successes in the Seventh Offensive; like its predecessors, it
eventually petered out.

Warmest of all Fitzroy's relationships on Vis was that with Commander Morgan-Giles, a fellow buccaneer, who was in charge of naval
operations. Morgan-Giles gloried in the title Senior Naval Officer, Vis
(SNOVIS); his assistants, for obvious reasons, were known as the
Seven Dwarfs. Giles had known Fitzroy since 1941 and was a staunch
admirer: 'The first thing that struck me on Vis was that Fitzroy was
at once every inch a brigadier *and* exactly the same with his old
friends – no side or rank-pulling. That combination is difficult to bring
off.'[46] Fitzroy had requested Giles as his naval aide, but the Admiralty
refused on the grounds that Giles had already spent too much of the war
'off the lead' on unorthodox missions. Fitzroy then took the matter to
the top, but still the appointment was blocked, this time by his uncle
Admiral Whitworth, Second Sea Lord. Fitzroy finally appealed to
Churchill on the letter of his brief, which was that he could have 'anyone' he wanted. The Prime Minister promptly overruled Whitworth.

Giles had done a lot of solid spadework, in Malta, Taranto and Bari,
before ever he came to Vis, so that his convoys of MTBs and other craft
were organized with high efficiency. He was aided, too, by disguised
intelligence from Ultra, which played a great part in winning the battle
for the Adriatic.[47] In 1943 the normal procedure was for Giles and his
men to run convoys between Bari and the mainland. They would land
arms and *matériel* at night, hide up during the day under camouflage,
then make the return journey the following night. In the early days
operations were hazardous; as contact with the Partisans could not be
made by radio, loudhailers were used, and this sometimes resulted in
shoot-outs between Partisans and the Royal Navy.

By 1944 Giles had almost complete command of the Adriatic. With
a huge fleet of high-speed launches, gunboats and destroyers at his
disposal – for by this time the Royal Navy was running out of operations in the Mediterranean – Giles instituted a tight blockade that
dismayed the Germans. Not only could they not prevent massive reinforcements reaching the Partisans, but they had themselves to run the
gauntlet of Giles's raiders to supply their own beleaguered troops in
Greece and Crete.

The first six months of 1944 saw the Dalmatian islands changing
hands all the time. The campaign was fought just as ferociously as the
struggle on land. Giles tells a story revealing the German fear of falling
into Partisan hands. A German ship with a concert party on board was

1. Fitzroy at Eton

2. In Moscow, 1938

3. Fitzroy in kilt at the
time of his election to
Parliament, 1941

4. An SAS convoy in the desert

5. In fancy dress in
Cairo, 1942

6. The Yugoslav situation as seen by the *Standard*, 1943

7. A female Partisan

8. The commander of the political and military mission to Tito, 1943

9. Wounded Partisans

10. A millionaire with the Partisans

11. Ante Pavelic in Croatia

12. Allied naval operations in the Adriatic

13. The cave at Drvar

14. Tito in his lair

15. The 'kilted pimpernel', London, May 1944

16. Subasic with Tito, Vis, 1944

17. A family gathering

18. Fitzroy as Under-Secretary for War, 1955

19. Fitzroy in his study, 1964

20. On the terrace of the house in Korcula

21. With Tito and Mrs Thatcher, Belgrade, 1977

22. With Sir Harold Wilson and Sir Geoffrey Howe, Great Britain-USSR Society

23. With 'Jimmy' at the Creggans Inn, Strachur

24. With Tito in the Marshal's last decade

threading its way down through the islands. The captain struck up a friendship with one of the pretty actresses, and the two went ashore to a secluded spot to make love. When they returned to the shore they found the Partisan flag fluttering over their ship; all their comrades had been killed. The captain shot first the girl and then himself, rather than be taken.

Although Giles's role was purely naval, he tells a story that indicates the political tensions on Vis over the question of King Peter. Giles's superior, Admiral Morgan, came over from Taranto on a tour of inspection and was introduced to Tito. Also in the party were Giles, Fitzroy and Velebit, acting as interpreter. Morgan asked Tito if he would like to see the Royal Navy bombard a rock that afternoon. Tito accepted, but asked for his 'Russian friends' to be allowed to come too. At this Morgan bridled, and said that the invitation was personal. Tito in turn became difficult and announced that in that case, *he* would not be going. Fitzroy and Velebit then poured oil on troubled waters: it was agreed that the Russians certainly ought to be invited to an 'official' rock bombardment, but this one was unofficial. Tito brightened at this diplomatic solution, and it was agreed that the Russians should be left behind. But just as the Admiral's ship, with Tito on board, left the jetty, a Russian jeep screamed up to the quayside and two secret service men literally jumped on board at the last moment. The Russians thought King Peter might be aboard the destroyer, and that Tito had been tricked into meeting him behind their backs.[48]

It is clear that many of the British on Vis did resent the Soviet presence there, and endorsed the Foreign Office line that the Maclean mission was doing the Russians' job for them. Fitzroy's reply to this is forthright: 'The Russians, by sitting back and letting the British help Tito, produced the opposite effect from that which they intended. By not helping the Partisans they did their own case no good, while we, by supporting the Partisans, ultimately won their friendship.'[49] Indeed, Tito himself was worried by the westward drift of his movement that resulted from the Soviet fainéant attitude, and sent Djilas on a mission to Stalin in early 1944 to 'balance' the Velebit embassy to the Allies.

While the Russians still offered little more than moral support, the British were honing the Partisans to a rare edge of military perfection. On Vis they became acquainted with ever more sophisticated hardware, especially mountain guns and howitzers. Over 1944 as a whole the Allies supplied to the Partisans over 100,000 rifles, 50,000 sub-machine-guns, 1,380 mortars, 324,000 mortar bombs, 636,000 grenades, 97,500,000 rounds of small-arms ammunition, 700 wireless sets, 175,000 suits of battledress and 260,000 pairs of boots.

The month from mid-June to mid-July 1944 slipped away comfortably. There was daily contact between Fitzroy and Tito, and sometimes

the Marshal would go to Fitzroy's villa for a swim. Characteristic portraits of the two of them on Vis are provided by different observers.
David Sutherland, who had last seen Fitzroy at Athlit Castle the year
before, had flown in for talks with Vivian Street and found Fitzroy
sitting under a tree writing. ' "Wait a minute, David, just got to finish
this," he said. A few more squiggles, then he said, "Take a look at
this." He handed me a telegram in which, in eight or nine sentences, he
had encapsulated the entire political situation in Yugoslavia. He had a
genius for that sort of thing, not just for seeing the wood for the trees,
but for putting it on paper. Vivian said to me, "These people from the
Foreign Office can do this sort of thing so much better than us." '[50]

Douglas Fairbanks, who was with the American 'beachjumpers' in
combined operations with Tom Churchill's Commandos, remembers
an occasion when Tito came to inspect them. The officers paraded in
their smartest uniforms and Tito complimented them warmly,
proposing to give them a token of his gratitude. The eager officers
craned forward, hoping for a ribbon, or perhaps the Partisan Star. Tito
motioned to his aide to bring a box, and drew out for each man – two
tins of anchovies.[51]

Normally Fitzroy appeared the model soldier and diplomat, but
sometimes the strains of office told on him. Morgan-Giles recalls a
ferocious dressing-down Fitzroy gave Slim Farish for taking
unauthorized leave. 'Fitzroy could be a martinet and was certainly not a
man to cross.'[52] Annette Street, Vivian's widow, who saw a lot of him in
Bari, also remembers his darker side.

> Nowadays you see a kind, happy, wonderful man. But when young he could be
> extraordinarily difficult. He was an awkward cuss. Once at Bari he decided it
> would be good to go for a ride. The *carabinieri* were roused to get six horses. Off
> we went into the hills. Extraordinary thing to be doing in the middle of the war,
> but there was no gainsaying him. His mania for exercise transcended the fact
> that we had loads of office work to do. But he wasn't upfront difficult like
> Randolph. It was always, 'I'm terribly sorry, do you mind?' If he said tonight,
> it had to be tonight.[53]

Fitzroy's leisure time in Bari throws light on the proposition that he
was a ladies' man. He was certainly no Lloyd George or Jack Kennedy,
but he always enjoyed the company of women, especially beautiful
ones, of whom there were plenty among the FANYs (Female Auxiliary
Nursing Yeomen) and secretaries in the Mediterranean capitals. A
great favourite of Fitzroy's was Hermione Ranfurly. Another was
Nina, the Latvian widow of Colonel Guy Tamplin – whom Brigadier
Keble had been accused of hounding to death in SOE Cairo. Mike
Parker remembers: 'Nina was a famous "merry widow" – pots of
money, had a whale of a time, everyone on the mission proposed to her,

but unsuccessfully, as she was looking for a title.'[54] Though there are some grounds for Fitzroy's 'womanizing' reputation, Annette Street thinks that the Fitzroy of 1944 was too stiff and formal to be a philanderer.

> None of the girls I shared a flat with in Bari – there were six of us – wanted to sit next to him at dinner, he was that awkward. We were six girls among hundreds of men, but Fitzroy was nowhere as regards the desirable male. He never made a pass – the last thing he would have done. Always polite and correct – in many ways still very much the Third Secretary – but it was considered a great triumph once when we got him to do the hokey-cokey. He could drink anyone under the table and could breakfast off *raki*, which none of the other Brits could. He always called the girls 'dolls' – 'must have plenty of good-looking dolls' was his watchword – but there was never anyone he showed much interest in. He was too absorbed in what he was doing.[55]

'I would have thought Fitzroy a most chaste man,' says John Henniker, 'but giving the impression that he wasn't. "Bring on the dancing girls" is simply an idiom of that generation. He's a very good old thing in most ways – a very moral old thing. He'd like to have been a Lothario in a kilt, but wasn't. He talked a lot about women, but it didn't come naturally.'[56]

The equable tenor of life on Vis, and the trips to Bari, came to an end towards the close of July when Tito accepted an invitation to visit 'Jumbo' Wilson at Caserta. In June Tito had rebuffed an identical overture when he learned King Peter was to be in Italy at the same time, fearing an 'accidental' meeting contrived by the British. As it was, the Caserta meeting also very nearly failed to take place. Fitzroy explains:

> The day before the aeroplane came over to pick him up – you could land by Dakota in Vis then – at the very last moment Tito came and had lunch in my mess. After lunch he said, 'There's something I want to talk to you about.' I took him up to my room upstairs in the little house I was living in and he said, 'I cannot go tomorrow to see the Commander-in-Chief.' I was naturally not at all pleased and said, 'You will do yourself nothing but harm by being rude to the Supreme Allied Commander.' To which he replied, 'It is more complicated than that.' I had no idea that there was any question of his being confronted with King Peter and I would have strongly opposed the suggestion had I known of it.[57]

Tito departed from Vis with extreme reluctance, for he feared not only British chicanery but also the possible effect on the morale of his fighters on the mainland. He took with him five staff officers, including his son, his skilled interpreter Olga, a nine-soldier bodyguard and, as always, Tigger.

General Wilson's first encounter with Tito was at the lunch so hilariously described by Fitzroy at the beginning of this chapter. In the end, the two got on so well that the bodyguards would go to drink beer in the canteen and Tigger would go off to the cookhouse.[58] Tito's demand for tanks was countered by an invitation to visit the Eighth Army tank maintenance workshop at Naples. When he saw that 12,000 men were employed in servicing and repairing tanks, he agreed that to maintain such behemoths was beyond the Partisans at that time. Wilson was impressed by Tito, but less by his staff officers, whom he found arrogant, and high on revolutionary voluntarism. 'In talking to Tito's senior staff officers I realized how little they understood the technicalities of keeping armour in action. I mentioned that even an armoured regiment would require a maintenance unit so that the tanks could be serviced after a certain mileage and he [Tito] replied, "When our men drive tanks they will go 500 miles easily and we do not want such an encumbrance." '[59]

While Fitzroy was at Caserta a cable arrived from Churchill to say that he would be in Naples in a week's time and wanted to meet Tito. For security reasons this news could not be divulged, so Fitzroy had to stall Tito, who grew increasingly restive as meaningful subjects for discussion with Wilson became exhausted. To keep him busy, Fitzroy took him to meet General Alexander at Lake Bolsena, where Trieste was discussed, and to Capri for tea with his friend Hermione Ranfurly.

The highlight of the interlude between the Wilson and Churchill conferences was the trip Fitzroy made with the Marshal to Rome. Tito wanted to see St Peter's; once again, the fanaticism of his bodyguards Bosko and Prlja led to embarrassment. Admittedly, their task was thankless: Italy at that time was teeming with Germans, devout Catholic Italians, Ustase refugees and many others who wanted Tito dead, and Tito did not make security easier by insisting on wearing his extraordinarily ostentatious Marshal's uniform. The consequences of an assassination while Tito was under British protection were too frightening to contemplate. So there was some justification for Bosko and Prlja following Tito into the great basilica. Fitzroy pointed out to Tito that the presence of bodyguards with sub-machine-guns at the ready would give offence, quite apart from being counterproductive since it would alert any would-be assassin that here was a prize worth taking. Tito saw the point at once and ordered his men out, but they stood their ground. 'Comrade Tito, for more than three years we have protected you against the attacks of Nazi enemies and we're not going to fail you now.' Tito lost his temper and yelled, 'You do what you're told! Get out at once.' By now people were gathering to see what the commotion was all about: priests, GIs, American hospital nurses. The situation could scarcely have been more embarrassing.[60]

After all the diversionary sight-seeing and stalling, Tito turned out to be much better informed than the British thought. As he and Fitzroy sat eating lunch in the garden of the Williams' villa in Capri, they looked up to see a heavily escorted York aeroplane coming in to land. 'Here comes Mr Churchill,' said Tito. He had known all along.[61]

The two met next day on the wide balustraded terrace of General Wilson's villa, which had once been a favourite residence of Queen Victoria. It was swelteringly hot. Fitzroy describes the scene.

Tito, resplendent in gold braid, red tabs and tight-fitting grey serge, had arrived first and was looking out across the glittering waters of the bay to where a plume of smoke rose lazily from the summit of Vesuvius, when suddenly he became aware of the Prime Minister of Great Britain advancing on him with outstretched hand. Mr Churchill was wearing loose white ducks and an open-necked shirt. His face was round and pink and at the same time awe-inspiring, his expression welcoming and friendly. He had long wanted to see Tito for himself.[62]

Pierson Dixon of the Foreign Office, a 'hostile witness' on Churchill's staff, put a slightly different slant on the meeting: 'Tito was cautious, nervous and sweating a good deal in his absurd Marshal's uniform of thick cloth and gold lace.'[63]

There were four main topics of discussion. First, Tito was laying claim to Istria, Trieste, Venezia Giulia and part of Carinthia. Tito's forces were likely to get there before the Allies and present them with a *fait accompli*, but Churchill warned that the Allies were as likely to be able to do the same to him. Second, there was the military imperative of cutting off the retreating Germans in the Balkans. Third, there was the continuing issue of how to resolve *de jure* recognition of Subasic and King Peter with *de facto* acceptance of Partisan hegemony. Fourth, looking ahead to the post-war situation, there was the question of the feasibility of a pan-Balkan federation. Churchill made it clear he would not recognize the Partisans unless they came to terms with Peter's government. The possibility of Allied landings in Istria was discussed amicably, but Tito made it plain that he was interested in *Yugoslav* federation only, not pan-Balkanism. Tito played his cards cleverly. He assured Churchill that he had no intention of forcing Communism on Yugoslavia, since he expected all Europe to be democratic after the war. Churchill asked whether he would mind going public on that statement, but Tito shrewdly ducked the challenge and claimed to be reluctant to take such a step at present, lest it should look as though the declaration had been forced on him.

Churchill lectured Tito on Communism, and on the collectivization of agriculture remarked: 'My friend Marshal Stalin told me the other day that his battle with the peasants had been a more perilous and formidable undertaking than the battle for Stalingrad. I hope that you,

Marshal, will think twice before you join such a battle with your sturdy Serbian peasantry.'[64] Churchill also told Tito the Allies would lose interest in him if he turned his guns against the Cetniks rather than the Germans. Only then did Tito's composure begin to fray. Olga Humo's skill in translation averted some of the worst storms, so much so that Churchill later presented her with a gold locket. The morning session ended with an encomium from Churchill on the Partisans' achievement, which the lugubrious Pierson Dixon thought quite undid the effect of his 'sermon'.

At lunch the morning's work was nearly undone more comprehensively: once again, the problem was Bosko and Prlja. Since the villa was large enough to provide separate washing facilities for each delegation, Churchill and Fitzroy disappeared down one corridor and Tito and his bodyguards down the other, at right angles to the first. Five minutes later the two parties made their way back, converging from different directions on the same corner. Suddenly the Prime Minister found himself looking down the barrels of two sub-machine-guns. A fan of Westerns, Churchill whipped out a gold cigar case about the size of a Colt automatic and levelled it at Tito's stomach. Fitzroy says:

> What he did not know (but I did) was that Bosko and Prlja, after three years as guerrillas, were men of lightning reflexes who took no chances and who, if they thought their Marshal's life was in danger, would gladly have wiped out all three of the Big Three with a single burst. For the space of a split second I saw their trigger-fingers twitch, and only had time to hope that I for one would not survive what came next. But then, Tito began to laugh. Winston, seeing that his little joke had been a success, laughed too. And Bosko and Prlja, observing that the danger had passed, lowered their guns. Following on into Queen Victoria's fusty dining room, I took out a large khaki handkerchief and wiped the cold sweat from my brow.[65]

There were three main meetings. Churchill told Tito of the wonderful reports he had received from Randolph about life with the Partisans. Tito, becoming more emollient, agreed to the full merger of Subasic's government and his own, pending a final resolution. A declaration was issued on 17 August and it fell to Fitzroy to warn King Peter that, if he did not endorse it, the Russians would attack Mihailovic as an ally of the Axis.[66] But the entente was greeted with dismay by hardliners on both sides. The Partisan commander Zujovic commented sourly, 'The English are clever! An escort of warships and naval manoeuvres laid on in honour of the Old Man and I see it's had its effect!'[67] The curmudgeonly Pierson Dixon on the other side complained that Churchill had been much too cordial. He provides us with a glimpse of Fitzroy in action on the return journey to Naples on 13 August: 'Halfway across Fitzroy Maclean met us by arrangement, bearing a letter from Tito and a report on a conference in the morning between Tito and our military representatives. Fitzroy was a brave sight, in his kilt, boarding the launch. The rest of the voyage was complicated, as the Prime Minister was trying to read Tito's letter and Fitzroy's report in the interval of saluting the destroyers.'[68]

What were the reactions of the two leaders when the dust had settled? Tito on the flight back to Vis with Subasic professed himself well pleased. Fitzroy remarked: 'A year ago the Partisans had scarcely been heard of outside their own country. Now he, their leader, the one-time jailbird, had been received as an honoured guest by one of the Big Three.'[69] Tito told Fitzroy he thought Churchill a very human kind of man, with whom one could make real personal contact. 'It was quite a big moment for him. He had never met Stalin or Roosevelt, had been living in the wilds for three years, and through no fault of his own had seen little of life outside Yugoslavia. To come face to face with Churchill was a great thing for him.'[70]

What of Churchill on Tito? According to King Peter, Churchill told him that he had found Tito agreeable and polite but with an under-current of arrogance.[71] It later became the orthodox view that Churchill had not been at all impressed by Tito, and it is true that the King Peter imbroglio had been hardening his attitude towards the Marshal all summer. 'Tito failed to live up to Churchill's expectations of what this hardy guerrilla was meant to be like,' comments Mark Wheeler. 'He wasn't as romantic and impressive as Churchill had expected and was proving reluctant to fit in with Churchill's pet schemes – beating the Russians to Vienna by going through the Lubliana Gap, or the landings in Dalmatia.'[72] But Fitzroy insists that Churchill got on well with Tito at the Naples conference, and that his later strictures on him were the product of hindsight and *ex post* rationalizations.

Fitzroy's own labours were certainly perceived in a favourable light. Churchill even introduced him into the inner circle of his Ultra advisors. Wing Commander Crawshaw, officer in charge of Ultra at Allied Forces' HQ, was invited to a high-level supper, at which the only other two guests were Harold Macmillan and Fitzroy.[73] This makes it seem unlikely that Fitzroy was as ignorant of Ultra as (according to the rules) he should have been, and does help to fuel the speculations of hostile critics who assert that Menzies and Fitzroy were always hand in glove, and (assuming British omniscience) that Fitzroy therefore 'must have known' that Drvar was about to be attacked by the Germans in May 1944. It seems to be Fitzroy's fate that canards about him, no matter how often refuted, resurface periodically with but a slight change of form. It is therefore good to be able to ring down the curtain on August 1944 with a solid sign of his superiors' approval: he was made a CBE.[74]

13

'Ratweek' and Finale

OCTOBER 1944–MARCH 1945

IN his writings Fitzroy reveals a great warmth for Yugoslavia and a fine appreciation of its people and their qualities, so it is not surprising that after the war he bought a house there. His wanderings in Serbia in the autumn of 1944 produced the following notable passage.

> I recall, too, without being able to place them in the general plan of our journey, numerous isolated scenes and incidents which have somehow stuck in my memory; cold clear water spurting from a pump on the hillside under the trees in a village where we stopped in the blazing heat of midday, one working the pump while the others put their heads under it; a vast meal of milk and scrambled eggs eaten ravenously by the open windows of a low, cool, upper room overlooking a valley; sleeping on the grass in an orchard by a little stream and waking suddenly to find Sergeant Duncan's hand on my shoulder: 'They're moving off, sir; they say the Germans are coming'; and then shouts of '*Pokret*! Get going!' and confusion and plunging horses and 'What's happened to the wireless sets?'; long dismal tramps in pitch darkness through pouring rain; discussions whether to push on or to stop in a village with a population reputed to be pro-German or riddled with typhus; speculating as to the meaning of black flags hung outside peasants' houses; knocking and being told that they mean that one of the family has just died of typhus; hoping this is bluff and sleeping there all the same, all crowded into one room; waking next morning to find the rain stopped and the house, where we had arrived in the middle of the night, surrounded by orchards laden with ripe plums; arriving in a village to find a wedding in progress and being swept, before we know where we are, into a *kola*, twisting and whirling in the sunshine on the green with the village maidens; lying at night out on the hillside in our sleeping-bags and listening to the wireless: the BBC, the nine o'clock news, Tommy Handley.

The Soviet Union, which has also always fascinated Fitzroy, intruded in this period as the Red Army attacked Belgrade. His description of an encounter with a Soviet officer and a couple of his sergeants has a different kind of appeal.

Finding that we spoke their language, [they] at once made us welcome. Soon all of us, including the family of peasants who owned the cottage, were sitting on the only bed, drinking hot milk and some kind of raw alcohol and eating black bread and listening to a detailed account, not only of the immediate military situation, but of the Lieutenant's own war experiences and of his early life and childhood in far-away Vologda. In a flash I was back in the Soviet Union: the taste of the food and drink; the stuffiness of the little wooden shack; the cold outside; the heat inside; the droning voices; the soft inflexions of spoken Russian; the stereotyped Russian jargon; and, above all, the smell: that indefinable composite aroma of petrol, sheepskin and vodka, black bread and cabbage soup, Soviet scent and unwashed human bodies, which permeates every inch of the Soviet Union and which Russians somehow manage to take with them wherever they go.

By the time Fitzroy returned to Vis, Paris had been liberated and the American commanders in Western Europe were talking sanguinely of having 'the boys back home' by Christmas. On the Balkan front it did not seem that the German nut could be so easily cracked, though the Red Army had entered Romania and was advancing rapidly towards the Danube and the frontiers of Yugoslavia. But it was obvious in London that the Wehrmacht was overstretched on this peripheral theatre of war, and that Berlin would very soon order its divisions to pull out. In early September Fitzroy and his aides worked on a plan, codenamed Operation Ratweek, which was designed to ensure that as few Germans as possible withdrew from Yugoslavia in safety. By land, sea and air the Allies and Partisans would make a concerted effort to disrupt enemy communications, causing chaos and netting thousands of prisoners.

The German position was in fact desperate. The Russians were advancing north-east of Belgrade while the Partisans were pressing from the south-east. Though few of the actors realized it, the role of Ultra was again crucial. Intercepted signals showed the German generals in disarray over the wisdom of keeping divisions idle along the Dalmatian coast, waiting for an Anglo-American invasion that would probably never come; the best Wehrmacht opinion held that Hitler was letting the shadow of this imaginary invasion prevail over the substance of Russian divisions at the gates of Belgrade. The critics were right. Ultra also proved Mihailovic's collaboration beyond all doubt. In revenge for the Allies' having 'handed the country over to Bolshevism', he was eager to assist German Army Group E's retreat through Sarajevo.[1]

Peter Moore and John Clarke did most of the detailed operational planning of Ratweek at Bari. Yugoslavia was divided up into sectors, a Partisan commander and a British officer attached to him were made responsible for each, and objectives were allotted. Difficult targets were made the responsibility of the RAF and USAAF.[2] German withdrawal would be bound to take place along the Vardar valley, so the Belgrade-Salonica railway was the chief target.

Once he was convinced that the planning for Ratweek was in its final phases, Fitzroy went to Tito's cave on Mount Hum to bid a friendly farewell; the two pledged a reunion soon in Belgrade. Some heads of mission would have stayed on in Vis, but Fitzroy yearned for further action in the field and was by now bored with the endless round of political wrangling featuring the eternal triangle of Tito, Subasic and King Peter. His plan was to join John Henniker in Serbia – which he had not seen – where Koca Popovic was the Partisan commander. Tito made straight the ways by despatching a personal signal to Popovic; he also sent with Fitzroy his chief troubleshooter General Zujovic, also known as Crni, 'the Black'. Fitzroy and Crni made arrangements to land by plane near Popovic's headquarters on the slopes of the Radan.

After a difficult landing by Dakota – which made Fitzroy think it might have been better to drop in by parachute – followed by a tiring ride on horseback through a wooded battlefield where bullets whined and pinged around them, Fitzroy and Crni made contact with Henniker, who was sleeping in an improvised wigwam made from parachute parts. Next day Henniker reported on the four months he had spent in Serbia. The Partisan cause had prospered for a number of reasons: the leadership of the Serb, Popovic; the supplies from the Allies, which allowed Popovic to arm volunteers he had previously had to turn away; and the abandonment of Mihailovic by King Peter, which cut the ground from under the Cetniks' claim to be fighting for the monarchy. Fitzroy already knew that Cetniks were deserting Mihailovic in droves and coming over to the Partisans, for in August he had received 'begging letters' from would-be converts to Tito's cause, asking for General Wilson to arrange a temporary non-aggression pact pending their ultimate fusion with the Partisans.[3] It was now clear that the Partisans were going to win the war against the Germans, and everyone wanted to be on the winning side.

Fitzroy next met Koca Popovic and co-ordinated operations with him, deciding which targets the Partisans could attack on their own and which needed RAF support. He then conferred by signal with Bill Elliott in Caserta. By the end of August preparations for Ratweek were complete. By a stroke of luck, the Germans began their withdrawal exactly when Ratweek had been perfected.

In the week that followed Fitzroy was an eyewitness of the near-incredible success of the operation. He and the Partisans watched with awe as fifty Flying Fortresses pounded a heavy concentration of German armour into ashes at Leskovac. As each Allied bombing raid reduced a further German target to rubble, the Partisan ranks were swollen by deserting Cetniks, convinced now that Mihailovic's game was up. From all over Yugoslavia reports came in of terrible damage to enemy communications, and especially to the Belgrade–Salonika and the Ljubljana–Zagreb railways. Each time the Germans tried to repair the damage, a squadron of Balkan Air Force fighters would come swooping down like angry bees. Fitzroy was in the thick of Partisan action, first in a bitter skirmish outside the town of Lebanc, then when advancing north towards the Toplica valley, and finally at the liberation of Prokuplje.

All this activity was greatly to Fitzroy's taste, so he was intensely annnoyed to be ordered out to 'find' Tito, who had disappeared from Vis. 'Mentally consigning BAF, Tito and General Wilson, and everyone else concerned to perdition'[4], he made his way to the landing strip at Bojnik.

On his arrival at Bari he found an angry telegram from Churchill, exclaiming at the way Tito had 'levanted' without a word to his allies. Mutual suspicion and cries of 'doublecross' arose once more. Reconstruction of the Marshal's dramatic exit revealed that on 21 September he had left Vis surreptitiously, made his way across the Adriatic, avoided detection by the RAF guards at Bari airfield and boarded a Soviet-piloted Dakota, in which he flew first to Romania and then to Moscow. Fitzroy describes the element of farce that always seemed to accompany Second World War dramas: 'At the last moment his dog Tigger, realizing that his master was going away, made such a fuss that Tito decided to take him too. A sack was put over his head to keep him quiet while the party was getting into the aircraft.'[5]

The Americans seem to have been better informed about Tito's likely intentions than the British. The American diplomat Robert Murphy, after a talk with Tito in August, was convinced that the Red Army would not enter Serbia but would confine their trans-Danube activities to Hungary, leaving the Partisans to deal with the Mihailovic heartland. After Tito's 'levant' he reported that the Marshal's aim was clearly to dissuade the Russians from entering Yugoslavia.[6] He was nearly right, but not quite. Tito was agreeable to the Red Army assisting in the capture of Belgrade, but he wanted the terms upon which his Soviet allies would tread Yugoslav soil clearly spelt out. He decided he had no choice but to go to Moscow and talk to Stalin, whom he had never before met. After his Naples talks with Churchill, it was also necessary for Tito to reassure a suspicious Stalin that he had not gone over completely to the Western camp.

The encounter between Tito and Stalin was not a notable success. Stalin had resented the independent tone of Tito's cables to Moscow over the past two years, and had allegedly stamped his foot with rage when he received the Neretva message in early 1943 ('If you cannot help

us, at least do not hinder us'). By continuing in the same vein in
Moscow and contradicting him on a number of points, Tito did nothing
to assuage Stalin's unease. He felt that Tito was getting above himself:
he resented his good looks, his spectacular uniforms, and the publicity
the Partisans had been getting.[7] There were, however, some areas of
accord. The two agreed to strive for a federated Yugoslavia, but conceded that they might have to leave Serbia as an independent country;
Stalin also went out of his way to make it clear that he understood and
approved British interests in the region. On the question of the Red
Army, Tito drove a hard bargain. He told Stalin he would give permission for Marshal Tolbukhin's forces to enter Yugoslavia for a finite
period only and that, although the Partisans would co-operate with the
Soviets, there was no question of their being under Tolbukhin's overall
command.[8]

If Tito had scored over Stalin in Moscow, he now had a lot of work to
do in mending fences with the British and Americans. Tito offered two
comments on his actions. One was that he had been advised by Moscow
that if he announced his intention openly, the Allies would stop him
leaving Vis or, worse, mete out to him the Sikorski treatment.[9] The
other was that he was under no obligation whatever to give an account
of himself to the Allies, and that their resentment was an impertinence.
'We are an independent nation,' he proudly told Fitzroy when explaining his flight to Moscow.[10] When Fitzroy pressed him, Tito responded
facetiously. 'Only recently Mr Churchill went to Quebec to see President Roosevelt and I only heard of this visit after he had returned. And I
was not angry.'[11]

Allied representations to Stalin fared no better. Stalin told Averell
Harriman that Tito had asked him to keep the visit secret, and when
Eden raised the matter with Molotov, his reply was lofty: 'He said
[Tito] was a peasant and did not understand anything about politics . . .
he had the secretiveness of his type and had not dared to impart his
plans to anyone.'[12]

With the exception of Macmillan, senior British figures reacted with
anger to Tito's 'treachery'. Churchill muttered about 'Balkan brigands'. 'When Tito flew to Moscow in September,' Mark Wheeler sums
up, 'Churchill's disillusionment increased. He became worried that
Britain would be deeply implicated in a Yugoslav civil war – as if there
were not already a civil war in which Britain was implicated, and which
had been going on for four years!'[13] Some observers have tried to claim
that Fitzroy himself lost caste because of these events and that, had he
been dogging Tito's footsteps in Vis instead of glory-hunting in Serbia,
the incident would not have occurred.[14]

Once he reached Bari, it was clear to Fitzroy that there was no point
in proceeding to Vis. He therefore returned to Serbia. Maps in the

operations room at Bari indicated that the corps under Peko Dapcevic, thrusting north-east through western Serbia, was likely to reach Belgrade before Koca Popovic. Dapcevic had reached Valjevo, so it was there that the Balkan Air Force landed Fitzroy a few nights later.

With him was Charlie Thayer, his old friend from the Russian days. Fitzroy had met in him the bar of Claridges in May and told him that the Anglo-American Mission had been split into two, with Donovan now organizing his own independent team; why not try for that? Fitzroy remembers: 'When I got to Chequers and saw Winston and Donovan, Charlie Thayer's fate was sealed!'[15]

Thayer had a vivid memory of the landing.

> Maclean turned to his liaison officer, Major Freddy Cole, who'd met us.
> 'Where's Tito?'
> 'Don't know.'
> 'Where's Arso [Jovanovic]?' Maclean asked.
> 'He arrived last night from Vis with half a dozen officers of the Supreme Staff and the Russian Military Mission.'
> 'Where's Peko?'
> 'He's here all right. Planning to move to Belgrade soon.'[16]

In Valjevo, which had been taken only after ferocious fighting, Fitzroy was surprised by the leniency with which the Partisans seemed to be treating the Nedic quislings, Serbian fascists and other pro-Axis elements. But he was also concerned by the subtly growing rift between Tito's men and the Allies. When senior Partisans like Crni arrived, Fitzroy tackled them about this. He reported to General Wilson: 'General Zujovic, who in many respects is Tito's right-hand man, is here. I have always found him sensible and I took the opportunity of speaking to him strongly on the present state of our relations with the Partisans. I said that in Tito's absence friction had reached such a pitch that we wondered if the Partisans were not seeking pretexts to sever all relations with Great Britain and the United States.'[17]

Zujovic (Crni) was conciliatory, but admitted there were problems. Why had there been a sudden falling-off in Allied supplies, in particular the withdrawal of two British supply ships? To the Partisans it looked very much as if the British were trying to use humanitarian aid as a political lever. There was also the recent incident, 'unfortunate' at best, of a BBC broadcast attributing Partisan successes during 'Ratweek' entirely to the *matériel* provided by the Allies. But the main problem was the US mission to Mihailovic. Once again Donovan was proving a thorn in Fitzroy's side. Zujevic reiterated Tito's bitter complaints, which the Marshal had also made in person to Fitzroy on Vis, about MacDowell's claim to be offering Mihailovic official aid from the

USA.[18] When Fitzroy remonstrated at the time with Wilson, OSS pretended that MacDowell had been trying to get out of Yugoslavia but had been prevented by the fighting. Fitzroy now complained bitterly to Bill Elliott: 'I learn privately from the Americans that aircraft was actually sent to bring out MacDowell some time ago, but that latter has refused on some inadequate pretext.'[19]

The upshot of Fitzroy's report was that General Wilson contacted Churchill, who in turn got Roosevelt to intervene with Donovan and order MacDowell's evacuation.[20] But Donovan rejected a British request that OSS evacuate Mihailovic, on the grounds that 'serious consequences' would ensue.[21] Still, Fitzroy felt reasonably satisfied, and even more so, two days after his talk with Crni, when Zujevic brought him a very conciliatory message from Tito. To show that his heart was still in the Partisan highlands, Fitzroy sent a message to General Popovi, commander of the Greek guerrilla forces, congratulating him on the liberation of the Peloponnese.[22]

In Valjevo Fitzroy and Thayer met Colonel Ellery Huntingdon, commander of the US military mission to the Partisans, who brought the bad news that Slim Farish had been killed in Greece. Thayer was constantly with Fitzroy in these October days and has left a revealing memoir.

We'd hardly arrived in Valjevo when Maclean announced we'd have to get horses. I knew from the old days in Moscow how much Fitzroy liked to ride, but I wondered whether it was worth all the trouble and expense of fitting up a stable.

'Indeed it is,' Maclean answered. 'Horses are absolutely essential in case the Germans make another raid on us.'

'But we've got jeeps now. Couldn't we escape in those?'

Maclean gave me a withering glance. 'When the Germans are raiding,' he explained condescendingly, 'the Partisans invariably hide in the deepest forests where jeeps can't go. Besides, we don't have to buy horses. We simply requisition them – and anyway, I need exercise if I'm going to keep fit. Come on, let's go and see Arso's supply officer.'

The supply officer soon produced a couple of diminutive animals that looked more like rabbits than horses, but by shortening his stirrups, Maclean was able to keep his long legs off the ground. That same day we had the horses saddled up for a 'reconnoitre' in the hills. When the horses turned up they were accompanied by four teenage roughnecks, also mounted and armed with tommy-guns.

'What in God's name are those thugs for?' I asked.

'They aren't thugs, they're our bodyguards. Always have bodyguards when you leave camp, you know.'

'What are we being protected from – wolves?'

'No, assassins,' Maclean retorted. We mounted up and trotted off into the wooded hills south of Valjevo.[23]

From Valjevo Fitzroy accompanied the Partisans on the advance to Arandjelovac, forty miles south of Belgrade. Here on 19 October they learned that the battle for Belgrade had begun. The Red Army was sweeping in from the north-east and south-east and the Partisans from the south. The Yugoslav capital, which had taken a pounding from the Luftwaffe in 1941, was now subjected to a far more awesome barrage by the RAF and USAAF. As the 1st Partisan Corps drove up from Arandjelovac to Belgrade, they found the villages full of the Red Army. Fitzroy had just been awarded the Order of Kutusov by the Russians, so he screwed the large silver and platinum star onto his battledress tunic. 'This, and the fact that both Charlie and I could talk to them in their own language, had an immediate effect on the Russians, who came crowding round the jeep whenever we stopped, fingering our weapons and equipment admiringly and proudly exhibiting their own.'[24]

They saw evidence in plenty, in the smoking hulks of disabled Soviet tanks, of the ferocity of the battle that had been raging just hours before. Twenty miles south of Belgrade they emerged onto the main road and joined a huge convoy of Soviet armour also flowing northwards. Fitzroy noticed that the Red Army lived off the land and that their trucks carried just petrol and ammunition.

> Of rations, blankets, spare boots or clothing there was no trace. The presumption was that such articles, if they were required at all, were provided at the expense of the enemy or of the local population. Almost every man we saw was a fighting soldier. What they carried with them were materials of war in the narrowest sense. We were witnessing a return to the administrative methods of Attila and Genghis Khan, and the results seemed to deserve careful attention. For there could no doubt that here lay one reason for the amazing speed of the Red Army's advance across Europe.[25]

Fitzroy also saw plenty of evidence of atrocities, and of prisoners slaughtered in droves. 'I saw a hundred or more corpses, lying in rows, one upon the other, like ninepins knocked over by the same ball. They had clearly not died in battle.'[26]

At the outskirts of Belgrade they ran General Peko to earth at his headquarters. They asked to be allowed into the thick of the fighting but Arso Jovanovic, Fitzroy's old enemy, intervened to say that he would not hear of the Allied Mission being allowed near the battlefield. The American head of mission, Huntingdon, cajoled, argued and threatened. Fitzroy weighed in on his side, and Arso dug in even more obdurately. Finally it was agreed that Peko's Chief-of-Staff would take them to the ancient Ottoman fortress, the Kalmegdan, to view the battle.[27]

Fitzroy, Street and Thayer were driven round Belgrade while the city was still under heavy shell fire. Street began to grow impatient with the zigzag line they were threading to the fort, which seemed to take them needlessly into the thickest fighting, but Peko's Chief-of-Staff would not be deterred. Finally they reached the grounds of the Kalmegdan, to find heavy skirmishing still going on in its gardens. Pressing through the trees they emerged on a terrace from which they looked out over an immense panorama of the Sava river: they had a bird's-eye view of the final stages of the battle for Belgrade. The Germans, driven back across the Zemun bridge, unaccountably failed to blow it up and were then routed in the suburb across the river by pursuing Russians. It was later learned that the Germans' demolition charges on the bridge had been disconnected by an old man who had won a gold medal for a similar feat in the Balkan war of 1912. Thayer describes their position at the Kalmegdan: 'I huddled with Maclean behind a large stone lion on the parapet, occasionally taking a peek over the lion's front paws. Maclean was much braver and rested field-glasses on the lion's back to get a good look at what was going on.'[28]

The spectacle was brought to an end when Russian gunners opened up from the Kalmegdan on the Zemun suburb, thus drawing counter-fire from the Germans. The Partisan Chief-of-Staff hurried his guests back to headquarters. But there was no stopping the irrepressible Fitzroy. Thayer tells what happened next.

Maclean and I went out to investigate. A piece of steel shrapnel hit the cobblestone street in front of me. I looked at Maclean.
    'Do you think it is very safe being out in this hail-storm?'
    'Very safe, no,' Maclean answered laconically. 'Safe enough, yes.'
    We walked on. Fortunately we hadn't gone far along the blacked-out street when we met a military patrol. They challenged us. We identified ourselves and asked where Corps HQ was located. They gave us a guide and in five minutes we were talking to Peko himself.
    'What's going on, Peko?' Maclean asked. 'Haven't heard such a row since the war began.'
    Peko looked a little embarrassed. 'It's nothing serious, I promise. It's just . . . well . . . you see, the troops are . . . are just sort of celebrating.'
    'Celebrating! Good God! Using up all that ammunition and supplies just to celebrate. It took us months to get that out to you,' Maclean protested.
    'Well, we're doing our damnedest to stop it, but the boys are in pretty high spirits. They know now that they've linked up with the Russians, they'll have all the supplies they need. It won't have to come from you any more.'
    The thrust went home and Maclean and I both winced. 'We understand, and will report what you've said to AFHQ. But just for your own sake you'd better make sure the Russians are in a position to supply you. We've been supplying Russia ourselves pretty substantially for the past few years. We hope they have enough to keep you going.'[29]

There was some justification for boisterous celebration: the week-long battle for the Yugoslav capital had involved bitter hand-to-hand fighting with an enemy who refused to admit defeat and performed prodigies of valour. Casualty lists showed 16,000 Germans killed and 8,000 captured. In addition, now that Belgrade had fallen, the Partisan army could appear openly in the field for the first time. On the debit side, the devastation in the city was appalling. There were bomb-sites everywhere, derelict tanks on the streets, and rough wooden crosses for the dead. On walls there still hung German notices announcing executions for aiding the Partisans. At night stray Germans would emerge from cellars and attics where they had holed up, and start trying to fight their way out of the city.

Fitzroy was housed in the Hotel Balkan, and could see Belgrade degenerating into a Hobbesian war of all against all. One afternoon he was listening to the radio when a drunken Russian soldier burst in carrying a sub-machine-gun. Laughing insanely, he silenced the radio with a burst from his gun. Fitzroy lifted the phone and asked for the Russian general, billeted upstairs in the same hotel. Two even tougher Russian soldiers soon burst into his room and led away the culprit. 'There was a bang, and that was the end of him.'[30] Another morning he found the Partisan sentry who had been detailed to guard his much-prized jeep standing over a dead Russian soldier. The sentry explained that he had shot the man as he tried to steal the jeep. Next morning Fitzroy found the sentry dead and the jeep gone.[31]

The Russian troops were out of hand. Tension between them and the Partisans had been acute even before the Germans had been driven from Belgrade, because each claimed to be doing the bulk of the fighting. Now, the Russian soldiery behaved liked the Hunnish conquerors of legend, and Yugoslav indignation led directly to the great rift in 1948. The Yugoslavs could perhaps have shrugged off the 1,204 cases of robbery with violence, but not the outrages committed on their women. There were 1,219 rapes, 329 attempted rapes, 111 rapes with murder and 248 rapes with attempted murder. As Fitzroy recorded sadly: 'To an eyewitness of the liberation of Belgrade there seems nothing inherently improbable about these statistics.'[32] One Russian officer actually raped a Partisan girl while she was delivering an important message at the height of the battle. It did not help, either, that a drunken Russian officer shot and wounded Tito's son Zharko in a Belgrade night-club. The Partisans were all the more shocked because they had thought of the Soviet Union as the fount of virtue.

When Tito arrived he had an angry confrontation with General Korneyev, with whom he had never enjoyed particularly warm relations. Doubtless remembering his many limping treks to Tito's cave, and the fangs of Tigger, Korneyev exploded over the 'slur' on the honour of the Red Army. Djilas actually caused an international incident by pointing out that not a single British officer had behaved like a beast, unlike their Russian counterparts.[33] There was a further furious altercation when Tito demanded of Marshal Tolbukhin that the detested Bulgarian troops be transferred forthwith from Yugoslavia to Hungary. There was general relief when the Red Army switched its attentions to the land of the Magyars.

Tito decided to hold a victory parade. The campaign for Yugoslavia was as good as over: the Partisans had liberated Serbia, Macedonia, Montenegro, Herzegovina, Dalmatia and most of Bosnia and Croatia. The Germans were in full retreat, though they were trying to hold onto the Sarajevo–Brod–Zagreb communication network while they prepared their ultimate line of defence in Croatia and Slovenia. The guerrilla phase of the war was finished; it now became an orthodox war of movement. Tito's political grip on the country was unchallenged; Mihailovic and his tattered remnants had retreated into the very Bosnian fastnesses where Fitzroy had first made contact with the Partisans.

On 27 October Fitzroy had his first interview with Tito since Vis. He was anxious for this moment as it was a week since he had received an urgent signal from General Wilson, asking for clarification on future joint operations.[34] Tito announced his new idea of a Council of Regents, to exclude King Peter; it was quite clear that this was a device to secure recognition from the Allies. Meanwhile he and Subasic would form a united front, with elements from both the Anti-Fascist Council and the Royal Yugoslav government.

It was time to move on to the more contentious issues separating the Allies and Tito. Fitzroy began by handing the Marshal a personal message from Churchill, which put him in a good mood for the rest of the interview.[35] They talked of the embarrassment caused by Tito's journey to Moscow, and Tito defended his position vigorously. He expressed vexation that King George VI had sent a message of congratulation on the liberation of Belgrade to 'our gallant ally King Peter' instead of to the Partisans who had done the fighting, although he claimed that Fitzroy's personal message of congratulation to him had done much to assuage the slight.[36]

Fitzroy was unable to make too much of the flight to Moscow: Churchill had by now given offence by a visit of his own. He had discussed the future of Yugoslavia with Stalin, without breathing a word of his intentions to Tito. This was the famous '50:50' agreement by which the two agreed to partition south-east Europe into spheres of influence: in Romania there would be a 90:10 ratio in favour of the Russians; in Greece the proportions would be reversed; Russia was to predominate 75:25 in Bulgaria, while in Yugoslavia and Hungary the split would be 50:50. Apparently Churchill simply jotted down the figures on half a sheet of paper, which Stalin then ticked with a blue pencil. Tito was convinced that the Big Two aimed at a political division of Yugoslavia, with the Red Army advancing from the east and Anglo-American landings on the coast. His conviction on this point vitiated Anglo-Yugoslav relations for the rest of the war.

Fitzroy knew there would be trouble once Tito got wind of this piece of Great Power high-handedness: 'I myself just heard about it by signal in Belgrade. I got to Belgrade on 20 October, which was the day when Belgrade fell. And I hardly had time to look round before I got a top secret signal from the Foreign Office to say that they had reached this agreement. I must say I was amazed and I also thought, when Tito finds out about this it is going to be very awkward.'[37]

Not until after the war did Fitzroy discover that, as always, Tito had been better informed than he realized. Tito knew, and Churchill knew that he knew. In a personal message to Tito at the beginning of December, Churchill appealed to the percentage agreement over difficulties some of Tito's commanders were making about British activities on the Adriatic coast. Tito's reply was conciliatory, but he made no reference to the agreement.[38] Churchill returned to the attack: 'As you know, we have made an arrangement with the Marshal and the Soviet government to pursue as far as possible a joint policy towards Yugoslavia, and that our influence there should be held in equal balance. But you seem to be treating us in an increasingly invidious fashion.'[39] Churchill informed Stalin that he had sent that cable to Tito and asked for his comments. Stalin said he wanted to consult Tito first, but a later reply from Tito to Churchill answered every point he had raised *except* the '50–50' agreement.

Tito was not alone in thinking that Churchill wanted to partition Yugoslavia. Fitzroy thought so too, and agreed with Tito that Churchill's action was insensitive: 'Of course, to say equal joint policies towards a country is not the same as saying, "We are going to split you up 50–50". The first time I discussed this awkward subject with Tito after the war, I did my best to explain it on the grounds that of course it did not mean anything like spheres of influence and that it seemed to me pretty silly anyway.'[40]

The best research seems to indicate that the '50–50' policy was not really a policy at all. To begin with, the sheet of paper hastily scribbled out at dinner could by no stretch of the imagination be called an 'agreement' in the true diplomatic sense; moreover, as Churchill explained to Roosevelt, this *ad hoc* arrangement was intended to last no more than three months. It seems likely that the entire '50–50' charade was simply a ploy by Churchill to get Stalin to reveal his hand on how far he expected the Red Army to advance in Europe. But it caused confusion and bad feeling. Bill Deakin said in 1974: 'What he was really after was to see where the Red Armies were going. He was not trying to divide up the Balkans. Maybe he gave the wrong impression; but all I can be sure of is what he thought he had done.' Fitzroy riposted: 'He gave me the wrong impression, all right.'[41]

On 2 November a draft agreement was signed between Tito and Subasic, along the lines intimated to Fitzroy at the 27 October meeting. When Fitzroy informed London, the reaction was far from favourable. Churchill was most annoyed with Fitzroy's first telegram, concerning the proposed Council of Regents, particularly as King Peter was complaining sullenly to Cadogan that Churchill had authorized the manoeuvre. When Fitzroy's second telegram of 2 November, announcing the Tito–Subasic agreement, was received, Churchill thought it high time he summoned the head of his political and military mission back to London for talks.[42]

While Subasic departed for Moscow for talks with Stalin, Fitzroy flew to London, where he arrived on 8 November.[43] He brought the Tito–Subasic accord with him for inspection by Churchill and King Peter. Fitzroy had a difficult meeting with the young king on 16 November, when Peter tetchily asked why Subasic had not contacted him direct, instead of sending the agreement with Fitzroy; the king hinted broadly that Tito must have suborned Subasic and tried to make propaganda from his visit to Moscow. Later he insinuated, absurdly, that Subasic had kept Fitzroy in the dark: 'When the news came through that Subasic was in Moscow shortly afterwards, even men like Brigadier Maclean were alarmed,' he claimed.[44]

If the political aspect of his work was as tiresome as ever, Fitzroy found the gathering military collision between London and the Partisans much more worrying. Churchill was always a man of extreme likes and dislikes, oscillating between excessive admiration and unjustified denigration. He continually changed his mind about Tito. Having previously regarded Tito as the archetype of hardy guerrilla leader, by the end of 1944 he was coming to view him as a somewhat unsavoury Balkan bandit, and a Communist to boot. He did not approve of Tito's independent tone, which made nonsense of the Moscow '50–50' agreement, and seemed unable to understand the force of Tito's objection that the agreement was an insult to Yugoslavia in the first place. And he had no patience with Tito's insistence that the British clear all troop landings with him. 'We shall land anywhere we like, whatever we like and as much of it as we choose.'[45]

It did not help to achieve a balanced picture that General Wilson had by now also taken against Tito. He was irked that Tito, having officially accepted his assurances on sensitive matters, continued to complain of Allied duplicity. He was also irritated that his urgent request to Tito to deny the Germans the bottleneck of roads radiating out from Sarajevo had been ignored. And when he asked permission to land British troops in the far north, in the Dalmatian ports, Tito responded with complaints about the American mission to Mihailovic. To supply the Partisan campaign against the retreating Germans in Bosnia, Wilson asked that the ports of Split, Zara and Sibenik be opened. 'On 19th November I followed this up by asking for a permit to land a British force of one armoured regiment and a field artillery regiment at Zara to help the Partisans, who were in difficulties. Tito was not willing to grant this and wanted equipment to be handed over to be used by the Partisans, an absurd request as the Partisans had not the trained personnel to handle and maintain it; I refused.'[46]

These were reasonable enough complaints on paper, but they ignored the nuances of the Yugoslav situation. It was simply not good enough for Wilson to tell Tito that the MacDowell mission was with Mihailovic to rescue baled-out airmen at the request of President Roosevelt; Tito was too well-informed, and he knew all about his detractors in the State Department. Wilson was also insensitive to Yugoslav pride and concern over sovereignty. Above all, he ignored Tito's fears about British intentions. The British campaign to destroy the Greek Communist ELAS guerrillas was at its height in November 1944, and Tito feared a repeat in Yugoslavia. This is why, though Tito initially authorized the British to land field artillery at Dubrovnik to harry the German retreat, he changed his mind at the end of November, unblocking the Germans' escape route. In the considered opinion of John Henniker, Wilson's reports on Tito did him nothing like justice.[47] A good example of Wilson's misperceptions arose over Trieste, to which Tito formally laid claim in September 1944. At this stage the Italians were happy to see this port fall into Tito's hands, and many Italian partisan groups placed themselves under his operational control in the autumn and winter of 1944.[48] Yet Wilson construed the situation as 'Partisan misdemeanours' in Italy, and complained to Fitzroy accordingly.[49]

Fitzroy therefore faced a great test of his diplomatic skills when on 6 December he returned to Belgrade with another personal message from Churchill to Tito. Those who accuse Fitzroy of having fallen under Tito's spell cannot have read his reports in December 1944. 'Tito struck me as looking tired and harassed. He is clearly overwhelmed with hopes of all kinds and is obliged to delegate responsibility to subordinates who are unwilling and unable to assume it. To this and to the great inexperience of Tito and his followers I attribute many of the problems which have arisen. Matters have been further aggravated by suspicions of our motives.'[50]

An exhausting round of talks with senior Yugoslavs made clear these suspicions. Fitzroy found Subasic less than coherent about his trip to Moscow, though he and Kardelj had been amused when Stalin admonished them to ensure free and fair voting in Yugoslavia: 'None of

your rigged elections!' Stalin had roared.[51] But the Partisan leaders'
preoccupation was the British suppression of Communist guerrillas in
Greece. Some Partisans suggested sending a corps of veterans to Athens
to turn the tide against the 'imperialists', and their attitude was
reflected in the pronouncements of the Titoist press. Fitzroy warned
Tito about 'unsatisfactory' propaganda towards Britain and the USA;
Tito distanced himself from his more extreme followers.[52]

He also apologized for his men's failure to co-operate with the British
in Dubrovnik, and for an incident when Crni was said to have 'insulted'
a Royal Navy ship. Yet it was clear that he still suspected the British of a
secret design to restore King Peter by force. He was not the only one to
draw the wrong conclusion. Mihailovic, too, began to think that the
Allies might pull his chestnuts out of the fire.

Fitzroy was worried about the way Wilson's attitude was pushing
Tito towards Moscow, militarily. That Partisans were fighting with the
Red Army in Hungary could be dismissed as a gesture of 'comradely'
solidarity: not so easily dismissed was the way the Russians were equip-
ping Tito's air force. It was supposed to be a corollary of the '50–50'
agreement that the Soviets would supply the Partisan army with *matériel*
while Britain trained and equipped the air force. But because of
Wilson's hawkish line the British were doing very little; even worse,
they insisted that this was because Tito was 'making difficulties'. Fitzroy sent cable after cable imploring London to rectify matters.[53]

December found Fitzroy embroiled in four crises, each involving him
in tough talking with Tito. There was the continuing crisis over Greece,
leading to much wild talk (which Tito staunchly repudiated) of a war to
clear the 'imperialists' from south-east Europe.[54] There was trouble
with local Partisan commanders, especially Crni whom Fitzroy tried
hard to get Tito to sack, because of their surly and uncooperative
attitude towards the British troops in Yugoslavia. A particular bone of
contention was the airfield at Zara: Wilson wanted it under British
command – the Partisans regarded that as an infringement of sovereignty.[55] Third, there was a clash over UNRRA food aid sent from
Britain to Yugoslavia. London insisted that there had to be observers,
to see that the food was not 'administratively absorbed' by some corrupt
local Partisan commander, and that Tito did not make its distribution
contingent on political acceptance of his party. Tito regarded this, too,
as an infringement of sovereignty. On 15 December General Alexander
wrote to Fitzroy: 'This is an intolerable state of affairs. Please inform
Marshal Tito that the food and ships are waiting to sail to relieve the
starving population of Dalmatia but in view of my orders from the
Combined Chiefs of Staff . . . my hands are tied in this matter.'[56]
Fitzroy wrote back gloomily that Tito preferred to starve rather than
accept British terms: he was adamant that he did not want his country

overrun by foreign bureaucrats. 'My experience has always been that in such matters it is necessary to take him personally over each jump in turn.'[57] Further talking revealed that Tito felt bitterly that his people were having to suffer because the British wanted to be bullies. Fitzroy had to mix firmness and cajolery in judicious measures before Tito finally agreed to a total influx of 300 extra Allied personnel.

The fourth crisis was the most difficult. While Fitzroy was in London in November, the British had become worried by the formation of a battalion of Greek Macedonians on the Yugoslav side of the frontier: the fear was that Tito might be intending to annex Greek Macedonia.[58] When Djilas and others spoke in December of the bloody suppression of Marxist comrades in Greece, it appeared that Tito might throw the Macedonian brigade into the struggle in Athens. Tito explained that the brigade had been formed from refugees from oppression in Greece, and would not be allowed to cross the border to take part in the civil war there.[59] But the affair blew up again when the commander of the Partisans in Macedonia, General Apostolski, ordered British Liaison Officers out of his territory. Fitzroy at once remonstrated with Tito, who replied that Apostolski had acted without authority and had now been ordered to retain his BLOs.[60]

In Belgrade Tito had taken up residence in Prince Paul's White Palace at Dedinje, on the outskirts of the city. Here Fitzroy visited him and together they explored the building from attic to basement. Tito adjusted easily to the good things in life, but he remained at a personal level as friendly and easy-going as before.

Fitzroy, chained Prometheus-like to the rock of diplomatic boredom, yearned to see more action before the war was over; he told Tito he was keen to leave Yugoslavia as soon as a proper government had been formed and regular diplomatic relations established between Britain and the new regime. Yet each week brought fresh developments that postponed that further into the future. In January 1945 Tito once again fell foul of the British military establishment, this time over a ghost from Fitzroy's past – Floydforce, brain child of David Stirling and Randolph Churchill. The battle with the Germans was still going on in the north, yet the British demanded that they be allowed to land Floydforce battalions in strength at Dubrovnik. This looked to Tito like the prelude to a British occupation of Dalmatia and restoration of King Peter. What did the British mean by it? And how dare they attempt such a thing without his authorization?

Fitzroy did not reveal that Churchill had arrogated to himself the right to land troops wherever he chose, without let or hindrance, nor that the Chiefs of Staff had recently advised him that they wanted no agreement with the Partisans that would limit their scale of operations in Yugoslavia. But Churchill had in effect let the cat out of the bag already by cabling Tito: 'We should be afforded complete freedom to move sea, land and air forces to any part of Yugoslavia where they could kill the most Germans.'[61] In private Fitzroy admitted himself puzzled by his own government's intentions. What did 'getting our foot in the door' mean, he queried? Did this portend general armed intervention by Floydforce?[62] Fitzroy insisted that the Allies should not land troops in Dalmatia or anywhere else without Tito's consent. He knew that terrible bloodshed could result. Stalin had already asked Tito in September 1944 what the Partisans would do if the British invaded in force, and Tito had replied that they would fight to the last man.[63] The more thoughtful Partisan leaders, like Velebit, were confident that the Allies lacked the resources for a successful invasion of Yugoslavia, but always Tito returned to his favourite theme: why the large numbers, if the British had no sinister intentions? And why did the British always land double the numbers for which they had secured authorization?

Some members of Fitzroy's mission were forthright in their views on Churchill's ham-fistedness. This is Hilary King: 'Certainly the numbers we thought it necessary to land for relatively small endeavours were breathtakingly large. They may have been reasonable by British standards, but not by those of the Partisans.'[64]

There was further controversy when HMS *Delhi* sailed into Split harbour without any prior warning. Confident of their welcome, the crew organized a children's party on board. But when they tried to land, they were driven back by machine-gun fire. Why, the Partisans asked, was the warship not going further north to where the fighting was? Why did it dock without permission? And why was it sitting in Split Roads with its guns pointing towards the city? Hilary King comments: 'I still don't understand why that ship was sent, in the light of Fitzroy's strongly worded and reiterated advice. It almost looks like a deliberate provocation, but was probably merely incompetence.'[65]

Even Fitzroy himself came briefly under suspicion. At the fall of Belgrade, Partisans found a German order that all members of the British Mission were to be shot. Then another directive was unearthed, that Fitzroy Maclean and Charlie Thayer, if captured, were instead to be treated well and sent up to headquarters. Thayer relates the sequel.

'What', asked Tito, 'does this mean?'

Maclean looked at me. I looked at Maclean. We both felt a bit crestfallen. Then Maclean had an inspiration. 'Jonny must be around.'

'Who's Jonny?' Tito asked, and we explained that he was a friend, but unfortunately on the wrong side of the front. Tito seemed satisfied, and we more or less forgot about the matter as the chances of getting captured by the Germans became more remote.[66]

Fitzroy's conjecture was correct. Jonny Herwarth von Bittenfeld had indeed been at the Yugoslav front and had written the special order – an order which might have had serious consequences for himself.

As if these suspicions harboured were not enough, the dreary saga of King Peter continued as well. In London, Peter continued to nag ministers about the Tito–Subasic agreement. He now said that although he accepted the accords of November and December, he objected to the method of choosing the Council of Regents and to the surrender of interim powers to Tito's National Council of Liberation. Foreign Office patience snapped. Two acerbic diary entries from Bruce Lockhart sum up the mood. 'King Peter raising niggling points about the Tito–Subasic agreement. He must be told he's got to hold his nose and swallow the medicine.' 'Eden saw . . . that silly little King Peter again, who's digging his toes in. A twig defying an avalanche, and a rather rotten twig too.'[67]

On 18 January 1945 Churchill told the House of Commons that a political settlement in Yugoslavia would be endorsed by HMG, whether King Peter liked it or not. This finally reassured Tito, and Fitzroy noticed that his manner became more jocular. On 22 January King Peter attempted a forlorn counter-attack and dismissed Subasic. But the sequel was closer to farce than drama. ' "Do what you can to keep Tito calm,'' telegraphed the Foreign Office, now thoroughly alarmed. But there was no need. Tito had never been calmer. The whole thing, he said, was "as good as a play''.'[68]

In the end the hapless King Peter was forced to take Subasic back; negotiations narrowed down to a protracted selection of the three Regents. The Big Three at Yalta instructed Tito and Subasic to come to a quick settlement but they made no mention of King Peter who, faced with this final humiliation, threw in the towel and retired from the scene. There were still Royal supporters who argued, illogically, that the young monarch was the only hope for democracy, but Fitzroy's 'end of term' political report concisely exposed that argument. He pointed out that the issue in Yugoslavia could not be democracy versus Communism, since 'Democracy, as we know it, has never existed. Periods of corrupt parliamentary confusion have been followed by periods of equally corrupt dictatorship.'[69]

With the merger of the Tito and Subasic factions, there was now a legitimate Yugoslav government with which Britain could establish diplomatic relations, so Ralph Stevenson prepared to fly in as ambassador. Effectively, Fitzroy's political role was over. Indeed, with the Allied armies already in Germany, the war was as good as over, too. The Wehrmacht left their evacuation of Bosnia too late and lost 100,000 dead and 200,000 prisoners – disaster of a magnitude not far short of Stalingrad.

Fitzroy's very last military function arose from a visit to Tito by

General Alexander, whose personal relations with the Marshal were
always as good as Wilson's were now bad. Alexander arrived in
Belgrade on 21 February and after talks with Tito toured the Srem
sector of the Yugoslav front. A party then formed for a trip across the
frontier into Hungary to visit Marshal Tolbukhin. Among the visitors
were Fitzroy, Charlie Thayer and Generals Lemnitzer and Airey.[70] At
Russian Army Group HQ they were received cordially, even lavishly.
'For three days we lived in a haze of vodka in a nameless village in
Hungary from which all the inhabitants appeared to have been
removed and their places taken by high-ranking officers of the Red
Army.'[71]

This visit with Alexander was the occasion for a risible incident. The
Russians pressed Fitzroy insistently to inspect Alexander's bedroom to
make sure that it was 'all right for a general'. In the end, to stop the
nagging, he agreed. The room was as well-appointed as could be
expected, but sprawled across the bed was a shapely blonde female Red
Army captain, wearing a pair of thigh-length boots ('lying to attention',
as Fitzroy puts it). 'Everything all right?' asked the eager-to-please
Russians. 'Everything is most certainly not all right,' Fitzroy replied.
'Get her out of here.'[72]

Alexander returned to Italy at the beginning of March, Fitzroy to
Belgrade, where on 7 March the Council of Regents was sworn in and
the Yugoslav government took office. Tito was Prime Minister, Velebit
his deputy, Djilas Minister without Portfolio. Subasic's title of Foreign
Minister looked imposing, but he was no more than a figurehead. On
12 March Ralph Stevenson arrived to take over Fitzroy's political functions; Air Vice-Marshal Lee assumed his military role. There was a
final friendly farewell with Tito then, a couple of days after his 34th
birthday, Fitzroy boarded the plane for England.

> Soon we were circling high above Belgrade. Looking out, I could see the road
> stretching away southwards to Avala and to the green, rolling country round
> Valjevo and Arandjelovac. Then we turned in the direction of the coast. Below,
> the snow was still lying on the mountains of Bosnia. The little paths wound in
> and out along the ridges. Dense forests reached down into the valleys. Here and
> there smoke went up from a cluster of huts. Then came the barren crags of
> Dalmatia, and the islands, bathed in sunshine; and before long we were flying
> far out over the Adriatic. Westwards.[73]

14

Fitzroy's Kindergarten

A distinctive feature of Fitzroy's life is the way the serious alternates with the comic, the tragic with the farcical. In Yugoslavia the black comedy was provided by Randolph Churchill and Evelyn Waugh, who played Falstaff, Pistol or Bardolf to the Hotspur or Northumberland, the Mortimer or Glendower of Tito and Mihailovic.

It was in Cairo in November 1943, while recruiting officers for his mission, that Fitzroy ran across Randolph Churchill again. He had last seen him hobbling out of the Alexandria military hospital after a near-fatal crash in David Stirling's car on the road from Benghazi. In a moment of self-knowledge, Randolph admitted he was in a cul-de-sac in Cairo, getting drunk, insulting generals at parties and embarrassing his father. Seeking redemption through action and austerity, he begged Fitzroy to give him a chance of salvation. Fitzroy agreed.

> For my present purposes he seemed just the man. On operations I knew him to be thoroughly dependable, possessing both endurance and determination. He was also gifted with acute intelligence and a very considerable background in general politics, neither of which would come amiss in Yugoslavia. I felt, too – rightly, as it turned out – that he would get on well with the Yugoslavs, for his enthusiastic and at times explosive approach to life was not unlike their own. Lastly, I knew him to be a stimulating companion, an important consideration in the circumstances under which we lived.[1]

Fitzroy knew Randolph's mercurial temperament all too well. And Randolph was no respecter of rank, having – as he had – immediate access to the Prime Minister. So Fitzroy made it a prime condition of engagement that Randolph must observe a strict respect for hierarchy. Meanwhile the generals objected that the Germans, once they knew of Randolph's presence in Yugoslavia, would redouble their efforts to net such an important prize; if they captured him, they would be likely to torture him – send his toes back in matchboxes, and so on.[2] Perhaps, too, at a deeper level, Winston Churchill felt uneasy at this conjunction of his real son with Fitzroy, arguably his ideal son.

These objections were overruled by Randolph's strenuous insistence, and he became Fitzroy's aide. To begin with, he rather overplayed the deference, making a point of beginning every utterance with 'Permission to speak, Sir?' Fitzroy became oppressed by the constant saluting and the over-formal 'Brigadier, may I have a word?', but realized it would be disastrous to let Randolph off the leash. Randolph's diplomatic début was hardly auspicious. When Velebit reached Cairo, Randolph bounded up to be introduced and said, 'Well, Major Velebit, it seems your Cetniks are doing some splendid work.'[3]

However, Randolph redeemed himself with a concisely written minute, dated Christmas Day 1943, which he took with him to Marrakesh and which was instrumental in stiffening his father's resolve against Foreign Office quibbles over Tito. And when Randolph parachuted in with Fitzroy on 19 January 1944, Tito was deeply flattered that, as he saw it, Winston Churchill had sent his only son to him. The other Partisans were more perplexed. The people of Drvar were confused as to his identity. Some thought he was Fitzroy's boss, others at first suspected he might be the great Winston Churchill himself, or some British equivalent of King Peter. But Randolph soon managed to offend his hosts by preaching to them against Marxism. Communism, he announced, 'is like a man talking on a cold day, it looks like he's breathing fire when he's really breathing ice.'[4]

Djilas was one of those who at first thought there must be an ulterior purpose to Randolph's presence, but ended by conceding that the appearance was the reality. 'He himself convinced me by his behaviour that he was a secondary figure . . . Randolph soon enchanted our commandos and commissars with his wit and unconventional behaviour but revealed through his drinking and lack of interest that he had inherited neither political imagination nor dynamism with his surname.'[5]

On one occasion a youth congress was held at Drvar and Fitzroy was invited to send a delegate. To his annoyance, the Foreign Office vetoed participation, on the grounds that it would be tantamount to recognizing the Partisans as the provisional government. Fitzroy saw that a great propaganda advantage was about to be lost and Randolph offered to step into the breach, using his own 'wild man' reputation as deniable cover. He had one of the Partisans write a speech in Serbo-Croat, full of acceptable bromides and clichés, which he then memorized and delivered without notes to a standing ovation.[6]

For all that, Randolph was difficult and quarrelsome. Those who shared a hut with him at night told of stertorous snoring and grampus-like apnea. He quarrelled on principle. The American Major Richard Weil was one of his targets. Randolph unwisely engaged him on the

subject of democracy, whereupon the intellectually gifted and studi-
ously courteous American reduced him to silence with his dialectical
skills. This was the first time his fellow-countrymen had seen the bom-
bastic Randolph at a loss. He grunted ungraciously, 'Well, you're the
first American I've met who has been capable of presenting a logical
case.'[7]

Eventually Fitzroy decided that Randolph must be put in his place
once more. He took advantage of April Fool's Day, asking Hilary King
to prepare a fake signal, complete with the right markings and call signs,
marked 'Personal and Private to Fitz, Decipher Yourself'. Fitzroy told
King to take the prepared cable to Randolph with the message 'Fitz has
received this, is embarrassed and doesn't know how to reply. Could you
draft a reply for despatch this afternoon?' The signal was a long one and
read as follows:

PERSONAL AND PRIVATE FOR FITZ FROM PM DISTURBING REPORTS HAVE
BEEN REACHING ME IN RECENT WEEKS ABOUT RANDOLPH'S CONDUCT. IT
HAS BEEN SUGGESTED THAT five groups corrupt CAN HARDLY BELIEVE THAT THIS
CAN BE TRUE. HAVE ALSO HEARD THAT HE HAS five groups corrupt. PLEASE TELE-
GRAPH IMMEDIATE YOUR RECOMMENDATIONS ON HOW TO PROCEED.

About three o'clock a flustered Randolph appeared, white-faced with
fury. 'He had worked hard for, as you know, he was a man who enjoyed
being extremely offensive. He loved polishing every phrase to get the
maximum wounding, unpleasant insinuation. He was eventually told
the whole thing was a hoax, turned on his heels with a scowl and said,
"Well, you got the better of me that time." '[8]

Randolph struck back by writing to Virginia Cowles (the journalist
who had visited Fitzroy in Moscow in 1939) to say that he thought
Fitzroy was in love with her and wanted to marry her. When Fitzroy
heard about this, and remonstrated with him, Randolph said: 'You
were very busy and I thought your exploits should be better known,
Sir.' Fitzroy thought he was safe, as she was in the United States, but
when he was on Vis with Tito in June a cable came saying 'Have
arrived in Naples. Am at your disposal.' The next thing was a sharply-
worded signal from General Wilson to Fitzroy, asking why he had made
an exception, in this single case, when he had previously refused to have
any war correspondents with the mission. The upshot was that Virginia
Cowles had her press credentials withdrawn.[9] Randolph was granted
leave when Fitzroy went with Velebit to Algiers but before he left put
forward two propositions. The first was, As the mission did not contain
any of his (Randolph's) intellectual equals (this despite having been
worsted in argument by Richard Weil), could he bring back 'a few
amusing chaps' to Yugoslavia? The other was that the mission needed

a good, solid, Catholic BLO to liaise with Catholics in Bosnia and, later, Croatia; this would benefit long-term British interests and counterbalance Communist influence. Fitzroy acquiesced.

Such was the genesis of Randolph's recruitment of Evelyn Waugh. The sequel was amusingly related by Christopher Sykes, who happened to be in White's Club in London in early May when Randolph burst in.

> 'Where's Evelyn Waugh? I've got to get hold of him! Where the devil is he?'
> 'I know where he is, and he can be with you here tomorrow morning.'
> 'You mean it?'
> 'I think I do, if you let me get to the telephone. Why do you need him?'
> 'Because', said Randolph, standing by the bar and in a very loud voice, 'my father has agreed to me taking charge of a mission to Croatia under Fitzroy Maclean. Fitzroy and I have been hunting for Evelyn everywhere, because I need him. I can't go to Croatia unless I have someone to talk to.'[10]

The necessary red tape took some time, and it was 2 July before Waugh got official confirmation that he would be accompanying Randolph to Croatia. Meanwhile Randolph had flown to newly-liberated Rome for an audience with Pope Pius XII on the future of Yugoslavia; he was surprised to find that the Pope had not heard of Evelyn Waugh. Churchill and Waugh arrived on the island of Vis on 9 July, in time to be present next day at a banquet in honour of Tito. Waugh took an instant dislike to Fitzroy, and noted in his diary for 10 July: 'All a little affected by wine in the evening. Maclean dour, unprincipled, ambitious, probably very wicked; shaved head and devil's ears. I read his reports in one of which he quoted Lawrence of Arabia saying it was a victory to make a province suffer for freedom.'[11]

Waugh then opened a sustained campaign against Fitzroy and Tito. His diary records his views. '*11 July*. Brigadier Maclean saturnine and Nazi. *12 July*. Changes of plan ended in Brigadier and Randolph not lunching with Tito and Brigadier going alone to Caserta to explain to Jumbo Wilson his protégé's rude behaviour.'[12] Waugh also recorded his impression that Tito looked like a lesbian. Thereafter he took to referring to Tito as 'she', insisting that he was a woman. A few days later, when Fitzroy formally introduced the newcomer to Tito, who was wearing exiguous swimming trunks, the Marshal shook hands with him and looked him steadily in the eyes. 'Captain Waugh, why do you think I am a woman?' he asked. Fitzroy reports that this was the one and only occasion he knew Waugh at a loss for a reply.[13]

It was an egregious mistake to bring Evelyn Waugh out to Yugoslavia. He had been allowed to go because it was thought that as a Catholic he would be ideally placed to build bridges to the Croatian leaders; it was true that Yugoslav Catholics were prepared to divulge things to him they would have kept from a non-Catholic. But both he and Randolph seemed to forget that they were part of a mission officially accredited to the Partisans. Waugh was an unregenerate opponent of 'godless Communism', and his detestation of the Partisans increased daily, fuelled by other mission members' and the British media's favourable perceptions of them.

On their first attempt to reach Croatia, the DC-3 carrying Randolph and Waugh crash-landed on an OSS-managed airstrip at Gajevi. Captain Benson, the veteran of the Huot incident the year before, pulled them clear of the wreckage before the plane exploded, killing several men.[14] The survivors were taken to Bari and thence to Rome to convalesce. Accidents with aeroplanes seemed to dog the mission.[15] It was 16 September before the ill-starred duo flew to Topusko in Croatia. There now began a saga of ill-will and recrimination that involved the Maclean mission in an immense amount of extra work. Waugh and Randolph soon concluded that they had, in fact, nothing in common. Waugh was stupefied to discover that Randolph, continually asserting that no one in the mission was his intellectual equal, had never heard of Sainte-Beuve. When Waugh pinned him down and insisted he say who Sainte-Beuve was, Randolph replied that she was an abbess renowned in medieval France for her sanctity.[16]

To soothe the ruffled feathers of Randolph, who cabled that he was 'Waugh-weary', Fitzroy sent out Freddie Birkenhead as the Number Two BLO in Croatia. This was a card Fitzroy had had up his sleeve for some time; Randolph had been Birkenhead's fag at Eton and it was thought that, even though he was nominally second-in-command to Churchill, the memory of those days would give him influence. The story is told in Bruce Lockhart's diaries:

> *27 July*: I gave luncheon today at the East India Club to Freddie Birkenhead whom Brendan [Bracken] wants to send to Fitzroy Maclean's mission with Tito. The telegram from Fitzroy has now arrived inviting Freddie to look after Randolph and Freddie is prepared to undertake this task. Freddie, who is diffident and lacks self-confidence, has been a failure with us. Yet he preferred to stay with us to accepting the post of Under-Secretary for India which the Prime Minister, his godfather, offered him. This is perhaps the best proof of his diffidence and fear of himself. On the other hand, though lazy, he has quite a good brain and has far better judgement than the other three members of the crazy mission to Tito: Fitzroy, Randolph Churchill and – worst of all in the lack of discretion – Evelyn Waugh.[17]

Lord Birkenhead arrived at Topusko with Major Stephen Clissold on 13 October, to find relations between Randolph and Waugh at rock-bottom. Waugh's diaries make the point.

27 October. A day of continuous rain. We did not leave the house. Further 'tiffs' with Randolph resulting in his making a further appeal to me for kinder treatment. It left me unmoved for in these matters he is simply a flabby bully who rejoices in blustering and shouting down anyone weaker than himself and starts squealing as soon as he meets anyone as strong. In words he can understand, he can dish it out, but he can't take it.[18]

To try to keep him quiet, Freddie Birkenhead and Waugh bet Randolph £10 he could not read the Bible right through in a fortnight. Randolph set to work and soon found the Bible 'full of quotations'. At odd moments Waugh and Birkenhead would hear snorts and grunts of disapproval. 'God, isn't God a shit.'[19] Soon even this distraction was not enough to constrain Randolph. On 19 November, after a memorable row between him and Clissold, Birkenhead and Clissold departed for Bari, having promised to secure Waugh's recall. Waugh was far from blameless himself. He insisted on wandering round Topusko in full-dress uniform, topped with a white duffle-coat. During air-raids he refused to take cover, and reproached Randolph with cowardice for doing so.[20] And he continued his tiresome personal vendetta against Tito. When Birkenhead reproached him, saying, 'Everyone knows he's a man, and a good-looking one at that', the dauntless Waugh replied, 'Her face is pretty, but her legs are *very* thick.'[21]

In Bari Waugh's immediate superior, Major John Clarke, was at his wits' end over radio traffic from Topusko. An 'urgent' signal from Randolph turned out to be about spares for his jeep.[22] Waugh excelled himself by sending trivial signals to headquarters at Bari prefixed by four 'Q's, so that a senior officer had to decode them. There were cases of colonels being got out of bed at four in the morning to decode signals about supplies of toiletries. Hilary King remembers one such instance.

> Evelyn Waugh sent frequent telegrams demanding a brand of high-quality toilet soap. The major in charge, a South African called Wilson, was tearing his hair out as there seemed to be a jinx on the soap. One day it would be loaded on the wrong plane, next day there was bad weather, and so on. Meanwhile Waugh's cables came pouring in . . . monopolizing half the radio traffic. It became a real scandal. Major Wilson was reduced to personally supervising its loading and briefing the crew. He . . . sent off a signal saying SOAP WILL ARRIVE ON THIRD PLANE. HOPE YOU ARE NOT TOO DIRTY. But this attempt at levity backfired, since next day there came in from Waugh a Personal and Private Message to the Commander-in-Chief, demanding immediate disciplinary action against the author of the telegram.[23]

Relations with the Partisans at Topusko were also tense because of the dispute over the presence of Floydforce on the west coast. Hostility grew to any Allied presence whatever. This was a situation calling for superlative diplomatic skills, but Waugh exacerbated Anglo-Yugoslav relations by overt contacts with Croatia's ultramontane Catholics. When the Partisans moved to expel him for meddling in Yugoslavia's internal affairs, Waugh appealed to his superiors in Bari. But they had enough on their hands already with the tensions over Greece and Tito's claim to Trieste and Venezia Giulia. Morever, they emphatically did not share the view that the Croatian Catholics – many of them Ustase supporters – merited Allied support. There were therefore good grounds for removing Waugh even before Randolph lent a hand.

Almost as soon as Waugh arrived, Randolph had begun lobbying for his recall. He demanded immediate action on Waugh, and blustered about 'Fitzroy's prolonged absence'.[24] The fact that Fitzroy was about his father's business cut no ice with Randolph. Finally John Clarke signalled at the end of November: 'Have discussed question of Waugh with Maclean. You should evacuate him soonest by whichever evacuation route you consider best.'[25]

Waugh was flown to Bari, where he spent most of December enjoying hospitality from Clarke at his villa in San Spirito. Then he reported for duty at Dubrovnik, having secured authorization from Fitzroy to report on the religious situation there. Peter Carey, later Press Attaché at the British Embassy in Belgrade, shared a house with him just outside the walls of Dubrovnik. 'One day when Waugh was out there was a knock at the door and outside was a shabby, unshaven Franciscan friar who handed over a sheaf of documents concerned with Partisan atrocities against the Church in Dalmatia.'[26] By the end of February Waugh had collected enough material, and requested permission from Clarke to go to Rome for an audience with the Pope on the subject.

After lengthy consultations with the Vatican, Waugh wrote his memorandum on Catholicism in Yugoslavia. But by this time Fitzroy's mission had been disbanded, so Waugh decided to return to London and present it to Fitzroy in person. Fitzroy passed on the violently anti-Partisan report to the Foreign Office, where it was received with stupefaction. Orme Sargent minuted:

> I would like Brigadier Maclean's views on this report as well as those of Mr Stevenson. This is an official report written by a military officer while on duty; and I see no reason why we should agree that the author should use it as propaganda against the government's policy. Not only must it not be published, but if he shows it to persons outside the Foreign Office and War Office he does so without consent and at his own risk.[27]

Ralph Stevenson's report from Belgrade, which arrived in London on 17 May, was a devastating refutation of Waugh's memorandum, containing detailed documentation on the role of the Catholic Church in the Ustase and other Fascist movements. Even Waugh's biographer concedes: 'Evelyn Waugh seems foolishly to have given way to the temptation to doctor his evidence.'[28]

By now the Foreign Office and War Office were incensed by Waugh's leaks to other English Catholics of information gathered in the course of his official duties. A move arose to court-martial him, though shrewder souls pointed out that this would simply make him a martyr, even if his case were to be heard *in camera*. It was thought best to concentrate on discrediting his findings, rather than the man himself. Fitzroy played a key role in this decision. His testimony to the Foreign Office at the beginning of April 1945 was grounded, not in loyalty to a member of his mission, but on the cold technicalities which appeal to mandarins. There might be difficulty in snaring Waugh under the Official Secrets Act, he pointed out, not least because he himself had received a copy of the report after he had ceased to be head of the mission and was therefore, technically, an 'unauthorized person'. Orme Sargent and the others accepted the force of his logic.

The fact that Fitzroy had done him a favour did not assuage Waugh's personal animus. He believed that Fitzroy was a 'Red', and sneeringly referred to the 'Maclean youth centre at Stalingrad'.[29] In a letter to Randolph Churchill in April 1946, written while he was reporting the Nuremburg trials, he described Ernst Kaltenbrunner, Chief of Secret Police and director of the SS, as 'the only obvious criminal in the dock . . . a cross between Noel Coward and Fitzroy Maclean [in appearance]'.[30] Later that year, when Waugh had Bill Deakin and his wife to stay at Combe Florey, he started the hare that Fitzroy had taken credit for Deakin's work and presented himself as first to make contact with Tito. Fitzroy later disposed of this argument: 'Even after all these years, the suggestion that I was trying to steal the credit for such an intensely unpopular decision [to support Tito] has a somewhat ironical ring.'[31]

Why did Fitzroy take on Randolph Churchill and Evelyn Waugh? Was it an error of judgement? Were there undeclared motives? Annette Street comments: 'Freddie Birkenhead, Waugh and Randolph! Very naughty of Fitz. I can't think what he was playing at, having those three.'[32] Mike Parker: 'Randolph and the others were useless from the day-to-day point of view of the mission. Waugh, of course, was a character of some distinction, and Fitzroy liked such people. You could see him watching you and you would think, Hello, I'm going to appear as Pilot Officer Prune in the next novel. Freddie Birkenhead was another one. Useless, but he had a title. Amazing how many titles he had. Henniker was the exception, a lord but a good soldier.'[33] Lord Henniker himself: 'Fitzroy was dazzled by Waugh's reputation and thought it would add to the aura of the mission. Freddie Birkenhead, too. Fitzroy was also convinced SOE would suppress his signals, so he had to have other lines out to the Establishment.'[34]

Of all the senior mission members, John Clarke saw most of Waugh. In his biography Christopher Sykes writes: 'His immediate superior in Bari was Major John Clarke, with whom Evelyn enjoyed pleasant relations . . . He immediately approved of Evelyn's plans for himself.'[35] But Clarke tells a different story – that he swiftly gave Waugh permission to go to see the Pope, 'To get rid of him!' On the entire Waugh/Randolph experience he is jaundiced.

> Fitzroy was a great meddler politically. Why did he think it was a good thing to have Evelyn Waugh? Why did he send him down to Dubrovnik to tickle up the RC clergy? This made my life a hell. Waugh stirred up a hornet's nest. I think Fitzroy was a stirrer. It all seems incredibly stupid. What was Fitzroy doing? . . . On top of that there were telegrams all the time from Fitzroy asking that Randolph be pulled out to accompany his father to Yalta. I was bombarded by cables. Meanwhile Waugh was sending messages that Randolph was moody and had gone off his rocker and fallen in love with a goose.[36]

Fitzroy stands by what he wrote about Randolph in *Eastern Approaches*. Of Waugh he says: 'I had received an advance copy of *Put Out More Flags*, liked it and thought it would be interesting to have a writer on the mission, especially one Randolph had requested.'[37] But Michael Lees believed that Fitzroy used Randolph, expertly, to get to the top. 'He was brilliant at it. He would send a signal to Churchill saying, I want X,Y,Z and by the way Randolph sends his love. Brilliant manipulation.'[38] It does seem clear that Fitzroy impressed Tito as a miracle-worker with instant access to Churchill, and that this access was partly thanks to Fitzroy's role as 'minder' to Churchill's turbulent son.

Another view is that Fitzroy thrives on 'psychic overload'. To deal with mavericks like Waugh and Randolph was to set himself extra challenges. Fitzroy's friend Sir John Astor comments: 'He could handle people like Waugh and Randolph who were very hard to handle, but he could do it because he was tough and controlled and ruthless. They realized that if they were out of line they'd be out. Also, Fitzroy was better educated than Waugh and Randolph.'[39]

One another possibility is worth exploring. It is clear that in 1944 Fitzroy was concerned about possible American dominance in Yugoslavia when Donovan cut loose from the Anglo-American mission and sent his own men in, a concern exacerbated by the pronounced pro-Mihailovic drift of OSS policy. It is conceivable that, consciously or unconsciously, Fitzroy wished to build up his mission into a powerful counterbalancing force and that one way to do this was to recruit 'names' from the various British élites.[40] The creation of a 'kindergarten' along the lines of Milner's experiment with John Buchan and others in South Africa at the turn of the century would have appealed to a man with Fitzroy's sense of imperial history. Sadly, when John Clarke refers to the wrangles by cable emanating from Topusko as 'kindergarten stuff', he is using the word only in its conventional sense.

15

Fitzroy: Right or Wrong?

T HE main thrust of the revisionist view of Yugoslavia is that
Britain backed the wrong horse: London should have continued
to support Mihailovic throughout 1944, and failed to do so because of
advice from Fitzroy Maclean.

The dramatic events in Eastern Europe in 1989 have convinced
unwary Cold Warriors that the Soviet power bloc was always a paper
tiger, which could have been faced down by resolute action at an earlier
date – such as the end of the Second World War. The current pervasive
spirit of anti-communist triumphalism has thus engendered a quite
unhistorical perspective, according to which Eastern Europe 'went
Communist' in the first place only through Western mistakes. Lord
Henniker describes this as 'rather nasty Right-wing bunk, which sees
everything in the 1980s as on the Right and thinks everything else
should have been [the same] in the past.' To hold this view, one must
believe 1945 to be the same as 1989; Stalin the same as Gorbachev; Tito
and his Partisans actuated by the values of consumerism; the demoralized Muscovites of the 1990s equivalent to the triumphant and euphoric
Red Army of 1945. Sir William Deakin calls this 'absolute nonsense';
Hilary King, 'mindless pap'; John Clarke, 'balderdash'; Mike Parker,
'tripe'. These are some of the more printable verdicts on recent
'reinterpretations' of Britain's role in Yugoslavia. One is tempted to
rest the case there, but Sir Richard Burton long ago pointed out that not
to answer criticism is always used by a disingenuous enemy as 'proof'
that the allegations, however absurd, are unanswerable.

Fitzroy's critics are by no means united on what they believe. David
Martin, for instance, seems to believe in a conspiracy of disinformation
orchestrated by the putative Soviet spy James Klugmann. He asks us
to believe in a spy so brilliant that he could prevent all information
about the Cetniks from reaching top British decision-makers, yet so
incompetent that he failed to destroy the incriminating evidence he

suppressed, leaving it to surface thirty years later in the Public Record
Office. Of the dozens of devastating critiques made of the 'Klugmann'
theory, those of Hilary King and Mark Wheeler stand out. Hilary King
points out that the most elementary knowledge of the technicalities of
signalling would have convinced Martin that his theory was untenable.
And what of Ultra, of whose existence Klugmann was unaware? How
did he manage to suppress that? Mark Wheeler points out that the
Klugmann conspiracy theory fails through simple chronology. By his
decisive confrontation with Brigadier Keble, Fitzroy removed SOE
from all but a transport and communications role in August 1943. How
could he have been manipulated by Klugmann, an operative of SOE
Cairo? Indeed, if Klugmann were the key, Fitzroy would be irrelevant,
since during the only period Klugmann could have had any influence
on policy he was with SAS in Palestine, with no thought yet of Yugoslavia. Those who want to elevate Klugmann are driven to dating the
decision to switch from Mihailovic to Tito further and further back in
time, until it disappears into absurdity.

The truth of course is that the revisionists are divided among themselves and have different targets. Martin's target is the British decision
to abandon the Cetniks; he is not interested in Fitzroy. By contrast,
Michael Lees' prime target appears to have been Fitzroy himself, which
is why Lees found the Klugmann theory unconvincing. The SOE angle
obviously had to be sacrificed if Fitzroy was to be put in the frame of
culpability. Lees' case was that Fitzroy was the begetter of Titoism. It
has to be conceded that some of Fitzroy's friends' hyperbole has not
helped his cause.

There are four competing propositions that can be advanced about
Fitzroy and Yugoslavia in the Second World War. One is that in choosing Tito we made the right choice, and Fitzroy was responsible; until
recently this could have been described as received opinion. The more
sophisticated, and I believe the correct, view, based on consideration of
Ultra, for instance, is that the right choice was made, but that it had
little to do with Fitzroy. A third view, David Martin's, is that we made
the wrong choice, but that Fitzroy was in any case marginal. The
fourth, Michael Lees', is that we made the wrong choice, and that
Fitzroy was responsible. British choices and Fitzroy's responsibility are
logically independent. As Martin concedes, even if we conclude that
the British should have supported Mihailovic, it does not follow that
Fitzroy was culpable. To sustain that, an extra layer of premises is
necessary. The argument narrows down to two areas. Did the British
make the right choice? And was Fitzroy Maclean responsible for that
choice?

A view the revisionists share is that, instead of supporting the Partisans, Britain should have supported Mihailovic and the Cetniks, or at

the very least both sides evenly. This view shows an ignorance of history. For nearly three years the British supported Mihailovic alone. The Foreign Office backed him in the teeth of mounting evidence of his inactivity. Even when there was overwhelming evidence from Ultra and the BLO reports that the Partisans were doing most of the fighting against the Germans, the mandarins still wanted to continue supporting the Cetniks.

Despite frequently reiterated claims that Britain knew nothing about the Partisans until Deakin and Maclean 'discovered' them in 1943, their existence as well as their power had been known for at least two years. SOE's Lord Glenconner wrote to the Foreign Office in November 1941 that to back the Partisans would be to back Moscow puppets.[1] This was at the time, be it noted, that our 'gallant ally' was fighting for its life outside Moscow. The head of SOE, the fanatically pro-Mihailovic Lord Selborne, was waging a losing campaign on the Cetniks' behalf as late as May 1944.[2] So blatant was the pro-Mihailovic bias in both SOE and the Foreign Office in 1943 that Mountbatten himself wrote to the Chiefs of Staff in May 1943 to ask how it could be squared with the Allies' professed admiration and friendship for the Russians.[3] It is interesting, incidentally, that Yugoslavia produced some strange bedfellows. Despite their fierce personal antagonism, Fitzroy and Brigadier Keble agreed that the only viable military policy was support for the Partisans. There was violent institutional rivalry between SOE and the Foreign Office, but in the higher echelons there was a shared ideological commitment to the cause of Mihailovic.

Charges and counter-charges fly back and forth about suppression and distortion via the BBC. Those who say Cetnik successes were suppressed suggest a conspiracy theory. Those who say that news of the Partisan victories was suppressed cite chapter and verse from the archives. In July 1942 Lord Glenconner wrote to the Southern Department of the Foreign Office: 'As we know . . . any activity in Yugoslavia should really be attributed to the Partisans, but, for practical purposes, we can see no harm in a certain amount of this going to the credit of Mihailovic.'[4] The Foreign Office's Douglas Howard, one of Mihailovic's doughtiest ideological champions, wrote to Political Warfare Executive, the propaganda service, to suggest that the Cetniks should be helped by either suppressing news about the Partisans or inventing some about Mihailovic.[5] In early 1943 SOE's Sir Charles Hambro suggested to Orme Sargent that Mihailovic be built up as a mythical figure; even the Foreign Office jibbed at this. Elisabeth Barker concludes: 'On the basis of the available documents, it seems fair to say that the original decision to back Mihailovic exclusively was taken by the Foreign Office and SOE, not for operational reasons, nor because they believed him to be the most effective resistance leader, but with the

longer-term political aim of *establishing* him as sole leader and inducing
the Communists to subordinate themselves to him, or at least of drawing off support from the Partisans.'[6]

The pro-Mihailovic policy was misguided in a number of ways.
Quite apart from increasing the risk of civil war, a ban on mentioning
the Partisans on the BBC would have revealed the Corporation as
biased, since Tito's activities were being widely reported in other
European media. The Foreign Office knew, too, as early as November
1941, that Mihailovic was making no moves against the Axis, since
British orders had been sent to the Cetniks but had been ignored.
Indeed Simovic, 'Prime Minister' of the Royal government-in-exile,
actually instructed the Cetniks to discontinue sabotage and guerrilla
attacks, and these instructions were broadcast over the BBC.

Extraordinarily, the Foreign Office decided at the end of 1941 to give
exclusive backing to Mihailovic when it was already known that he had
lapsed into inactivity and was even considering collaboration with the
Germans against the Partisans. It was also known that he had close
contacts with Nedic, a quisling in overt collaboration with the
Germans. The dishonesty of the Foreign Office was matched by
Mihailovic's. On 26 December 1941 Simovic passed Eden a message
from Mihailovic saying, 'I have succeeded in ending the internal fighting *provoked by the other side*' (my italics). He had not ended the fighting,
and it had not been provoked by the other side. But the Foreign Office
argued that even if he was lying he should be supported, to impress on
the Partisans that it was Mihailovic the British government was backing. Eden in fact took it for granted that the civil war was over and
persuaded the War Cabinet and Chiefs of Staff to send aid exclusively to
Mihailovic. This was done on condition that the truce between Partisans and Cetniks should hold – a lame proviso: as the Foreign Office
had taken Mihailovic's word for it that hostilities had ceased when in
fact they had not, they were unlikely to insist on verification that the
truce was holding.[7]

The flaws in British policy towards Yugoslavia did not end there.
Eden persuaded Churchill to commit a squadron of long-range bombers for use exclusively in Yugoslavia. These, however, had to be
diverted to Ceylon early in 1942 to deal with the Japanese threat.
Elisabeth Barker comments: 'The British therefore found themselves in
the rather ridiculous position of publicly backing a physically and morally weaker party in an internal Yugoslav struggle, without the power of
supplying arms which were essential if the weaker party were to succeed.'[8]

Pro-Mihailovic suppression and disinformation went on during 1942
and 1943. The British media quite unfairly built up the legend of
Mihailovic as the great resistance leader; Partisan exploits were

automatically attributed to him. As a result of rivalry between SOE and SIS, intercepts about the Partisans, which were available to the War Office from 1941 onwards, were not available to SOE Cairo until 1942 and not to many top officials in SOE London until the spring of 1943. Elisabeth Barker says: 'It seems to me that it was not just a question of SOE withholding information, but that the Foreign Office knew perfectly well during 1942 what was going on. There was masses of information on the Partisans from one source or another. And SIS must also have had quite a lot of information.'[9] Even in terms of the official archives, April 1943 is the last date at which 'ignorance' can be offered as an excuse, since in that month Major Michael Maclaglan wrote a widely circulated report detailing the progress of the Partisans since 1941.[10] It is clear that those in Britain who counted knew perfectly well what the situation was, but were constrained by the official policy of supporting the Royal Yugoslav government-in-exile and its 'Defence Minister' Draza Mihailovic.

By August 1942 concealment of the truth had become embarrassing. All sources available to the Political Warfare Executive showed very little resistance in Serbia but a lot of activity outside the areas controlled by Mihailovic. Additionally, evidence of Cetnik collaboration with the Axis powers was mounting. A meeting was called in Whitehall on 8 August 1942 to discuss possible responses to a Soviet dossier alleging such collaboration. The mandarins found nothing in the dossier they did not already know, but they faced a problem of credibility if they continued to deny what the rest of the world knew. To keep their critics at bay, the Foreign Office advised contacting the Partisans – whose existence they had until then implicitly denied – while maintaining support for and recognition of Mihailovic. Even the idea of contacting the Partisans offended Selborne and the zealots of SOE. They put up stiff resistance to the idea of intelligence reconnaissance; they knew only too well what the British envoys would find. It is from August 1942 that we can date the first real divergence between SOE and Foreign Office over Yugoslavia.

The problem now arose of how to broach the new Foreign Office line over the BBC. An ingenious solution was reached. Yugoslav Resistance forces were thenceforward described as 'Patriots', cunningly conflating Partisans with Cetniks. The long-term effect was to add to Tito's post-war bitterness against the British.

Colonel Hudson, who had been with Mihailovic, was debriefed on his return, but his report was not what the Foreign Office wanted to hear. 'I consider him perfectly capable of coming to any understanding with either Italians or Germans which he believes might serve his purpose without compromising him.' By now it was obvious that Mihailovic was collaborating with the Italians, but Orme Sargent in the

Foreign Office minuted: 'I do not think the time has come to break with Mihailovic and still less to give direct assistance to the Partisans.' The Foreign Office decided on the classic stall: 'more research is needed'.

Colonel William Bailey was now sent to investigate the Yugoslav situation. He quickly learned that Mihailovic's policy was abstention from serious action against the occupying forces. Determined to preserve Serbia from the threatened ten-for-one retaliation by the Germans against any guerrilla 'atrocity', and to avoid Serbian casualties such as were suffered in the First World War, the Cetnik leader was following a policy of trimming and expediency. That part of his programme, though shot through with flawed mysticism, intransigent stubbornness and a fundamental lack of clarity, might have been justifiable. But Mihailovic wanted to avoid reprisals on the civilian population, not from humanitarianism but for hard-headed political reasons: he feared such reprisals would cost him the support of the Serbian peasantry, which he needed if he was to consolidate his position in the heartland and in time extend his control over the whole country. Mihailovic could not see that the idea of restoring King Peter to an unchanged Yugoslavia was an illusion. The whirlwind of the world had carried him away before ever he stood in the dock in Belgrade.

Mihailovic's treatment of Bailey hardly helped his ailing cause. When the Italian forces capitulated in 1943 Bailey knew nothing of it, any more than Deakin, now with Tito, did. Yet Mihailovic roundly accused him of lying. Mihailovic exulted whenever there was an aerial drop from the British; when there was not, Bailey recalls, 'I was again relegated to the end of the baggage train or put in a billet very close to the point at which the Germans might attack us. This happened more than once. Then things would go a little better. The BBC would say something complimentary about him, and I would be invited to dinner.'[11] According to Bailey, nearly all Mihailovic's signals – the ones supposed to have been suppressed by SOE Cairo – were concerned with the minutiae of military administration. On 28 February 1943, piqued at not receiving the supplies he felt were his due, Mihailovic delivered an extraordinary outburst in Bailey's presence. He attacked Allied policy towards his movement and his country; he had his own agenda, independent of British wishes; it was imperative for him to liquidate his enemies – Partisans, Croats, Moslems, Ustase – in that order – before dealing with the Axis forces, and no action or threat from the Allies would make him alter his policy one jot; he did not need the democracies and, if necessary, he would get all he wanted from Italy. 'He seemed to be so obsessed', Bailey comments, 'by what he regarded as the Communist threat to his country and people that he could unashamedly argue that the protection given by the quisling Serb government in Belgrade, and even perhaps that given by the Germans themselves, was preferable to a composition with the Partisans.'[12]

Mihailovic eventually sealed his own fate by failing to respond to a request from General Wilson to attack, before 29 December 1943, two vital railway bridges within the area he claimed to control. Bailey sums up: 'There can be no real quarrel with the final decision to leave Mihailovic to his fate . . . Mihailovic himself made it impossible for the British government to go on regarding him as [the] central figure of resistance in Yugoslavia.'[13] As a political and military leader, Mihailovic was outclassed by Tito. 'We had built up Mihailovic into something which he never remotely thought he was himself,' Fitzroy says. He also had unrealistic expectations of the British, and knew nothing of the daily battles in London with Air Marshal 'Bomber' Harris to get any planes at all for Yugoslav operations: until 1943 there were just four Liberators available for all operations from Egypt, and often these had to cover all operations in the whole of the Balkans.[14]

Mihailovic was the wrong man for his task: Bailey sums up.

> On Mihailovic's side, there were certain characteristics which militated against cooperation between himself and the Allies: an innate Slav mysticism which, combined with his professional loyalty to his king and country, dictated his overall objective, namely, to hand back the country to the former, intact both geographically and constitutionally; a cognate Slav fanaticism, which made him indifferent to the consequences of his actions; an almost pathological obsession with military administrative procedures; a fanatical hatred, inculcated firmly during his military training, of anything such as Communism which, in his narrow view, was inimical to the interests of the monarchy – essentially Serbian – and to a lesser extent the Church – essentially Orthodox; and finally, his inability to appreciate that the military, political and social set-up in Europe had changed irreversibly since the halcyon days of the First World War, the Salonika front, and the subsequent restoration of quasi-absolute monarchy in virtually all the countries of south-eastern Europe; in other words, his failure to realize that the clock could not be put back.[15]

Even figures sympathetic to Mihailovic concede that he was the wrong horse to back. The British Liaison Officer George Taylor says: 'By November 1942 it was fully realized by SOE Cairo that in fact Mihailovic's primary concern, his overriding, overwhelming concern, was not with carrying on the war against the Germans and Italians, but with what the ultimate power situation in Yugoslavia would be when the war came to an end.'[16] That being the case, it is astonishing that the British continued to provide exclusive military aid to Mihailovic for a further twelve months.

The British could leave the enigma (in so far as it was one) of Mihailovic unresolved as long as the fate of Yugoslavia was a long-term concern. But in 1943 the country became a vital military area as the battle for the Mediterranean reached its critical stage. British military leaders could not afford the luxury of ideological crusades. This is an issue never squarely faced by the Mihailovic apologists, who subordinate the entire struggle against Fascism to the causes of Serbian nationalism, the Orthodox Church and Serb monarchy. When the Chiefs of Staff sought enlightenment from Ultra, it became clear that there had been a mine of information previously available about the Partisans which had been suppressed. The Ultra specialist, Ralph Bennett, comments:

> It can hardly be a coincidence that Ultra signals about the Balkans greatly increase in number from the moment that London and Cairo begin to take a greater interest in the area in the spring of 1943. It cannot yet be actually proved that material of the type which was now regularly signalled had been available in equal measure earlier, but had been hidden from the eyes of those in the Middle East who might have used it to inform themselves better about the way the Axis was being forced to concentrate men and equipment in the Balkans; but it is almost impossible to escape this conclusion.[17]

Nineteen forty-three, the year of decision in the Mediterranean, brought the pro-Mihailovic lobby in London into the open. Before victory in North Africa it had not been feasible for the Allies to give large-scale aid to anyone in the Balkans. Now that they had that option, they had to make sure they gave it to a genuine fighting force: in 1943 at Neretva, Durmitor and elsewhere, Tito showed that the Partisans were such a force. The military issue could not be fudged as in 1942, the year of the 'Long March' and of obscure withdrawals. Total war exposed the hollowness of Mihailovic's repeated protestations. The general rising of half a million Serbs that he had been promising for two years still looked as far distant as the Second Coming.

We are bound to ask, next, did Mihailovic collaborate with the Axis powers? No serious historian doubts that there was collaboration with the Italians and, later, the Germans. Some of the best evidence is provided by historians sympathetic to the Cetniks,[18] yet it has always been denied in the pro-Cetnik literature, which seeks to evoke sympathy for a man who was a 'victim of the Communists' (or executed for treason, depending on the point of view). The most zealous supporters of Mihailovic hold that he made no accommodations with the Axis. Thus John Plamenatz: 'Though Mihailovic was in occasional contact with the Serbs in Dalmatia, there is no evidence that he urged them to get arms from the Italians to fight the Partisans . . . Mihailovic . . . never sought Italian help against the Partisans, neither directly nor through subordinates, nor did he advise anyone else to do so.'[19]

A more subtle defence concedes collaboration by his subordinates but alleges either that it took place without his knowledge or that, if he knew, he was powerless to stop it.[20] This looks less convincing when one reflects that Churchill tried to get other Cetnik leaders to overthrow Mihailovic in 1944 but was unsuccessful since all the rivals approached claimed that Mihailovic was too powerful to be toppled.

In fact, copious evidence exists of Mihailovic's personal collaboration with both Germans and Italians.[21] General Mario Roatta, commanding the Italian 2nd Army, expressly justified the use of Mihailovic's troops against the Partisans as being the most intelligent way to advance the policies of the Axis in Yugoslavia.[22] Against German misgivings he claimed he could not do without Cetnik support, and opposed German demands that the collaborating bands be disarmed; in this he was supported by the Wehrmacht general, Walter Warlimont.[23]

But the most telling evidence of Mihailovic's direct collaboration with the Germans is provided by Ultra. The best known intercept to reveal it was the Abwehr message of 1 December 1943, decrypted by Bletchley on 4 December 1943, which prompted the exclamation from 'NID 12' himself that here at last there was irrefutable evidence that Mihailovic was personally involved in collaboration with the Germans.[24] Of this Fitzroy remarks: 'Though in reality hostile to the Germans and Italians, they [the Cetniks] drifted inevitably into a policy of collaboration with them. Having started as patriots they had, from the best of motives, become something like traitors.'[25]

The ill-considered American mission to Mihailovic in 1944 encouraged him to collaborate more overtly, in the belief that American endorsement meant the Allies would overlook such peccadilloes. The deepest study of the Cetniks to date suggests that 'There is reason to believe that MacDowell did encourage the officers to think they had American backing for the pursuit of anti-Partisan projects. There is even strong evidence to suggest that MacDowell led Mihailovic to believe that the Russians would not enter Yugoslavia and that Mihailovic took this as proof that at least part of the country would fall in the non-Communist "sphere". With that sort of external support, the Cetniks could make one last deal with the Germans before they left the Balkans, in order to gain the upper hand in Serbia.' Matteo Milazzo concludes: 'Collaboration . . . if born of mutual desperation and wild miscalculation, was collaboration nonetheless.'[26]

In sum, then, it is difficult to see how any rational person can assert that, after 1943, the British should have backed Mihailovic and not Tito. Even if a blind eye is turned to Cetnik collaboration, Mihailovic was useless militarily and interested only in the future of Serbia. Should the defeat of the Axis have taken second place to his aims? Could allies against Fascism never be Communists? By the logic of that argument, the Soviet Union should not have been admitted as an ally either. To support the Partisans was the right decision.

Can Fitzroy be held responsible? This is a *post hoc ergo propter hoc* fallacy: Churchill made his final decision to switch support to the Partisans after receiving the Maclean 'blockbuster'; therefore, it is alleged, it was that report which made him change his mind. However, this makes Fitzroy more important than he really was. He had two clearly defined tasks in Yugoslavia: militarily, to find out exactly what supplies and *matériel* the Partisans needed; politically, to find ways in which Britain could play a part in the future evolution of the country. Churchill did not send Fitzroy to Tito for him to decide on his own initiative whether support should be switched to the Partisans. Churchill already knew from Ultra what the situation was, and his mind was as good as made up before September 1943. This is admitted even by some of the most vociferous pro-Cetnik critics of British policy. Here is David Martin: 'Mihailovic had for all practical purposes been abandoned by the beginning of September 1943.'[27] Bill Deakin comments:

> Michael Lees' story that I and Fitzroy persuaded Churchill to abandon Mihailovic in December 1943 is utter nonsense. Churchill had already taken his decision on the basis of the Ultra intercepts. But he had to make it *appear* that there had been a conventional decision-making process in order to protect this most secret source . . . Churchill took the final decision at the Teheran conference before he had even seen the Maclean blockbuster. Mihailovic as such wasn't even discussed at the villa. If what Lees says is true, is it conceivable that there is no record *anywhere* that a decision was taken to abandon Mihailovic after the meetings in the villa?[28]

Fitzroy's critics sometimes use as 'collateral evidence' the way he carried out his brief and the numbers he quoted in his report. In particular they single out the mistaken estimate of 30,000 Partisans in Serbia in October 1943 – a figure Fitzroy himself later corrected. We are asked to believe that if this one figure had been different, history would have been otherwise. But the error was picked up at once by the Foreign Office, and deluded nobody. Writing on 25 November, Orme Sargent minuted that the FO accepted Fitzroy's estimates for Slovenia, Croatia, Dalmatia and Bosnia, but 'As for the rest of Yugoslavia, and especially Old Serbia, we feel that Maclean's estimate of Partisan strength is exaggerated.'[29]

Fitzroy is also accused of underrating the strength of the Mihailovic movement in Serbia. But his critics can be accused of overrating the importance of Serbia, both in the fight against the Axis and in its antipathy to Communism. Hugh Seton-Watson has scouted the widely prevalent idea of a conservative Serbia and a Communist rest of Yugoslavia. He points out that there were more pro-communists in Serbia than elsewhere, and many thickets of anti-communism in Croatia and Slovenia; these facts were masked by the circumstance that the officer corps in the Yugoslav army was overwhelmingly Serbian.[30] As for the anti-Axis struggle, Matteo Milazzo remarks: 'After the Italian capitulation, the Mihailovic movement no longer represented a serious factor in occupied Yugoslavia, with the limited exception of Serbia. As far as the Germans were concerned, the main battleground was still the western half of the country, where Tito's Partisans had seized the initiative.'[31] An Ultra intercept of 24 September 1943, showing increased Cetnik activity in south-west Serbia, was greeted with joy by the pro-Mihailovic ideologues of the Foreign Office but, as Ralph Bennett comments, 'Some of the sabotage in south-west Serbia at this time was organized by British Liaison Officers acting contrary to Mihailovic's instructions, and so was presumably known to the Foreign Office.'[32]

Another charge laid at Fitzroy's door is that he did not follow the instructions in his original brief, and seek to prevent civil war in Yugoslavia. Nobody seems to have asked how realistic this part of the brief in fact was. Could Britain have prevented civil war? Was this prescription not simply another in the long line of Palmerstonian delusions about British power in the 1940s? Fitzroy himself comments: 'I got instructions, to which I cannot say I paid all that much attention, to impress on Tito the advisability of coming to terms with Mihailovic. Just as Bailey got the same parallel, complementary instructions to do the same the other way round. But we both came to the conclusion the policy was inoperable.'[33]

It was not just that Fitzroy was marginal to Churchill's decision-making over Yugoslavia. What Britain decided was marginal to the future of Yugoslavia. Tito would still have prevailed whatever the British had done. Even had Mihailovic not collaborated with the Axis, and had Britain wished him to prevail in post-war Yugoslavia, the British would have had to ally themselves with the Germans to destroy the powerful Partisan movement. As Fitzroy says, 'Supporting Mihailovic would have led to a worse situation than in Greece. I always said, if your top priority is not to beat the Germans but to defeat the Reds, you'd better throw in twenty divisions on the German side and work out the consequences later.'[34]

The only effect of British support for Mihailovic would have been to increase the bloodshed and postpone the inevitable. Only if the British and Americans had landed in overwhelming strength before the Red Army reached Yugoslavia would the outcome have been different, but the Allies lacked the capacity for this sort of operation in the Balkans in 1943 and 1944, even if they had seen any point to it. The British military operation to crush the Communists in Greece in 1944 was a near-run thing, and they had there to contend with forces only one-tenth the strength of the Partisans. Even had there been a successful Anglo-American invasion, the end result would not have been democracy. Milazzo comments: 'Had Mihailovic's officers and the Serbian civilian nationalist leaders triumphed in some sort of decisive Allied intervention on the Greek model, the restoration of the monarchy would surely have been accompanied by violent political purges and a reign of Serb vengeance.'[35]

Tito's victory in Yugoslavia was inevitable. One could cite many opinions on this point, but four will suffice. They are taken, respectively, from a 'neutral' SOE operative, a naval officer, a diplomat, and the most distinguished contemporary English-speaking historian of wartime Yugoslavia.

Bicknam Sweet-Escott, a doughty defender of SOE against Fitzroy's strictures, says: 'In Yugoslavia, if we had done as some suggested and never helped the Partisans at all, it would not have saved the royalist government . . . What seems to be beyond question is that to take the short-term military view and to help the Partisans was the only practical course . . . and that last but not least, whatever the reasons may have been, the German troops in Yugoslavia were too tied up there to be used against us when we invaded Italy.'[36] Sir Alexander Glen, veteran of Watkins' last expedition in Greenland and friend and admirer of Mihailovic, concurs:

> It is difficult to believe that earlier supplies to the Cetniks would have been used with consistency against the Germans, and not more regularly in that other war, which did not invite reprisals, against the other enemy, the Communists. The Pan-Serb views at Cetnik headquarters combined so bitterly with loyalty to the monarchy in a Slav mysticism, that I would incline to the opinion that, even had the Cetniks alone received effective support earlier, the final outcome would not have been changed, but the Civil War would have been still bloodier . . . It is difficult to resist the conclusion that for the Partisans the outcome would have been the same with or without Allied aid. In the latter case, the cost to them would have been heavier, almost certainly much heavier, and the Civil War would have been longer and more terrible. But I believe the Partisans would still have won.[37]

Sir Reginald Hibbert, Balkan expert and veteran of the guerrilla war in Albania in the Second World War, says:

> Fitzroy Maclean went into Yugoslavia when Tito had already found himself and was imposing himself on the world, so Maclean didn't have to invent Tito. It was more a question of discovery and clarification. So Maclean was in a sense an auxiliary in the process. Maclean was simply helping him to do the job properly. In Albania this never happened, because no effective leader emerged and created an effective movement for the British government to latch on to. There we were at sixes and sevens, as we didn't know who to support. Whereas in Yugoslavia Tito made it absolutely obvious who we should support. The other thing is the revisionist school that says we turned Yugoslavia Communist

unnecessarily. But this comes back to the decisions of the Allied leaders in the summits of 1943. The essential point is that by the end of 1943 there was no alternative. All we could do with our resources was make sure we kept Greece in the West. There was no way we could stem Tito and the only sensible thing was to ride with the punch, so to speak. It is a perversion of history to suggest that the Partisan movement was foisted on Yugoslavia, either by the Russians or by us. If it was foisted on them by anyone, it was by the Germans. One cannot sufficiently overemphasize the destruction of Yugoslavia by the Germans, the destruction of the country's institutions and the terroristic edge the German army used to consolidate its power. It is also absurd to think that Britain was omnipotent and had a free field of operation. It is true that in 1939 the Foreign Office thought it could dispose of the fortunes of nations in Europe, but by 1943 such confidence has gone, and by 1944 there is even a hint of perturbation – not Maybe we cannot do everything, but Can we do anything?[38]

The historian Mark Wheeler suggests some psychological reasons for the revisionists' would-be denial of the obvious.

Tito would have prevailed whatever the British did. The most horrible error of Lees, Martin and the other revisionists is that they make Allied actions decisive. Allied aid helped Tito, as did the Red Army, but it accelerated a process that was anyway inevitable. Serbs today cling to the exculpation the revisionists offer them. They didn't make their own bed – the British did it for them! This fits in with the tradition of 'perfidious Albion' in Eastern Europe – the British have a uniquely competent and uniquely evil secret service, et cetera. In the Balkans there is a constant motif that one is not responsible for one's own fate, that malign foreign influences, especially the British secret service, are manipulating them. Balkan peoples like to believe they are not in charge of their own destiny and that dark forces are running them. Of course, like all clichés, this one contains some truth, just as the most intriguing cases of paranoia contain a good deal of rationality. Historically, and above all in the nineteenth century, the Great Powers *did* determine their destiny.[39]

There is something risible in the revisionist model of wartime decision-making, where a single flawed individual, peculiarly susceptible to Slavic charm, puts in a bogus report to the Prime Minister and then uses his own charm to inveigle him into embracing the policy contained in that report. To believe it we have to accept that Fitzroy Maclean was naïve, that Churchill was more so, that Churchill had access to no other information, that the Americans endorsed the policy, though there was no rationale for it; and that the driving force for the policy was the Communist sympathies of Winston Churchill and Fitzroy Maclean! It is relevant, I think, to examine the credibility of the witnesses. Some of the finest academic historians have gone on record as stating that the Maclean policy in Yugoslavia was the correct one: Elisabeth Barker, Ralph Bennett, F. H. Hinsley, Sir William Deakin, Mark Wheeler,

Hugh Seton-Watson. Who is there of this stature on the revisionist side?

What would have happened if Fitzroy Maclean, not Brigadier Armstrong, had been sent to Mihailovic? Again, this assumes that the reports from the BLOs were the only factor taken into account by Churchill. Given Churchill's military aims, the information he was receiving from Ultra left him no choice but to back the Partisans, however eloquent and skilled the advocacy for the Cetniks. Mark Wheeler writes: 'If Maclean had gone to Mihailovic, things might have been different because of his contacts and entrées into élite circles. If he had shared Bailey's view, he might have been able to convince the British that the breakup of Yugoslavia and the establishment of a Serbian state should have been a British aim.'[40] But, after some initial dithering, a united Yugoslavia *was* a British aim, and it became more strongly so once Roosevelt suggested detaching Serbia as a Russian satellite. More importantly, perhaps, from 1941 on it was also one of Stalin's cherished aims.[41] Those who claim that Britain had a clear field of power in wartime Yugoslavia ignore not just the strength of Tito and the Partisans, and the weakness in resources of the British, but also the might of the new arbiter of Balkan destinies in the 1940s, the Red Army.

'Ruthlessness, but never at the expense of integrity.' Pamela Egremont's words about Fitzroy are exemplified by two quotations. The first concerns the reluctance with which, as a known anti-communist, he reached his conclusions. He wrote on 27 December 1943 to Orme Sargent: 'I am afraid that my reports may have made unpalatable reading. It is certainly disappointing to find that we have been backing a wrong and thoroughly discredited horse all this time, and I know that some people tend, not without some justification, to find the Red bogey disquieting. Personally, however, I feel encouraged by what I have seen in Yugoslavia.'[42] The second concerns his fairness to Mihailovic.

Mihailovic behaved impeccably by his own lights, as his first loyalty was to Serbia, the Serbian royal family, the Serbian church and the Serbian social system. It would be an enormous mistake to suggest that Mihailovic was anything other than an honourable Serbian officer. He was up against what he called 'the gale of the world', which swept him away. Also up against something much tougher and abler. He was attempting an almost impossible task, to keep the Serbian church and the Serbian monarchy in being. He worked out, after they [the Cetniks and the Partisans] had originally fought alongside each other, and the Germans had massacred hostages on an enormous scale, that if things went on like that, by the end of the war there would be nothing left of the Serbian monarchy or church or anything of Serbia. Therefore the right thing was to coast along, collaborate against the Partisans and change sides at the last moment. That was a reasonable calculation. But it's a basic fact that you can't have a Resistance that does not resist. Tito's policy was the right one and the winning one. To have a Resistance that collaborates is a truly Balkan situation.[43]

16

The Year of Decision

1945–1946

A PARADOX of Fitzroy's career is that, while he is an undoubted man of the Right, his achievements have been more clearly appreciated by those on the Left. Basil Davidson, African historian, writer, and wartime major with the SOE and the Partisans, took exception to many of the 'anti-Left' passages in *Eastern Approaches*, but here summarizes generously Fitzroy's wartime achievements.

> I enormously admire the exremely effective way he accepted the challenge of liaising with Tito – a very difficult challenge against his own political feelings. He behaved with great dignity, great courage and great good sense, and those are three things you don't often get together. He was never at a loss in situations that were often very difficult. Fitzroy stands out head and shoulders above all of us because he understood the politics. He coped with it and stood up to the real situation, without compromising his own position, with quite extraordinary vigour and good sense. I relate it to his personality as a Highland aristocrat. A man like that doesn't have to explain himself and is not concerned what people think about him. Unlike many others, he had a complete command of the situation in Yugoslavia from the moral and military point of view. He didn't do it in any overbearing way but by sheer force of habit: that was the way he had grown up. He was given command and so he exercised it. He didn't shilly-shally, calculate personal advantage or weigh up what his superiors would think if he did X. A very complete soldier and, what is rarer, a very good diplomat. Above all, Fitzroy had the gift of leadership. People shy away from talking about that very much misused concept, and it's true that it's difficult and anomalous, but Fitzroy *did* have the gift of leadership, which meant he had the gift of evoking and using loyalty. I've always thought it relates to his Highland background, where a laird is accustomed to looking after his clan, his dependants and those inferior in rank.

Fitzroy's critics claim that the dark side of his leadership qualities is a certain martinet or prima donna quality. Fitzroy's defence is that people habitually mistake softness for weakness, and that only overt toughness compels respect, above all on the battlefield.

Nobody is ever as confident as he pretends to be, me least of all. I accept that I
was probably sharper and tougher when young. I saw Tito getting mellower as
he got older, so I can accept it about myself. I'm much less self-confident and
self-assured than people think, but I think that applies to everyone. I remember
complimenting Winston on a speech, and how even a great man like that
seemed touchingly and genuinely moved by the compliment. One of the problems for great men is that others rarely compliment them, since they assume the
greatness must be obvious to the possessor. But it doesn't work like that. Tito
said to me about [General] Alex[ander] that he could see he was a real fighting
soldier and not a stuffed shirt. I repeated this to Alex and he was tickled pink,
even though he was Supreme Allied Commander at the time, and you'd have
thought he needed no plaudits from anyone.

In 1945 Fitzroy was at the peak of his fame and achievement, fêted as
the 'kilted Pimpernel' and the 'Balkan Brigadier'. Major Franklin
Lindsay, the American commanding officer of the Allied Military Mission to the Partisan forces in the Stajerska area, met him at about this
time. He had not expected to like him, for his briefing from OSS had
contained the following note: 'The so-called Allied mission is in reality
not "Allied" at all, but it is strictly British, and American officers
assigned to it are more or less on "detached duty" status with it. The
Command of the Mission is strictly British. I didn't like it but Brigadier
Maclean has said that that is the way it is, and no one on an equal or
higher level denies it.' Early in 1945 Lindsay was promoted to Colonel
and went to Belgrade to replace Charlie Thayer as head of the American
military mission.

> For the first time I now met Brigadier Maclean, for whom I had worked most of
> the previous year. He was a very tall and thin Scot. At only 34, he was already
> at the upper end of the age bracket into which most Partisans and Allied officers
> fell. Although I found him warm and friendly, many of the Yugoslavs said they
> found him impassive and aloof. Milovan Djilas described him as 'this reserved,
> cold-blooded Scot'. Shortly after arriving in Belgrade I was invited to dine one
> evening at Maclean's mess. All his officers appeared to be old friends and
> several had been together in North Africa fighting against Rommel's forces.
> These British officers who were drawn to irregular operations seemed not only
> to have been together in early wartime operations, but also to have had many
> close school and family ties. In contrast, in three years overseas, I had met only
> one person I had known before the war. A day or two after the dinner I was told
> quite informally that as a 'colonial' I had apparently passed the test of social
> acceptability and that I would be invited back.[1]

Major Basil Davidson had formerly been, with Bill Deakin, Brigadier
Keble's right-hand man in SOE. He had been with the Partisans in a
backwater on the Hungarian border, and like Lindsay saw a lot of
Fitzroy in the period after the fall of Belgrade. Fitzroy showed great

sensitivity in bringing Davidson 'in from the cold', inviting him to a formal dinner with Tito where he was the youngest officer present.

> I was very impressed with Fitzroy as a personality. He had a great capacity for winning confidence, not on the basis of rapid talk or great personal charm – he may have had that, but it wasn't evident. Remember, we were in harsh times, and charming people were out of place. I was impressed by his complete political grasp. He understood very well what was at stake, which was a great relief to me because I had been dealing with people who were at sea politically and in confusion. Here was someone on top of it all, who grasped the point of it. Next, I was impressed by his generosity of spirit. He's a generous man because he showed great sensitivity to my position in a group of about forty Partisans for over a year. I was feeling very lost and lonely and he took me under his wing and made me feel one of his mission. He gave me a valuable feeling of belonging after a year of isolation. To find Fitzroy so friendly and generous was marvellous.[2]

Vladimir ('Vlatko') Velebit ended the war with a profound admiration for Fitzroy, which has never altered.

> I know that a number of British, American and Yugoslav quasi-historians are now busy writing a lot of nonsense about the sinister role Mr Churchill and Fitzroy have played in twisting the fate of Yugoslavia. But that is pure malicious imagination and political speculation. In my opinion Fitzroy did a splendid job. His reports are masterpieces of understanding a very complicated and confused political situation. I would even venture to say that Fitzroy has often demonstrated a more profound insight into Yugoslav affairs than many Yugoslavs.[3]

Yet in March 1945, on his return to England, Fitzroy faced a personal challenge. What do war heroes do when the fighting ends? How do they find a niche in the routine of peacetime life? It is true that Fitzroy had a role as MP for Lancaster, but it was one he had assumed out of convenience. He could not be sure that politics was the right *métier* for him. If it was not, what was? The Diplomatic Service? But it was unlikely they would want him back after his somewhat cavalier leavetaking in 1941. In any case, could he really accept the rule of 'Buggins' turn', having run his own show for two years? In his early thirties he had been Britain's ambassador to Tito in all but name. It was just conceivable, of course, that Churchill might twist the mandarins' arms and force Fitzroy on them as youngest-ever actual ambassador to Yugoslavia. But that would mean resigning his seat in the House of Commons, in which case could he claim that he had fulfilled his obligations to the people of Lancaster?

In May 1945 it was far from clear that all chance of getting into the fighting had now gone. That month Fitzroy and Churchill dined with

David Stirling, newly released from Colditz Castle, and discussed what Stirling called the 'Chungking Project'. This was the notion of forming a brigade commanded by Stirling, with Fitzroy as his Number Two, to be raised from among released prisoners-of-war, especially from Colditz; there would be three regiments, two from SAS veterans, the other from OSS men, to win American approval. The idea was to go beyond Wingate and his Chindits by operating in China itself, cutting off supplies to Malaya, sabotaging industrial centres in Manchuria, and seizing ports to enable American forces to land. As expected, the scheme appealed to Churchill, and planning was at an advanced stage when the dropping of the atom bombs on Hiroshima and Nagasaki brought the Pacific war to an abrupt end.[4]

So it was that the political once again prevailed over the military in Fitzroy's life. As VE day approached, so did a general election. As Churchill wrote to Fitzroy, 'I am expecting of course you and Randolph to defend your seats with vigour in these two months. All necessary permissions will be given to Members and Candidates, subject only to battle conditions.'[5] Fitzroy was slightly nervous about the electors' response to him after such a long absence. Occasionally during his wartime work, this anxiety had surfaced. Writing to a fellow MP in December 1943, Fitzroy declared: 'I take this opportunity to let you know I am in the pink. I hope you are too and that my constituents are also in good form and not too angry with me for neglecting them.'[6]

The Parliament elected in 1935 would normally have expired by November 1940 but, after the formation of Churchill's wartime coalition in May 1940, it was prolonged by annual Prolongation Bills. Churchill wanted it to continue until the end of the war with Japan, but the Labour leader Clement Attlee insisted a new parliament be elected in the 1944–45 session, now that the principal task of the coalition – the defeat of Germany – had been accomplished. On 23 May, therefore, Churchill formally asked the king to dissolve Parliament, and infuriated Labour by proposing himself for election as Prime Minister of a 'National' Government.

While Fitzroy was MP for Lancaster, his two friends Randolph Churchill and Julian Amery were members for Preston. These Lancashire constituencies were, coincidentally, the English Jacobite heartland through which Fitzroy's hero Prince Charlie had marched exactly two hundred years before. Now and later Fitzroy and Amery often made the five-hour train journey from London together, trying to devise ways of beating rationing and having a decent lunch. On one occasion Winston Churchill was due to speak in Preston, on his whirlwind tour through the Midlands and the North. Twenty thousand people packed the main square to hear Churchill's stirring rhetoric, but his train was late so Fitzroy had to speak in his place – an ordeal for a man who has always detested public speaking. [7]

Since Churchill was universally acknowledged as the saviour of his country, it seems surprising that the British electorate turned him out so decisively in 1945. But the reasons for the Tory defeat are clear. Primarily the Conservatives were associated with peacetime unemployment, and nobody wanted a return to the bad old days. There was also a fear that the Tories themselves would ditch Churchill, as he might prevent a return to the domestic policies of the thirties. Another strand of opinion was that Churchill was a great wartime leader, but unreliable in peacetime, and critics pointed to his dubious record over Ireland, the General Strike and much else. Most of all, the hordes of returning servicemen had seen something of the world, had imbibed new ideas through the Army Education Corps, and were not prepared to return to the old class-ridden ways. They no longer thought that there was a class naturally fitted to rule, or that 'gentlemen' knew best. All research confirms that the result of the election had been determined by the beginning of 1945, and that the mood of the electorate was set long before the campaign began.

In 1945 there was a gap between political consciousness and social conditions. The electorate might be more sophisticated than ever before, but their material circumstances were still straitened. The Lancashire in which Fitzroy campaigned was in many ways still the county of Gracie Fields and *Sing as We Go*, as a contemporary report of Churchill's tour in the *Manchester Guardian* makes clear: 'Many moments still live in the minds of those who took part – and not least impressive will be the memory of the young children who lined the route, of the scurrying music of their clogs as they raced to new vantage points like a flight of eager starlings.'[8] Especially dated forty-five years on is the Conservative candidates' presentation of themselves as 'officers and gentlemen'. One Tory hopeful proposed himself to the electors as follows: 'His most thrilling week-end was when he shot and killed a tiger which had for months killed the coolies' cattle; a few hours later he was in an earthquake which damaged his bungalow, and a few hours later still a coolie was murdered within a hundred yards of his bungalow. On another occasion he shot four python snakes, the largest being eighteen feet long.'[9] Fitzroy, after his basic training with the lads from the Gorbals, was much too shrewd to misread the feelings of ordinary people in this way.

Most of the polling took place on 5 July, but there was an unprecedented three-week wait before the results were declared. In twenty-three seats polling was delayed, and there was a huge service and proxy vote to be counted.[10] It was not until 27 July that the full result was known. Labour had won 393 seats – a majority of 146 over all other parties. The Conservative (National) party was reduced to a mere 213, one of which was Fitzroy's. He had a safe seat, and he also benefited from a below-average swing to Labour in Lancashire.

Why did Fitzroy fight the election of 1945? After all he had, in Churchill's words, used the Mother of Parliaments as a public convenience, and for him politics had outlived its usefulness. He was at the height of his fame, and the glittering prizes beckoned. He had been very nearly the youngest brigadier of the war; it was now possible that he might be the youngest ambassador somewhere, or the first British representative at the United Nations. But Fitzroy felt his honour was involved. He had promised the people of Lancaster that he would come back and work for them after the war, and a Highlander's word was his bond. Besides that, as a like-minded fellow MP, Douglas Dodds-Parker, explains: 'This may sound pompous, but people like Fitz and I really thought after the war that by going into politics we might this time win the peace, having lost it after winning the First World War. Also to do something about better living conditions, unemployment. What concerned us most was the moral rather than the financial waste.'[11]

Why did Fitzroy not receive higher honours in the aftermath of the war? There is a general consensus among his friends that he was ill-requited, and that he himself was disappointed that he received no more than the standard decoration – the CBE for a brigadier, the MBE for a colonel, and so on. The right decoration for Fitzroy was clearly the DSO. Why, then, did he not receive it?

Some think it is because he 'allowed' Tito to 'levant' in 1944, or because he was a victim of the Cold War, when a shadow fell on all those who had had close wartime links with Communists. Fitzroy himself inclines to this view. 'Jumbo Wilson put me in for a military KBE, but I would not have wanted that. From 1945 to 1948 I was in disgrace because of my links with Tito.'[12] Others thought that, as Head of the Mission to Tito, Fitzroy fell between two stools: neither clearly a military figure, nor manifestly a political one. Douglas Dodds-Parker explains:

> Unfortunately, anyone not in regular military service was resented by both military and politicians on the grounds of usurpation of functions. Fitzroy . . . [was] at once quasi-military and quasi-political. He was not in action in Yugoslavia, through no fault of his own. Politicians dislike 'funnies', as do regular soldiers. Moreover, Fitzroy's close personal relationship with Churchill was resented in some quarters, and it has to be said he had made enemies by going above heads. If Fitz had wanted a DSO, he should have stayed with SAS.[13]

Yet others point out that Britain is notorious for squandering resources and talents. Lord Henniker says: 'This is the key thing, it is a peculiarly British failing and links with the cult of the amateur and all that. There's no question but that Fitz should have been an ambassador somewhere. Bill Deakin too has been enormously wasted.'[14] Sir Peter Carey endorses this: 'Maclean was underused. British governments and institutions are notoriously bad at using talent. The individual has to push in a rather hard-faced manner, and Fitzroy didn't knock hard enough on the door.'[15]

Fitzroy's career suffered when Churchill, who had thrown him a broad hint that there was a job for him at the War Office, was turned out. He now had no immediate career objective. For eighteen months or so he tried to make his mark in the House of Commons. His first major Parliamentary question showed his lack of inexperience, for it admitted of only one answer.

FITZROY MACLEAN: Is it the intention of His Majesty's Government in all circumstances to safeguard our interests in South Persia and the Persian Gulf?

MR LAW: The answer to Brigadier Maclean's question is in the affirmative.[16]

On 3 August 1945 Fitzroy took the oath of office as a newly-elected MP. He was one of several brigadiers sworn in that day: others were Selwyn Lloyd, Otho Prior-Palmer, Toby Low, Ralph Rayner, Frank Medlicott and Anthony Head. They were men of proven competence and reliability of whom the Party managers had high hopes.[17] Much play was made of 'the brigadiers', as if they were Dumas' musketeers, and the Speaker always addressed them as 'honourable and gallant members'. But the Labour front bench liked to poke amiable fun, and Hugh Dalton jibed: 'We'll reduce all the Tory brigadiers to the ranks when the Red Revolution comes.'[18]

There was a friendly, non-partisan atmosphere in the House of Commons between 1945 and 1950. More than the usual mutual respect was enjoyed between front and back benches, many members having served together in the wartime coalition. Both sides were wedded to the Beveridge Plan, and Labour later proved as committed to the Cold War alliance with the USA and to NATO as the most right-wing Tory could have wished. It is true that the Tories were unhappy with Labour's plan to nationalize the 'commanding heights' of the economy, and Fitzroy was not convinced that public ownership was the answer for the working class, but for the time being he and many other Conservatives were half-inclined to let Labour have its head temporarily. Some guilt was felt about the mass unemployment of the 1930s, and Labour argued that everything but nationalization had already been tried. On Scottish affairs Fitzroy was especially inclined to be emollient. As between John Buchan and Jimmy Maxton in an earlier era, there grew up a wary respect between Tories like Fitzroy and Douglas Dodds-Parker, and Labour's Glasgow members like Buchanan and McGovern.

Fitzroy also admired the new Foreign Secretary, Ernest Bevin, and was quite prepared to describe Prime Minister Attlee as 'a great man'. But he was sceptical of Labour's claim that it would handle the Soviet government better since 'Left would speak with Left'. His Yugoslav experiences, especially during the battle for Belgrade, led him to doubt that ideology would transcend nationalism. He also thought that the entente between Labour and the British trade unions and the corporatism it seemed to portend could not last, since the unions would find themselves trapped between the State in its capacity as employer and the State as friend and associate of the unions. He warned that the right to strike was enshrined under capitalism, but might be lost under socialism.

A long letter to *The Times* in October, expounding this theory, provoked an angry rejoinder from the union boss John Clynes, who described it as 'a medley of ill-informed and unhelpful stuff'. Fitzroy replied by arguing that nationalization of the docks was not in the workers' interest since they would then find themselves in the same position as the troops, who were at present (during the 1945 dock strike) obliged to do a docker's work for a fraction of the money. After teasing trade unionists as being potentially, under socialism, 'enemies of the people', Fitzroy pulled rank in a different way on Clynes. 'While I do not pretend to Mr Clynes' intimate knowledge of the inside workings of trades unions and the Labour Party, I feel that I can claim a wider first-hand experience of the practical workings of the Socialist state at various stages of its development than he or most members of his party.'[19]

Fitzroy was learning the art of political street-fighting, and his next exchanges in the House showed a marked improvement on his first efforts. He pressed Bevin on the Soviet role in the Allied Control Commission in Hungary, then in November returned to the question he had first posed in June about safeguarding imperial interests in Persia. This time, when Bevin gave a bland assurance, Fitzroy was not satisfied – though he got no further. FITZROY MACLEAN: Will the Right Honourable Gentleman say how he proposes to carry out this assurance in this particular case? BEVIN: I cannot divulge all the strategy of the Chiefs of Staff and everybody else concerned to the honourable and gallant member in answer to a question.[20]

November 1945 found Fitzroy in energetic mood. He made a forceful contribution to the debate on Russia in the House on the 22nd, praising Bevin for his firmness towards those erstwhile allies and reiterating his firmly held conviction that the Russians admire strength only and despise those who take a liberal line towards them. 'The leftist complexion of members opposite did not necessarily endear them to our Russian allies. Parlour pinks and other left-wing diversionists inspired neither admiration nor respect in Moscow.' He taunted the Labour government with their election promises of cordial relations with the Soviet Union; in fact, relations were at their worst 'since the pact of 1941, the product of Tory statesmanship.'[21]

A week later, at the Conservative Party Conference, Fitzroy moved a resolution on behalf of his Lancaster constituency to improve the machinery for putting across the Conservative point of view and for divining public opinion. He emphasized the failure of the Tory party at the 1945 election to understand the popular mood or catch the imaginations of ordinary people.[22] This was perhaps the first appearance in the annals of the Conservative party of the now-familiar doctrine that there is nothing wrong with Tory policy but presentation and image-making.

Fitzroy could regard 1945 as a satisfactory year on the public front; it also brought him happiness in his private life, when he was introduced to the Honourable Mrs Alan Phipps, Lord Lovat's daughter and widow of the Royal Navy Lieutenant Phipps lost off Leros in 1943. Married at eighteen and now with two children, Veronica Phipps had lived for two years in an agony of suspense, her husband officially classified as 'missing'. It was only when returning servicemen began to reach England early in 1945, and an eyewitness came forward who had seen Phipps killed in the fighting, that she could allow herself to mourn.

Veronica was a beautiful but boisterous young woman, now 26, and when Fitzroy first met her at a dance someone remarked, 'That's the noisiest girl in London!' Their second meeting, at dinner with David Stirling and his sister on 23 August, was the critical one.[23] The couple found they had things in common, for Veronica had been helping her brother Hugh Fraser to fight the general election. The Fraser campaign was covered for *Life* magazine by the 28-year-old John Fitzgerald Kennedy, whom the Frasers came to know well. 'If anyone had told me that Jack Kennedy would one day be President,' Veronica says, 'I would have roared with laughter.'[24] Fitzroy and Veronica lingered over the dinner table after the Stirlings had left. They went on to a night-club and got home in the small hours. Next day Fitzroy rang and asked her to dinner. By this time, Veronica confesses, she was 'slightly interested'. There followed the proverbial 'whirlwind courtship' which was such a feature of the war years and their immediate aftermath. By October the two were engaged.

Early in November Fitzroy departed for Switzerland to tell his parents. When war broke out his mother and father had decamped from Florence to Montreux and there they had looked after some Cameron Highlanders who escaped south after Dunkirk. Fitzroy's maternal grandmother, who died in 1941, had also moved to Florence between the wars, and owned a flat in the city centre. The plan was that Major and Mrs Maclean would move back to Florence and live in the flat, but meanwhile Montreux would be ideal for a honeymoon venue in that era of post-war austerity and scarce foreign currency.

Engaged in October, Fitzroy and Veronica were married on 12 January 1946. Veronica sums up the prelude to marriage.

> We got engaged when I was still only half-healed from Alan. It took a long time to accept that he was really dead, and I was only half-ready for marriage. We had a three-month engagement and literally dated each other for a fortnight only, but I am impetuous. After all, I married Alan after only a fortnight. I relied on instinct both times to tell me, 'This is it'. Something deeper than genes and almost against my will. My initial feeling was that I wouldn't have minded an affair with Fitz, but he insisted on marriage. Then something said, 'Yes, this is the right thing'. We drove round and round Hyde Park Corner while he proposed. I asked him whether he wouldn't prefer a love affair. He said, no, he wanted marriage.[25]

After the wedding, the couple departed for Switzerland on 17 January and were away until the beginning of March. A notice in *The Times* made it clear that they did not want to be disturbed. 'No correspondence will be forwarded, but letters addressed to Brigadier Maclean at the House of Commons will be dealt with by his secretary.'[26]

It was particularly gratifying for Fitzroy that Veronica and his parents struck up an immediate rapport.

> I got on splendidly with [Fitzroy's mother], and she was always so extraordinarily generous. Whenever we went out to see them, she would press into my hand not just the cost of our journey but a little extra with which I could buy a dress or something. It was a very different kind of family from mine. The Maclean/Royle family never criticized each other. In the Lovat household people always did, and there was a total free-for-all. We rowed a lot to begin with, as I was so used to brothers and sisters and was used to answering back. He soon got used to the Lovat way and yelled back at me!

Many war heroes came back in a highly disturbed state, and Veronica confirms that her first two years of marriage were not easy, not just because of the difference in temperament and family culture but because Fitzroy was still highly-strung, half-alert for the cry of 'Pokret!' 'For two years he was very tense, still "coming down to earth" after the war. If he woke in the night, he would instinctively roll out of the bed and onto the floor.'[27]

Fitzroy returned to London in time for a defence debate featuring all the brigadiers. He dilated on his favourite theme, southern Persia, 'the most vital and weakest spot in imperial defence'. A month later, in a debate on the Trade Disputes Bill, he reproduced his most cherished domestic argument: that under a socialist government trade unions become the servant of established authority, not its enemy.[28] Next he and Veronica looked at houses in Lancaster; he had promised his constituents he would live among them. They found a delightful house at Yealand Conyers to the north of Lancaster, which they bought for £12,000.

By June 1946 Fitzroy was emerging as a vigorous champion of empire, even as governments showed signs of the retreat that in twenty years ended the British presence east of Suez. Fitzroy deplored all moves to withdraw from empire on several grounds: that it would create a power vacuum others would exploit; that it would render meaningless the sacrifices and heroism of past generations; and that precipitate moves to abdicate responsibility would jeopardise the security of the countries the British were leaving, or their UN trusteeship role there. Fitzroy bitterly opposed British withdrawal from Egypt, and repeated his conviction that adversaries admire strength. The Egyptians, he claimed, 'like most eastern (and a good many western) peoples . . . are not impressed by what they interpret, perhaps unjustly, as a display of fumbling or weakness.' At this time, too, the future of India was at issue. In a debate in December Fitzroy asked what the government would do if the main parties on the subcontinent could not reach agreement; he warned that to abdicate responsibility meant handing India over to civil war, which would further diminish the reputation of the West in Asia.[29]

In 1946 when General Douglas MacArthur, viceroy of Japan in all but name, invited a delegation of five MPs to visit the Far East as his guests Fitzroy was one of these, and he relished the opportunity to visit a part of the world of which he had hitherto seen only the Sino-Russian border. The delegation arrived at Irakuni, thirty miles from Hiroshima, on 18 September and next day began a fact-finding tour of Tokyo. Fitzroy was principally concerned with the contingent of British troops stationed in Japan, which the Labour government was proposing to withdraw. 'Even in these days of itinerant Cabinet Ministers, the British soldier is still our best ambassador,' he said, though without effect. Later Fitzroy flew over to the China coast to visit military installations. In Nanking he could hear the booming guns of the advancing Communist army.

True to his propensity for getting 'in harm's way', Fitzroy soon found a genuine trouble-spot, Korea, which he visited after the MacArthur-sponsored tour of Japan. Seoul he found 'a strange jumble of Japanese-built skyscrapers and ancient Buddhist temples'. The political situation was even more jumbled. At Yalta it had been decided to return Korea to independence after the final defeat of Japan; in the interim there was to be a five-year trusteeship by the Big Four (Britain, USA, USSR and China) and a joint Soviet-American Commission to establish a provisional Korean government. At the Moscow Conference of December 1945 a further decision was taken: American and Russian troops would occupy the two halves of the country, Americans south and Russians north of the 38th Parallel. By now, Fitzroy found, relations between the Soviets and the Americans had all but broken down. The Commission had met just once, in March 1946, and had immediately fallen out over the meaning of 'democratic'. With South Korea torn by strikes and riots and a strong Soviet military presence in the North, it was clear that war was probable rather than possible.[30]

The trip to the Far East enabled Fitzroy to see at close quarters the 'American Caesar', General Douglas MacArthur, whose quasi-imperial proconsular style was already a legend. During the war Fitzroy had dealt with Wilson and Alexander. He had seen nothing of the notorious military showmen; though Charlie Thayer had been taught to ride by Patton. General Montgomery was disliked by the SAS, having criticized their exploits in the desert. 'However,' says Fitzroy with disarming frankness, 'I met Monty after the war, and he said I was the one man he had always wanted to meet, so that changed my opinion somewhat!' But MacArthur was almost as big a figure as Monty. Alanbrooke, Chief of the Imperial General Staff, told Fitzroy that in his opinion MacArthur was the greatest general of the Second World War.

Fitzroy discovered that all the legends were true. MacArthur acted like the Mikado and bade fair to displace Hirohito himself as the true emperor. He kept the delegation of British MPs waiting for half an hour in a semi-circle – in the stance petitioners for favour were wont to adopt at the ancient Japanese courts. The Japanese may have loved MacArthur's imperial antics, but the British were less impressed. They would have sympathized with Eisenhower, who said drily that not only did he know General MacArthur, but he had studied dramatics under him in the Philippines. Fitzroy heard that MacArthur had been plagued by a Filipino ex-mistress, who as a result had been found in a 'concrete overcoat' in California. 'One of our delegation, the Reverend Gordon Laing, said that he had never met anyone like MacArthur, who was so self-evidently a good man. Knowing what I knew, I allowed myself a silent dissent.'[31]

It was a not altogether happy Fitzroy who flew home to London in October. Somewhat forlornly he raised Japanese and Korean issues in the House before Bevin and his Minister of State, Hector McNeil. McNeil stonewalled, sheepishly (though correctly) describing all such issues as primarily matters of US foreign policy, out of British hands. But Fitzroy drew blood in a debate on Japan on 27 January 1947. When McNeil confirmed that British trade was still on a government-to-government basis, Fitzroy nonplussed him by revealing that representatives of American insurance firms and car manufacturers were present in Japan in large numbers, gobbling up actual and potential markets. A flustered McNeil managed an inadequate answer which drew cries of 'Oh' from the Opposition benches. Unconvincingly claiming that American businessmen were in Tokyo merely to 'service the troops', McNeil continued: 'I have no knowledge about motor representatives. As to the others it is true that they are there, but not in a representative capacity.'[32]

It must be admitted that Fitzroy languished in Parliament. He did not find the life of an MP to his taste, and it was difficult for him to adjust to the boredom of civilian life.

> I had high expectations, and there were high expectations of me, because of what I had done in the war. But I didn't enjoy it and never felt marvellous when I got to my feet. I also found I lacked talent for and pleasure in making speeches. I suppose this was because I'd been formed as a diplomat. A diplomat is told to look at both sides of the case, sum up and reach a conclusion. The politician is told to look at one side only. I didn't get on with the Parliamentary way. You know, don't be concise, say it over and over again in different ways. All this was alien.[33]

In these years Fitzroy was also disturbed by the criticism that came his way for having 'misled' Churchill over Tito. This was the time of revenge killings in Yugoslavia and the trial and execution of Mihailovic. He tended to avoid the House of Commons while this controversy was at its height. Veronica comments:

> He's not a clubbable man and not a Commons man, and never was. Now he thinks he would love to have had a brilliant parliamentary career and was unlucky that Churchill lost in '45. But Fitz did not enjoy committees and has never been anyone's Parliamentary Private Secretary. He has a lot of pride, and didn't want that. But it's the only way back-benchers get on. But in those days Fitz didn't listen to me – nowadays he does – even though my family has politics in their blood and he didn't. I always had an instinct that he should have done different things in the House. I wanted him to go back into the Foreign Office and become an ambassador. He wouldn't have it, and perhaps it would have been a mistake. He never had enough nasty qualities to get on, and couldn't make speeches full of cant and humbug. Like everyone who writes, he writes sentences that mean something. And he hated wheeling and dealing, or intriguing, or using people, which is the essence of politics. The combination of having had a brilliant war and being honourable told against him.[34]

Fitzroy's career seemed to have reached an impasse. The breakthrough involved Yugoslavia.

17

Tito Lends a Hand

1945–1949

'JONNY' VON HERWARTH tells of being with Fitzroy in Lancaster when Veronica, who was driving, crashed the car into a red bus. Fitzroy, winking at von Herwarth, said, 'I never did like the colour red.' His critics have always claimed that he didn't mind red if it went with the 'Black Lamb and Grey Falcon', to use Rebecca West's image of Yugoslavia. Some see Fitzroy's role in Anglo-Yugoslav relations during 1947 and 1948 as even more important than his wartime mission. Vlatko Velebit comments: 'Fitzroy played a very important part in the after-war period in furthering Anglo-Yugoslav relations, and this period is not covered by any historian.'

Fitzroy had noticed straws in the wind indicating that Tito might one day break with Stalin. Even his famous report of 6 November 1943 included these prophetic words: 'Events will show the nature of Soviet intentions towards Yugoslavia; much will also depend on Tito and whether he sees himself still in his former role of Comintern agent, or as the potential ruler of an independent State.' What he saw of Russian behaviour in Belgrade in October 1944 strengthened his belief that Yugoslav and Soviet interests might some day diverge. However, in the comradely euphoria following the Red Army's successes, Fitzroy hedged his bets. His final report from Yugoslavia in February 1945 excluded almost all possibility that Tito's new state would or could be anything but a Moscow satellite. 'Both Tito's personal background and the present trend of events in Europe have undoubtedly convinced him that in all major questions of policy Yugoslavia must henceforward take her line from the Soviet Union . . . its internal institutions will bear an ever increasing resemblance to those of the Soviet Union, and its foreign policy will be dictated from Moscow.'

He was not alone in this conclusion. The OSS intelligence officer Major Franklin Lindsay believed that international Communist ideology would always be a stronger force than the nationalism of the

Yugoslav Communist Party. In his final report in 1945 he wrote: 'The basic policy of the present Government is the complete orientation of Yugoslavia into the Russian sphere. This policy is being implemented primarily by the Yugoslav Communists and is not being directed locally by Russian representatives . . . the top Yugoslav leaders are so thoroughly indoctrinated with Soviet policies and methods that there is little or no need for day-to-day directives from Moscow.'

Tito's break with Moscow, when it came in 1948, can be seen in retrospect as a pivotal moment in history. It was the first crack in the Soviet monolith and, Fitzroy thinks, the first step in a causal chain that led eventually to the collapse of Communism. One of the few lessons history does teach is that once an iron tyranny – whether Stalin's Russia or the South Africa of apartheid – relaxes its grip, it is on a slippery slope. Fitzroy grasped this earlier than most. Tito opted for Communism without Stalin. Khruschev pushed the process a stage further. Brezhnev tried to slam on the brakes, but by then it was too late. Fitzroy is fond of quoting an aphorism of Jean-Paul Sartre's that sums the whole thing up: '*C'est la déStalinisation qui déStalinisera les déStalinisateurs.*' 'The process', Fitzroy says, 'was to reach its logical conclusion twenty years after Khruschev's dismissal with the emergence of Mikhail Sergeyevich Gorbachev.'

Since March 1945 relations between Tito and the British government had been worsening, and that trend was accelerated by the 'forty days' of tension (from 3 May) over Trieste.[1] The Allied armies and the Partisans converged on the area almost simultaneously, and New Zealand units of General Alexander's 15th Army Group faced Tito's men in an anxious stand-off. Trieste, Venezia Giulia and Carinthia were all regions claimed by Yugoslavia, and after a brilliant *blitzkrieg* of their own in north-western Yugoslavia in April, the Partisans were infuriated to be denied the area by Alexander's forces advancing northeast from Padua. Tito felt that the British had treacherously stolen 'his' victory, and the rival armies glared at each other in a state of uneasy truce. Then the British brought up reinforcements and the Partisans were forced to back down.[2]

Tito was angry that Stalin had done nothing to help him press his claim, especially as he was also forced to evacuate Klagenfurt and Villach on the Austro-Yugoslav border. When Tito withdrew his men, all Stalin said was, 'You did right.' Suspicions that Stalin was more interested in constructing a Popular Front government in Italy, which would have been jeopardized if he had backed Tito over Trieste, did not improve Soviet–Yugoslav relations. Stalin's assurances to the Austrians over Carinthia also looked to Tito like a doublecross.

The British left Yugoslavia under a cloud. The last troops out were a patrol of LRDG, the Long-Range Desert Group. The Partisans had spent much of May clearing the last vestiges of foreign 'imperialism', and finally the British soldiers were given an ultimatum: clear out or be arrested. One LRDG patrol leader signalled: 'I would prefer to be picked up by the Navy rather than slaughtered by these garlic-eating bandits.'[3]

Tito set to work to repair the ravages of four years of war. Of a population of some sixteen millions, over a million had lost their lives in battle, massacre, concentration camp or from war-related disease,[4] fatalities equivalent to those of Poland or the USSR. Half a million more were wounded or disabled. Countless men, women and children were suffering from tuberculosis. A hundred and seventy thousand were prisoners-of-war, 320,000 were internees, and 270,000 were in labour camps outside the country. Fifty-three thousand others had been forcibly evacuated and another 350,000 recruited into enemy forces. The average age of the killed and missing was 22. The labour force had been decimated, and tens of thousands of technicians and skilled workers lost; one estimate of the dead counted 90,000 skilled workers and 40,000 intellectuals, bureaucrats and administrators.

On top of this, a quarter of the pre-war aggregate of agricultural wealth had been lost. Two-thirds of the livestock and horses had perished, and even greater proportions of small livestock. In the livestock breeding areas of Bosnia, Herzegovina and Montenegro, 85 per cent of the pre-war livestock and 90 per cent of poultry had been destroyed. A quarter of all vineyards and orchards were ruined. The same was true of agricultural implements: destroyed were 1,530 tractors, 2,485 steam engines, 12,800 threshing machines, 380,000 ploughs, 8,200 harvesting machines, and 485,000 peasants' carts. Meanwhile 48 million cubic metres of wood had been felled and 260,000 young trees and 35,000 hectares of cultivated woodland destroyed. Sixty-five per cent of the pre-war mining industry was in ruins. Trade had been paralysed during the war, especially since the German looting of the National Bank's gold reserves and privately-owned valuables, including Church property. Insurance companies and public ultilities had been paralysed for four years. Losses from the railways included 28,000 trucks, 15,000 waggons, 3,000 passenger carriages and 587 locomotives looted or destroyed. Most of the railway tracks and bridges had been destroyed or damaged, to an estimated value of 1½ million dollars. Shipping and motor transport had been virtually wiped out: 3,000 seagoing ships had been sunk or impounded.[5]

Tito's government announced a Five-Year Plan, which did not enjoy Russian support. The pro-Soviet Hebrang was sacked from the Politburo for his vociferous criticisms. Stalin wanted Yugoslavia as a satellite agricultural state servicing the Soviet Union, a provider of raw materials and a monopoly outlet for Soviet heavy industry. He wanted a

Soviet–Yugoslav bank under a Russian director-general, which would have throttled Yugoslavia's own economic development. It was a pity that, faced with such problems, Tito could not look to the West for support. Slight traces of Fitzroy's influence can be discerned in 1945 in the Foreign Office report that 'placed' Tito as moderate nationalist first, Communist second[6] but in general Fitzroy's pro-Tito stance was unpopular, and his perception of the uselessness of Dr Macek and his reformist Yugoslav Peasants' Party as an alternative to Communism merely drew this barb from his old enemy Bruce Lockhart: 'This seems to me too servile an attitude towards Tito or/and Russia. Apparently we think that Macek is a dead letter because that foolish young man Fitzroy Maclean says so.'[7]

Hostility to Fitzroy increased as the Cold War began in earnest. Tito's treatment of Mihailovic in 1946 hardened attitudes further. The closing stages of the war had turned into a nightmare for the Cetniks. As they withdrew from Bosnia, hoping to reach Austria, many were slaughtered by the Ustase and many more by the Partisans. In March 1946 Mihailovic himself was lured back into Serbia by faked signals showing popular support for him there, captured, and then executed after a show trial.

Two of Mihailovic's supporters, Greenwood and Greenlees, both members of the mission to Mihailovic, wrote to *The Times* implicitly criticizing Fitzroy, thus initiating a controversy that has not ended yet. Fitzroy pointed out that the allegedly moral case for Serbian hegemony was being confused with military realities; in other words, they were in effect arguing that the cause of Serbia should have taken precedence over the entire Allied project to destroy Nazi Germany. He reiterated that Mihailovic's inactivity and collaboration were undeniable, citing Jasper Rootham's recently published *Miss Fire*, and scoffed at his critics' figures for Cetnik strength, pointing out that they included both active collaborators and those who, it was claimed, would join in 'when the time was ripe – neither of which categories were of much use to the Allies.'[8]

Fitzroy still had his admirers in the Foreign Office, whose policy after 1945 was not to seek to displace Soviet influence there (in any case impossible), but to maintain existing contacts against the day when these might be properly exploited.[9] There was no common Western policy towards Yugoslavia; in fact, Britain and the United States had conflicting aims, but the head of the FO, Sir Alexander Cadogan, wanted Britain to keep a toe in the Yugoslav waters.[10] Even after the elections of mid-November 1945 had entrenched Tito and the Communists in power and finally excluded the royalists, on whose behalf so much effort had been made, the British still sought to keep in touch with Yugoslav decision-making.[11] Yugoslavia was simply too important to be sulked over; it must be 'business as usual' if Britain were ever to challenge Soviet influence.[12] Naturally the Foreign Office was not happy about the trend of events. Despite Tito's assurances to Fitzroy in February 1945, British economic interests, in shipping and mining, were nationalized by a decree in August 1945 expropriating all mineral wealth.[13] Yet it was still British policy to try to make inroads on the Yugoslav economy, so as to prevent the emergence of a Soviet-style closed economic system there. For a long time, however, all attempts to get an economic agreement between the two countries foundered on the question of compensation to British nationals, which Tito refused. There was also continuing tension over Trieste.

This was the context in early 1947 when the Foreign Office decided to make use of Fitzroy's expertise. Perhaps the most serious issue of all those bedevilling relations was that of Yugoslav displaced persons (DPs). The devastation wrought by the war left a total of eighteen million refugees, many in camps across Europe. There were some 70,000 Yugoslav DPs in jointly-administered Anglo-American camps in Italy and Austria, awaiting screening to see if they should be classified as political refugees or as war criminals. There were also Ukrainians, whose future fate clearly depended on negotiations with the USSR. At Yalta the Allies had agreed to repatriate to the Soviet Union all war criminals who had fought on the eastern front but fled for sanctuary into the western zones. In Yugoslavia, they had formally undertaken to repatriate for trial Ustase and other quislings.[14] The Yugoslavs were convinced the British were welching on the deal. In particular, there had been an angry correspondence between British and Yugoslav Foreign Office officials about alleged British collusion in the escape of Yugoslavia's 'most wanted man', Ante Pavelic, dictator of the wartime Fascist state of Croatia. The Yugoslavs, despite British denials, insisted that Pavelic was in the British zone in Austria – they were right, he was – and that the British Army was protecting him. Although the British embassy in Belgrade issued a formal denial of these charges in August 1946, earlier that year Orme Sargent minuted a reminder that the Yugoslav government felt deeply about the quislings and were not just using the issue as a bargaining counter in negotiations.[15] But lack of manpower, a pro-Croat clique in the Foreign Office, and the uncooperative attitude of the Americans, who loathed Tito, made tracing the guilty all but impossible. By the end of 1946 no more than a handful of 'most wanted' war criminals had been repatriated to Yugoslavia.

Just before Christmas 1946 Ernest Bevin formally raised the matter with his senior officials.[16] It now seemed that 20,000 or so Yugoslav DPs in Italy would be handed over to the Italian government on 8 February 1947 when the Italian peace treaty, normalizing relations with the

Allies, was signed. The Italians had made it clear they could not guarantee to stand firm against Yugoslav demands that the entire 20,000 be sent back to Yugoslavia. But the refugees included, as well as the Ustase, some 13,000 Cetniks and other dissidents who would be shot as soon as they were deported. Britain had no wish to repeat the events of 1945, when 'wanted men' were handed back to the Soviets and the innocent suffered with the guilty.[17] Yet the existing situation could not be allowed to continue. The Foreign Office was afraid that even if the Ustase and others were not handed back, extremists among them would launch cross-border raids into Yugoslavia, prompting Titoist retaliation.[18]

The Italians were prepared to guarantee that the DPs would not be sent back by force, provided the Allies paid for their maintenance. This was agreed. The next stage was a British mission to sift through the camps for quislings. The mission was to be a delicate blend of humanitarianism and *realpolitik*, designed to protect the innocent and also to allay Tito's fears that the Allies would simply grant amnesty to the war criminals most wanted by his regime.[19] Bevin therefore had to find a man acceptable both to the Cold Warriors and to Tito. He would have to deal not only with the Yugoslav DPs, but also with the Ukrainians claimed by the Soviet Union. Only one man fitted the bill: Fitzroy Maclean.

Veronica Maclean remembers a winter's evening at Yealand Conyers, when the butler mysteriously announced two gentlemen to see Brigadier Maclean. 'When they left, Fitz told me they had offered him a job which meant spending six months in Rome and six in Austria. I said, "Yippee, let's go!" You can have little idea how miserable post-war austerity was, and how glad people were to get away from Britain. He then tried to recruit his old staff and was very successful, even though most of them were newly married with young children. They too were glad to get away from cold and rationing. There were so many small kids along on the mission that we nicknamed it "Operation Cow and Gate".'[20] Fitzroy recalls the circumstances of his appointment.

Veronica and I were living in Lancashire at the time. A Colonel Finlay from the War Office and Professor Royce, an American, came to see me and asked if I would take this problem on. They dangled the bait of a brevet rank as major-general and the promise that I could pick anyone for the mission I liked. The idea of this was exciting after a boring year in the House of Commons. The prospect of six months in Rome and six in Austria looked very appealing in the post-war austerity of England. I think on looking back it was a mistake to take the job. The Conservative whips told me that Labour was offering a permanent pair, so there were no problems on that score, but that, if I took the job, if it succeeded the Labour Government would get the credit, and if it failed I would be blamed. Also, having been an MP for five years when nobody saw me, if after just one year I was to decamp again, well . . . I think this was sound advice and I should have buckled down to Health, Education, Local Government, et cetera, but the temptation was too great.[21]

Even though Fitzroy overcame his own misgivings, his support for Tito during the real war was seen as a liability in a Cold one by certain arch-conservatives who doubted his 'objectivity'.[22] Nor were the Americans pleased by the appointment; they too saw Fitzroy as a man easily influenced by Tito.[23] In fact, by 1947 the State Department's principal concern was to renege on their agreement with 'Stalin's creature' to repatriate the Ustase. They wanted to dump the whole affair in the lap of the Italians.[24]

Fitzroy saw the Junior Ministers at the Foreign Office, Hector McNeil and Christopher Mayhew, and later Bevin himself. McNeil was a former journalist and fellow-Scot, later Secretary of State for Scotland. Mayhew remembers the occasion well:

> In those days government decision-making was devolved quite far down, so that Under-Secretaries sometimes had the most tremendous jobs to do. The question was, what to do? Some of these people in the camps were the worst sort of war criminal, others were merely anti-Communists who had taken a wrong turn in the war. But we were pledged by all kinds of treaties and UN resolutions to return anyone against whom there was a war crimes charge or a prima facie one of active and wilful collaboration with the enemy. We couldn't send them all back as they'd be executed without trial, and there had already been controversy about the Cossacks in 1945. We needed someone to sort out the sheep from the goats and the obvious person to do this was Fitzroy Maclean, who spoke the languages, knew the political background, and could sort out a war criminal from a tough anti-Communist fighter, Croat, Ustase or whatever . . . When Fitzroy came to see me he agreed to take it on, but said that he was only a brigadier and would like to be a major-general. Slightly tongue-in-cheek. I was quite prepared to make him a lieutenant-general if he would relieve me of this appalling task![25]

Fitzroy took on Stephen Clissold, who had been with Evelyn Waugh and Randolph Churchill in Croatia during the war, and also many of his old friends, including Annette Street. As his personal assistant he selected a former liaison officer with Mihailovic, Michael Lees, who in later years became his bitterest critic. 'Finlay and Royce recruited me,' Lees remembered. 'The idea was supposed to be to get balance by having a commission comprised of people who had served with both Partisans and Cetniks . . . Only afterwards did I learn that Fitzroy Maclean was heading up the mission.'[26]

Most of Fitzroy's team went out to Rome by special train and took their families. Many, like himself, were recently married, so the train was full of new brides and babes-in-arms, including Fitzroy's own son Charlie, born in late 1946 and named after Prince Charles Edward. Mrs Rhoda Cockerell, the children's nanny, made her debut on this trip. Another close connection was Jeanne Thomlinson, later Fitzroy's private secretary and wife of Stephen Clissold. When the Macleans arrived in Rome, they booked into the royal suite of their hotel.

There followed what Fitzroy describes as a 'funny six months'. Italy was not gripped by the austerity that was suffocating England, so day-to-day living was relatively easy. Veronica remembers intense cold, followed by intense heat, to the point where she took the children to the cooler climate of Florence and rented a villa. 'We enjoyed the whole adventure, even though I am afraid to say that I behaved badly by taking a trip to Venice.'[27]

The problem of sifting displaced persons was a nightmare, and the tasks assigned to Fitzroy's team bewilderingly heterogeneous. Apart from identifying war criminals, the mission had to determine which DPs were prima facie eligible for aid from international bodies. It scarcely helped that there were already two relief organizations, and after July 1947 a third: to the Inter-Governmental Committee on Refugees (IGGR) and the United Nations Relief and Rehabilitation Commission (UNRRA) was added the International Refugees Organization (IRO), also under UN auspices. On top of the identification and winnowing processes, Fitzroy's team had to provide the DPs with all available information about the conditions that would await them if they accepted the amnesty offers and simply went home.[28]

Fitzroy's mission had two objectives: find the guilty and protect the innocent. Some of the team tracked 'most wanted' men; others sifted records to establish that nothing adverse was known about individual refugees. A few, like Stephen Clissold, did both. But the mission's two aims were often in conflict. Already among British decision-makers there was an ambiguity of purpose. On the one hand, Cold War anti-communists argued that 'my enemy's enemy is my friend', and on that basis were prepared to condone known Fascists as 'freedom fighters'. This group based its defence of wanted men on the principle that only citizens of the Soviet Union as at 1939 (before the absorption of the Baltic states and the hegemony over Eastern Europe) should be returned. Thus, no citizen of any Eastern European country, no matter how egregious his war crimes, could be returned, and tens of thousands of people the Allies had agreed at Yalta to send back to the Soviet Union would be excluded. On the other hand, the socialists, liberals and Jewish lobbies argued that it was morally unacceptable that the Klaus Barbies and Ante Pavelics should be allowed to escape punishment for their crimes, simply because this now suited Western *realpolitik*.

The most obvious bone of contention was the Ukrainians. Many had

served with the SS and some even bore SS tattoos. By the laws of
international justice, and particularly following the precedent set by the
Nuremberg trials, they had to be sent back. But the Allies knew this
meant certain death. They therefore drew a threefold distinction
between actual war crimes (uncondonable), membership of the SS (a
'grey area'), and the mere bearing of arms against Soviet forces (which
could be justified as nationalism or freedom fighting). The Allies were
more generous towards people they accepted as Soviet citizens in international law (the Ukrainians) than to their own kind. William Joyce
('Lord Haw Haw') and John Amery were executed as traitors for their
advocacy of the Nazi cause. Those in Eastern Europe who had actually
taken up arms for that cause were to be given the benefit of every
doubt.

The Allies soon showed their hand. In January 1946 the State
Department ruled that only those Ukrainians who were both citizens
and residents of the Soviet Union after 1939 should be handed over.
This placed in the 'grey area' most of the Ukrainian 'Galician SS'
Division who had been in the British camp at Rimini since May 1945,
men in an entirely different category from those tens of thousands of
petty collaborators, prisoners-of-war and ordinary political refugees
who had been mistakenly repatriated to the Soviet Union in 1945, and
thus condemned to death or imprisonment – making the West for a
short time an accessory in Stalin's post-war massacres.[29]

Fitzroy was at once plunged into a tumult. As a result of the State
Department ruling, British administrators would now have to screen
8,000 or so men in the Galician Division before September 1947 when
the camp would be turned over to the Italian government. Late in
January, Fitzroy and his assistants arrived at Rimini.[30] The conditions
they found were farcical. Bored and surly British guards made it clear
that they resented overseeing DPs and wanted to get home to Britain
like 'the rest of the Army'. Consequently, people came and went into
and out of the camp almost at will. Lack of manpower meant the
screening was perfunctory. Only 200 men out of a muster-roll of 8,272
were interviewed. Fitzroy had with him no one competent in Ukrainian
dialects; his men therefore used camp inmates as interpreters, conducted no cross-examinations, and simply accepted the Ukrainians'
word for what they had been doing during the war. His team reported to
London that 'The short history of the division was supplied entirely
by the Ukrainians themselves and we had no information of any kind
against which they could be checked . . . Some of the real villains . . . if
there are any, may be sheltering behind these innocuous-sounding
units, but that is a risk we have to take.'[31]

Fitzroy concluded that the Ukrainians were affable and harmless. He
cabled London for advice on how to protect them from falling into

Soviet hands once the Italian government took over the camp. He suggested removing them entirely from Italy to a British-controlled zone before the ratification of the treaty. This suggestion at once flushed from cover the two opposing cliques within the Foreign Office. Rightists proposed bringing the entire Galician SS to Britain 'for rigorous screening'. An international campaign began attempting to prove that the Ukrainians, SS regalia notwithstanding, were simply anti-Soviet freedom fighters. Leftists protested at this evasion of the Yalta obligations,[32] but the right won, and anti-communism, not criminality, became in reality the criterion for sorting out the DPs. In 1945 the British had preferred that an innocent majority should perish so that a few guilty might be punished; in 1947 they decided that war criminals among the Ukrainians should be protected so that the innocent might live.

On this occasion there was a meeting of minds between Fitzroy and the Foreign Office. The mandarins did not want the embarrassment of a rigorous examination of the Ukrainians, and hoped that those who had confessed to volunteering for the Germans would take the hint and decamp; there were few guards to stop them.[33] Misgivings were expressed at the time that anti-communist ideology was being manipulated by war criminals for their own ends.[34] In 1947 such worries were stilled by assurances that the Ukrainians had been brought to Britain for further screening. But in fact they were not even subjected to normal immigration formalities, let alone exhaustively screened.

In a recent study, Mark Aarons and John Loftus write: 'William Wilkinson of the Foreign Office insisted that "it is unlikely that any war criminals will be found". Perhaps he knew that no one was really looking. In his many memoranda Wilkinson insisted that the Ukrainians had already been screened by Brigadier Maclean at Rimini. Unfortunately, both Maclean and Wilkinson were relying on the prisoners' own information. The "never in the SS" cover story was soon rebutted by the Ukrainians themselves.'[35] They quote from a Rome news agency in 1947:

Galician Division in Britain . . . A dispatch from Rome comments on the statement made by Mr Hector McNeil, British Minister of State, about Hitler's so-called Galician Division, 8,000 members of which have been brought to Britain from Italy. Mr McNeil claims that a Soviet Commission took part in the screening of these 8,000 men from the Western Ukraine and that no war criminals have been discovered among them. This statement has occasioned considerable surprise in Rome Press circles, since the 'Galician Division' was notorious for its cruelty and belonged to an SS formation. No Soviet representatives took part in any check-up of these 8,000 men, as the British military authorities invariably replied with a refusal when approached by Soviet representatives on this subject. Mr McNeil's statement is clearly intended to mislead public opinion.[36]

Fitzroy stands accused of sacrificing justice to expediency and turning a deaf ear to inconvenient evidence. It is said that many Ukrainians in the camp at Rimini, confident of British anti-Sovietism, admitted that they had volunteered to fight for the Germans – an admission that made them liable to repatriation under the Yalta agreement. Some, it was said, even boasted of their SS rank. Aarons and Loftus conclude: 'Fortunately none of the prisoners was stupid enough to confess to war crimes, and so none was discovered. Despite his assistant's recommendation that it would take many months to screen each person in the camp properly, Maclean informed the Foreign Office in February that his investigation in Rimini would be completed by the middle of March.'[37]

Several comments are in order here. First, Fitzroy was genuinely convinced there were no war criminals in the camp at Rimini. He based this conviction on simple probability. 'By 1947 there were very few war criminals in any of the camps. By then most of them had been got out, because of course most of them bobbed up again in the Argentine where they formed an independent Croat enclave. A tiny handful might have pushed their luck and taken their chance in the camps, but on the whole I thought it unlikely.'[38] Count Nikolai Tolstoy supports Fitzroy.

> I would take the line that there were very few war criminals among the Ukrainians. They were engaged in so much sustained heavy fighting that they would need to have committed the war crimes in the heat of battle, and once you start down that road, which nation is innocent? More particularly, I don't see when the Ukrainians in the Rimini camp would have had the occasion to commit war crimes. Most of them were new recruits, since the original Galician SS Division was all but wiped out at the battle of Brody in 1944.[39]

Tolstoy's contention is denied by Mark Aarons and John Loftus, who point out in their book *Ratlines* that, the British government having decided to let the Ukrainians settle quietly in Britain without probing into their backgrounds, the head of the Ukrainian Union caused some embarrassment by revealing in 1948 that many members of the Galician SS Division had in fact been volunteers, not draftees. In alarm lest worse revelations might pour forth, the Home Office checked the status of the Ukrainians against the records held by American Intelligence but not released at the time, and had their worst fears realized. The resulting conflict between Home and Foreign Offices was averted only by a deal whereby the most notorious war criminals among the Ukrainians were offered citizenship in Canada.[40]

For Fitzroy, it should be pointed out that probability was clearly on his side, and he was working against the clock. He had to produce a solution before the Italian treaty was ratified, and could not have screened properly, even with ten times the staff and watertight security at Rimini. Nikolai Tolstoy estimates, judging from the Cossack experience, that it would have taken two years to screen the Galician SS Division adequately. Fitzroy had made this clear to the Foreign Office before leaving London, and they had accepted it. His priority was to prevent a repeat of the tragic events of 1945. That the Ukrainians were not properly screened in Britain cannot be blamed on Fitzroy. Nor can the *raison d'état* of protecting ex-Nazis for reasons of Cold War expediency.

Anti-Soviet personnel on the mission were delighted. Michael Lees remembered working with a certain Roy Farran, who fudged paperwork to allow Cossacks to melt away into Italy in obscurity. Lees explained that the Cossacks had fought with him in northern Italy, together with a battalion of the SAS and the Italian partisans, and he was therefore disposed to be on their side.

We flew out from a freezing Britain in the last Dakota and it was freezing cold in Rome. I had a gammy leg and was in bad shape after being wounded in northern Italy in late '44. I worked away on the Ukrainians. I must have spoken to at most two Yugoslavs the whole time. We tried to give the benefit of every doubt and classify people as political rather than economic refugees. The only ones excluded were Germans coming from Germany and trying to get to the USA by posing as Volkdeutsch from Yugoslavia. A lot of the Ukrainians found homes in England. Nearly all of them got to England except for two or three who were thought to have been concentration camp guards.[41]

The hectic pace of Fitzroy's life in 1947 is clear from his diaries: '*7 March*, depart Rome. *9 March*, arrive London. *2 May*, depart Rome. *3 May*, arrive Lausanne.' After the Ukrainian episode, he now had to deal with 12,000 or so Yugoslav DPs. This task, for which he and his team were much more fitted by qualifications and experience, involved both screening Yugoslavs still in the camps and tracing war criminals who had fled to Rome and Genoa.

When the Ukrainians were sent to England, the 12,000 Yugoslavs were moved to Germany: in both cases the immediate motive alleged was to take the financial burden off the Italian government. In 1945 Lord Carrington was responsible for a DP camp in the Rhineland containing largely Cetnik and Ustase refugees, and he was horrified by the behaviour of those appealing to the West for clemency. 'Murder between the factions was frequent. Atrocities against the local population if, as sometimes happened, the inmates of the camps went on unauthorized sprees in the countryside, were equally common.'[42] It was in fact very difficult for anyone to keep adequate control over these camps. There was a shortage of guards, and by this time British troops were so demoralized by battle fatigue and post-war 'burn-out' that any camp commandant who ordered his men to enforce the rules strictly

might have had a massacre on his hands. As a result the DPs in the
camps largely set up and administered their own 'city-states'. A sub-
machine-gun could be bought for a kilo of coffee, and brigands and
deserters in the Italian hills had plenty of them. Most DPs were armed
to the teeth.

Despite this, Fitzroy made a point of going into some of the camps
himself.

> The Cetniks, more than 10,000 of them, the strength of a division, were the big
> problem. Being Serbs, the first thing they did – there were a lot of American
> deserters and the remains of the Italian Resistance more or less armed – was
> trade in their rations for tommy-guns. So the first thing we knew there were
> 10,000 armed Yugoslavs facing one British battalion, very tired and wanting to
> go home, some Italians who had never liked fighting and some Americans who
> by then were practically gangsters, buying and selling everything. A man
> called General Damianovic took command of the Serbian outfit. They had
> their own guards, they even had their own wireless transmitter which broadcast
> to Yugoslavia saying, wait for it, we're coming to get you, you bastards. Tito
> didn't much like this. There were a lot more equally strange refugees. On top of
> it all was an Italian government about to fall or to give up on the problem or to
> send them all back by force.[43]

Lack of manpower still bedevilled the Mission, as it combed through
suspected Yugoslav war criminals. Jeanne Clissold recalls:

> It was a case of interrogating and building up card indexes. Stephen and
> Desmond Clarke were the principal interrogators. They had the list of wanted
> war criminals and all the Yugoslavs provided. With their own knowledge of
> Yugoslavia, if anyone looked dodgy they interrogated them separately. If it was
> obvious that someone was not a suspect, the other members of the team inter-
> rogated them in a rough and ready way. Desmond had a wonderful card-index,
> said he used to go to sleep with it. If the people were run-of-the-mill Cetniks,
> unless there was evidence agreed by the British and the Americans that they
> had been guilty of war crimes, they were safe. It was the people on the list we
> wanted. Any results went to Fitzroy, who was on a higher level, dealing with
> telegrams to London, contacts with the Americans, generally heading up. The
> team had to clear their conclusions with him.[44]

Most of the Yugoslavs Fitzroy and his men found in the camps were
Cetniks, at best guilty of collaboration with the Axis. The real villains,
the Ustase, some of whom had committed horrific war crimes, had
already by and large got clear of Italy, or at least out of British-
controlled zones. The second part of Fitzroy's task was to trace these
men, and in particular Ante Pavelic, but the complexity of the task
cannot be understood without a recapitulation of events that had taken
place in London and Italy since 1945.

In July 1945 Tito's ambassador in London had asked the Foreign Office what had become of Pavelic, since they knew he had been taken prisoner by General Alexander's troops at Klagenfurt in Austria.[45] The British denied that Pavelic had ever been in their hands (and it is true that most Foreign Office personnel were unaware that he had), considered that Pavelic must be in the American or Russian zones, and asked their allies to co-operate in the search for him.[46] Tito's government attacked Britain's duplicity, claiming to have provided the precise address in Austria where he was living in freedom. The Foreign Office reiterated its innocence and protested that the entire anti-British campaign in Yugoslavia was based on a mirage.[47]

Belgrade next accused the British of colluding with the Holy See to protect Pavelic and the Ustase; they passed on intelligence that Ustase leaders were moving from Austria to Italy dressed as monks. The Foreign Office described these accusations as groundless and once more asked the Americans to report any sightings of Pavelic.[48] Charges and denials continued throughout 1946.[49]

In fact, it was true that the Vatican had sheltered Pavelic. In April 1946 he left Austria disguised as a Catholic priest and was taken by sympathisers to Rome, where he was housed in a monastery owned by the Brotherhood of San Girolamo, a Croatian college attached to the Vatican. Fitzroy explains: 'Many of the clergy in the Croat college were strongly nationalist and were inclined to overstep the mark. In 1947 my Mission's Intelligence branch submitted an important report on the role played by one Father Krunoslav Draganovic, director of the college. In 1945 Draganovic toured the DP camps in Austria and set up an intelligence organization establishing contacts between the chief Ustase representatives in the camps and San Girolamo. This led to the formation of a fully-fledged intelligence service.'[50]

This intelligence service established a method for getting Pavelic and the Ustase war criminals to safety in South America – by routes later dubbed the 'Ratlines'. In the camps Draganovic, supposedly on pastoral visits, handed out false ID documents to the Ustase, who travelled in disguise to San Girolamo where the production of false passports was a thriving industry. With these passports the Ustase could get genuine exit papers from the International Red Cross (whose Croatian representative was Draganovic), and with Red Cross passports they could obtain entry visas from the Argentine government. The Argentine dictator Juan Peron was keen to build up the rabidly anti-communist Croatians as a praetorian guard against Communism in Argentina, and 35,000 entry visas were to issued to the Croats.[51] The activities of Draganovic and San Girolamo continued throughout 1946 and 1947; they could not have done so without Vatican connivance. Fitzroy says: 'I think that most people in Rome who were interested knew that San

Girolamo and especially Draganovic were working to get Croatian criminals out of Europe. This was an open secret in the intelligence community.'[52]

It was late 1946 before the British concluded that most of the important Yugoslav quislings were being sheltered by the Catholic Church, and that nothing could be done unless the Vatican were cajoled into co-operation, since the alternative was to invade the territory of the Vatican City and face a major diplomatic incident.[53] Embarrassed by their own impotence, the British and Americans disingenuously suggested that Tito apply direct diplomatic pressure on the Vatican; meanwhile, they laid all the blame for Pavelic's disappearance on Draganovic.[54]

The upshot was a Yugoslav request for Draganovic's extradition in 1947.[55] Fitzroy meanwhile was determined that the Ustase and Draganovic should not have things all their own way. Members of his mission patrolled suspect Franciscan monasteries – the followers of St Francis having had a lamentable record of forced conversions to Catholicism in Croatia between 1941 and 1945. Annette Street remembers: 'We used to lurk outside the monasteries. The theory was that as the Vatican had been good about British POWs, they'd do the same about fleeing Ustase and Croats. These people were known to go, in disguise as Franciscans, to sister houses, leaving the Vatican for the purpose, and that was our chance. I remember I used to have my glasses on, glued to their feet to see whether they had on the statutory sandals.'[56] Annette's husband Vivian, Fitzroy's Number Two in wartime Yugoslavia, meanwhile established conclusively that Pavelic had left Austria in April 1946 and had since been sheltered at San Girolamo.[57] Fitzroy's team also chalked up one of the few successes recorded by Western intelligence in their campaign against the Ustase. In March 1947 Major Stephen Clissold swooped on Genoa after a reliable tip-off that several wanted war criminals would be on the Buenos Aires-bound SS *Philippa*. Clissold's men arrested sixteen prominent Ustase, including General Vladimir Kren, formerly head of Pavelic's airforce.[58] The mass arrest of one hundred men outside San Girolamo a few weeks later was a second success.

By the middle of 1947 Fitzroy and his team had uncovered most of the secrets of San Girolamo and the 'Ratlines'. Among the Ustase war criminals they identified as having been spirited away by Draganovic and his acolytes were Father Dragutin Camber, an officer in Pavelic's personal bodyguard who had presided over a massacre of Serbians; Dragutin Toth, Pavelic's Minister of Finance; Lovro Susic, his Minister of National Economy; Vilko Pecnikar, a general in his bodyguard; and Vjekoslav Vrancic, who had been responsible for Croatia's concentration camps and secret police. They also discovered that Pavelic had funded the 'Ratlines'. The role of the Vatican in sheltering Ustase war criminals was also clearly established.[59] Fitzroy summed this up in his report to London of 17 October 1947: 'There is incontrovertible evidence that some of the most notorious war criminals were issued . . . with the San Girolamo identity card under an entirely false name and were thus enabled to obtain Italian residence permits, visas, and other documents allowing them to emigrate.'[60]

The Vatican involvement particularly irritated Fitzroy's liaison man at the Foreign Office, Wallinger, to whom he made his reports. Wallinger would not accept the claims of pro-Ustase diplomats at the Vatican that Draganovic was a 'rogue male', operating without the knowledge or consent of Pius XII.

> While we cannot condemn the charitable attitude of the Church towards sinful individuals we feel, however, that there has been much evidence to show that the Vatican has permitted the encouragement, both overt and covert, of the Ustashi [*sic*]. This wholly undesirable organization has not only been collectively responsible for vile atrocities on an immense scale during the war but has ever since its inception made use of murder as a normal political weapon. There is surely all the difference between shelter to, let us say, dissident Slovene priests, and giving positive aid to a creature like Pavelic.[61]

It was not just the Vatican's clandestine support for the Ustase – crowned with triumph when Pavelic got away to Argentina in 1947 – that eventually wore down Fitzroy's team in their hunt for war criminals. Allied intelligence was honeycombed with Ustase sympathisers. In his October 1947 report Fitzroy recorded bitterly that Draganovic usually had advance warning of any operation to arrest war criminals; in some cases he was even provided with lists of those to be arrested. Many Allied officers co-operated openly with him: Fitzroy instanced a British officer at Military and Intelligence HQ in Rome who leaked to Draganovic details of every search-and-arrest operation.[62]

The USA was also pro-Ustase. After penetrating San Girolamo, Fitzroy and his team found evidence implicating US Intelligence in successful Ustase escapes to South America.[63] By mid-1947 there was considerable distrust between the Foreign Office and the US State Department. The British suspected that American insistence that Italian police be involved in attempts to catch Ustase war criminals, when it was well known that many were themselves Ustase sympathisers, was in fact sabotage. Every time the British suggested cutting the Gordian knot over Pavelic by staging a raid on Vatican City territory and risking the diplomatic consequences, the Americans insisted that any such initiative must come from the Italian authorities.[64]

Though Fitzroy was not at first aware of it, there were influential figures in the British government too who believed that it would be better to keep former Nazis on ice, as part of the West's anti-communist crusade. As it was cynically expressed at the time, 'increasing the pool of freedom fighters' meant beating the deadline of 'R-Day', when the Italian government would take over responsibility for the remaining DPs. Fitzroy's mission would have to be nudged towards just 'going through the motions'. By 1947 the British government was quite prepared to help the Vatican smuggle the Ustase out of Europe, even reclassifying 'blacks' (known war criminals) as 'greys' (Nazi collaborators). But Fitzroy, the Aristides of the piece, was an obstacle. Mark Aarons and John Loftus have written recently:

> As much as he liked the Ukrainians, he had a fanatical hatred for the Croatian Ustashi [*sic*]. Maclean was very thorough in screening Yugoslav Nazis. He had no need to rely on phoney histories supplied by the prisoners. He knew – firsthand – what Pavelic's supporters had done. As head of the screening mission, Maclean's stubbornness could wreck the scheme for getting Nazis out of Italy. Worse, he was beginning to realize that his own British superiors were leaking his top-secret screening reports to Father Draganovic, who tipped off the Ustashi before they could be arrested. The good brigadier was beginning to suspect too much. The situation was simple: circumvent Maclean with a higher authority. There were always a few friendly Americans willing to lend a hand.[65]

Indeed, the secret policy endorsed by the Allies in June 1947 was that all Nazi screening should henceforth be done by a Joint Review Committee. Fitzroy himself was back in London at this time.[66] He declares himself unaware of behind-the-scenes machinations, though he also denies partiality for the Ukrainians and bias against the Ustase. 'The implication is vaguely racist, that I preferred Ukrainians over Croatians. Completely untrue. What you can say is that having seen Stalin's terror at first hand I was far from convinced by the formulaic Soviet charges against the Ukrainians. On the other hand, I had seen the Ustase atrocities with my own eyes and knew very well that most of Tito's repatriation demands were fair.'[67]

Faced with so many obstacles to his pursuit of Ustase war criminals, Fitzroy concentrated on the 12,000 Yugoslavs in the DP camps. He now had to square London's demands with those of Tito. With limited manpower having to perform diverse duties, Fitzroy soon decided he was faced with a sisyphean task. Since the political consequences of failure were so acute, he considered that the best chance for a settlement of the DP issue lay in an *ad hoc* agreement with Tito, making use of their wartime friendship, and he therefore requested permission to travel to Belgrade for this purpose.[68] The Foreign Office dithered. There had been an ugly incident when a Yugoslav consul, visiting one of the DP camps to try to identify 'most wanted' men, had been murdered when he was supposed to be under British protection. Bruce Lockhart, describing a conversation with Orme Sargent, described the atmosphere: '[Orme Sargent] was very critical of our soldiers in Italy over the problem of the Yugoslavs. The Army was very pro-Italian and anti-Yugoslav. This was understandable, but it did not help when they kept the Yugoslavs in military formations and included among them real quislings whom we had agreed to hand over . . . We now had to get the Yugoslavs out of Italy for their own safety, because when the treaty was signed Italy might very easily hand them over to the Yugoslavs in exchange for the numerous Italians whom the Yugoslavs held.'[69]

Eventually Fitzroy received permission to go to Belgrade. He was given the difficult brief of reducing British commitment to the DP problem as well as alleviating Tito's grievances.[70] He found Tito tense and abstracted, but when he introduced Veronica the old Tito reasserted himself. He gave her a diamond ring, and suggested they should ride together since, he asserted, both he and Fitzroy had put on weight alarmingly since their days in the Bosnian hills, and badly needed exercise. After an early breakfast they mounted three very powerful and highly-strung horses and galloped away like the wind. Veronica's mount bolted, and the trio careered through woods and villages where the inhabitants cheered wildly; an escort of fifty cavalrymen meanwhile tried to keep up with them, as well as Tito's personal physician, who repeatedly galloped alongside Tito to warn him that his heart was not very strong and that he would kill himself. Tito brusquely waved him away.[71]

In *Disputed Barricade* Fitzroy, referring to both himself and Tito in the third person, wrote: 'They spent long hours riding together through the forests of Slovenia. Tito had put on weight since the war, but showed himself both physically and mentally as alert and energetic as ever. At Brdo, Tito lived in a charmingly furnished country house, once Prince Paul's summer residence, where he and his closest associates spent the summer months. Kardelj and Marko Rankovic were there with their families. Prlja, Tito's wartime bodyguard, now drove the Marshal's immense touring car. Tigger, beginning to get a little grey round the muzzle, was more sedate than in the days when he used to snap at General Korneyev's ankles in the cave at Drvar.'[72]

The rapport between Tito and Fitzroy was still strong. By going straight to an old friend at the top, Fitzroy cut through the 'atmosphere of intrigue, controversy and blackmail' that had characterized the negotiations about DPs.[73] Tito told him the slump in Anglo-Yugoslav relations was a result of their countries being helpless appendages of the two superpowers. Perhaps partly for this reason, the Bled treaty, signed on 8 September 1947, shows considerable independence on both sides. This agreement was a great personal triumph for Fitzroy, since it freed the British from their earlier undertaking to repatriate the Ustase without asking further questions, and set a definite time-limit on further requests for the handover of quislings. The Foreign Office was delighted with his achievement,[74] but the US State Department was displeased by the UK's unilateral initiative, and particularly annoyed that Fitzroy had conceded Tito's demand for the removal of Yugoslav DPs in Austria to the Anglo-American zones in Germany without consulting Washington.[75]

After his visit to Belgrade, Fitzroy moved his headquarters from Rome to Wurtensee near Klagenfurt in Austria. Annette Street remembers Klagenfurt as a polyglot gallimaufry of refugees, 'people littering the pavements, all muddled up, some of them even French on the move from concentration camps.'[76] Fitzroy's main task now was to administer the resettlement of the Yugoslav DPs in Germany and Austria and to arrange in other cases for their onward transit to Australia and South America. This meant liaising with the top echelons of Anglo-American administration, both military and civilian. His wartime contacts paid dividends. Sholto Douglas had been Commander-in-Chief of the RAF in the Middle East and had backed Fitzroy all the way on Balkan Air Force and other matters between 1943 and 1945; now he was military governor of the British zone of occupation, and was able to smooth Fitzroy's path through the bureaucratic jungles.[77]

By the end of 1947 Fitzroy's DP mission had achieved what it could and began to wind up. Michael Lees returned to the British Council before Christmas that year. 'I worked amicably with Fitzroy. He did a reasonable job.'[78] Not everyone thought the twelve months had been worthwhile. Annette Street recalls: 'My section certainly never caught anybody, and I doubt if many people were brought to book.'[79] Jeanne Clissold was annoyed that the work of the mission was misrepresented. 'The object of our work has been reversed, whether purposely or by mistake. Its aim was to prevent the innocent or even the greyish from being handed back and tried and shot. People have said its object was to hand back war criminals. But the package agreed between us, Tito and the Americans was about a very small list of agreed war criminals; thereafter they would not make a fuss about the ones we let go. Obviously there was a bit of a dispute about who should be on the list and who not, but nowadays you find this absurd belief that *no one* should have been on it.'[80] Since Fitzroy is an interested party, the last word should perhaps go to Christopher Mayhew.

I hadn't time to look at the ones he released. I went through the ones he recommended for repatriation and signed them, after making sure the proper procedures had been gone through. I couldn't do anything else, as my judgement was worth nothing against that of experts. We sent back about 40 or 50, who I assume were executed. This was the roughest, toughest part of the Cold War. We were criticized by the Yugoslavs for not sending them all back, and by some UK Communists, but most of the criticism was that we ought to have done this before and that 1948 was very late in the day. I announced the findings in the House in 1948 and paid tribute to Fitzroy. He was quite indispensable.[81]

Fitzroy's claim to historical significance rests on his relationship with Tito; and the Bled agreement he engineered may have been the last straw in the Marshal's turbulent relationship with the Soviet Union. British unilateral action may have irritated the USA, but Tito's independent style certainly infuriated Stalin, and Fitzroy's presence in Belgrade during the agreement's gestation aggravated matters. One of Stalin's propagandists, Mdivani (once again a significant name in Fitzroy's life), wrote an article in *Literaturnaya Gazeta* in October 1947 alleging that Fitzroy had had foreknowledge of the German paratroop assault on Drvar in May 1944 which he failed to pass on to his supposed friend. Tito protested to Moscow that there was not a word of truth in this allegation,[82] but the Soviet propaganda machine continued to target Fitzroy. At the 1949 Budapest trial of seven Hungarian Communist 'deviationists', the former Tito confidant Lazar Brankov asserted that Tito and his comrades had been 'turned' by Fitzroy in 1943, and that after that date they had worked assiduously for the western imperialists. Yet Brankov unwittingly turned his own testimony into farce when he went on: 'Western liaison officers were highly experienced secret service men whose real aim was to carry out a plan of Mr Churchill's for turning Yugoslavia into a bourgeois capitalist state, as a nucleus round which other European countries were to be grouped . . . They were headed by Brigadier Fitzroy Maclean, Major Randolph Churchill . . . the American officer Colonel Hamilton and two named Firo and Farts.'[83]

The dispute between Tito and Stalin had a long history. Tito resented Stalin's lack of support over Trieste, especially when Stalin made it clear that the Italian Communist Party ranked higher in his scheme of things than the Titoists. Most of all, Stalin opposed Tito's independent line and his refusal to turn his country into an economic vassal. The Kremlin inveighed against Yugoslav plans for a customs union with Bulgaria and Romania, and for political federation with Bulgaria. When Albania in early 1948 requested two Yugoslav divisions to defend her southern border against the Greeks, and Tito agreed, Stalin accused him of trying to 'swallow' Albania and ordered that the arrangement be cancelled. In February 1948 Stalin forced a Yugoslav delegation in Moscow to sign a 'Treaty of Consultation', in effect depriving Yugoslavia of all independence in foreign policy.

Tito refused to rescind his plans for union with Bulgaria. Thereafter Yugoslav–Soviet relations plummeted. All Russian civilians in Yugoslavia were ordered home and military advisers withdrawn, because of Titoist 'hostility'. In his famous letter of 27 March 1948, Stalin rehearsed all his grievances. He reverted to Djilas's famous 'insult' to the Red Army, which evidently still rankled; he complained that Soviet officials in Yugoslavia were subject to constant surveillance, as if they were enemy aliens; he criticized the Yugoslav Communist Party for being undemocratic and sneered at the 'socialism' of a country which retained a residue of capitalism in peasant villages. Most insultingly, Stalin pretended to be outraged that Tito's chief negotiator in the recent discussions over Russo-Yugoslav stock was 'the British spy', Vlatko Velebit.

Thunderstruck by this outburst, Tito and his comrades nevertheless determined to resist. A plenary meeting of the Central Committee of the Yugoslav Communist Party was called for 12 April. Tito had the pro-Soviet Hebrang and Zujovic expelled from the Politburo. A spirited reply was sent to Stalin, accusing him of interference and spying. When Stalin attempted the *coup de grâce* against Tito, he found opposed to him the power of an entire state and a united Yugoslav Communist Party. 'I will shake my little finger and there will be no more Tito',[84] Stalin had boasted, but when he shook his finger nothing happened. Invasion was too risky against the battle-hardened Partisans, even if he could be sure the West would not intervene. He had to content himself with excommunicating Yugoslavia from the Communist world church, at a Cominform meeting in Bucharest on 28 June 1948.

Bewildered by the turn of events and disorientated by the sudden prospect of 'going it alone', Yugoslavia sought moral and material aid from the West. On paper the outlook for rapprochement was not good. Britain and the USA were no more pleased than Stalin was about Tito's apparent ambition to absorb Bulgaria and Romania. Tito had defied the British by supporting the Greek Communists, and the disputes about Trieste and Carinthia still lingered on. Tito was violently unpopular after the trials of Mihailovic, and of the Catholic Archbishop Stepinac, who had blessed Pavelic's death squads in Croatia. The Foreign Office continued to regard Tito as a Soviet puppet even after unmistakable evidence that he was not.[85] Finally, there were particular conflicts with the USA over gold deposited in New York, assets expropriated in Yugoslavia and the shooting down of an American plane in 1946.

There was deep suspicion, too, on the Yugoslav side. Djilas was obsessed with the machiavellianism of the British Secret Service, and other Titoists knew little of Britain and the British. The English-educated Dedijer was ambivalent in his attitude to his mentors, and the

most sympathetic, Velebit, had known no English at the beginning of
the war. Even the British Communists who had once been on Tito's
side, like James Klugmann and Kenneth Syers, came out for Stalin
once the rift was overt. The one real link with Britain was the men who
had so impressed Tito during the war, especially Bill Deakin and
Fitzroy Maclean.

Fitzroy and Deakin provided a bridge over which Tito could pass
towards trust of the British and eventual political non-alignment.
As early as March 1944 Fitzroy had written: 'Much will depend on
whether Tito sees himself in his former role as Comintern agent or as
the ruler of an independent Yugoslav state.'[86] Fitzroy had always
thought the latter more likely, and 1948 proved him right. Now he had
to convert sceptical members of the British élite to his view.

At Fitzroy's urging, after 1948 Bevin and his officials operated a
policy they called 'keeping Tito just afloat'. This meant providing Tito
with just enough aid to survive, but not so much that it would give
comfort to the Soviets if they managed to oust him by coup or invasion.[87] To promote this policy Bevin sent a delegation to Belgrade at the
beginning of March 1949. But Tito insisted on credits and payment
agreements – precisely the form of accord the British, now under heavy
pressure from the Americans to desist from their policy, did not want to
grant. Bevin once more turned to Fitzroy, who arrived in Belgrade in
May 1949 as an unofficial, private visitor. His mission was to discover
exactly what Tito wanted and what Britain could get in return. Tito
remained adamant in his demand for credit, but agreed to close his
frontier with Greece so that Yugoslav 'volunteers' could not infiltrate
that country to take part in the fighting there.[88] This was an important
concession: it effectively ended the Greek civil war, in September 1949.
In return a five-year Anglo-Yugoslav trade agreement was signed, and
Tito's demand for a credit of £8 millions guaranteed. For a long time
the Americans knew nothing of Tito's concession, and were therefore
annoyed by the Foreign Office's apparent 'surrender' to him.

Yugoslavia's experience between 1945 and 1949 triumphantly vindicated Fitzroy's view that Tito was nationalist first and Communist
second. How should we assess his overall contribution to Tito's change
of bearing? There is a strong case for saying that the real significance
of Fitzroy's wartime mission to Tito was not that it recommended
assisting him rather than Mihailovic – a decision Churchill had taken
independently of Fitzroy's advice – but that it bore a long-term fruit in
1948. Sir Alexander Glen's assessment is as follows:

> Had a break with the Russians not taken place, the personal bonds which were
> forged would probably have had no further meaning . . . but . . . I believe that
> Tito particularly, as well as some of his colleagues, were not uninfluenced by
> what they had learnt of the West from Fitzroy Maclean, Bill Deakin and Vivian

Street . . . Perhaps the association had outlived its usefulness to Tito in 1945, perhaps it was renewed for purely cynical reasons. I believe there is something more, something which could be a tribute to all four of them. In that case, this country has not realized the measure of what Maclean, Deakin and Street achieved.[89]

Sir Reginald Hibbert, who has made a close study of Eastern Europe in 1948, agrees.

I actually think it very possible that but for the confidence provided Tito by Fitzroy Maclean the Yugoslavs would never have had the steel to stand up to Stalin. It was because Tito and his commanders felt they commanded respect elsewhere than in Russia that they had the spirit, cohesion and know-how in 1948. It was Western mistakes in Albania that led to Hoxha's isolation. Had we had a Tito in Albania or a Fitzroy Maclean to liaise with him, all would have been very different. Things were so touch-and-go for Yugoslavia in the postwar years that a small balance in the weight, like Maclean's relationship, was actually vital.[90]

18

A Career in Politics

1948–1956

F ITZROY'S political interests were almost entirely concerned with defence and foreign affairs. In the years between 1948 and 1954, before he became a Junior Minister, he was able to watch at close quarters two of the most successful post-war Foreign Secretaries: Ernest Bevin and Anthony Eden, both in different ways men after his own heart, the former a founder of NATO, the second a man who had resigned as Foreign Secretary over his opposition to appeasement. Fitzroy believes that ex-diplomats or diplomats *manqués*, like Eden, always make the best Foreign Secretaries. For this reason he has a very high regard for his fellow Etonian Douglas Hurd.

Surprise has sometimes been expressed at the vehemence of Fitzroy's right-wing opinions during these years. His detestation of Stalin and lament for the vanishing empire may partly explain this, but it may also be that the disintegration of the pre-war world he had known and loved created a yearning for order. The defection of Burgess and Maclean to the Soviet Union in 1951 seemed to open up a fresh vista of chaos. If a Foreign Office training could not guarantee loyalty to the Establishment, there was a question mark against all the old certainties. Fitzroy's jaundiced response to this scandal revealed perennial mistrust of the secret services and astonishment at the gullibility of those who had helped the deserting duo to early preferment.

On the first point: 'I recall before the war attending a meeting of the Chiefs of Staff in the course of which its [SIS] representative, an undeniably bright but still relatively junior officer, boldly declared that the work in which he was engaged was far too secret to be discussed in the presence of such people as the Chief of the Imperial General Staff, the First Sea Lord and the Chief of the Air Staff. And, to my amazement, got away with it.' On the second, he recalls two incidents from 1947 and 1948: 'In Washington the then Ambassador, Lord Inverchapel, himself a strange, flamboyant character, had been loud in his praises of his brilliant First Secretary [Maclean]. "Donald's a sweetie," he would say cosily to me. And to me, a casual visitor, he declared that my namesake was the best Head of Chancery he had ever known.' In 1947, when visiting Hector McNeil, Minister of State at the Foreign Office, in connection with the DP mission, he found Guy Burgess at the outer office as McNeil's private secretary. 'Things, I reflected rather pompously, thinking back to before the war, were not what they had been in my day.'

On the Berlin airlift crisis of 1948 and 1949 Fitzroy was hawkish in the House of Commons. He argued that brinkmanship was superior to vacillation, the gravest crisis preferable to a policy of drift.[1] At this time Fitzroy (strangely, in the light of his Yugoslav experiences) still adhered to the doctrine of Kremlin-controlled 'international Communism'. As the Chinese Communists routed the last remnants of Chiang Kai-shek's Kuomintang forces and Red China became a fact of political life, Fitzroy, impatient with niceties of abstract theory, argued in a bluff Tory manner that the true touchstone of Marxism was not 'dictatorship of the proletariat', 'social praxis' or any other such notion, but readiness to be subservient to the Kremlin; Stalin's dilution of the theory of Marx and Lenin itself proved that.[2] Fitzroy also embraced the 'domino' theory. In the House on 21 July 1949 he argued that China was the most important theatre of the Cold War, on which the fate of all Asia depended, and once the last Nationalist oasis in south-west China fell to Mao, the Communist tide would sweep through Thailand, Malaya and Burma.[3]

Fitzroy was confident enough in 1949 to clash with both Attlee and Christopher Mayhew, his former ally in the Displaced Persons affair and now Minister of State at the Foreign Office. In March, with the backing of Harold Macmillan, he pressed Mayhew hard over the recent arrest of a British military attaché in the embassy in Prague. Fitzroy was annoyed that the ambassador seemed to have caved in to the Czechs by agreeing that the attaché should be expelled, and suggested that a vigorous government protest would be more appropriate.

Fitzroy questioned the Prime Minister about conflicting government pronouncements on the UK economy and the extent of our dependence on the USA. Attlee replied that the Chancellor's latest statement had been made only after consultation with himself and the Foreign Secretary. But Fitzroy pressed on.

FITZROY MACLEAN: 'Is the Prime Minister aware that during the past five or six days no less than seven more or less conflicting statements on this subject have been made, consciously or unconsciously, by members or representatives of the government, none of the statements being made in this House, and that the effect produced in the USA and elsewhere has been bewildering and deplorable?'

ATTLEE: 'If the honourable member would send me his collection, I would be glad to have a look at them' (laughter).[4]

But a few minutes later Fitzroy drew an admission from Attlee that the Under-Secretary of State had indeed blurted out indiscreet remarks on economic policy before consulting the British ambassador in Washington.

All of this indicated a conscientious, hardworking Opposition member who hardly merited the incessant sniping from old enemies like Bruce Lockhart, who continued his private vendetta with this diary entry in 1948: 'The only other guests at Binderton were the Palmers . . . Palmer is a young man who won a DSO and Bar during the war. He is a Palmer of the Reading biscuit firm and is very nice. He has a poor view of Fitzroy Maclean's intelligence.'[5]

In 1949 Fitzroy became a best-selling author with *Eastern Approaches*, the story of his life from 1937 to 1945. The idea of writing a book about his experiences was sown during a visit to General Alexander's headquarters in Italy in 1944. One of Alexander's friends, the war artist Edward Seago, was looking for fresh commissions and casually suggested that as Fitzroy had had an interesting life, he might care to write it up, using Seago's war illustrations, old and new. Seago recommended Billy Collins, head of the publishing house of that name, and after the war Fitzroy got in touch with them and proposed a book in three parts: the first dealing with Russia between 1937 and 1939; the second with the war in the desert; and the third with the mission to Tito. Collins agreed to the idea in principle, so Fitzroy went away to write.[6]

The fluency of Fitzroy's prose gives the impression that it has flowed effortlessly from his pen, but his clarity is the result of much careful craftsmanship, and multiple drafts. The first and last thirds of the book were relatively easy to write, as he had described his Russian and Yugoslav travels at length in despatches, but he had little except his memories to work on for the desert war.

To type up his final drafts he again employed Jeanne Thomlinson. She remembers 1948 well. 'I would come up to London, stay with my brother, get a batch and take it home. That went on for six months. At one point he had a wild idea I might combine secretary with governess, but I knew him well enough to know that it wouldn't work.'[7]

At last, towards the end of 1948, the book was done. Fitzroy proudly took the typescript over to Billy Collins, who seemed to have forgotten their earlier conversation and was disconcerted to find the book in three parts. He promised to get one of his readers to 'look at it' and to report back within a week. Collins duly came back: he wanted to scrap the first two parts, thus saving 100,000 words, and expand the last 50,000 into 70,000 words. 'That's the length we like our books to be,' he said, rather patronizingly. Fitzroy was disappointed; he asked for time to think the matter over.[8]

Secretly piqued that Collins wanted to geld his book, especially as he was convinced the best material was in the first two-thirds, Fitzroy cast around for a solution. He remembered his old friend Peter Fleming and asked him to cast an eye over the typescript, unaware that Fleming was not only an author but doubled as a reader for Cape. A week later a contract for the book arrived from Cape, proposing a royalty of a flat 20 per cent. Fitzroy was naïve about publishing in those days and did not realize that this was an unheard-of offer for a first book. He rang up to ask Peter Fleming about it. 'A 20 per cent royalty. Is that good?' Fleming answered urbanely, 'It's what we gave Hemingway for his fourth book, so you can take it from me it's exceedingly good.' Feeling residual loyalty towards Collins, Fitzroy then asked them for an offer on the three-part book as originally agreed. No reply came, so he signed with Cape. Because of Billy Collins's dithering, Peter Fleming had carried off the non-fiction scoop of the year.[9]

Eastern Approaches went into seventeen editions in hardback alone and sold over a million copies worldwide. After more than forty years, the writing is as fresh as ever. *Eastern Approaches* is to quotidian historical process what edited highlights are to the full ninety minutes of a football match: all the boring bits have been left out. The book bubbles with humour and anecdote, and plays down the physical courage that lay behind Fitzroy's exploits. The critics were ecstatic in their praise. Fitzroy's reputation as wit and raconteur was made.

Eastern Approaches surprised those who, having seen the austere, serious side of Fitzroy's personality, thought they had the whole picture. Many who are now admirers confess that their first impression of him was unfavourable, and that by no stretch of the imagination would they have perceived him as a humorous man. Lord Henniker admits: 'I was surprised . . . I wouldn't have thought it at all the sort of book he would have written. My first thought was that he must have spent a lot of time polishing it, as the Fitzroy I knew was extremely laborious. It's far too insouciant and light-hearted. The young Fitzroy was hardworking, solid, plodding, not at all mercurial, a very serious young man. Very intelligent, of course, but I hadn't detected the wit and humour.'[10]

Why did Fitzroy wait eight years before producing another book? He explains: 'After *Eastern Approaches* I was asked to write a lot of articles and reviews, which it was quite possible to combine with being an MP, and of course I still went on travelling around a lot so I had plenty of material; but up to 1957, and to a lesser extent thereafter, I was still hoping to get into government, which would have absorbed all my energies.'[11]

Others suggest that Fitzroy did intend a sequel to *Eastern Approaches*, but failed to find a suitable subject. In 1951 he frequently saw Freya

Stark; indeed he and Christopher Sykes were favourite friends of hers. She loved his Tito anecdotes, and welcomed his presence in her house as an antidote to less affable visitors, like A. L. Rowse the Elizabethan scholar, whom she described as 'an arid little combative man'. Fitzroy consulted Freya Stark on a speech he had written about the Middle East, and later she wrote to Stewart Perowne, to whom she was briefly married, as follows: 'Fitzroy tells me he is now really happy only when writing, and I think I was right in *Perseus* to say that loving and creating are the only two happinesses that last.'[12]

The publication of *Eastern Approaches* also gave Fitzroy a higher profile, when he had been in some danger of becoming 'yesterday's man'. In particular, he saw more of Winston Churchill, who vetted the book and asked Fitzroy to make one change. In March 1949 Fitzroy was one of six back-benchers who lunched with Churchill at Hyde Park Gate.[13] The near coincidence of the Yugoslav break with Moscow and the publication of the book gave Fitzroy a new lease of life as a Balkans expert.

In March in the House of Commons Fitzroy described the situation in the Balkans as the worst for ten years. 'My former associate Marshal Tito is not a very popular figure. He has lost some friends and I do not know that he has made many new ones. What matters to us is whether a country is bound hand and foot or whether it shows some degree of independence. The decision whether or not a person is a Communist depends on Moscow, and Moscow has said that Tito is not a Communist. Tito is showing some degree of independence. The question is: how long will that last, and how long will Tito last?'[14]

In November Fitzroy re-entered the fray and urged the democracies to show themselves as tough as Stalin. The West was engaged in a Cold War which the enemy was waging with all the ruthlessness and bitterness of a real war. He did not believe Stalin wanted war at present, but that did not mean he would not in the future. The Yugoslav rebellion against Moscow had fundamentally changed the political, economic and strategic picture in south-east Europe. The British seemed unaware that much hinged on the outcome of the struggle between the Kremlin and Tito and that if Yugoslavia was crushed, Moscow's authority would be vindicated; if Yugoslavia survived, it would encourage others to break away and would explode the myth of Soviet invincibility. With this in mind, Fitzroy urged the House to oppose the withdrawal of British troops from Greece, since that would surely be taken as a sign elsewhere in the Balkans that His Majesty's Government had no interest in the area. This drew a dismissive cry of 'Nonsense' from Bevin.[15]

Fitzroy's profile as hawkish Cold Warrior and his unflinching support for Tito made him a marked man in the eyes of Stalin and his followers. By 1949 he was Public Enemy Number One and 'most

wanted war criminal' in Albania, on the grounds that he had master-
minded Tito's defection to the West by 'turning' him in 1944. A more
specific accusation arose when in 1948 an Albanian 'confessed' that
Fitzroy had hired him to assassinate Enver Hoxha. Notoriety even
brought *Daily Worker* journalists up 'doorstepping' at his house near
Lancaster. Sir Reginald Hibbert, expert on Albania, unravels this
tangle:

> In the first place, it is possible that they confused the two Macleans. Billy
> Maclean, so like Fitzroy in so many ways, really had spent time in Albania and
> the Albanians were unlikely to have been able to differentiate between the two
> Macleans. Then you have to remember the relations between Tito and Hoxha.
> Tito undoubtedly wanted to overthrow Hoxha in 1948 so that he could bring
> Albania into a Yugoslav federation. Hoxha made his name by opposing that.
> Now, since Fitzroy was Tito's ally, Hoxha would have deduced that Britain
> was manipulating Tito in its own aim of destabilizing Albania, especially as by
> that time we had started on that foolish destabilizing exercise. Hoxha put two
> and two together. He knew that the British were after him and that Tito was
> also, in a different way. What more natural than that he should link the two and
> then see Fitzroy Maclean as the *éminence grise*.[16]

Once, much later on, Fitzroy and Veronica nearly made the mistake
of driving across the border from Serbia to Albania. Had they crossed
the checkpoint, Fitzroy would certainly have been arrested and very
possibly executed, though Fitzroy tends to dismiss the entire incident:
'When Tito broke away, Moscow proceeded to purge all the governments of the satellites. My alleged "contract" on Hoxha was all part of
that. Albania became the spearhead of Stalinism and they put this
wretched man up to it. I put it to the Russians that, if they knew I was
trying to murder Tito during the war – which later they would have
liked better than anything – was that why they gave me the Order of
Kutusov? Tito, to do him justice, when shown the article saying I was
an assassin, flew into a great rage.'[17]

The Soviets kept up their propaganda campaign linking Tito with
British 'spies', principally Fitzroy. In 1951 Molotov described the Par-
tisans as 'spies and provocateurs who betrayed their people and sold out
to the Anglo-American imperialists, re-established the capitalist system
and deprived the people of their revolutionary victory'. Tito replied
in kind: 'They have been murdering in Albania, Bulgaria, Hungary,
Romania, Poland and Czechoslovakia, not to mention Russia itself.
They had exterminated whole communities – the Crimea Tartars, the
Chechens of the Caucasus, the Germans of the "Volga Republic".
Tens of thousands of Estonians, Latvians and Lithuanians had been
uprooted to perish in the forests of Siberia. And it was these practition-
ers of genocide who were now accusing and threatening Yugoslavia.'[18]

Fitzroy's staunch support for Tito paid off. In 1950 the Yugoslavs played host to a major delegation from the Labour Government.[19] Then in January 1951 Djilas himself came to London to buy arms with which to combat the Soviet threat. At a meeting in Hyde Park Gate, Djilas twitted Churchill: 'In 1945 you said that Tito had tricked you. We Yugoslav Partisans considered that a great compliment.' Churchill always liked that kind of talk. He winked and said with a laugh, 'I don't remember having used those words, but I was so angry at all of you that I could have said something worse.' He continued in the same friendly vein: 'It was a mistake to say that and it shall never happen again.'[20] But even as Fitzroy's efforts to cultivate good Anglo-Yugoslav relations were being so well rewarded, snipers were denigrating him. In March Bruce Lockhart entered in his diary: 'Fitzroy Maclean took Pijade [the Yugoslav Foreign Minister] to see Anthony [Eden]. I discovered that Anthony did not think much of Fitzroy either as a man or as a politician.'[21]

The climax of Fitzroy's behind-the-scenes lobbying was Tito's own visit to London in February 1952 for the funeral of King George VI. Antonia Fraser tells a revealing story. 'This was one of the first state occasions since the war and I was in a party looking down on Edgware Road from a flat belonging to Douglas Woodruff. Fitzroy and Veronica were there. Just as the dignitaries were coming, I was pulled away from my position at the window by an iron hand. It was Fitzroy. "That's Tito!" he shouted, much more interested in the Marshal than anyone else in the procession. He then gazed fixedly at Tito from the window. I never got to see Tito or anyone else!'[22]

At the beginning of the 1950s, and especially after the Conservatives returned to power in 1951, Fitzroy was much exercised about Red China and the Korean war. He fought a long campaign in the 'Letters' columns of *The Times* against recognition of Red China, and was less than gracious in conceding defeat when the Labour Government bowed to the inevitable in May 1950.[23]

It was the Korean war, above all, that troubled Fitzroy at this time. Naturally there was controversy about whether the hidden hand manipulating the North Koreans was Peking's or Moscow's. In a series of debates in the House in July 1950 Fitzroy threw himself into the fray with more than usual gusto. In the 19 July debate he intervened no fewer than five times to press Labour ministers on the alleged sale of arms to Mao's China. It was the failure of the British to stand with their American allies against recognition of Red China, he claimed, that had encouraged Stalin to order the North Koreans to cross the 38th parallel. If Stalin wanted a Third World War, no amount of appeasement could stop him. By the same token, replied his opponents, neither could any amount of bellicosity. Fitzroy at any rate agreed with his critics that

Stalin was a cautious and calculating man who would go to war only if guaranteed a cheap and easy victory. 'As to the likelihood of the Chinese Communists eventually "turning Tito", I agree that such a possibility cannot altogether be excluded.'[24] Fitzroy was not at his best in these debates, and sometimes went over the top. In a not very convincing defence of American policy on Formosa he claimed that its aim was to 'neutralize a strategically important island which would otherwise by now have become a fresh jumping-off place for future Communist aggression.' His critics pointed out that a glance at the map would reveal that the only place you could jump off to from Formosa was the Chinese mainland, which was already in Communist hands.[25]

Fitzroy was sounder on purely European policy. In 1950 a great debate raged within the Foreign Office on the Schumann plan for an integrated European iron and steel community – the embryo from which the EEC eventually grew. Arguments about loss of sovereignty identical to today's echoed in Whitehall. Herbert Morrison thought the Durham miners 'wouldn't like it'.[26] The British ambassador in Paris, Fitzroy's old friend and colleague Sir Oliver Harvey, thought it a revolutionary proposal which should not be allowed to fail; the union of Germany and France would remove the principal cause of European conflict over the past hundred years. Fitzroy backed Harvey; he argued the plan must be a consummation devoutly to be wished, since the Russians hated it so.[27]

Between August and November 1950 Fitzroy and Veronica toured south-east Europe and the Middle East, taking in Greece, Yugoslavia, Turkey and Iran and travelling every stage of the journey by road or rail.[28] He claimed to find universal concern over Korea and used his findings to counter the criticism of those who said that Asia was a US sphere of influence and should be left to the Americans.[29]

In 1951 Fitzroy shifted his focus of concern from Korea to Iran, where the Mossadeq government, after overthrowing the Shah, threatened British interests at the Abadan oilfields with a large-scale nationalization programme. Fitzroy once more took a hawkish line and again he made extensive tours through the nation-states of the Middle East. He was an early advocate of regional agreements, like the Baghdad Pact, designed to check Soviet influence in the Middle East.[30] But Korea was never far from his thoughts. In a debate on Korea in the House on 26 February 1952 he accused the Labour opposition of sabotaging British foreign policy by starting a 'scare' that Chiang would cross from Formosa with his armies and open a second front on the Chinese mainland: 'The China scare is harmful and artificial. A cooked-up motion had been tabled as a direct result of stresses and strains within the Labour Party. It was a sop to the yapping Cerberus Mr Bevan.'[31]

Bevan made his counter-attack in a debate on 14 May 1952, and

Fitzroy's parliamentary skills this time appeared to advantage. Fitzroy was speaking of NATO, arguing that at the moment it fell into the category of Becoming rather than Being. 'As somebody had said, NATO was like the Venus de Milo, plenty of shape but no arms.' This crack drew laughter, so Fitzroy warmed to this theme. 'There were signs', he continued, 'that the bipartisan policy had been thrown to the wolves, to the big bad wolves of Ebbw Vale and Bishop Auckland, hungry jackals who came yapping along in their wake.' This too drew ministerial laughter, and in a trice Bevan was on his feet to reply that whenever the problem of the Soviet Union was approached, it was almost impossible for some members not to do so in an Antichrist state of mind.[32]

Fitzroy has always been strongly pro-American, unwilling to criticize the USA even in cases, like Suez, where Washington humiliated its cousin. By the day of the great debate on responsibility for the continuing Korean conflict, 29 June 1952, it was widely whispered that the Labour government had been pressurized by the Americans into branding the Chinese Communists as aggressors. When the USA resumed bombing targets in North Korea while peace negotiations were in progress, and without consulting their allies, concern over American intentions became acute even on the Tory benches. Speakers as various as Tom Driberg, Hartley Shawcross and Chuter Ede voiced misgivings. Ede expressed a widely held view: 'The course of truce negotiations, no matter how protracted they may be, should not be jeopardized by the use of unnecessary force while these negotiations are proceeding.' This brought Fitzroy charging out of his corner. 'I welcome these attacks against very important military targets. By helping to convince the enemy that aggression does not pay, they may help to accelerate the conclusion of an armistice and the end of negotiations.'[33]

The years 1951 and 1952 saw East–West tensions at their worst. It was widely felt that a third World War was only a matter of time. This was a perception Fitzroy shared with General de Gaulle (who, interestingly, was also convinced from the very first days of the Second War that the Allies would prevail; de Gaulle thought that when the war between the West and the Soviet Union broke out, France would welcome him back as a saviour). In this atmosphere, when Cold War seemed likely to become hot, Fitzroy dreamed of playing once again a role in enemy-occupied territory. In 1952, just after his forty-first birthday, he visited Stewart Menzies, head of SIS, and suggested that he should go to Yugoslavia (which was sure to be overrun by the Red Army in the event of war) and resume his relationship with Tito and the Partisans. Menzies promised to consider the suggestion. A few days later he called Fitzroy into his office and proposed a 'stay behind' role for him in Turkey, since the Russians were thought certain to invade that country through the Caucasus. 'By this time MI6 had taken over SOE's operational role. I was sent off with Veronica in a Land Rover to do a recce over likely Turkish terrain . . . But I shudder to think how the affair might have ended had it been for real, as the man who briefed me was Philby!'[34]

Nineteen fifty-three saw the end of the Korean war, the Coronation of Queen Elizabeth II, and the first ascent of Everest. The 'roof of the world' has always fascinated Fitzroy, and the Hillary/Tenzing conquest of Everest gave him the chance to intervene on behalf of a monarch – always a cause dear to his royalist heart. During a somewhat self-congratulatory debate on Everest in the House on 17 June, Fitzroy punctured the narcissism of the proceedings by asking why news of the conquest of the peak had been withheld from the King of Nepal by the British embassy in Kathmandu until after he had already learned of it from other sources. He finally wrung reluctant regrets from a frosty Selwyn Lloyd.[35]

In 1953 Fitzroy took part in routine debates on education and the future of British colonies in south-east Asia. He also helped to set up an Anglo-Turkish society to improve trade and cultural relations, and was appointed its first chairman.[36] Yet his principal concern now was Egypt and the Suez canal. Harold Macmillan later noted: 'Certain members of the party, led by Charles Waterhouse and Ralph Assheton, with the active support of Fitzroy Maclean and Julian Amery, were totally opposed to a British withdrawal from the Canal.'[37] Fitzroy made that plain in a debate on 11 May 1953. The Suez Canal was the key to the problems of the entire Middle East, he said; of course it was expensive to maintain a British military presence there, but it would be far more expensive to our long-term interests if we simply cut and ran.[38]

The Suez issue came to a head in December 1953. Fitzroy was one of thirty-nine back-bench Tory MPs who tabled a motion opposing any resumption of talks with Egypt.[39] The most vociferous of these members were Julian Amery and Viscount Hinchinbrooke. Prime Minister Churchill, now 80, decided to appeal personally to this group not to rock the boat. He, 'Rab' Butler and Antony Head, Army Minister, attended a private meeting of the Tory MPs Services Committee and brought some powerful arguments to bear. Churchill pointed out that the H-Bomb had made bases like those in the Canal Zone obsolete, and that it would cost £50 million a year to maintain them. But none the less, at midnight on 12 July 1954 the Suez group informed the government that they would vote against any treaty with Egypt that involved abandoning the bases.

Churchill pressed on nevertheless. On 27 July he announced an agreement whereby Britain would evacuate the Canal Zone within twenty months. The Suez group remained defiant. One of them,

Captain Waterhouse, held above his head a copy of the Cairo agreement. 'This piece of paper is not worth anything to us.' Two days later the crucial debate took place. Fitzroy, however, was now one of four apostates, together with Messrs P. Bell, W. H. Bromley-Davenport and P. Marshall.[40] In the debate Fitzroy declared himself unhappy with the agreement but did not presume, he said, to know better than the Prime Minister: if Churchill thought quitting the bases was sensible, he, Fitzroy, was prepared to take his word.[41] 'I could not vote against Winston,' Fitzroy explained later, and indeed it would have been difficult for a man of honour to betray the mentor to whom he owed so much. But when, at the end of 1954, Churchill gave Fitzroy a junior post in the government, the suspicion arose that his apostasy was the result of an 'understanding' with the Prime Minister. Enoch Powell was another who had second thoughts on this matter. He voted with the Suez group on 29 July but in October told his former comrades with some asperity that, as far as he was concerned, once Britain agreed to withdraw from the Canal Zone, the fight was over.[42] Powell too was accused of currying favour with Churchill and was widely tipped as first choice for Under-Secretary of War, but it was Fitzroy who was given the position. There was some ill-feeling among Tory back-benchers. Lord Henniker remembers: 'Julian Amery thought Fitzroy had let him down over Suez. He once said to me, "I think I've made the most ghastly mistake over the future of the British Empire. It's bound to collapse as I've just taught Fitzroy to speak." Well, in fact he hadn't.'[43]

The genesis of Fitzroy's appointment to office was his long-standing relationship with Churchill. 'I remember spending a weekend at Chequers with Antony and Dot Head. Churchill had an old-fashioned gramophone and was playing a lot of old-fashioned records someone had given him – mainly marches, Band of the Grenadier Guards, that sort of thing. Veronica and Clemmie were chatting, as only Veronica can chat. Churchill turned on them and said, "You silly women, these tunes may not mean much to you but they mean a lot to me." At which he burst into tears. They mopped him up and patted his head.'[44]

Churchill handed over the prime ministerial baton to Eden in 1955. Just before he retired, he summoned Fitzroy, who relates the circumstances. 'You know, when there's a new government you're rather hoping you'll get a job and you hope for the telephone to ring. I'd been sent for twice by him but, it turned out, for other reasons: once to be godfather to his youngest granddaughter and the next time to represent him at some service at Westminster Abbey, which was very nice but not quite what I was hoping for. Then, third time lucky.'

Fitzroy had Lord Lloyd staying with him at Yealand Conyers when they were both called to London. 'Veronica got out our little car to take us both to the station. Halfway down a hill about two miles outside

Lancaster the car ran out of gas. You can imagine the frustration and the humiliation at the thought of turning up at Number 10 late. Anyway, I flagged down the next car and they very kindly got us to the station. When we got to London, we rushed over to the interview. Winston said to me, ''I've always wanted to give you a job ever since I came back to power in '51 but they (meaning the whips) wouldn't let me. Now I'm old and finished and I'm going to give it to you whatever they say. How would you like to be Under-Secretary of State for War?'' '[45]

This was a post Churchill himself had occupied early in his career, and Fitzroy jumped at the chance. 'For me it was a marvellous job. I'd always been very close to the Army and brought up with the Army as a child and got on well with soldiers.' His friend Antony Head, Secretary of State of War, was delighted to have Fitzroy as his deputy, though rather piqued at the high-handed way Churchill had made the appointment; he had not been consulted, and arrived back from an official tour in Singapore to find a *fait accompli*. But this was typical of Churchill's methods. The Prime Minister's penchant for favourites and a tendency to nepotism attracted adverse comment, especially as his son-in-law Duncan Sandys was appointed Minister of Housing and Local Government in the same shake-up, thus becoming the second youngest member of the Cabinet at the age of 46.

In the early fifties the great issue for an Army minister was conscription. Fitzroy recalls: 'It was a critical time for the Army because there was a general tide running in favour of abolishing conscription, but both I and Antony Head as well as Field-Marshal Harding were for retaining it.'[46] Harding, Chief of the Imperial General Staff until 1955, when he went to Cyprus as governor-general, worked particularly well with Fitzroy but not all the 'top brass' liked a situation where the top two in the War Office had extensive experience of soldiering.

> Our system is based on the idea that it's very unusual and even undesirable to be an expert in your field of ministerial office. Head was an exception and so was I. But a lot of civil servants take the *Yes, Minister* line that it's better for a Minister not to know too much. I remember that the soldiers and generals didn't like to be sent for by Antony Head, who'd retired as a brigadier five years earlier, and cross-questioned on the sorts of things he wasn't supposed to know about. Civil servants, I think, prefer a Foreign Secretary who talks the kind of French Winston used to. What he has to do is sum up his advisers, in all senses. Personally, however, I think that someone with some military experience, even if it's only National Service, is better than the reverse.[47]

Fitzroy settled in quickly, and appointed T. L. Iremonger, MP for Ilford North, as his Parliamentary Private Secretary. But it was January 1955 before he was called on to show his Parliamentary mettle as a junior minister. Asked what proposals he had to increase Regular Army recruiting, Fitzroy made a crisp reply. He explained that the recent decline was due to the 1952 figures having been abnormally high. New 22-year engagements had been introduced; furthermore, because of a 'birth bulge' there had in 1952 and 1953 been an exceptionally large intake of National Servicemen, from whom a good proportion of the regulars was drawn. But Fitzroy assured the House that Britain could meet its commitments at existing manpower levels, and that recruitment would soon pick up once the effects of better barracks, superior married quarters and higher pay filtered through.[48]

There was another debate in February 1955 over an opposition amendment to the Army Bill, concerned with the arrest and punishment of Army transgressors, to abolish the death penalty in the Army. Fitzroy argued that it did not take account of the fact that treason under civilian law attracted a mandatory death penalty, nor that other clauses of the Bill prescribed capital punishment in cases of failure to suppress a mutiny. He pointed out that the Bill did not seek to impose the death penalty where it did not exist before, but rather tended to restrict the opportunities of attracting it, and to impose a number of safeguards that did not previously exist. Nor could the death penalty be imposed lightly, as the decision of a court martial had to be unanimous. After all, there had to be *some* method for dealing with a deliberate traitor. On a free vote the Opposition amendment was defeated by 205 votes to 10.[49]

In this debate Fitzroy had the vociferous support of the Labour member George Wigg. Wigg, later Harold Wilson's *éminence grise*, was a jug-eared ex-colonel, well-known for his remark that he would hate the Tories' guts, if they had any. Apart from the Army, he had two other passions: spies and horse-racing. Their common passion for the Army often enabled Fitzroy and Wigg to make common cause, but Wigg was no charmer and his enemies were legion. 'Wigg's paranoid, he thinks everyone hates him,' Fitzroy told his friend Jakie Astor, adding: 'He's quite right, they do.'[50]

Fitzroy's ministerial career was largely concerned with minutiae. Many would have found these tiresome and longed for a post that was more challenging, with a higher profile, but Fitzroy's love for the Army in all its manifestations sustained him. He particularly enjoyed the opportunity to visit military bases overseas. One such visit, to Malaya and Singapore, was more than usually interesting. Apart from renewing acquaintance with Peter Moore, now a brigadier, Fitzroy got on famously with General Gerald Templar, 'the tiger of Malaya', whose distaste for politicians was notorious.[51] He also met the novelist and physician Han Suyin, author of *A Many Splendoured Thing* and a renowned beauty though at the time (during the emergency campaign against Communist guerrillas) suspected at Government House of

being a Communist sympathiser. 'Of course he had some ideas different from mine,' Han Suyin says: 'I saw the guerrilla war in Malaysia
from the point of view of the people who were confined in villages
behind barbed wire. They had no medical care, but I went to see them.
Fitzroy Maclean saw it from a more idealistic point of view, as order
versus disorder, as the perpetual war against those who in the name of
Communism seize power. But he was a man of courtesy, of knowledge
too.'[52]

Peter Standish, who was Fitzroy's Private Secretary, travelled with
him in the summer of 1955 to Nepal and Malaya.[53] Fitzroy loved Nepal
and packed in as much travel as he could manage. One night, in
Kathmandu, he wanted to see the sights. 'He didn't mean the tourist
sights, but wanted to wander into dark alleys, seedy bars and opium
dens. He loved it and the locals loved him. There was no sense of danger
or that anything could happen to him.'[54] Standish was afraid they could
end up stabbed in a back-alley, but Fitzroy was unconcerned.

Back in London conscription was still a contentious issue. He and
Head persuaded the new Prime Minister Anthony Eden to stand firm
against Labour demands for the abolition of National Service or for the
reduction of the period of service; in this he also had the support of the
powerful Defence Committee chaired by his friend 'Bobbity', Lord
Salisbury, said to have been the last bastion of truly independent influence in a Tory party dominated by the machine and the whips. Fitzroy
remembers the laborious toil of the Army Council, of which he was
vice-chairman under Anthony Head. 'Our actuaries worked out that
we would never get the necessary numbers from the Regular Army
alone. There was a gap of something like 40,000 between what our
commitments would be and what we would have, even if we reduced
conscription from two years to eighteen months. The Navy and Air
Force would have managed all right, they could get their numbers. But
the Army couldn't. In the end Antony Head went to Cabinet and
threatened that not only would we both resign but [so would] all the
Field-Marshals and Generals as well. That stopped them.'[55]

In July 1955 Labour called for National Service to be reduced by
twelve months on the grounds that conscription was a denial of the
fundamental rights of man. Fitzroy explained that the government did
not like conscription (true, if hardly indicative of his own position), but
that it was a necessary evil as long as tensions continued. A twelve-
month reduction of service would shake 150,000 men out of the Armed
Forces and even a six-month reduction would lead to the loss of 72,000
men.[56] Making no progress by frontal assault, Labour took to guerrilla
warfare and asked for pay parades to be abolished in favour of pay
packets; Fitzroy replied that parades would still be necessary even if
pay came in packets. They also brought forward cases of organized

bullying, which Fitzroy was meticulous in following up and examining. One case, involving misdemeanours at the Army Apprentices School at Chepstow, was brought to his attention by Fenner Brockway, his old rival in the 1941 Lancaster by-election. Yet Brockway was nothing if not a man of honour, and was impressed enough by Fitzroy's conscientious investigation to declare openly that he would not press for a formal inquiry.[57]

Some of Fitzroy's work was scarcely to his taste. He had to work out the administrative details for the withdrawal from Suez he had so strenuously opposed the year before.[58] He laboured hard to improve the training and conditions of National Servicemen, in an attempt to cut the ground from under his critics' feet,[59] but was always vulnerable to the freak accident or the rogue sergeant-major that gave Labour the opportunity to portray the Army as a monstrous system of inhumanity run by dolts.

In 1956 Fitzroy acquired a new Private Secretary in place of Peter Standish. The new man, John Blelloch, with just two years' experience of the Civil Service behind him, was expecting a strict disciplinarian or a fire-eater. What he found surprised him. 'Fitzroy Maclean was not at all what I expected. I envisaged a glamorous war-hero who'd done amazing things in the mountains with Tito. My impression, though, was of a huge, slightly vague bear of a man, not a dynamic killer slaughtering Huns. He was lovely to work for, very kind and forgiving when I made mistakes. He was a master of writing prose and had the most wonderful handwriting. I learned how official English should be written. He had a very wide range of contacts and so I got invitations to all sorts of social occasions. He was always very humorous, though never ribald, and always enjoyed a joke.'[60]

John Blelloch remembers the workload in 1956 very clearly. 'Fitzroy signed the huge correspondence personally. Traditionally, the Junior Minister handled all parliamentary correspondence and that with the public. Much of it was to do with reservists, but there was plenty about servicemen. At that time it was basically a conscript army that was deployed. Many anxious mums writing about their sons. A citizen army with scope for complaints about haircuts and so on. After call-up it was usually, why have I been called up? Afterwards it was, why am I kicking my heels, what's happening about my job, university place.'[61] In debates Fitzroy was pressed hard on the Regular Army practice of sending 16-year-old band boys to trouble spots like Cyprus, where they might be shot. The possibility of emotive tabloid headlines was clear, yet Fitzroy refused to budge from the conventional Army view.

Willie Hamilton, the well-known anti-royalist, asked about a sentence of 84 days' imprisonment imposed on a private in the parachute regiment who had refused to make a jump from a balloon. Fitzroy knew all about the 'white-knuckle' aspects of paratrooping from his own experience, and was a little impatient with the question. Men were sent on a six-week course and could withdraw at any time. After that it was understood they *had* to jump when ordered, including from balloons, and this requirement was reflected in extra pay. 'It is well known that refusal to jump after training is a serious offence.'[62]

Many men would have quailed under the relentless barrage of trivia to which an Under-Secretary of War had to address himself. An old adversary, Marcus Lipton, had the better of an exchange in the House on 4 June 1956. Lipton began with a seemingly innocent question about why the town of Banbury was out of bounds to troops. Fitzroy replied blandly that 'certain troops were involved in discreditable activities in Banbury'. Lipton then asked why British troops were banned while American ones were not. Fitzroy answered that the banning had taken place after consultation between Western Command and the Banbury police, but they clearly could not bind Americans. Lipton then shrewdly gave the impression of a government afraid to take strong measures against the American 'guests', by revealing that the original trouble was a 'punch-up' between British and American soldiers.[63] Three weeks later George Wigg also drew blood with a question revealing that nine WRACs had acted as ushers at the Antique Dealers' Fair. This conjured visions of the private sector using Army labour free for its own profitable pursuits. Fitzroy admitted that the arrangements had been wrongly authorized because of a 'misunderstanding', and would not be repeated.[64]

Yet in retrospect, Fitzroy saw these months of 1956 as a halcyon period. After July 1956 the entire country was in the grip of the Suez crisis. John Foster Dulles, US Secretary of State, is one of the few American politicians for whom Fitzroy is prepared to express open distaste. It was Dulles's veto of a World Bank loan for the construction of the Aswan Dam that led Egypt's President Nasser to nationalize the Suez Canal Company. The Prime Minister, Anthony Eden, it is now generally agreed, overreacted. Patient diplomacy, especially with the co-operation of the Americans, could have achieved results. But Eden talked wildly of 'this vital trade artery' and made absurd comparisons of Nasser with Hitler. Almost from the first, despite intense American opposition, Eden determined on a military solution to the conflict with Egypt.

Suez polarized public opinion in Britain as nothing since has. At first outrage against the 'tinpot dictator' Nasser, fanned by the tabloids, ranged the majority behind Eden. But as the crisis became protracted and some of the practical consequences of a military adventure – not least the prospect of alienating opinion in the Arab world, with consequent threat to British oil supplies – impinged on the public, the tide of opinion turned. By the time Eden finally launched 'Operation Musketeer' to re-occupy the Canal Zone, he was somewhat isolated. In the House of Commons passions ran high, as Labour indicted the Eden government for moral turpitude. There were demonstrations in the streets of London. President Eisenhower warned Eden against precipitate action. Finally, Eden's diaphanous collusion with the Israelis lost him credibility. A plan was cooked up with the French premier Guy Mollet and the Israelis, whereby Israel would invade Egypt, and Britain and France would then step in 'to separate the combatants'.

Suez split the country between those who hankered after Britain's imperial greatness, entertaining illusions about British power and freedom of action in foreign affairs, and those who could see that the imperial mantle had already passed across the Atlantic. Many of Fitzroy's friends, like John Henniker and Jakie Astor, vehemently opposed Eden's policies; but Fitzroy, ex-member of the Suez group and advocate of a continuing imperial role for Britain, was among the 'gung-ho' group who backed Eden all the way. In retrospect Fitzroy has no regrets about his stance.

> I have no quarrel with sending the expedition, but several things were wrongly done. We let the enemy see our hand too clearly. The big mistake was to declare war and then have a large gap between announcing the expedition and landing it. Another thing that was heavily criticized was that we started to bomb the Egyptians before the troops landed. Yet another thing was that the Labour Party was badly handled. In the summer they were basically on our side and in favour of an expedition. Then the mood in the country changed and a lot of people lost heart. Gaitskell and the Labour Party came down against it. So we went in at the worst possible moment and in the worst possible conditions.[65]

But Fitzroy's interest in the Suez crisis was not purely ideological. He was up to his eyes in extra work. 'The thing hung fire over the summer. I remember that we got the Queen's authority to mobilize at Goodwood, as we had to send down there and get her to sign things in the Royal Box. Of course we now know that Eden was a very sick man, but the contrast between the work at our level and what happened in Cabinet was astonishing. Nothing happened or nothing seemed to happen for months. The expedition was waiting to go, all the tanks were on board ships at Liverpool, but there was all this dithering. Antony Head became Secretary of State for Defence, and John Hare came in as my boss at the War Office.' John Blelloch confirms the exponential increase in workload.

> Fitzroy didn't have as much of a role in the planning of the operation as Antony Head, for example, did. But it was a very, very fraught time for us. As

a Resident Clerk at the War Office for a month I got almost no sleep, taking
messages all night and then working during the day. My memory of the impact
on Fitzroy is not quite what you might expect. What happened was an absolute
flood of parliamentary correspondence concerning reservists, National Servicemen and regulars. People writing to their MPs in their thousands. Sounds
mundane, but was important. My memory of the time, therefore, apart from
being up at night more or less continuously, was of dealing with this mass of
correspondence. Hundreds of letters a week. Initially reservists, tens of thousands of them, kicking their heels between July and November and generating
this mass of correspondence in the office. But our office wasn't in the thick of
the ops. Not at all, that was the tightest of nets. Head may have talked to
Fitzroy informally.[66]

In the end Eden fulfilled the worst fears of his critics. The Israelis
invaded Egypt, the British and French 'intervened to part the combatants' and invaded the Canal Zone, and the Russians took advantage of
the chaos in the Western world to put down an uprising in Hungary.
Harold Macmillan had been an early enthusiast for military action, but
in November, as the first of the British troops touched Egyptian soil, he
came to Cabinet with news of a catastrophic run on the pound. 'First
in and first out' was Harold Wilson's scathing characterization of
Macmillan's conduct. Confidence in sterling could be restored only by
an IMF loan, but Eisenhower, furiously angry with Eden for acting
without Washington's consent, threatened to block the loan unless
British forces were withdrawn at once. There followed an ignominious
withdrawal. Christmas 1956 was the blackest of black nights for those
who still purported to believe in the reality of the British Empire.
Fitzroy sums up his feelings about Suez.

> The Russians and the Americans together brought all the pressure they could
> to bear and the government decided to pull out, which to my mind was
> disastrous. I know that Winston in his retirement felt the same way – that
> having once gone in we should have stuck it out to the end, but the pressure
> from abroad was *very, very strong*. I had had a very good idea of what was going
> on, because Antony Head was a close friend and I had lots of contacts in the
> Army itself, so I was far from badly informed. I was in no way shocked at what
> was happening. I gather that some of the books on Suez suggest that the
> military operation was muddled by Anthony Head or by the military. It cer-
> tainly wasn't, everything went remarkably well. It was all extremely efficient
> and the whole operation would have been completed successfully if we hadn't
> pulled out.[67]

Despite the reservations allegedly expressed to Bruce Lockhart, Eden
had treated Fitzroy with consideration and had co-opted him as an
extraordinary member of the Cabinet for a few special sessions on
defence. Fitzroy, for his part, found Eden a scarcely adequate

replacement for Churchill. 'I thought of resigning when we pulled out of Suez, but Eden was in such a shaky state that I thought it would be disloyal. I remember having to answer some convoluted question about the squirrelling-away of millions of horseshoe nails, and thousands of cans of paint going dry. I went to see Eden and spent an hour with him, trying to get him to address the issue, but he was obviously a sick man. Personally I liked him . . . He was charming and highly intelligent, but his *métier* was diplomacy rather than politics.'[68]

When Eden, broken and seriously ill, resigned in December 1956 and Harold Macmillan took over as Prime Minister, it was clear that Fitzroy's own career was at the crossroads. Macmillan, it appears, was willing to keep Antony Head on as Secretary of State for Defence, provided he agreed to steer through the Commons a bill abolishing conscription and basing future British defence on nuclear deterrence. This Head refused to do, and Macmillan had presumably expected such a response for, as Fitzroy relates: 'Antony Head was an experienced operator and as he went out of Number 10 he looked at the Private Secretary's diary – he was good at reading upside down – and he saw that the time allowed for his interview was exactly five minutes – hardly the quota of time one would have allocated to a man one expected to take the job.'[69]

The writing was now on the wall for Fitzroy also, and the dolorous stroke fell as expected. Macmillan's stated reason for dismissing Fitzroy was as follows: 'I was sorry to lose Fitzroy Maclean, but he really is so hopeless in the House that he is a passenger in office . . . a great pity, since he is so able.'[70] In any case, Macmillan knew well enough that there would be no place for a champion of conscription in an administration where Duncan Sandys, the new Defence Secretary, was about to produce a White Paper announcing the switch to nuclear deterrence. But there are some who feel that it was Fitzroy's wholehearted support for the Suez adventure that led to his downfall. Sir Douglas Dodds-Parker, a fellow Tory MP, comments:

I don't think Fitzroy would ever have been welcome in political circles except under Churchill. But the reason for his sacking was Suez, without a doubt. Selwyn Lloyd and Heath were the two determined to get rid of the pro-Suez lot, even though they themselves had defended the line loyally. I myself had to deny collusion with the Israelis when everyone knew it had occurred. The Israelis and the French were boasting of it! Heath particularly, as Chief Whip, tried to get his friends in and the 'old Tories' out. I was replaced by someone later convicted of gross indecency. That's how good Heath's judgement was! You say Julian Amery's appointment to Fitzroy's job works against my thesis, as Amery was pro-Suez, but Amery played an important role in getting rid of Eden.[71]

Within the space of a year, Fitzroy had lost one job and missed the chance of three others. Dodds-Parker had suggested to Eden that Fitzroy be appointed ambassador to Yugoslavia if he agreed to leave the House; Eden seemed agreeable, but then the matter was pushed aside by the Suez crisis.[72] In 1955 Fitzroy was also on the short list as a possible governor of Malaya. Finally, late in 1956 Eden agreed to his promotion as Antony Head's deputy at the Ministry of Defence, and the necessary paperwork had already been done when Macmillan came in.[73] The net result was that at the age of nearly 46 Fitzroy was a 'failed' Minister, relegated to the back benches. His career as a metropolitan English politician was over. For salvation he looked to the land of his fathers.

19

Scottish Laird

IT has been said that in Britain talking about money is regarded as 'bad form' – worse form, indeed, than talking about sex. But Fitzroy's biography would be incomplete without some mention of this most basic of all human concerns. From an old, well-connected family Fitzroy became what the historian David Cannadine called one of the few 'aristocratic' war heroes. He inherited no fortunes – he has earned his money from writing and has inherited some. His marriage to a Lovat daughter did not bring much in the way of liquid assets, for the great Scottish families, though rich in land, are vulnerable to death duties. Indeed, in the 1940s it was the custom in upper-class circles for the groom's family to provide a kind of 'reverse' dowry for the bride.

In 1957 Fitzroy's purchase of the Strachur estate used up much of his financial means. Nowadays, it is true, he possesses considerable wealth in land and flocks – for he has farmed sheep shrewdly and successfully, and of course he also owns his hotel in the Highlands. Veronica worked hard at the Creggans Inn and friends think it has made money for them. Fitzroy's son Jamie is more sceptical. 'My feeling is that Strachur House is just too big and just too much of a responsibility. Its financing? If you want my opinion, it's all done with mirrors.'

Fitzroy is not interested in making money for its own sake. 'One can't imagine him with a career at Hambro's,' says Jakie Astor. 'He's not commercial. He likes what money brings, that's all.' Douglas Dodds-Parker claims that money did not feature as an ambition for his (and Fitzroy's) generation. 'Our ambition was to serve, not make money. Take the Indian Civil Service. Its maximum pension was set at £1,000 a year in 1947 and it was still at the same level in 1957. So no money to be made there. It was job satisfaction and working with like-minded people. That was the ethos of the British Empire. An unimaginable contrast with the television presenters of today. Fitzroy and I were just as happy having bread and cheese with people of like mind as dining in the Savoy Grill.' Yet Fitzroy has a keen sense of the worth of money and how easily it can dribble away. 'I never travel anywhere in the world where I am not paid to do so,' he boasts. This accounts for the narrow track of his journeys – usually to areas where he has acknowledged expertise. Lord Henniker, himself a considerable landowner in Suffolk, sees Fitzroy's attitude as 'lairdly' in a limited sense. 'I do a lot of charitable work, which Fitzroy wouldn't do. I have lots of kids running in and out of my house and Fitz wouldn't do that. Where Fitz sees local lairds as a good thing, I don't think most local gentry are like that.'

Another aristocrat enters a defence for Fitzroy. Here is Lady Hesketh's view: 'Fitzroy, unlike most West Highlanders, is money-minded. That's good, because I get fed up with the fainéant aspect of some West Highlanders. His money-making is in a good cause, to hand on his beautiful home to his family. He's not a self-indulgent man. Yes, he likes a good bottle of wine, but he's not comfort-loving the way most people are. His only indulgence is travel.'

Fitzroy took his dismissal from office stoically; he bore no ill-will towards Macmillan, and his assessment of him as a politician is also characteristically generous. 'At the beginning of 1957 when Eden resigned the Tory party was at a very low ebb and I think Macmillan pulled it together magnificently. He was an extremely cunning politician and I have no doubt that we won the 1959 General Election very largely on his political nous . . . My main reservation was over the 1957 Sandys White Paper, introducing a policy of streamlined nuclear forces, which was a nonsense, really. It became more and more obvious that what we needed for the next twenty years were men on the ground in a lot of places.' But Fitzroy is inclined to blame the Prime Minister who bore the chief responsibility. What happened was that Field-Marshal Dick Hull, who succeeded John Harding as Chief of the Imperial General Staff, produced one report for us in the War Office to the effect that you couldn't get enough men by voluntary recruiting alone. Then he produced Hull report Mark 2 for Macmillan which said the exact opposite and was what Macmillan wanted to hear. The Sandys reforms left an aching void of some 40–50,000 men, and from then on there was no doubt that the Army was short of men for a very long time.'[1]

However spirited Fitzroy's tributes to Macmillan, it is clear that his own dismissal closed an era of his life. For nearly sixteen years he had represented Lancaster and been a conscientious constituency MP. Allan Garnett, who was then a member of Lancaster's Young Conservatives, remembers Fitzroy as very popular with the young Party faithful. His electioneering style leaned heavily on the alleged form-filling bureaucracy of the Labour Party, but this went down well in the largely rural constituency. Like many others, Garnett remarked on the gap between the war-hero image and the self-effacing reality. 'The man we knew was modest, shy and retiring but with an aura, a very definite presence. From time to time he would disappear on his travels to Eastern Europe and, on his return, would speak to the YCs about what he had been up to. In fact, we had the view that he was much too "nice" a man to be involved in the no-holds-barred politics of the time, much less the Richard Hannay type of exploits we knew were commonplace to him.'[2]

There were not many opportunities to promote specifically local initiatives in the House in the post-war decade, but Fitzroy seized any that presented themselves. In a debate on road transport in 1954 he lobbied hard for a by-pass in his constituency to relieve congestion between Warrington and Carnforth, describing the A49 to A6 link as the most dangerous stretch of highway in the country.[3] Five years later the Preston by-pass became Britain's first section of motorway. Fitzroy is quite sure that with Veronica's help he was an efficient constituency member, and that his 'surgeries' gave satisfaction.

> One of the advantages I had, being a back-bench member, was that I had seen politics from the other side, both as Minister and Civil Servant. I knew how the system worked and I knew how to get an answer. If one of my constituents brought me a problem, I would write a civil servant's brief on the problem, then write to the Minister concerned and say, I've had such and such a case drawn to my attention and could you answer the points in my 'minute'. Because Ministers are used to having information processed to them in a certain way, I found my system worked brilliantly. Our government departments take enormous trouble over these sorts of things, quite rightly – it's a very important part of their work and it's what makes the big difference between us and a lot of other countries where no notice at all would be taken of such representations.[4]

The Maclean house at Yealand Conyers was the background to most of the childhood memories of Jeremy and Suki, Veronica's children by Alan Phipps. Jeremy provides an encapsulated memory of the decade from 1946:

> I remember going to Fitzroy's wedding at the age of five. My nanny gave me money for the collection but I upset her by saying, 'I'm going to Mummy's wedding'. I knew right from the start that Jamie and Charlie were half-brothers. Until the age of eight, before going to prep school, I had a governess and was often banished to the nursery for being too noisy. When we did see Fitzroy he tended to lock himself in the library and write. My sister and I saw little of him until we went to Scotland. My school report was always read and discussed closely by my mother, but only vaguely by Fitzroy. When I got a

report from Ampleforth saying that I had learned very little history but could cast a pretty dry fly, my mother was impressed but my stepfather wasn't. I remember her influence at school but not his. But he did train me how to behave at dinner parties. He taught me to talk to adults. He said, try and be as inquisitive as possible about your next-door-neighbour. He's bound to have a fascinating story to tell. You just have to press the right button. I was at a disadvantage in not having my natural father. I suppose I was upset not to have the normal closeness. But I respected the fact that [Fitzroy] was a very busy man. I knew he liked me and loved me. But he was difficult to relate to until one was in one's late teens. He was more relaxed once he became an established writer and politician.[5]

Fitzroy's stepdaughter Suki Paravicini got more attention. 'I was lucky to be the only girl among three boys, and was spoiled by Fitzroy. I was coached by Edith Cooper, his political right arm in Lancaster, and other governesses. I had a very Edwardian upbringing. I didn't go to school until I was 14, and I had been dying to go for years before that. But in those days, if you were a girl and had a pretty face and could speak languages, that was it. My education was lopsided – lots of Latin, French and later German and Italian. I was very lucky, as he adored having pretty girls to stay. He was not so keen on young men unless they were going into the diplomatic service.'[6]

Suki later 'came out' as a débutante. In retrospect she sees the fifties as a curiosity, an era when in the upper classes parents and children (invariably under the aegis of a nanny) were species apart. She did not have dinner with her parents until she was 17: '. . . there was very much a green baize divide between adults and children.' Consequently it was the nanny, Rhoda, who was the great moral influence in Suki's early years; Fitzroy was a creature for occasional 'fun' excursions, visits to Lady Astor, the Tower of London. In some ways the true father-figure was the butler Mr Cockerell, who was always present. But Suki saw a side of public figures kept hidden from their leaders and constituents: Lord David Cecil used to eat scones with the children during 'nursery tea'; Julian Amery, nicknamed 'the Chinese bishop', told them he had a see in China *ex partibus* and liked to eat mice dipped in honey; Lord Salisbury's *gravitas* took the form of soda-siphon fights with Fitzroy.

Suki went through the usual teenage rebellion.

Fitzroy was never very good with small children, couldn't stand the noise. For very many years he was under a lot of strain. In the early years I don't think writing came easily to him. He really had to shut himself away and have absolute silence. A door was closed between the side of the house where his study was situated and the nursery/kitchen side. I resented the fact that he was tetchy. As an only child he was spoiled and always got his way and I think he expected the same in later life. But I wouldn't say I was disillusioned, as I probably wasn't 'illusioned' in the first place. The father-daughter relationship was very close, but there was never that blood tie, which is indefinable, so I didn't need to be disillusioned as a real daughter might be.[7]

Fitzroy's impatience with the very young is confirmed by his natural children. Jamie Maclean remembers: 'You can say that my father has been through three stages in his life: tense when young, all right when middle-aged, and mellow in old age. He was certainly quite tense in the fifties. He didn't like children except to play with – looking after them was the job of mother, nanny and butler. I remember as an under-five having a tantrum because I'd broken a toy. He came roaring in, furious, not with me, but with the nanny for not keeping me quiet. He had been in the study writing an article.'[8]

Fitzroy's marriage to Veronica has endured the vicissitudes of political life. The legion of Veronica's admirers take the view that the marriage has been the making of Fitzroy, unfreezing some of the more austere aspects of an ambitious young man. There are those who feel that before Veronica the serious and the humorous sides of his personality operated independently, and that only after his marriage did he achieve integration. As a couple they have achieved integration in another sense, too, having devised a relationship where their lives work both individually and together. Veronica and Fitzroy spend large segments of their lives away from each other, but this does not indicate a marriage of convenience – reunions are always joyful.

The fact that Fitzroy and Veronica cross swords publicly and are even prepared to have blazing rows in the presence of third parties has encouraged speculation that the marriage might be less than sound, and it is true that Veronica once in exasperation told Suki that but for the fact that she saw Fitzroy only at weekends, the marriage might not have survived. To some extent the altercations are a clash of two strong personalities. To some extent, also, their sensibilities rub each other the wrong way. Veronica is an improviser who can make decisions on the wing. Fitzroy is slow but sure. If people can be divided into those who prefer to get it done and those who prefer to get it right, Fitzroy is assuredly in the latter category. Veronica rattles out words at machine-gun speed, whereas Fitzroy is angry if he is not allowed to speak. Jeanne Clissold, who observed them at close quarters for a number of years, says: 'Fitzroy speaks slowly and that can be dull. He doesn't think fast on his feet, unlike Veronica, who's both a good and a fast speaker.'[9]

Lady Maclean herself attributes their many clashes in part to their different childhood experiences. Fitzroy was an adored only child in a household where stability was the norm. The world came to him; he did not have to go to it. Veronica, on the other hand, was a member of a large family where one had to shout to be heard. Fitzroy had to adapt to the massed battalions of the Lovats, but he managed. Veronica recalls:

'My family had a happier relationship with Fitz than with Alan, my first husband. They overpowered Alan and were not used to sailors. My family takes a lot of standing up to, and Fitz was able to do it.'[10]

Perhaps Fitzroy, nearly 35 when he married, had been a bachelor too long and had become set in his ways.

> Fitz really enjoys the verbal battles we have had. Our arguments have made the children very calm and peaceful, even though they ran during our rows. More often than not Fitz was right. The arguments made him human and removed a lot of Foreign Office stiffness. But in the early days we *were* intolerant of each other. Obsessed and besotted with each other as we were, we locked horns, partly out of a difference of traditions. I was brought up in the tradition that you didn't allow the facts to stand in the way of a good story. But Fitzroy, the scholar and stickler for detail, couldn't bear the inaccuracies. We both learned from each other. He has become less austere and I have become more accurate.

These clashes took their toll of those around them. Even close friends often found the altercation and bickering tiresome. Veronica's cousin Christian Hesketh comments: 'It's been a very successful marriage, but most wives wouldn't have stood him for a second. Fitzroy was peevish, a nagger. "Why haven't you done X? I told you I didn't like Y. I don't have soup with my fish", that sort of thing. Luckily Veronica is a mercurial person, a wonderful housekeeper, very good organizer, not an intellectual but full of ideas and go, and just as Highland as himself. Other things told against the marriage. He didn't want his children brought up as Catholics, which in those days you had to do. All these things made for more aggro. They're still bickering and so it will go on . . . To an outsider it would have seemed an uneasy relationship, which it certainly wasn't.'[11]

Were Catholicism and the education of the children issues? Lady Maclean comments: 'Fitz didn't like it that the children were brought up as Catholics, for this was the rather austere church of Pius XII. But with ecumenism and his trips to the Outer Hebrides, he's seen that Catholicism is a broad Church. He's an Episcopalian and we've come to a happy centre in religion. Since he had agreed to bringing the children up as Catholics, reluctantly, I also reluctantly agreed they could go to Eton. Neither Jamie nor Charlie were happy at Eton. I wish they had gone to Ampleforth. I think schools like Eton are dangerous. It's like sending a 12-year-old to university.'[12] Both Jamie and Charlie were rebellious teenagers, and Veronica is sure that the principal trigger for this was an unsatisfactory experience at their father's school.

How did the children react to the quarrelsome parents? 'It was only at the age of 14, when friends came to stay, that I began to realize that not everybody acted like that' Suki Paravicini says. 'I had thought it perfectly normal. Once, when I was 17, the boys borrowed a tape-recorder and taped one of the altercations while we were driving. We played it back to them later and they couldn't believe it was them.'[13]

Jeremy Phipps remembers: 'I found the rows embarrassing and sometimes used to stay in Lancashire with my mothers' friends to get away. Most of them were political or academic shouting matches, but it was embarrassing when others were present. Charlie found it particularly wearing and on one occasion pretended to be sick, complete with squirted soda from a siphon, to distract attention and break up the wrangle.'[14] Charlie agrees that the altercations were tiresome but adds: '. . . I see it as a safety-valve for two intense, powerful people.'[15]

In middle age people frequently go through crises of identity, and in 1957 Fitzroy finally faced up to a dilemma he had hitherto never satisfactorily solved. Was he primarily a Highlander, or was he a member of the *English* Establishment? By moving his home and family to the Highlands, Fitzroy proved that was where his heart really was.

He put down secure roots in Scotland, the land of his forefathers. Consciously, he wanted to establish his position in the historical tradition of the Macleans. Unconsciously, he may have been reacting to the rootlessness of his childhood. Placing himself firmly as a link in the great chain of Highland being became even more important as dynastic overtones suggested themselves, for in June 1957 Fitzroy was awarded a baronetcy for his political and public services.[16]

The idea of a move to Scotland had been germinating for years. While he was still Under-Secretary of State for War, he was walking one day across the Horse Guards ('where I always seem to have meaningful encounters') when he ran into Bernard Ferguson, who had served with Wingate. Ferguson told him he had just been offered the safe seat of Bute and North Ayrshire, then held by the Deputy Speaker, Charles MacAndrew, who was going to the Lords. However, Ferguson had decided that a political life was not for him and had declined the offer. This was just the chance Fitzroy was looking for. Getting the nod from Ferguson, Fitzroy went straight to the House, found MacAndrew in the chair, and asked about his chances of succeeding to the seat. MacAndrew promised his full support. Shortly afterwards Alec Cameron, chairman of the Bute and North Ayrshire Conservative Association, came down to London to take informal soundings.[17]

These developments first manifested themselves publicly after Fitzroy's dismissal by Macmillan. It was announced that for purely personal reasons Brigadier Maclean would not be standing for Lancaster again; a month later the news broke that he had been named as prospective candidate for Bute and North Ayrshire. The adoption procedure went off without a hitch and, defending a 9,000 majority, Fitzroy looked certain to be a Scottish MP at the next general election.[18]

There were some rumblings of discontent about the ease with which Fitzroy had switched his base. David Lambie, the Labour candidate who had fought MacAndrew in 1955 and was to take on Fitzroy unsuccessfully in 1959, 1964 and 1966, thought that Central Office and Veronica's family connections between them had played too big a role. 'The local Tory party wanted someone local, someone who would work in the constituency. MacAndrew had not been seen much in the constituency. But Fitzroy wasn't that sort of person either. Because of the power of the Lovats Fitzroy was forced on the constituency. The Lovats shouldn't have used their power in that way. In those days Central Office of the Tory party had more power to impose than nowadays.'[19] Antonia Fraser is sceptical. 'Power of the Lovats? The only politician in the family was Hugh [her own ex-husband], who had no clout in the west of Scotland and had himself decided to go south of the border. He was told that to be a laird's brother would arouse great resentment in Scotland, and that was why he never tried for the Inverness seat and went to the Midlands. He certainly took the line that there was *no* power of the Lovats. Anyway, the decision to go to Scotland to the new constituency and become Scots was all Fitzroy.'[20]

The second stage in Fitzroy's relocation to Scotland was the purchase for £40,000 of Strachur House and the surrounding estate in the Argyllshire village of the same name. In June 1957 Fitzroy bought 7,500 acres in all. The estate included the 20-room Strachur House with 300 acres, Inverglen Farm and 600 acres, the Creggans Inn, whose licence was transferred to Fitzroy, and a further huge acreage of timberland. Three months later he sold his house in Yealand Conyers.[21] Being based in Strachur partly answered the objection that he was an 'imposed English MP'.

The constituency of Bute and North Ayrshire was a geographical oddity, consisting of the Isles of Arran and Bute and a mainland strip of North Ayrshire. Rothesay, on the Isle of Bute, was the chief town, and there are all kinds of relatively inaccessible crannies, like the tiny island of Millport opposite Largs. It was a very difficult constituency to represent and campaign in because of the water. To live in any one of the three areas would have been to give offence to the other two; Fitzroy's solution was to live just outside the constituency, but within easy reach of all three localities.

Taking over the Creggans Inn (then only a quarter the size it is today) meant adding hotelier to the multiple roles Fitzroy had filled in his career. Fitzroy and Veronica were no more than enthusiastic amateurs, and the first thing was to find a manager. Rhoda Cockerell, the nanny, had a sister who was just retiring as matron of an enormous military hospital in Nigeria, and it had always been her ambition to run a hotel. She jumped at the chance of becoming manageress. At the very last moment, however, the Queen Alexandra's Royal Army Nursing Corps decided it would not find a suitable replacement for the outgoing matron in Nigeria, and cajoled her into staying on. In the end Fitzroy and Veronica decided to manage the hotel themselves, short-term. Rhoda Cockerell, her husband the butler and Jeanne Thomlinson, Fitzroy's secretary, doubled as hotel staff for a while. In the early days a visitor could have witnessed the interesting spectacle of Sir Fitzroy Maclean, Bt., former head of the political and military mission to Tito, taking guests' bags upstairs and being tipped for his trouble. Fitzroy comments: 'Those six months were awfully useful because we learned a lot about running hotels and, with just six bedrooms and a dining-room that seated no more than twenty people, we could cope. Then at the end of six months Rhoda's sister finally retired from the Army and was able to come and take over.'[22]

There have been only five managers in thirty-five years. The second and third manageresses put in fifteen years' service each, which is a tribute to Fitzroy and Veronica as employers in an industry notorious for the rapidity of staff turnover. The early worries concerned money, not personnel. In their first year the hotel made a profit of £1,500 – a reasonable sum in the mid-fifties. Encouraged, Fitzroy put in another twenty rooms, then another storey, then a set of dormer windows. The turnover shot up from £5,000 a year to £50,000, but the profit of £1,500 became a loss of £5,000. 'We were innocents abroad. All we knew was what food we liked, and we imagined everyone else would like it too. That part of it was fine, the hotel was always full and everyone was happy. Then we got the accountants in and they told us we weren't charging enough. We also learned some of the hidden snags to the hotel business, one of which is that it takes years to build up and that with a bad manager the whole thing can go right down in a matter of months.'[23]

How did the move to Scotland affect the children? Basically, Jeremy welcomed the move and Suki deplored it. 'Suki wasn't all that pleased about going to Scotland,' says Jeremy Phipps,

> . . . she . . . was at an age [16] when uprooting is not welcome. I, on the other hand, was delighted because of the hills and the sport. The move changed the sibling rivalry in my favour. Fitzroy was delighted that he could talk to me about the landscape and explain the meaning of Scotland to me. I was happy there and had never been really comfortable in Lancashire. Also, I was rather jealous of Fitzroy's partiality for Suki. Fitzroy thoroughly enjoyed it when Suki was coming out and enjoyed showing this beautiful stepdaughter on the London scene. I thought that unfair but thought it was one of the advantages of being a girl. But at least by moving to Scotland I felt that something was working in my favour. Also, once Fitzroy got to Scotland, with an estate and countryside, he relaxed more.[24]

Jamie remembers Strachur as the beginning of his happy relationship with his father, for it was there that Fitzroy started to read to him. 'As an MP's children we were not roped into garden fêtes and stuff like that. But my father used to read M. R. James ghost stories to me at an age when I was probably too young to be read material like that. As an impressionable seven-year-old, I was terrified having to go to bed, after spending a highly enjoyable time in my father's study. But I have to say that Strachur itself was not at all menacing.'[25]

Making Scotland his permanent base also obliged Fitzroy to regularize his position within his clan. In the fifteenth century the clan Maclean had split into two main branches. Fitzroy's family was descended from the Macleans of Ardgour, while the clan chiefs descended in the line of the Macleans of Duart, who also held the hereditary title of Keeper of the Castle of Dunconnel until they were deprived of that office in favour of the Campbells of Argyll after the Glorious Revolution. In the twentieth century a crisis of succession arose when Alexander Maclean of Ardgour died in 1932, leaving a widow and five daughters. Immediately litigation ensued through the Lyon Court, Scotland's court of chivalry, to determine whether a woman could succeed as chief. There was a further complication in that the land accompanying the title was entailed, to exclude women. Fitzroy's father's eldest brother Henry now seemed clearly the male heir in default of heirs male of Alexander. The protracted litigation cost thousands of pounds and poisoned relations in the extended Maclean family. The case hinged on the technical point whether chiefs, recognized by the Lord of the Isles in medieval days, had rights that prevailed over chieftains, recognized by the joint monarchs of England and Scotland after 1603. But in reality, says Fitzroy, 'the battle was between two women: Alex's widow and my uncle Henry's wife'.[26]

The matter was further complicated by the fact that Fitzroy's uncle Henry had no children, but his case was aided by recognition from the clan chief Maclean of Duart ('Chips' Maclean) and the Maclean Clan Association. In the end Henry Maclean did indeed win the case, but shortly afterwards a new Lyon King-of-Arms was appointed, who switched the judgement to one of Fitzroy's cousins. Henry Maclean retaliated by making Fitzroy his heir over the head of the cousin (the son of Henry's younger brother; Fitzroy's father, Charles, was the third of the brothers). Meanwhile the eldest of Alex's five daughters, Catriona, who had no children, named her nephew Robin as Maclean of Ardgour, by deed poll.

When Fitzroy received his baronetcy, he had no wish to stir matters further. But a baronet must take a title, and at first Fitzroy chose to style himself Baron Maclean of Strachur. This, however, was deemed unsatisfactory, as Strachur lay in Campbell territory and there was already a perfectly good Campbell of Strachur. Fitzroy took soundings with 'Chips' Maclean, the Clan Association and Malcolm Innes, the new Lyon King-of-Arms, whose father's reversal of judgement had caused so much confusion. They decided to revive an ancient chieftainship: the captaincy of Dunconnel and the Isles of the Sea. The previous 'keeper' of Dunconnel, 14th in that line, had been the Jacobite Sir John Maclean, deprived of his hereditary office in 1691. Fitzroy then had to square the arrangement with all interested Macleans, including Robin of Ardgour and the owner Lord Sandys, an Englishman who had no particular sentimental attachment to the title. It says much for Fitzroy's talents as a diplomat that he was able to achieve his ends without ruffling feathers; but it was 1980 before a document granted him the 'sovereignty' of Dunconnel – now a ruined castle on Mull – together with the hearthstone of the original castle. Henceforth he was Captain and Keeper of Dunconnel.

All of this may seem to the outsider like much ado about nothing, but Veronica's cousin Christian Hesketh remarks: 'Fitzroy has tremendously strong clan feelings. Kin means much more to Scots than to the English. There are times when Fitzroy even gets agitated because Strachur is Campbell territory, which in a way makes his house a Campbell house, but its proximity to Mull and the west coast makes it all right. I like his Highland pzazz. Nobody in the world but a Highlander would think it worthwhile to get himself made Keeper of Dunconnel. He has registered a coat-of-arms over which he has gone to a lot of trouble.'[27]

The late 1950s brought a third significant development in Fitzroy's life. Although he had earlier stoutly denied the assertion of Gilbert Murray, the classical scholar and tireless worker for world peace, that the death of Stalin heralded a change in the Soviet Union,[28] Fitzroy gradually conceded much of Murray's position, particularly after his trip to the Soviet Union in June 1958, his first visit for nearly twenty years.

The following year Macmillan played a shrewd electioneering card by going to Moscow and being photographed with Khruschev; he came back to England wearing a fur hat, and the impression disseminated by the Tory propaganda machine that he was now a 'world statesman' is thought to have contributed to his victory in the October 1959 general election. On his return Macmillan called Fitzroy to Number 10 to discuss the formation of a body that would foster genuine cultural links between the two countries. At that time all educational and cultural exchanges between Britain and the Soviet Union were handled by the Anglo-Soviet 'Friendly Societies', which were widely thought to be no more than front organizations for the Communist Party. Doyen of these exchange schemes was Dr Hewlett Johnson, Dean of Canterbury, not actually a Communist but proud of the soubriquet 'the Red Dean' which he had picked up during the Spanish Civil War.[29] Johnson was the cynosure of Soviet eyes, as a revealing anecdote makes clear. The Master of Pembroke College, Oxford was showing the Soviet Cultural Attaché round the college and pointed out Dr Samuel Johnson's teapot. 'This is the teapot from which Dr Johnson poured so many cups of tea,' said the Master. A light came into the attaché's eye. 'Oh, that is very helpful. Our people are most interested in everything connected with Dr Hewlett Johnson.'[30]

It was to combat Hewlett Johnson and his acolytes that Fitzroy and others of like mind came up with the idea of a Great Britain–USSR Society, which would run exchange programmes with non-Communist British hosts. After all, Fitzroy explained, 'What was the point of Russians coming to Britain to get their own propaganda served up to them? That could be more efficiently done by staying in Russia.'[31]

It was important that the new organization have a bipartisan approach, and on the Labour benches a man whose mind had been working along similar lines was Christopher Mayhew, Fitzroy's 'employer' on the 1947 Displaced Persons mission.[32] Earl Attlee (as he now was) agreed to be President and Fitzroy was appointed Executive Chairman of the new organization; he was chosen over Mayhew as there was a Tory government in power.

In 1959 Fitzroy made another trip to the Soviet Union, this time with Mayhew, as a kind of reconnaissance mission. Fitzroy had shown his anti-Soviet colours clearly between 1939 and 1941, but he was as a lamb compared with Mayhew, who describes himself openly as 'an experienced cold warrior'. Mayhew had a virulent distaste for Hewlett Johnson and felt that the Communist-to-Communist exchanges hitherto had merely succeeded in netting new recruits for the Soviet security services. The two men had diametrically opposed views on policies east of Suez, but Mayhew always felt warmly towards Fitzroy for having helped him out in Yugoslavia in 1947. Mayhew relates: 'We were both very robust. We weren't paid by the government so we had nothing to lose. We laid on a lot of visits and student exchanges, which encouraged the dissidents of Leningrad. I remember sitting round a table with Fitzroy and all these ghastly Stalinist bureaucrats, Soviet culture-vultures, et cetera. Making toasts and winking at each other, being disliked by the Russians. They knew what we were up to and we knew they knew.'[33]

The Great Britain–USSR Society proved a great success. Once established, it worked closely with the British Council and the Foreign and Commonwealth Office, through which it received an annual grant-in-aid. In time it drew in the great and the good to membership of its council. Its chairman usually had a distinguished record in Soviet affairs, but the office of president was even more prestigious. Fitzroy became the third president, in the late 1960s. Mayhew was rather disappointed not to be offered the post, as by that time there was a Labour government, but George Brown 'took against' him on the basis that his fervent support for the Palestinians made him 'too controversial'. Fitzroy in turn handed over the presidency to Harold Wilson in the 1970s.

John Roberts, the present Director of the Great Britain–USSR Society, found ex-president Fitzroy too much of a prima donna for his taste. 'Fitzroy, a freelance buccaneer, does not understand the problems of organizations and wants quick *ad hoc* solutions. He also wants to be top gun. He made a lot of waves when he retired as president by wanting a splendid title. I objected that we had too many titles and functions as it was. Soon we would be like the LSO with Music Director, Principal Conductor, Emeritus Conductor, Conductor Laureate and all the rest of it. Too many titles lessen any organization's credibility.'[34]

Naturally, there have always been cold warriors who think that any form of contact with the 'evil empire' is unjustifiable, and Fitzroy concedes that both he and the Society went through bruising times in 1968 when Brezhnev sent the Red Army into Czechoslovakia to suppress Alexander Dubcek's experiment with 'socialism with a human face', and again in 1979 when the Soviets invaded Afghanistan. He feels, however, that the record of cultural links speaks for itself, and that no apologies are necessary.

In 1957 Fitzroy brought out his second book, *Disputed Barricade*, a lengthy analysis of Tito and Titoism. The book's gestation had not been easy. Jeanne Clissold, who typed his first four books and large segments of the others, says: 'Fitzroy always wrote many drafts and cannibalized them, but it could be a nightmare when all the different drafts got mixed up. *Eastern Approaches* was fairly straightforward, but the worst one, the really terrible one, was *Disputed Barricade*.'[35] Many who had thrilled to the high adventure of *Eastern Approaches* eight years earlier found the book a disappointment, of interest only to specialists. Jeremy Phipps remarks: 'I was thrilled by *Eastern Approaches* as a boy and was expecting something similar, but I found *Disputed Barricade* much heavier going.'[36] Reviewers, however, found much to admire.

As his political hopes faded and the Soviet Union opened up to Western travellers, Fitzroy increasingly turned himself into a travel writer. Nineteen fifty-eight saw the publication of *A Person from England*, an account of early British travellers in Russia inspired by a whirlwind tour through the Soviet Union in June that year. *The Times* reviewer unerringly put his finger on Fitzroy's dilemma: 'What do such people as the heroes of these stories find to do nowadays? Can it be only to write up the powers of their predecessors?'[37]

The next thirty years, as Fitzroy converted himself to something like a professional traveller, produced a spate of books on his journeys into the remoter parts of the Soviet Union, as well as general histories of Russia and works of popular sociology. The later books always won respectful reviews from the critics, but friends and close observers usually found them wanting. 'He makes quite a lot go a long way. I used to tell him he'd written the same book every five years', says Jakie Astor; and Peter Carey 'found the travel books disappointing and turgid, not very well assembled in terms of material. The historical part of his travel was not well presented'; 'Not great literature or great history and not poetic. Says more about him than his subject', is Linda Bullard's comment.

To some extent the disappointment reflects a debate about what travel writing should be. Pamela Egremont, a close friend whom he influenced to become a traveller, comments: 'I wouldn't travel with Fitzroy, quite apart from the consideration that with him there could be just one master. I have my own way of travelling and it's not Fitzroy's. I don't take a camera and I like to stay for ten days in an ostensibly dull place and soak up the atmosphere. In his first travels Fitzroy did that, but nowadays it's always to make a film or a book. He wants constant excitement or good material for his books and films – good copy, in a word – and this is the difference between now and *Eastern Approaches*.'[38]

Yet in many ways Fitzroy is superbly equipped to be a great traveller. He can rough it and accept hardships, can tolerate the boredom of cancelled flights and long bus journeys better than most, and always goes prepared. He has a preferred area of operations – the Soviet Union from Europe to Siberia – and is a good linguist. He is also an accomplished enough photographer to have had his work published in the *Sunday Times* and other newspapers. A true traveller prefers to make his way in little-known areas but has an expertise within those areas. It is quite clear that tourism as against travel has no interest for Fitzroy.

Moreover, he is a romantic – an essential qualification for the true traveller. It was the Romantic movement and the cults of the picturesque and sublime that vastly expanded the range of what appeals to travellers. Until Rousseau's time there had been no sentimental love of nature, and until Scott's no spirit of enquiry into 'all sorts and conditions of men'. Before the Romantic movement, travellers were interested in the ways in which Man had conquered Nature; after it, the interest shifted to the ways in which Nature could not be conquered. Byron described travel as life's most powerful excitement after ambition; for him its purpose was to heighten sensation and intensify the sense of being alive. Childe Harold seeks change at any cost, even death.

Fitzroy seeks out danger to a point which might be mistaken for a 'death wish'. Alistair Milne puts this into perspective. 'I think Fitzroy is to the twentieth century what Burton was to the nineteenth. Like Burton, taking huge risks in uncharted areas. He likes danger – that's a key. Always did. That's why he found Parliament so boring and preferred Russian or Yugoslav affairs. Another person with this taste for danger is David Attenborough. The more they told him the Komodo dragon was dangerous, the more he wanted to go. Fitzroy has the same instinct. Rather carnivorous, you might say – the more dangerous it is the better.'[39]

Fitzroy's career as traveller acquired a fresh dimension in the 1960s when he turned himself into a film-maker as well as writer. This is a difficult transition to make, and the opportunity was provided by Grace Wyndham Goldie, the dynamic Controller of BBC Television in the fifties. Fitzroy describes their meeting. 'As you know, MPs get on telly a lot. I met Grace through my appearance on some television programme. She had a stable of young talent called ''Grace's young men'' – people like Alistair Milne, Donald Baverstock, Paul Fox, who all later became big figures in television. She was an enormously determined lady and had a terrific word of command and built the BBC up – it was her whole life, though there was a husband somewhere in the background. We became friends.'[40]

Fitzroy appreciates powerful and dynamic women and his feeling for Grace Wyndham Goldie is like his later admiration for Mrs Thatcher. 'He likes people who speak their mind, especially women', comments Jeanne Clissold. 'He was very fond of Grace Wyndham Goldie even though she tore him off a strip once or twice.'[41] Michael Gill, the BBC producer with whom Fitzroy later worked in Russia, claims to remember one of these 'strip-tearing' occasions.

I think it was 1958. At that time I was PA in what was then called Talks Department of the BBC and was working on *Monitor*. For some reason I was in the hospitality room when Grace Wyndham Goldie came storming in. Then Fitzroy came in with the producer of *Panorama*. As soon as he entered, in a crowded room full of strangers, Grace did her party trick, which was to remove her spectacles in an imperial manner. She went up to Maclean and said, 'Fitzroy, you really must be less wooden in the way you talk and present material.' Fitzroy, who was twice her size, listened attentively and said he would do his best. That's one side of him. I thought it was endearing that even though so gifted he was remarkably modest.[42]

Fitzroy explained to Goldie that he would like to shoot a film about Central Asia himself. This was an unusual request, and it is doubtful that anyone with less panache than Fitzroy could have got away with it. But it was the sort of aplomb that appealed to Goldie and she kept his plan in the back of her mind. Finally, in 1962, approval and funding were given for a programme about Soviet Turkestan. Fitzroy was confident that with his Soviet contacts he could get approval for filming. The pilot film was to be about Samarkand and Bokhara, with plans for a follow-up on Georgia if the pioneering effort was successful. Goldie introduced Fitzroy to Alistair Milne, then a producer on the highly successful *Tonight* programme. To train Fitzroy as cameraman Milne selected Slim Hewitt.

No more incongruous 'odd couple' could be imagined than Fitzroy the patrician Etonian and Slim Hewitt, the acerbic cigar-chomping Cockney. Whenever *Tonight* needed a particularly cynical view of the world, they would encourage Hewitt to come out from behind his camera and deliver a jaundiced commentary on mankind's follies and foibles. An Army Film Unit cameraman in the war, and later one of *Picture Post*'s star stills photographers, Hewitt soon graduated to film and cinematography.[43] Fitzroy confounded expectations by getting on extremely well with him, but his apprenticeship on the Bolex – a little hand-cranked 16 mm camera of the time – was arduous. Alistair Milne recalls: 'Fitzroy went out on his own to do the filming in Bokhara. I'd never seen the walls of Bokhara before and I remember having to view them through Fitzroy's amateur filming. The first results were terrible because Fitzroy would not stop shooting, and kept panning in an amateurish way. A year later Slim Hewitt went out and they did a film on Georgia together. This was the first time anything had been seen of Georgia since World War II.'[44]

Fitzroy remembers learning to shoot film as being full of problems. 'Slim Hewitt came up to Strachur. There was an old man lived in one of the cottages who used to cycle across the bridge and would try to pose balancing on his bicycle in the belief that we were taking still photographs. No matter how many times we told him, he never grasped the principle of movies. Later on I used to practise in the zoo, which was good because you could film people as they looked at the animals without their noticing you. If you tried filming courting couples in Hyde Park you were likely to get into a lot of trouble. I've always said that even if what I shot wasn't high-class stuff, at least it was useful to me in understanding the problems of cameramen.'[45]

As well as learning cinematography, Fitzroy also acted as narrator and presenter on his documentaries. He attracted much the same criticism as in the House of Commons.'He was never very good at talking to camera,' says Alistair Milne. 'He's a rather *louche* performer in that respect.'[46] The producer John Purdie, with whom Fitzroy worked in the 1980s, agrees. 'He's a bit set in his ways and can't change his style, which isn't right for television. He considers what he says. He's not given to a flip approach, so needs a lot of producing. He's not easy on camera. His manner is too patrician, not relaxed enough. But as an adviser he was excellent and full of ideas. Sometimes you had to wean him off a choice that was made for hedonistic reasons rather than the best for the programme. But once overruled, he would accept it.'[47]

Fitzroy's determination to succeed in television demonstrates his formidable willpower. He practises incessantly until he reaches his required standard, and in this way has mastered golf, tennis and photography. His life is a testament to Balzac's dictum that there is no great talent without willpower. His combination of taking pains, circumspection and physical courage makes an unbeatable combination and often comes across as ruthlessness. 'Marvellous at convincing people that their interests would be served by doing what was in his interest,' is Pamela Egremont's way of putting it.[48] But Alistair Milne takes a harsher view. 'Fitzroy has a ruthless streak. One of his great characteristics is to be relentless in pressure to get people to go his way . . . A man of tremendous stamina and mental energy. A bit like Grace herself – she bored away until she got her own way.'[49]

Fitzroy was well capable of requiting any rebuffs from media men or women. Jeanne Clissold cites a case: 'I remember once the BBC coming to record. The production girl hadn't done her homework and we were getting the usual BBC nonsense about how we must hurry to avoid overtime, simultaneously with insistence that we break for tea. That's not Fitz's way of working at all. I often worked very late, very often because he wouldn't be hurried. He thought people should work at what they were doing until they finished it properly. I was sitting in the kitchen out of the way and he came in once and said, "It's very funny in there and I'm being as awkward as I know how." Which is *very* awkward.'[50]

By the early sixties, then, Fitzroy was acting a number of roles at once: MP, doyen of Anglo-Russian relations, hotelier, writer, traveller, film-maker. There are those who think that constant activity is a sign of underlying depression or, as Robert Louis Stevenson puts it: 'Extreme *busyness*, whether at school, college, Kirk or market, is a symptom of deficient vitality; and a faculty for idleness implies a catholic appetite and a strong sense of personal identity.'[51] Identity is always under threat from a multiplicity of roles, but nobody could accuse Fitzroy of deficient vitality, and it has always been his belief that the route to happiness in the vale of tears is always to have too much to do. It is interesting to find two distinguished Scotsmen so much at variance.

20

Farewell to Politics

F ITZROY'S political orientation often puzzles observers, but this is because we are used to Toryism in its post-war guise, when the Disraelian element has been increasingly discarded. In fact Fitzroy is a *Scottish* Tory of a traditional hue. 'I'm a romantic Tory,' he confesses.

This implies a backward-looking world view, but there is nothing of the reactionary in Fitzroy. His pursuit of 'intimations' and his view that theory is simply an 'abridgement' of practice, not a guide to it, bring him close to the empirical Tories like Hume, Burke and Oakeshott. The two political thinkers most often quoted by Fitzroy are Burke and Lenin, whose dictum 'who, whom' expresses in a nutshell the view of politics as the study of power. Some have criticized as rather naïve Fitzroy's belief in the possibilities of meritocracy within societies stratified on hereditary principles, as when he remarks in *Holy Russia*: 'As in Victorian Britain, there are plentiful opportunities for the working class, the proletariat, if sufficiently shrewd and industrious, to better themselves, to improve their position and, given time and opportunity, to climb to who knows what heights on the social ladder.'

There is a Burkean flavour to many of Fitzroy's social utterances. 'With time, experience has shown, the steam goes out of crusades, but never out of human nature.' An unchanging human nature, with biology forever having the better of culture, is one of the givens of Fitzroy's philosophy. 'My basic criticism of whatever you like to call it – State Socialism, Communism – is that it doesn't take sufficient account of human nature and it doesn't work and it is therefore very vulnerable to ordinary life. Stalin made it work in a sort of way by total terror, but as attempted by ordinary so-called Social Democrats socialism doesn't work. I'm glad to have lived long enough to have seen that so conclusively proved. That's one of the reasons I became a Conservative and have always been a Conservative. Human nature is an enormously powerful force and in the end makes hay of any system that tries to leave it out of account.'

But he resists any suggestion of 'original sin' conservatism, that human beings are essentially a bad lot, and that socialism goes wrong because it takes too idealistic a view. 'Human beings, I believe, are capable of wonderful things, as I saw again and again in the war. But if you have a system that doesn't take into account their ambitions, feelings and other aspirations, then it won't work.'

His remarks on everyday politics are always amusing and refreshingly down-to-earth. Fitzroy must be the least snobbish member of the British Establishment. He defends John Major against the charge that a 'bank manager' background is inadequate for political leadership. 'I see no reason why accountants should not be just as good leaders as historians or classical scholars.'

Almost as soon as Fitzroy became a Scottish MP, Harold Macmillan offered him a peerage. Fitzroy turned it down on two grounds. In the first place, the House of Lords seemed to contain all the undesirable aspects of the Commons with none of its advantages. Second, he considered it would anyway have been hypocritical, after his pronouncements of delight at representing a Scottish constituency, to decamp almost immediately for the Lords.[1]

After his move to the Bute and North Ayrshire seat, Fitzroy became a back-bench MP of classical stripe. He confined his parliamentary interventions to defence and Army matters and issues affecting Scotland. He continued to urge that conscription was necessary for Britain's defence, and that cuts in conventional forces 'justifiable' by the nuclear umbrella were disastrous. That Fitzroy eludes easy political classification is clear from his utterences on defence. He continued to believe that the Soviet Union was the West's principal military enemy, but he parted company decisively with those who put their trust in an 'independent' nuclear deterrent for Britain.

Fitzroy always saw more clearly than others who opposed nuclear weapons that there were no easy solutions. Anti-nuclear campaigners often opposed conscription as well, which to Fitzroy was nonsense. He never believed in the efficacy of civil disobedience against a ruthless foe and, since he is not a pacifist, it seemed obvious to him that the choice narrowed to nuclear deterrence or conscription. This issue could not be fudged. Fitzroy also considered that well-armed and numerous conventional forces offered a defence second to none. Steeped in diplomacy and *realpolitik*, he saw through the scaremongering of pro-nuclear zealots who argued that the Soviet Union could compel British surrender by threatening to use nuclear weapons against a non-nuclear island. Fitzroy realized that all statesmen, even the most morally repugnant like Stalin, pursued rational aims and that for a whole host of reasons, deriving from political realities, not sentiment or morality, doomsday scenarios did not apply to the real world.

The tenor of his remarks over fifteen years as a Scottish MP is remarkably consistent. He always vigorously opposed a British nuclear deterrent while, as an advocate of the North Atlantic Alliance, he argued that it was for the Americans to decide where they wanted to site their nuclear bases to meet a perceived threat. In some quarters this was seen as being 'soft on the Americans': Fitzroy had thus now been accused of complaisance towards Yugoslavia, the Soviet Union and the USA.

Fitzroy was always very clear that the Sandys White Paper of 1957, taking Britain down the path of an 'independent' nuclear deterrent, was a wrong turning. In a debate in February 1959 he argued that Britain could not afford the endless cycle of 'rocket and counter-rocket' and that an extra 20,000 men in the Army would do more than Blue Streak or any other missile to enable the nation to play its part in the world.[2] In a debate in March 1960 he drew laughter from his fellow members when, arguing that nuclear defence was a costly disaster, he said: 'How could Britain afford to compete? It was not a question of keeping up with the Joneses, but of keeping up with the Rocket-fellers.'[3] But at the same time he would have no truck with CND or nuclear disarmers who wanted a neutral Britain. Nineteen sixty was the year the Labour Party Conference first alarmed centrist Labour MPs by committing the party to unilateralism. When in December 1960, the turbulent Reg Prentice, later to convert from Labour to Thatcherism, argued for US Polaris bases in Holy Loch, Fitzroy gave him full support.[4]

In tandem with his opposition to Britain's independent deterrent, Fitzroy argued time and again for an increase in Army numbers via conscription. The crux of the problem, as he explained patiently over and over again, was the 'contradiction' between the 200,000 the 1957 Hull Committee had fixed as the minimum for fulfilling Britain's commitments and the 165,000 Government actuaries reckoned as the absolute maximum obtainable by recruiting. Repeatedly Fitzroy stressed that the shortfall in Army numbers could have only one result: British overseas commitments would have to be curtailed.[5] His Parliamentary comments on defence became increasingly strong; with the passage of years it became obvious that his own party was marginalizing him while his views were borne out by events. In 1962 he voted against the government's Commonwealth Immigration Bill, partly out of dissatisfaction with the legislation itself but mainly as a way of showing distaste for the Army Reserve Bill. To Opposition cheers he accused the Tory government of having wasted the House's time for the past five years by its cynical attitude to Army recruiting.[6] In a debate in March 1963 he declared: 'It should be clear even to the layman that the development of a credible nuclear deterrent, and in particular the development of a delivery system, was economically beyond Britain.'[7]

Fitzroy was dismayed by the way, every time he urged the government to take seriously its manpower commitments to NATO lest the Americans pull out from Europe in disgust, the government apparently responded by withdrawing garrisons east of Suez to bolster the British Army of the Rhine. He made it clear that he wanted a strong British contingent in NATO and a formidable presence worldwide. To the predictable government protests that they could not afford both, Fitzroy answered that they seemed able to afford the much more expensive luxury of NATO commitment and an 'independent' nuclear deterrent.[8]

The Labour government of 1964 to 1970 fulfilled all Fitzroy's worst fears, persisting with the nuclear deterrent while withdrawing east of Suez. Far from increasing the size of the Army via conscription, the Army now reduced its volunteer strength. This brought the Army issue right into Fitzroy's back yard, since among the victims of retrenchment were some of the most famous Scottish regiments. In 1962 their numbers had been cut from six to four; 1967 saw them halved again. Fitzroy was aghast. The one area where recruitment had never been a problem was Scotland. Cynics spoke of the impetus of unemployment, but Fitzroy believed the reputations of the Scottish regiments, resting in part on a fierce local pride incomprehensible to England, was the true explanation. In an era of falling recruitment he could think of no better way of accelerating the disastrous trend than abolishing celebrated regiments like the Argyll and Sutherland Highlanders and the 2nd Battalion, Scots Guards. In despair at the way that the government, by 1967, seemed set on merging all the old Scottish regiments into two large conglomerates, he suggested ironically that Harold Wilson and Denis Healey, the Defence Secretary, should produce a 'government tartan' to match.[9]

By 1970 Fitzroy was becoming tired of the way those advocating conscription were portrayed as benighted backwoodsmen. He called for the issue to be lifted above party political point-scoring and for conscription to be treated sensibly, not simply used as a smear word. Here, as elsewhere, he was too subtle. In a debate in March 1969 he said Denis Healey was right to point out that Britain's defence choice was now continuing nuclear escalation or surrender to the Russians. Few noticed the ironical stress he gave to the word 'now'. Exactly a year later in another defence debate Fitzroy made the point explicit: nuclear defence left the narrow choice of suicide or surrender.[10]

On foreign affairs generally Fitzroy was nothing like as vociferous as he had been in the immediate post-war decade, and his pronouncements were fewer. He opposed withdrawal from Aden, the last outpost east of Suez, and called for a tough line towards Spain over Gibraltar. Initially, at least, he supported US involvement in Vietnam, but then in warfare Fitzroy is invariably a hawk, having supported the Korean, Vietnam, Falklands and Gulf conflicts.[11] In 1968, on the occasion of the Soviet invasion of Czechoslovakia, he neatly conflated the themes of opposition to Soviet military power and the necessity of supporting Tito during the war. He stressed that the West needed to express strong feelings over Czechoslovakia to prevent the Russians trying the same thing elsewhere, possibly in Yugoslavia, and argued that what the world had just witnessed in Czechoslovakia would have been seen in far worse form if the advice of the pro-Mihailovic faction had been heeded.[12]

Fitzroy was a supporter of the EEC from the earliest days, and in 1972 was among a delegation of MPs to the European Parliament in Strasbourg. He has always been a devoted royalist, a favourite at the Palace and a special friend of the Queen Mother, so that when Willie Hamilton and others brought the Royal Family under heavy fire in a debate in December 1971 over increasing the Civil List, Fitzroy was one of the foremost in the fray. He defended the increase and challenged Labour MPs to say whether they favoured a republic, the presidency of which would cost more. His growing television expertise, both as film-maker and presenter, enabled him to make a thoughtful contribution to the debate in October 1972 on televising Parliament. Fitzroy argued that film editing, a necessary part of visual presentation, would distort reality, and he referred to the sensational material in the last Parliament: 'There was the leader of the Liberal Party being assaulted by MPs, Miss Bernadette Devlin pulling the Home Secretary's hair, and MPs singing the Red Flag . . .'[13]

Between 1959 and 1974 Fitzroy also performed valiantly on Scottish affairs, speaking in regional debates, in defence of Scottish regiments and Scottish soldiers killed by the IRA in Northern Ireland, writing about the depopulation of the Isle of Arran as a result of government neglect.[14] His Labour opponent in the Bute and North Ayrshire constituency, David Lambie, pays tribute to his work: 'At that time we were experiencing grave economic difficulties. Shipyards closing, steelworks in difficulty and ICI, which in wartime employed 12,000, cutting back. We put pressure on ICI to get government investment through regional bodies. Fitzroy Maclean worked well with us and exerted tremendous pressure behind the scenes with ICI, the Scottish Office and the Department of Industry. We ended up with one of the biggest investments, guaranteeing 800 jobs – the nylon plant at Ardeir. Eight hundred permanent jobs and another 800 indirect jobs via contractors. Sir Fitzroy must take a lot of the credit for his pressure and for working so well with a Labour borough council and a Labour county council.'[15]

However, Fitzroy's rapport with the Labour opposition in Scotland took time to mature. Like many people who have encountered him, David Lambie formed an unfavourable impression initially. But, also like most, he ended as an admirer. 'I met him just before the 1959 election. I had built up an image of him on the strength of *Eastern Approaches* and was disappointed. He came across, well, to put it bluntly, like a great big public schoolboy. A gentleman, of course, but very quiet, looked as though he wouldn't say boo to a goose. I began to wonder whether what I had read was correct. But after a while I realized I was quite wrong; he was in fact a man of steel.'[16] Lambie drew blood early in his gladiatorial combats with Fitzroy in the constituency by claiming he was better known in Mongolia than in Arran. The tag 'MP for Outer Mongolia' stuck, and did Fitzroy harm. It was all very well for him to rest on the authority of Burke, who famously declared that he had been elected to represent Bristol in the House of Commons, not the House of Commons in Bristol, but Scottish constituents did not see it that way.

The logistics of visiting such a geographically awkward constituency as Bute and North Ayrshire in the early sixties, certainly for an MP without a private helicopter, were formidable. Even commuting from the House of Commons to Strachur House was a consideration in those days. It involved a train journey to Glasgow, a slow train to Gourock and then a ferry to Dunoon, where Veronica or one of the hotel staff would meet him in a car for the drive to Strachur. Yet transport difficulties and David Lambie's highly effective guerrilla campaign were not the only factors constraining Fitzroy as a Scottish MP. When he moved to Scotland, he did not appreciate what a factor the Catholicism of his wife and children would be north of the border. But the Orange Lodge was a powerful force in Scottish politics and, after the Anglo-Irish agreement signed by Mrs Thatcher and Garrett Fitzgerald, advised its members to vote Labour. 'Agent Orange' was one factor in Fitzroy's declining majority in the constituency during 1959 to 1974.

Additionally, the very *Zeitgeist* was against him. The sixties cannot have been the happiest time for a man wedded to notions of order, hierarchy and discipline, but overlying all this was a new mood of nationalism in Scotland. Scott's famous reference to 'the national disposition to wandering and adventure' underlined the fact that Scottish assent to Union with England was always provisional. One of the factors predisposing some Scots to accept the Act of Union in 1707 had been the prospect of gaining access to imperial markets. In a wider sense, Scots were only ever content with the Union as long as there was an empire to absorb their energies. Following the loss of empire, Scotland confronted the kind of uncertainty about its role that Fitzroy experienced in microcosm. A symptom of that was the rise of the

Scottish Nationalist Party and the sensational victory in the mid-sixties of its candidate Winnie Ewing in the Labour stronghold of Hamilton. Fitzroy's response to the Hamilton result was characteristically nuanced. 'Though it was argued at the time that this was no more than a protest vote, it was a protest vote on a scale which made a powerful and in some ways salutary impact on the whole political scene and gave the old-fashioned parties serious food for thought.'[17]

Fitzroy suffered from the Scottish Nationalist backlash not just because he was a Tory but because he was perceived as an 'Anglo', in the demotic: in other words, a Scot whose connections were mainly in England and whose power base was the London metropolitan Establishment. Scottish nationalism, sixties liberalism, anti-Catholicism, the 'MP for Outer Mongolia' tag and a general decline in the fortunes of the Conservative party in Scotland, all amplified one another. Faced with these obstacles to a smooth passage as constituency MP, Fitzroy determined to give the lie to the canard that he was a part-timer, an amateur or a political dilettante. In addition to his normal constituency work he set out to gain a reputation as the soldier's friend. He and Veronica drew up a card-index system for following up specifically military complaints from constituents who had written to them; this involved tabling Parliamentary questions, chasing departments for replies, and evolving a method for follow-up to ensure constituent satisfaction. In addition, if ever there was a free weekend, he and Veronica would conduct a mid-term canvass, either on one of the islands or in three or four streets in the mainland, where they would assiduously knock on every door in the street.[18]

Veronica was Fitzroy's secret weapon in more ways than one, since she made a lot of money for the local Conservative Association from her cookery book. Always herself interested in cooking, she invited constituents to send in menus on their headed writing paper, added some of her own, and then got Fitzroy to write a jokey foreward telling how he had balloned from eleven stone to sixteen as a result of her cooking. The royalties were donated to the party association, not just swelling its coffers but effectively publicizing the human side of its parliamentary representative.

Fitzroy fought for Scottish interests to the end of his Parliamentary career; his last battle was over the Hunterston Ore Terminal. In 1973 in the House Fitzroy vigorously opposed the Hunterston project on the ground that it 'would charge the character of the Middle Clyde. It will blight and pollute one of Scotland's brightest beauty spots and deprive industrial Scotland of its principal playground.'[19]

By 1974 the attractions of a political career had palled. Cynics have suggested that Fitzroy left politics because the Tory majority in Bute and North Ayrshire was declining; but he was never in any danger of losing his seat, at least not until the constituency was reorganized, David Lambie concedes:

> We used to say, when Labour wins Bute and North Ayrshire, we'll only have the Ulster constituencies left to win. I ground Fitzroy down to a 2,000 majority but after that the vote was inelastic, as there were so many old-age pensioners. But I brought the majority down each time. We had a good relationship, though . . . In fact I often found myself defending Sir Fitzroy against the SNP . . . I found it difficult to fight such an incumbent as he was too nice and I couldn't go for the throat. But the candidate who replaced me and fought him in 1970 was no respecter of persons and was vicious with him. He didn't like these young kids who kicked him, and that could have been a factor in his decision to quit. Maybe if I had still been the [Labour] candidate, he'd still be the MP![20]

Fitzroy handed over as Conservative candidate in 1974 to John Corrie, a Kirkudbright farmer, who lost the constituency to Labour when it was reorganized.

What general conclusions can we reach about Fitzroy as a politician? There is a general consensus that he was not really a political animal. John Blelloch contrasts him with his friend and successor at the War Office, Julian Amery. 'Fitzroy was in politics by accident. Having got into it, he enjoyed the company and the ambience of the House of the Commons rather than the job. Everyone in the House liked and respected him, but he could never impress the House the way Amery could. Both were war heroes and linguists, but one was a natural politician and the other was not.'[21]

Fitzroy did not impress in the House because he was a poor speaker and insufficiently partisan. Fitzroy himself laments the fact that he was never as effective in debate as in a committee room or as a political journalist.[22] Jakie Astor comments: 'He was not a through-and-through politician, he simply enjoyed bits of the House. He didn't take politics very seriously, as he saw through the charade. He didn't enjoy speaking in the House. Christopher Hollis and I used to amuse ourselves by listening to Fitzroy speak. He was so slow, and mumbled, and the lack of range in his voice was monotonous. You'd think his speeches would be witty and dynamic, but he was slow and pedantic. What he did like was meeting people and getting close to the centres of power. He's not an exhibitionist, but he does like being in the spotlight.'[23]

Perhaps the Commons is an uncongenial place for adventurers or *condottieri*. Roy Jenkins, who was paired with Fitzroy after 1959, comments: 'Fitzroy was not in the same category as other adventurers, since he was a long-term MP. I doubt if more than fifteen per cent of Members sit for as long as thirty-three years. But I agree that Fitzroy's heart was never in the House of Commons and he was always half in, half out.

I remember once he was alarmed when "Crossbencher" in the *Daily Express* revealed his poor division record. I pointed out that division records meant nothing, and that my record was even worse.'[24]

More even than most MPs, Fitzroy had friends right across the political spectrum. He was always a particular favourite of Harold Wilson's. In 1968, Wilson was wandering around the Commons disconsolately just after sacking George Brown as Foreign Secretary, and came across Fitzroy. At once he poured out his bitterness towards Brown – a bully who pitched into ambassadors when he knew they could not answer back.[25] This was just one of many such cross-bench encounters. Fitzroy's lack of partisanship is usually ascribed to his diplomatic training. Another diplomat, Sir Reginald Hibbert, describes him as a committee man. 'At meetings he managed to make very sensible points very firmly in a way that didn't ruffle feathers and, whether it was liked or not, did not carry an ideological load. I think things go wrong if people are too pro-Communist or too anti-Communist. Emotion should be kept out of it. Fitzroy and Tito is a case in point. What was remarkable was the way he could put his pro-Tito point in such a way that people of all persuasions, from right-wing Americans to left-wing British, were persuaded by his arguments. I don't agree that this is the Foreign Office training, because not everyone in the FO is like that. There are strong ideologues there.'[26]

Outside the House and on the campaign trail, Fitzroy did not like the rough-and-tumble of politics, the open meetings, baby-kissing and dealing with hecklers. David Lambie remembers the campaign in Ayrshire in the sixties.

> In those days political meetings were exciting because of the hecklers. Groups of young people followed one around from meeting to meeting. I loved it, but he hated it. He was not good at answering questions. But I found that the enemy is useful, especially when one is trying to defend a party line in which one doesn't believe. When I was a candidate and Fitzroy was the MP, most people thought it was the other way around, as he was so self-effacing and I seemed to be able to answer all the questions at these all-party candidate versus MP sessions. My own idea is that Veronica should really have been the MP. She was outspoken and vibrant and would have gone down well in Scotland. I would certainly have been able to attack Veronica better. She'd have counter-attacked.[27]

Some people think Fitzroy's Achilles' heel as a politician was his versatility. The party hack is preferred, especially in the era of machine politics, to the multitudinous man, and party whips care little for the individual reputation of members they see only as lobby fodder. Versatility is often the sign of the easily bored, and some of Fitzroy's critics think that an inability to concentrate on any specific objective, as much as his travels and adventures, marks him out as a twentieth-century Burton.

His friends, on the other hand, tend to think that the fault lay not in Fitzroy but in his having been born into the twentieth-century British political culture, which seems almost to make a fetish of squandering talent. The former Liberal leader Jo Grimond is of this persuasion. 'He was not . . . conformist, especially about the Army . . . Promotion in the Tory party remains something of a mystery to me. The party was not really so rich in talent that it could leave such members as . . . Fitzroy on the back benches.'[28]

Fitzroy was also part of the 'awkward squad' in that his views could not be categorized as Right or Left, as could those of so many of his party colleagues. Roy Jenkins, who observed him for twenty-five years, found him enigmatic. 'Fitzroy's politics are difficult to place. Ideologically he has an easy-going attitude to match his personal manner. Whether he has an ideological core, I don't know. He's a man out of his time . . . Often one doesn't know what Fitzroy *does* take seriously.'[29]

Fellow-Scot Alistair Milne adds a Scottish dimension: 'I never thought he was very interested in British politics, even when at the War Office, where he had some expertise. His mind was always towards the East. I think the generality of British politics actually bored him. He was interested in East–West relations and large concepts, of which he knew quite a lot from the thirties to the fifties. He's no Thatcherite. If anything, he's always expressed very cynical views about the conduct of politics generally.'[30]

Though in many ways he had the attributes of charm and ruthlessness that should have produced a successful politician, the consensus is that Fitzroy stayed in politics chiefly because it opened doors for him, built contacts and enabled him to write and film without the limitations that would have hedged him about in the Foreign Office. He was interested in power, but once he realized that Western politics involved very little power, he lost interest.

21

Traveller in the Soviet Union

F ITZROY is a self-confessed hedonist, and all who travel with him
tell stories of his zest for life and its pleasures. 'Fitz is a real "heavy
grubber" ', says Tony Isaacs. 'Eats constantly. We had to take a snack
box on our travels. Drinks a lot, too. In Georgian restaurants they ask,
how many bottles of wine do you want, and they mean *each*, not per
table.' John Purdie agrees: 'Fitzroy has elevated being a trencherman
to an art form. He has this compulsion about eating what's on your
plate. If you leave anything – and I warned the crew about this – he'll
stretch across and say, "I'll just have that piece of meat." He's got this
almost Calvinistic notion that nothing must be left.'

The appetite for food and drink was clear in *Eastern Approaches*, where
the pages often crack and sizzle with culinary delights: eggs, milk, fresh
bread, chickens, roast sucking-pig, cream cheese, pastries, wine,
peaches, grapes. Thus does Fitzroy describe his Serbian cook in the
autumn of 1944:

> We needed a cook and so I took him on; after which we enjoyed, for the rest of
> our brief stay in Arandjelovac, almost the best food I have ever tasted, perfect
> alike in its admirable materials and skilful preparation. Pork, for which Serbia
> is rightly famous, dominated our diet, the juiciest, tenderest, most succulent
> pork imaginable. There was roast pork, and grilled pork chops, and pig's
> trotters and sucking-pig and bacon and ham and innumerable kinds of pork
> sausages, all swimming in the very best butter and lard. It may sound monoto-
> nous; it may even sound slightly disgusting. But at that time and in that place,
> after years during which such things had existed only in one's dreams, it was
> highly enjoyable. We felt that we were at last enjoying the fruits of victory.
>
> Nor was the preparation of pork by any means the only branch of his art at
> which this admirable man excelled. The richest soups; the most delicious
> omelettes; the most luscious preserves; layer upon layer of the lightest pastry
> mingled with the freshest cream cheese; all these delicacies, washed down by a
> variety of excellent wines, were lavished on us daily.

Fitzroy recalls another gastronomic high point, from his visit with Field-Marshal Alexander to Marshal Tolbukhin's headquarters in Hungary in February 1945: 'Sweet Crimean champagne had succeeded the vodka and had in turn been replaced by sticky brandy from the Caucasus. Enormous sturgeon, roast turkeys and whole stuffed sucking-pigs, gaping hideously, followed closely on a great bowl of iced caviar and a formidable array of hot and cold *zakuski*. Now an elaborate iced cake, surmounted by allegorical statuettes and patriotic symbols worked in pink sugar, had made its appearance and yet more bottles and glasses.'

'He's amazingly good at ferreting out where you can get good food', John Purdie concludes. 'It's the foraging mentality of the SAS. And the only time I saw him in a genuinely bad mood was when he was kept waiting for his food.' Some wonder whether Fitzroy's gulosity should be accounted cause or effect of his marriage, for Veronica is acknowledged as an outstanding cook.

Since the late 1950s Fitzroy has established himself as Britain's leading interpreter of the Soviet Union to the general public. On scores of separate trips he has criss-crossed the vast territories of the USSR, from the Baltic to Siberia; almost the only region he has not visited is the remote Siberian Tunguska area, scene of a mysterious comet impact with earth in 1908. His first post-war return to the Soviet kaleidoscope, the heart of his outer life for the last thirty years, was in 1958. He revisited the scenes of his youth, exhilarated by jet travel which allowed him to fly nearly 2,000 miles in three and a half hours. He found Samarkand and Tashkent less exciting than in 1938, perhaps because he was twenty years older, but perhaps partly because the speed and ease of the journey reduced their exotic aura. Yet his favourite city, Bokhara, was still closed to foreigners. Fitzroy got round this obstacle by flying back to Moscow, wangling an invitation to a reception with Khruschev, then making a nuisance of himself with the First Secretary until he was given the necessary permission.[1] He wound up his 1958 tour by flying back from Bokhara via Tashkent and Baku. This was the first of many trips, including an extended journey to Soviet Asia and China, taking in Irkutsk, Ulan Bator and Peking.

During the sixties he had at least three strings to his Russian bow. His work for the Great Britain–USSR Society necessarily took him to Moscow. Commissions for travel books took him further afield. Film-making and television work involved both the glamour of Samarkand and Soviet Central Asia and the inner 'dark continent' of the apartment blocks and housing estates of Kiev, Leningrad and Tomsk.

Since Fitzroy is more self-effacing in his Soviet travel books than in *Eastern Approaches*, the best witnesses are those who accompanied him. Laurence Kelly, another writer on Russian subjects, was with him in

Moscow in 1958 at the British Trade Fair, when Fitzroy was surrounded with old friends including Frank Roberts, then Ambassador. Kelly remembers: 'The Argyll and Sutherland Highlanders were playing on the forecourt of the Embassy and there were lots of teenage Soviet girls crawling around to see what was under these kilts. On top of the pediment a party was going on. To show how acceptable he was to his hosts, Fitzroy was wearing the order of Kutusov. The diminutive Mikoyan was next to Fitzroy – the long and the short of it, you might say. Mikoyan didn't know what to make of Fitzroy's wearing that decoration. In the end he looked up at him, jabbed him in the solar plexus and said, "I've got that too".'[2]

When Fitzroy travelled outside urban areas, he took with him his 'small kit'. His 'large' camping kit was kept permanently ready in leather straps at Strachur, and there were strict rules that nobody was ever allowed to touch it; the children were not even allowed in the room where it lay. Like all good soldiers, Fitzroy guarded his kit fiercely. The 'small kit' is a couple of night-bags containing shirts, underwear, two cameras and assorted *vademecums*. Travelling with Fitzroy and Sir John Lawrence for the Great Britain–USSR Society in 1974, John Roberts discovered exactly how useful Fitzroy's impedimenta could be when, consigned by bureaucratic bungling to an express with no restaurant car, they were presented by embarrassed Intourist guides with a cardboard box containing vodka and various tins. Fitzroy delved into his kit and produced three vodka glasses, a tin-opener, a bread-knife and divers other implements. Lawrence and Roberts teased him until he surprised them still further by coming up with a joke set of dentures.[3]

The television producer John Purdie found that Fitzroy's fetishes were excitement, novelty and danger; he nearly lost his life in the Black Sea.

> He's an obsessive swimmer. Has to swim every day. I'd hate to be in the middle of the Sahara with him. You'd find his attitude would change because he couldn't get a swim in. At the end of winter we were by the Black Sea. The sea was rough, with waves six to eight feet. We were walking along the beach and Fitzroy suddenly announced that he was going to have a dip. I wondered what I was supposed to do if he was washed out to sea. The waves were crashing in on the rocks. He got in, kept disappearing in the waves, with me wondering when the inevitable was going to happen. Eventually he dragged himself back onto the shore, got dried and declared the dip fabulous. From what I saw he must be a very, very strong swimmer. He's made of steel![4]

On another occasion Fitzroy and Purdie were diverted to Tomsk, a city closed to foreigners. They arrived at eleven at night, having already been buffeted for two hours in a snow storm on Aeroflot, which does not enjoy the highest reputation in the aviation industry. The temperature at Tomsk was $-40°F$. The passengers slithered with their heavy baggage over a runway to a freezing waiting room where they waited for three hours for another plane. Once again they had to carry bags onto the tarmac through a howling blizzard. Once on the plane Fitzroy calmly took a swig of Scotch from his hip-flask. Purdie remembers:

> I was flaking. But here was this craggy old mountain sitting there, taking a dram and saying, fine, we're on our way again. His physical stamina is astonishing. You have to keep reminding yourself of his age. The wilder it is, the tougher it is, the more he likes it. We've shared bedrooms in Outer Mongolia in appalling conditions. Always, when the alarm went off at five in the morning, Fitz was up before me and ready to go. He's fearless, too. Get on anything with a wing on it. He almost welcomes it if there's an edge there of danger . . . Fitz is not interested in frills. He doesn't care how rough, even if you say we have to sleep on the floor. He then at once sets about getting the necessary provisions. In Siberia we'd stay in a log cabin and Fitz would arrange tea and local delicacies.[5]

Another producer, Michael Gill, remembers interminable waits for trains in wayside halts and stations in Kazakhstan. 'Fitzroy would say, "It'll be many hours yet, no point in wasting time." Then out of his bag would come a volume of Greek or Latin and he would sit on this filthy floor reading away quite happily.'[6]

Fitzroy's larger-than-life persona was often thrown into even greater relief by 'smaller than life' Soviet *apparatchiks*, Intourist guides and KGB 'minders'. Stories of his jousts with Soviet officialdom are legion. In Russia once on a trip with his wife he rounded on an Intourist girl for being obstructive. Fitzroy berated her to the point where she put her hand over her face, burst into tears and rushed away. Veronica remonstrated with him for going too far and suggested that he say something emollient to her when she came back. 'That would defeat the object of the exercise,' he replied.[7] Fitzroy's ruthlessness is never gratuitous, but if he wants something he considers it reasonable to have he will not be constrained by 'wet', 'liberal' or '*bien-pensant*' considerations.

In Tblisi in 1979 with a third producer, Tony Isaacs, Fitzroy angered the authorities by taking photographs of some police violence. He and Isaacs were arrested.

> At the police station Fitzroy was just right, neither too tough nor too soft, the perfect diplomat. He switched films and put a blank roll in the camera. But Fitzroy's penchant for taking inconvenient snaps got us our visas cancelled and we were given twenty-four hours to leave. Fitzroy blamed this on the hostility of our KGB minder, a young fat pig of a man called Valentine. Fitzroy was bitterly disappointed as it meant we wouldn't be able to shoot the Georgian carnival. Valentine was with us in the car and suddenly Fitz lost his temper. He

rounded on him. 'I've been a great friend of Russia for more than forty years. As a young man I fought the Fascists. I have been awarded the Order of Kutuzov.' The red-faced Valentine was so taken aback by this flood of invective that eventually Fitzroy browbeat him to get back on the phone, so that we got our visas extended for two days.[8]

Michael Gill, in the course of six trips to the USSR with Fitzroy in 1981 and 1982, often found himself involved in battles of wits between Fitzroy and the Soviet authorities. He and Fitzroy would use all the normal means of baffling the bugs in their hotel rooms, running baths, talking in languages other than English, turning up the radios. They took to planning their moves on benches near Moscow University, only to spot cameras with zoom lenses and unidirectional microphones zeroing in on them. The American producer Jerome Gary would often take them to parties given by young female Communists, who seemed to have an insatiable appetite for good-looking capitalists. At these parties Gill and Fitzroy would whisper asides to each other amid the general conversation, effectively thwarting eavesdroppers.

Fitzroy's deep knowledge of things Russian and his insight into the 'wrinkles' in the Soviet system proved invaluable to all who filmed with him. 'Fitz kept my morale up when dealing with Russian officialdom', Purdie testifies. 'Like all larger-than-life people, he deals in great generalisations. "Shout at them, they like to be shouted at" was one of his catch-phrases . . . We were always changing rooms in hotels when it was "impossible". Fitz would sit down in the foyer and make it clear he wouldn't move . . . half an hour later there would be a much better room on the floor we wanted . . . "They're lying", Fitzroy would say, "they've always got somewhere." '

Fitzroy knew his way around Moscow in more senses than one. He loved walking through endless suburbs, navigating his way to an interesting restaurant or art-gallery. As he himself puts it, 'Discovering where to go in Moscow and what to eat and drink and what to avoid is a painfully acquired but thoroughly worthwhile art.'[9] Tony Isaacs remembers an occasion when this know-how was particularly valuable. Dining with Fitzroy, he was accosted in the lavatory by a black-marketeer who became threatening when Isaacs brushed aside his importunity. Isaacs doubled the man up with a couple of blows, then returned to Fitzroy and asked what to do next. 'We walk. Very fast,' replied Fitzroy. They set off for a five-mile circular tour to their hotel via the back streets.[10]

Fitzroy went with John Purdie to one of Moscow's up-market restaurants, elegant and sumptuous. Inside was the usual Muscovite chaos, waiters ignoring diners, queues for tables. Because of the arthritis that progressively lamed him after the mid-eighties, Fitzroy sat on a serpentine sideboard, his legs dangling. Suddenly someone got up from a table and walked towards them, staring intently at Fitzroy. 'I thought, here comes trouble. The man came up to us and said, "Fitzroy Maclean?" "Yes," said Fitzroy. "Yevgeni Yevtushenko, the poet," said the man. "I am sitting here. I look across. I think, there is only one man in the world who would sit on a sideboard. Has to be Fitzroy Maclean." ' Fitzroy and Purdie were invited to his table, where he was sitting with the beautiful daughter of Sophia Loren and Carlo Ponti. Purdie recalls: 'What an evening! Loren's daughter in her twenties and Yevtushenko in his fifties, flirting with her. Champagne and vodka flowing like the Volga. Most of the conversation about relations between the sexes, what men want from women and vice versa. But it was Fitzroy's unique posture on the sideboard that struck the spark of recognition.'[11]

Fitzroy never tires of his beloved Georgia. This, from *Eastern Approaches*, is typical of his attitude to Georgians: 'They combine a truly Mediterranean expansiveness and rivalry with the dash of the High-lander. As a race they are strikingly good-looking: the men dark, wiry and aggressive in their long cloaks and sheepskin hats on the side of their heads; the women high-breasted and dark-eyed, with straight classical features.'[12]

Fitzroy has always held, like Montesquieu, that mountain peoples are folk apart, and that there is a special congruence between Georgians and the Highlanders of Scotland. The Georgians have the same impres-sive warrior history as the clansmen. There is also a classical parallel: in Georgia, as in Ancient Greece, there is the tradition of the toastmaster, the *tamada*, who has the right to call on any guest at a feast, to compli-ment him or ask for a speech. The tradition of going round the table singing praises is Homeric or recalls the Argonauts at Colchis, and certainly one would have to go back to classical times to find this in Europe. Laurence Kelly says: 'Fitzroy in the atmosphere of Georgian bards and toastmasters comes to life like a sunflower before the sun and makes the most charming speeches in reply. He complimented one toastmaster by saying he'd been thirty years in the House of Commons and had never heard such a graceful speech. Also, Fitzroy's ability to drink people under the table is important in Georgia. There are so many toasts you have to respond to, you need to be a drinker.'[13] John Purdie adds: 'Fitzroy likes their high-spiritedness and their partiality for a dram. He's got a great eye for women, and Georgian women *are* beautiful. He likes the food, the wine, the women, the song. For Fitz Georgia is wine, women and song with mountain air, the perfect combination.'[14]

The Georgians repay their champion with great affection. Whenever a Georgian dance or theatre company comes to Britain, Fitzroy will be on hand. He loves to have large companies of Georgians at Strachur, to impress them with the ethos of chivalry and martial valour in the High- lands, and to demonstrate the toughness of Scots by swimming in ice-cold lakes or picnicking in the rain. Thelma Holt remarks: 'The Georgians thought Strachur House was a typical British home! Also they think Fitzroy comes from a nation not subjugated: Scotland. They slightly misunderstand that and romanticize it. But the skirl of the pipes and the swirl of the kilt impresses them, as does his hardiness.'[15]

If Georgia has sometimes been described as being like Scotland before the Jacobite rising, so has Montenegro, in Fitzroy's other favourite country, Yugoslavia. Here too are warrior cults and clan bonding, chivalry and primitive notions of honour: 'revenge is its greatest delight and glory.'[16] So why has Montenegro never captured Fitzroy's affections in quite the way Georgia has? Perhaps it is because the Georgian sensibility is essentially romantic, nostalgic and backward- looking, wedded to tradition, order and hierarchy. The Montenegrin, on the other hand, is rebellious and revolutionary. Djilas's English biographer Stephen Clissold sums up: 'The Montenegrin character is . . . single-minded, violent and much given to hero-worship. Hence it has a natural affinity with what is popularly taken as Marxism– Leninism. When a Montenegrin rebel meets Marxism–Leninism, the recognition is instantaneous and satisfying.'[17]

John Purdie recalls an occasion when the Georgian and Yugoslav motifs converged. 'We sat outside in a restaurant at Tbilisi. From the corner of my eye I could see a smartly dressed fellow staring at Fitz. I felt a twinge of paranoia. Was this KGB? Eventually, the man came over and asked if my companion was Fitzroy Maclean. He introduced him- self as a high ranker in the Yugoslav Foreign Ministry and told me that Fitz was a hero in Yugoslavia. I introduced them.'[18]

Fitzroy's Russian travels fit into four categories: trips to make a film or for a book; rarer trips to areas unknown to him; pure pleasure trips to his beloved Georgia; and last, trips to take the temperature on behalf of the British Government. Fitzroy's advocacy was instrumental to the famous Thatcher–Gorbachev entente. After a visit to Russia in 1985, Fitzroy was called in to Number 10 and quizzed about the new bearings in Soviet society under the reforming First Secretary Gorbachev. Fitzroy advised the Prime Minister to put all her political money on the leadership in the Kremlin. Shortly afterwards Mrs Thatcher made her well-known pro- nouncement that Gorbachev was a man she could do business with.

Despite Fitzroy's skill as go-between, promoter of understanding and interpreter of the Soviet Union, his Russian work has attracted almost as many critics as his wartime exploits with Tito. Indeed, anti- communist triumphalism has singled out his rapport with the Russians as a continuation by other means of his wartime 'mistakes'. There are several strands in the critique, so that it needs careful disentanglement.

The first complaint is that Fitzroy is too complaisant towards the Soviet Union, too much a Foreign Office man at heart. This is a persistent criticism from one wing of the Great Britain–USSR Society. Sir John Lawrence, his contemporary at Eton, says: 'Fitzroy always thought the Soviet system was more stable than I did. I always took the line that the Christian religiosity of the Russian people was enormously important, could never be eliminated, and would eventually remove the tyrants. When I made this point in an article in 1978 in *The Times*, Fitzroy thought it injudicious and thought I should have published it anonymously. It seemed to me that he never appreciated what a mess [the Soviet Union] was and based on what rotten foundations'.[19] John Roberts, Lawrence's ally, supports this. 'I think John understands the spirit of Russia better than Fitzroy [who] suffers from the fatal romantic attachment of the true Tory for those in power, whoever they are, Communist or whatever. Because he has so many friends in the upper Soviet echelons, he tends to be uncritical.' Roberts talks of Yuri Lubimov, the Brechtian director who brought satirical dissident theatre to the UK and was threatened with retribution by the Soviet Embassy in London. 'I dined with Fitzroy and Lubimov. Lubimov, a brilliant wit and conversationalist, made a number of cracks against the Soviet system that made Fitzroy uncomfortable. In a recent piece in the *Sunday Times* Fitz is praising as his guides and mentors the kind of people who in Eastern Europe are now behind bars.'[20]

However, it would be a grievous mistake to think that Fitzroy is alone in believing one can do business with people about whom one has severe moral reservations. Even within the Great Britain–USSR Society there are luminaries, the present chairman Sir Curtis Keeble among them, who take the same view as Fitzroy. Another mandarin, Sir Reginald Hibbert, offers a rebuttal of the Roberts–Lawrence view: 'Fitzroy Maclean is one of the people in this country who has consistently taken a balanced view of Russia and Eastern Europe. He's never made the ghastly mistake of thinking that if you disapprove of Communism the thing to do is break off relations with the Soviet Union. Fitzroy is an example of how you can be loyal to your country and yet get on with its official enemies. It's quite a feat to be respected by the other side while not compromising a whit.'[21]

Another criticism of Fitzroy is that his books, in effect if not in intention, peddle the Moscow line on internal Soviet affairs. The student of Kazakhstan and Dagestan, Robert Chenciner, complains that Fitzroy skates over unsatisfactory Soviet treatment of its Muslim population, is too friendly with Moscow place-men, treats Party hacks as figures of genuine importance, passes judgement after spending too little time in an area, and writes books that have no thesis or line.

Maclean's writing is, in the bad sense of the word, journalistic, in that he's more interested in 'good copy' than the full story. His work is the romantic sensibility of the ego interacting with the environment, not the detached classicism of the true student. He's fond of Russian Orthodoxy, to which he gives a better write-up than to Islam. Arguably the best thing the Russian Revolution did was to get rid of Orthodoxy, which was racist and anti-Semitic and kept the people in subjection for centuries. It was the only religion that had no revival as it had never changed. Maclean is enamoured of the incense of the Russian Orthodox Church and regards the Asiatics as illiterate savages. He is serving up a hegemonic view of Russian superiority, derived both from nineteenth-century Russian literature and from modern Soviet propaganda. In a word, Maclean is a good PR man for Intourist.[22]

Chenciner's strongest criticisms are reserved for Fitzroy's love of the Georgians, though we must bear in mind his pro-Muslim bias. He describes Fitzroy's hope for an independent Georgia under a monarchy as a 'total fantasy', citing Georgia's need of oil from Azerbaijan and the large racial enclaves of Azeris and Armenians within the Christian borderlands. 'Why are the Georgians Maclean's favourites? They are Christian, they're good-looking, which he goes for, they're a nice racial type, they're flashy. Another attraction is the monarchy. Georgia is a sexist and racist society, and in the last ten years we've seen a lot of Georgian chauvinism in all senses. Maclean sees Georgia through a Homeric/Highlander filter and ignores its racism and sexism. He goes for fake sovcult phoney popular culture.'[23]

What is one to make of these criticisms? In the first place, many of them cancel each other out. Chenciner reprimands Fitzroy for favouring Russian Orthodoxy over Islam, but Lawrence says Fitzroy does not stress Russian Orthodoxy enough. The Left sees Fitzroy as a Cold Warrior, sneering at the achievements of the Soviet Union; the Right sees him as a dupe of the Kremlin. These propositions cannot coexist. In some quarters the objection seems to be that Fitzroy did not go to the USSR and denounce the Soviet system. But foreign relations and travel are not based on morality or confined to desirable governments. And as a transmission belt between the Soviet élite and the British Establishment, Fitzroy could not afford the luxury of berating his Russian contacts. An obscure British scholar in some Islamic republic of the USSR may get away with insulting his hosts; a man of Fitzroy's stature could not.

Perhaps the most dishonest criticism of Fitzroy is that of right-wingers who claim they 'always knew' the Soviet Union was brittle and would collapse. The high tide of anti-communist triumphalism after 1989 has provided retrospective justification to people who even ten years ago could not have prophesied the death of the Soviet monolith within the century. We hear little nowadays of all those studies published in the Brezhnev era assuring us that the Soviets were pre-pared to fight a nuclear war rather than abandon Eastern Europe.

To return to the parallel drawn earlier between Fitzroy's record in the Soviet Union in the last thirty years and his wartime feats with Tito: in both cases we confront a totally unjustifiable avalanche of criticism directed against honourable actions undertaken by an honourable man.

22

The Elder Statesman

T HE SOVIET UNION has not been Fitzroy's only destination in
the past thirty years. He has also toured the length and breadth of
North America, attending clan reunions in Canada, where the Scot-
tish tradition is strong, and stomping the lecture circuit in the USA.
He first visited the Eastern seaboard in January 1948, returned in
1957, and then from the early 1960s on was a fairly constant visitor.
As an ambassador for the English-Speaking Union and the British
Tourist Association he has performed prodigies of public relations.
Americans like him and he likes them, and, like most people on the
lecture circuits of the USA, he has tales to tell. Public speaking in
America is not a question of (to use an Americanism) 'phoning in one's
lines' – an invitation to speak in Dallas can mean addressing 1,500
'blue rinses' or sixty world experts on the Soviet Union: the exact
nature of the audience may not be known until the day. Fitzroy tended
to prefer the English-Speaking Union circuit because their schedule was
less demanding – some of the bigger agencies insisted on three lectures
a day.

Chairmen of university departments so drunk that they fell onto the
platform were not unusual, but even the veteran of a hundred such
encounters found a television phone-in hosted by an East Coast university more than a little surreal. It was in the late 1960s, and the technology for such encounters had not then been perfected. Fitzroy was
taking part in a four-way debate on foreign affairs with Paul Reynaud,
Kurt von Schuschnigg and Alexander Kerensky. As each celebrity
spoke, an enormous screen relayed his image to an audience of 1,500
students. No sooner was Fitzroy into his stride than an angry woman
came on the line with a query about her laundry. The more the president
exhorted the woman to get off the line and allow the distinguished Sir
Fitzroy to speak, the more querulous she became about her lingerie.
The exchanges between irate woman and exasperated president became

more impassioned, and the phone-in was eventually abandoned in a chaos of mutual recrimination.[1]

'Fitzroy leads British Tourist Authority missions overseas with the same panache as he showed in the Yugoslav mountains,' comments Sandy Glen.[2] It was when Glen was chairman of the BTA that the two men saw most of each other. Glen, at a party for hoteliers at the Hyde Park Hotel, was surprised to see the familiar tall figure among those present. When he heard about Creggans Inn he at once recruited Fitzroy for PR work in the USA. Tourism to Britain went through a particularly thin time during the three-day week of 1973, and to arrest the decline Glen put together a number of parties of contrasting envoys to tour the States and promote Britain. 'Fitzroy's party, I remember, contained a very attractive American woman who owned a stately home, Brian Redhead, and young Rocco Forte, just 21, in his first job outside Pa's influence.'[3] Fitzroy by common consent performed well on morning television chat shows from New York to Texas, but caused consternation among thermostatically minded Americans by plunging into a Houston swimming pool in ice-cold temperature and a swirling yellow fog.

This passion for swimming once almost exhausted Fitzroy's nine lives. In Hawaii in 1981 for a conference, Fitzroy swam out among the giant Pacific rollers – something not even the strongest swimmer should do. Near his hotel was a small bay fringed by a coral reef. A sailor would have looked closely at the way the sea was making before plunging in, but Fitzroy the old soldier had not yet learned about the power of the sea. 'Veronica said, which was fatal, don't go out too far, so of course I went out quite a long way and then found I couldn't get back.' The tide turned and the current carried him onto the coral reef. Then a tropical storm arose suddenly and he had to cope with great waves. On the shore Veronica was with some American friends, almost within shouting distance of her husband, but it was quite clear he could not get back to them. Time was too short to hire a helicopter: in the end, Veronica opted for prayer.

Fitzroy describes his ordeal out in the ocean. 'Things got worse and worse, and the waves bigger and bigger. I was out there for one and a half hours. For the last half-hour I was convinced I'd had it. I had a long time to think about death. Most of it about death duties and had I done the sensible thing. Finally, the biggest wave you ever saw got hold of me just as I was approaching the coral reef, picked me up and swept me right across it. I did something without knowing what it was – body-surfing – right on top of the wave and eventually arrived at the other side of the bay, where I was able to put my foot down and touch the bottom. A very narrow squeak indeed.'[4]

Fitzroy used his extensive American contacts to drum up business for the Creggans. Strachur became a favourite venue for American conferences sponsored by the Rockefellers, the Smithsonian Institute and others. Meanwhile Fitzroy built up links with the American commanders at the Holy Loch base. After 1974 he was chairman of the Community Relations Committee, set up to foster good relations with the US Navy, who rented cottages in the Strachur area, and for whose wives' committees Creggans was a favoured spot. But the American trade in Scotland in general fell off disastrously after the Lockerbie tragedy in 1988. Over the past three years it has been European visitors who have dominated the Scottish tourist industry.

Until 1988 the Creggans Inn was a spectacular commercial success. Some said the energetic Veronica was the driving force, but the inn has always been important to both, and not just in a sentimental sense. Fitzroy shrewdly combines business and showmanship, dressing up in Highland trews, dispensing his own brand of malt whisky (MacPhunn's, around which he has woven an apocryphal story), displaying his talent as wit and raconteur. Alistair Milne reports a scene from 1987: 'There was a whole party of US Senators and their wives there – about thirty of them – who had been bussed in from Glasgow. Fitzroy gave them a dram or two, then put on his show, dressed in kilt and sporran, showed them locks of Prince Charlie's hair, and so on . . . He's a tremendously impressive man for hospitality.'[5]

Fitzroy's luck is proverbial, and it held one night in the 1970s when he was walking back from dinner in a Piccadilly hotel to his flat in Knightsbridge. He took the pedestrian subway to get across Hyde Park Corner and was accosted by two muggers. Fitzroy is uncertain about the exact sequence of events, except that his legs were tripped and he lost consciousness. He awoke to find his wallet gone and himself covered in blood. He limped back to Lowndes Square expecting to find stab wounds, but after taking a bath found there was not a mark on him. Puzzling about the vast quantity of blood, he reasoned that instinct must have taken over and his old commando training asserted himself. The inference was that there was a badly-wounded mugger wandering around London that night. But he *was* lucky, since conventional wisdom holds that resistance to the urban mugger invites a possibly fatal knifing.

Fitzroy has also been fortunate in that his two natural children and two stepchildren have all emerged into adulthood having developed satisfactory relations with this particularly dominant father-figure.

Some have speculated that Suki, now in her third marriage, may have been hampered in her relations with men by having such a powerful male role-model. She laughs this off: 'Does anyone really know why anyone does anything?' She is quite clear that her affinity with Fitzroy comes from shared interests: languages, and a passion for puns and

verbal humour. Jeremy Phipps goes out of his way to scout any suggestion that the strong paternal role-model influenced him into a career
in the Army. 'Trying to please Fitzroy by going into the Army? No,
because initially I tried to please my mother by going into the *Navy*, as
that's where my father had been. It was only after I failed Dartmouth
that I went into the Army, and even here the two great influences were
my uncle, Mervyn Phipps, who had served in the 7th Hussars, and
Suki's first husband, who had done National Service in the 3rd
Hussars.'

Phipps joined the Army as a private in 1960, then went to Sandhurst
and saw service in Aden and Germany and with the SAS, eventually
rising to Fitzroy's old rank of brigadier. He confirms that he achieved
real rapport with Fitzroy when he himself became a seasoned traveller.
'The Army similarity is a bit of a red herring. I joined the cavalry in
peacetime. Fitzroy joined the infantry in wartime. Entirely different
worlds. But I've always been grateful to him for his best advice, which
was not to go straight to Sandhurst but to spend some time in the ranks
first. He said, wisely, that that way you learn how soldiers tick and how
they really see officers. The best officers understand their men from the
roots up. I spent six months at Catterick before going to Sandhurst, and
I've always been pleased I did that.'[6]

Charlie, heir to Fitzroy's baronetcy, seemed when young the exact
opposite of all that Fitzroy typified. Disdainful of physical exercise,
aesthetic, Charlie became a hippie and seemed uninterested in Strachur
and its associations until he reached middle age. Ironically, what
changed his mind was an event that caused Fitzroy a lot of soul-
searching. Charlie spent many years in the USA and there met his wife
Debbie, who is black. Fitzroy wondered whether the cultures would
mix and, in particular, once Charlie and his family decided to move
back to Strachur, whether the conservative people of Argyll would
welcome a black American. Jamie Maclean observes: 'He was worried
that the children would not be in either world, black or white. He was
pessimistic where we were optimistic . . . But there was a complete
turnaround. Debbie lived in Strachur House for a year with my parents – not easy, as they need and demand a lot of space – and they
forged a good relationship. It's remarkable how well they get on
together.' In fact, Debbie proved as astute and charming a diplomat as
Fitzroy himself. Her integration into the world of the Macleans has
been notably successful. In addition, marriage to Debbie has persuaded
Charlie of the importance of tradition and the need to hand on a family
treasure like Strachur House.

Even Jamie, now a London art dealer, more critical of Fitzroy than
the others, makes plain at all points his love and admiration for his
father.

I think, as I think the other three do, that Fitzroy is wonderful, remarkable and original, but we get fed up with hearing it from his contemporaries. His advice to me, as he read yet another dismal school report, was always sound. 'Jamie, what you will get if you go on getting bad reports is a very dull office job. If you want an exciting job you have to get good reports.' He said this in a very dull, repetitive matter-of-fact way – he had to repeat it, as my reports were all bad. I have to accept that what he said was very wise. You *do* get an interesting life by working hard and you *don't* get it just by waiting for it to happen. We reached a compromise whereby I would be allowed to go to art school provided it was a *Scottish* art school. Here is a minor grievance against my father. I went to Edinburgh College of Art and it didn't work out. I feel I would have done better south of the border, so that I very slightly feel I was manipulated for my father's private ends. He could say, 'Look at my son, he's being educated in *Scotland*'.[7]

Fitzroy has always combined work with a gargantuan social life, in the manner of Henry James. All who encounter him speak of his charm. Charm is more highly prized among Celts than Anglo-Saxons, who tend to suspect it and look for the manipulation it conceals. It also appeals more to women, and there can be little doubt that Fitzroy is more at home in their company than he is with other males. 'Fitzroy . . . prefers female company,' says Jakie Astor.[8] This is a paradox, for one would normally expect a fire-eating ex-SAS war hero to be a 'man's man'. But the judgement is confirmed by women. Pamela Egremont remarks: 'All women find him attractive. First of all as the hero and warrior. Then, he likes women, not just to go to bed with. He likes their company and the way their minds work.'[9] Thelma Holt, the theatrical producer, agrees. 'He has great charm and is a ladies' man. He always notices what you're wearing. Always comments. If you're feeling terrible, he'll cheer you up. I and Veronica share a characteristic of an overlapping tooth – not generally considered attractive. Fitzroy pointed this out and said: ''The most attractive women in the world always have a crooked tooth.'' No one ever said anything like that to me before. Whenever I grin at myself in the mirror, I think of Fitzroy.'[10]

Some women feel that Fitzroy's charm conceals a reserve, which his critics would call coldness. Antonia Fraser says, 'I wouldn't confide personal problems to him. We would have great talks about Scottish history . . . But I never thought of Fitzroy as an intimate person.'[11] Americans, particularly, who always complain about the British 'cool', can find this reserve disconcerting. Linda Bullard, who first met him in Washington in 1964 and has been friendly ever since, once wrote in her diary that people thought she and Fitzroy were having an affair, so close did they seem; her comment: 'What a laugh! In fact he was never interested in me as a real person with problems. If I said to him, ''I'm

worried about this child or that child'', he wasn't interested. I soon
realized it wasn't the kind of friendship Americans are used to, where
you bare your soul and expect love and attention and get support. He
didn't want to know me very well and I assumed he didn't want to know
anyone very well.'[12]

Fitzroy's attraction to women and his mania for exercise come together in a love of dancing, and this has given rise to a lot of amused but
adverse comment from his friends. Jakie Astor says, 'He walks on the
dance floor rather than dances, treats it as a form of exercise. He used to
dance women into the ground. We used to see him sleepwalking on the
dance floor, clasping some pretty girl so closely to him that she could
hardly breathe. About an hour and a half non-stop on the dance floor,
moving slowly.'[13] Antonia Fraser comments: 'Hugh [Fraser] and I
used to call it the dance of death. Dancing until 4 a.m., but absolutely
silent.'[14] Linda Bullard remembers her first meeting with Fitzroy, at an
extraordinary traditional occasion for the 'Old Washington' socialites
called 'the Dancing Class'. 'I remember dancing with him and thinking
he was the worst dancer I'd ever known. I thought it was more like
dancing with a mattress. He liked the hugging, but all he did was shift
from one foot to the other. But remember that I was trained as a dancer,
so I'm hypercritical. I was impressed by Fitzroy's grasp of the sensuous
appeal of dancing. This clearly shows him as a Scot rather than an
Englishman.'[15]

Fitzroy also enormously enjoys his role of Highland laird and gentleman farmer. As a sheepfarmer he liked nothing better than to take
special friends to sheep sales at Dalmailly and other agricultural markets, where the authentic flavour of the old Highlands could still be
perceived. Fitzroy likes to treat the Highlands as a kind of integrator of
all that is most important to him. So his close rapport with the Queen
Mother derives from their common Scottish ancestry, he recognizes a
kinship with his fellow highlanders in Georgia, and he encourages the
SAS to train on his grounds. On one occasion a major SAS exercise
involved one squad protecting Fitzroy in Strachur House while another
tried to capture him. The entire operation was conducted with the
utmost realism but, it is almost unnecessary to add, given 'Fitzroy's
luck', the defending squad won.

For better or worse, Fitzroy's name will always be linked with Tito's.
Having once made up his mind about the Marshal, he never allowed
anti-Tito propaganda in the West to sway him from his friendship.
Indeed, as Alistair Milne comments, 'He could sometimes be very
boring about Tito. That was an obsession and he was always trying to
get us to make more films about Tito. After Tito died and I was Director-General, he wanted us to make a film about Tito's life with him.'[16]

Only a handful of incidents disturbed the even tenor of Fitzroy's friendship. One was the Djilas affair, a long-running saga that began in the late 1950s. Perplexed by the break with the Soviet Union in 1948, Djilas reasoned that, if his certainty that Stalin was an international socialist rather than a nationalist dictator was wrong, perhaps he was wrong about the nature of Communism itself. His doubts and self-doubts found expression in a long series of articles in the official Titoist organ *Borba*. Periodically Djilas asked Tito if he approved of his new line and Tito, who never read the articles, lazily gave him the nod. Djilas began to argue that the Communist Party was a mausoleum, that its officials formed a corrupt 'new class', and even went on to insult the Party wives. Finally the middle echelons could stand it no more and protested to Tito, who was thoroughly alarmed to find what it was he had condoned. Tito also knew he must carry the Party with him, for it was the Party's rock-solid support only that had enabled him to resist Stalin in 1948. Djilas was brought to book and jailed when he refused to recant. Fitzroy intervened, pointing out that the imprisonment of Djilas was making him into a martyr and that socialist opinion in Britain was running strongly in his favour. At first Tito angrily rebuffed the overture as unwarranted foreign interference in an internal Yugoslav matter. But when Fitzroy pointed out that he would be saying the same thing if Djilas was sitting in the presidential suite and Tito in jail Tito thought again, and released Djilas soon afterwards. Unfortunately, this encouraged Djilas to redouble his attacks on Yugoslavia's Communist Party.

Djilas was not Tito's only problem. Throughout the 1950s and 1960s he implemented 'self-management': decentralized decision-making, concern for profitability, demand for Western know-how and markets. Even this limited economic liberalization proved difficult to reconcile with centralized planning. Worse still, self-management stimulated purely local interests and fissiparous nationalist passions. At the end of 1971, in alarm at the threat to 'democratic centralism', Tito withdrew his support from the decentralization process and began a drastic purge of the most 'deviationist' local parties, especially that in Croatia, prior to reimposing stricter centralized control. Once the Croats had been brought to heel, Tito, half-Croat himself, turned on Greater Serb chauvinism and its 'rotten liberalism'. Party leaders in Slovenia, Macedonia and elsewhere were eliminated, ideological orthodoxy tightened, and greater emphasis placed on 'democratic centralism'.

At this final stage of Tito's career, in the 1970s, Fitzroy saw more of his friend than at any time since the 1940s. During the Heath premiership he accompanied Tito to Dalhousie University in Nova Scotia to be given an honorary doctorate. Fitzroy was approached by Dalhousie ('run by a Maclean Mafia', he jokes) to see if he could persuade Tito to accept the degree; for services rendered, Fitzroy too would be honoured. Tito accepted and flew up to Nova Scotia after meeting President Nixon at the White House. Before the ceremony Fitzroy commented to his old friend how good it was to be honoured by a 'non-aligned' nation rather than one of the super-powers or their satellites. Tito responded by making a statesmanlike speech on Yugoslavia's role in the world. At the Lieutenant Governor's reception which followed, Fitzroy mentioned that he was due at Buckingham Palace for lunch the day after next and would have to cut his celebrations short. Tito was due at the same lunch and offered a lift in his private jet. The result was that Fitzroy crawled onto the plane next morning at 6 a.m. 'feeling like death' – this, from the iron man, is quite an admission.

On the plane Tito told Fitzroy of the world tour he was just completing – the visit to Nixon had followed one to Emperor Hirohito of Japan. It was while crossing the Atlantic that Fitzroy noticed all was not well between Tito and his wife.

> I was trying to keep awake, trying to hoist in what he was saying in Serbo-Croat, and generally doing my best. Tito remonstrated with his wife for standing up and gazing out of the window. There's nothing there but sea, he said. 'No, there's the whole of Nova Scotia,' she said. Then she said to me pointedly, 'He likes being right.' I thought, what a mistake to make. Breakfast arrived, and Tito looked at his watch and said, 'Seven a.m. Canada time, that's one p.m. London time. Time for a whisky.' Enormous breakfasts of scrambled eggs and large measures of whisky were produced. Soon Mrs Tito was at it again. 'That's your second whisky,' she said. I thought again, you're making a fatal mistake. Sure enough, soon afterwards Mrs Tito disappeared or, rather, was 'administratively reabsorbed'.[17]

There was a sequel to this tale. When Fitzroy was in Yugoslavia in 1977, CBS offered to commission him to interview Tito provided he was prepared to ask what had happened to Mrs Tito. Fitzroy declined on the grounds of his friendship, so it was left to the redoubtable Walter Kronkite to put that question to the Marshal. Tito replied that at 85 his nerves were still strong, but not strong enough to endure the constant assaults on them by his ex-wife.

Fitzroy's next major encounter with Tito took place in 1977 when Mrs Thatcher, then Leader of the Opposition, visited Belgrade.[18] Tito and the virulent anti-communist Thatcher found conversation difficult at first. Since Mrs Thatcher had just been to China, Tito talked of that country, then engulfed in the controversy over Madame Mao and the 'Gang of Four'. 'Of course,' said Tito, looking her straight in the eye, 'I don't believe in women interfering in politics.' Mrs Thatcher at once snapped back, 'I don't interfere in politics. I *am* politics.' According to Fitzroy, 'Tito was simply delighted, and after that the two of them got on like a house on fire.'[19]

Tito liked to test the mettle of visiting dignitaries. When Fitzroy accompanied Prince Charles on his official visit to Yugoslavia, he took Tito some of his celebrated MacPhunn malt whisky. At the official reception Tito served Chivas Regal, to the chagrin of the Prince, who accosted Tito. 'Can't we broach some of Fitzroy's malt?' 'Oh no,' replied Tito, 'we keep that for special occasions.'[20]

Margaret Thatcher's visit to Belgrade in December 1977 was memorable for Fitzroy since he has always been one of her greatest admirers. For once he found himself accompanying someone with even more energy than himself, who could walk *him* into the ground. With awestruck admiration he recalls her stamina and zest for work.

> We flew to Paris and spent a happy evening at the Embassy there. Then we got up at dawn and flew to Belgrade, where there was snow on the ground. She shot out of the aeroplane, placed a wreath on the Tomb of the Unknown Soldier, then laid another at the British War Cemetery. That set the pattern for the days ahead. Conversations with Tito, visiting factories and supermarkets, where she mastered all the detail and soon knew the price of everything. Remember that we'd had four hours sleep, had been going since 7 a.m. and flown from Paris. Then came Press conferences and a television interview. In the evening we were taken to dinner by the Mayor of Belgrade and then on to a gypsy night-club, where I witnessed the unlikely spectacle of a gypsy fiddler gazing into her eyes and playing 'Yes Sir, That's My Baby'. She ate and drank everything that was put before her and meanwhile the Town Clerk was becoming attentive too – a little too attentive. All this while the Mayor, who had been to the LSE, carried on a high-class conversation with her about economics. We got home at 1 a.m. and she was still going strong. The British Ambassador said 'It would be awfully nice if you could meet the clerical staff at the Embassy.' 'What time do we start tomorrow?' she asked. 'Seven a.m.,' came the answer. 'Right. Make it 6 a.m. We mustn't miss them on any account.' Amazing. She kept up that pace for the best part of a week.[21]

When Tito died in 1980 at the age of 88, Fitzroy was among the dignitaries invited to the funeral. Leonid Brezhnev, Willi Brandt, Margaret Thatcher (now Prime Minister), the Duke of Edinburgh, the US Vice-President (Carter's absence was generally considered a diplomatic blunder), Bill Deakin and a host of leaders from the Third World came to Belgrade. Fitzroy was invited to do the English commentary at the funeral, to be broadcast around the world. Thelma Holt remembers: 'The commentary he did then was great and shows another side of him. He did it beautifully, nothing sombre, nothing funereal.'[22]

Fitzroy rates Tito, after Churchill, as the greatest political leader he has known. But he is magnanimous and generous in his assessment of all political figures. Mrs Thatcher he considers 'a very great Prime Minister', though he expresses severe reservations about her wisdom in pressing on with the hated Poll Tax. 'That really was unbelievable, disastrous – you'd think they would have been able to work that out. I mean, it was done out of pure zeal . . . She can be very stubborn.'[23]

He is fond of Harold Wilson, too. 'I think I am one of the few people who can say he has spent a weekend in Samarkand with Harold Wilson,' he says with a smile.[24] John Roberts, usually a critic of Fitzroy, tells a revealing story about the 25th Anniversary Dinner of the Great Britain–USSR Society. By this time Harold Wilson was suffering from Alzheimer's Disease. He proposed a toast to the Queen and then to the First Secretary of the Soviet Communist Party. A few minutes later he got to his feet and proposed the health of the Queen again. Realizing what was happening, Fitzroy quickly intervened, improvised a second round of toasts, then got the guest speaker Sir Geoffrey Howe to his feet at once.[25]

When he reached seventy, the media showered honours on Fitzroy. In April 1981 he appeared for the second time on *Desert Island Discs*; it was even rumoured that, had Roy Plomley lived, he intended to invite Fitzroy for an unprecedented third appearance.[26] As his luxury item Fitzroy chose pencils, pen and paper, and his 'desert island' book was *War and Peace* in Russian. His love of Russian language and literature is such that his bedtime reading is the Sherlock Holmes stories in the language of Pushkin. Later there were numerous television and radio appearances, star turns on the *Wogan* programme, and so forth. But perhaps the most notable event was Eamonn Andrews' *This is Your Life* programme devoted to Fitzroy in December 1984. As always, the surprise 'biography' had to be sprung on the victim. An obscure books programme was set up as the pretext for his presence at the television studios and all seemed set fair when, one week before the scheduled transmission, our hero decided London was too hot and abandoned his Knightsbridge flat for Argyll, declaring that an appearance on a minor books programme did not warrant such discomfort. In consternation, Veronica played the only card that would bring her husband back to London on the required date. She phoned Fitzroy's good friend the Queen Mother, explained the situation, and asked her to insist on his presence at lunch that day.

Fitzroy was obliged to accede to such a request, and travelled down to London. The Queen Mother played her part well and delayed his departure on one pretext or other. Fitzroy became uneasy and agitated. Meanwhile, at Teddington Studios matters were scarcely proceeding smoothly. Sandy Glen had cautioned Eamonn Andrews against giving a lunch for such a bibulous group as Fitzroy's old friends, but Andrews went ahead anyway. The result was some not inconsiderable intoxication by 3 p.m. Fearing that matters were getting out of hand, Andrews' staff suggested putting the guests to bed in the studio accommodation quarters and locking them in until the programme began. But locking in ex-commandos is always a forlorn hope. Within five minutes all were out again, heading for the hospitality room.

By the time Fitzroy had torn himself away from the Queen Mother's lunch, it was time to head for the studio. Fitzroy was in a foul mood because he had not been able to go home between engagements. He suspected that something was wrong only when his limousine entered Teddington Studios and he saw Douglas Fairbanks, Jr waiting to meet him, which hardly suggested an esoteric programme for bibliophiles. Fitzroy confesses that he was genuinely astonished by the sequel. After the programme a lavish dinner went on until 2 a.m. Celebrating his achievements as a war hero seemed all the more appropriate when the Macleans returned to Lowndes Square in the small hours to find that Veronica had locked her keys indoors. The fire brigade was called and Fitzroy had to climb up a fireman's ladder to break into his own flat.[27]

Fitzroy has always enjoyed his contacts with the world of show business and the media. Favourite movie stars, all of whom he met at one time or another, include Alec Guinness, Lauren Bacall and Shirley Maclaine. The walls of Creggans are covered with photos of showbiz visitors to the inn, including Michael Caine, Roger Moore, and Michael Winner, and Fitzroy also numbers among his friends Susannah York and Gayle Hunnicutt. His taste for showbiz he shared with Tito, who liked nothing better than to entertain Hollywood stars like Richard Burton and Elizabeth Taylor on his island retreat of Brioni.[28] Fitzroy also wrote a treatment for and was historical advisor on Veljko Bulajic's film *Battle of the Neretva*, made in 1970. The cast included Yul Brynner, Orson Welles, Hardy Kruger, Franco Nero, Kurt Jurgens and Sylva Koscina. 'Pretty good nonsense, though quite amusing to watch, and the Germans [Kruger and Jurgens] excellent.' At the 'wrap' dinner the ravishingly beautiful Koscina sat between Fitzroy and Tito. The filming gave Fitzroy an opportunity to renew his acquaintance with Orson Welles, whom he had first met on a train in Italy. Welles played a thinly-disguised Mihailovic. 'The filming involved some breathtaking journeys to remote locations on winding roads and hairpin bends,' Fitzroy recalls. 'Orson Welles took it all in his stride but Yul Brynner, who played the explosives expert, panicked and insisted on being conveyed by special train. Brynner was not popular with the Yugoslavs. In his hotel he roared impatiently for ice, and the Yugoslav waiter was so disgusted that he got a huge block of it and dropped it on his toe.'[29]

As he approached his eightieth birthday Fitzroy showed no signs of slowing down. At the age of 78 he and Veronica fulfilled a long-standing ambition by travelling by truck and train from Gilgit in Pakistan along the old Silk Route to Kashgar in Chinese Turkestan – in the opposite direction from that taken by Peter Fleming in his famous journey.

There followed a train journey across China in the notoriously uncomfortable 'iron rooster' – an experience assuaged at the end by 'the most luxurious hotel I have ever stayed in', the White Swan in Canton. His 79th birthday found him accompanying Veronica to Nepal and to the Kingdom of Lo, a walled city 12,000 feet up in the Himalayas, reachable only by ladder. Later in 1990 there were trips to Yugoslavia, the Caucasus and Tibet. A typical week in London in December 1990 involved hosting a dinner party for visiting Russians, a theatre visit to see the visiting Georgian company, dinner at Buckingham Palace, dinner with a delegation of visiting Yugoslavs, dinner with the MPs John Smith and Norman Tebbit at the 'Other Club', two six-hour sessions with his biographer, an interview with Jasper Ridley for his forthcoming biography of Tito, plus innumerable phone calls to television companies about his planned programmes on the Scottish clans and the proposed dramatization of *Eastern Approaches*.

On 11 March 1991 he celebrated his 80th birthday in style. Sixty guests were invited to a dinner at the British Embassy in Paris hosted by the ambassador, Sir Euan Fergusson, whose ambition to become a diplomat was first fired by *Eastern Approaches*. Then the restless Fitzroy was on his travels again, first to Georgia, and later to Yugoslavia to take informal soundings for the EEC on the prospects for ending the disastrous civil war there.

'I am grateful that I have been granted more than my biblical span of three score years and ten, for otherwise I would not have seen the momentous changes in Eastern Europe,' Fitzroy says.[30] He welcomes both the liberation of the former satellite states and the dismemberment of the Soviet Union itself, satisfying occurrences to a man who helped Tito to knock the first chips off the monolith. But he did not welcome Gorbachev's downfall at the end of 1991, and sees social unrest and even civil war ahead in the bleeding *disiecta membra* of the former Soviet Union. His favourite project, the restoration of the monarchy in Georgia, also seems unlikely now.

The threatened break-up of Yugoslavia, on the other hand, fills him with profound gloom. Fitzroy has always believed that the unified Yugoslavia achieved by Tito was a genuine act of statesmanship, and deplores the double standards of those in the West who encourage every act of separatism in Eastern Europe, in defiance of the conventional wisdom that nowadays only large-scale units are economically viable. There is something bizarre about Western attitudes to nation-states east of the Danube, he believes. The northern states of the USA fought to prevent the secession of the southern states – a right of secession that was clearly implicit in the 1787 Constitution. In Britain politicians fight tooth and nail against an independent Scotland or a united Ireland, on the grounds that Scotland and Northern Ireland are part of an indissoluble United Kingdom. Yet as soon as a separatist politician arises in Eastern Europe or the former Soviet Union, he is at once acclaimed by the Western media and given the title 'president'.

Croat separatists know that Fitzroy has no patience with their aspirations – hardly surprisingly, given his knowledge of the Ustase state between 1941 and 1945. One of them told Sir Peter Carey: 'Fitzroy Maclean has quite the wrong views, he wants to hold Yugoslavia together.'[31] Fitzroy makes no bones about this and is prepared to express his views even against official disapproval in Serbia and Croatia. Recently he was filmed for Yugoslav television at the memorial in Sarajevo where Prinzip assassinated Archduke Franz Ferdinand in 1914. He spoke as follows: 'The Serbians who refused to be separated from their brethren the South Serbians started a war that cost ten million lives. In common humanity you now owe it to the shades of the departed to stick together, so that all those millions may not have died in vain.'[32] The controllers of Yugoslav television swallowed hard, but put the speech out unaltered.

Fitzroy is also critical of many opinions about Yugoslavia expressed in the West. To those who claim that the assault on Croatia is an attempt by the Communist old guard to retrieve their former position, he says that Titoism is scarcely a factor in the struggle between Serbia and Croatia: it is the spiritual descendants of the Cetniks and the Ustase respectively who are battling it out. He talks of the many profound problems overlooked by the Western media, among them that of the Albanians domiciled in Yugoslavia, 'a problem so intractable that not even Pavelic or the Nazis with their gas ovens would be able to solve it. But in the *brouhaha* over Croatia, when do we ever hear of this?'[33] An even thornier problem is that of Bosnia. Bosnia's population is made up of 50 per cent Slav Muslims, 30 per cent Bosnian Serbs and 20 per cent Bosnian Croats, all inextricably intermixed, especially in the towns. Any break-up of Yugoslavia involves dividing such a Bosnia between Serbia and Croatia. He is deeply depressed by all that has happened in Yugoslavia and its impending break up. This, he accepts, is now an accomplished fact, and he believes that the component parts must now be recognized as sovereign states. He hopes, however, that as they are, for geographical reasons, going to have to exist side by side in future, they will at least try to work out a system of peaceful coexistence rather than remain permanently at loggerheads.

Yet Fitzroy knows that rationality is not usually to the forefront in politics. Sometimes he entertains an apocalyptic vision of Yugoslavia dissolving into bloodshed with all former Tito supporters, including himself, being rounded up and shot. 'It would be a good and dignified end,' he muses.[34] He remains the romantic hero.

Conclusion

F ITZROY MACLEAN has achieved success as diplomat, soldier, traveller, author and man of the media. In an age of specialization, when 'Renaissance man' has come to mean 'dilettante', such a career is suspect. 'An amateur in a world of professionals', 'a man with an obsession about being typecast', are typical criticisms from those disposed to bridle at the name of Fitzroy Maclean. There is a larger class prepared to give him his rightful place as a latter-day Burnaby or Burton, but these in turn are often sceptical about the project of assessing Fitzroy's life and exploits. Some claim his achievement is unique and only to be comprehended by a similar high-flyer. There is an element of *reductio ad absurdum* here, for that logic would require biographies of Roosevelt by Churchill, Wittgenstein by Russell, Bernstein by Previn, or Orson Welles by Peter Ustinov. Every human being is full of contradictions; what matters is how felicitously these elements are resolved in living. By this standard Fitzroy's life has been unusually successful, for he has integrated the contradictions better than most.

Each of Fitzroy's critical attributes, or the criticisms made of him, can be offset by an equal and opposite quality. The charge of dilettantism looks facile in the light of the careful and painstaking way he prepares every aspect of his life, from travelling to writing. The accusation that he is easily bored and impatient of detail does not stand up against the witness of those who have travelled with him, who to a man testify to his stoicism and patience in the face of the manifold difficulties that beset voyagers in Central Asia. The charge that he is unwilling to submit to the discipline of hierarchies is contradicted by those who speak of his readiness to take direction from a film producer or his meekness in accepting criticism from an expert. Any thought of 'vaulting ambition, which o'erleaps itself' is dispelled by an examination of his political career, where he failed mainly because he did not have the driving ambition of a Thatcher or a Heseltine.

His famous love of danger, too, has to be qualified. He is too full of zest for life to harbour any form of death-wish. He likes to think through an adventure and to see how much risk can be accommodated while still achieving the end result. Here we return to the proposition that true courage involves forethought and the rational calculation of risks, rather than the blind instinct of 'dissociative reaction', when hesitation on the borderlands of terror and cowardice can lead to a freak reaction like the single-handed storming of a machine-gun nest – an action more properly described as being taken while the balance of the mind is disturbed. Fitzroy can be seen at his best in his barefaced effrontery towards the Italian sentries in Benghazi, which required flair and aplomb but was a necessity arising from the moment, not a reckless act of egocentric bravado putting the entire mission in jeopardy. Fitzroy has luck, the first attribute of the successful soldier; he also has a sixth sense, in the very moment of action, of what will work and what will not.

The historian J. H. Plumb once told Michael Gill, the film producer, that the modern world lacked valour, gusto and hope. Gill replied that he had just been to Russia with the only man he knew who had all three. Undoubtedly the great period in Fitzroy's life was between 1941 and 1945, when he gained his credentials as war-hero, uniquely combined the roles of soldier and diplomat, and established the interest in Yugo-slavia and the Soviet Union that has sustained him ever since. Many war heroes emerged from the conflict unable to find a niche in civilian life and condemned ultimately to drink, despair and early death. Fitzroy felt he owed it to the spirits of his fallen comrades to live life to the full and never to despair. 'The secret of life is having too much to do' is his credo, and he has been true to it.

Fitzroy's has been the fate that often befalls great adventurers: an action-packed early life, in contrast to which the rest of his career appears an anti-climax. He was 34 when the high adventures came to an end, and in this he resembles Burton, all of whose important exploits were behind him by his late thirties. Fitzroy is also superficially similar to his hero Bonnie Prince Charlie, whose fourteen months in Scotland in 1745 and 1746 were followed by more than forty years of decline. However, insists Fitzroy, 'the difference is that I got married and lived happily ever after, whereas the poor Prince made a disastrous marriage and took to the bottle.' Yet Fitzroy's later life can be seen as a kind of coda to his heyday in the epoch of the dictators. Even in his writing he could never match the success of his first book, *Eastern Approaches*. To achieve a glittering triumph with one's first creative endeavour can be a mixed blessing, as Orson Welles discovered after *Citizen Kane*.

The two most fundamental drives in Fitzroy's life were the Army and Scotland. The military tradition was bred in the bone. John Purdie remarks: 'The Army is crucial . . . To Fitzroy the hardihood of the clansman or the squaddie who can shave in cold water is an important element in being male, but that breed is disappearing, which is why he laments the passing of National Service.' John Henniker adds: 'One of the things motivating Fitzroy was to prove that he could be as big and macho as the big, bad, fire-eating Highland chiefs. In terms of their culture, doing well academically, getting prizes at Eton, a First at Cambridge, a place in the Foreign Office, all this was rather wimpish. Soldiering and adventuring was the really important thing. I think the wish to be seen to be a true Maclean scion was one of the powerful motives. He was going to prove he was a big, bad Highland chieftain.'

But unlike David Stirling, Paddy Mayne and many of the other SAS heroes, Fitzroy is an intellectual, and it is this that enabled him to achieve equilibrium in the difficult transition to peacetime while so many of his comrades lapsed into depression. Yet some even of the intellectual survivors of the Second World War, like Kenneth Allsop and Spencer Chapman, found the adjustment too great and in the end killed themselves. Fitzroy is tough and self-controlled, both physically and mentally. Harold Macmillan, updating the concepts of *noblesse de la robe* and *noblesse de l'épée*, spoke of the distinction between the warrior and the cardinal. Few men are both, but Fitzroy is one of the few. This aligns him with scholar-soldiers like Allenby, who could recite passages of the Classics in the original, or the poetry-loving Wavell, rather than with the self-destructive intellectual commandos like Orde Wingate or T.E. Lawrence.

The congruence of man of action and man of intellect is not the only striking mark of Fitzroy's integration as a human being. More surprising, perhaps, is that this man's man – who surely epitomizes Monty's conception of the man you would go into the jungle with – is also a ladies' man who enjoys their company most.

Scotland is as important to Fitzroy as the Army. Some Scots may regard him as an 'Anglo' and scoff at his '*passé*' obsession with the clans, plaid and tartan, but David Lambie the Labour MP puts this issue in perspective: 'We accept him as a good Scotsman, even as a great Scotsman, but not as a politician.'

Fitzroy is sometimes compared with two other notable twentieth-century Scotsmen, John Buchan and Compton Mackenzie. Mackenzie was Veronica's girlhood hero, and a friend and admirer of her mother Laura Lovat. His love of Barra stands comparison with Fitzroy's for Strachur; like Fitzroy he was devoted to Prince Charlie and wrote about him; and in many ways he had in the First World War a career not dissimilar to Fitzroy's in the Second. But Mackenzie was a deliberate controversialist, whereas Fitzroy tends to be dragged into controversy against his will. Mackenzie's volumes of memoirs are full of his wrangles

with secret service chiefs and the top brass; Fitzroy, by contrast, omit-
ted from *Eastern Approaches* any mention of his celebrated battle with
Brigadier Keble and SOE.

Buchan resembles Fitzroy only in his undistinguished political career
and his ability to penetrate the inner portals of the Establishment. Their
sensibilities were poles apart, and Fitzroy admits that though he always
enjoyed Buchan's novels he regards the man himself as a second-rater.
Buchan's sensibility was in some ways closer to that of Wilfred
Thesiger: both were fishermen, prepared to wait hours for a salmon,
which Fitzroy would regard as a waste of time. Where Fitzroy and
Compton Mackenzie were privateers who believed that rules were there
to be broken, Buchan almost certainly never broke a rule in his life. He
was a repressed romantic, but he played the game according to a book of
rules drawn up by an English élite.

Fitzroy's penchant for breaking rules, so clear in Russia between
1937 and 1939, was still very much to the fore in the 1980s, as John
Purdie remembers: 'In the Soviet Union I was forever noticing his
roguishness. He'll break every rule in the book, from No Smoking
upwards. He bought tins of snuff in Uzbekistan, then in meetings with
Soviet VIPs when there were prominent No Smoking notices displayed,
he'd take the snuff out and pretend to be smoking. Because he has such
an inbuilt sense of hierarchy and order, that's why – every so often,
when it's not going to break the house, he likes bending the rules and
being a naughty boy. It's the schoolboy or *enfant terrible* side. He's an
adolescent, he does have this amazingly youthful approach to anything.
You don't feel you're talking to an old man, more like a teenager who'll
do anything, be into anything.' Thelma Holt agrees: 'He's both larger
than life and ageless. In spite of his eminence and intelligence, in some
ways he's never reached maturity, he's a little boy, he likes play and
fun.'

Some of Fitzroy's friends claim that at a deeper level, his classical
education and his love of Russia might be even stronger influences on
him than the hereditary pull towards Scotland. This claim in turn
subdivides into a debate as to whether he is really classical or romantic
in temperament. Is he a man of the eighteenth century or the nineteenth, a clan chief or a Scot of the diaspora, a Highland warrior or the
Scotsman forced out to the corners of the Empire? Some stress his love
of Russia, his special feeling for Pushkin's poetry, the time he puts in
every day on the Russian language. A Soviet official once told him,
'Ideologically and politically we know you're hopeless, but we also
know that you love our country.' On the other hand, the Greek and
Latin classics have certainly influenced Fitzroy. The clarity of his prose
style he attributes to his close study of Thucydides, while if there is a
classical character who resembles Fitzroy in his mixture of martial

valour, diplomacy, cunning and shrewdness, it is surely Odysseus. Jamie Maclean emphasizes the classical side of Fitzroy: '. . . our tastes in painting are so very different. I have a broad range, but his appreciation ends with Turner. He's very much an eighteenth-century man and I don't think he's much interested in periods before and after. His interest is focused on the eighteenth century, very conservative, very classical, like his interest in architecture. This fits in with his classical education, as the eighteenth century was the era when the study of the classics was most admired. Fitzroy will go as far as the early Romantics, but a perfect illustration of his taste would be a Piranesi engraving of a ruined Roman temple.'

Yet the high noon of Empire in the nineteenth century might have provided an outlet for Fitzroy's talents and energies. In the twentieth century he is a man out of his time. Even the pro-Imperial statements of the 1940s and 1950s, the gung-ho enthusiasm for Suez (and later for the Falklands conflict and the Gulf War), which can be read superficially as reactionary, can be seen in a profounder sense as lamentation for a Golden Age. He yearns for a time when the individual adventurer made a difference, when the dead hand of economic forces and multinational corporations was not on everything. The charismatic leader is Fitzroy's *beau idéal*, the romance of Bonnie Prince Charlie and the clan chieftains his inspiration. One of the reasons for his rapport with Tito may have been his perception of him as a representative of a bygone culture of charismatic leadership, to which he could relate easily. And we are always being reminded by Hugh Seton-Watson and other authorities of the similarity between parts of wartime Yugoslavia and Scotland before the '45.

Fitzroy is often called a 'buccaneer', but such men are usually impatient of detail; Fitzroy is not. He works hard to get things right. His writing, for example, is the result of conscientious craftsmanship, and his near-total recall is a great help. Annette Street, who worked for him in the 1940s, remembers: 'If you were typing his handwritten drafts up and changed one preposition, he noticed. He had a wonderful command of the English language. I worked for a lot of bright people, Christopher Sykes and others, but I never met anybody else who wrote in longhand but remembered every last thing he'd written. He claimed it was his Foreign Office training, but in that case why are all FO people not good writers?'

Fitzroy can also take a long time to come to a final conclusion, which has earned him the reputation of being slow. But Jeanne Clissold thinks this masks an ability to make interesting links. 'Also an ability to decide that X was not the right thing and change it. A lot of changing of minds. Not so much indecisiveness as second thoughts, and the idea that there was a better plan. He was sometimes a very long time making up his mind. Once he had, he would not be indecisive unless he thought of a better plan. But he so often did. I think he was a perfectionist. Get it right rather than get it done.' Jeanne Clissold also remembers that the Cockney charlady at his Lowndes Square flat in the late 1940s – she who was interviewed by the *Daily Worker* in connection with the Albanian allegations that Fitzroy was a master spy – said that Fitzroy knew to within an inch where everything was in his room, and that if moved, it would cause 'a regular D'Oyly Carte'.

The contradictions multiply; immense shrewdness and a somewhat cynical view of humanity are counterbalanced by an almost Panglossian world-view. John Henniker says: 'Fitzroy has not much idea what people are like deep down. He has political street-wisdom, but in many ways he's rather an innocent. He doesn't know who's doing him down. In Yugoslavia he didn't know what any of us were propelled by. He wouldn't understand Bill Deakin at the deepest level. He wouldn't know what made him tick. I wouldn't have expected Fitz as Prime Minister to show genius in picking his ministers. His idea is a few old friends on a mission and he favours those in his club, or regiment. All of which makes me think that his wonderful team in Yugoslavia was more luck than judgement. Fitzroy is lucky, and he does have a nose for who's doing him good.'

Fitzroy is also a solitary who likes nothing better than to be in his study working on a book, or stalking the heather alone. Yet he can appear to be the most extrovert and gregarious of men. John Blelloch remembers Hugh and Antonia Fraser's wedding in 1956. 'I said to Fitzroy, "There'll be hundreds of people there, Minister, you should think yourself lucky you're not an usher." He replied, "Not only am I an usher but I am Captain of Ushers, much as d'Artagnan was Captain of Musketeers." '

At Hugh Fraser's funeral Fitzroy most clearly revealed his sentimental side. Antonia Fraser remembers him delivering the oration: 'At the end he was almost in tears and couldn't go on. It was remarkable to see someone like Fitzroy in tears publicly. One realized he was emotional deep down, a real Celt.' Pamela Egremont's conclusion is judicious: 'Ruthless? Yes, but never at the expense of integrity. Hard-nosed but tender-hearted. Ruthless and sentimental, the way you see in nineteenth-century novels.'

The polarity that most impressed John Purdie was that between humour and cantankerousness. 'Occasionally he can be bad-tempered and even a difficult old bugger, but I didn't mind that and saw it as a spicy side to him. You could always get him out of it by cracking a joke. A terrific sense of humour. If you can go with that, you're fine. You can cut straight to the man. The key to him is, when he gets cantankerous or irascible, treat him with humour. He responds quickly.'

'I would be very surprised if anyone found a dark side in Fitzroy,' said Linda Bullard. The dark side most frequently alluded to by those who know him is ruthlessness. 'Fitz is ruthless, and can be fairly brutal,' remarked Alistair Milne. The producer Michael Gill, who travelled with Fitzroy in Russia, remembers that Fitzroy jettisoned him and switched to another company when Goldcrest ran into trouble. 'He was quite right from his point of view; my not being involved in it was the price of his getting the money. Films are all about money, so this did not end my friendship, but it did make me realize he could be ruthless.' Christian Hesketh says: 'Romantics and adventurers like Fitzroy are not usually admirable in the normal sense. Under the charm and affability Fitzroy is a hard man. He can be incredibly selfish and manipulative, and if it's a conflict between your interest and his, and his prevails, he has no worries or doubts on that score.' John Henniker adds: 'My quarrel with ruthlessness is that it's so often self-destructive. Fitzroy never understood that it's counterproductive to antagonize the little man by going over his head, as you simply make unnecessary enemies.' Fitzroy himself answers his critics thus: 'Ruthless? That's a compliment. What's the difference between ruthless and realistic? I don't think there are many bleeding corpses on my path. Again, if I had been that ruthless, surely I would have done better in terms of the glittering prizes.'

Fitzroy believes in hierarchy, order and social stratification, yet can get on as well with the dustman as with the Queen Mother. He likes all kinds of people and is fascinated to observe how many different kinds of talents there are in the world. He is a supporter of the Establishment, though himself neither stuffy nor self-important. No dyed-in-the wool lover of the Establishment would have had Fitzroy's weakness for plausible pirates like Robert Maxwell and Aristotle Onassis. 'I like the Establishment in that I'm a keen monarchist. I like what has been built up in this country over a thousand years, and its flexibility. In some ways our class system is a bad thing, but not in all. There is always a circulation of élites within the Establishment, it's not just the hereditary principle. The aristocracy has never managed to divorce itself from ordinary people here. I'm amused to see how the rebels of the sixties – people like Paul Johnson and Woodrow Wyatt – have come round to my way of thinking.'

His inner life is more difficult to pin down. Jakie Astor remarks: 'I think Fitz is after a bit of fun. He has no deep down philosophy. He's not a great Tory or a great Communist or anything like that.' That makes him sound frivolous and light-weight, but Fitzroy cleaves to the H.L. Mencken dictum that a belly-laugh is worth a thousand syllogisms. Besides, it is not true to say that he believes in nothing, as if he were a Flaubertian nihilist. He is a devoted Episcopalian, with a spiritual mentor half his age in the form of Allan Maclean. John Purdie observed in Russia that Fitzroy went to church every Sunday and assumed it was merely the way of the 'man in the manor house', but Fitzroy's Christian belief, though he doesn't talk about it, is deeply held.

Fitzroy Maclean is a controversial figure in 1992 as Yugoslavia and the territories that made up the Soviet Union slide into anarchy. The air is full of anxiety about the destabilizing consequences of a dismembered Yugoslavia and, especially, of the break-up of the Soviet Union. Nobody in the West likes the present state of anarchy but, as Fitzroy has pointed out all along, in this life you do not get all you want, and the West can now decide whether it preferred the tense but predictable relationship with Communist regimes to the nightmarish uncertainty of nuclear-armed crackpot 'republics'.

Fitzroy's enemies accuse him of many things. He 'created Tito virtually singlehanded' (though who then commanded at the Battle of Neretva must remain problematical). He was 'soft on the Soviets' during the Khruschev and Brezhnev years; he produced a bland, acceptable image of the Soviet Union for his western readers. He ruthlessly cut out Bill Deakin and others from credit for the achievement in Yugoslavia. He discarded friends when they were no longer any use to him. He had too keen an eye for pretty women, a womaniser *manqué* if not in fact. By careful montage one can assemble a picture of a fairly unpleasant man. It would, however, bear no relation to the real Fitzroy Maclean; it would omit his courage, his wit, his charm, his humour, his intellect, and his humanity.

His place in history rests on his work in Yugoslavia during the war. Here he showed greatness, not just in his mastery of his political and military task, but in his integrity. What Fitzroy found in Yugoslavia in 1943 did not accord with his own *a priori* political convictions. A lesser man might have doctored evidence to suit his political prejudices; Fitzroy reported what he found. For this his enemies on the Right will never forgive him, and they judge him by criteria they would not apply to other situations. A recent television programme on the historical background to the crisis in Northern Ireland unveiled singular political cowardice in the years from 1914 to 1921. Successive Secretaries of State for Northern Ireland were asked to comment; their remarks were masterpieces of evasion. 'I refuse to pass judgement on my predecessors'; 'It's impossible to say what I would have done as I wasn't there'; 'It's easy to judge with hindsight'; 'We have to deal with things as they are now, not as we would like them to be'. These doctrines are forgotten when it comes to Yugoslavia in the War. The Right must weigh Fitzroy in the balance, and always find him wanting.

Fitzroy has been misunderstood by people who can understand an out-and-out Communist or an out-and-out Right-winger, but not a non-ideological eclectic. If the ability to get on with all kinds of people is 'vertical' tolerance, the ability to get on with all shades of political opinion can be construed as 'horizontal' tolerance. Fitzroy possesses both. His Foreign Office reports from 1939 to 1941 reveal a genuine detestation of the Soviet government, but he was prepared in the 1950s and afterwards to work amicably with Soviet officials. This realism has often been denounced. There has over the past thirty years been a strain of opinion stressing the 'realism' of economic contacts with, for instance, South Africa while advocating moral crusades against China and the Soviet Union, accommodation with whom is somehow not 'realistic'. If the United States engages the Soviet Union in an arms race and spends its enemy into terminal crisis, this – the result of a crusade – is taken to mean that the Soviet Union was always ripe for defeat by a determined opposition. Failure to squeeze South Africa economically, resulting in the survival of the regime there, is then taken as evidence for the 'realistic' view that South Africa's ruling élite was always indestructible.

It has for many years been Fitzroy's fate to be subjected to double standards and selectively applied logic. Just as his enemies cannot agree whether he was duped by Tito (the Right in England), or whether he duped Tito (the Stalinists), so they cannot decide whether he should be regarded as a hardline Cold Warrior, or as an apologist for the Soviet Union. One critic will say that Fitzroy Maclean is 'too right-wing'; another that he is not right-wing enough. Fitzroy's approach to reality is eclectic. He buys no overall package. Eclecticism is always suspect to those who demand partisanship, and it is the fate of the judicious to make enemies at both ends of the political spectrum. Equilibrium and balance will always be perceived as sitting on the fence. But Sir Fitzroy Maclean is bigger than his critics, and his achievements will endure when they are all forgotten.

Sources

———

THE principal oral sources are the hundreds of hours of interviews taped with Sir Fitzroy Maclean and those who have known him at various stages in his life. The principal written primary sources all come from the Public Record Office and consist of the Foreign Office, Cabinet and War Office papers for the relevant period. Not the least important source for Fitzroy's life is his own *oeuvre*, as follows:

EA	*Eastern Approaches* (1949)
DB	*Disputed Barricade* (1957)
PFE	*A Person from England* (1958)
BB	*Back to Bokhara* (1959)
CHS	*A Concise History of Scotland* (1970)
BN	*The Battle of Neretva* (1970)
TBB	*To the Back of Beyond* (1974)
CEE	*To Caucasus, the End of all the Earth* (1976)
HR	*Holy Russia* (1978)
TNS	*Take Nine Spies* (1978)
JBT	*Josip Broz Tito: A Pictorial Biography* (1980)
IOS	*The Isles of the Sea* (1985)
PSU	*Portrait of the Soviet Union* (1988)
BPC	*Bonnie Prince Charlie* (1988)

Chapter 1

1. Sir Iain Moncreiffe, *The Highland Clans* (2nd edn, 1982), pp. 166–70.
2. *IOS*, p. 16.
3. Michael Lynch, *A History of Scotland* (1991), p. 291. See also Paul Hopkins, *Glencoe* (1986).
4. *CHS*, p. 163.
5. Frank McLynn, *Charles Edward Stuart* (1988), p. 120.
6. Fitzroy Maclean to author, interview, 29 December 1991.
7. Ibid.
8. Lady Maclean to author, interview, 29 December 1991.
9. Suki Paravicini to author, interview, 25 June 1991.

10. Lady Maclean to author, interview, 29 December 1991.
11. Fitzroy Maclean to author, interview, 29 December 1991.
12. Fitzroy Maclean to author, interview, 14 October 1990.
13. Fitzroy Maclean to author, interview, 13 April 1991.
14. Fitzroy Maclean to author, interview, 14 October 1990.
15. Suki Paravicini to author, interview, 25 June 1991.
16. J. F. Crace (1877–1960) retired from Eton in 1935, aged 58, after 34 years' service at the school. For the 'overfondness', see Michael Shelden, *Orwell* (1991), p. 78.
17. *Eton College Chronicle*, 5 May 1960.
18. Fitzroy Maclean to author, interview, 14 October 1990.
19. Quoted in Philippe Daudy, *Les Anglais* (1991), pp. 62–3.
20. Sir John Lawrence to author, interview, 16 August 1991.
21. 'Randolph as Commando', in Kay Halle, ed., *Randolph, The Young Pretender* (1971), p. 88.
22. A. J. Ayer, *Part of My Life* (1977), p. 60.
23. *Eton College Chronicle*, 27 September 1928.
24. Lady Maclean to author, interview, 29 December 1991.
25. Fitzroy Maclean to author, interview, 29 December 1991.
26. Fitzroy Maclean to author, interview, 14 October 1990.
27. *TNS*, p. 241.
28. Fitzroy Maclean to author, interview, 14 October 1990.
29. Fitzroy Maclean to author, interview, 17 October 1991.
30. Ibid.
31. Fitzroy Maclean to author, interview, 14 October 1990.
32. Fitzroy Maclean to author, interview, 17 October 1991.

Chapter 2

1. *EA*, p. 16, pp. 11–12, pp. 14–15.
2. Fitzroy Maclean to author, interview, 14 October 1990.
3. Michael Davie, ed., *The Diaries of Evelyn Waugh* (1976), p. 675 (under 7 April 1947).
4. *EA*, p. 16.
5. Sir Frank Roberts to author, interview, 6 November 1990.
6. Fitzroy Maclean to author, interview, 14 December 1990. Nemesis finally overtook the ageing playboy-diplomat. Clerk was invited to dine at Buckingham Palace: he was proud of his *savoir-faire* in social engagements, and the invitation was the acme of his social aspirations. Unaccountably, he forgot about the party, neglected to attend, and was never asked again.
7. John Harvey, ed., *The Diplomatic Diaries of Oliver Harvey 1937–1940* (1970), p. 291 (under 20 May 1939). The Establishment is a close-knit circle: Phipps was the father of Alan Phipps, Lady Maclean's first husband.
8. For Roberts see *The Diaries of Bruce Lockhart*, p. 763 (under 22 April 1960). For his own account, see *Dealing with Dictators* (1991).
9. Fitzroy Maclean to author, interview, 14 October 1990.
10. Sir Frank Roberts to author, interview, 6 November 1990.
11. *EA*, p. 16.
12. Alexander Werth, *The Last Days of Paris* (1940), p. 137.
13. Fitzroy Maclean to author, interview, 14 December 1990.
14. Ibid.

15. See Anthony Cave Brown, *The Secret Servant* (1988), pp. 140, 254-5, 406-8, 445-6, 581.
16. Written statement by Fitzroy Maclean to author.
17. Fitzroy Maclean to author, interview, 6 March 1991.
18. Fitzroy Maclean to author, 14 October 1990. It is interesting to see that A. J. P. Taylor, with whom Fitzroy once clashed in the pages of *Picture Post* over the future of Germany, concurred in this high estimate of Simon: 'Simon was not second-rate or failing in health. He had a cold, unattractive personality, but he was very able.' (A. J. P. Taylor, *Letters to Eva* (1991), p. 196).
19. *EA*, p. 14.
20. Fitzroy Maclean to author, interview, 13 April 1991.
21. Fitzroy Maclean to author, interview, 14 October 1990.
22. Ibid.
23. Ivar Bryce, *You Only Live Once* (1984), p. 30.
24. Fitzroy Maclean to author, interview, 14 October 1990.
25. J. E. Dreifort, *Yvon Delbos at the Quai d'Orsay* (Lawrence, Kansas, 1973), p. 206.
26. Ibid., p. 47.
27. Basil Liddell Hart, *Memoirs* (New York, 1966), 2 vols: ii, pp. 127-8.
28. For further details on these events, see United States Documents on Foreign Affairs (hereinafter *USD*), 1936, ii, pp. 447-9; Cordell Hull, *Memoirs* (New York, 1948), p. 476; *Les Evénements Survenus en France 1933-45* (Paris, 1951), pp. 216-19.
29. Jules Moch, *Rencontres avec Blum* (Paris, 1970), p. 195.
30. *TNS*, p. 242.
31. Hugh Thomas, *The Spanish Civil War* (1960), p. 531.
32. Pierre Cot, *Le Procès de la République* (New York, 1944), pp. 343-4.
33. Fitzroy Maclean to author, interview, 14 October 1990.
34. Fitzroy Maclean to author, interview, 14 December 1990.
35. *EA*, p. 16.

Chapter 3

1. *EA*, p. 19.
2. *TNS*, p. 30.
3. Fitzroy Maclean to author, interview, 17 January 1991.
4. *HR*, pp. 174-5.
5. Fitzroy Maclean to author, interview, 17 January 1991.
6. *EA*, p. 80.
7. See Charles Thayer, *Bears in the Caviar* (1952).
8. George F. Kennan, *Memoirs 1925-1950* (1967), p. 62.
9. Ibid., p. 81.
10. Fitzroy Maclean to author, interview, 9 December 1990.
11. Ibid.
12. Fitzroy Maclean to author, interview, 14 October 1990.
13. Charles Thayer, *Hands Across the Caviar* (1953), p. 160.
14. Von Herwarth to author, conversation, 31 July 1991.
15. Von Herwarth, *Against Two Evils* (1981), p. 70.
16. Von Herwarth to author, conversation, 31 July 1991.
17. *Against Two Evils*, p. 80.
18. 'At the British Embassy the member of the Mutual Admiration Society who seemed to be most likely to report fully on any statement I might give him was

Fitzroy Maclean.' (Ibid., p. 125.)

19. E. L. Woodward & Rohan Butler, eds, *Documents on British Foreign Policy 1919-1939*, 3rd Series, Vol. 2 (1949), pp. 140-1.
20. In a letter to von Herwarth on 3 June 1978, Fitzroy wrote: 'My recollection is that you also emphasized most strongly the need for the British to take a firm line with Hitler over Czechoslovakia. You said that the Czechs' will to resist would depend very largely on the attitude of the French and ourselves and also told me that there were a number of German generals who would be more inclined to stand up to Hitler if we adopted a really resolute attitude.' (*Against Two Evils*, op. cit., pp. 127-8.)
21. *Against Two Evils*, pp. 128-9.
22. Chilston to Collier, 22 July 1937, FO 371/21095
23. John Harvey, ed., *The Diplomatic Diaries of Oliver Harvey 1937-1940* (1970), p. 158 (under 2 July 1938).
24. Ibid., p. 256 (under 19 February 1939). 'I saw Virginia Cowles today back from the Soviet Union - very disappointed and horrified at what she saw - great inefficiency, complete ignorance of the outside world, no foreigners hardly there, almost complete seclusion. I asked her about the chances of Russia joining up with Germany: she said that the German Embassy there were always urging the advantages of this, pointing out the resemblances the two systems have now, but that Hitler was obstinately opposed - thank goodness. She said our new ambassador . . . had astonished them by talking Russian.'
25. Fitzroy Maclean to author, interview, 3 March 1991.
26. Ibid. Muggeridge's account of Russia is in *Winter in Moscow* (1934).
27. Fitzroy Maclean to author, interview, 14 December 1990.
28. Fitzroy Maclean to author, interview, 14 October 1990.
29. *EA*, p. 28.
30. *HR*, p. 190.
31. *EA*, p. 29.
32. Fitzroy Maclean to author, interview, 14 October 1990.
33. See Robert Conquest, *The Great Terror* (1968).
34. *EA*, p. 25.
35. *TNS*, pp. 173-4.
36. See also S. J. Taylor, *Stalin's Apologist* (1990).
37. *HR*, p. 193.
38. *EA*, p. 88.
39. Ibid., p. 90.
40. Ibid., pp. 94-5.
41. Harold Eeman, *Clouds over the Sun* (1981), pp. 33-4. It is possible, however, that Eeman is presenting Fitzroy in a bad light, since elsewhere in his book there seems to be a rumbling hostility to him. Talking of his trips to Central Asia Eeman says: 'He was reticent about these trips and indeed most of his remarks were laconic.' For Eeman's experiences in the USSR see also *Inside Stalin's Russia* (1977).
42. *EA*, pp. 119-20.
43. Arkady Vaksberg, *The Prosecutor and the Prey* (1990), p. 109.
44. Maclean to Weinberg, 9 November 1937, FO 371/21108.
45. See the voluminous correspondence in FO 371/21107.
46. See Maclean to Weinberg, n.d., FO 371/21098.
47. Fitzroy Maclean to author, interview, 14 October 1990.
48. Ibid.
49. Ibid.
50. *HR*, p. 193.

51. Fitzroy Maclean to author, interview, 14 October 1990.
52. R. S. Hudson was one of the 'malcontents' (the others being Lord Strathcona, the Marquess of Dufferin, Kenneth Lindsay and Harvey Crookshank) who wanted to resign over the triple issues of Munich, inadequate rearmament and failure of agricultural policy (see *Harvey Diaries*, op. cit., p. 227). For Hudson's Moscow mission see ibid., p. 259 (under 9 March 1939).
53. For Ian Fleming in Russia, see John Pearson, *The Life of Ian Fleming* (1966), pp. 87–8.
54. Fifty years later, when Wilhelm Rust landed in a plane at Red Square, having evaded drunken frontier guards, Grover wrote to the press from South Africa to point out that he had done the same thing in 1938.
55. Fitzroy Maclean to author, inteview, 14 October 1990.

Chapter 4

1. Fitzroy Maclean to author, interview, 17 January 1991.
2. *EA*, p. 43.
3. MacKillop to Eden, 14 June 1937; Collier to MacKillop, 24 June 1937, FO 371/21107.
4. Fitzroy Maclean to Roy Plomley, 11 April 1981, in *Plomley's Pick* (1982), p. 110.
5. *EA*, p. 63.
6. Ibid., p. 78.
7. Chilston to Eden, 24 December 1937, FO 371/21105.
8. Fitzroy Maclean to author, interview, 14 October 1990.
9. Fitzroy Maclean, written statement to author.
10. Fitzroy Maclean to author, interview, 14 December 1990.
11. *EA*, p. 137.
12. Ibid., pp. 141–2.
13. Ibid., p. 154.
14. George Curzon, *Russia in Central Asia* (1889), p. 9.
15. *EA*, p. 167.
16. Fitzroy Maclean to author, 17 January 1991.
17. Embassy to Litvinov, 19 December 1938, FO 371/22301.

Chapter 5

1. 'The one Briton whom I decided I could alert to the possibility of a Soviet-German agreement was my friend Armin Dew, who had just succeeded Fitzroy Maclean' (Von Herwarth, *Against Two Evils*, op. cit., p. 152).
2. Ibid., p. 74.
3. Fitzroy Maclean to author, interview, 14 April 1991.
4. Ibid.
5. Robert Cecil, *A Divided Life. A Biography of Donald Maclean* (1988), p. 49.
6. *TNS*, p. 237.
7. Fitzroy Maclean to author, interview, 10 October 1991.
8. This was a common Foreign Office view at the time. See *Harvey Diaries*, op. cit., p. 246 (under 19 January 1939).
9. E. L. Woodward & R. Butler, eds, *Documents on British Foreign Policy 1919–39*, 3rd Series (1949–55), iv, pp. 160–1.

10. See P. Sevostyanov, *Before the Nazi Invasion* (Moscow, 1984), *passim*.
11. *Soviet Documents on Foreign Policy*, 3 vols (Oxford, 1951–3), iii, pp. 377–80; see also *Cadogan Diaries*, p. 231; N. Bethell, *The War Hitler Won* (1972), Chapter 9.
12. See *Harvey Diaries*, pp. 230, 237 (under 6, 29 February 1939).
13. File N 5736/G (1939) has now been withdrawn from public inspection in the Public Record Office. Large portions of it were, however, reproduced in the *Independent*, 26 February 1990. It must be said that the 'weeders' did not do a very efficient job, since there is extensive discussion of N 5736/G in other files which makes it possible to reconstruct the gist of Fitzroy's memorandum.
14. Maclean memorandum, 9 January 1940, FO 371/24843.
15. Maclean minute, 24 December 1939, FO 371/24844.
16. Collier minute, 26 December 1939, FO 371/24884.
17. Fitzroy Maclean to author, interview, 14 October 1990.
18. L. Woodward, *British Foreign Policy in the Second World War* (1970), i, pp. 11–42.
19. A. J. P. Taylor, *English History 1914–1945* (1965), pp. 571–2.
20. Maclean memorandum, 2 February 1940, FO 371/24845.
21. Maclean minute, 1 January 1940, FO 371/24843.
22. Maclean minute, 9 March 1940, FO 371/24845.
23. Maclean minute, 13 March 1940, FO 371/24845.
24. Cadogan minute, 26 March 1940, FO 371/24887.
25. CAB 65 W.M. 76(40), 27 March 1940.
26. Minutes of meeting of 8 April 1940, FO 371/24888.
27. Maclean minutes, 12 December 1939, 2, 6 January, 15, 18, 30 March, 25, 26 April 1940, FO 371/24843–5.
28. Maclean minute, 15 May 1940, FO 371/24844.
29. Fitzroy Maclean to author, interview, 17 January 1991.
30. Kenneth Young, ed., *The Diaries of Sir Robert Bruce Lockhart*, 2 vols, ii, 1939–1965 (1980), pp. 48, 66 (under 17 March, 10 July 1940).
31. Anthony Beevor, *Crete, The Battle and the Resistance* (1991), p. 54.
32. Maclean minute, 29 May 1940, FO 371/24844.
33. *Cadogan Diaries*, op. cit., p. 365 (under 21 March 1941).
34. Maclean minute, 4 July 1940, FO 371/24844.
35. *HR*, p. 146.
36. J. Erikson, 'Threat Identification and Strategic Appraisal by the Soviet Union 1930–1941', in E. R. May, ed., *Knowing One's Enemies: Intelligence Assessment between the two World Wars* (Princeton, 1984).
37. *Documents on International Affairs* (1954), pp. 68–72.
38. Maclean minute, 24 September 1940, FO 371/24845.
39. Maclean minute, 14 October 1940, FO 371/24845.
40. Maclean memorandum, 2 October 1940, FO 371/24845.
41. Maclean memorandum, 31 October 1940, FO 371/24845.
42. Ibid.
43. See in general G. Gorodetsky, *Stafford Cripps's Mission to Moscow* (Cambridge, 1984).
44. See the copious Maclean minutes on this subject from 29 May to 4 December 1940 in FO 371/24843.
45. Maclean memorandum, 19 June 1940, FO 371/24844.
46. Maclean minute, 3 January 1941, FO 371/29463.
47. Fitzroy Maclean to author, interview, 17 January 1991.
48. Peter Clarke, *A Question of Leadership* (1991), p. 203.
49. Fitzroy Maclean to author, interview, 14 April 1991.
50. Cripps to Halifax, 16 August 1940, FO 371/24845.
51. *Cadogan Diaries*, p. 321 (under 17 August 1940).

52. Maclean minute, 20 August 1940, FO 371/24845.
53. Maclean minute, 1 August 1940, FO 371/24844.
54. Cripps to FO, 13 October 1940, FO 371/24845.
55. Maclean memorandum, 21 June 1940, FO 371/24844.
56. Maclean memorandum, 4 July 1940, FO 371/24844.
57. See Maclean minutes, 4, 23, 24 January, 4 February 1941, FO 371/29463.
58. *Lockhart Diaries*, pp. 101–2 (under 3 June 1941).
59. See B. Whaley, *Codeword Barbarossa* (Boston, 1973), Chapter Nine.
60. Fitzroy Maclean to author, interview, 9 October 1990.
61. See especially Dmitri Volkogonov, *Stalin: Triumph and Tragedy* (1991).
62. Lord Bullock to author, 17 April 1991.
63. See FO 371/29590.
64. Fitzroy Maclean to author, interview, 6 March 1991.

Chapter 6

1. Fitzroy Maclean to author, written statement.
2. Ralph Barker, *One Man's Jungle* (1975), p. 177.
3. Fitzroy Maclean to author, interview, 15 April 1991.
4. *EA*, p. 186.
5. Ibid., pp. 186–7.
6. Fitzroy Maclean to author, interview, 15 April 1991.
7. *EA*, p. 187.
8. Fitzroy Maclean to author, interview, 14 October 1990.
9. Brian Roberts, *Randolph* (1985), p. 193. The well-known bandleader Vic Oliver had married Churchill's daughter Sarah.
10. *The Times*, 29 September, 7 October 1941.
11. Fenner Brockway, *Towards Tomorrow* (1977), p. 136.
12. Fitzroy Maclean to author, interview, 14 October 1990.
13. Ibid.
14. *The Times*, 17, 22 October 1941.
15. Fitzroy Maclean to author, interview, 14 October 1990.
16. Fitzroy Maclean to author, interview, 9 December 1990.
17. Peter Matthiessen, *African Silences* (1991), p. 30.
18. Fitzroy Maclean to author, interview, 9 December 1990.
19. For Stirling, see Virginia Cowles, *The Phantom Major* (1958).
20. Waugh to Laura Waugh, 25 December 1940, in Mark Amory, ed., *The Letters of Evelyn Waugh* (1980), p. 149.
21. Anthony Beevor, *Crete, The Battle and the Resistance*, p. 195.
22. Written statement to author; also Fitzroy Maclean to author, interview, 13 April 1991.
23. See W. B. Kennedy Shaw, *The Long-Range Desert Group* (1945).
24. Vladimir Peniakoff, *Popsky's Private army* (1991 edn, foreword by General Sir John Hackett).
25. *EA*, p. 191.
26. Ibid., p. 197.
27. General Berger to author, 3 August 1991.
28. Colonel David Sutherland to author, interview, 5 March 1991.
29. Fitzroy Maclean to author, interview, 13 April 1991.
30. Len Deighton, *Alamein and the Desert War* (1967).
31. Written statement to author.

32. Fitzroy Maclean to author, interview, 13 April 1991.
33. Fitzroy Maclean to author, interview, 17 January 1991.
34. *Letters of Freya Stark*, iv, p. 136.
35. Alan Moorehead, *African Trilogy* (1944), p. 189.
36. Fitzroy Maclean to author, interview, 17 January 1991.
37. Trefor E. Evans, ed., *The Killearn Diaries 1934–1946* (1972), pp. 220–1 (under 28 March 1942).
38. Fitzroy Maclean to author, interview, 13 April 1991.
39. Fitzroy Maclean to author, interview, 17 January 1991.
40. *Killearn Diaries*, 8 December 1940.
41. Bickham Sweet-Escott, *Baker Street Irregulars* (1976), pp. 74–5.
42. *Killearn Diaries*, 24 March 1941.
43. Charles Johnston, *Mo and other Originals* (1971), p. 5.
44. Artemis Cooper, *Cairo in the War, 1939–1943* (1989), p. 219.
45. Johnston, op. cit., p. 17.
46. Ibid., p. 3.
47. Ibid., p. 4.
48. Cooper, *Cairo*, op. cit., p. 221.
49. Ibid., p. 223.
50. Fitzroy Maclean to author, interview, 17 January 1991.

Chapter 7

1. *EA*, p. 201.
2. Kay Halle, *Randolph Churchill. The Young Pretender* (1971), pp. 89, 160. See in general Fitzroy Maclean, 'Randolph as a Commando', ibid., pp. 88–91.
3. Johnny Cooper, *One of the Originals* (1991), p. 45.
4. *EA*, p. 214.
5. Some stories have it that Randolph panicked and began shooting at the car: see Roberts, *Randolph Churchill*, op. cit., p. 203.
6. Cooper, *One of the originals*, op. cit., pp. 46–7.
7. *EA*, p. 221.
8. Ibid., p. 222.
9. Anita Leslie, *Cousin Randolph* (1985), p. 67.
10. *EA*, p. 225.
11. Fitzroy Maclean to author, interview, 17 January 1991.
12. 'Randolph as a Commando', in Halle, op. cit., pp. 88–91.
13. John Lodwick, *The Filibusters* (1947), p. 19.
14. Fitzroy Maclean to author, interview, 17 January 1991.
15. *EA*, p. 244.
16. Ibid., p. 249.
17. Hilary King to author, 3 May 1991.
18. *EA*, p. 256.
19. Fitzroy Maclean to author, interview, 17 October 1991.
20. Anthony Beevor, *Crete, The Battle and the Resistance* (1991), p. 40.
21. For Bullard, see his *Letters from Teheran: An Ambassador in World War Two Persia* (1991). Fitzroy made friends with him and even borrowed his copy of Dostoevsky's *The Idiot* (WO 202/138).
22. Geoffrey Thompson, *Front Line Diplomat* (1959), p. 185.
23. Fitzroy Maclean to author, interview, 17 January 1991.
24. Ibid.

25. Fitzroy Maclean to Roy Plomley, 11 April 1981, in *Plomley's Pick* (1982), p. 113.
26. Field Marshal Lord Wilson, *Eight Years Overseas 1939–1947* (1950), p. 146.
27. Gault to FO, 4 January 1943, FO 371/35120.
28. Fitzroy Maclean to author, interview, 17 January 1991.
29. Artemis Cooper, *Cairo*, op. cit., p. 233.
30. Colonel David Sutherland to author, interview, 5 March 1991.
31. Lord Jellicoe to author, interview, 27 February 1991.
32. Fitzroy Maclean to author, interview, 13 April 1991.
33. Ibid.
34. *EA*, p. 277.
35. Winston Churchill, *Closing the Ring*, p. 102.

Chapter 8

1. *Daily Express*, 3 January 1969.
2. Fitzroy Maclean to author, interview, 9 December 1990. Stalin, however, professed himself convinced that Sikorski had been assassinated by British Intelligence (Milovan Djilas, *Conversations with Stalin* (New York, 1962), pp. 64–72).
3. Ralph Bennett, *Ultra in the Mediterranean* (1989), p. 334.
4. Winston S. Churchill, *Closing the Ring*, v, pp. 410–11.
5. Brief of 20 July 1943, FO 371/37610.
6. *EA*, p. 280.
7. *Cadogan Diaries*, op. cit.
8. *EA*, pp. 280–1.
9. Churchill to Eden, 28 July 1943; Sargent minute, 30 July; Eden to Selborne, 2 August; Churchill to Wilson, 3 August; Eden minute, 4 August; Selborne to Eden, 5 August; Eden minute, 6 August; Eden to Wilson, 9 August 1943, FO 371/37610.
10. Hugh Seton Watson, 'Afterword', in Richard Auty and Phyllis Clogg, eds, *British Policy towards Wartime Resistance in Yugoslavia and Greece* (1975), p. 284.
11. Ibid., p. 290.
12. *EA*, p. 281.
13. S. W. Bailey, 'British Policy towards General Draza Mihailovic', in Auty and Clogg, *British Policy*, op. cit., pp. 59–92 (at p. 67).
14. Ibid., pp. 75–6.
15. Elisabeth Barker, *British Policy towards South-eastern Europe in the Second World War* (1976), pp. 36–8, 148.
16. Churchill, *Closing the Ring*, v, p. 410; William Deakin, *The Embattled Mountain* (1971), p. 223–4; Michael Howard, *Grand Strategy* (1972), iv, pp. 482–3; F. H. Hinsley, *British Intelligence in the Second World War*, Vol. 3 (1979), i, p. 149.
17. Churchill to Eden, 28 July 1943, FO 371/37610.
18. C. M. Woodhouse, 'Summer 1943: the Critical Months', in Auty and Clogg, op. cit., p. 134.
19. *HC Debates*, 5th Series, col. 778, 24 May 1944.
20. Auty and Clogg, pp. 222–3; Fitzroy Maclean to author, interview, 9 December 1990.
21. Bickham Sweet-Escott, *Baker Street Irregulars* (1976) p. 170.
22. Ibid.
23. FO 371/37579; Bennett, *Ultra and Mediterranean Strategy* (1989), p. 334; Churchill, *Second World War*, iv, p. 828.
24. Hugh Seton-Watson, 'Afterword', in Auty and Clogg, p. 292. Seton-Watson

calls Keble 'resolute and ambitious' (p. 290), but cannot take his defence further.
25. Beevor, *Crete*, op. cit., p. 267.
26. Xan Fielding, *Hide and Seek* (1954) p. 99.
27. Xan Fielding, op. cit., pp. 98, 105–06; Artemis Cooper, *Cairo in Wartime*, p. 263.
28. Fitzroy Maclean's own statement, in Auty and Clogg, pp. 223–4; Fitzroy Maclean to author, interview, 9 December 1990.
29. *Lockhart Diaries*, pp. 296–7 (under 18 April 1944). Cf. also ibid., p. 21.
30. Fitzroy Maclean to author, 14 October 1990.
31. Hilary King to author, interview, 14 April 1991.
32. Auty and Clogg, pp. 224–5; Fitzroy Maclean to author, 9 December 1990.
33. Auty and Clogg, p. 226; Fitzroy Maclean to author, 9 December 1990.
34. 'Trotsky' Davies, *Illyrian Adventure* (1952), p. 42.
35. Field Marshal Lord Wilson, *Eight Years Overseas 1939–1947* (1950) p. 169.
36. Auty and Clogg, pp. 164–5.
37. Hugh Seton-Watson, 'Following Sweet-Escott', in Auty and Clogg, p. 211.
38. Lord Henniker to author, interview, 12 June 1991.
39. For the importance of Protville before Bari in Italy became available, see D. Hamilton-Hill, *SOE Assignment* (1973), pp. 54–61.
40. Fitzroy Maclean to author, interview, 9 December 1990.
41. Ibid.
42. Franklin Lindsay to author, 21 October 1991.
43. *EA*, p. 299.

Chapter 9

1. Edmond Paris, *Genocide in Satellite Croatia 1941–1945* (Chicago, 1961).
2. See Kruno M. Dincic, 'Tito et Mihailovic', *Revue d'Histoire de la deuxième guerre mondiale*, 29 (1958), pp. 3–31; Rodolojub Colakovic, *Winning Freedom* (1962), p. 147.
3. The similarity of Tito's Partisans to Mao's Red Army does not end there. In both cases the Communists faced a mortal enemy (the Kuomintang being the Chinese analogue of the Cetniks) much more interested in destroying the Reds than in fighting the Axis enemy. For an explicit comparison of the two Communist experiences, see Chalmers Johnson, *Peasant Nationalism and Communist Power. The Emergence of Revolutionary China 1937–1943* (Stanford, 1962).
4. For a detailed assessment of the Communist Party in Yugoslavia in these years, see Fabijan Trgo, ed., *The National Liberation War and Revolution in Yugoslavia 1941–1945: Selected Documents* (Belgrade, 1982); Mark Wheeler, 'Pariahs to partisans to power: the Communist Party of Yugoslavia', in Tony Judt, ed., *Resistance and Revolution in Mediterranean Europe 1939–1948* (1989), pp. 110–56.
5. See Mario Roatta, *Otto Millioni di Baionette* (Milan, 1946); William Deakin, *The Brutal Friendship: Mussolini, Hitler and the Fall of Italian Fascism* (1962).
6. Milovan Djilas, *Wartime* (1977), pp. 226–44.
7. See William Deakin, *The Embattled Mountain* (1971).
8. Stephen Clissold, *Whirlwind* (1948), pp. 86–7.
9. Deakin, *Embattled Mountain*, op. cit., pp. 210–21; Basil Davidson, *Special Operations Europe* (1980), p. 123; Vladimir Dedijer, *With Tito through the War* (1951), pp. 319–20.
10. Sir William Deakin to author, interview, 27 June 1991.
11. Ibid.
12. Velebit on *This is Your Life*, 13 December 1984.

13. *DB*, p. 233.
14. Ibid., p. 103.
15. Ibid., p. 233.
16. Lord Henniker to author, interview, 12 June 1991.
17. Mike Parker to author, interview, 3 August 1991.
18. Ibid.
19. Brigadier Peter Moore to author, interview, 23 april 1991.
20. Lord Henniker to author, interview, 12 June 1991.
21. Mike Parker to author, interview, 3 August 1991.
22. Fitzroy Maclean to author, interview, 29 December 1991.
23. *DB*, p. 140.
24. *EA*, p. 338.
25. Sir William Deakin to author, interview, 27 June 1991.
26. Maclean mission to Cairo, 26 September 1943, WO 202/335.
27. See telegrams of 10 and 17 October 1943, FO 371/37613.
28. Fitzroy Maclean to author, interview, 17 October 1991.
29. *EA*, pp. 363–4.
30. Rafo Ivanevic on *This is Your Life*, 13 December 1984.
31. Alexander Glen, *Footholds against a Whirlwind* (1975), pp. 146–7.

Chapter 10

1. Michael Rose minute, 15 October 1943, FO 371/37613.
2. Stevenson to FO, 4 October 1943, FO 371/37612.
3. Telegrams and minutes, 30 October–3 November 1943, FO 371/37614.
4. Maclean report, 6 November 1943, FO 371/37615.
5. David Stafford, *Britain and European Resistance 1940–1945* (1980), p. 270.
6. 'The most practically useful single Balkan item, in all probability, was one dated 3 October which estimated Partisan numbers in the Split–Dubrovnok area at between 160,000 and 200,000, for this was the section of coastline most accessible from the naval and air supply base of Vis, which was reconnoitred and developed in September and October.' (Bennett, *Ultra and Mediterranean Strategy* (1989), p. 344.)
7. Wilson, *Eight Years Overseas*, op. cit., p. 169.
8. Elisabeth Barker, *British Policy in South-East Europe in the Second World War* (1976), p. 64.
9. Bennett, *Ultra and Mediterranean Strategy*, p. 338.
10. W. Hubatsch, ed., *Kriegstagebuch der Oberkommandos der Wehrmacht* (1963), iii, pp. 1252–5. For a concise guide to Weichs, see Samuel W. Mitcham, *Hitler's Field Marshals and their Battles* (1988), pp. 205–21.
11. Telegram, 5 November 1943, FO 371/37614.
12. John Harvey, ed., *The War Diaries of Oliver Harvey* (1978), pp. 319–20.
13. WO 202/143 and 332.
14. Barker, *British Policy*, op. cit., p. 39.
15. Bentinck minute, 16 November 1943, FO 371/37617.
16. Morrison to Eden, 6 December 1943, FO 371/37615.
17. Patrick Howarth, *Intelligence Chief Extraordinary. The Life of the Ninth Duke of Portland* (1986), p. 178.
18. F. W. D. Deakin, 'The Myth of an Allied Landing in the Balkans during the Second World War', in Auty and Clogg, *British Policy*, op. cit., pp. 93–116 (at p. 107). Cf. also Michael Howard, *The Mediterranean Strategy in the Second World*

War (1968). John Ehrmann, *Grand Strategy* (1956), v, p. 112, remarks: 'So far as 1943 is concerned, the Balkan campaign with substantial Allied forces is a myth.'

19. Ehrman, *Grand Strategy*, op. cit., v, p. 554.
20. Churchill, *Second World War*, v, pp. 121, 411; Martin Gilbert, *Winston Churchill. Road to Victory* (1986), p. 640; Ehrman, *Grand Strategy*, op. cit., v, p. 81.
21. Mark Wheeler to author, interview, 12 March 1991.
22. Robert Murphy, *Diplomat among Warriors* (New York, 1964), p. 220.
23. Keith Eubank, *Summit at Teheran* (New York, 1985), pp. 296, 305, 331.
24. Cairo to FO, telegram, 20 November 1943, FO 371/37616.
25. Moscow to FO, telegram, 31 October 1943, FO 371/37614.
26. Fitzroy Maclean, statement in discussion in Auty and Clogg, op. cit., p. 275.
27. Sargent minute, 17 November 1943, FO 371/37615.
28. FO minute, against Roosevelt to Churchill, 19 May 1944, FO 371/44290.
29. *EA*, p. 391.
30. Ibid., p. 398.
31. Deakin, *Embattled Mountain*, op. cit., p. 254.
32. Sir William Deakin to author, interview, 27 June 1991.
33. Ibid.
34. Barker, *British Policy*, p. 119.
35. Fitzroy Maclean to author, interview, 9 December 1990.
36. Donovan received instructions from the Joint Chiefs of Staff on 7 September 1943 to 'show preference among resistance groups or prospective successor govern-ments only on the basis of their willingness to co-operate and without regard to their political program.' (Anthony Cave Brown, *The Last Hero* (1982), p. 353).
37. Louis Huot, *Guns for Tito* (New York, 1945) describes his activities.
38. Cave Brown, op. cit., p. 447.
39. Vladimir Dedijer, *With Tito* (1951), p. 197.
40. Cave Brown, op. cit., p. 449.
41. Hilary King to author, 3 May 1991.
42. Cave Brown, op. cit.
43. Ibid.
44. Mark Wheeler to author, interview, 12 March 1991.
45. Sir William Deakin to author, interview, 27 June 1991.
46. Hilary King to author, 3 May 1991.
47. Cave Brown, op. cit., p. 452.
48. *EA*, p. 298.
49. See R 12265 in FO 371/37616.
50. Deakin, *Embattled Mountain*, p. 260.
51. Maclean to War Office, 13 December 1943, WO 202/138.
52. *EA*, pp. 401–2.
53. Ibid., pp. 402–3.
54. For a sympathetic view of the Karadjordjevics, see Neil Balfour and Sally Mckay, *Paul of Yugoslavia* (1980).
55. Cadogan to Eden, 28 May 1943, FO 371/37593.
56. Mark Wheeler, 'The British, King Peter and the path to Tito's Cave', in Richard Langhorne, ed., *Diplomacy and Intelligence during the Second World War* (Cambridge, 1985), pp. 184–218 (at p. 187).
57. Stevenson to FO, 5 November 1943, FO 371/37614.
58. Minutes of meeting of 7 November 1943, FO 371/37184.
59. Telegram and minutes, 11–15 November 1943, FO 371/37615.
60. Telegram and minutes, 14–21 November 1943, FO 371/37615.
61. Correspondence between Stevenson, Dew and Sargent, 21 December 1943, FO 371/37619.

62. Maclean and Stevenson to FO, 24, 25 December 1943, FO 371/37619.
63. Minutes by Dew, Sargent and Eden, 26–28 December 1943, FO 371/37620.
64. Sir William Deakin to author, interview, 27 June 1991; cf. also Martin Gilbert, *Road to Victory, Winston S. Churchill 1941–45* (1986), p. 601.
65. Julian Amery, *Approach March* (1973), pp. 270–2.
66. Gilbert, *Road to Victory*, op. cit., p. 602.
67. Sir William Deakin to author, interview, 27 June 1991.
68. Peter II of Yugoslavia, *A King's Heritage* (1955), pp. 121, 137, 139.
69. Ibid., pp. 139–40.
70. *EA*, p. 406.
71. Colonel John Clarke to author, interview, 13 March 1991.
72. Gilbert, *Road to Victory*, p. 614. Among Fitzroy's Christmas contacts was Sir John Dashwood, whom Fitzroy met at dinner at Shepheards's Hotel. Dashwood, Vice-Marshal of the Diplomatic Corps and premier Baronet of Great Britain, was on his way back to Ankara to plug the leak later shown to have been the result of operations by the master spy 'Cicero'. (*TNS*, p. 212.)
73. On 21 December Randolph wrote to his confidante Laura Charteris: 'I am just off to Italy to join Fitzroy'. (Anita Leslie, *Cousin Randolph* (1985), pp. 79–80.)
74. Tom Churchill, *Commando Crusade* (1987).
75. Diana Cooper, *Trumpets from the Steep* (1960), p. 175.
76. *EA*, pp. 412–13.
77. Churchill, *Second World War*, v, p. 416; Gilbert, *Road to Victory*, p. 640; Woodward, *British Foreign Policy*, iii, p. 315.
78. Warren F. Kimball, ed., *Churchill and Roosevelt, The Complete Correspondence*, 3 vols (Princeton, 1984), ii, p. 668.

Chapter 11

1. *EA*, p. 423.
2. Ibid., p. 428.
3. Fitzroy Maclean to author, interview, 13 April 1991.
4. Lord Henniker to author, interview, 12 June 1991.
5. Mike Parker to author, interview, 3 August 1991.
6. Annette Street to author, interview, 23 April 1991.
7. Brigadier Peter Moore to author, interview, 23 April 1991.
8. Farish's two reports are conveniently reproduced in David Martin, *The Web of Disinformation* (1990), pp. 331–44.
9. Mike Parker to author, interview, 3 August 1991.
10. Colonel John Clarke to author, interview, 13 March 1991.
11. Fitzroy Maclean to author, interview, 9 December 1990.
12. Hilary King to author, interview, 14 April 1991.
13. Elisabeth Barker, 'Some Factors in British decision-making over Yugoslavia 1941–44', in Auty and Clogg, *British Policy*, op. cit., p. 26.
14. Mark Wheeler to author, 19 April 1991.
15. WO 202/337.
16. Lindsay Rogers, *Guerrilla Surgeon* (1957), pp. 81–2.
17. Lord Henniker to author, interview, 12 June 1991.
18. Colonel John Clarke to author, interview, 13 March 1991.
19. Mike Parker to author, interview, 3 August 1991.
20. *DB*, p. 251.
21. Maclean to FO, 14 March 1944, FO 371/43587.

22. Fitzroy Maclean to author, interview, 13 April 1991.
23. David Martin, *Web of Disinformation*, op. cit., p. 341.
24. Mike Parker to author, interview, 3 May 1991.
25. Ibid.
26. *EA*, pp. 436–47.
27. Deakin, *Embattled Mountain*, op. cit., pp. 264–5.
28. Rogers, *Guerrilla Surgeon*, op. cit., p. 96.
29. *DB*, p. 251.
30. Fitzroy Maclean to author, interview, 13 April 1991.
31. *DB*, p. 254.
32. Fitzroy Maclean to author, interview, 13 April 1991; *DB*, p. 254.
33. Maclean to Churchill, 18 March 1944, CAB 66/48 WP 44, 17 April 1944.
34. Djilas, *Conversations with Stalin*, op. cit., p. 103.
35. Fitzroy Maclean to author, interview, 13 April 1991.
36. Cave Brown, *Last Hero*, op. cit., pp. 453–4.
37. Berle, Assistant Secretary of State, memo, 26 January 1944, FRUS 1944 Vol. 4 (Europe), pp. 1339–40.
38. Macreagh to Hull, 21 February 1944; Donovan to Hull, 2 March 1944, FRUS 1349–50, 1353–54.
39. Alfred D. Chandler, ed., *The Papers of Dwight D. Eisenhower, Vol. 3; The War Years* (Baltimore, 1970), p. 1815.
40. Hull to counsellor of mission at Algiers, 8 July 1944, FRUS ibid., p. 1387.
41. Murphy, *Diplomat among Warriors*, op. cit., p. 221.
42. Political adviser to Hull, 31 October 1944, FRUS 1944 Vol. 4, pp. 1415–16.
43. *DB*, p. 324.
44. Matteo J. Milazzo, *The Cetnik Movement* (Baltimore, 1975), p. 174.
45. 'I recently saw an extremely peremptory telegram sent by Jumbo Wilson to Maclean, saying, in effect, you have no right to keep these people out. Of course, not even Churchill could have kept OSS *secret intelligence* people out, whether out of Yugoslavia or anywhere else.' (Mark Wheeler to author, interview, 13 March 1991.)
46. Hilary King to author, 3 May 1991.
47. Ibid.
48. Fitzroy Maclean to author, interview, 14 December 1990.
49. Telegram and minutes from Howard, Sargent, Eden and Stevenson, 25 January–4 February 1944; Churchill to Tito, 5 February 1944, FO 371/44246.
50. Tito to Churchill, 9 February 1944; Maclean to Churchill, 10 February 1944, FO 371/44247.
51. Churchill, *Second World War*, v, pp. 420–1; Gilbert, *Road to Victory*, op. cit., p. 690; *The Times*, 23 February 1944.
52. FO 371/442499.
53. A notable historian of Yugoslavia has said of King Peter: 'Importuning King Peter was like wrestling a tar baby. It was easy to make an impression, but impossible to make it stick.' (Mark Wheeler in Langhorne, ed., *Diplomacy and Intelligence*, loc. cit., p. 208.)
54. Mark Wheeler comments: 'The Serbs' odd views about wartime marriages were of a piece with their abysmal failure to manage their own affairs.' (Ibid., p. 310.)
55. Maclean to Churchill, 9, 13 March 1944, FO 371/44250.
56. Djilas, *Conversations with Stalin*, op. cit., pp. 70–2.
57. Tito to Churchill, 26 March 1944; Maclean to Churchill, 27 March 1944, FO 371/44251.
58. Churchill to Eden, 1 April 1944, FO 371/44309.
59. 'When early in 1944 the British sent liaison officers to the Partisan units in

Serbia – until then regarded as Mihailovic's private stronghold – and could see the rapid strides Tito was making there, it became clear beyond doubt that in practice he would control the whole country at the end of the war.' (Barker, *British Policy*, op. cit., p. 170.)
60. Maclean to Elisabeth Barker, 28 August 1974.
61. Velebit, *Memoirs*, p. 220.

Chapter 12

1. *The Times*, 3 May 1944.
2. R 7213/44/92 in FO 371/44290. This meeting received a somewhat fanciful gloss in Hugh Dalton's memoirs. On Churchill he writes: 'He had Fitzroy Maclean down to Chequers the other day with one or two others recently returned from the Balkans, and harangued them for four hours about the merits of the Yugoslav and Greek bandits. None of them could get a word in edgeways to report to him what had actually happened.' (Ben Pimlott, ed., *The Second World War Diary of Hugh Dalton 1940–45* (1986), p. 743.)
3. Kenneth Young, ed., *The Diaries of Sir Robert Bruce Lockhart*, Vol. 2, 1939–65 (1980), p. 305.
4. Pimlott, *Second World War Diary of Hugh Dalton*, op. cit., p. 745.
5. *Lockhart Diaries*, op. cit., pp. 10–11.
6. Velebit, *Memoirs* (Zagreb, 1983), pp. 222–30.
7. *EA*, p. 447.
8. R 6399/11/92 in FO 371/44270.
9. Mark Wheeler, 'The British, King Peter and the Path to Tito's Cave', loc. cit., p. 212.
10. The saga can be followed in FO 371/44310 and 44311 *passim* and in FO 371/44290.
11. Churchill to Tito, 25 May 1944, FO 371/44365.
12. Fitzroy Maclean to author, interview, 17 January 1991. Fitzroy was not allowed to include the story in *Eastern Approaches*, doubtless because of the implicit criticism of the king's godson King Peter, so he was miffed to find that Wheeler-Bennett had secured permission to use it in his *Life* of King George VI.
13. SOE advisor at FCO to Hilary King, 3 December 1982. For the insecurity of the Partisan cipher, see WO 202/332.
14. Churchill to Roosevelt, 18 May 1944, in F. Kimball, ed., *Churchill and Roosevelt. The Complete Correspondence* (Princeton, 1984), iii, pp. 131–2. For Churchill's unexpurgated version, see *Second World War*, v, pp. 477–8; Gilbert, *Road to Victory*, p. 779.
15. David Stafford, *Britain and European Resistance 1940–1945* (1980), p. 169.
16. 'The Balkan peoples who know little of the problems of seapower judge the war on the progress by land. They see that, on their own admission, we are stuck in Italy and that the Russians are already in Rumania after a remarkably rapid advance.' (*Lockhart Diaries*, ii, p. 292, under 29 March 1944.)
17. Statement by Fitzroy Maclean in Auty and Clogg, *British Policy*, op. cit., p. 242. The evidence for Stalin's advice is in V. Dedijer, *Tito Speaks* (1953), p. 234.
18. WO 106/3284.
19. WO 202/303 and 304; also WO 106/3284, *passim*.
20. On the Shornikov mission, see FO 371/ 44272.
21. Hilary King, 'The British Mission at Drvar', unpublished paper presented to the

Anglo-Yugoslav Historical Colloquium, Imperial War Museum, 14 December 1982.

22. Djilas, *Wartime*, pp. 387–89.
23. *Literaturnaya Gazeta*, 22 November 1947, quoted in *DB*, p. 351.
24. Wilson, *Eight Years Overseas*, op. cit., p. 213.
25. WO 106/3287.
26. Cave Brown, *Last Hero*, op. cit., pp. 459–65.
27. Hinsley, *British Intelligence in the Second World War*, op. cit., iii, Pt. 1, p. 165; Gilbert, *Road to Victory*, p. 979.
28. Hinsley, ibid., p. 166.
29. WO 202/332 and 8458.
30. Ralph Bennett, 'Fitzroy Maclean', *Journal of Contemporary History* 22 (1987), pp. 195–208.
31. Bennett, *Ultra in Mediterranean Strategy*, op. cit., pp. 348–9.
32. I wish to acknowledge my profound debt to Hilary King for guiding me through this maze, and in particular to thank him for his unpublished paper cited at note 21.
33. The theory that Menzies 'knew all' is advanced in Anthony Cave Brown, *The Secret Servant, The Life of Sir Stewart Menzies* (1988), p. 543.
34. Churchill to Eden, 31 May 1944, FO 371/44311; Eden minute, 30 May 1944; Rose minute, 2 June 1944, FO 371/44257.
35. Wilson, *Eight Years Overseas*, op. cit., p. 225.
36. Woodward, *British Foreign Policy in the Second World War* (1962), pp. 344–5.
37. Churchill, Stevenson, Eden and Cadogan minutes, 4–7 June 1944, FO 371/44291.
38. Maclean to Wilson and Churchill, 6 June 1944, FO 371/44258.
39. FO 371/44258.
40. FO 371/44259, 44312; Djilas, *Wartime*, p. 395.
41. FO 371/44291.
42. Minutes by Dew, Eden, Sargent, Reed, Cadogan, 19 June 1944, FO 371/44312.
43. *EA*, p. 457.
44. Admiral Sir Morgan-Giles to author, interview, 7 March 1991.
45. J. Slessor, *The Central Blue* (1956), pp. 597–606.
46. Admiral Sir Morgan-Giles to author, interview, 7 March 1991.
47. S. W. Roskill, *The War at Sea*, 3 vols (1954–61), iii, p. 305; Bennett, *Ultra in Mediterranean*, op. cit., pp. 344–5, 347.
48. Admiral Sir Morgan-Giles to author, interview, 7 March 1991.
49. Fitzroy Maclean statement in Auty and Clogg, *British Policy*, op. cit., p. 241.
50. Colonel David Sutherland to author, interview, 5 March 1991.
51. Brian Connell, *Knight Errant* (1955), p. 189.
52. Admiral Sir Morgan-Giles to author, interview, 7 March 1991.
53. Annette Street to author, interview, 23 April 1991.
54. Mike Parker to author, interview, 3 August 1991.
55. Annette Street to author, interview, 23 April 1991.
56. Lord Henniker to author, interview, 12 June 1991.
57. Fitzroy Maclean statement in Auty and Clogg, op. cit., p. 242.
58. Wilson, *Eight Years*, op. cit., p. 226.
59. Ibid., pp. 226–7.
60. Fitzroy Maclean to author, interview, 13 April 1991.
61. *DB*, p. 275.
62. Ibid.
63. Gilbert, *Road to Victory*, p. 890.
64. *EA*, pp. 465–6.

65. Fitzroy Maclean to author, interview, 13 April 1991.
66. King Peter, *A King's Heritage*, op. cit., p. 162.
67. Stephen Clissold, *Djilas: The Progress of a Revolutionary* (1983), pp. 150–1.
68. Gilbert, *Road to Victory*, p. 890.
69. *DB*, p. 277.
70. Fitzroy Maclean to author, interview, 9 December 1990.
71. *A King's Heritage*, op. cit., p. 160.
72. Mark Wheeler to author, interview, 13 March 1991.
73. Ronald Lewin, *Ultra goes to War* (1978), p. 148.
74. *The Times*, 1 September 1944.

Chapter 13

1. Bennett, *Ultra in Mediterranean Strategy*, p. 351.
2. Maclean to Air Vice-Marshal Elliott, 8 September 1944. Air Ministry Papers 23/852.
3. See R 13201/8/92 in FO 371/44262 and R 18689/11/92 in FO 371/44280.
4. *EA*, p. 497.
5. *DB*, p. 280.
6. Murphy to Cannon, 8 September 1944; Murphy to Hull, 23 September 1944, FRUS (1944). Vol. 4, pp. 1404, 1410–11.
7. *DB*, pp. 280–4.
8. Averell Harriman to Roosevelt, 12 October 1944, FRUS (1944), p. 1013–14.
9. Stephen Clissold, *Yugoslavia and the Soviet Union 1939–1973* (1975), p. 104.
10. Tito, *Sabrana Djela* (Collected Works), 33, p. 213.
11. *DB*, p. 291.
12. Anthony Eden, *The Reckoning* (1965), p. 482.
13. Mark Wheeler to author, interview, 13 March 1991.
14. Sir Douglas Dodds-Parker to author, interview, 9 July 1991.
15. Fitzroy Maclean to author, interview, 9 December 1990; see also Charles Thayer, *Hands Across the Caviar* (1953), pp. 10–11.
16. Thayer, *Hands Across the Caviar*, p. 19.
17. Maclean to Wilson, 8 October 1944, WO 202/220.
18. Maclean to Wilson, quoted in Murphy to Hull, 3 October 1944, FRUS (1944) Vol. 4, pp. 1415–16.
19. Maclean to Elliott, 8 October 1944, WO 202/220.
20. Clarke to Maclean, 14 October 1944, WO 202/220.
21. Murphy to Hull, 15 November 1944, FRUS (1944), p. 1422.
22. *The Times*, 9 October 1944.
23. Thayer, *Hands Across the Caviar*, op. cit., p. 25.
24. *EA*, p. 505.
25. Ibid.
26. Ibid., p. 508.
27. Thayer, op. cit., p. 35.
28. Ibid., p. 42.
29. Ibid., pp. 46–7.
30. Fitzroy Maclean to author, interview, 13 April 1991.
31. *EA*, pp. 522–3.
32. *DB*, p. 308.
33. Djilas, *Conversations with Stalin*, op. cit., pp. 82–3; *Wartime*, p. 417.
34. Wilson to Maclean, 20 October 1944, WO 32/18517.

35. Maclean to Churchill, 27 October 1944, WO 202/220.
36. *The Times*, 31 October 1944.
37. Maclean statement in Auty and Clogg, *British Policy*, op. cit., p. 240.
38. FO 371/44292.
39. Churchill to Tito, 3 December 1944, FO 371/44293.
40. Maclean statement in Auty and Clogg, op. cit., p. 247.
41. Ibid.
42. David Dilks, ed., *The Diaries of Sir Alexander Cadogan 1938-1945* (1971), pp. 677-8 (under 2, 3 November 1944).
43. *The Times*, 9 November 1944.
44. King Peter, *A King's Heritage*, op. cit., pp. 163-5.
45. Gilbert, *Road to Victory*, pp. 1065-6.
46. Wilson, *Eight Years Overseas*, op. cit., p. 239.
47. See Henniker report, 14 May 1946, WO 32/18517.
48. C.S.R. Harris, *The Allied Military Administration of Italy 1943-45* (1957), pp. 308-9.
49. FRUS (1944) Vol. 4, pp. 1425-6.
50. Maclean to Churchill, 7 December 1944, WO 202/220.
51. *EA*, p. 520.
52. Maclean to Churchill, 8 December 1944; Maclean to Sacmed, 9, 10 December 1944, WO 202/220.
53. Maclean to Sacmed, 8 December 1944; Slessor to Maclean, 13 December; Maclean to Churchill, 9 December 1944, WO 202/220; Maclean to Sacmed, 1 January 1945, WO 202/252.
54. Maclean to Sacmed, 10, 27 December 1944, WO 202/252.
55. Maclean to Hawksworth, 16 December 1944, WO 202/220.
56. Alexander to Maclean, 15 December 1944, WO 202/220.
57. Maclean to Sacmed, 16 December 1944, WO 202/220.
58. Eden note, 23 November 1944, FO 371/43649.
59. Maclean to FO, 16 December 1944, FO 371/43649.
60. Velebit, *Memoirs*, p. 346.
61. Alexander to Maclean, 27 December 1944, WO 202/220.
62. Maclean to Sacmed, 12, 13 January 1945, WO 202/252.
63. Dedijer, *Tito Speaks* (1953), p. 235.
64. Hilary King to author, interview, 14 April 1991.
65. Ibid.
66. Thayer, *Hands Across the Caviar*, p. 161.
67. *Lockhart Diaries*, pp. 692, 695 (under 3, 15 January 1945).
68. *EA*, p. 527.
69. Maclean report, February 1945, FO 202/254.
70. *The Times*, 3 March 1945.
71. *EA*, p. 528.
72. Fitzroy Maclean to author, interview, 14 April 1991.
73. *EA*, p. 532.

Chapter 14

1. *EA*, p. 408.
2. Fitzroy Maclean to author, interview, 6 March 1991.
3. Anita Leslie, *Cousin Randolph*, op. cit., p. 78.
4. Roberts, *Randolph Churchill*, op. cit., p. 257.

5. Djilas, *Wartime*, p. 369.
6. Hilary King to author, interview, 14 April 1991.
7. Ibid.
8. Ibid.
9. Fitzroy Maclean to author, interview, 6 March 1991.
10. Christopher Sykes in Halle, op. cit., pp. 46–7; cf. also Sykes, *Evelyn Waugh* (1975), p. 243.
11. Michael Davie, ed., *The Diaries of Evelyn Waugh* (1976), p. 571.
12. Ibid., p. 572.
13. David Pryce-Jones, *Evelyn Waugh and his World* (1973), p. 135.
14. *News Chronicle*, 24 July 1944; Davie, *Diaries*, op. cit., p. 573.
15. Another recruit, Air Commodore Viscount Carlow, was killed in a plane crash when flying out to join the mission (Lord Drogheda, *Double Harness* (1978), p. 8).
16. Sykes, *Evelyn Waugh*, p. 268.
17. *Lockhart Diaries*, ii, p. 333; cf. also p. 352 (under 8 September 1944).
18. Davie, *Waugh Diaries*, p. 587.
19. Ibid., p. 591.
20. Fitzroy Maclean to author, interview, 14 April 1991.
21. Pryce-Jones, *Evelyn Waugh and his World*, op. cit., p. 151.
22. Randolph Churchill to Parker, 10 November 1944, WO 202/244.
23. Hilary King to author, interview, 14 April 1991.
24. Maclean to Randolph Churchill, 2 November 1944; Randolph Churchill to Parker, 16 November 1944, WO 202/244.
25. Clarke to Churchill, n.d.; Clarke to Churchill, 28 November 1944, WO 202/244.
26. Sir Peter Carey to author, interview, 9 May 1991.
27. Sykes, *Evelyn Waugh*, p. 276; cf. also Davie, *Waugh Diaries*, p. 625 (under 13 April).
28. Sykes, op. cit., p. 278.
29. Waugh to Tom Driberg, 11 August 1945, in Mark Amory, ed., *The Letters of Evelyn Waugh* (1980), p. 210.
30. Ibid., p. 226.
31. Davie, *Waugh Diaries*, pp. 651–2 (n.).
32. Annette Street to author, interview, 23 April 1991.
33. Mike Parker to author, interview, 3 August 1991.
34. Lord Henniker to author, interview, 12 June 1991.
35. Sykes, *Evelyn Waugh*, p. 271; cf. also Davie, *Waugh Diaries*, p. 616 (under 25 February 1945).
36. Colonel John Clarke to author, interview, 13 March 1991.
37. Fitzroy Maclean to author, interview, 14 April 1991.
38. The late Michael Lees to author, interview, 27 March 1991.
39. Sir John Astor to author, interview, 21 March 1991.
40. Cave Brown, *Last Hero*, p. 454.

Chapter 15

1. FO 371/30220.
2. Selborne to Churchill, 11 May 1944, FO 371/44290.
3. Mountbatten to Chiefs of Staff, 17 June 1943, FO 371/37609.
4. Glenconner to Pierson Dixon, 3 July 1942, FO 371/32469.
5. Howard to Elisabeth Barker, 2 March 1943, FO 371/37580.
6. Auty and Clogg, *British Policy*, op. cit., p. 33.

7. Ibid., pp. 3–33.
8. Elisabeth Barker, *British Policy*, op. cit., p. 160.
9. Auty and Clogg, op. cit., p. 237.
10. FO 371/37586.
11. Bailey statement in Auty and Clogg, p. 250.
12. S. W. Bailey, 'British Policy towards General Draza Mihailovic', in Auty and Clogg, op. cit., pp. 59–92 (at p. 83).
13. Ibid., pp. 86–7.
14. Maclean statement in ibid., p. 252.
15. Bailey, loc. cit., pp. 88–9.
16. Statement by George Taylor in Auty and Clogg, op. cit., pp. 229–34 (at p. 230).
17. Bennett, *Ultra in Mediterranean Strategy*, op. cit., p. 338.
18. See J. Tomasevic, *The Chetniks* (Stanford, 1975), esp. pp. 209–11; Matteo J. Milazzo, *The Chetnik Movement and the Yugoslav Resistance* (Johns Hopkins, 1975), esp. pp. 90–112.
19. John Plamenatz, *The Case of General Mihailovic* (1946), pp. 18–19.
20. See Michael Lees, *The Rape of Serbia* (1990) and David Martin, *The Web of Disinformation* (1990). Even the Americans, who for reasons of their own were disposed to deny Mihailovic's personal collaboration, accepted as incontestable the evidence for collaboration between the Italians and the senior Cetnik commanders. See Biddle to Dept. of State, 2 January 1943, in FRUS (1943) Vol. 2, (Washington, 1964), pp. 962–4.
21. See WO 208/2006, *passim*; Deakin, *Embattled Mountain*, p. 144; Clissold, *Whirlwind* (1949), p. 72; Mark Wheeler, *Britain and the War for Yugoslavia 1940–1943* (Columbia, 1980), pp. 105–9; W. R. Roberts, *Tito, Mihailovic and the Allies* (Rutgers, 1973), pp. 35, 367.
22. Mario Roatta, *Otto Millioni di Baionette* (Milan, 1946).
23. W. Hubatsch, ed., *Kriegstagebuch des Oberkommandos der Wehrmacht* (1963), iii, pp. 168–75.
24. F. W. Hinsley, *British Intelligence*, op. cit., Vol. 3, Part 3, Chapter 3 deals with this in detail.
25. *DB*, p. 269.
26. Milazzo, *The Chetnik Movement*, op. cit., pp. 169–71, 174–5.
27. Martin, *The Web of Disinformation*, op. cit., pp. 144–5.
28. Sir William Deakin to author, interview, 27 June 1991.
29. Sargent to Hollis, 25 November 1943, FO 371/37616.
30. Hugh Seton-Watson, statement in Auty and Clogg, op. cit., p. 276.
31. Milazzo, *The Chetnik Movement*, op. cit., p. 162.
32. Bennett, *Ultra in Mediterranean Strategy*, op cit., p. 343.
33. Maclean statement in Auty and Clogg, p. 239.
34. Fitzroy Maclean to author, interview, 17 January 1991.
35. Milazzo, p. 187.
36. Sweet-Escott statement in Auty and Clogg, p. 19.
37. Glen, *Footholds against a Whirlwind*, op. cit., pp. 185, 190.
38. Sir Reginald Hibbert to author, interview, 28 February 1991.
39. Mark Wheeler to author, interview, 12 March 1991.
40. Ibid.
41. See FO 371/44290; cf. also the discussion in Auty and Clogg, p. 275–6.
42. Maclean to Sargent, 27 December 1943, WO 202/138.
43. Fitzroy Maclean to author, interview, 9 December 1990.

Chapter 16

1. Franklin Lindsay to author, 21 October 1991.
2. Basil Davidson to author, interview, 7 January 1992.
3. Vladimir Velebit to author, 9 September 1991.
4. Anthony Kemp, *The SAS at War* (1991), p. 226.
5. Gilbert, *Road to Victory*, op cit., p. 1072.
6. Maclean to J. P. L. Thomas, 17 December 1943, WO 202/138.
7. Julian Amery to author, interview, 19 March 1991.
8. *Manchester Guardian*, 28 July 1945.
9. R. B. McCallum, *The British General Election of 1945* (1947), pp. 106–7.
10. Ibid., p. 269.
11. Sir Douglas Dodds-Parker to author, interview, 9 July 1991.
12. Fitzroy Maclean to author, interview, 17 October 1991.
13. Sir Douglas Dodds-Parker to author, interview, 9 July 1991.
14. Lord Henniker to author, interview, 12 June 1991.
15. Sir Peter Carey to author, interview, 9 May 1991.
16. *The Times*, 7 June 1945.
17. D. R. Thorpe, *Selwyn Lloyd* (1989), p. 102.
18. Ben Pimlott, ed., *The Political Diary of Hugh Dalton 1918–40, 1945–60* (1986), p. 512.
19. *The Times*, 25 October, 3 November 1945.
20. *The Times*, 1, 22 November, 6 December 1945.
21. *The Times*, 23 November 1945.
22. *The Times*, 29 November 1945.
23. Private diary, 1945.
24. Lady Maclean to author, interview, 29 December 1991.
25. Ibid.
26. *The Times*, 18 January 1946.
27. Lady Maclean to author, interview, 29 December 1991.
28. *The Times*, 5 March, 3 April 1946.
29. *The Times*, 5, 6 June, 13 December 1946.
30. *The Times*, 6, 19 September, 24 October, 1, 14 November, 5 December 1946.
31. Fitzroy Maclean to author, interview, 29 December 1991.
32. *The Times*, 28 January 1947.
33. Fitzroy Maclean to author, interview, 9 December 1990.
34. Lady Maclean to author, interview, 29 December 1991.

Chapter 17

1. *War Diaries of Oliver Harvey*, op. cit., p. 382 (under 10 June 1945).
2. For an eyewitness account see Geoffrey Cox, *The Road to Trieste* (1947), esp. pp. 193–249.
3. Michael McConville, *A Small War in the Balkans* (1986), pp. 3–4.
4. The exact figures are disputed. Fitzroy reproduces the official list of 1,685,000 dead (*DB*, pp. 341–2). But a recent careful study levels this down to 1,014,000 (Mark Wheeler, 'The Communist Party of Yugoslavia', in Tony Judt, ed., *Resistance and Revolution in Mediterranean Europe* (1989), p. 151).
5. Basil Davidson, *Partisan Picture* (1946), pp. 331–2.
6. See FO minute of 26 July 1945, FO 371/44823.
7. *Lockhart Diaries*, ii, p. 486–7 (under 8 August 1945).

8. *The Times*, 19 June 1946.
9. See Eden to Churchill, 18 January 1945, FO 371/48816.
10. Cadogan to Prime Minister, 20 June 1945, FO 371/48812.
11. Paper on the Yugoslav elections, 14 November 1945, FO 371/48874.
12. Sargent to Stevenson, 24 November 1945, FO 371/48874.
13. See FO 371/48854. For the assurances, see Maclean to FO, 14 January 1945, FO 371/48851.
14. See Foreign Office Policy Documents, 29 March 1945, FO 371/57734; Secretary of State to Kirk, 11 October 1945, FRUS (1945), v, pp. 1265–6.
15. Sargent minute, 27 March 1946, FO 371/49499.
16. Minutes of meeting of 23 December 1946, FO 371/66600.
17. See Nikolai Tolstoy, *The Minister and the Massacres* (1986).
18. FO memorandum to Cabinet, 23 May 1946, FO 371/57710.
19. Cabot to Secretary of State, 15 May 1947, FRUS (1947) Vol. 4, pp. 797–800.
20. Lady Maclean to author, interview, 29 December 1991.
21. Fitzroy Maclean to author, interview, 9 December 1990.
22. Rendel minute, 4 January 1947, FO 371/66600.
23. Washington to FO, 14 February 1947, FO 371/66605.
24. Washington to FO, 20 May 1947, FO 371/67376.
25. Baron Mayhew to author, interview, 1 March 1991.
26. The late Michael Lees to author, interview, 27 March 1991.
27. Lady Maclean to author, interview, 29 December 1991.
28. *The Times*, 29 January 1947.
29. Nikolai Tolstoy, *The Secret Betrayal* (1978).
30. Report on Ukrainians in SEP Camp No. 374, Italy, 21 February 1947, FO 371/66605.
31. Ibid.
32. Minutes of 7 March, FO 371/66606.
33. WR 58 of 12 March 1947, FO 371/66605.
34. See correspondence and minutes under WR 2353, 19 June 1947, FO 371/66712.
35. Mark Aarons and John Loftus, *Ratlines* (1991), p. 198.
36. Ibid., p. 197.
37. Ibid., p. 195.
38. Fitzroy Maclean to author, 1 November 1990.
39. Count Nikolai Tolstoy to author, 17 January 1992.
40. *Ratlines*, op. cit., pp. 199–200.
41. The late Michael Lees to author, interview, 27 March 1991.
42. Lord Carrington, *Reflect on Things Past* (1988), pp. 64–5.
43. Fitzroy Maclean to author, interview, 9 December 1990.
44. Jeanne Clissold to author, 5 November 1990.
45. Note of 3 July 1945, FO 371/48890; note of 30 August 1945, FO 371/48892.
46. See FO 371/48892 and 48893, *passim*.
47. FO 371/48894, *passim*.
48. Correspondence and telegrams, 10–14 January 1946, FO 371/59399.
49. British Embassy, Belgrade to FO, 9 June 1946, FO 371/59408; Yugoslav Embassy, London, to FO, 2 August 1946, FO 371/59415; British Embassy to Yugoslav Ministry of Foreign Affairs, 21 August 1946, FO 371/59417.
50. Fitzroy Maclean to author, 26 November 1990.
51. Telegram from Rome to Caserta, 25 February 1947, FO 371/67372; FO to Screening Mission, Klagenfurt, 14 August 1947, FO 371/67386; Maclean to FO, 16 May 1947, FO 371/67378; FO to Klagenfurt, 30 July 1947, FO 371/67384; Klagenfurt to FO, 29 September 1947, FO 371/67393.
52. Fitzroy Maclean to author, 1 December 1990.

53. Note of 21 November 1946, FO 371/59423.
54. Telegram and minutes, 14–18 December 1946, FO 371/59423.
55. Note of 26 July 1947, FO 371/67384.
56. Annette Street to author, interview, 23 April 1991.
57. Vivian Street to FO, 5 June 1947, FO 371/67380.
58. *Ratlines*, op. cit., p. 109.
59. FO 371/59415 and 67376, *passim*; British political adviser, Caserta, to FO, 26 February 1947, FO 371/67372; Special Refugee Commission to FO, 23 October 1947, FO 371/67398. See also FO 371/59400, 59406, 59412 and 59415, *passim*.
60. Maclean to Wallinger, 17 October 1947, FO 371/67398.
61. Wallinger to Perowne, 5 December 1947, FO 371/67402.
62. Maclean to Wallinger, 17 October 1947, FO 371/67398.
63. FO memo, 10 September 1948, FO 371/72563 E.
64. Warner note, 19 June 1947, FO 371/67385; letters and telegrams, 17–25 July 1947, FO 371/67385–7.
65. *Ratlines*, op. cit., p. 205.
66. Private diaries, esp. 3 June and 16 July 1947.
67. Fitzroy Maclean to author, 1 December 1990.
68. Maclean to FO, 23 February 1947, FO 371/66603.
69. *Lockhart Diaries*, p. 597 (under 3 May 1947).
70. Instructions for Maclean, 16 June 1947, FO 371/66664.
71. Fitzroy Maclean to author, interview, 9 December 1990.
72. *DB*, p. 350.
73. Maclean to FO, 25 August 1947, FO 371/66669.
74. See text of agreement, 8 September 1947, FO 371/67402; FO to Washington, 5 September 1947, FO 371/66670.
75. Anne J. Lane, 'Coming to Terms with Tito: the policy of the British Foreign Office towards Yugoslavia, 1945–1949', Ph.D. dissertation, London University, 1988.
76. Annette Street to author, interview, 23 April 1990.
77. Fitzroy Maclean to author, interview, 13 April 1991.
78. The late Michael Lees to author, interview, 27 March 1991.
79. Annette Street to author, interview, 23 April 1991.
80. Jeanne Clissold to author, interview, 5 November 1990.
81. Baron Mayhew to author, interview, 1 March 1991.
82. Vladimir Dedijer, *Tito Speaks*, op. cit., p. 216; Stephen Clissold, *Yugoslavia and the Soviet Union*, op. cit., p. 169.
83. *The Times*, 19 September 1949.
84. This *bon mot* was revealed by Khruschev in his famous speech to the Twentieth Communist Party Congress in Moscow in February 1956. See Clissold, *Yugoslavia*, op. cit., p. 259.
85. See FO 371/72578, *passim*.
86. Maclean to Churchill, 18 March 1944, CAB 66 (48), WP 44.
87. Lane, loc. cit.
88. See FO 371/78768, *passim*; Campbell minute, 12 May 1949, FO 371/78739.
89. Glen, *Whirlwind*, op. cit., p. 192.
90. Sir Reginald Hibbert to author, interview, 28 February 1991.

Chapter 18

1. *The Times*, 23 September 1948.
2. *The Times*, 3 February 1949.

3. *The Times*, 22 July 1949.
4. *The Times*, 2, 25 March 1949.
5. *Lockhart Diaries*, p. 666 (under 17 July 1948).
6. Fitzroy Maclean to author, interview, 13 April 1991.
7. Jeanne Clissold to author, interview, 5 November 1990.
8. Fitzroy Maclean to author, interview, 13 April 1991.
9. Peter Duff Hart-Davis, *Peter Fleming. A Biography* (1974), p. 310.
10. Lord Henniker to author, interview, 12 June 1991.
11. Fitzroy Maclean to author, interview, 13 April 1991.
12. Freya Stark to Stewart Perowne, 26, 28, 30 July 1951, in Lucy Moorehead, ed., *The Letters of Freya Stark*, vi, pp. 241–2.
13. Martin Gilbert, *Never Despair. Winston Churchill 1945–1965* (1988), pp. 453, 461.
14. *The Times*, 24 March 1949.
15. *The Times*, 17 November 1949.
16. Sir Reginald Hibbert to author, interview, 28 February 1991.
17. Fitzroy Maclean to author, interview, 9 December 1990.
18. Stephen Clissold, ed., *Yugoslavia and the Soviet Union 1939–73. A Documentary Survey* (Oxford, 1975), pp. 239–40.
19. British Embassy to FO, 26 September 1950, FO 371/88340.
20. For details of the Djilas visit, see FO 371/95539 and 371/95488.
21. *Lockhart Diaries*, p. 728 (under 25 March 1951).
22. Lady Antonia Fraser to author, interview, 22 April 1990.
23. *The Times*, 10, 24 January; 26, 29 April; 5, 15, 25 May 1950.
24. *The Times*, 6, 11, 20 July; 1, 14 August 1950.
25. *The Times*, 18 August 1950.
26. Edwin Plowden, *An Industrialist in the Treasury* (1989), p. 91.
27. *The Times*, 27 June 1950.
28. Private diaries, 1950.
29. *The Times*, 15 December 1950.
30. *The Times*, 9 February, 13 March, 23, 27 June, 31 July, 26 September 1951; 7 February 1952.
31. *The Times*, 27 February 1952.
32. *The Times*, 15 May 1952.
33. *The Times*, 30 June 1952.
34. Fitzroy Maclean to author, interview, 17 October 1991.
35. *The Times*, 18, 25 June 1953.
36. *The Times*, 15 May, 21 June, 14 July 1953.
37. Harold Macmillan, *Tides of Fortune* (1969), p. 502.
38. *The Times*, 12 May 1953.
39. For a detailed study of the Suez group and the events of 1953–4, see D. A. Farnie, *East and West of Suez* (Oxford, 1969).
40. Ibid., p. 711.
41. *The Times*, 30 July 1954.
42. See the extended discussion in Andrew Roth, *Enoch Powell. Tory Tribune* (1970).
43. Lord Henniker to author, interview, 12 June 1991.
44. Fitzroy Maclean to author, interview, 9 December 1990.
45. Fitzroy Maclean to author, interview, 13 April 1991.
46. Ibid.
47. Fitzroy Maclean to author, interview, 14 October 1990.
48. *The Times*, 18, 23 October; 4 December 1954; 26 January 1955.
49. *The Times*, 10 February 1955.
50. Sir John Astor to author, interview, 21 March 1991.
51. John Cloake, *Templer, Tiger of Malaya* (1985), p. 336.

52. Dr Han Suyin to author, 29 June 1991.
53. For Fitzroy's work on military policy in Malaya 1955–6, see WO 32/15540.
54. Ex. inf. John Blelloch, interview, 9 July 1991.
55. Fitzroy Maclean to author, interview, 13 April 1991.
56. *The Times*, 26 July 1955.
57. *The Times*, 9, 11 November 1955.
58. See WO 32/15546.
59. WO 32/15591.
60. John Blelloch to author, interview, 9 July 1991.
61. Ibid.
62. *The Times*, 16 May 1956.
63. *The Times*, 5 June 1956.
64. *The Times*, 20 June 1956.
65. Fitzroy Maclean to author, interview, 13 April 1991.
66. John Blelloch to author, interview, 9 July 1991.
67. Fitzroy Maclean to author, interview, 13 April 1991.
68. Fitzroy Maclean to author, interview, 17 October 1991.
69. Fitzroy Maclean to author, interview, 13 April 1991.
70. Alistair Horne, *Macmillan 1957–1986* (1989), p. 10.
71. Sir Douglas Dodds-Parker to author, interview, 9 July 1991.
72. Ibid.
73. Fitzroy Maclean to author, interview, 29 December 1991.

Chapter 19

1. Fitzroy Maclean to author, interview, 13 April 1991.
2. Allen Garnett to author, 16 July 1991.
3. *The Times*, 16 February 1954.
4. Fitzroy Maclean to author, interview, 13 April 1991.
5. Jeremy Phipps to author, interview, 10 July 1991.
6. Suki Paravicini to author, interview, 25 June 1991.
7. Ibid.
8. Jamie Maclean to author, interview, 18 June 1991.
9. Jeanne Clissold to author, interview, 5 November 1990.
10. Lady Maclean to author, interview, 29 December 1991.
11. Christian, Lady Hesketh to author, interview, 27 November 1990.
12. Lady Maclean to author, interview, 29 December 1991.
13. Suki Paravicini to author, interview, 25 June 1991.
14. Jeremy Phipps to author, interview, 10 July 1991.
15. Charlie Maclean to author, interview, 29 December 1991.
16. *The Times*, 13 June 1957.
17. Fitzroy Maclean to author, interview, 9 December 1990.
18. *The Times*, 11 January, 22 February, 8 April 1957.
19. David Lambie to author, interview, 13 February 1991.
20. Lady Antonia Fraser to author, interview, 22 April 1991.
21. *The Times*, 20 March, 6 June, 17 September 1957.
22. Fitzroy Maclean to author, interview, 13 April 1991.
23. Ibid.
24. Jeremy Phipps to author, interview, 10 July 1991.
25. Jamie Maclean to author, interview, 18 June 1991.
26. Fitzroy Maclean to author, interview, 29 December 1991.

27. Christian, Lady Hesketh to author, interview, 27 November 1990.
28. *The Times*, 15 April 1954.
29. See Hewlett Johnson, *Searching for Light* (1968).
30. *Lockhart Diaries*, p. 732 (under 28 June 1951).
31. Fitzroy Maclean to author, 1 November 1990.
32. See Christopher Mayhew, *Time to Explain* (1987), pp. 135–45.
33. Baron Mayhew to author, interview, 1 March 1991.
34. John Roberts to author, interview, 24 June 1991.
35. Jeanne Clissold to author, interview, 5 November 1990.
36. Jeremy Phipps to author, interview, 10 July 1991.
37. *The Times*, 30 October 1958.
38. Pamela, Lady Egremont to author, interview, 9 April 1991.
39. Alistair Milne to author, interview, 30 October 1990.
40. Fitzroy Maclean to author, interview, 13 April 1991. Cf. also private diaries, 30 August 1960; 15 May, 22 June 1961.
41. Jeanne Clissold to author, interview, 5 November 1990.
42. Michael Gill to author, interview, 12 February 1991.
43. Alistair Milne, *Director-General. The Memoirs of a British Broadcaster* (1988), p. 18.
44. Alistair Milne to author, interview, 30 October 1990.
45. Fitzroy Maclean to author, interview, 13 April 1991.
46. Alistair Milne to author, interview, 30 October 1990.
47. John Purdie to author, interview, 26 November 1990.
48. Pamela, Lady Egremont to author, interview, 9 April 1991.
49. Alistair Milne to author, interview, 30 October 1990.
50. Jeanne Clissold to author, interview, 5 November 1990.
51. Robert Louis Stevenson, *Works* (Edinburgh Edition), xi, p. 85.

Chapter 20

1. Fitzroy Maclean to author, interview, 17 October 1991.
2. *The Times*, 27 February 1959.
3. *The Times*, 2 March 1960.
4. *The Times*, 17 December 1960.
5. *The Times*, 17, 26, 29 November 1960; 8 March, 12 July, 26 September, 18, 21 October, 2, 3 November, 8 December 1961.
6. *The Times*, 26 January 1962.
7. *The Times*, 6 March 1963.
8. *The Times*, 20 March, 19 November 1963; 22, 27 April 1964; 5 March 1965.
9. *The Times*, 6 June 1962; 5 May 1967; 16 July 1968.
10. *The Times*, 5 March 1969, 2, 5 March 1970.
11. *The Times*, 21 July 1965; 25 May 1966; 28 July 1967.
12. *The Times*, 27 August, 22 November 1968.
13. *The Times*, 23 July, 22 December 1971; 20 October, 22 November 1972.
14. *The Times*, 11 November 1959; 18 December 1962; 4 December 1963; 17 May 1969; 17 March 1971.
15. David Lambie to author, interview, 13 February 1991.
16. Ibid.
17. *CHS*, pp. 213–15.
18. Fitzroy Maclean to author, interview, 13 April 1991.
19. *The Times*, 22 February, 12 December 1973.
20. David Lambie to author, interview, 13 February 1991.

21. John Blelloch to author, interview, 9 July 1991.
22. Arthur F. Seldon, *Churchill's Indian Summer* (1981), p. 308.
23. Sir John Astor to author, interview, 21 March 1991.
24. Lord Jenkins of Hillhead to author, inteview, 27 June 1991.
25. Fitzroy Maclean to author, interview, 28 December 1991.
26. Sir Reginald Hibbert to author, interview, 28 February 1991.
27. David Lambie to author, interview, 13 February 1991.
28. Jo Grimond, *Memoirs* (1979), p. 177.
29. Lord Jenkins of Hillhead to author, interview, 27 June 1991.
30. Alisdair Milne to author, interview, 30 October 1990.

Chapter 21

1. *PFE*, pp. 38–81.
2. Laurence Kelly to author, interview, 14 January 1991.
3. John Roberts to author, interview, 24 June 1991.
4. John Purdie to author, interview, 26 November 1990.
5. Ibid.
6. Michael Gill to author, interview, 12 February 1991.
7. Jeanne Clissold to author, interview, 5 November 1990.
8. Tony Isaacs to author, interview, 26 October 1990.
9. *PSU*, p. 34.
10. Tony Isaacs to author, interview, 26 October 1990.
11. John Purdie to author, interview, 26 November 1990.
12. *EA*, pp. 45–6.
13. Laurence Kelly to author, interview, 14 January 1991.
14. John Purdie to author, interview, 26 November 1990.
15. Thelma Holt to author, interview, 15 November 1990.
16. Stephen Clissold, *Djilas. The Progress of a Revolutionary* (1983), pp. 5–54.
17. Ibid., p. 12.
18. John Purdie to author, interview, 26 November 1990.
19. Sir John Lawrence to author, interview, 16 August 1991.
20. John Roberts to author, interview, 24 June 1991.
21. Sir Reginald Hibbert to author, interview, 28 February 1991.
22. Robert Chenciner to author, interview, 4 April 1991.
23. Ibid.

Chapter 22

1. Fitzroy Maclean to author, interview, 15 April 1991.
2. Glen, *Footholds*, op cit., p. 262.
3. Sir Alexander Glen to author, interview, 3 March 1991.
4. Fitzroy Maclean to author, interview, 14 April 1991.
5. Alistair Milne to author, interview, 30 October 1990.
6. Jeremy Phipps to author, interview, 10 July 1991.
7. Jamie Maclean to author, interview, 18 June 1991.
8. Sir John Astor to author, interview, 21 March 1991.
9. Pamela, Lady Egremont to author, interview, 9 April 1991.
10. Thelma Holt to author, interview, 15 November 1990.

11. Lady Antonia Fraser to author, interview, 22 April 1990.
12. Lady Bullard to author, interview, 3 March 1991.
13. Sir John Astor to author, interview, 21 March 1991.
14. Lady Antonia Fraser to author, interview, 22 April 1990.
15. Lady Bullard to author, interview, 3 March 1991.
16. Alistair Milne to author, interview, 30 October 1990.
17. Fitzroy Maclean to author, interview, 14 April 1991.
18. *The Times*, 4, 5, 6, 7 December 1977.
19. Fitzroy Maclean to author, interview, 14 December 1990.
20. Fitzroy Maclean to author, interview, 3 March 1991.
21. Fitzroy Maclean to author, interview, 14 April 1991.
22. Thelma Holt to author, interview, 15 November 1990.
23. Fitzroy Maclean to author, interview, 14 April 1990.
24. Fitzroy Maclean to author, interview, 14 December 1990.
25. John Roberts to author, interview, 24 June 1991.
26. For the interview, see Roy Plomley, *Plomley's Pick* (1982), pp. 110–14. Fitzroy's records were: 1 'Barren Rocks of Aden' (Band and Drums of the Black Watch); 2 'As Time Goes By' (Russell Scott, Organ); 3 Tchaikovsky, *Swan Lake* (Ansermet, OSR); 4 'Lili Marlene' (Lale Anderen); 5 Haydn, *Trumpet Concerto in E Flat* (Maurice André, Lopez-Cobos, LPO); 6 Mozart, 'Voi che sapete,' from *Le Nozze di Figaro*; 7 Beethoven, *Piano Concerto No. 5* (Ashkenazy, Solti, CSO).
27. Fitzroy Maclean to author, interview, 5 May 1990; Sir Alexander Glen to author, interview, 3 March 1991.
28. See Melvyn Bragg, *Richard Burton* (1988), pp. 435–6.
29. Fitzroy Maclean to author, interview, 14 April 1991.
30. Fitzroy Maclean to author, 21 November 1990.
31. Sir Peter Carey to author, interview, 9 May 1991.
32. Fitzroy Maclean to author, 26 November 1990.
33. Fitzroy Maclean to author, 1 November 1990.
34. Fitzroy Maclean to author, interview, 14 April 1991.

Bibliography

Aarons, Mark & Loftus, John, *Ratlines* (1991)
Addison, P., *The Road to 1945: British Politics of the Second World War* (1975)
Amery, Julian, *Sons of the Eagle* (1948)
—— *Approach March* (1973)
Amory, Mark, ed. *The Letters of Evelyn Waugh* (1980)
—— ed., *The Letters of Anne Fleming* (1985)
Anderson, T. H., *The United States, Great Britain and the Cold War 1944–1947* (1981)
Armstrong, John, *Ukrainian Nationalism 1939–1945* (New York, 1955)
Auty, Phyllis, *Tito* (1970)
—— & Richard Clogg, eds., *British Policy towards Wartime Resistance in Yugoslavia and Greece* (1975)
Ayer, A.J., *Part of My life* (1977)
Baerenstein, Lars, Intridis, John & Smith, Ole, eds., *Studies in the History of the Greek Civil War* (Copenhagen, 1987)
Balfour, Neil & McKay, Sally, *Paul of Yugoslavia* (1980)
Banac, Ivo, *With Stalin against Tito: Cominformist Splits in Yugoslav Communism* (Cornell, 1988)
Barker, Elisabeth, *Macedonia: Its Place in Balkan Power Politics* (1950)
—— *British Policy towards South-eastern Europe in the Second World War* (1976)
—— *Churchill and Eden at War* (1978)
—— *The British between the Superpowers 1945–1950* (1986)
Barker, Ralph, *One Man's Jungle* (1975)
Barker, Thomas M., *Social Revolutionaries and Secret Agents* (Boulder, Colorado, 1990)
Beevor, Anthony, *Crete, The Battle and the Resistance* (1991)
Beevor, J.G., *SOE: Recollections and Reflections 1940–45* (1981)
Beloff, Max, *The Foreign Policy of the Soviet Union* (1966)
Beloff, Nora, *Tito's Flawed Legacy* (1975)
Bennett, Ralph, *Ultra in the West* (1979)
—— *Ultra and Mediterranean Strategy 1941–1945* (1989)
Bernstein, Serge, *Le 6 Février 1934* (Paris, 1975)
Bethell, Nicholas, *The War Hitler Won* (1972)
Blanch, Lesley, *Journey into the Mind's Eye* (1968)
Bohlen, Charles, *Witness to History* (New York, 1973)
Bower, Tom, *The Pledge Betrayed* (1981)
Boyle, Andrew, *The Climate of Treason* (1979)
Bragg, Melvyn, *Richard Burton* (New York, 1988)

Brockway, Fenner, *Towards Tomorrow* (1977)
Brown, Anthony Cave, ed., *The Secret War Reports of the OSS* (New York, 1976)
—— *The Last Hero. General William Donovan* (1982)
—— *The Secret Servant. The Life of Sir Stuart Menzies* (1988)
Bryce, Ivar, *You Only Live Once* (1984)
Bullard, Reader, *Letters from Teheran: an Ambassador in World War Two Persia* (1991)
Bullock, Alan, *Ernest Bevin, Foreign Secretary 1945–1951* (1983)
—— *Hitler and Stalin* (1991)
Calvocoressi, Peter, *Top Secret Ultra* (1980)
Cannadine, David, *The Decline and Fall of the British Aristocracy* (1990)
Carr, E. H., *A History of the Soviet Union*, 14 vols (1950–1978)
Carrington, Lord, *Reflect on Things Past* (1988)
Cecil, Robert, *A Divided Life. A Biography of Donald Maclean* (1988)
Chandler, Alfred D., ed., *The Papers of Dwight D. Eisenhower, Vol. 3 The War Years* (Baltimore, 1970)
Churchill, Tom, *Commando Crusade* (1987)
Clarke, Peter, *A Question of Leadership* (1991)
Clissold, Stephen, *Whirlwind* (1948)
—— ed., *Yugoslavia and the Soviet Union 1939–1973. A Documentary Survey* (1975)
—— *Djilas: the Progress of a Revolutionary* (1983)
Cloake, John, *Templer, Tiger of Malaya* (1985)
Cohen, Stephen F., *Bukharin and the Bolshevik Revolution* (1974)
Colakovic, Rodoljub, *Winning Freedom* (1962)
Connell, Brian, *Knight Errant* (1955)
Conquest, Robert, *The Great Terror* (1968)
Cookridge, E. H., *Inside SOE* (1966)
Cooper, Artemis, *Cairo in Wartime 1936–43* (1989)
Cooper, Diana, *Trumpets from the Steep* (1960)
Cooper, Johnny, *One of the Originals* (1991)
Cot, Pierre, *Le Procès de la République* (New York, 1944)
Courtney, G. B., *The Special Boat Squadron in World War Two* (1983)
Cowles, Virginia, *The Phantom Major* (1958)
Cox, Geoffrey, *The Road to Trieste* (1947)
—— *A Tale of Two Battles* (1987)
Craig, G. A. & Gilbert, F., eds, *The Diplomats 1919–1939* (New York, 1965)
Curzon, George, *Russia in Central Asia* (1889)
—— *Persia and the Persian Question* (1892)
Dalton, Hugh, *The Fateful Years* (1957)
Daudy, Philippe, *Les Anglais* (1991)
Davidson, Basil, *Partisan Picture* (1946)
—— *Special Operations Europe* (1980)
Davie, Michael, ed., *The Diaries of Evelyn Waugh* (1976)
Davies, 'Trotsky', *Illyrian Adventure* (1952)
Deakin, F. W., *The Brutal Friendship. Mussolini, Hitler and the Fall of Italian Fascism* (New York, 1962)
Dedijer, Vladimir, *With Tito through the War 1941–1944* (1951)
—— *Tito Speaks* (1953)
—— *The Beloved Land* (1961)
Degras, J., ed., *Soviet Documents on Foreign Policy*, 3 vols (Oxford, 1953)
Deighton, Len, *Alamein and the Desert War* (1967)
Dilkes, David, ed., *The Diaries of Sir Alexander Cadogan* (1971)
Djilas, Milovan, *Conversations with Stalin* (New York, 1962)
—— *Land without Justice* (1968)

—— *Wartime* (1977)

Douglas, Roy, *The Advent of War 1939–1940* (1978)

—— *From War to Cold War 1942–1948* (1981)

—— *New Alliances 1940–1941* (1982)

Douglas, William Sholto, *Years of Combat* (1963)

Dreifort, J. E., *Yvon Delbos at the Quai d'Orsay* (Lawrence, Kansas, 1973)

Drogheda, Lord, *Double Harness* (1978)

Dubief, Henri, *Déclin de la Troisième République* (Paris, 1976)

Eden, Anthony, *Facing the Dictators* (1961)

Edmonds, R., *Setting the Mould; the US and Britain 1945–1950* (Oxford, 1986)

Eeman, Harold, *Inside Stalin's Russia* (1977)

—— *Clouds over the Sun* (1981)

Ehrmann, J., *Grand Strategy* (1956)

Eubank, Keith, *Summit at Teheran* (New York, 1985)

Evans, Trefor, ed., *The Killearn Diaries* (1972)

Farnie, D. A., *East and West of Suez* (Oxford, 1969)

Feis, Herbert, *Churchill–Roosevelt–Stalin* (Princeton, 1967)

Ferguson, Robert, *Henry Miller* (1991)

Fermor, Patrick Leigh, *A Time of Gifts* (1977)

Fiennes, Ranulph, *Feathermen* (1991)

Fielding, Xan, *Hide and Seek* (1954)

Foot, M. R. D., *SOE in France* (1966)

—— *Resistance: European Resistance to Nazism 1940–1945* (1976)

—— *SOE 1940–1946* (1984)

Fotich, C., *The War We Lost* (New York, 1948)

Fraser, D., *Alanbrooke* (1982)

Getty, J. Arch, *Origin of the Great Purges: the Soviet Communist Party Reconsidered* (Cambridge, 1987)

Gilbert, Martin, *Road to Victory. Winston S. Churchill 1941–1945* (1986)

—— *Never Despair. Winston S. Churchill 1945–1965* (1988)

Gladwyn, Lord, *Memoirs* (1972)

Glen, Alexander, *Footholds against a Whirlwind* (1975)

Glendinning, Victoria, *Rebecca West. A Life* (1987)

Gorodetsky, G., *Stafford Cripps' Mission to Moscow* (Cambridge, 1984)

Grimond, Jo, *Memoirs* (1979)

Gromyko, Andrei, *Only for Peace* (1979)

—— *Memoirs* (1989)

Hagen, Walter, *The Secret Front. The Story of Nazi Political Espionage* (1953)

Hamilton-Hill, D., *SOE Assignment* (1973)

Hailsham, Lord, *A Sparrow's Flight* (1990)

Haines, Joe, *Maxwell* (1988)

Halle, Kay, *Randolph Churchill. The Young Pretender* (1971)

Harris, C. R. S., *Allied Military Administration of Italy 1943–45* (1957)

Hart, Basil Liddell, *Memoirs* (1965)

Hart-Davis, Peter Duff, *Peter Fleming. A Biography* (1974)

Harvey, John, ed., *The Diplomatic Diaries of Oliver Harvey* (1970)

—— ed., *The War Diaries of Oliver Harvey* (1978)

Herwarth, J. Bittenfeld von, *Against Two Evils* (1981)

Heuser, B., *Western Containment Policies in the Cold War: the Yugoslav case 1948–53* (1989)

Hibbert, Reginald, *Albania's National Liberation Struggle* (1991)

Hinsley, F. H., *British Intelligence in the Second World War* (1981)

Hollingworth, Clare, *Front Line* (1990)

Hopkins, Paul, *Glencoe* (1986)

Bibliography

Hopkirk, Peter, *Foreign Devils on the Silk Road* (1980)
—— *The Great Game* (1990)
Horne, Alistair, *Macmillan 1894–1956* (1988)
—— *Macmillan 1957–1986* (1989)
Howard, Michael, *The Mediterranean Strategy in the Second World War* (1968)
—— *Grand Strategy* (1972)
Howarth, Patrick, *Intelligence Chief Extraordinary. The Life of the 9th Duke of Portland* (1986)
Hubatsch, W., ed., *Kriegstagebuch des Oberkommandos der Wehrmacht* (Berlin, 1963)
Huot, Louis, *Guns for Tito* (1945)
Ivanovic, Vane, *Memoirs of a Yugoslav* (1977)
James, Robert Rhodes, *Anthony Eden* (1986)
Jenner, R. & List, D., *The Long Range Desert Group* (1983)
Johnson, Chalmers, *Peasant Nationalism and Communist Power: the Emergence of Revolutionary China 1937–1945* (Stanford, 1962)
Johnston, Charles, *Mo and other Originals* (1971)
Jones, William, *Twelve Months with Tito's Partisans* (1946)
Jordan, William, *Conquest into Victory* (1969)
Judt, Tony, ed., *Resistance and Revolution in Mediterranean Europe 1937–48* (1989)
Kemp, Anthony, *The SAS at War* (1991)
Kennan, George F., *Memoirs 1925–1950* (1967)
Khruschev, Nikita, *Khruschev Remembers* (1977)
Kimball, Warren F., ed., *Churchill and Roosevelt. Complete Correspondence* (Princeton, 1984)
Knezevitch, Z., *Why the Allies Abondoned the Yugoslav Army of Mihailovic* (Washington, 1945)
Kolko, Gabriel, *The Politics of War: the World and US Foreign Policy 1943–1945* (New York, 1970)
Korbel, J., *Tito's Communism* (Denver, 1951)
Kostunica, Vojislav & Cavoski, Kosta, *Party Pluralism or Monism: Social Movements and Political Systems in Yugoslavia 1944–1949* (New York, 1985)
Lacouture, Jean, *Leon Blum* (1982)
Lamb, Richard, *Churchill as War Leader* (1991)
Langhorne, Richard, ed., *Diplomacy and Intelligence during the Second World War* (Cambridge, 1985)
Lawrence, C., *Irregular Adventure* (1947)
Leeper, Rex, *When Greek meets Greek* (1950)
Lees, Michael, *Special Operations Executed* (1986)
—— *The Rape of Serbia* (New York, 1990)
Leslie, Anita, *Cousin Randolph* (1985)
Letley, Emma, *Maurice Baring* (1991)
Lewin, Ronald, *Ultra goes to War* (1978)
Lincoln, John, *Achilles and the Tortoise* (1958)
Lodwick, John, *The Filibusterers* (1947)
Lovat, Lord, *March Past* (1978)
Lowenheim, Francis L., Langley, Harold D., & Jones, Manfred, eds., *Roosevelt and Churchill. Their Secret Wartime Correspondence* (1975)
Lynch, Michael, *Scotland: a New History* (1991)
McCallum, R. B., *The British General Election of 1945* (1947)
McConville, Michael, *A Small War in the Balkans* (1986)
McIan, R. R., *The Clans of the Scottish Highlands* (1980)
McLynn, Frank, *Charles Edward Stuart* (1988)
Macmillan, Harold, *Tides of Fortune* (1969)

Martin, David, *Patriot or Traitor: the Case of General Mihailovic* (Stanford, 1978)
—— *The Web of Disinformation* (New York, 1990)
Matthiessen, Peter, *African Silences* (1991)
May, E. R., ed., *Knowing One's Enemies, Intelligence Assessment between the two World Wars* (Princeton, 1984)
Mayhew, Christopher, *Time to Explain* (1987)
Medvedev, Roy, *All Stalin's Men* (1983)
Messenger, Charles, *The Middle East Commandos* (1988)
Milazzo, Matteo J., *The Chetnik Movement* (Baltimore, 1975)
Milne, Alistair, *The Memoirs of a British Broadcaster* (1988)
Mitcham, Samuel W., *Hitler's Field Marshals and their Battles* (1988)
Moch, Jules, *Rencontres avec Blum* (Paris, 1970)
Moncreiffe, Iain, *The Highland Clans* (2nd edn, 1982)
Moorehead, Alan, *African Trilogy* (1944)
Moorehead, Lucy, ed., *The Letters of Freya Stark. Vol. 4 Bridge of the Levant 1940-43*; *Vol. 6 The Broken Road 1947-52* (1977; 1981)
Muggeridge, Malcolm, *Winter in Moscow* (1934)
—— *Chronicles of Wasted Time* (1973)
—— *Like it Was* (1981)
Murphy, Robert, *Diplomat among Warriors* (New York, 1964)
Nicholson, Harold, *Diaries and Letters 1939-45* (1970)
North, J., ed., *The Alexander Memoirs* (1962)
Owen, David Lloyd, *Providence Their Guide* (1980)
Palmer, Stephen E. & King, Robert R., *Yugoslav Communism and the Macedonian Question* (Connecticut, 1971)
Paris, Edmond, *Genocide in Satellite Croatia 1941-1945* (Chicago, 1961)
Pearson, John, *The Life of Ian Fleming* (1966)
Peniakoff, Vladimir, *Popsky's Private Army* (1991)
Peter II of Yugoslavia, *A King's Heritage* (1956)
Pimlott, Ben, ed., *The Political Diary of Hugh Dalton, 1918-40, 1945-60* (1986)
—— ed., *The Second World War Diary of Hugh Dalton 1940-45* (1986)
Pitt, Barrie, *The Western Desert* (1981)
—— *The Special Boat Squadron* (1983)
—— *The Crucible of War* (1986)
Plamenatz, John, *The Case of General Mihailovic* (1946)
Plomley, Roy, *Plomley's Pick* (1982)
Plowden, Edwin, *An Industrialist in the Treasury* (1989)
Porter, Ivan, *Operation Autonomous: with SOE in Wartime Romania* (1989)
Pritt, D. N., *Light on Moscow* (1939)
—— *Autobiography* (1966)
Pryce-Jones, David, ed., *Evelyn Waugh and His World* (1973)
Quayle, Anthony, *A Time to Speak* (1990)
Read, Anthony & Fisher, David, *The Deadly Embrace* (1988)
Rendel, G. *The Sword and the Olive* (1957)
Roatta, Mario, *Otto Millioni di Baionette* (Milan, 1946)
Roberts, Brian, *Randolph* (1984)
Roberts, Frank, *Dealing with Dictators* (1991)
Roberts, Walter R., *Tito, Mihailovic and the Allies 1941-1945* (New Jersey, 1973)
Rogers, Lindsay, *Guerrilla Surgeon* (1957)
Rootham, Jasper, *Miss Fire* (1946)
Rose, Norman, *Vansittart. Study of a Diplomat* (1978)
Roskill, S. W., *The War at Sea* (1961)
Roth, Anthony, *Enoch Powell. Tory Tribune* (1970)

Rothwell, V., *Britain and the Cold War 1941-1947* (1986)
Seago, Edward, *With the Allied Armies in Italy* (1945)
Seldon, Arthur F., *Churchill's Indian Summer* (1981)
Sevostyanov, P., *Before the Nazi Invasion* (Moscow, 1984)
Shaw, W.B. Kennedy, *The Long Range Desert Group* (1945)
Shelden, Michael, *Orwell* (1991)
Slessor, J., *The Central Blue* (1956)
Smith, A.C., *The German Campaign in the Balkans* (1953)
Soames, Mary, *Clementina Churchill* (1979)
Soulie, Michel, *La Vie Politique d'Edouard Herriot* (Paris, 1962)
Stafford, David, *Britain and European Resistance 1940-1945* (1980)
Strenson, John, *A History of the SAS Regiment* (1984)
Suyin, Han, *My House has two Doors* (1982)
Sweet-Escott, Bickham, *Baker Street Irregulars* (1976)
Sykes, Christopher, *Evelyn Waugh* (1975)
Taylor, A.J.P., *English History 1914-1945* (1965)
—— *Letters to Eva* (1991)
Taylor, D.J., *Stalin's Apologist* (1990)
Thayer, Charles, *Bears in the Caviar* (1952)
—— *Hands Across the Caviar* (1953)
Thesiger, Wilfred, *A Life of My Choice* (1987)
Thomas, Hugh, *The Spanish Civil War* (1960)
Thompson, Geoffrey, *Front-Line Diplomat* (1959)
Thorpe, D.R., *Selwyn Lloyd* (1989)
Tolstoy, Nikolai, *The Secret Betrayal* (1978)
—— *The Minister and the Massacres* (1986)
Tomasevich, J., *War and Revolution in Yugoslavia 1941-1945: The Chetniks* (Stanford, 1975)
Trgo, Fabijan, ed., *The National Liberation War and Revolution in Yugoslavia (1941-1943) Selected Documents* (Belgrade, 1982)
Ulam, U., *Tito and the Cominform* (Harvard, 1952)
Vaksberg, Arkady, *The Prosecutor and the Prey* (1990)
Van Creveld, Martin, *Hitler's Strategy, the Balkan Clue* (Cambridge, 1973)
Velebit, Vladimir, *Memoirs* (Zagreb, 1983)
Vickers, Hugo, *Cecil Beaton. The Authorized Biography* (1985)
Volkogonov, Dmitri, *Stalin. Triumph and Tragedy* (1991)
Vucinic, W.S., ed., *At the Brink of War and Peace: the Tito–Stalin split in a Historical Perspective* (New York, 1982)
Vukmanovic, Szetozac, *The Struggle for the Balkans* (1990)
Warner, Philip, *The SAS* (1971)
Webster, Jack, *Alistair MacLean* (1991)
Werth, Alexander, *The Last Days of Paris* (1940)
West, Rebecca, *Black Lamb and Grey Falcon* (New York, 1941)
Whaley, B., *Operation Barbarossa* (Boston, 1973)
Wheeler, M.C., *Britain and the War for Yugoslavia* (New York, 1980)
Williams, Ronald, *The Lords of the Isles* (1984)
Wilson, D., *Tito's Yugoslavia* (1979)
Wilson, Field-Marshal Lord, *Eight Years Overseas* (1948)
Windt, Harray de, *A Ride to India* (1891)
Wittner, L.S., *American Intervention in Greece* (New York, 1982)
Woodhouse, C.M., *Apple of Discord* (1948)
—— *The Struggle for Greece 1941-49* (1976)
—— *Something Ventured* (1982)

Woodward, E. L., *British Foreign Policy in the Second World War* (1962 & 1970)
Woodward, E. L. & Butler, Rohan, eds, *Documents on British Foreign Policy 1919–1939* (1949)
Wright, Peter, *Spymaster* (1987)
Wyatt, Woodrow, *Confessions of an Optimist* (1985)
Young, Kenneth, ed., *The Diaries of Robert Bruce Lockhart 1915–1938* (1973)
—— , *The Diaries of Robert Bruce Lockhart 1939–1965* (1980)
Zapantis, A. L., *Hitler's Balkan Campaign and the Invasion of the USSR* (New York, 1987)
Zayas, Alfred M. de, *The Wehrmacht War Crimes Bureau, 1939–1945* (Nebraska, 1990)
Ziegler, Philip, *Diana Cooper* (1981)
Zilliacus, Konni, *Tito of Yugoslavia* (1952)

Index